Oracle
E-Business Suite 12
Tuning Tips & Techniques

About the Author

Richard Bingham is an Applications Architect currently working in the Oracle Developer Relations Team, helping customers and partners build customizations, extensions, and integrations on the Fusion Applications platform. Richard joined Oracle in 1999 and, prior to moving to Oracle Product Development, was part of Oracle Support, delivering and developing support services across a range of applications products, with a large percentage of time devoted to E-Business Suite.

Between graduating with a BSc in Geology and joining Oracle, Richard worked as a developer, an analyst, an implementer, and a systems manager (as well as a doorman and an offshore mud-logger—just Google it). Richard is a certified ITIL V3 practitioner, a member of the Chartered Institute of Management, and an accredited assessor for the UK Institute of Customer Services, awarding professional certifications to a wide range of organizations.

About the Technical Editors

Scott Mikolaitis is an Applications Architect at Oracle Corporation and has worked at Oracle for over ten years. He works on prototyping and standards development for the SOA technology in Oracle Fusion. Scott also enjoys working with Web Services in Java as well as Jabber for human and system interaction patterns. He spends his spare time on DIY home improvement and gas-fueled RC cars.

James Phipps is a Senior Principal Technical Support Engineer in Oracle E-Business Suite Customer Support. He spent 19 years at Oracle Corporation, working the last 9 years in Oracle Support. His focus in Oracle Support has been on the E-Business Suite modules of Product Information Management, Product Hub, Inventory, Bills of Material, and Engineering. He is involved in on-demand hosted environments, Oracle problem-solving methods (ODM), and best practices and tools within the support community. Before Oracle Support, James spent 10 years in Oracle Consulting implementing and supporting the Oracle Applications and custom solutions.

ORACLE® *Oracle Press*™

Oracle
E-Business Suite 12
Tuning Tips & Techniques

Richard Bingham

Mc Graw Hill Education

New York   Chicago   San Francisco   Athens   London   Madrid
Mexico City   Milan   New Delhi   Singapore   Sydney   Toronto

Library of Congress Cataloging-in-Publication Data

Bingham, Richard (Richard John)
    Oracle E-Business Suite 12 tuning tips & techniques / Richard Bingham.
      pages   cm
    ISBN 978-0-07-180980-1 (alk. paper)
    1. Oracle E-business suite.   2. Electronic commerce—Computer programs.
    3. Management information systems.   I. Title.
    HF5548.32.B56   2014
    658.8'72028553—dc23
                                                            2013028306

McGraw-Hill Education books are available at special quantity discounts to use as premiums and sales promotions, or for use in corporate training programs. To contact a representative, please e-mail us at bulksales@mcgraw-hill.com.

Oracle E-Business Suite 12 Tuning Tips & Techniques

1234567890   DOC DOC   109876543

ISBN   978-0-07-180980-1
MHID   0-07-180980-5

Sponsoring Editor	**Technical Editors**	**Production Supervisor**
Paul Carlstroem	Scott Mikolaitis	Jean Bodeaux
Editorial Supervisor	James Phipps	**Composition**
Patty Mon	**Copy Editor**	Cenveo Publisher Services
Project Manager	Sally Engelfried	**Illustration**
Hardik Popli,	**Proofreader**	Cenveo Publisher Services
Cenveo® Publisher Services	Claire Splan	**Art Director, Cover**
Acquisitions Coordinator	**Indexer**	Jeff Weeks
Amanda Russell	Jack Lewis	

To my wife, Kate, for always encouraging me to actually do what I dream of; to my daughter, Charlotte for showing me how everyday life can be an adventure if you just try; and to my son, Gabriel, for refreshing our lives with his bristling sense of fun.

Contents at a Glance

Contents

Acknowledgments

I would like to thank everyone who helped turn this from a nice idea into a real book. I couldn't have completed the work without the help and support of all these people.

First and foremost are Scott Mikolaitis and Jim Phipps for their technical reviews and editorial feedback—you guys are the best at what you do and this book benefited greatly because of you.

I'd also like to thank the E-Business Suite ATG Product Management team for their help and support. Also, the Oracle Enterprise Manager development team deserves a special mention with a great deal of their product vision essential to this book and with whom I continue to enjoy collaborating and brainstorming ways to evolve enterprise application management. I nearly joined your team and suspect I still may in the future.

Special thanks goes to the Oracle E-Business Suite Support team, with whom I shared many years of hard work and which helped me lay the foundations of where I am headed today. Special mention goes to Christian Elsner and Petra Doering for making the time especially enjoyable. Also, Frank Höhne for providing access to his systems, which supported many test and trials, from which most of the fabulous screenshots were taken. I'd also like to recognize the backing of this project by the support management team, especially Kuldeep Chaudhuri and their glorious leader Medi Goker, who during my time transformed Oracle Applications support into a dynamic team of passionate and creative individuals providing truly next-generation services. I never thought support could be so exciting!

Finally, all at McGraw-Hill Education, especially Paul Carlstroem, who appreciated what I was trying to achieve here and stuck with this project when others had doubts.

Introduction

Improving the overall management of an E-Business Suite system has historically meant either an expensive consulting engagement or a set of in-house best practices that never gets publically shared. This book tries to address that, and with about 2300 companies running E-Business Suite, there is a huge need to move from just "getting by" with administrative tasks to actually delivering on the promise of lower Total Cost of Ownership (TCO) and achieving what is often known as "operational excellence."

These days, just managing an enterprise application like E-Business Suite is not enough, as business users demand more mobility, usability, and productivity from their applications, often based on the high expectations set by consumer apps. This pressure is also combined with many in-house business and IT development teams determined to adopt cutting edge technologies to keep pace with the competition. Done right, enterprise applications that are managed in a strategic, flexible, and effective manner will remain key contributors to business success. Done badly...well, let's not consider that.

Chapter 1: Technical and Functional Summary   In the first chapter, you'll learn the basics of E-Business Suite, both the functional breadth and the main components of its technology architecture and stack. To complement this chapter, the constituent products of E-Business Suite are explained in simple terms in the appendix.

Chapter 2: Successful Enterprise Application Management   As a counterpart to Chapter 1, in this chapter you'll learn the foundations of enterprise application management. We look at all the areas that are most important and impactful to delivering truly effective service to end users. The first two chapters combined give the base platform upon which we build going forward.

Chapter 3: Oracle E-Business Suite Management Lifecycle   We then move into considering how you might build a strategy around this platform. We look at many different popular lifecycle management models, and I explain how parts and concepts can be applied to enterprise application management. Taking these bits and pieces, we put together what we call a Fusion Lifecycle Model that can then be applied. For your implementation, you can either adopt this model or use it to build your own.

Chapter 4: The Oracle E-Business Suite Management Toolbox This chapter introduces Chapters 5 to 9, explaining how all the different features, options, and services can be generally categorized as tools and how they can be deployed in the parts of the management plan.

Chapter 5: A Reliability Management Toolbox In this chapter, we discuss reliability and consider many ways in which you can bullet-proof your E-Business Suite instances, including what tools to use when something bad happens.

Chapter 6: An Availability Management Toolbox This chapter reviews the concept of availability and how to monitor and manage E-Business Suite accessibility and overall uptime.

Chapter 7: A Performance Management Toolbox In this chapter, we analyze the best approaches to managing the speed and performance of E-Business Suite. It's well known that nothing hurts end-user adoption of an application as much as poor levels of responsiveness.

Chapter 8: An Optimization Management Toolbox Complementing the preceding sections, in this chapter we look at optimization and how the application and its management should be continuously made to evolve and improve. This includes fulfilling long-term strategy goals as well as having the tools in place for short-term flexibility in response to shifting priorities.

Chapter 9: A Governance Management Toolbox In the final toolbox chapter, we nail down the key aspects of application governance and the many different ways in which you can properly secure and control E-Business Suite.

Chapter 10: Getting and Staying Healthy In this chapter, we look at the different ways to measure the success and performance of the management plan and how other aspects of system health should be included beyond the five key areas.

Chapter 11: Being Future-Ready In the concluding chapter, we look at the future of E-Business Suite and consider ways to develop its application management based on constantly changing and evolving priorities, technologies, and systems.

Intended Audience

With the bulk of the content in the toolbox chapters, IT staff such as help desks and system administrators can use this book to learn the options available to help them get the most from their E-Business Suite systems. It may also act as a reference or a training resource.

In addition, systems analysts and leaders from both IT and the business will benefit from the first and last chapters as they strategize and plan the evolution of both their applications portfolio and the related technology and infrastructure investments.

As such I hope the varied content attracts a broad audience and provides something for everyone.

This book is an addition to the fabulous E-Business Suite product documentation. In the product's latest form (Release 12.x), it is broken into categories based on usage, greatly enhancing how easy it is to find information to help complete the real-world tasks that apps DBAs commonly get stuck with. The documentation is divided into sections on architecture, install, upgrade, integration, development and personalization, lifecycle management, reporting, and system administration. Even within the latter broad category, the standard Administration Guide is now broken down into separate subguides for each of the main activities: configuration, maintenance, and security. This certainly makes it much more usable than ever before.

There are also several fabulous books on E-Business Suite Administration, such as the *Oracle R12 Applications DBA Field Guide* (Coqui, 2010) by Elke Phelps, focusing on the detailed administration utilities and features that sysadmins need to perform day-to-day actions, such as stopping and starting, installing, patching, and upgrading. This is all very important, and this book too has many of these low-level details; however, we approach them with a higher level of thinking, considering not only *how* to perform these tasks, but also *when* and *why*.

Why Listen to Me?

As is traditional in nonfiction books, I would like to take a few paragraphs to authenticate my role as author of this book. I hope the "About the Author" page has already given you some substance that attests to my worth; however, as an Englishman, I think it is somewhat polite to introduce myself fully. Prior to joining Oracle, I had various roles that centered on using, administering, and developing enterprise business applications. One of my first post-graduation jobs was as a consultant, supporting a massive financial services IT system rollout, catching the last year of what was a five-year project. I also held another role early in my career as a systems administrator and went on to become the project manager for an implementation of a retail system across an international chain. As time progressed, I moved into applications development, using various technologies to create and extend internal systems to support core business processes.

When I first joined Oracle, I started supporting vertical industry applications. After setting up and training teams to support various niche solutions, and with some rationalization after the Internet bubble burst, I took my broad experience into E-Business Suite. There I was able to apply my creativity to find lots of new ways to help my colleagues deliver better services.

After nearly a decade in the trenches, helping thousands of different Oracle Applications customers, I had served my time and in doing so gained a reasonable grasp of the common challenges and gripes, never losing the ability to be excited and enthusiastic in envisioning how they might be improved.

Next, in one of my more insightful moves, I jumped at an opportunity to get on board with the development of Fusion Applications. Using my experience, I was asked to spearhead the work related to something known as *supportability*—making sure the product was as easy to support as possible. After a couple of years on the design side, a realization came to me: this combination of new technology, new applications, and new management tools is so different from our existing applications products that our customers are going to need some extra help.

So, with "write a book" still on my bucket list, and a few failed attempts on other topics, the planets aligned because I now had a subject I knew well in an area that was a hot topic. The affiliated publisher was excited, and I was on my way. What happened next was even more surprising. In researching and developing the book, I somehow invented a generic model for enterprise application management. I saw this as mostly common sense, a broad amalgamation of everything you'd need for success, based on the well-recognized practices I knew from experience and had validated and completed with extensive research.

Indeed, the more I looked the more it became clear that this complete picture didn't really exist anywhere else, and it became obvious that while the book describes the management-related features of a product, there is also great value in the way it describes approaching application management best practices.

Needless to say, after completing my first book on Fusion Applications, I realized that I had an opportunity to share the exact same model with the Oracle E-Business Suite community that I had worked with for so long. So in conclusion, I feel like this was the book I was always supposed to write, and that I just went about it in a slightly cart-before-the-horse way.

CHAPTER
1

Technical and Functional Summary

O racle Applications began life back in 1987. After eight years of successfully selling the database and development tools and watching almost every customer use these in business application development, Oracle decided it could help (and profit) by writing the most common business applications and distributing those to its clients. Initially the Applications division was seven employees who started by building the first accounting module, General Ledger, followed by Purchasing.

The Payables product was then added, and just two years later (1989) Oracle Applications Release 4 included Receivables, Fixed Assets, and Revenue Accounting. By the end of 1989, more features were added, with Release 6 including basic manufacturing products and the first Human Resource Management System (HRMS) application. With Release 7 in 1990, more manufacturing products were released, to include Oracle Inventory and Order Entry.

By 1993, Release 10 was available, which leveraged the client/server architecture and became the well-known *character version* (10C). This saw Project Accounting added to the current list of products: General Ledger, Accounts Payable, Accounts Receivable, Purchasing, Order Entry, Fixed Assets, Revenue Accounting, Inventory, Engineering, Bills of Material, Manufacturing Resource Planning, Capacity Planning, Master Scheduling, Work in Process, and Human Resources with Personnel and Payroll.

The *Smart Client* (10SC) version followed a year later (1995), adding multimedia support including graphics, charts, spreadsheets, voice annotation, and video. The product list was extended to include applications for sales force automation, electronic commerce, data warehousing, customer service, and workflow.

In 1996, Oracle introduced the first browser-based self-service applications, such as Oracle Web Customers, Oracle Web Suppliers, and Oracle Web Employees. These products ran on the new Oracle Web server, the very first commercial product to support persistent database connections over the Internet.

By 1998 and Release 10.7, we saw significant expansion of the Financials, HRMS, and manufacturing products, as well as the addition of business intelligence capabilities. This also saw the first introduction of Oracle Business Online, an early application hosting service that marked Oracle's pioneering industry leadership in what we now see as cloud services.

In 1999, I joined Oracle, just prior to the release of 11*i*. Oracle then also renamed Oracle Applications to Oracle E-Business Suite (EBS), helping mark the fact that the products were now comprehensive and integrated enough to run entire business operations over an Internet-enabled platform. This release also added several Customer Relationship Management (CRM) applications, exposing new ways to deliver customer services and sales. There were more than 45 products in 11*i*, and all were web-enabled, meaning that client PCs required only a browser to access them. In 2001, Oracle published the fact that through its own use of E-Business Suite it saved more than $1billion.

Although more products and features were added in 11*i*.X and Release 12, the next five years were dominated by the acquisition of other Enterprise Resource Planning (ERP) product vendors. Most notably, these included PeopleSoft (with J.D Edwards) in 2004, Retek and G-Log in 2005, and Siebel in 2006. Obviously, this still goes on today. These sister products and suites were added under the Applications Unlimited commitment to continue feature development and evolution for years to come.

By 2007, Release 12 came out, adding 18 new products and with 2,442 enhancements to the existing features. This also included the new Application Integration Architecture (AIA), allowing E-Business Suite to be quickly and easily connected to complementary applications and external

1987	Release 1	*General Ledger*	
	Release 2	*+ Purchasing* *+ Payables*	
	Release 3		
	Release 4	*+ Receivables, Fixed Assets, and Revenue Accounting*	
	Release 5		
1990	Release 6	*+ Core HRMS*	
	Release 7	*+ Inventory and Order Entry*	
	Release 8		
	Release 9		
1993	Release 10	*+ Manufacturing and Human Resources Personnel and Payroll.*	

Client-Server

Multimedia

Business Intelligence Business Online Hosting

Release 10.7 / Release 11.0 (1998)

Web-enabled > 45 Products, including CRM

Major Acquisitions

AIA / Release 12 (2007)

Fusion Strategy

Release 11.5 (11*i*) (1999)

Release 12.1 (2009)

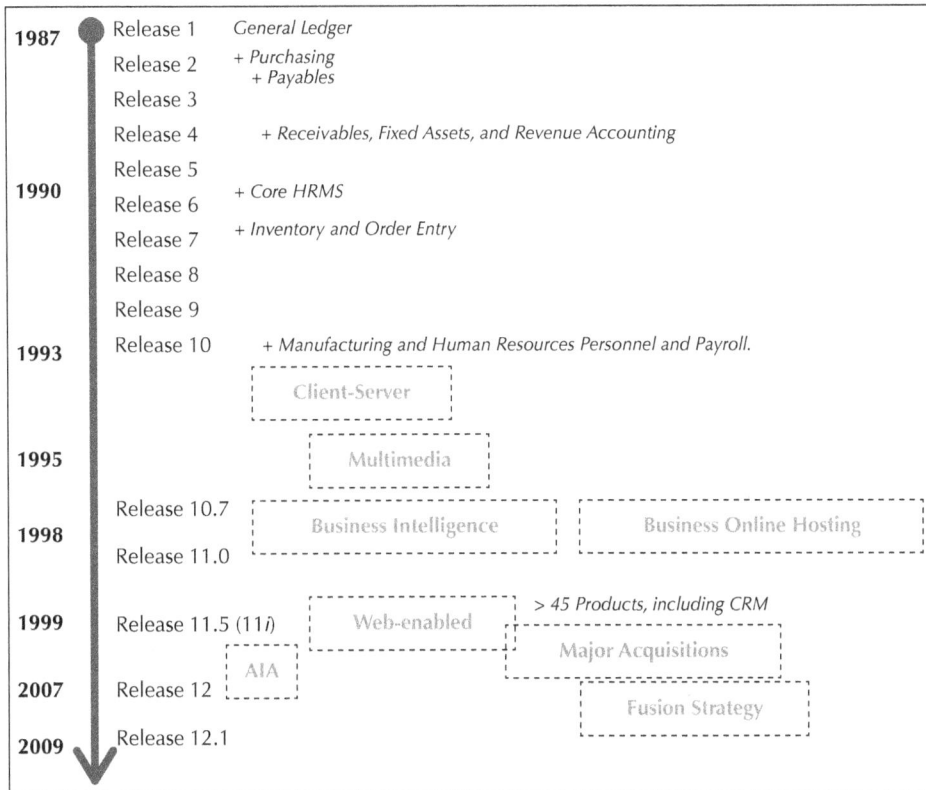

FIGURE 1-1. *The origin of Oracle Applications*

systems. That year also saw the initial formation of a Fusion Applications strategy, with the aim of designing and building a new suite of applications using the best parts of each Oracle-owned product suite, based on the latest technologies available (many through acquisition).

In 2009, we saw Release 12.1, the most recent version of E-Business Suite, which focused on adding products around value-chain planning and talent management, together with some technical architecture adjustments. So while Figure 1-1 illustrates this long evolution, and Release 12.2 is just around the corner, we've also now seen the first few releases of Fusion Applications, the next generation solution and already part of the applications architecture of some E-Business Suite customers.

Oracle E-Business Suite Functional Summary

You are unlikely to be new to E-Business Suite; however, the breadth of the product is such that it's worth including a summary as it may help shine light onto what is often seen as a *black hole of functionality* to those that do not use it. It's also true that most people involved with EBS have to specialize, and as such this chapter may enlighten folks across their normal work and knowledge silos.

The theory goes that it's impossible to manage what you don't really understand, or at least it isn't ideal, especially in these modern times of "service-based metrics" where it's the end users who measure IT on the successful provision of business features, not on the delivery of IT technologies or even software applications.

One more point: some of the names in E-Business Suite can be easily misinterpreted. For example, Universal Work Queue could be a technical messaging feature (it isn't); Install Base might be related to the software installation (again, no); and One-to-One Fulfillment sounds like it's related to delivering parcels to customers (it's not). Oh, and Oracle Treasury is *not* an application for would-be pirates!

Rather than take ten pages to give the details here, a summary of all the E-Business Suite products currently available as of Release 12.1 is provided in the appendix, where each product is described briefly to give administrators and managers an idea about what they are used for.

Functional Core Components

Now let's go one level deeper, beyond the business features and processes and into some of the functional components that underpin much of the E-Business Suite system.

As illustrated in Figure 1-2, the Functional Core Components are not quite technologies and not quite business product functionality; they fall in between. As such, it is sensible for System Administrators and Application Managers to have a reasonable understanding of them, should adjustments or related investigations be required.

As mentioned, it's unlikely you are new to E-Business Suite, so you may be aware of most of the information in the upcoming sections. Feel free to skip ahead; however, it might be a mistake to make too many assumptions about the dozens of components involved. The following sections include a useful overview, with a simple explanation of the main areas of functional coverage. So while similar information is available in parts of the product documentation, such as

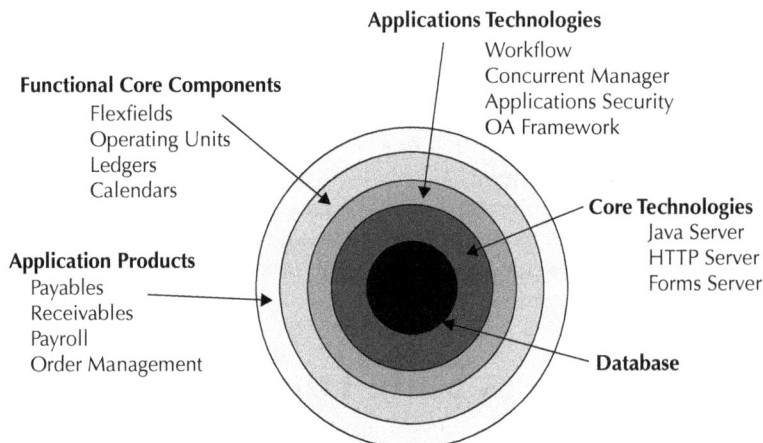

Applications Technologies
Workflow
Concurrent Manager
Applications Security
OA Framework

Functional Core Components
Flexfields
Operating Units
Ledgers
Calendars

Core Technologies
Java Server
HTTP Server
Forms Server

Application Products
Payables
Receivables
Payroll
Order Management

Database

FIGURE 1-2.   *The layers of Oracle E-Business Suite*

The Concepts Guide for E-Business Suite, here there are more illustrations and examples, as well as a clearer focus on the important principles in the context of system management.

Business Structures

Functional setup is based on the physical and logical divisions within an organization. These are mapped into E-Business Suite so that data can be properly associated to those structures. This allows effective entry of data, clear security segmentation, and full compliance with legal and reporting requirements. A very simple example is the way the fictional company known as Vision Corporation is comprised of the units Vision-UK, Vision-France, and Vision-USA.

These structures are commonly quite complex, just like the organizations themselves. They can vary depending on their uses and even overlap; for example, the way the HRMS legislation and reporting is implemented might be slightly different from the Finance and Accounting functions. This flexibility is fully supported by E-Business Suite through the use of various components and configurations.

What follows is a summary of the main parts used to represent and manage these structures; however, these are not all the objects available, nor are they directly related to each other.

Organizations

As the upper level in the hierarchy, this is the overall container for the business structure. Each organization has a *classification*, such as Business Group, HR Organization, Inventory Organization, GRE/Legal Entity, and Company Cost Center. These define what information is associated with the organization and what it can do.

Operating Units

While not used in HRMS, operating units define a division of the company that performs day-to-day activities like the buying (via Purchasing) and selling (via Order Management) of goods and services as well as the associated accounting (via Payables and Receivables). Operating units are tied to an organization and inherit the associated data as well as having some basic configurations of their own. Each E-Business Suite user is commonly assigned to one or more default operating unit. These units require some financial configuration, such as association with a ledger (see the section, "Ledgers") for managing accounts, a financial calendar, and a default currency. They are also assigned to a Legal Entity for tax and fiscal reporting. Operating units are logical objects, and therefore may span one or more actual physical location.

Business Groups

Business groups are a type of organization and most often represent a country. Business groups are primarily used by HRMS functionality for person assignment, although they are regularly used and displayed in other product areas also.

Legal Entities

Legal entities represent the designated legal employer in HRMS and are also used extensively in Financials. Officially, a legal entity administers transactions in compliance with national laws. This is usually another top-level object under which a hierarchy structure exists.

Ledgers

Formally known as Set-Of Books in Release 11, a ledger is a division that can be held financially accountable for its own activities. Ledgers are commonly assigned to legal entities and are used to manage and balance accounts. Ledgers can be grouped into sets and may have subledgers whose transactions are posted into the overall parent for balancing at the end of an accounting period (for example, a quarter or year).

Chart of Accounts

While specific to financials, the chart of accounts component is exposed in all places where transactions need to be associated back to the accounting function. The chart of accounts is simply a list of internal account numbers to which transactions are associated, such as a cost center code. These are implemented using the E-Business Suite technology known as flexfields, discussed in a later section.

Multiple-Organization Access Control (Multi-Org or MOAC)

In essence, Multiple-Organization Access Control allows processing and reporting across operating units. This allows more flexibility to perform actions and analysis across the organization to better synchronize tasks and identify opportunities like reduced redundancy and improved economies of scale.

Seed Data

E-Business Suite comes with a wealth of data ready for use. These are not fictitious organizations (unless you've installed the Vision demo data) or related structures, but common values that everyone uses. Much of this is accessed through the *Functional Administrator* responsibility, and here are some basic items explained.

Lookups

Lookups are functional datasets commonly used to classify objects, such as the list of different 401K Investment Options shown in Figure 1-3. They are comprised of lookup code values that

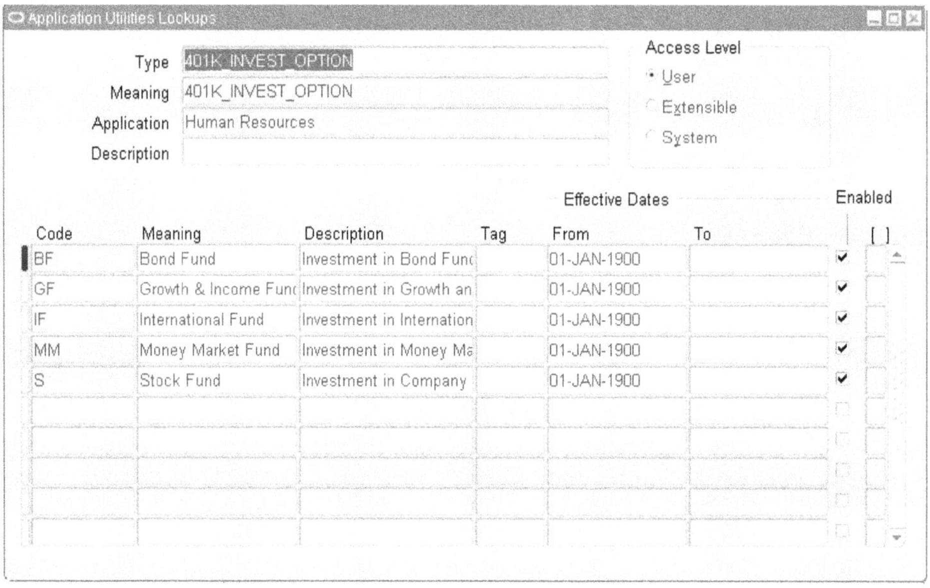

FIGURE 1-3. *Definition of the lookup and values for the 401k Investment Options list*

may be associated with custom names and descriptions, while retaining the associated functionality. Lookups are used for most of the types, classes, and codes used throughout E-Business Suite. New lookups can also be added to support customizations.

Messages
Messages are shown to the end user when they perform a specific activity, including confirmation messages, information messages, warning messages such as the one shown in Figure 1-4, and error messages. They are stored in the database and can therefore be personalized or added to, to suit individual needs, should additional code be implemented.

List of Values (LOV) Data
Lists of values examples might be taxation countries as shown in Figure 1-5, currencies or units of measure, and while most of these are seeded out-of-the-box, they can be adjusted by looking at the setup options available within the closest related product.

Profile Options
Almost the entire functional configuration that controls how the features operate is controlled by profile options. These values can be entered at different levels, with the most commonly used ones being *site* to apply to the whole system, *product* to apply inside one specific named product only, or *user* to apply to one specific named user. Figure 1-6 shows an example in which the default site level value for Need-By Time for deliveries is set to midnight, but for user CBAKER the value is a more realistic 09:30 A.M.

Name	Language	Application	Number
MRC_PO_ERROR_DURING_INSERT	US	Purchasing	0
MRC_PO_ERROR_DURING_UPDATE	US	Purchasing	0
MRC_PO_INVALID_CONVERSION	US	Purchasing	0
MRC_PO_INVALID_PARAM	US	Purchasing	0
MRC_PO_INVALID_PSOB_ID	US	Purchasing	0
MRC_PO_NO_RSOB	US	Purchasing	0
MRC_PO_PARAM_REQD	US	Purchasing	0
MRC_PO_PERIOD_CHECK	US	Purchasing	0

Current Message Text

The transaction/balance conversion type or date on the Reporting Book Initialization window or the first MRC Period in the Assign Reporting Ledger window has not been defined in &TABLE for the primary Ledger &PSOB_ID. Please verify these values in the Assign Reporting Ledger window.

FIGURE 1-4.   *Definitions of the Multiple Reporting Currency (MRC) messages*

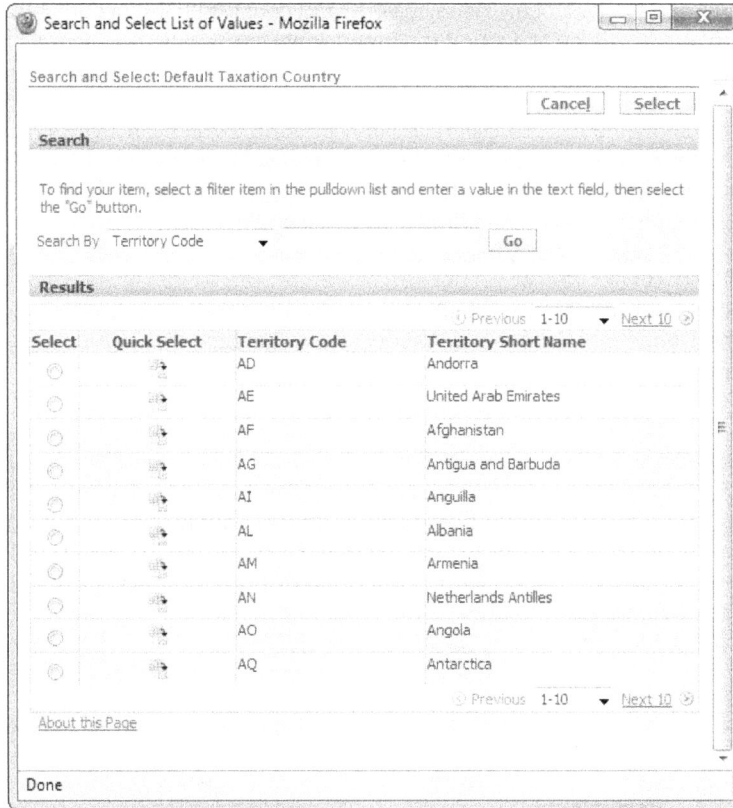

FIGURE 1-5. *The list of values for default taxation country*

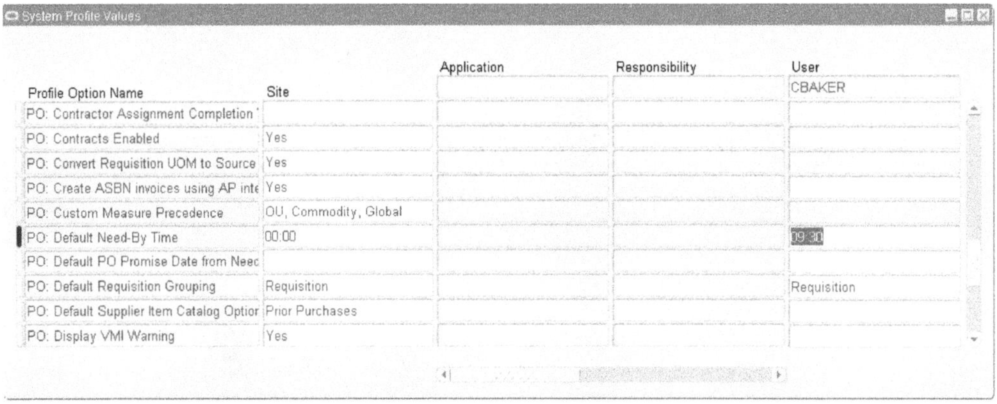

FIGURE 1-6. *Profile option values for Need-By Time*

Flexfields

There are two types of flexfields, *key* and *descriptive*, both of which provide abstract data composition on top of predefined column attributes to meet the individual needs of the business. A flexfield is made up of several distinct fields, known as *segments*.

For a *key flexfield*, each segment has a value chosen from a predefined set. All the segments concatenated together (often with hyphens between them) form the final flexfield value. The segment values can also have rules and relationships between then, so that only a valid combination can be chosen. As shown in Figure 1-7, account codes associated with business transactions are a common way to see these used in E-Business Suite.

Descriptive flexfields are different in that, while still composed of segments, they are "spare fields" that are available in a page or form for the entry of additional data that might be useful. These fields are supported by the corresponding database tables so that the record always has the entered value associated with it. Obviously, custom logic can also be added to validate and process the extra data if needed; however, as shown in Figure 1-8, it's commonly implemented as an associated descriptive attribute, such as color, size, or volume.

Flexfields are core functional structures that should be implemented carefully with consideration of future requirements, as they should not be significantly changed once they are set up. While flexfields are part of implementation planning, and therefore outside the scope of this management book, they are considered further in Chapter 9.

Trading Community Architecture (TCA)

Transaction data is usually denormalized so that duplication doesn't occur, storage is optimized, and updates need only be made in one place. The same applies to setup data, such as supplier and customer records, where a duplication would lead to poor performance and potential data

Requisitions	Orders	Agreements	Deliverables	Negotiations	Suppliers

Orders > Standard Purchase Order >

Distribution 1 (Standard Purchase Order 7444)

Operating Unit	**Vision Operations**
Line	**1**
Schedule	**1**
Quantity	**100000**
Unit	**Each**
Amount	**1,000,000.000**

Delivery

Destination Type	**Inventory**
Subinventory	
Requester	
Deliver-To Location	

Billing

PO Charge Account	**01-000-1410-0000-000** Company-Department-Account-Sub-Account-Product
PO Accrual Account	**01-000-2220-0000-000** Company-Department-Account-Sub-Account-Product

Contract

FIGURE 1-7. *Key flexfields used for the account fields on the purchase order billing*

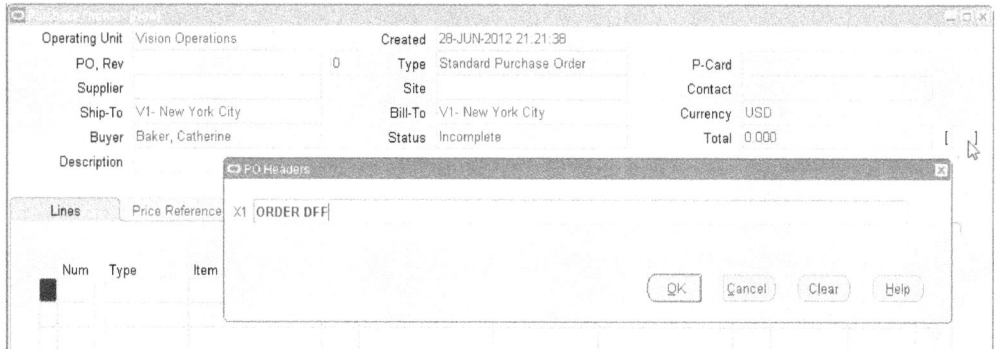

FIGURE 1-8. *A descriptive flexfield capturing extra information on a purchase order header*

inconsistency. Maintaining this *single source of truth* is at the core of Master Data Management. For many entities in E-Business Suite this is done through a single data model known as the Trading Community Architecture (TCA).

Physical objects such as people and companies are represented as *parties* and have one or more relationships among themselves and other parties in the model: for example, the employee relationship that exists between a person party and a company party. A party will also have one or more locations such as addresses and contact details. These are recorded as *party sites*. Figure 1-9 illustrates the general concepts here.

TCA is leveraged inside almost all E-Business Suite products, bringing a standardization and simplicity to help ensure functional data integrity.

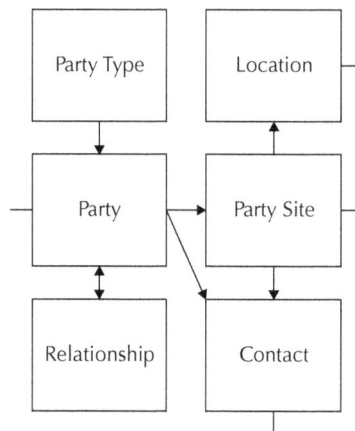

FIGURE 1-9. *The core entities of the Trading Community Architecture*

Although this level of detail will remain invisible to the business end user, the applications administrator will benefit from a basic understanding of this model. Uses include analyzing functional setup issues, managing customizations (for example, additional reports), and managing the applications database.

Approval Management Engine (AME)

While a somewhat pseudo-technology, the Approval Management Engine (AME) component allows business experts to create rules to generate one or more approvers for use with workflow processing. A simple example shown in Figure 1-10 is a requisition that needs approval before it's sent to a supplier. Depending on the item, price, and total cost of the order, how much approval is needed and by whom will vary. AME supports several different types of approval, including parallel processes using complex hierarchies or groups.

It works fairly independently to E-Business Suite and each business process uses it as-and-when required, passing in a context and accepting a list of approvers in return.

Most E-Business Suite approval processes support the use of AME; however, some also still support their own mechanisms for generating approver lists. Generally speaking, AME provides much more functionality and flexibility than the proprietary methods.

Oracle E-Business Suite Technical Summary

Much has already been written about the technologies inside E-Business Suite. Most are standalone products in their own right, and of course if you are already running E-Business Suite instances you'll be intimately familiar with most of them. What I do here, however, is provide a summary in case anything remains a little unclear, and we can demonstrate how these work together at runtime.

To that effect, we'll first review the main technical components, starting with the front end of the application and working our way through the technology stack layers therein.

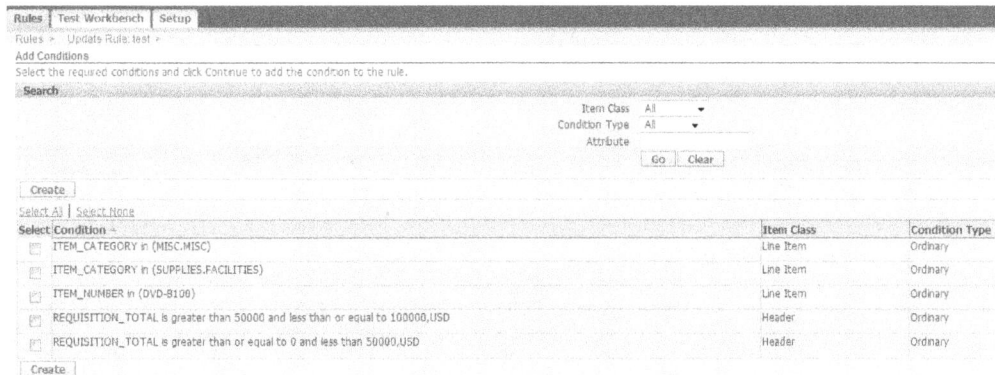

FIGURE 1-10.   *Conditions defined in an AME rule*

Oracle Forms

While Release 12 saw an increase in the movement from an Oracle Forms user interface (UI) to a browser-based one, some parts of the application remain available in the original style. There are various reasons for this (beyond the reengineering involved), including the fact that many forms interfaces are optimized for fast data entry, and some forms would gain little by moving to a browser-based interface. As shown in Figure 1-11, the different page types can be identified by their different icons: Releases is in the classic Oracle Form's UI and PO Change History is in HTML.

Oracle Forms relies on the browser having a Java plug-in available; if no plug-in is available, it provides one for download and install. Once installed, the Forms server sends some initial Java executable files to the client browser plug-in, called an *applet*. These Java executables are run by the applet to provide the technology for forms to be displayed and for features like menus, buttons, and some graphs and charts. Once the base forms executables are running, the specific form is sent to the client, built, and displayed. While quite fast, you can see this happening in your browser when you first connect to an E-Business Suite form, and if you enable the Applet Console you'll see exactly what is going on. Figure 1-12 gives an overview.

When first implemented, this technology allowed a rich user experience without the need to apply and manage local PC software installation of the forms (beyond the applet). Over the years, the technology embedded in browsers has increased to the point that downloading programs to provide rich user interfaces is no longer required, and fairly simple HTML and JavaScript pages can provide equally, if not more, powerful features. That said, E-Business Suite has many hundreds of forms and those built before such evolution occurred remain in the product today.

HTML-Based User Interface

Once browser technologies got to the point of supporting a rich user interface, Oracle created a development platform with which to implement these pages. At that time E-Business Suite was the lead Oracle application and therefore this became known as the *Oracle Application Framework* (OAF) and is the standard for all non-Oracle Forms pages.

OAF is based on an open standards design pattern, known as the Model View Controller (MVC) architecture. In very simple terms, the Model is the back-end part of the process representing the business data and logic, the View is made up of the user interface components, and the Controller is the glue that makes them work together; that is, the Model is triggered by actions in the View. This is illustrated in Figure 1-13.

Purchase Orders
- Purchase Order Summary
- Purchase Orders
- Releases
- PO Change History
- Exceeded Price Tolerances
- Pending Purchase Order Changes
- Manage Deliverables

FIGURE 1-11. *Different icons for the Oracle Forms and Oracle Applications Framework pages for managing purchase orders*

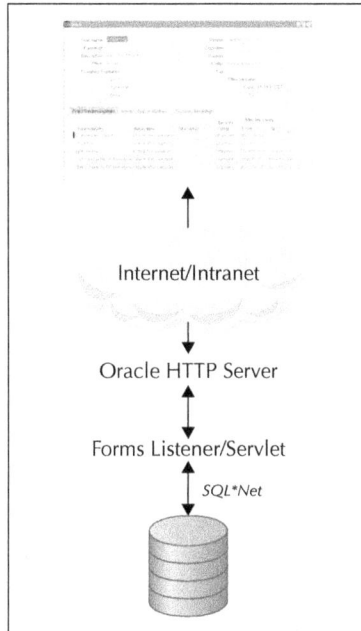

FIGURE 1-12. *The technical flow of Oracle Forms*

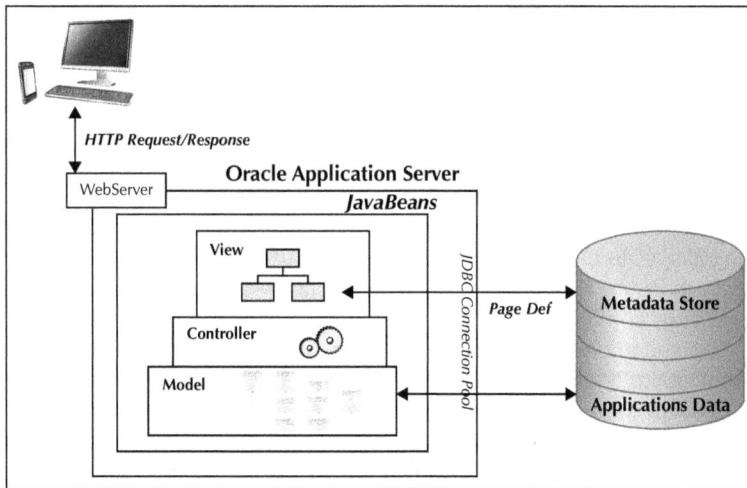

FIGURE 1-13. *Overall flow of the MVC architecture*

The View (user interface) is made up of a library of technologies and standard components for generating consistent forms, pages, and reports. These components are all designed and developed using Oracle's own JDeveloper tool, with each page composed of *regions*, which themselves contain *items*, such as fields, buttons, and images. A page works through a mixture of XML MetaData Services (MDS), a standard library of JavaBeans, and a rendering engine known as UIX; however, detail on exactly how this works is beyond the scope of this book. The Oracle Application Framework Developers Guide gives more detail if required.

The Model (business data and code) is constructed of a set of objects that are executed by *Oracle Business Components for Java* (Oracle BC4J), essentially a runtime platform that is deployed inside the Java Virtual Machine.

- View objects (unrelated to the View in MVC) can be considered queries to get data from the database. The result set is placed into attributes that can be used for display or processing.

- Entity objects implement the business logic associated with a database record, such as the validations performed before updating a supplier record as embedded in the entity object's code. They could be seen as wrappers around database records, ensuring quality and integrity are retained while making the more detailed processing relatively simple.

- Application modules are container objects that help relate other objects together so they run effectively. For example many of the queries to collect the data displayed in a page will be held as view objects inside one application module. Application modules also implement controller-triggered code and help control database transaction (through the OADBTransaction object).

The Controller is the code that gets invoked when a button, link, or other item is used on the page. The initial process, say from a Submit button press, flows through one of the standard handlers (processRequest, processFormRequest, or processFormData) and invokes the controller code class associated with that page region. Obviously, controller code is only the tip of the code execution flow; however, it acts as the standard gateway in which to capture end user events and actions.

User Interface Personalization

As mentioned previously, there is a component called *MetaData Services* (MDS) that is integral to the generation of the HTML returned to the client browser. This is a store (usually in a database) of each page definition; however, the interesting part is that it can store a definition at multiple levels. The base definition is created upon install, but if a particular user decides to personalize their page, it will store those changes against that user. Whenever they request the page again, it applies the changes to the base definition, resulting in the custom page.

As shown in Figure 1-14, the levels are known as the personalization context, and adjustments can be kept at any combination of function, industry, location, site, organization, and responsibility. In reality, they tend to be set at a responsibility, organization, or site level.

The fact that the original page definition never gets overwritten means that these are upgrade safe, and mistakes can easily be reverted and reapplied after correction.

We'll revisit managing personalization in later chapters, and more detail on the capabilities can be found in the Oracle Application Framework Personalization Guide.

Generally speaking, Oracle Forms-based pages cannot be personalized in the same way as HTML pages can; however, they can be customized to fit a specific need. More detail on how to customize Oracle Forms can be found in Oracle E-Business Suite User Interface Standards for Forms-Based Products at http://docs.oracle.com.

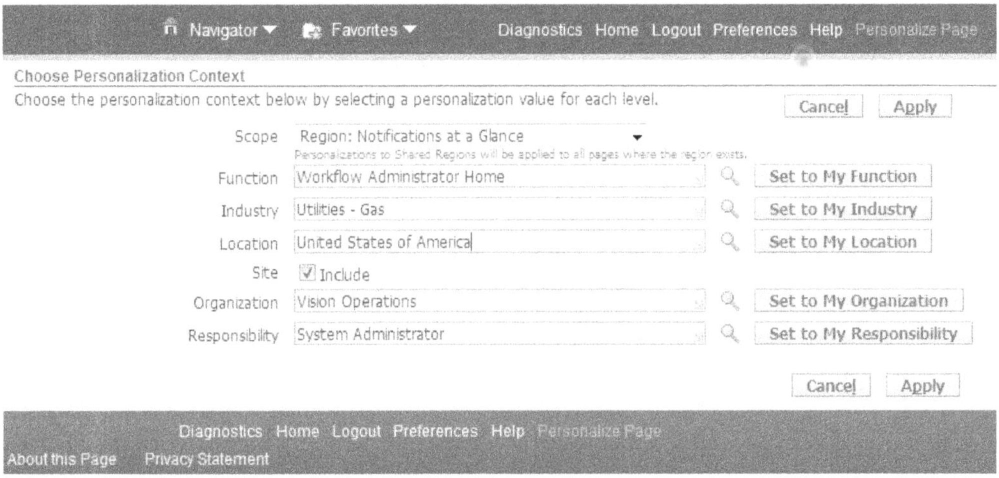

FIGURE 1-14.   *The levels of the personalization context*

Business Intelligence

Like all parts of E-Business Suite, Business Intelligence, the component that sits over the application and helps turn transactional data into summaries, charts, and analytics upon which business decisions can be made, has evolved over time.

In Release 12, Business Intelligence essentially takes two forms:

- **Daily Business Intelligence (DBI)**   Introduced in the 11*i*10 and later releases, DBI leverages the use of Oracle Database structures known as *materialized views*, which act as a kind of data warehouse for use by reporting. Strictly speaking it's not a full data warehouse technology, but it has several similar concepts, including *dimensions* to support viewing data based on different criteria and an *incremental refresh* for copying data from transactional tables into reporting tables. An example of a DBI dashboard page is given in Figure 1-15.

  At one point this solution evolved slightly into something known as *Fusion Intelligence*, but this was really a stepping stone to the current solution.

- **Oracle BI Applications**   Unlike DBI, which is included with E-Business Suite, the latest set of packaged Business Intelligence solutions for Oracle E-Business Suite is a separate set of products. Each integrates with E-Business Suite and supports other Oracle Application products such as Siebel and PeopleSoft, bringing data from multiple sources together for full enterprise-wide analysis. An example is given in Figure 1-16.

  BI Applications uses the full set of Oracle's latest Fusion Middleware and Oracle Business Intelligence Enterprise Edition (OBIEE) technologies to provide a separate platform for data warehousing and management. Oracle BI Applications is comprised of a full suite of preconfigured reports, dashboards, and analytical features for all common requirements, based on the core application products such as Sales, Service, Supply Chain, and Order Management, Human Resources, and Financials, and they feature powerful drill-downs through summarized data to get to actionable results.

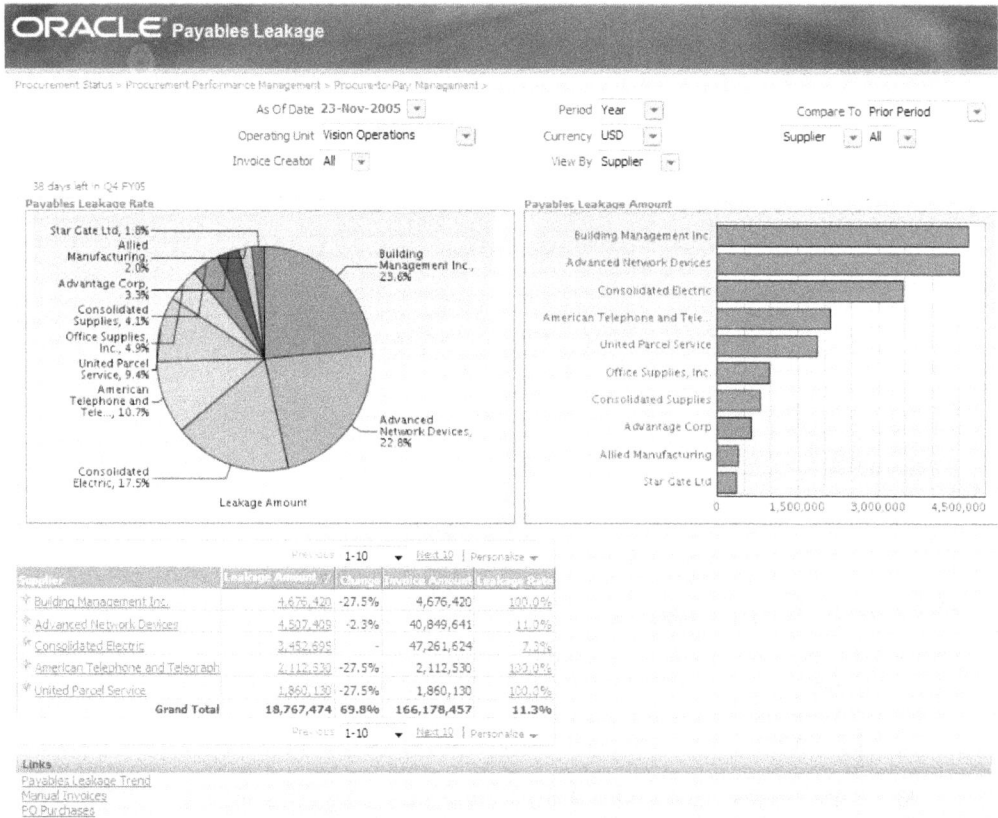

FIGURE 1-15. *The Payables Leakage dashboard in DBI*

In addition to these main two solutions, the *Enterprise Performance Management* suite of intelligence applications also sits over Oracle's Applications data (E-Business Suite included) and leverages Hyperion's Essbase technologies to deliver advanced solutions and features for strategy, planning and budgeting, profitability, and financial reporting.

Reports

While similar to Business Intelligence, reports are stored or printed as documents based on a specific purpose, normally as part of a legal, regulatory, or business process requirement. Examples might be copies of orders, invoices, contracts, and payroll documents.

In the past, E-Business Suite used the Oracle Reports technology to design and generate these documents. With Release 12, the Oracle Reports server component is gone; however, many of the traditional style reports are still generated, albeit by a newer component.

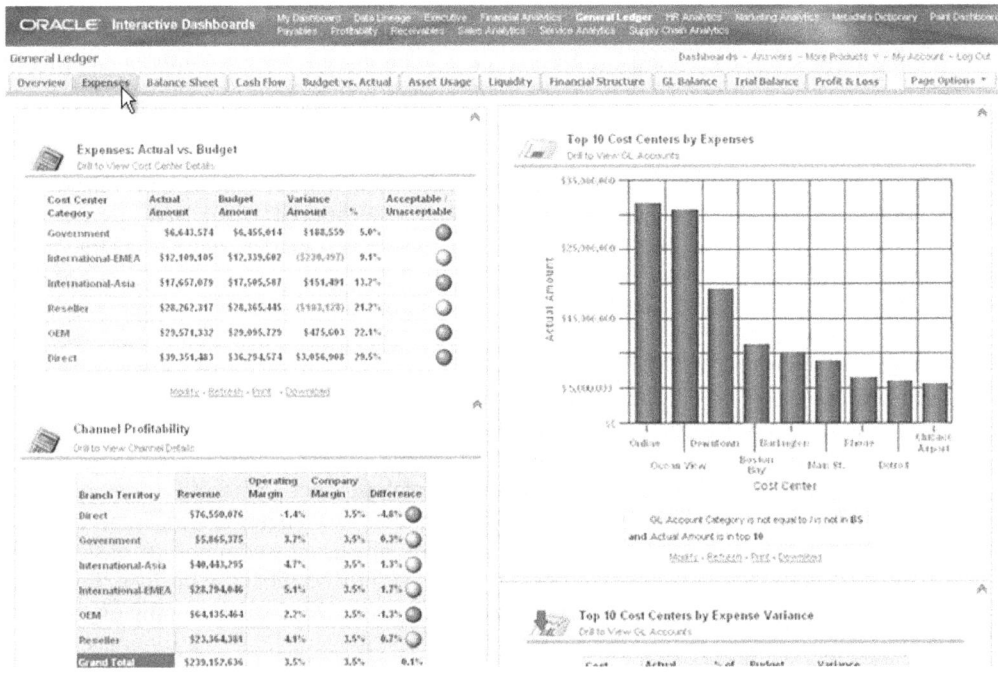

FIGURE 1-16. *The General Ledger expenses dashboard in BI Applications*

This new reporting engine was integrated from E-Business Suite 11*i* onward. Originally known as XML Publisher and now evolved into BI Publisher, it uses a simple XML template definition file, stored against each document type. These templates can be created and adjusted in tools like Microsoft Word and uploaded into E-Business Suite directly for immediate use. This simplicity and flexibility means reports are richer and formats are easier to manage, plus it adds more options for format and storage (for example, as PDF files).

Oracle Web Applications Desktop Integrator

Another part of the client technology, Web Applications Desktop Integrator (Web ADI) provides integration between E-Business Suite and sets of predefined Excel spreadsheets, Word documents, and Microsoft Project files. Some of this comes prebuilt, but the functionality also supports the creation of new Microsoft Office files and their integration with E-Business Suite.

These tools are commonly used for client-side analysis activities as well as the ability to quickly and easily load data into E-Business Suite. Microsoft Office has predefined templates that govern the mapping of fields to database records and provide functionality logic and look-and-feel standards, so that data always works with E-Business Suite.

Web ADI is used commonly with CRM applications for mobile workforce integration, HRMS applications for standard forms and letters, and financial applications for data analysis and managing project schedules.

The Middle Tier

Having looked at the main components related to the user interface and client, let's move to a brief overview of how these components communicate with the server-side components. This should help you envisage the process flow by continuing down a sequential tour of the components-based execution flow.

First, let's consider OA Framework pages. As mentioned previously, the back-end business logic triggered from button presses, menus, and links on the UI are handled through the Oracle Business Components for Java (BC4J) layer, itself represented by the "model" of the MVC architecture. This *glue*, implemented as XML object definitions and code in Java classes, handles a large percentage of the business logic, such as retrieving data and making basic updates. However, for detailed and voluminous processing activities it invokes APIs from other technology components, such as Concurrent Manager and Workflow.

Next, let's consider the flow for Oracle Forms. With E-Business Suite Release 12, by default the *Forms Listener servlet* handles the communication between client and server, routed via the HTTP server (different from "socket mode," which is used for direct client-to-server communication). This JVM-based servlet allows for better resource and connection management. The forms servlet still leverages a direct Oracle Net connection with the database once the form is running, and the logic is either embedded in the form or in the associated PL/SQL packages. Oracle Forms also makes calls to other components for large pieces of work, usually using a common set of standard APIs.

The next steps in the execution process depend entirely on what the business logic is doing. Activities range across many other servers, processes, and components running on the middle-tier, each providing different E-Business Suite services. The following table is a summary of the main components:

Component	Full Name	Description
OACORE	Oracle Applications Core	An OC4J (JVM) group used for executing OA Framework applications
OAFM	Oracle Applications for Fusion Middleware	An OC4J (JVM) group used for running all Fusion Middleware extensions such as MapViewer and Web Services
FORMS-C4WS	Oracle Applications Forms	An OC4J (JVM) group used for running the Forms Services
OPMN	Oracle Process Management and Notification	Used to stop, start, and manage the preceding JVM processes
JTFF	Fulfillment server	Used by CRM's one-to-one fulfillment product
ICSM	Interaction Center Server Manager	Used for CRM products to manage telephone calls
AOL/J	E-Business Suite implementation for common components	Utility Java components, programs, and libraries
CMAN	Connection Manager	Used for forwarding network connections (proxy server)
OHS	Oracle HTTP Server	Web server for handling initial connections and static files

Component	Full Name	Description
MWA	Mobile Web Application server	Used mainly inside the Supply Chain products (for example, Warehouse Management) for tailoring data entry pages run on commercial mobile devices
FMS	Forms Metric server	Used for load balancing multiple Forms servers
DISCO	Oracle Discoverer	Optional report creation layer and tooling, somewhat outdated
SMTP and WFMAIL	Operating system mailer and Workflow Java Mailer	Used for sending and receiving business notifications (for example, approval requests), usually as part of Workflow processing
ICM, PMON, FNDSM, FNDLIBR, RRA, OPP	Various components of concurrent processing	Managers and programs that control the scheduling and execution of background processing

Applications Technology

Many E-Business Suite features use technical components that were explicitly developed to provide that function, often because at that time the technology required was simply not available. The more common features are described in the following table.

Some of these have existed for many years and inherit somewhat legacy nomenclature, such as FND, which stands for "Foundation," or AOL, which stands for "Application Object Library." Others are based on the newer technologies or more recent additions—for example, OAM, "Oracle Applications Manager." In this book we'll group these together under our Applications Technology layer.

Title	Example	Description
Applications DBA Utilities	adpatch, adconfig, and adadmin	Various tools for applying patches and adjusting options and configurations
Application Online Help (iHelp)	"Defining Units of Measure"	The infrastructure and content of the end users' help system
Applications Loader	FNDLOAD	Tools for loading system values and data
Application Lookups	401K_INVEST_OPTION	Lists of standard types and codes used in application pages and forms
Applications Worklist	Notifications of approval required	All Workflow notifications are summarized on an online page within which actions can be taken directly

Title	Example	Description
Applications Profile Options	DEFAULT_COUNTRY	The main configuration and setup feature used across application products
Flexfields	Accounting, Item Category	Configurable fields offering a flexible data model
Applications Security	AOL/J	E-Business Suite Security infrastructure
Schedulers and Concurrent Requests	FNDLIBR	Tools for managing data-intensive batch processing
Oracle Applications Manager	OAM	Overall E-Business Suite Management Console and features (including license manager)
Common Modules	AK	Utility features for building custom pages and labels
Applications Utilities	AU	Features and resources to support the Oracle Forms deployment and runtime

There are many important components in this layer, and we'll look at their effective management in the subsequent chapters.

Basic Process Flows

The flow diagrams shown in Figure 1-17 give a very basic idea of how the technical components I described work together within E-Business Suite. Again, the intention here is not to describe every last moving part but to ensure the basic concepts are well understood so that we can drill into more specifics in later chapters.

Concurrent Processing

Sometimes deployed on what is known as the *Management server*, concurrent processing is the main component in E-Business Suite for running asynchronous programs, more traditionally known as batch processing. The need for this comes from functionality that involves extensive data processing, resource intensive activities, or specific actions that need to be scheduled to begin at specific times.

Rather than present a long-winded definition of the concurrent manager pieces, the following list, along with Figure 1-18, simply illustrates the key parts and how they work together.

- Programs are registered in the concurrent processing library for execution.
- Work shifts define specific dates and times when each concurrent manager executes.
- The Conflict Resolution Manager ensures that incompatible concurrent programs are not run together.
- The Internal Concurrent Manager (ICM) controls all concurrent manager processes, including startup, failure, and shutdown.

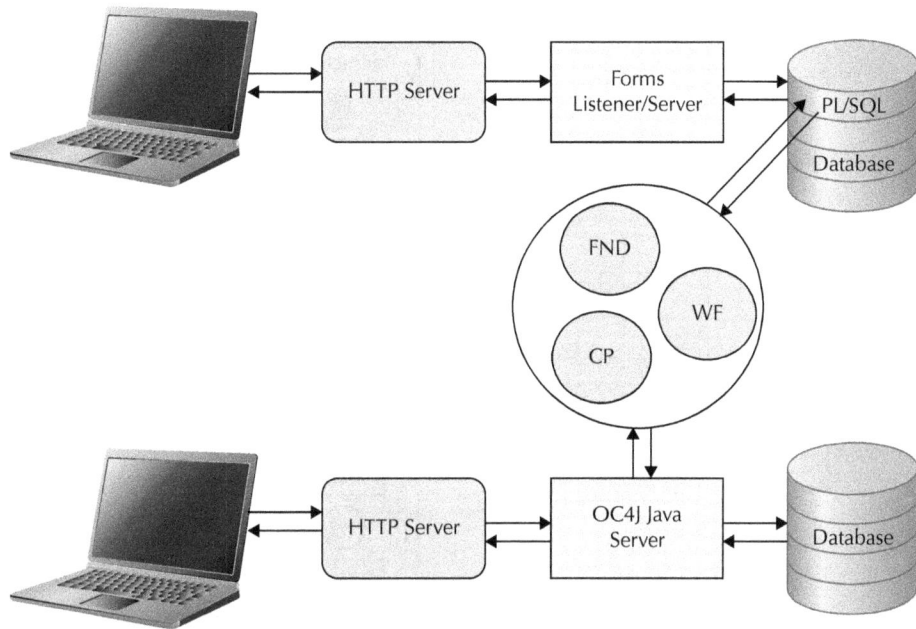

FIGURE 1-17.   *Basic processing flows for Forms and OA Framework*

- The ICM process launches service managers on the processing nodes and these do the ICM work locally, based on the predefined work shifts.

- A Standard Manager is an agent for handing requests for general purpose concurrent program execution.

- A Transaction Manager is a special type usually used for synchronous program execution, where immediate real-time results are required. An example is the generation of a report for display.

- The target processors (or workers) run a specific concurrent program controlled by a manager.

- Various types of programs can be run by concurrent managers, with some executed by the same system process as the manager (for example, PL/SQL) and others as spawned child processes (for example, reports and C programs).

- Jobs are entries in Oracle Advanced Queue tables used by concurrent processing.

- Concurrent Managers write both log and output for a job, the first as an activity record and the other containing any specific result intended (or it may be empty). It uses a process called the Report Review Agent to manage these files and pass them back to the requesting components, such as Oracle Forms.

- Parallel Concurrent Processing is available to share the load across RAC or similarly clustered nodes.

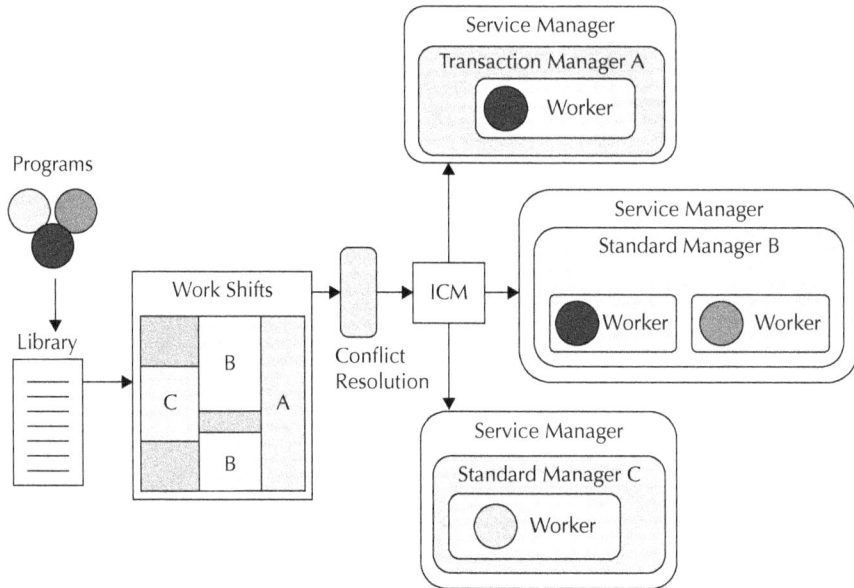

FIGURE 1-18. *Key components of the Concurrent Processing architecture*

This may be the briefest description of the E-Business Suite Concurrent Manager ever, but we'll drill into more detail as required as we visit its tuning and troubleshooting throughout this book.

Oracle Workflow

Broadly speaking, Workflow executes and manages a sequential process flow. While this can be a technical process, the majority of use cases are for functional business processes, such as approving an expense report. Each stage of the process executes a specific *activity* (such as a program), and depending on the result, a subsequent process gets called. Workflow in E-Business Suite is an entire subsystem that sits alongside E-Business Suite and is leveraged by many parts of the functionality. Oracle Workflow has for a long while been available within the database as a standalone product for use in custom applications.

Using our expense workflow example, the E-Business Suite code that validates and commits the new expense report to the database will also make a call to Oracle Workflow with parameters that tell it to invoke the first node of the appropriate approval process. This first node will commonly analyze the transaction data and run the appropriate process, either leveraging a tool like Approval Management Engine (AME), or itself sending notifications to the right person. Workflow then waits until a response comes back (from AME or from a direct notification) and, based on the result, moves to the next node in the process flow, which might be either to request additional approval or simply to call the code that updates the expense report and pass it to the accounting team for reconciliation and payment.

Workflows can quickly get complex when all manner of real-world scenarios are mapped into the process, such as the exceptional cases when normal processing shouldn't occur, the additional processing of data required based on specific outcomes, or the support of practical things such as the vacation of an approver, as illustrated by the vacation rules feature shown in Figure 1-19.

Oracle Workflow is a mature part of the E-Business Suite platform, and while its underlying technology is based on older PL/SQL-based processing it has been proven powerful enough to handle high volumes of throughput while flexible enough to satisfy the needs of most organizations.

We'll be looking at Workflow in depth in many chapters to come, since the efficient execution of processes controlled by E-Business Suite is right at the top of the Application Manager's goals.

The Oracle E-Business Suite Database

Interestingly enough, the person tasked with managing an E-Business Suite installation is often referred to as an "Apps DBA," even though the overall proportion of the role that is related to true

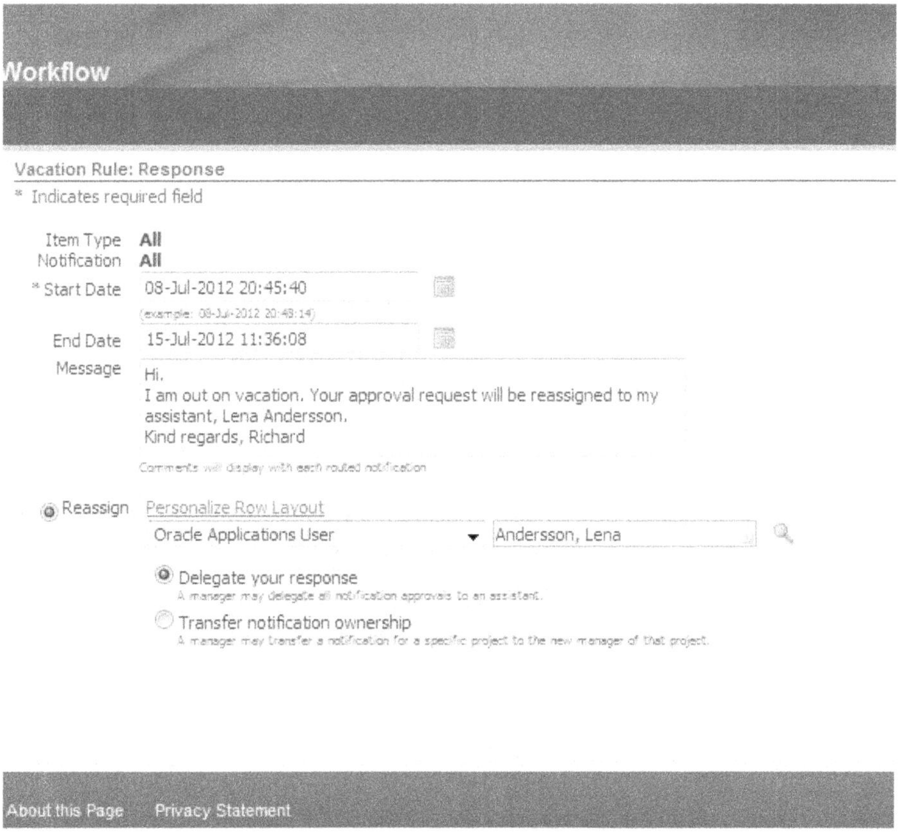

FIGURE 1-19. *Simple Workflow feature creating a vacation rule*

DBA tasks has diminished significantly as the technology has evolved. An obvious example is Automatic Storage Management (ASM), where the database extends resources as required, rather than requiring reactive manual involvement.

With Release 12, E-Business Suite requires a standard deployment of the Oracle Database system with very few special requirements. This is a good thing, since it means all the features and capabilities of the best-in-class database platform are at the disposal of the application features. Examples include leveraging Real Application Clusters (RAC) for multinode scalability or materialized views for powerful Business Intelligence.

The implementation and configuration of the E-Business Suite database is, however, carefully designed to offer the best in data management and processing. We'll look at this in detail throughout this book and focus on the important and newer features, configurations, and tools that must be used to deliver true Applications DBA excellence.

The Applications Filesystem

E-Business Suite maintains a specific way of laying down the files within the hardware servers it uses. Just like the other architectures, this has evolved over the years to both accommodate the introduction of new technology components and to try to gain management effectiveness. With Release 12 this can be summarized as follows:

The Database Tier

- **APPS_ST**   To hold the actual data files
- **TECH_ST**   To hold the ORACLE_HOME for the database product code

The Application Tier

- **APPS_ST**   For the APPL_TOP for all the E-Business Suite features code and the COMMON_TOP for utility code, such as that for Concurrent Manager.
- **TECH_ST**   For the two required ORACLE_HOME's for the code for the various technology products involved (for example, Oracle Application Server).

New in Release 12 is the concept of having a *shared application tier*, meaning that the respective APPS_ST and the TECH_ST nodes can be reused by multiple instances of E-Business Suite. When this is done, the only things that are unique to an instance are found under an INST_TOP directory, which mainly includes logs and configuration files. This greatly improves the opportunity to reuse all standard parts of the provisioned environment, saving of space, resources, maintenance, while improving consistency and automation opportunities.

We'll look at the various deployment options in more depth in later chapters and focus on discovering the related management opportunities available.

Oracle E-Business Suite Security

Security is a very big area, and much of Chapter 9 is devoted to understanding how to get the most effective strategy and tooling for securing E-Business Suite. Indeed, a comprehensive discussion of

E-Business Suite security should be an entire book on its own, so this section is a super-simple background overview of a few main principles. Security can be broken into two sections:

- **User Login**   The *authentication* of usernames and passwords has, up until Release 12, been done mainly inside E-Business Suite, using its native security features. While this remains at the core of Release 12, more options are now available to integrate with industry standard authentication tools, such as Microsoft's Active Directory LDAP server, as well as capabilities from within the E-Business Suite technology stack, such as Oracle Application Server's Single Sign-on.

- **Access to Features and Data**   The *authorization* of users once logged in, controlling what data they can see and what tasks they can perform, is also controlled entirely inside E-Business Suite.

Both *function security* (what users can do) and *data security* (what data they can do those things to) are controlled by E-Business Suite *responsibilities,* provisioned to users either explicitly or automatically. At a very simple level, this is how it works:

- **Function Security**   Governed by *menus*, themselves containing *functions* that control a specific task or action. Menus are linked directly inside the definition of each *responsibility*.

- **Data Security**   Controlled by *grants*. These are records that tie up a *security context* (a responsibility and an operating unit) with a *data security object* (like a table record, supplier, or user) and a *set* (a permission or a menu). This combination therefore has all the ingredients to ensure business data is secured.

Of course, the HRMS products have a slightly different take on some of the security principles, and while the same core structures remain, it has some product-specific features and options.

Release 12 provides many new features that ensure the overhead of administering users is kept to a minimum, including a whole new product, known as *User Management* (UMX). As shown in Figure 1-20, This includes features such as the industry standard *Role Based Access Control* (RBAC), where predefined roles are used to assign all the security required to fulfill a specific job within the organization.

Integration Technologies

While E-Business Suite is a complete set of Enterprise Application products, most organizations have specialist needs and various different software applications that help support them. This therefore brings an integration requirement. Another common situation is a splintered IT landscape where multiple business divisions are running different applications that should work together to make the overall business operate more efficiently.

In the past, E-Business Suite integration was a complex matter, involving complex customizations that were very sensitive to change. However, in the last five years or so multiple platforms have been built that offer a host of solutions that are easier to implement, more declarative to build, and have

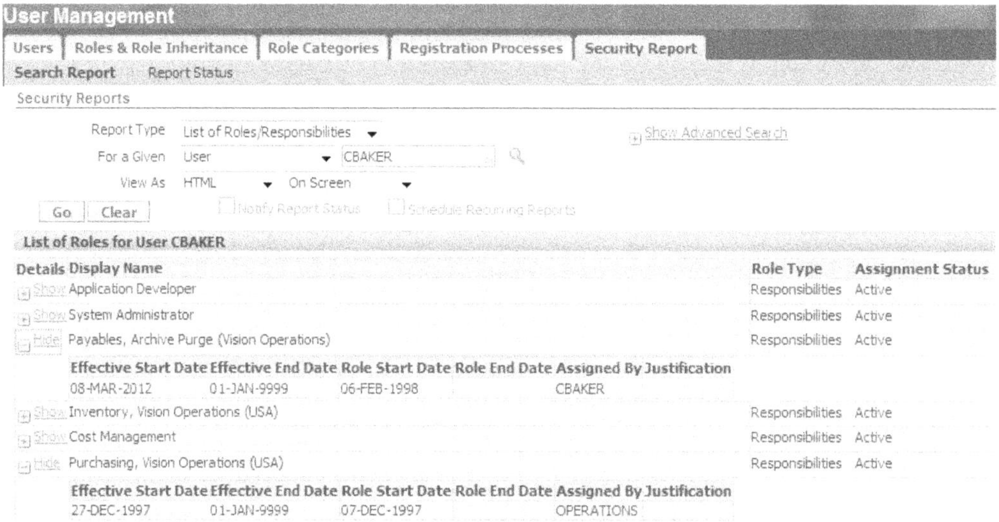

FIGURE 1-20. *The security report screen in the new User Management product*

proven to be as resilient. We'll look at these in more depth in Chapter 8, but here are a few of the main solutions:

- **Application Integration Architecture (AIA)**   A complete platform for integration between Enterprise Applications, it provides open standard business object definitions and implementation tooling, as well as a rich set of out-of-the-box integrations.

- **XML Gateway**   A native extension to many business processes, this tool permits the communication of various business transactions as Internet-based messages either directly to and from trading partners, or via a message routing hub.

- **Integrated SOA Gateway**   Introducing the latest in standards-based Oracle SOA technology, this tool exposes native E-Business Suite processes as Business Process Execution Language (BPEL) activities with web services that can be integrated with those from external sources to create a complete execution flow.

- **eCommerce Gateway**   Somewhat more traditional, this tool allows Electronic Data Interchange (EDI) messages to be generated, communicated, and consumed by related E-Business Suite products. It supports the common code message standards (EDIFACT, ASC X12, and so on) through integration with EDI translators.

The Management Infrastructure

To round off our E-Business Suite technology tour, it seems an ideal time to briefly introduce the Application Management tools that we'll be focusing on throughout this book. You'll already be familiar with some of these, and for those we'll look at recommended ways to get even more out of them. We'll also introduce some tools you might not have had the chance to use and demonstrate the major benefits they can bring to your E-Business Suite ecosystem. Here are a few examples:

- **Oracle Applications Diagnostic Framework (ODF)** The core troubleshooting capability inside E-Business Suite, this tool is well known but rarely used to its best abilities.
- **Oracle Applications DBA Utilities (AD)** Scripts and programs that are used for maintenance duties but can be extended to drive management excellence.
- **Oracle Applications Manager (OAM)** Incorporating all the management and administration features that are embedded inside the E-Business Suite product itself. This forms the heart of the management tooling, but effective and creative use has been proven to deliver unexpected benefits.
- **Oracle Enterprise Manager (OEM)** This best-in-class management tool has dozens of native features for complete management of the entire E-Business Suite technology stack.
- **Oracle Enterprise Managers Application Management Suite for Oracle E-Business Suite** A set of extensions to Enterprise Manager that helps deliver better overall application management as well as efficient and effective day-to-day operation.

Technical Evolution

It's interesting to also consider how the E-Business Suite technical components have evolved over the last few releases, from 11*i* into Release 12, and while we focus on Release 12 in this book, those still running 11*i* instances will likely appreciate a short summary of some of the key technical differences:

- Re-architecture of the applications filesystem, helping differentiate the data, techstack, and product code to support for flexible deployments
- Movement from the Apache HTTP and JServ servers to the Oracle Application Server components
- Introduction and expansion of Oracle Applications Manager functionality
- Expansion of support for newer security technologies, such as LDAP and Single Sign-on
- More migration and new features based on the OA Framework technologies
- More support for parallel and scalable features in Concurrent Processing
- Introduction of SOA technologies, supporting more business process integration
- Retirement of Oracle Reports, replaced by wholesale use of Oracle XML Publisher
- Evolution of the Business Intelligence solutions, with increased focused on Oracle BI Applications

As we move forward, it's well publicized that Release 12.2 will leverage the Fusion Middleware technology stack, including deploying the OC4J Java components of E-Business Suite via the WebLogic Server platform. This incremental adoption of the latest Oracle and Industry standard technologies opens up many opportunities for improved system management, as well as to gain practical experience of the technologies behind Fusion Applications, the eventual E-Business Suite successor that we'll discuss more in Chapter 11.

Summary

In this chapter I laid the foundations for our in-depth discussion of managing E-Business Suite. We started with some background information by looking at a history of Oracle Applications and how they have evolved to where we are today. Next, I highlighted the functional breadth of E-Business Suite (which is supported by a full blown product-by-product explanation in the appendix). Finally, I dove into the technology stack that supports E-Business Suite, where I covered each main part of the execution flow, including the user interface, the middle-tier components, the applications tier, and the database.

CHAPTER
2

Successful Enterprise Application Management

Y̶ou might be wondering how I gathered enough real-world information together to be able to advise anyone on how to manage their own application deployments. While it's true that every deployment is different (and some wildly so), there are a host of common themes and guidelines that should be shared for the benefit of everyone involved.

This section is not actually Oracle-specific and the details here could be applied to any enterprise application. In fact, I formulated these principles while I helped design the management solutions for Oracle's newest application suite, Fusion Applications. So, while the details in Chapter 5 onward are very specific to E-Business Suite, the model in which they are applied is built from proven best practices of the past together with recommendations that support the future as well.

My personal history with enterprise application goes back to my first post-graduate job as an assistant to the project team on a very large implementation project for an insurance policy administration application. Since then I've been a data analyst, an application developer, a DBA and, especially relevant to this discussion, an Application Systems Administrator and Manager.

Over the years I have worked with a range of enterprise applications, including homegrown solutions, best-of-breed niche products, and the larger Enterprise Resource Planning (ERP)-like packages such as E-Business Suite.

On top of these real-world experiences, I have spent over a dozen years helping Oracle support some of the largest organizations on the planet and ensure their own enterprise applications are successful. This hasn't been restricted to E-Business Suite either, and I've been involved in many different applications products, tools, and integrations.

Objectives: A Definition of Success and Failure

Wouldn't it be great if enterprise applications like E-Business Suite were simple systems made up of manageable groups of components easily configured to provide the precise functionality required for business operation excellence? Small software systems are actually like this, mostly closed-loop systems with modular code running over a modern, manageable, industry standard platform. Real business applications simply cannot be like this, and for some very understandable reasons.

- Real-world business operations of larger organizations are complex, constructed of hundreds of work processes and often many exceptional situations to handle.

- Real-world business structures are complex, including broad regional and international variations that need accommodating.

- Software evolves over time, adding code to deliver more features and capabilities. The more lines of code added, the more complex the system becomes.

- Each feature has its own configuration that works over the top of a base set of common configuration for the application core. As features grow, the options to configure them grow.

As a result, controlling the whole enterprise application is a bit like herding cats, where just as you get the full management of one area complete, a business change or software change means another area needs addressing. This book aims to provide an insight into what you need to do to understand the key focus areas and how you can use the E-Business Suite data and tools available to manage them now, as well as adjust to the inevitable changes to come.

Success

Clearly a subjective matter, and very much based on the perspective of those involved with the enterprise application. Consider what makes a successful patching strategy: the IT department (and vendors) would say that keeping the system as updated as possible is the optimal solution so that all known issues are eliminated. On the contrary, the business users would probably prefer a more static system, with less frequent changes and without regular and costly acceptance testing.

Success should therefore be measured against predefined and agreed targets, and as such those responsible for the enterprise application must have a defined management plan. We'll look at what goes into building this in detail in the next chapter.

Failure

While technical measures can define success, the real litmus test of failure is the impact to the business operation. These generally fall into the following broad categories:

- **Inefficiency**   Tasks are slow to perform
- **Mistakes**   Failures lead to costly delays and fixes
- **Frustration**   Tasks are complex, repetitive, or overly laborious

To help define and measure success, most organizations try to leverage some form of a service level agreement (SLA) between the business users and the IT team managing the application. These agreements very precisely define what the expectations are and exactly how they will be measured. SLAs do miss some of the aspects of planning and continuous management improvement, but we'll look at this in the next chapter.

Participants and Roles

In order to understand everything about managing E-Business Suite, or any enterprise application for that matter, let's quickly review the roles most commonly involved today.

The Systems Administrator (sysadmin)

The systems administrator is the staple of the IT department. The person in this role provides general installation, configuration, and troubleshooting for any and all technologies in use. This commonly focuses around operating systems, execution platforms, as well as more specific specializations such as networking, storage, and hardware. A traditional systems administrator would probably not be an Oracle Applications technology stack expert, but since E-Business Suite ultimately runs over the operating system and hardware, many of the traditional sysadmin skills remain essential.

Database Administrator (DBA)

At the heart of the enterprise application is the database, commonly one single instance that contains all the data for transaction data, processing, setups, and so on. Some enterprise applications also have other supporting database instances or similar data-related components like data warehouses, and all these together require a set of specialist management skills.

Traditionally, it's the database administrator who is the person most associated with looking after enterprise applications, due to their inherent data dependency. This, however, is changing somewhat for two reasons. First, processing is increasingly moving away from the database itself to more specialist components, leaving the database as just information storage. Second, the tools to manage the database are increasing in maturity, to the extent that most database systems can be fully managed from a graphical console, and increasingly all maintenance type tasks are automated.

Clearly, DBA skills remain essential to enterprise applications, and a reduction in emphasis in this area provides an opportunity for focus in other value-add activities.

Network Administrator

The connectivity that surrounds and runs through modern enterprise applications is only increasing, and in order to manage this, a reasonable level of understanding and skill by the network administrator is required. Some examples of networking touch-points are

- Distributed computing platforms, such as Service Oriented Architecture (SOA)
- Clustering of multiple software servers for performance and high-availability deployment
- Multisite data storage, which is increasingly required for regulatory compliance
- Extensive integrations to other internal and external application systems
- Multiplatform mobile device integration
- Ensuring access is controlled and appropriately secured

So, while the network administrator role is traditionally considered outside enterprise applications, as the related components and their connectivity become spread across the network (and Internet) this is changing.

Security Administrator

While security assurance is part of all IT operational roles, most large organizations have a dedicated information security group assuming the overall responsibility, headed by the security administrator. As distributed systems and remote access continues to proliferate, protecting intellectual property and corporate data from prying eyes is a high priority to everyone, from boardroom to basement, and increasingly to the public relations team!

As the business backbone, enterprise applications like E-Business Suite contain security management services that provide support for embedding safeguards, ensuring the use of compliant procedures, and monitoring for violations.

The Help Desk

The help desk team that handles and triages calls from end-users will commonly have a division that specializes in supporting all the corporate applications, including systems like E-Business Suite. They require at least basic knowledge and appropriate tooling so they can resolve as many of the easier issues as possible, such as rectifying usage mistakes, managing core data—like user accounts or making small configuration adjustments. The more complex issues and errors will get routed on to experts and respective component owners.

It's not scalable to train the central IT help desk to handle all aspects of E-Business Suite maintenance and management, but with some effective triaging and routing of problems, it can alleviate large amounts of administration and work for those down the line. We'll look at some good practices, tools, and techniques in later chapters.

Business Analysts

Today's analysts must understand the needs of their organization and be able to translate those into requirements that can be matched to IT and software solutions, commonly focused around enterprise applications like E-Business Suite.

As the flexibility and configuration options continue to increase in off-the-shelf applications (and their technology) the business analyst must have an insight beyond just the capabilities of the tooling. This is because implementing a complex solution in order to meet a very specific business need has repeatedly led to unwieldy IT deployments that are hard to manage and very costly to maintain. Many times, analysis of the logic behind a preexisting business operation reveals an opportunity to simplify the process itself, thereby simplifying the IT solution and reducing the associated costs.

Super Users

Everyday users of an enterprise application like E-Business Suite are concerned only with their business tasks and are shielded from the complexities involved in implementing and maintaining the application in the most appropriate way for them to complete those tasks.

There is commonly a set of senior roles who assume some of the functional ownership, taking responsibility for tweaking setups to make improvements and helping to resolve day-to-day business issues. As organizations constantly evolve, such as with mergers and acquisitions, this role extends well beyond initial deployment. A simple example might be adjusting the document approval hierarchy and rules so that business transactions are processed more efficiently.

These super- or power-users are provided additional privileges to access tools and data to fulfill these duties. They are often defined based on subject matter expertise, such as having one per organizational department or per subdivision within the application itself, such as for Financials, Manufacturing, and Human Resources.

A New Hybrid Role

The enterprise application manager (or management team) needs to be a jack-of-all-trades, possessing a range of skills and knowledge from the roles mentioned so far. That said, the shallow level required shouldn't make this impractical and allows for the specialization on E-Business Suite's own unique component set—items such as Concurrent Manager, for example.

Just to be clear, and as you can observe from Figure 2-1, the discussion here centers on job roles, not specific individual people. This means that one role might cover a whole team of people, such as the help desk, whereas other roles form only part of one person's responsibilities, such as a system administrator who is also responsible for information security.

You'll see later how, with the right tools and practices, the roles involved in E-Business Suite management can be enhanced so that the outcome is one of continuous improvements rather than just keeping the lights on.

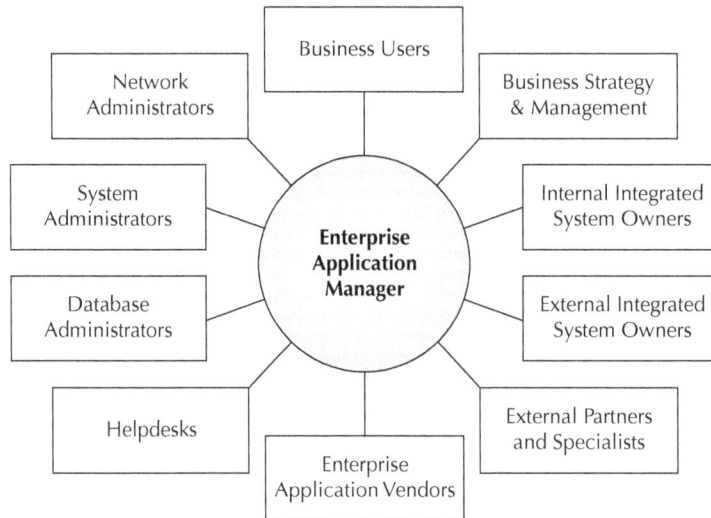

FIGURE 2-1.   *The roles around the enterprise application*

Cloud Manager Role

With the increasing popularity of cloud-based enterprise application consumption (also called Software-as-a-Service, or SaaS), you might be thinking, "But none of this applies if I've got a cloud solution." Big mistake! Just like any service delivery, you need to continuously monitor to make sure the vendor is delivering the things you expect and need, and take action if they don't.

Don't let it be the end users that report issues to you (that's very expensive); the effective solution is to be proactive. What a cloud service gets rid of are the humdrum daily management tasks, but it actually requires something new: really good service management. We'll touch on managing cloud services in Chapter 11.

The Enterprise Application Model: Five Core Principles

Making sure all aspects of managing a larger software application like E-Business Suite, which might have thousands of users in multiple countries and be central to the day-to-day running of an entire organization, is a huge and daunting task.

Like all of these monstrous tasks, chunking (breaking it down into smaller more manageable parts) is a great solution. To do this we'll use the five tenets of enterprise application management shown in Figure 2-2, discuss each in turn, and then in subsequent chapters provide clear illustrations of how the techniques and tooling from E-Business Suite can be leveraged to execute in those areas.

FIGURE 2-2. *The five principles of enterprise application management*

Reliability

Let's start the discussion with our own definition of reliability:

To ensure that the features consistently operate as intended.

It hardly needs spelling out, but successful organizations don't run unreliable business applications. Indeed the quality of the business operation is directly influenced by the quality of its infrastructure, including the business applications. Lack of reliability has the following obvious effects:

- It frustrates business users who cannot complete their assigned tasks efficiently and to their own satisfaction.

- It stifles the completion of core business processes, such as halting production, slowing sales generation and fulfillment, and impacting payments and revenue collection.

- It inhibits external integration, such as unreliable supplier invoice processing creating the foundation for an increasingly negative relationship.

Obviously, some failures in code execution may be caused by product defects (bugs), but for mature products like E-Business Suite this is less frequent, and it's more often due to setup and configuration issues and environmental issues like service interruptions, data issues, invalid usage, and bad custom code.

Within the reliability principle there are three main actionable areas, illustrated in Figure 2-3, where management excellence can be achieved.

Resource Management

Many failures occur at the point of resource interruption or depletion, with common limits bound to items like hardware (CPU, memory, I/O, disk, and so on), infrastructure (networking throughput/bandwidth, and bottlenecks or capacities of integrated systems), and pure configuration-based resources such as the JVM heap size.

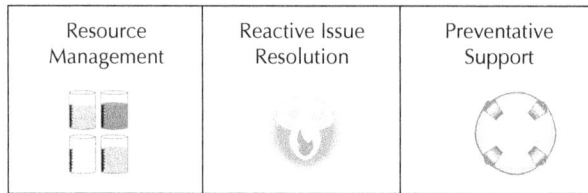

Resource Management	Reactive Issue Resolution	Preventative Support

FIGURE 2-3. *Components of reliability management*

It is therefore down to the application manager to implement the appropriate capacity planning, to understand the resource dependencies of the application features, and to include active monitoring containing items like threshold-based alerts and automated recovery rules.

With many different technology stack components in E-Business Suite, resourcing and monitoring this infrastructure is especially complex. We'll consider each area and the best tools available in Chapter 6.

Reactive Issue Resolution

Processing failures, errors, and other problems will inevitably occur, whatever the cause may be, and the more complex or cryptic their symptoms the more likely they'll involve those responsible for the enterprise application. Generally speaking these fall into two broad buckets:

- **Questions** These issues tend to be "how do I ..." type enquiries. While most questions based on functional processes should be handled by business domain experts (super users or the helpdesk), occasionally the requirement involves working with a lower level component. Examples might be, "How do I add a new field to this page?" or, "How do I remove this mistaken entry from the system?"

- **Break-fix problems** Warnings, errors, and unexpected results do occur from time to time. Unless the cause is a user's mistake that is readily explained, the application manager is often required. Ideally the symptoms, known as a *problem signature*, point close to the root cause (and solution). However, skills in troubleshooting, researching, execution analysis, and general technical know-how remain essential.

Preventative Support

Efforts to determine known solutions before they actually become serious problems are rarely a waste of time, and modern enterprise applications (like E-Business Suite) come with features that provide access to this kind of information.

Known solutions come in the form of patches, scripts, and a whole host of diagnostic tools that check the system for known issues such as code bugs, bad configurations, and missing or corrupt data.

Obviously, the extent of the system reliability is dependent on the proliferation of internal problems like these, so a proactive enterprise application manager will leverage tools and processes to make sure information is frequently reviewed and preventative actions are taken. Don't assume this will occur, however; dedicated time should be set aside to be proactive. Keeping above the curve creates a healthy system and avoids dropping into the hamster-wheel of handling one problem after another.

Other Reliability Engagements

Other problem-based tasks that the enterprise application manager will occasionally get involved in include

- Following up on service level agreement violations
- Acting as liaison for the troubleshooting of integrated systems
- Acting as liaison with infrastructure teams to validate their reliability issues and solutions
- Effectively routing problems to other subject matter experts
- Creating and sharing important knowledge and experience
- Engaging in future application development and evolution

Chapter 6 delves into understanding, monitoring, and managing reliability for E-Business Suite. In Chapter 11, we'll look at best practices for dealing with the reactive workload and demonstrate practical ways to prevent it from giving the feeling of constantly firefighting and allow more time for other value-add activities.

Availability

Let's start our discussion with a definition of availability:

Ensure that all features are available whenever and wherever.

Just as with the need for a reliable application, an application that is rarely available is frustrating. Clearly, lack of availability can be an extreme case of reliability issues (that is, an especially catastrophic failure), but there may be a number of other causes for general availability problems, such as:

- Scheduled and emergency maintenance
- Network accessibility issues
- Performance issues
- Application integration issues

It's also interesting to note that these days few organizations have alternative offline procedures to complete tasks that are normally completed in the enterprise application, except perhaps a few in military and medical industries.

As shown in Figure 2-4, there are three main areas of availability focus in respect to enterprise applications.

Continuity

Unexpected situations do occur, notwithstanding acts of God, and the enterprise application manager must maintain a detailed plan to provide uninterrupted service, especially for those features that are core to the business operation.

Organizations should already have something called a *Business Continuity Plan*, which in the case of IT will refer to a detailed disaster recovery plan, but it will also include the planning for non-IT related areas such as personnel, facilities, and crisis communication and reputation protection.

By definition, a disaster recovery plan includes the resumption of applications but also includes all data, hardware, communications and networking, and other key IT infrastructure. This is formulated based on the Business Continuity Plan's definitions of the priority of the business

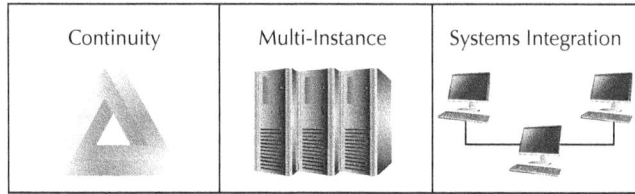

Continuity	Multi-Instance	Systems Integration

FIGURE 2-4. *The components of availability management*

processes that must be maintained. Then, for those dependent on IT, pairs of metrics are created, namely the *recovery point objective* and the *recovery time objective*—these are quite simply what functions need restoring and by when. Once these requirements are clear, subject matter experts and feature owners work out and test the most effective solutions and procedures.

In addition to these principles, the real world dictates that budgetary data should also be introduced. While it would be ideal to have the very best high availability tooling for all processes, the cost of maintaining this for an event that might never occur needs factoring in. It would also be nice to be able to factor in the probability and likelihood of each particular disaster type, but these are so speculative that it's rarely practical.

So, based on these factors, the disaster recovery plan is constructed, signed off on, tested and verified, and implemented. Obviously, dry runs and ongoing continuity management (taking backups, managing storage, testing failover) also needs factoring into the overall application management duties.

Industry standards and best practices are available for disaster recovery; Figure 2-5 shows the *Seven Tiers of Disaster Recovery*, illustrating the categories of restorative solutions that may be considered, starting with simple tape backups (stored on-site, then off-site), on to RAID-type disk

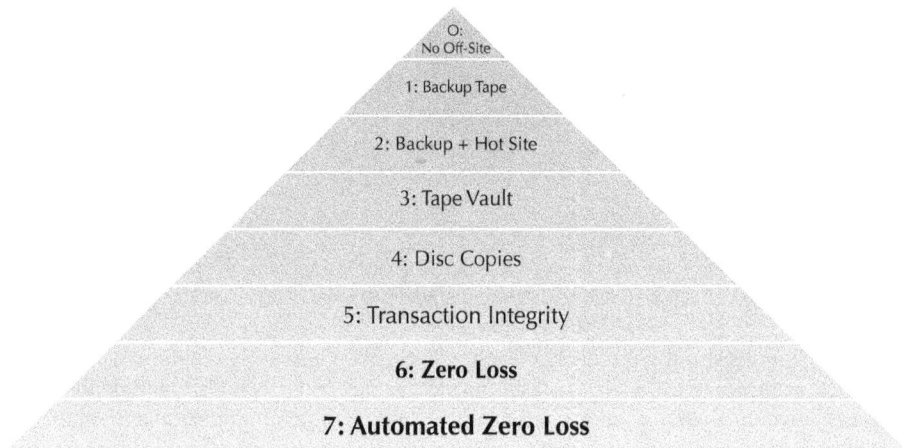

FIGURE 2-5. *The Seven Tiers of Disaster Recovery*

mirroring, to online storage and recovery via Storage Area Networks (SANs), and all the way into real-time redundancy and automated fail-over capabilities.

Specialist third-party providers do exist for complete disaster recovery management (for example, complete site redundancy), allowing standardized solutions to be used for the many applications an organization may have. This helps support broad IT landscapes and can simplify the task considerably. However this will also add additional costs and, of course, applying broad services may not support all organization-specific requirements.

Although the detailed process for defining a complete disaster recovery plan for your organization is beyond the scope of this short discussion, the Oracle technology stack under E-Business Suite has various high-availability tools available, and we'll look at these and related strategies in Chapter 6.

Multi-Instance Availability

In addition to managing the availability of the live production instance, organizations will commonly require multiple additional instances for various purposes, such as testing and custom development. Creating and maintaining the availability of the following three types is recommended, and there may be several instances of each.

- ■ **Preproduction instance**   A complete copy of the production instance, it replicates the same setup and data for use in areas such as training new users and testing new features and datasets. It is usually carefully controlled and refreshed regularly. While a formal preproduction instance may seem like overkill, the extra confidence and production-like verification of changes are significant advantages.

- ■ **Test instance**   This is a sandbox-type instance, used for many different purposes such as trying new setups, testing new features and custom developments, and testing the impact of patches and upgrades. Its data will be periodically refreshed from the other instances, and active test execution should be supported by usage guidelines.

- ■ **Development instances**   Provisioned for use by development teams to deploy their new extensions and customizations, these may also be used for trailing advanced technical configurations as well as new integration solutions. Also periodically refreshed with trail data, they should be controlled so that the complex and expensive development work is properly managed.

Systems Integration Availability

While E-Business Suite supports hundreds of core business processes, integration with organization-specific applications is commonplace, and clearly that connectivity needs managing, including deployment, monitoring for issues, and troubleshooting failures. Therefore, the key integrations need to be designed with availability management in mind, well written and tested, and properly understood and documented. We'll look at management solutions to support E-Business Suite's integration capabilities in various chapters throughout the rest of this book, but let's briefly describe what I mean and some of the overall capabilities.

Internal Systems Integration   This is the integration of E-Business Suite with other applications running in the organization. This may be a legacy system that performs a core function or smaller specialist solutions and homegrown programs to support a specific need. Examples include shop-floor manufacturing programs, service administration tools like insurance policy management, or other solutions like website order capture and those used at a physical point-of-sale.

In addition to links to other applications, it's common to integrate the enterprise application into general worker productivity solutions, such as portal-based dashboards, custom administration and productivity tools, and expert knowledge systems. Although these integrations may seem smaller, the same standardized management approach should be taken to ensure their successful availability.

In discussing integrations, I should mention Oracle's Application Integration Architecture (AIA), which allows E-Business Suite to integrate to other Oracle and third-party applications by introducing a layer of industry standard definitions and related technologies such as Services Oriented Architecture (SOA).

External Systems Integration   Moving beyond internal integrations, enterprise applications like E-Business Suite are designed to support reducing costs by automatically sharing information with external parties, including customers, suppliers, and various other partner organizations. Examples include orders for acknowledgment and fulfillment, shipment notices for future deliveries, invoices for paying, and manufacturing production plans for scheduling.

These transaction-based messages passed between integrated systems need processing in an efficient and fault-tolerant way to avoid manual intervention that may put a high-volume organization at a virtual standstill. In addition, integration may not be peer-to-peer, as central integration hubs exist (such as banking services, tax-calculation engineers, Amazon Marketplace or eBay, and Oracle's own B2B supplier network) that bring significant business benefits while often extending the application manager's role.

Also increasing dramatically in popularity is a hybrid integration scenario where parts (or all) of the enterprise application are hosted by a third-party provider, eliminating much of the overall maintenance overhead. Where this is used extensively, the enterprise application management role becomes mainly concerned with managing the integrations to and from the hosted systems. Most organizations adopt a mixed approach, where some services are provided as cloud-based, while legacy or core parts are kept in-house. Managing this is something we'll revisit in Chapter 12.

Performance

Once again, we'll begin with our own definition of performance:

**The ability to ensure that all work can be completed
within an acceptable timescale.**

It's well known that poor performance (anything beyond immediate response) is the biggest reason for web-application drop-off and failed enterprise application user adoption. Indeed, after just a few seconds we all start to re-press buttons, re-click links, and generally become impatient. While the reason for slightly slower performance may be logical, such as a large and complex transaction, users do not care and resent having to use a system that doesn't respond quickly.

It helps to encourage software developers to create a better user experience that promotes the consideration of new technologies and forces the enterprise application manager to make sure the service is adequately resourced and configured. Together, the focus on speed helps drive overall productivity, which is never a bad thing.

Let's discuss enterprise application performance in a little more detail here and then, in Chapter 7, we'll look at specific monitoring and troubleshooting tools that exist for use with E-Business Suite.

Performance Types

Enterprise application performance data can be grouped into three distinct types, and understanding these can help you envision a more complete picture for implementing performance management plans and solutions.

- **Failures** Connections and processes take an extended period of time to complete, or never actually do, and an internal timeout or low-level termination occurs. While these hangs, freezes, and technical errors should be appropriately handled by the application code, they may still cause severe consequences within an enterprise application, such as data corruption, unexpected process termination, and the loss of the entered data.

- **Peaks and troughs** Performance thresholds should be set against anticipated load and, when violated, investigation should occur to determine why. Clearly, bad performance represents a trough in most measurements; peaks in performance may signify underutilized resources that could be redeployed elsewhere.

- **Bottlenecks** Performance data should be interpreted against the execution of a business process flow, such as the process of the creation of an order. This data can then be analyzed to determine which parts of the key processes may represent a bottleneck and, if improved, will deliver the most value to business users.

Let's also look at a quick overview of the areas where performance management is especially important for the management of an enterprise application, as this does differ from how a system administrator or DBA would approach the same subject. This demarcation, illustrated in Figure 2-6, may also help prevent the duplication of effort.

Business Process

Business process performance is measured against service level agreements (or something similar) that are related not to IT metrics but to those from business task completion. The enterprise application manager therefore needs to understand how technology performance affects the

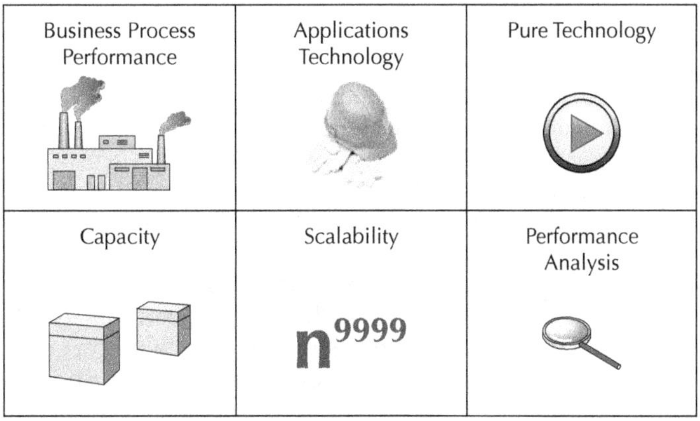

Business Process Performance	Applications Technology	Pure Technology
Capacity	Scalability n^{9999}	Performance Analysis

FIGURE 2-6. *The components of performance management*

features and functions end users see. Examples include transaction creation time, data processing time, and approval processing, in addition to infrastructure pieces like e-mail notification delivery.

Although logical on the surface, these items are tough to measure accurately, since end user functionality is made up of many technologies and code execution processes, bound by different datasets and configurations, all called in different usage scenarios. As a simple example, a report showing on-hand inventory for one small store might be quick to calculate, but the same report requested for the full organization that includes many stores, warehouses, and in-transit items will take considerably more processing effort.

Applications Technology

Working down a level in the technology stack, the measurements of applications technology performance help support the analysis of business process performance. However, where there are gaps, these detailed metrics can be used to quickly identify a performance problem in the application (and then the manifestation of that can be extrapolated).

Examples include the response times for the application UI pages, application program execution metrics, internal engine performance data, and internal applications connectivity rates.

As we go deeper into the technology, subject matter experts may be consulted. This means root causes and solutions can be quickly identified without the enterprise application manager either testing solutions that might have undesirable consequences or spending a long time reading up.

Pure Technology Performance

At the bottom of the technology stack are the basic components, like databases, software servers, operating systems, networking switches and routers, and of course, server hardware. Clearly, these will be monitored for performance, again feeding into reports and analysis of the layers above and still accessible in native view for areas that don't easily roll up for root cause analysis and troubleshooting.

These application foundations come with sets of performance management and monitoring tools of their own, and the enterprise application manager just needs to focus on understanding what they show (and knowing where to go if they don't) and integrate the data with the holistic management plan.

The Capacity for Performance

Beyond looking through the technology stack for performance metrics, the enterprise application manager needs to ensure that the system has the resources available to deliver the performance targets set. Indeed, the cause of performance issues is split between reliability problems like software bugs or configuration mistakes and inadequately provisioned resources of one kind or another.

While some resource sizing guidance comes from the vendor's minimum system recommendations (and similar benchmark data), there should be a full *Capacity Plan* available that explains both the current values, the knobs-and-dials that affect which features, and some aspect of projected system load calculated from system usage profiles (with near-, medium-, and long-term projections). This plan should form the heart of nonreliability-related performance management and should be constantly reviewed and maintained to keep it current, especially as the profile and needs of the business alter (for example, a merger brings in 50 percent more users).

The resources involved in the Capacity Plan should also be managed in terms of their lifecycle, and as such the enterprise application manager needs to actively monitor not only what resources to help maintain performance, but also where these stand in their maturity.

Interestingly, the average lifespan of hardware servers is estimated at between three and five years, and together with all the other components (storage drives, network routers/switches, and so on), plus the software installed (operating systems, database, middleware, applications), recording the component and overall reliability using a measure like mean time to failure (MTTF) becomes an interesting factor to consider. We'll look at lifecycles in Chapter 4.

Scalability

In enterprise applications, scalability describes how the allocated resources are used based on changes in load (also known as *utilization*), and how efficiently additional resources can be added or removed. In the modern IT landscape, innovations such as virtualization and cloud-related dynamic resource allocation technologies provide new options for organizations to better manage their resource infrastructure.

Most enterprise applications are built to leverage scalable architectures and components, and I'll illustrate some of these in Chapter 7.

Performance Analysis

In addition to monitoring, the enterprise application manager should engage in regular statistical analysis methods to compare and contrast performance metrics between systems, configurations, time, and numerous other environment variables. This represents an optimization project, something we'll discuss shortly and look at in detail in Chapter 8.

Likewise, performance management must be set up properly so that all the moving parts are passively monitored and require intervention only when problematic trends and early-warning alerts are triggered. Clearly, no one will sit and watch charts and graphs all day, so the better this is implemented the better the overall management will be. Chapter 7 will illustrate the options for E-Business Suite.

Optimization

Once again, let's start by defining what optimization means in this context.

To ensure that the software helps meet the organizational expectations and objectives.

By reducing the administration overhead of managing the reliability, availability, and performance of the enterprise application, there should be more time for positive tasks that help improve the service delivered to the business, such as offering productivity features, increased processing efficiency, or perhaps offering new business intelligence insights.

The six types of activities that fall into the optimization category are illustrated in Figure 2-7 and described here, with Chapter 8 detailing the techniques and tools available within E-Business Suite to achieve results.

Improvement Projects

The expectations of the enterprise application need to be static for the purpose of management and reporting (such as for SLAs), but this should be fixed for the short to medium term only; a strong desire to evolve and expand the targets and capabilities is an essential part of the management strategy.

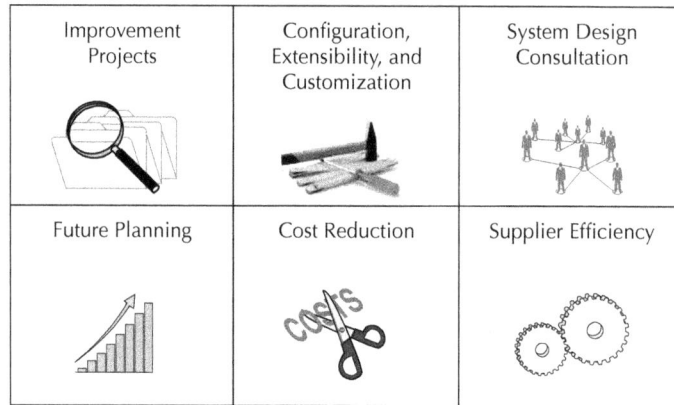

FIGURE 2-7. *The components of optimization management*

Resources should be dedicated to analyzing the areas where the benefits from improvements will be the greatest, determining a precise set of requirements, and researching the potential solutions.

Some examples include adopting new business features (where expertise permits); making adjustments in configuration to existing software, hardware, and supporting infrastructure; and making (certified) changes to the underlying technology stack.

Future Planning

The IT landscape is in constant change as organizations look to gain advantages from better internal services and solutions. Packaged enterprise applications like E-Business Suite are also constantly evolving, with new releases adding new features all the time.

The application manager needs to ensure he or she is aware of what is coming and optimize the plans, such as making sure that changes complement (and don't exacerbate) other changes, such as technology upgrades or business process alterations.

Configuration, Extensibility, and Customization

Enterprise applications need to be flexible in order to meet the needs of different organizations across varied industries. While essential, this flexibility adds considerable management complexity, and high quality control and knowledge systems are essential to optimize the associated additional costs.

Here are some examples of the areas where the enterprise application manager needs to ensure appropriate tools and techniques are employed.

- **Planning** Before building any new solution, there should be consultation on its manageability and an effort should be made to uncover any hitherto unforeseen risks.
- **Documentation** All alterations to the standard application must be documented based on a standard, to ensure consistency and completeness. The resulting knowledge must be kept and maintained in a single repository with good accessibility when required.

- **Standards** All additional code should be based on well-known development standards defined by both the enterprise application vendor (for example, OA Framework for E-Business Suite) or internally by the organization. This includes items such as:

  - Design patterns

  - Development languages and methodologies

  - Correct use of utility and common code libraries

  - Exception handling and diagnostics

  - Developer IDEs and toolsets

  - Comprehensive system testing processes and tools

Supporting customizations can add significant management costs and, while really this falls into governance, it's important to make sure that the best tooling and processes are employed—that is, it should be something that can be optimized in most organizations.

System Design Consultation

Almost all changes to the infrastructure around and within the enterprise application should go through a due diligence check for impact and risk assessment.

With such broad functionality, technology, and user interactions in modern enterprise applications, it can be hard for those not engaged directly with the enterprise application to appreciate how different changes may have an impact. A simple example might be network security adjustments that could easily block integration messaging without proper consultation and testing against the enterprise application.

Cost Reduction

In today's economy, organizations must squeeze as much value from their IT investments as possible, and the flipside of optimizing gains is reducing costs, especially as it's commonly known that more than 70 percent of the IT budget is spent on maintaining existing systems and applications.

Interestingly, the two most expensive parts of an enterprise application in terms of ongoing overhead are the electricity consumption it entails and the payroll of those supporting it. The good news is that application and infrastructure vendors are aware of this, and modern management tooling does have some interesting measurements of power consumption and utilization rates, as well as analysis of problem management. The analysis of this data provides the potential for cost optimization, especially with the increase in alternative outsourcing solutions available.

Supplier Efficiency

Enterprise applications are never self-contained or stand-alone systems; they're driven by data moving in and out and run over a broad IT infrastructure. As such, many of the dependent components are owned by other parties, and the better the working relationships, the better the whole management process operates. Examples include outsourcing and cloud service companies, implementation partners, specialist consultants, hardware and networking vendors, and the packaged enterprise application vendor themselves.

The same is true internally, where internal teams like IT divisions, business departments, or project teams control important knowledge or access to dependent components. The more open and collaborative the interactions between these team can be, the more optimized the management becomes.

Governance

For one last term, let's start with defining what we mean by governance.

To ensure that features and data are available only to authorized users.

As ultimate custodian and guardian of the application, the management process must address various aspects of governance in a complete yet pragmatic manner. We'll address the tools to do this in Chapter 9, but as illustrated in Figure 2-8 there are four main dimensions to consider.

Security

Security is clearly exceptionally important, even more so than availability. While the enterprise application manager may not include the entire information security role, it will include many aspects of enforcing and governing the tools and techniques put in place. Here are a just a few areas of security related to enterprise applications (indeed, few aspects are not related!):

- **Business user security** Monitoring and auditing of the granting of appropriate data and function access to users, either automatically or as part of administrative duties.

- **Intrusion detection** Preventing unauthorized access to functions or data, from either internal or external origins. Should these be attempted, early warning systems should trigger alerts and ideally prevent any further exploitation. This also includes ensuring audit data supports post-incident investigation.

- **Network security** Normally beyond the remit of the application itself, the interception of traffic as its flows between integrated systems does occur, and as such, an appropriate liaison with related experts is needed and may include implementation of safeguards and monitoring.

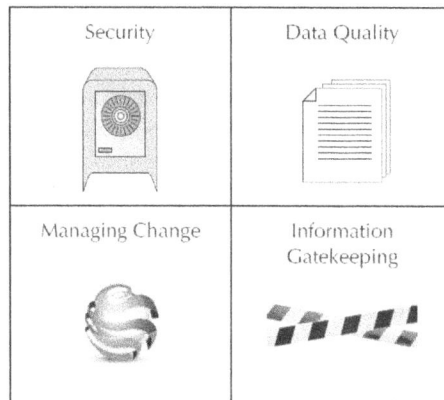

FIGURE 2-8. *The components of governance management*

- **Exported data**   The discovery of sensitive datasets from lost laptops and flash drives are frequently headline news, so careful consideration needs to be made by both IT and business managers as to how data can be exported and by whom. The enterprise application manager should consider implementing best practices like audit trails and data encryption. This includes not just data dumps like backups or archive files, but creating standard guidelines for corporate data republished in formats like reports, e-mails, blog posts, wiki pages, and other media.

- **Integration**   Clearly all the entry and exit points of the enterprise application should apply the same security rules.

- **Physical security**   While definitely outside the day-to-day responsibility of the application manager, controlling access to the related hardware and infrastructure remains part of an effective application management plan.

Data Quality

While a DBA might be the expert on the database technology, the data stored by the enterprise application also needs a certain amount of management to help ensure things like security and processing speed. This means looking out for potential duplication, redundancy, and corruption, as well as trying to understand and optimize data utilization.

As you'll see in Chapter 9, modern enterprise applications like E-Business Suite have *Master Data Management* (MDM) tools that address common problems such as stale and duplicated business data—for example, suppliers that exist in payment systems, order processing, and external marketing tools. As these three identical records get updated independently, it becomes hard to be sure which is accurate.

MDM tools help identify duplication, consolidate and cleanse old data, and create a single-source-of-truth record. They then synchronize that record (and future updates) across all of the application features, keeping everything consistent.

MDM solutions may also extend into data quality, as a system with poor data quality will be of little use to anyone. Outdated, corrupt, missing, or simply incorrect data can occur, usually as a factor of overly complex processes and the introduction of external factors like integrations and customizations.

Early warning signs of data issues that may be candidates for optimization can be found through looking at reliability patterns, such as errors in certain data-intensive work, or studying the performance and data usage profiles.

Similarly, causes of data issues are varied, such as severe failures midprocess that leave training or orphaned records, mistakes in data manipulation scripts, imported data from poor quality sources, unvalidated data coming through integrations, and abandoned or incomplete feature setups that leave malformed reference data.

Another aspect of what we're calling data quality here is old data that isn't needed anymore and should be either archived or purged from the system. Without proper management, this can grow and grow until it starts to impact the resources available to the system. Examples include logs, reports, processing records, and export files.

We'll look at the technology stack and E-Business Suite's own tools for data management and consider how to make sure you have all of them configured and scheduled for use at appropriate points in the upcoming chapters.

Information Gatekeeping

Information gatekeeping is not security, which includes data authentication and authorization, and it's not data management, which is about the quality and organization of all data. Information gatekeeping is about how effectively the right information is provided to the right person at the right time and in the right way.

Sure, the majority of this is built into the enterprise application itself, but custom reporting, flexible dashboards, business intelligence, enterprise performance management, and all manner of other solutions exist that center around making sure the roles and requirements that exist within each unique organization have what they need to be effective.

This isn't limited to business data either; technical staff need information to be able to do their jobs, such as resolving reliability issues and analyzing performance. Also, many organizations have to report very specific compliance data to regulatory authorities and internal review boards.

So as these tailored information solutions (including third-party solutions) are applied over the enterprise application, there is an important requirement to assist in the design, implementation, and management of these tools. The role demands to both satisfy the requests from the business, while balancing the implicit costs and manageability of the solutions available.

Managing Change

Just keeping the enterprise application running means constant change, from patches and updates to new features and adjusted business needs. All this change needs management, usually not especially involved; often record keeping and configuration management is adequate.

Change management is a major focus in IT, and most vendors provide tools and methodologies to help. The use of these often centralized tools to plan, track, and audit changes within the enterprise application is another important governance task.

One specific aspect of enterprise application change that is often overlooked by those outside involvement is that change implies both technology changes (patches, configurations) as well as more functional changes (process setup changes or large scale data changes).

Obviously, changes need controlling to ensure that certification standards are adhered to, change requests are reviewed against intended designs, and other guidelines are followed, such as the policy regarding the introduction of third-party software.

Changes obviously need proper review and sign-off by subject matter experts, and while sometimes this is the enterprise application manager, other times it will require deeper technology knowledge (such as a request to open a firewall port for a new integration) as well as functional and business assessment (such as changing approval process rules).

While this book does not include detailed instructions on installation, deployment, and upgrades, clearly these are significant change management events, and the use of best practices and planning is strongly recommended. Some of the dozens of tools we'll discuss in this book can be leveraged in these cases, but we won't go into detail, because to make an incomplete attempt to cover this large area would simply add confusion and be of little practical use.

Flexible Principles

When discussing these principles we often use vague unbounded statements, including words like "intended," "expected," and "acceptable." This is necessary because every E-Business Suite implementation is unique and therefore must establish its own detailed definitions based on its unique requirements and relative priorities.

For example, one organization might specify that the complete production instance availability should be no less than 99.9 percent (known as "three nines") of the scheduled up time, whereas another organization might break it down to say the customer facing CRM-related features are critical and need 99.99 percent availability ("four nines"), whereas other back-office features are fine with 99.0 percent ("two nines").

Similarly, specific key features will be important to different organizations, for example, the performance of the Payables invoice submission process should always be between 0 and 2 seconds for an organization that has many sensitive suppliers to pay, but it is of no special concern to most other organizations, where it falls into a general performance requirement of all forms responses in less than four seconds.

The idea of flexible principles can be applied to each of the five principles we've discussed— *Reliability, Availability, Performance, Optimization and Governance*—and of course, this kind of detailed breakdown can get unwieldy to manage. However, we'll look later at some tools that are specifically designed for this purpose.

Summary

Having looked at exactly what we mean by managing an enterprise application and the different parties and stakeholders involved, it's clear that assigned individuals or a team needs a broad understanding of complex technologies, clarity about the organization's real-world business processes and objectives, and the extraordinary ability to be able to translate one into the other.

We defined a model, as shown again in Figure 2-9, that allows us to consider and design a management plan that includes all the key aspects of enterprise application management, and we discussed the five main principle areas so you'll know precisely what we're trying to achieve.

With the basic E-Business Suite overview given in Chapter 1, and the new model for application management in this chapter, we can move forward to look at exactly how it can be applied to quickly achieve real-world results.

FIGURE 2-9. *The five principles of enterprise application management*

CHAPTER
3

Oracle E-Business Suite
Management Lifecycle

A s the IT industry matures, the more popular models for managing the related infrastructure have become those based on an evolutionary approach, recognizing that success comes from maximizing the existing investment over the complete lifespan of each component. This allows for both real-time management and some degree of future planning.

To illustrate why this works, let's take the analogy of the simple human lifecycle. Visualize how an infant changes into a child, grows to become a teenager, and then matures into an adult. By understanding and analyzing each of these phases of progression, it's easy to gain a clear and more complete understanding of the entity in question.

The real key to successfully leveraging these generic lifecycle-type models in application management is to absorb the underlying knowledge they provide and then to build on top your own specific set of requirements and goals that are accurate, measurable, and directly applicable.

As outlined in the broad IT solution lifecycle shown in Figure 3-1, these models help organizations to make the right decisions early, provide a path to follow as solutions are constructed and implemented, and even assist with decommissioning when components are no longer of use.

These models also allow individual systems to be easily recognized based on their maturity through the lifecycle and ensure that appropriate considerations and actions are being taken at each evolutionary stage. IT is a dynamic field, and software tools are becoming more and more like replaceable commodities. The challenge this presents is overcome by lifecycle-based models as they provide a guided path and tracking mechanism that managers can use to ensure that their systems remain up to date and are the best they can be for the business.

IT management has traditionally been rather ad hoc, based around internal processes and procedures that have evolved over time, often through bitter experience. With the advent of more IT management lifecycle models, any organization now has access to what is generally regarded as industry best practices, as validated by the fact that the most successful organizations frequently admit to their use.

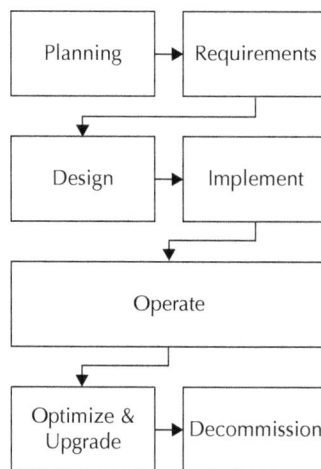

FIGURE 3-1. *A basic software application lifecycle*

Generally speaking, lifecycle models are also reasonably complete, representing the standard needs of most organizations, and can be applicable to both the Chief Technical Officer (CTO) and the software engineer. For IT management in particular, the wealth of all-encompassing frameworks that are appearing proves they're certainly in vogue. It remains early days for many of these models, however, and their evolution continues as they adapt to the new technologies and operating models they attempt to support.

Example Lifecycle Models

Let's take a look at some of the more popular lifecycle models that are used by IT departments today. The most common areas where well-used lifecycle models exist are in the related worlds of software development, information management, performance management, and IT service management.

In addition to providing useful general background information, this section helps illustrate the key parts and components of lifecycle models, and from this we can begin to formulate our own model for use with enterprise applications.

Software Development Lifecycles

Clearly, applications originate from, and evolve through, a development process, so it makes sense to look at this to begin with. Most of the dozens of different development lifecycle approaches terminate after the go-live date of the software application, carefully avoiding getting involved in maintaining and supporting the products they create.

Another factor is that with an enterprise application, the development methodologies that may get used in its initial creation may need to change as the product evolves, especially in products like E-Business Suite where architectures, technologies, approaches, tools, and even coding languages have changed significantly since its inception. It's also true that when a product suite spans many different development teams, the development methodologies can vary somewhat, even while sticking to the same design patterns.

The different development methodologies and lifecycles have their own strengths and weaknesses, and their suitability is often best determined by the properties of the task at hand. Since most development models originate from the generic Software Development Lifecycle (SDLC), let's look at a few popular examples.

The Waterfall Model

This traditional model, first described in the 1970s, is based on a sequential set of predefined activities that logically feed off each other to achieve an end result.

As shown in Figure 3-2, the process begins with the analysis and specification of the base requirements, upon which a full design is written. This is then implemented through coding, and integrations are built. The system is then tested and validated before live deployment to end users and the final maintenance stage is reached. A detailed review marks the end of each phase and is used to validate that all work is complete so the next phase can begin.

Although reasonably comprehensive and offering a logical process flow, the waterfall model is often criticized because of its structured and formal nature. This is usually based on the fact that retrospective adjustments are difficult to implement because past phases cannot be easily revisited. We'll consider these points later on.

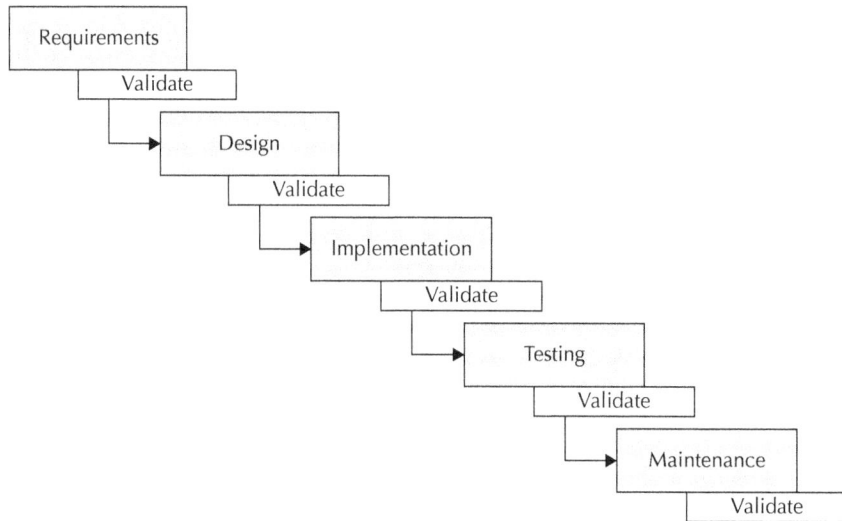

FIGURE 3-2. *The waterfall development lifecycle*

Iterative Development

Replacing the sequential nature of the waterfall model are several development approaches that perform each task in the development process several times, refining and improving the final solution each time. These lead with what is commonly known as Rapid Application Development (RAD) models.

This works by defining basic outlines first and, upon basic code completion, very early testing by users provides clear feedback on any major changes and extensions that are needed. The repeated cycling through the requirements, design, testing, and evaluation phases uses small subsets of features, allowing each iteration to be relatively quick.

The goal is to spend as little time as possible investing time and expense in writing large portions of code that might have to be reworked. The repeated testing inevitably also helps ensure the final product truly meets the users requirements. Although traditionally limited in their project scope, iterative development projects are often continuously expanded, building on past successes and finally resulting in reasonably broad results.

As an example, agile development models include feedback mechanisms between iterations, further reducing the traditional structures that can prevent testing information flowing back into the process.

One example is the extreme programming model, which starts by taking the understood requirement and building the basic test plans to be used later. By outlining these validation routines early on, you can immediately focus the development effort. Then, after the routines are implemented (and the test plan run), the other stages such as design are completed. This seems odd compared with sequential methods, but it is surprisingly effective and popular.

Another popular method, shown in Figure 3-3, is the scrum model, which has requirements listed out into a *backlog* and specific items that are chosen to be completed within a short coding

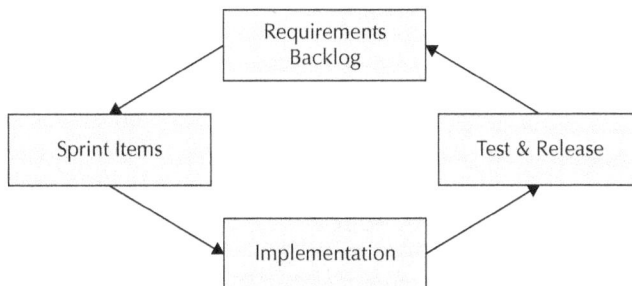

FIGURE 3-3. *An outline of the scrum agile model*

window, commonly just a few weeks long, known as a *sprint*. Once this is complete, a short testing cycle is done, and then the next set of items from the backlog is determined and addressed.

Again, note how this circular process aims to break down complex applications requirements into approachable chunks, so step-by-step progress is made and continuously validated.

Application Lifecycle Model (ALM)

From the name alone, the application lifecycle model (ALM) sounds like the most applicable model to managing enterprise software applications; however, upon closer inspection, you can see that this is not entirely the case. ALMs are based on the same principles as the rest of the models in this chapter: for an enterprise application to be properly managed, it must be based on a predefined set of rules, activities, and processes.

Unfortunately, there are no universal ALM models, and the majority of ALM content tends to focus on specific software vendor tools, such as Microsoft's Visual Studio Application Lifecycle Management and Oracle's own Team Productivity Center for JDeveloper. These include powerful IDEs with extra extensions for testing suites, source code management, project management, collaboration and task scheduling, and tools to manage deployment to and monitoring of test environments.

With ALM there is a strong bias toward internally developed applications, putting the most detail on the upstream development phases and substantially less on the post-deployment management activities.

The areas of focus for all ALM implementation include the following capabilities:

- Project management and collaboration
- Requirements management and analysis
- Modeling and design based on standard workflows and architectures
- Central build, test, deploy, and release management
- Change and configuration management
- Defect management

Unsurprisingly, ALM models often resemble the basic product lifecycle management (PLM) processes used in the creation of physical goods. The traditional steps, starting with idea conception, running into design and creation, and finally to service (including maintenance), do seem to have been translated across to the software development realm and ALM.

One recent evolution of ALM is that they now include the ability to support cloud computing, specifically Platform-as-a-Service (PaaS), where applications are created and deployed on purpose-built third-party hosted systems. This capability, supported by technologies such as Service Oriented Architecture (SOA), should ultimately help standardize the features of ALM so that PaaS vendors provide a core set of ALM capabilities that the most popular development tools support.

So although some basic outline principles are relevant here, the ALM model and its implementations currently don't venture downstream into the kinds of actions and activities that are included in managing a prepackaged enterprise application. The worlds of application development and application management remain sadly disconnected.

Application Performance Management (APM)

One model that often gets mentioned in the same context as ALM is Application Performance Management. This is much closer to the topic of application management but is specific to performance, and again, is very specific to the features offered by tool vendors.

Generally speaking, the following activities are covered by APM:

- **User experience monitoring**   Tracking performance of pages, regions, and clicks
- **Application component discovery, modeling, and monitoring**   The way the technical components of the application make up the business functionality
- **Business transaction management**   The performance of business tasks and processes, as measured from application metrics
- **Application data analytics**   The monitoring of application data records

Oracle's Enterprise Manager includes features that support all of these areas, and we'll look at them specifically in Chapter 8. So, while this is relevant to our discussion, it's actually not a lifecycle model, and doesn't commonly focus on any of the four areas outside of performance management.

Cloud computing also has impact on APM capabilities, where applications delivered as Software-as-a-Service (SaaS) run against service agreements that can be of value only when the appropriate service monitoring tools are provided. Again, we'll visit what is on offer from Oracle in later chapters.

Information Lifecycle Management (ILM)

ILM may be applied at various levels, such as an individual document's life from creation, distribution, use, maintenance, and disposition; however, it's also possible to apply it to the data within enterprise applications. Here it represents the lifecycle of datasets, over time and according to use. Specific datasets are assigned a maturity phase value based on its profile, and while the following are most commonly used, the exact values may vary to fit with organizational needs.

As illustrated in Figure 3-4, data ranges from active to expired. Active data is available online and is made up of active documents and records, such as orders, items, and people. Semiactive data represents reference data that is associated with active documents and records. Examples

Active Use	Semi-Active Use	Historical Data	Archived Data	Expired Data

FIGURE 3-4.   *The phases of information maturity*

might include trading partners, reference agreements, terms and conditions, and general enterprise structures. Historical data is documents, records, and reference data that must be kept for occasional use. This data is normally important in performance reporting that includes meeting regulatory requirements. Data in the archived division is no longer used for day-to-day work but must be kept for potential reference and is often focused around regulatory and legal compliance. Finally, expired data has no feasible purpose and should be considered for removal.

ILM's primary use is to identify specific volumes of data and to map these to data storage architectures, tools, and devices. The volume of both structured and unstructured data is ever increasing, and it's well known that high-performance storage costs roughly ten times more than archive type media. This fact, coupled with the fact that modern access mechanisms present less of a challenge to fully distributed data, means that while ILM is not an all-encompassing management model, it is a powerful model to leverage within aspects of enterprise application management. We'll look at E-Business Suite data management and optimization in more detail in Chapter 8.

IT Service Management (ITSM)

Most large organizations are looking at (or already using) IT service management (ITSM) for their technology infrastructure management. This uses a service-based approach to manage the IT department's provision of tools to business users to help them complete their tasks and meet their goals.

The broad aim of ITSM is to quantify and monitor IT resources properly, in terms that relate to day-to-day operations, and to be able to measure the quality of the services therein. By trying to more closely align IT with business operations, problems and areas that need improvement are much more easily identifiable.

For the uninitiated, this can be an odd way of looking at things, so let's briefly consider how IT elements can be defined as *services*. Certainly some business users require the delivery of certain core IT features so they can complete their daily tasks, such as the ability to create orders in a purchasing system. In addition, many business users also get significant benefits from IT when the tools provided help them perform their own operational analysis and create new business insights. An example might be determining the most cost-efficient supplier to place the order against. Each of these requirements can be defined as services, and as such the related tools can be measured in terms of their availability and effectiveness in satisfying the users' expectations.

ITSM service quality is usually measured through the use of service level agreements (SLAs) that define precisely what the service is and what the minimum acceptable performance quality should be. SLAs are traditionally very detailed, and it often takes substantial negotiation involving all parties before a definition is reached and an agreement is made effective. An SLA for ITSM services will commonly include the following:

- Overview and scope (with both IT and business perspectives)
- Performance measurements and expectations

- Tracking and reporting on service delivery
- Problem management and resolution process
- Violation terms and procedures
- Duties and responsibilities (for both producer and consumer)
- Security and legal considerations
- SLA review and expiration terms

Since the provision of IT services may also come from outside an organization, such as from outsourcing partners and cloud computing providers, the same ITSM model is often applied, with similar associated SLAs.

ITSM forms a set of core principles and is actually implemented based on the use of one of a number of framework models. Let's take a look at two of the common models used, and see what we can apply to enterprise application management.

Information Technology Infrastructure Library

Information Technology Infrastructure Library (ITIL) is a public framework for implementing ITSM in an organization. In its current version (v3) it is based on a set of five books that aim to orient the provision of IT services based on a service lifecycle: strategy, design, transition, operation, and improvement. As illustrated in Figure 3-5, it provides an outline to help organizations link their operational requirements to suitable approaches and more complete solutions.

The first phase of the ITIL lifecycle is *service strategy* and provides a central space in which organizations can evaluate the kinds of services they might want to consume to achieve operational excellence. The phase focuses on the definition of a service portfolio that explains what will be delivered and to whom, and the business value and risk of each. It should also include aspects of the service's ongoing management, including a financial consideration.

The second phase takes each of these services and defines a *service design*. This forms a translation of the business requirements into an IT solution. Like any good design, it includes aspects of integration, security, availability, and capacity. Here you see positive aspects of true application management being built into the design. However, although ITIL is a framework that explains the areas and disciplines of importance, it provides little detail on precise implementation.

The third phase, *service transition*, accepts the design as input and helps guide the solution as it moves into implementation. Although usually concerned with deployment, it also incorporates hardware architectures, documentation, and training for a more complete service solution. This phase has some more important concepts for setting up a high-quality enterprise application management platform, especially the inclusion of change and configuration management, as well as control of release processes, testing and validation, and of course storing a repository of known solutions as part of knowledge management.

With the solution built and implemented, the *service operation* phase proceeds, which is concerned with managing and maintaining delivery based on the parameters of the SLA. This is very much at the heart of day-to-day enterprise application management as well. For example, in Chapter 5 you'll see how E-Business Suite's reliability management tools and features support event, incident, and problem management.

The final ITIL phase rolls into the mix the concept of *continual service improvement*, so that the service provided today grows to meet the demands of tomorrow. This should be a major focus for packaged enterprise applications such as E-Business Suite; Chapters 8 and 10 show how optimization and health checking are essential parts of effective management.

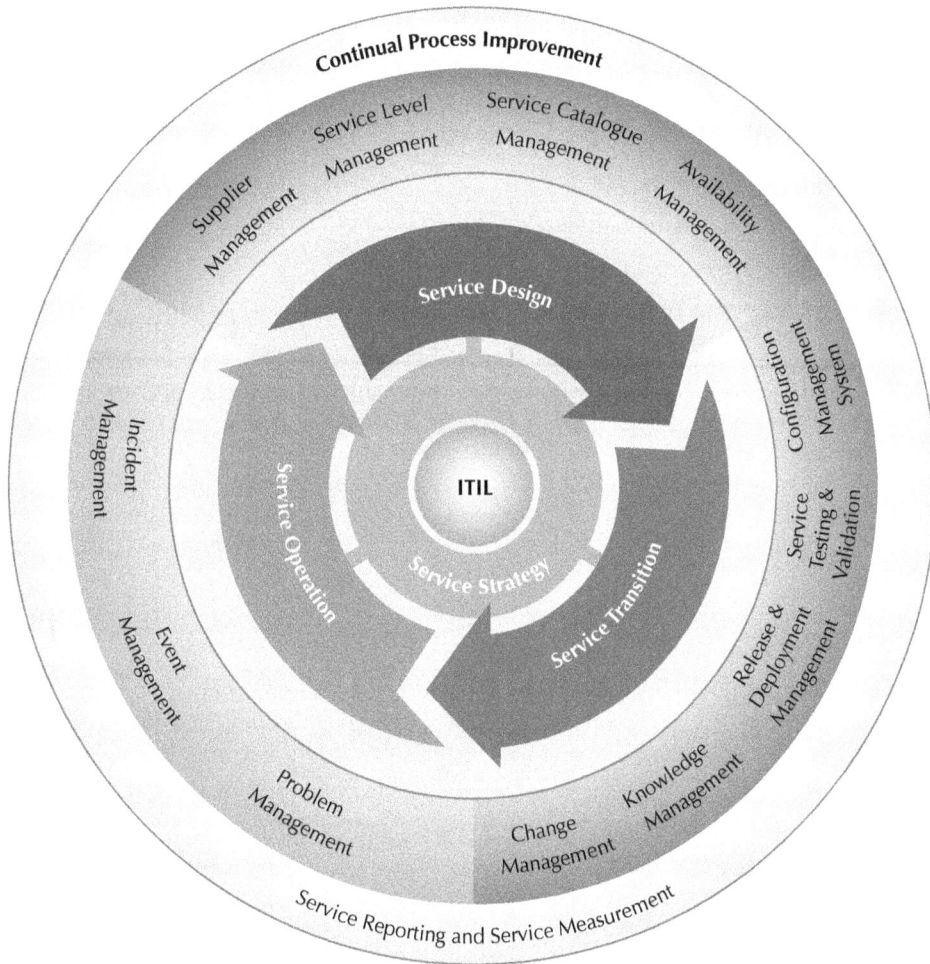

FIGURE 3-5. *The main components of the ITIL framework*

ITIL is exceptionally popular, especially in larger organizations, and although it is not a totally prescriptive guide to follow as it lacks detailed steps, it certainly helps organizations get a grip on sprawling IT infrastructures across all areas; desktop, networks, hardware, and homegrown and packaged applications.

Like all ITSM models, it allows for a clear rationalization of investments, both in terms of bottom-line financial costs and vital resources such as time and effort. In these cost-conscious times this often represents a consolidation and rationalization, but optimizing the IT service catalog to emphasize those with the most business impact will help organizations increase the visibility of the contributions that IT makes, and thereby also prioritize the provision and expansion of key value-added services for the whole organization's benefit. It need not all be doom and gloom!

COBIT Control Objectives for Information and Related Technology (COBIT) is also ITSM compliant; however, it has a more prescriptive focus by providing a clear set of measurements for IT managers and auditors to be able to interrogate and monitor the performance and governance of IT resources.

Within its current set of 210 specific measurements, spread across 34 IT processes, COBIT's coverage is similar to ITIL's, although it uses four core lifecycle-type phases or domains:

- Planning and organization
- Acquisition and implementation
- Delivery and support
- Monitoring and evaluation

Mapping has been done between ITIL and COBIT, highlighting the commonality. While COBIT validates the high-level processes that should be considered by application management, it is again intended for use against the whole IT infrastructure and therefore lacks a great amount of applicable detail.

One extra thing to note is that COBIT is certainly more focused around governance than ITIL is, a fact emphasized by its official endorsement for use in meeting the Sarbanes-Oxley (SOX) regulatory compliance. We'll look at more examples of applying enterprise application governance in Chapter 9.

Applying Generic Lifecycles

Although we didn't find an existing model that fully fits enterprise application management, the few example lifecycles discussed so far do show some methods and activities that will apply. In this section, we will summarize what we can take forward into defining our own model.

First, let's look at a few potential contributions the models discussed may offer.

- Software development lifecycles illustrate how understanding requirements is critical, followed by creating a properly detailed design. The iterative methods also highlight how regularly testing and revisiting the design allows for quicker improvement to the overall solution.

- ALM offers an application-focused model and provides a high-level, end-to-end lifecycle flow. Although many phases are not applicable for prebuilt enterprise applications, ALM may be useful when implementing extensive configurations or extensions that often represent a considerable project themselves.

- APM provides insight into methods to ensure effective performance and is definitely of value as part of an application management model.

- ILM offers a deep insight into application data and represents a helpful model that the enterprise application manager can use to orchestrate this part of his or her work.

- ITSM models like ITIL demonstrate how business user requirements should be very clearly understood, so that application functions and features are managed based on well-understood and recorded expectations. COBIT also introduces the importance of service control based on regulatory and internal governance guidelines.

Taking a more critical view, some key factors negate the complete use of any one of these models to deliver complete enterprise application management:

- Software development and ALM focus on the upstream design and build phases only, making them less relevant to packaged enterprise applications.

- ITSM models apply across the whole of IT management and do not focus on enterprise application–specific factors or requirements.

- APM and ILM cover only a small part of enterprise application management, not the whole picture.

Like any model designed to be applied in varied situations and organizations, there is plenty of inherent simplification and summarization. Generally speaking, some of these models touch on both enterprise applications management and IT lifecycle best practices; however, rarely do they tie the two together or offer comprehensive detail. So the only thing to do is to design our own model!

A Fusion Lifecycle Model

In true Oracle style, by taking the best bits of existing concepts and recommended practices and creating something new, we'll use the Fusion prefix. There are a couple of other good reasons for this. First, this model was initially developed after analyzing the best way to manage Oracle Fusion Applications, and since the principles apply to any enterprise application, it's therefore the same model. A second good reason to use this name is that inevitably existing E-Business Suite users will look to migrate to Fusion Applications (see the recommendations in Chapter 11), and this transition represents a great opportunity to address your entire enterprise application management. It's therefore a model for now and for the future.

The intention here is to take the enterprise application management principles defined in the preceding sections and build a method by which they can be actually implemented. This model is not intended to be all-encompassing or especially complex, but based on the lack of any reasonably useful equivalent, it should represent a good starting point. It will at least help get your organization thinking about the right topics in the right way.

It's worth noting that this new model could be considered a subset of ALM or ITIL, or a superset of APM, dropping in quite nicely as an extension where applicable. Indeed, ITIL does actually have a standard "application management" activity categorized as an associated function, but again, it provides no usable detail.

The easiest way to begin to explain the new model we're proposing is to provide an overall diagrammatic representation (Figure 3-6), and then to discuss the key parts one by one.

The process of enterprise application management ideally begins (#1 in the figure) as part of the standard enterprise application implementation process, spawned around the same time as the overall solution design is created and well before the deployment phase. Clearly, for the majority of E-Business Suite users this is long past; therefore, this could coincide with an upgrade (for example, to Release 12.x), or a similar major project.

The resulting application management design (#2 in the figure) should be comprehensive and completed in a formal method to help ensure complete coverage of the five separate (although interconnected) plans. The design creation should include the use of structured methods to gather requirements and expectations from all the key stakeholders involved with the enterprise application. The results of this are then analyzed to ensure associated service delivery costs are acceptable, and

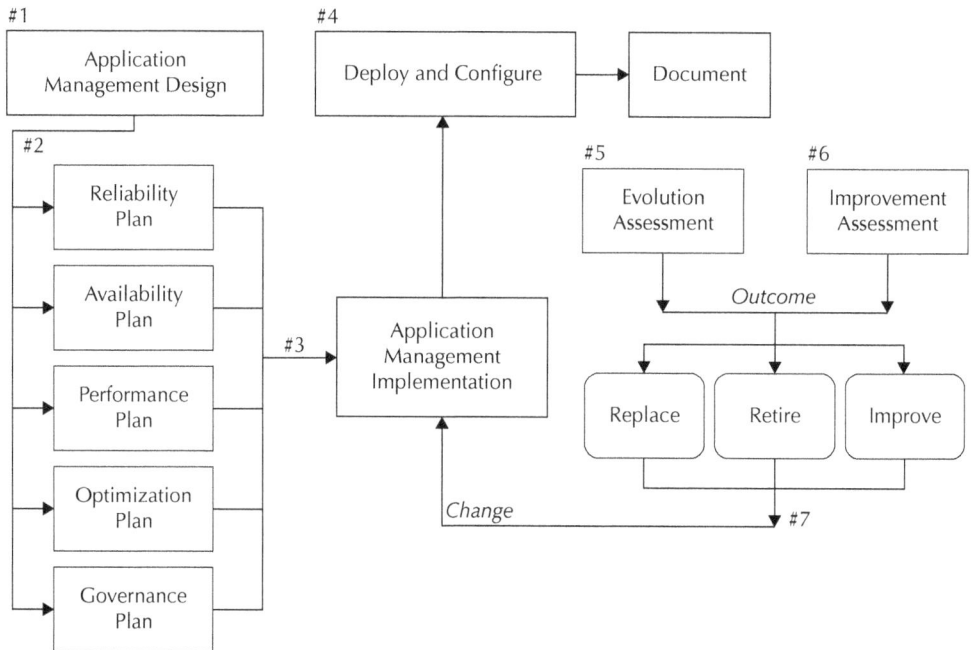

FIGURE 3-6.   *The Fusion Enterprise Application lifecycle model*

once documented, the final design (plans and associated services) is reviewed and signed off by all parties.

Application management implementation, the third phase of this model (#3 in the figure), is a kind of subsection to the design and is focused on making sure suitable tools, processes, and procedures are implemented so that the content of the five plans can be properly resourced. When using the ITSM approach to IT management (including the enterprise application), this is also where the service definition would occur, so that each discrete part of the provision of the enterprise application to end users is encapsulated and can be properly designed, executed, monitored, and measured.

Obviously, each organization will want to develop its own unique implementation design that fits its own needs and structures. Care should of course be taken, since all too often the system management plans and intentions are good but are not backed up by adequate resources (people and equipment), inevitably resulting in poor implementation and execution.

Interestingly, the converse is also occasionally true, where fabulous tools are implemented but with little or no clear intention on their purpose or most effective use. Having a dedicated implementation phase based on a clear design helps make sure the right balance is met.

The fourth phase (#4 in the figure) is spawned as part of the enterprise application deployment, upgrade, or whatever the associated project may be. It represents getting the management tools, processes, and procedures set up and ready for use. Although this might sound somewhat trivial, it is actually a complex task. In addition to establishing clear and efficient process and procedures (which is never easy), this step often requires considerable expertise in configuring complex software tools while maintaining security and not affecting the systems they monitor. Just to illustrate the complexity involved, let's look at a few example activities:

- The installation and provisioning of additional software with suitable resources and security
- The configuration of the nodes, servers, applications, and processes that are to be monitored
- The insertion of minimum and maximum thresholds for alerting mechanisms
- The entry of personal contact details, including availability and contact procedures for use by the alerting mechanisms
- The setting up of emergency contingency plans and procedures
- The creation of regular maintenance policies and procedures (including patching)
- The setting up of all availability, reliability, and performance targets from the design
- The setting up of sample frequency, record taking, and data longevity
- The adoption of security policies and procedures for system management and audit, with many being mapped based on existing business and regulatory rule sets
- The allocation of suitable resources for proactive improvement and optimization-based projects

Of course, it's possible that only core parts of a complete management design will be implemented initially and that additional iterations will be done for each subsequent management piece as additional tools and resources (including time) become available. It's also worth noting that at this stage, the full base specification for the system (configuration, architecture, and so on) should be carefully documented.

Once the enterprise application management design is in execution mode, the rest of the model is concerned with continuous improvement, ensuring that the process evolves with the changing expectations of business users, IT staff, and advancements within the enterprise application itself. Our model also includes two feedback loops that iterate on different frequencies.

The first phase of assessment, evolution assessment (#5 in the figure) is run only occasionally, possibly quarterly or semiannually, and consists of an in-depth and formal look at the enterprise application management. It considers various influencing factors, such as:

- A 360-degree review of delivery against targets (that is, SLAs), including deep root cause analysis of unexpected results or incidents
- Changes to the IT landscape, such as new services, tools, and systems whose intention is to run alongside (or integrate with) the enterprise application
- Changes to enterprise application features being used by business users, such as new datasets and new business objects that may affect processing or storage
- Forthcoming changes to the business organization that are represented within the enterprise application and how they may potentially affect usage profiles
- Creation of (or changes to) configurations, invasive personalizations, and customizations that have either occurred or are planned
- Existing or forthcoming upgrades and updates to the enterprise application, its technology stack, and all related hardware and networking

The second phase of assessment, improvement assessment (#6 in the figure), is run much more frequently and evaluates the output of the day-to-day management results. This could be performed monthly, with key stakeholders reviewing a set of performance reports to pinpoint problems in service quality (possibly against SLAs). The output of this should be either the reapproval of existing management activities or stakeholder-agreed adjustments to expectations, targets, or the enterprise application itself. Most changes are minor adjustments and fine-tuning.

All significant outcomes of both assessment and review exercises usually fit into either a replacement, a retirement, or an improvement proposal that then feeds back into the original application management implementation process (through #7 in the figure). This then ensures their proper deployment and configuration, as well as central documentation (via change management).

Clearly, the two assessment loops (#5 and #6) ensure that each of the five application management principles are revisited and applied, where the improvement assessment focuses the reactive items of reliability, availability and performance, whereas the evolution assessment focuses more on proactive governance and ongoing optimization.

Summary

In this chapter we considered several different applications-related lifecycle models and how parts of them will help us implement and operate a foolproof method of running a complete enterprise application management process. We looked at software development lifecycles, application lifecycle models, application performance management, and information lifecycle management.

We also looked in a little more depth at IT service management, and how both ITIL and COBIT offer some good general best practice approaches to managing technology components for delivering business value. However, although both also mention application management, they fail to provide any real usable detail.

Finally, using the best parts of the models we reviewed, we proposed a new model for enterprise application management. This includes a process-based flow for implementing our five core principles defined in the last chapter, as well as a cyclical method for continuous improvement and evolution.

Now that we have a workable model to apply our principles, let's see what tools, techniques, and services exist to realize this all in an Oracle E-Business Suite environment.

CHAPTER
4

The Oracle E-Business
Suite Management
Toolbox

T he five toolbox chapters that follow represent the core substance of this book, offering details on specific tools, features, and services to help manage Oracle E-Business Suite. The details provided are based either on their provision specifically within the product or as external utilities that are especially well suited for use in an E-Business Suite environment.

The main purpose of this book is to bring together the wide range of management capabilities available, in a directly applicable and practical format. To do that, we'll look at a multitude of capabilities from many sources and with many items being useful for more than one management task.

Why a Toolbox?

The toolbox analogy is frequently used for a set of software utilities that can be used for a specific purpose. Although there is the obvious comparison to the toolbox needed for car maintenance, let's also look at another area of IT for a similar example. Application programmers and developers commonly use a collection of tools to do the various tasks within their jobs. Many are embedded in their core applications, such as their Integrated Development Environment (IDE), but many more are additional general purpose utilities, such as debuggers, scripting platforms, documentation tools, template sets, and version control applications.

The enterprise application manager also needs a wide range of tools to implement his or her management plans, from reliability to governance, and the resources inside this toolbox are intended to fit the most common use cases and situations. This also includes both proactive and reactive management tasks. In some cases, additional utilities may be needed that are not listed here, but almost all of the tools we'll discuss can be used in a flexible manner to provide information in most scenarios.

Clearly, it's impossible to cover every potentially useful tool, and they do evolve over time. Therefore, this discussion focuses on a core set of features, functions, capabilities, and services, and the details in the last two chapters provide more consideration of evolving management requirements.

The toolbox structure serves as a guide of what to use and when, so that upon addressing a specific situation such as a reliability issue, you should be able to recall the related tools and techniques, or at least reopen this book and review it quickly. The structure should therefore act as a reasonable reference guide, as well as the foundation for some basic training.

Toolbox Structure

The next five chapters retain the focus, purpose, and intent of the preceding enterprise application management discussion. Specifically, we will look at the tools in the context of each of the five enterprise application management principles from Chapters 3 and 4. This has a couple of benefits. First, it works in a hands-on approach, with this book acting as a quick reference. Second, it allows us to build out the design for E-Business Suite management by putting real detail into the Fusion model we defined in Chapter 3. Simply stated, this structure helps ensure that the design plans actually match the execution; not ensuring this is a common cause of ineffective application management. As a quick reminder, we'll use the following as our toolbox sections:

- **Reliability**   Tools that help manage features so they consistently operate as intended. This includes monitoring for (and ideally avoiding) general problems and errors.

- **Availability**   Tools that help maintain feature access. This is essentially ensuring that all services and components are up and running.

- **Performance**   Tools that help spot the early signs of poor performance and provide facilities to help resolve any mismatch against expectations.

- **Optimization**   Tools that help facilitate additional contributions to organizational objectives and improvements.

- **Governance**   Tools that help manage the security, integrity, audit, and general quality of application features and data.

In addition to these broad categorizations, a further subdivision is also made, corresponding broadly to the layers that exist within the application, as discussed in Chapter 1. This is shown in Figure 4-1.

The first subsection of each category, the business process, provides tools that are best applied within the management of the highest-level application functions and features, essentially focused around business process completion, such as creating sales leads, matching invoices to orders and receipts, or on-boarding new employees. Many of the corresponding tools may be accessible by business users so that they can be involved and ideally self-manage certain parts of the application.

The next subdivision is the application technology layer, working under the aforementioned features and functions. This is a vital dependent layer that often provides in-context information that helps us understand processes and analyze management metrics.

The final subdivision is the platform technology layer, upon which all the components run. Examples are application servers, web servers, forms servers, and database servers. Management issues in these core components and their underlying operating systems, hardware, and networking do sometimes arise; therefore, appropriate management tooling is most certainly required.

Using these three layers should help the applications manager traverse the technology stack when working on a specific problem or project, commonly important when looking for the type of information needed to move toward a truly effective solution.

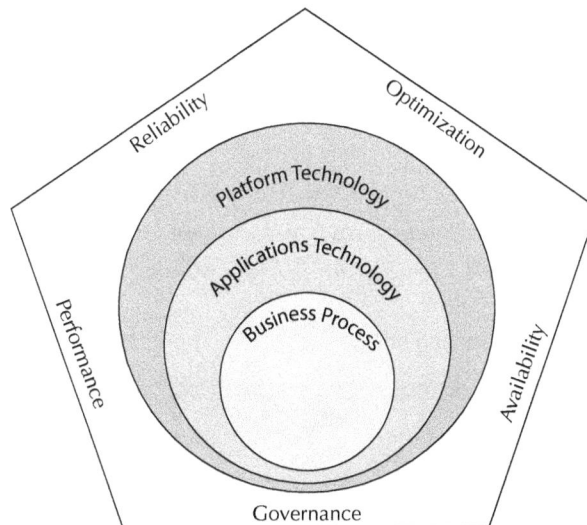

FIGURE 4-1.   *The sections and layers of the enterprise application management toolbox*

Toolbox Scope

Let's define a few boundaries for our toolbox discussion, so that it's very clear what kinds of utilities are included and how the related chapters are structured. As mentioned, we will discuss specific capabilities that exist within various tools, and their explicit use in E-Business Suite management.

The documentation references cited throughout the discussions can be used to find details on all aspects of the tools, specifically including their installation and configuration. The intention is therefore not to discuss tools comprehensively, but to highlight the features that help satisfy the requirements of effective application management.

As you read this chapter, you'll notice that although some tools have specific use cases and therefore apply in only one area (such as performance metrics), other tools have a wider range of features and are applicable in several places (such as logs).

As with installation and configuration, we'll defer to the documentation to cover the basics of administering the E-Business Suite instance, such as the starting and stopping of components. This way, we can take a more holistic look at overall application management and then drill down into examples of using specific features.

Although the majority of the tools mentioned are additional software programs, the discussion does include other types of tools such as services, recommended practices, techniques, and procedures. Table 4-1 provides a broad summary of some of those we'll be looking at.

Several basic capabilities exist within the standard technology stack and related resources available for use. The list of potential tools, services, and features that *could* be of use is infinite, and it's neither practical nor sensible to attempt an exhaustive listing. As such, we'll focus on core processes and the key moving parts, in the same way the application manager would initially prioritize his or her approach.

Similar to Enterprise Application Management itself, the tooling is not static. You'll recall in our Fusion Enterprise Application Management model we deliberately included two built-in

Oracle Applications Manager (OAM)	Applications AD/autoconfig
Diagnostic logging	Relational database management system (RDBMS) management tools
Oracle Diagnostic Framework	Remote Diagnostic Agent (RDA)
Authorization and authentication management	Master Data Management (MDM)
Reactive and proactive support services	Real User Experience Insight (RUEI)
Oracle Enterprise Manager, including the Application Management Suite	Business Intelligence management
Problem and incident management	Applications Integration Architecture (AIA), SOA Gateway, and Business Process Execution Management
Application Server Administration	Recovery, high availability, and failover
Governance, risk, and compliance	Command line utilities and scripts

TABLE 4-1. *Sample of the Toolbox Content*

continuous feedback loops to ensure that all the tools and services are reviewed and made to evolve with requirements, expectations, and the application itself.

Alternative Views

Although we're using our own lifecycle structure to lay out the toolbox, the same information could be oriented in other ways according to specific–use case needs or preferences. One example might be to arrange and look at the tools with less emphasis on planning and more on equipping adequately for reactive work, such as prioritizing reliability management. This is not to say it would include different content—it's just a different viewpoint. In this case, the following categorization might be interesting to consider:

- **Monitoring**   How to identify problems across the whole system
- **Analysis**   How to dig deeper when things go wrong or for proactive health checking
- **Knowledge**   Tools and resources to promote ideas and good practices through better understanding
- **Support Services**   Where to look to get additional help

Another alternative, and a more traditional view, is to consider how to manage each technology stack one piece at a time. Using this approach and based on the outlines provided in Chapter 1, the following might be used to organize the tooling required for success:

- Managing the application features
- Managing the application tiers and middleware
- Managing the applications database
- Managing security
- Managing batch processing
- Managing business intelligence
- Managing diagnostics
- Managing high-availability, backup, and recovery

Although useful, these additional views are more fragmented and therefore complex to execute when compared with our holistic model. Our model first sets out the goals covering all the key aspects of enterprise application management, and then implements them into a lifecycle model that makes sure they are applied and constantly reviewed and audited.

Summary

So, while short, this chapter has now provided a practical method for building out and applying our enterprise application management lifecycle model.

Now armed with this, and the preceding chapters that offered both details on the E-Business Suite architecture and the components and objectives of Enterprise Application Management, we can begin our deep dive into E-Business Suite and turn all this theory into a useful reality.

CHAPTER
5

A Reliability
Management Toolbox

R eliability management, the subject of our first toolbox chapter, is traditionally where enterprise application staff spends most of their time: troubleshooting errors, solving problems, handling questions, and completing general requests from end users or the help desks that support them.

This is never going to disappear entirely; unexpected failures will always happen with broad and complex enterprise applications. However, I hope the information in this chapter will help you catch these failures sooner rather than later, reducing their impact and keeping the resolution time to a minimum.

What Is Application Reliability?

If you fail to complete a task because the system isn't working as expected and you're using it as intended, then it's unreliable. The more frequently this happens, the more unreliable it is, and users quickly begin to both complain and try alternative workaround methods—both very undesirable results!

You'll recall that in Chapter 2 we defined "reliability" as the following:

To ensure that the features consistently operate as intended.

The American National Standards Institute (ANSI) defines "software reliability" as *the probability of failure-free software operations for a specified period of time in a specified environment*. This is interesting, and maybe somewhat optimistic, as this official definition emphasizes reality-based boundaries together with a scientifically derived measurement.

This is all fairly obvious, and just as with the analogy of an unreliable car, unreliable applications will not always get you from A to B. However, because this book is intended for management staff (the equivalent of the auto repair shop owner), we need to cover all aspects of problems and be a bit more specific. Let's define a couple more terms that we'll use throughout this chapter:

- **Failure**   The program operation doesn't meet its users' expectations.
- **Fault**   A defect in the program execution that causes a failure.

As mentioned in the previous ANSI definition, faults lead to failures, and failures lead to poor reliability.

Causes of Poor Reliability

There are essentially five broad categories that most failures fall into:

- **Code bugs**   Where faults in program code result in runtime failure. Causes include human error, poor design, and insufficient testing.
- **Unexpected data**   Bad data created or introduced into the application, or code unable to process certain values. An example is given in Figure 5-1, where a bad value entered in the previous form wasn't well handled. We'll look at methods to help ensure data quality in Chapter 8.
- **Setup errors**   Enterprise applications like E-Business Suite are so flexible that, in their willingness to meet all businesses needs, implementation mistakes are sometimes made. Likewise, many of the more complex features are designed for use by domain experts, and infrequent users may attempt operations that are outside the intended design. These

types of problems are commonly caused by insufficient training and implementation documentation, usability issues, lack of system testing, poor configuration management, and a deficient change control process. We'll look at this area more in Chapter 9.

■ **Capacity problems** Sometimes the resources required to operate effectively get unexpectedly depleted. Once they're gone, the application is disrupted. Unmanaged changes in application usage, poor configuration management, or insufficient monitoring are usually to blame. This area also includes potential hardware and dependent infrastructure failures. Since these kinds of issues usually take down parts or all of the system, we'll look at them when we discuss availability and performance in Chapters 6 and 7, respectively.

■ **Integration issues** While environmental issues shouldn't affect software reliability in the same way as they would physical systems, for enterprise applications as a whole the internal components and integrated systems may behave in unexpected ways, destabilizing program code. An example might be an application-to-application integration that returns an unexpected response message (or no message at all).

In this chapter, our take on reliability is concerned with the more serious failures, as opposed to warnings or alerts that, while annoying, still permit the user to complete their task.

Considering the causes of reliability issues and failures logically progresses into a discussion about the ability of an application to be *fault tolerant*, where issues are categorized into those that can be safely retried, perhaps after a simple correction, and those where the right thing to do is to halt the process before things get worse. Speaking of getting worse, where fault tolerance is low (and reliability is poor), the discussion inevitably moves into the realm of availability, which is the subject of the next chapter. Most modern application systems do have catch-all fault handlers that add a certain tolerance and robustness, and some even trigger diagnostics, but in reality they're rarely immediately informative or very user friendly. Broad messages like E-Business Suites own, "An unexpected error has occurred. Please contact your system administrator," do little to enhance the experience of reliability issues.

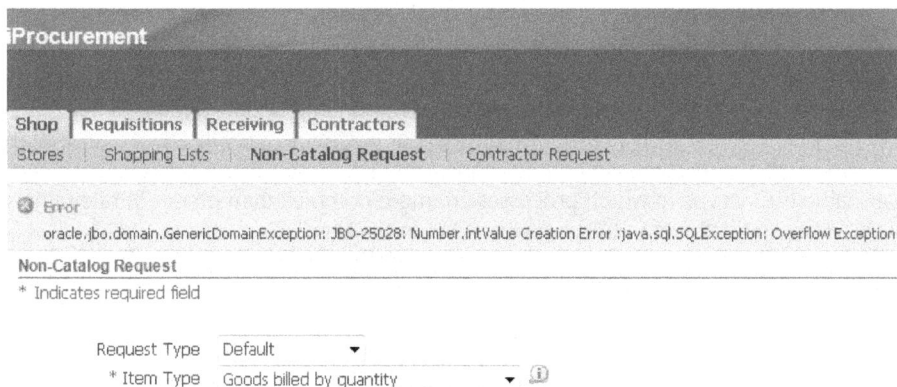

FIGURE 5-1. *A failure that prevents progress*

Measuring Reliability

There is a branch of engineering known as *reliability theory*, devoted to calculating the probability that a device will perform as intended over a specific period of time in known conditions. This definition is stated as a complex mathematical function. A subset of this is software reliability, which looks at applying similar models to complex application systems with the view to help manage and even predict failure. The challenge is that attempts at quantitative calculations are exceptionally complex, exacerbated by the huge numbers of variables involved.

Several of these mathematic theorems have been created, such as the early Jelinski-Moranda model, which uses complex statistical functions together with a broad set of assumptions to try to predict software failure rates. Generally speaking, these have had success in academic circles only because their lack of usability and flexibility to include real-world factors renders them too complex to add value back to the busy operation of a data center.

Also, many of these models are based on measurements from other engineering disciplines, such as hardware reliability, and return a probability of failure over a certain period of time. The problem with this is that software execution is only slightly influenced by degrading physical processes. Indeed,most software failure is related to poor coding or faulty design, both very hard to calculate or identify through mathematics.

On the flipside, other less theoretical attempts are routed in the software development process looking at items like failure density (per thousand code lines) based on rigorous testing, and execution complexity scores based on code scanning. While a bit more practical, they require significant investment to come up with some results.

Moving forward, let's look at some of the more usable parts of this area to try to understand and measure E-Business Suite reliability. Most measurements of this kind are based on two main data sources:

- **Software code analysis** The complexity and size of the code base strongly influences the likelihood that failures will occur. This touches on software quality engineering, again another separate discipline.

- **Historical failure data** How regularly the system has failed in the past should help predict how frequently it's likely to fail in the future. This includes calculating well-known metrics like *mean time to failure* (MTTF) and *mean time between failures* (MTBF).

We'll look at software code analysis first. Clearly, we cannot run debugging and analysis scripts against the source code of a packaged application with compiled code—that's just not practical. However, as users of the system, we can glean a reasonable understanding of the execution steps of our key operations, such as processing orders or posting ledgers. If we can understand the steps involved (such as user interface actions, concurrent processes, and workflows), we can make a reasonable estimate as to which processes are more complex than others. While fairly simplistic, this is a start and better than burying your head in the sand!

Next, application reliability is of course ultimately measured by the end-user's experience, based on his or her perception of any interruptions, failures, or instabilities. Much of this activity is already measured, using the various tools and logs that record errors, failures, crashes, and aborted transactions. This chapter provides details on all the various tools for capturing and analyzing reliability metrics.

I should also mention there are so many types and severities of failure that not all are easily machine traceable. Examples include ease-of-use, functional setup issues, and slow but nonfatal performance. As such, good reliability measurements should be a combined analysis of quantitative

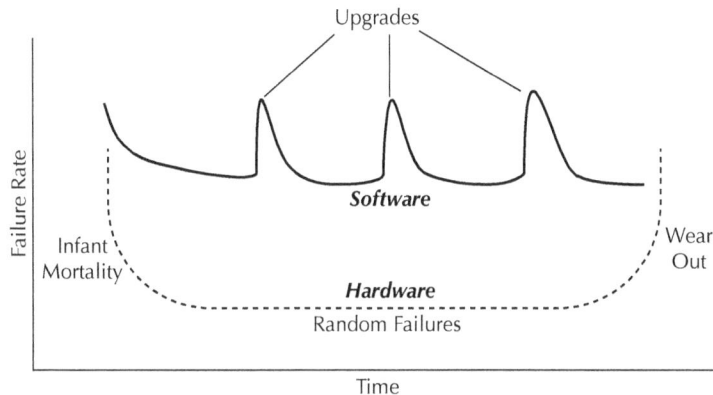

FIGURE 5-2. *The contrasting reliability curves for software and hardware*

and qualitative metrics such as incomplete transactions, error rates, help desk ticket volume, and feedback from endusers.

Software reliability data supports the logic that failures generally peak when new code is introduced, such as after upgrades. As illustrated by Figure 5-2, this is in contrast with hardware reliability's *bathtub* profile, which has a failure peak in the initial breaking-in period that then drops as the hardware runs consistently well until the components finally begin to degrade, and failures rise again.

When it comes to enterprise application management, reliability is an important metric. However, measurement and data collection can be very challenging, and areas like IT service management prefer to use a cut-and-dried availability measurement than try to decipher what might constitute a service failure. That said, enterprise application users will not tolerate an available yet unreliable service; therefore, it's critical to keep well informed of both reliability metrics and the end users' experiences and perceptions.

Managing Reliability

Making a dedicated effort to address ongoing reliability as a core area of application management is quite demanding, especially when dealing with packaged applications like E-Business Suite. This is because initially it may seem that failures are generally unpredictable and therefore unmanageable, being at the mercy of the users, the implementation, the product design, and the code quality.

While some of this is true, the more successful organizations understand that there are still many proactive steps that can be taken to negate the frequency and impact of any failures that may occur. So while this chapter provides details on related tools and features, just before we dive in, let's consider a couple of best practice areas to put the tools into context.

Interpret Error Quality

Great applications inform end users when something is (or could be) problematic, helping ensure more success in task completion. Obviously, not all possible scenarios can be accounted for, but errors should be meaningful and ideally actionable in some way so that end users can get the problem resolved quickly and effectively, limiting the overall impact.

As you'll see shortly, E-Business Suite does allow the supported customization of the warning and error messages that may be shown to end users when they take an action, such as submitting a page. This presents a small but not insignificant opportunity to build on top of the existing product quality. The same quality control should apply to messages used by custom code and integrated systems.

Often native software errors are meaningless to most end users and, while it might give a programmer a clue as to a fix required, this involves lots of expensive steps that are not always necessary. These errors also obliterate user confidence in the software, and the industry analyst firm IDC was once quoted as saying, "Two out of three IT projects are challenged or worse, due in large part to user adoption issues."

Effective reliability management requires a good understanding of the messages associated with the most important tasks (and customizations), and actions to make sure they are as effective as possible. We'll look at how to do this in the "Application Messages" section later in this chapter. Improvements may also include enhancing training or the availability of reference material.

Know the Symptoms

Great troubleshooting happens when the manifestation of the problem is readily matched to either a short list of potential causes, or a few effective diagnostic tools that will quickly do the same. Rather than repeat that high quality messages greatly reduce the time to resolution (and therefore the impact of reliability issues), let's look at it from the other way around, using problem symptoms in troubleshooting.

We'll use two examples. First, the error message shown previously in Figure 5-1 is a great example of a technical error message that doesn't help end users at all. It does, however, have some unique symptoms that may assist in effective troubleshooting:

- It tells us what part of the technology is involved (JBO being related to Oracle Application Framework).

- It has a unique message ID (25028) for which we can easily find matching known solutions or related recommended troubleshooting steps.

- It says what kinds of errors occurred (JBO's GenericDomainException and a SQLException).

- It gives us some detail on what the code was trying to do (JBO raised a Number.intValue Creation Error cause by the SQL Overflow Exception).

This example illustrates how we can get a good start on troubleshooting simply by recognizing the symptoms presented. The next stage is linking this identification to actions that are likely to produce meaningful results.

For the second example, we'll use a hypothetical situation that is a little less clearcut. Let's say that end users are reporting that processing is slow for a particular process, such as the approval of expense claims. The challenge here is to quickly determine what the symptoms are. There is no error here; this is a more subtle failure that needs investigation using measures of items such as response times to page requests, database transaction processing times, notification and workflow processing metrics, and even functional activities like ensuring that it's not just one manager being slow to reply to e-mails. In a case like this, a good reliability management plan ensures sufficient metric visibility, including access to tools that show exceptional peaks, troughs, and patterns. This may all seem rather optimistic in a system as broad and complex as E-Business Suite, but it's a great goal to aim toward.

Preventative Action

Rather than constantly having to look for corrective actions to current issues, great enterprise application managers devote time researching known issues and assessing which ones are likely to surface in their operational environments. Once they determine the most important set, they schedule the application and testing of those solutions to avoid potential interruptions. The trick here is justifying the cost involved in applying solutions for issues that may never actually occur. My recommendation is to use a change management process that includes recording detailed proposals for use in risk assessment. This sounds complex and convoluted, but it need not be so. Including simple details such as the following can help justify the applying proactive solutions:

- The origin of the preventative measure
- A sentence or two on its impact if not applied
- An estimate of the likelihood of occurrence
- A review of the costs involved in the application

So, in addition to equipping yourself with reactive tools, consider learning more about your organization's most important business processes and system usages, and work with the related business operations teams as required.

Fast Fail and Automation

Another great practical approach to managing reliability is to ensure problems are caught as early as possible—ideally automatically—where a part of the system knows that an error has occurred and captures the appropriate details for follow-up.

Also worth noting is that in functional business applications not all problems are software errors or exceptions, so there should also be a method for end users to report a problem with an equivalent quick and easy mechanism that captures the same details. This might be a secondary system or simply a great self-serve, in-house process to get help or quickly raise high-quality help desk tickets.

The ultimate goal is to automate as much of the failure resolution process as possible, reducing the administrative overhead and leveraging machines' power to process complex but expected information. Few truly autonomic systems can self-heal without human intervention; indeed, the most effective solutions are hybrids that deliver a selection of likely solutions, with final verification and solution approval given by the administrator. E-Business Suite itself offers no fully autonomous management tools; however, Enterprise Manager contains diagnostic frameworks and alerting capabilities that are getting close. You'll see these throughout this, and subsequent, chapters.

Take Meaningful First Action

Managing reliability means not only putting systems in place, but also ensuring that their supporting processes are efficient and effective. The obvious next stage after a failure occurs is for a meaningful action to happen, such as the collection of comprehensive information and the appropriate routing of the issue.

One important example of this is that an environment must be available in which detailed reliability investigation can occur. This is often not the live production instance, but a secondary recently cloned system where changes in logging, configuration, and even patch levels can take place without extensive change management processing that reduces resolution time.

Trying to cover every reliability eventuality is a massive task, with inordinately complex rule-based logic associated with it. In fact, it would be madness to try. Ultimately, it's down to the reliability management plan to keep basic resolution processes measured, monitored, and tuned to be both practical and effective. The recommendation is to consider the most likely and the most impactful potential problem types, then build a skeleton set of processes around the capabilities and tools. From this humble beginning, you can rapidly expand and evolve the processes as real experiences occur, just as described by the continuous feedback loops in our original Fusion management model.

Leverage Industry Best Practice

Reliability management has a lot in common with the Information Technology Infrastructure Library (ITIL) problem and incident management processes, with the same principles of handling issues based on clearly defined elements in a general process flow. I recommend you look at the details of the ITIL processes, as defined in its service operation book. Going beyond the tooling, but associated with ITIL recommendations, in Chapter 10 we consider many best practices for running a healthy and effective help desk operation.

Our definition of reliability management is more wide-reaching than just problem management and includes not just the reactive work illustrated in Figure 5-3, but also the management of the

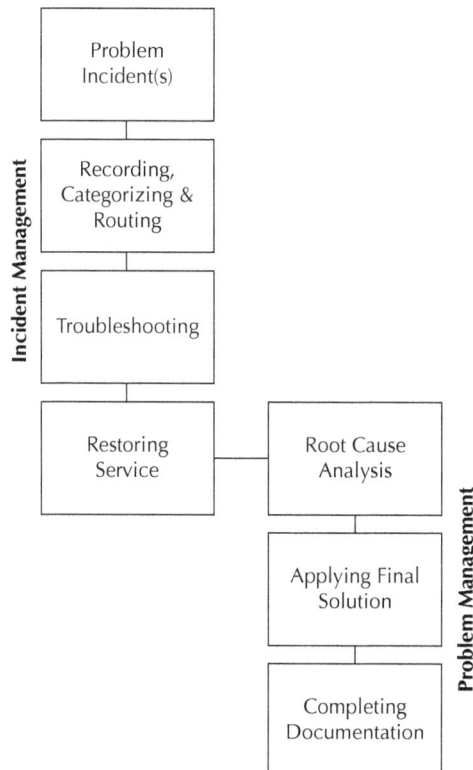

FIGURE 5-3. *The reactive problem management process flow based on ITIL standards*

overall system performance and the proactive identification of reliability patterns and trends to help implement preventative measures.

The identification of reliability patterns and trends is especially important as so often those overwhelmed with the constant volume of high priority issues are left with no time to consider how to negate the incoming flow with actions such as proactive health checks.

Reliability Tools

The remainder of this chapter focuses on troubleshooting tools in E-Business Suite, complemented by methods to help identify any missing solutions to known issues, so that their ill effects are never even encountered.

As mentioned before, all the tools and techniques are divided by the layer within which they mainly apply, starting with the Business Process Layer, which covers items that end users or functional administrators might use.

We follow this by reviewing the capabilities that exist within the Applications Technology Layer, the foundation upon which the features rely for many core utility services.

Finally, we dig deeper into the Platform Technology Layer where we consider the options that exist for use within the base architectural components such as the application server or the database.

It is worth clarifying that some of these tools are universal or may be used in different ways at different times, so don't be surprised to see them appear again in several layer sections.

In essence, to execute on a real reliability management plan, this division makes the most practical sense, and Table 5-1 summarizes the types of tools we'll review for reliability management in each of the three layers.

Business Process	Applications Technology	Platform Technology
Online help	Oracle Applications Manager (OAM)	Problem and incident management
Application messages	Oracle Workflow	Oracle Forms
Functional setup	Concurrent Manager	Java and the application server
Functional diagnostics	Oracle Forms	The database server
Functional scripts and utilities	OA Framework	Health recommendations and the Compliance Framework
FND: diagnostics	Business Intelligence	Remote Diagnostic Agent (RDA)
Applications logging	Oracle Diagnostic Framework	OS, hardware, and networking
Patching functional products	My Oracle Support: health recommendations and utility scripts	Platform technology
Working with My Oracle Support	Oracle Enterprise Manager	
Oracle Enterprise Manager		

TABLE 5-1.   *The Reliability Toolbox Manifest*

Table 5-2 shows the same manifest items again but reordered into two simple categories based on their most common usage. The intention here is to offer a chapter index that applies to whatever situation you are currently in, as opposed to the general sequential reading structure given in Table 5-1.

Business Process Layer

This section includes a collection of tools for troubleshooting the business functionality that falls under the Business Process Layer, such as hiring employees, paying salaries, approving promotions, or paying bonuses. The focus here is to illustrate capabilities for business users and those that assist them, such as help desks, and it should be clear that the use cases included are just examples. It's down to you to use the most applicable tool to each scenario you face.

Online Help

The online help is a powerful tool to address reliability issues and offers two methods of help. First, as a rich resource of information it should always be leveraged to address problems that may be related to functional configuration or usage. Second, it can be customized and extended so that areas users find consistently challenging are further explained and supported by additional material.

Monitoring and Troubleshooting	Managing
Health recommendations and the Compliance Framework	Oracle Applications Manager
FND: diagnostics	Working with My Oracle Support
Online help	Oracle Workflow
Problem and incident management	Oracle Forms
Application messages	Functional setup
Functional diagnostics	Concurrent Manager
Remote Diagnostic Agent	Java and the application server
Applications logging	OA Framework
Oracle Diagnostic Framework	Business Intelligence
Functional scripts and utilities	OS, hardware and networking
Patching functional products	Platform technology
My Oracle Support: health recommendations and utility scripts	Oracle Forms
	The database server
	Oracle Enterprise Manager

TABLE 5-2. *The Reliability Toolbox Based on Use Case*

The online help is accessible from throughout E-Business Suite and contains a fairly uniform content structure. It's also available for use offline as a stand-alone library zip file, with the same content published in both HTML and PDF file formats.

As shown in Figure 5-4, the online help can be browsed using a simple hierarchy in the Contents tab. You can also use a keyword in the Search tab, which includes an advanced search that allows a slightly more complex word sequence as well as the option to include only one data source—a specific product. The result selected for display is shown as part of the third View Topic tab.

All application products contain roughly the same types of content, including the following that are most applicable to reliability:

- **Setup and implementation**   Includes details on configuring the system to operate as intended.

- **User features**   Includes basic explanations of how the features are intended to support real business tasks.

- **Reference guides**   Includes integration resources and technical details such as rules logic and explanation of the key database structures like tables and columns.

In addition, the E-Business Suite help can be customized and extended as organizations see fit using the tools under the Application Administrator responsibility. This is a popular feature, since it allows you to tailor the text to fit specific user bases, as well as internal business processes. It's also sensible to implement custom help to support any extended or custom functionality.

In terms of reliability, a best practice is to always review the help available for areas where regular end-user problems occur. Then, if you deem it appropriate, adjust or add to the standard text to try to guide users through the difficult process, highlight common mistakes, or at least let them know what to do if problems do occur. This simple action can save many support calls and help capture the all-too-valuable information right where the problem occurs.

Precise details on adjusting the help files are available in the central document Oracle E-Business Suite System Administrator's Guide—Configuration (Part Number E12893-04).

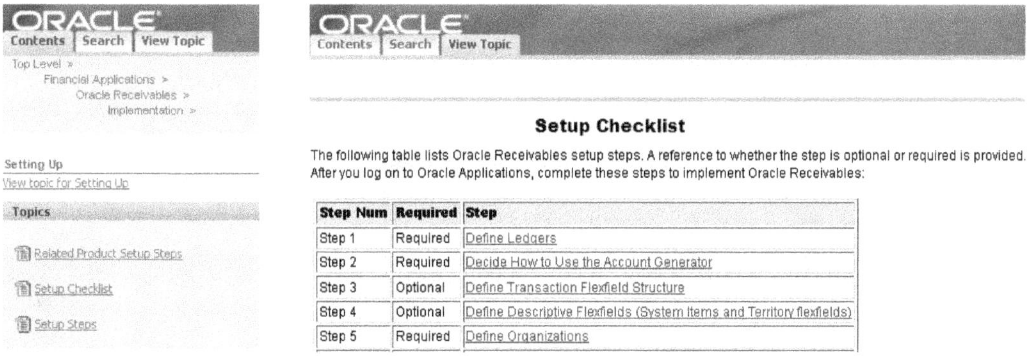

FIGURE 5-4.   *The online help for Oracle Receivables setup, accessible via a contents hierarchy browse*

Application Messages

When E-Business Suite provides a response to an end user action, such as submitting a transaction, the actual text shown can be adjusted. At runtime the text values originate from database records that can be queried back and changed as required.

Figure 5-5 shows an example, where the confirmation message "Your item category has been created" shown to an end user matches the record ICX_CAT_CATG_CREATE_CONF. The form to see these records is found under the Application Developer or Functional Administrator responsibilities, under the Application section, with the title Messages, as illustrated in Figure 5-6.

In the same way that online help can be adjusted and extended to help end users avoid getting into reliability issues, the messages shown to them can be optimized. A good example might be an error type of message that could be adjusted to ask them to make sure they have the related setup completed properly, or even a message that points users to the page to complete a missing value, such as an exchange rate. While the seeded messages are intended to be as descriptive as possible, it is common for organizations to expand on these, especially where the standard terms and processes are used differently in their own implementation. These messages are also translatable, so that any additional text can be added for users of other languages.

Complete details on using messages can be found in the Oracle E-Business Suite Developer's Guide (Part Number E12897-04) under the Message Dictionary section.

Functional Setup Vital to ensuring E-Business Suite's reliability is making sure that the product features are implemented in a way that is complete, corresponds to user's expectations, and is valid based on its design. Much of this is verified before the go-live date, such as trying to submit an order in Chinese yen where there are no exchange rates set to the implemented base currency of U.S. dollars, for example. The form simply prevents you from making this mistake. While the maturity of E-Business Suite means most checks for common gotchas are hardwired in, some of them are not, as they may limit some other valid use case and therefore restrict system flexibility.

In troubleshooting reliability problems, it is relatively common to need to check and verify the implementation details, including the various values in the functional setup.

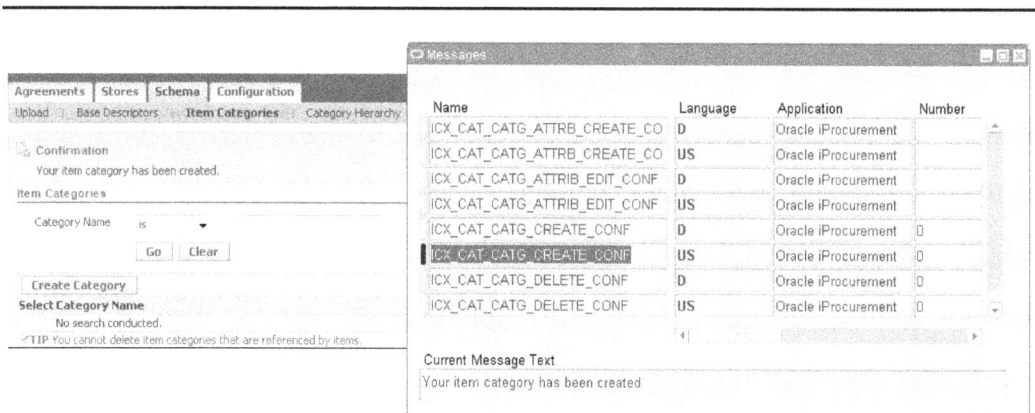

FIGURE 5-5. *A message at runtime and the same defined in the database, as shown in Oracle Forms*

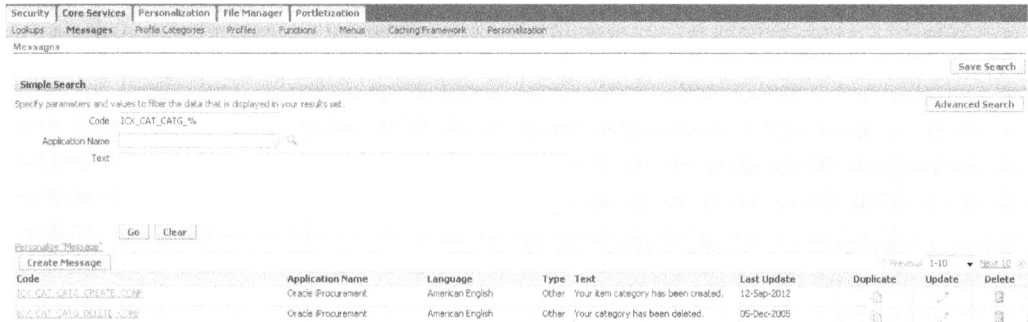

FIGURE 5-6. *The same message as shown in the OA Framework page under the Functional Administrator responsibility*

There are essentially two resources to use for accessing functional setup data in a broad native fashion. First are functional diagnostics, which we'll focus on in the next section; second is Oracle E-Business Suite's iSetup.

iSetup creates setup data extracts that are available for analysis in iSetup's built-in reporting tools. This provides *standard reports*, which provide details of data objects that exist within the context of a particular product, examples being setup options, templates, and data types. Figure 5-7 shows

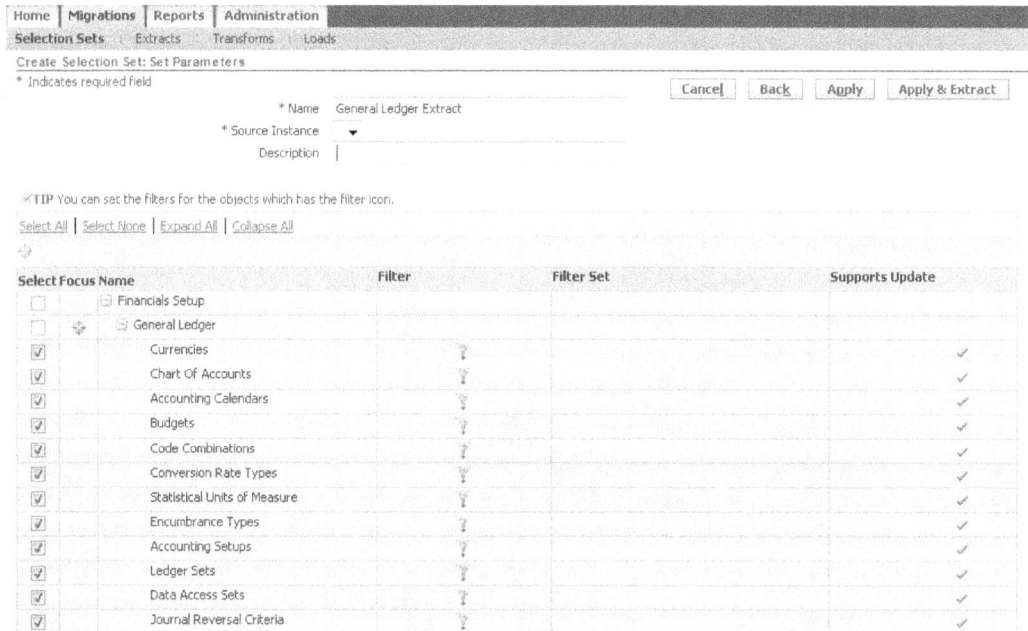

FIGURE 5-7. *iSetup extract creation showing the data available for General Ledger*

examples from General Ledger, where the selection sets for General Ledger are chosen and then used as the basis for data extraction, upon which reports are run. Reports allow quick access to all the key setup data for a particular product, which is very helpful during troubleshooting of functional issues.

In addition to standard reports, iSetup also supports *comparison reports*, in which two data sources (extracts) are compared to help highlight the differences. Configuration creep often leads to reliability issues, and when a gold instance is available this simple comparison check is recommended.

Obviously, dumps of functional setup and configuration data are only as good as their interpretations, so it requires either access to product domain experts or equivalent resources such as the following:

- Documentation that explains the setup processes and dependencies. For E-Business Suite these are often in the form of PDF implementation guides.

- Help content, as mentioned previously, that includes detail on setup related to specific functionality as well as many useful setup checklists.

- Oracle University courses that cover all core E-Business Suite products, including both setup and usage. These are available as in-class training, live virtual classes delivered over the Internet, and self-paced training (commonly on CD although it's moving toward video on-demand).

Functional Diagnostics   Functional diagnostics are the business task–related tests available as part of the Oracle Diagnostic Framework (ODF) embedded inside E-Business Suite. If you have administered any E-Business Suite instance since Release 11 onward, you will most likely have come across these before. They're accessed through the Application Diagnostics responsibility and provide around 400 executable tests, organized by application product.

Tests fall into various different categories depending on what they do, with common types being data collections, setup validators, and data integrity checks. As illustrated in Figure 5-8, once the application is chosen, tests are grouped based on subject domain, here showing that for Payables Setup there are two tests. Test are run individually or added to a batch. These are then run either immediately or scheduled for a later time.

While more often used to collect information when troubleshooting an existing problem, I also recommend you run a batch of tests together at specific times for more preventative purposes, such as checking the accounting setups and ledger postings before running the financial period close.

In addition, E-Business Suites' ODF supports adjusting the organization of existing tests, plus the registration of custom programs (Java, PL/SQL, and XML) as new diagnostics tests. This flexibility means proactive administrators can prepare checks and extra diagnostics in readiness of supporting their most sensitive and important functional processes.

Diagnostic tests are secured by normal E-Business Suite security and offer no administrative or data-changing functionality. Therefore, it is most prudent to grant access to tests to those who might be able to use them in dealing (or preventing) reliability issues, such as implementers, functional managers, business analysts, and knowledgeable endusers. This should also involve a certain amount of dedicated training so that these users are able to understand the test output and take appropriate actions. Equipping functional users with the tools to avoid and resolve functional problems is a basic essential for effective reliability management.

More details can be found in the Oracle Diagnostics Framework User's Guide (E12895-03) and the complete Release 12 catalog of diagnostic tests is listed out in My Oracle Support Note 421245.1.

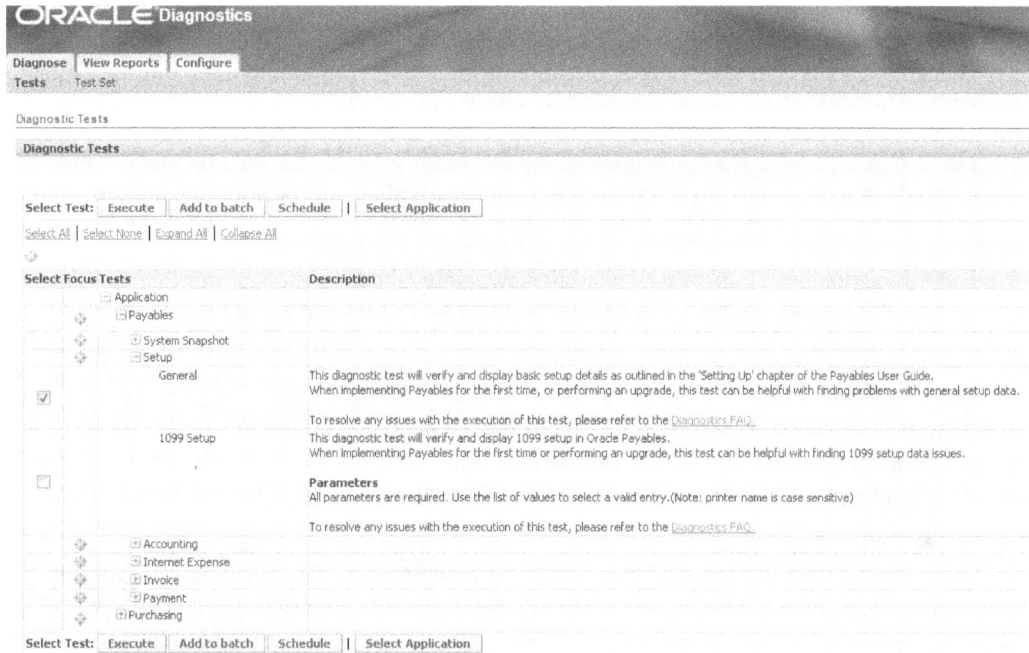

FIGURE 5-8. *Payables setup diagnostic tests*

Functional Scripts and Utilities   Sometimes the tests in the Oracle Diagnostics Framework are not specific enough to investigate certain types of problems, and while this central catalog and execution system is the right place to start, there are many other scripts available. These commonly originate from special requests or situations where particular pieces of information are needed as part of system diagnosis. Some of these scripts are used to gather information to help explain a particular situation or setup so that data in an unexpected state can be resolved.

Here are some examples from different product families, with the corresponding My Oracle Support note number in brackets:

- FIN: Script Catalogue for Receivables Support Transaction and Reconciliation Issues (974434.1)

- FIN: Funds Capture Configuration Data Gathering Script (794542.1)

- FIN: General Ledger: Script to Check Contents of GL_INTERFACE Table (77684.1)

- SCM: Sample Script of Receiving Open Interface (245334.1)

- SCM: Script to Cancel an Existing Order Line Using OE_ORDER_PUB (746798.1)

- CRM: Script to Verify Territory Setup for Task Assignment (840166.1)

- HRMS: Personal Information Data Collection Script (275483.1)

- HRMS: Data Collection Script (HRMS120.sql & HRMS121.sql) (453632.1)

The smart application manager will spend some time looking for these types of scripts, both for those functional areas where reliability issues are often found and for those areas where they have the most impact. While not always immediately identifiable, the best way to collect and check for scripts is to select the applicable product and component area and then look for troubleshooting documents or items with "script" in the title.

Keeping a good selection of bookmarks (a My Oracle Support feature) with these potentially useful scripts is strongly recommended. The use of these tools will probably involve collaborating with others with specific business and functional expertise, but it's worth the investment to help maintain maximum reliability and quick issue diagnosis.

FND: Diagnostics   E-Business Suite offers two general diagnostic features that are often used for troubleshooting issues and are accessible within the user interface, enabled by the profile option FND: Diagnostics.

These two features are illustrated in Figure 5-9, highlighted by boxes, with the About This Page link in the bottom left of every OA Framework page, and the Diagnostics link in the top right. Both of these tools provide output that is more technical in nature, but because they are exposed to end-users, they are included in this section.

The Diagnostics link provides the following features:

■   **Show Log**   This provides pages for searching and viewing the core E-Business Suite log files. It works only with the Applications and System Administrator responsibilities and links into Oracle Applications Manager pages. From these pages it is also possible to set the logging configuration.

■   **Set Trace Level**   This enables and configures the database tracing for that particular user's session. Once enabled, it shows trace numbers that can be used to find the respective files created on the database host machine.

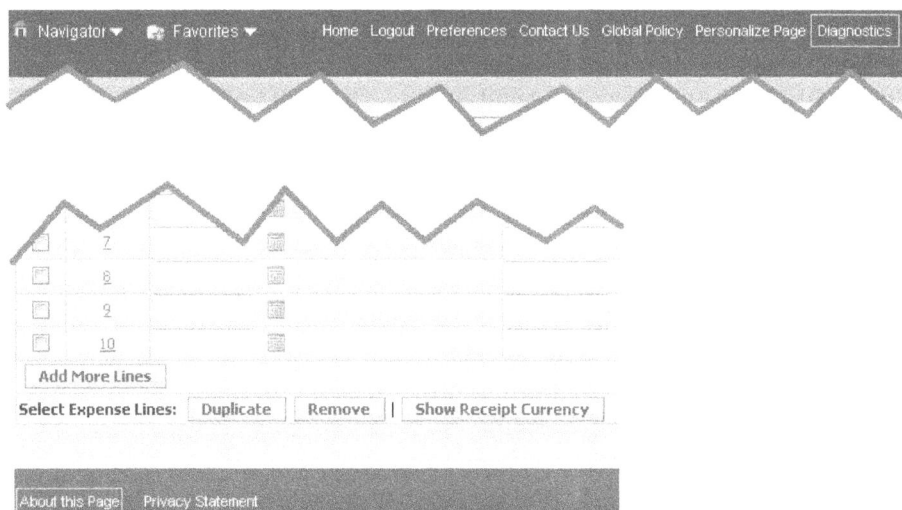

FIGURE 5-9.   *Links for the About this Page and Diagnostics features*

- **Show Log on Screen**   This enables and configures application logging for the user session and routes the output directly to the bottom of each OA Framework page. It's exceptionally helpful for user interface debugging but may lack the complete detail that persistent applications logging has when set via its own dedicated profile options (see the next section for more information).

- **Show Pool Monitor**   This provides lots of information about the execution environment within which the particular application and user activities are being completed. We'll look at this in more depth in other sections, but the ability to view the loaded Application Modules at any moment in time, the underlying JVM property values, and real-time memory data is significant, specifically for investigating reliability issues for functional processes.

The About this Page link reveals even more detailed information about the inner workings of the system, specifically all the components operating behind the current page. This is an exceptionally helpful resource for investigating reliability issues and, as shown in Figure 5-10, it exposes a wealth of information. The seven tabs across the top are relatively self-explanatory, exposing details about the page and the system under each. We'll look at many of them in context in other sections. Here are some of the highlights, related to functional reliability management.

- The Page tab has basic details, including the page version and page definition that shows the hierarchy of OA Framework components such as regions, tables, rows, cells, text, and so on that make up the page. It also shows the associated controller code names that are used when each page and region is requested or submitted.

- The Page tab also has details on flexfields and translations used by the page, plus a section hidden by default entitled "Business Component References Details." This is expanded in Figure 5-10 and, as you can see, contains the names and version of the code behind the user interface, including Application Modules, View Objects, and Controllers. You'll also note that the View Objects are hyperlinked and, when clicked, will display the associated SQL query (and attributes), plus details and versions of any associated entity objects and all related Java implementation classes. Armed with this information, it's relatively easy to search My Oracle Support for matching functional issues and looks for missing patches with higher related component versions.

- The Personalization tab displays the adjustments or customizations made to the page or related code components, providing they were done in accordance with the E-Business recommendations. As custom adjustments and new code are a regular cause of reliability issues, this is a great way to quickly see if there is something extra to investigate.

- The Page Context tab is a helpful way to see the environment within which a user is operating and can reveal misconfiguration and improper setup, which are often causes of unexpected reliability issues. This tab shows current details such as responsibility, organization, language, time zones, and some detailed applications security data that can explain why a user might not be able to see a specific page, region, or option.

Applications Logging   While logging is definitely a low-level technical tool, any tool that helps in either avoiding issues or resolving those that occur as quickly as possible is of interest, particularly because we're concerned with the reliability of the application's functionality (such as creating sales leads, booking orders, running payroll processing, and so on).

About Page: Oracle iProcurement: Shop

| Page | Personalization | Page Context | Technology Components | Java System Properties | Profiles | Patches |

/oracle/apps/icx/icatalog/shopping/webui/ShoppingHomePG 120.12.12010000.2

Page Definition

Focus Name		Controller	Application Module View Object View Attribute
⊞ pageLayout: Oracle iProcurement: Shop		ShoppingHomeCO	RequisitionAM

Business Component References Details

Retained Application Modules

Application Module

oracle.apps.icx.por.req.server.RequisitionAM

Application Modules

Application Module	Substitute	Load Lazily	Version
oracle.apps.icx.por.reqmgmt.server.ReqMgmtAM		Y	ReqMgmtAMImpl.java 120.17.12010000.3
oracle.apps.icx.por.req.server.RequisitionAM		Y	RequisitionAMImpl.java 120.21.12010000.3

View Objects

View Object	Substitute Entity Object
oracle.apps.icx.poplist.server.AdvSearchableStoresVO	
oracle.apps.icx.poplist.server.SearchableStoresVO	
oracle.apps.icx.por.reqmgmt.server.ReqTotalVO	
oracle.apps.icx.icatalog.shopping.server.StoreInfoVO	
oracle.apps.icx.por.reqmgmt.server.FullyReceivedVO	
oracle.apps.icx.icatalog.shopping.server.DisplayStoresVO	
oracle.apps.icx.icatalog.shopping.server.LanguageInfoVO	

Controllers

Controller	Version
oracle.apps.icx.icatalog.shopping.webui.SearchBoxCO	120.17
oracle.apps.icx.icatalog.shopping.webui.ShoppingCartCO	120.4
oracle.apps.icx.icatalog.shopping.webui.ShoppingHomeCO	120.27
oracle.apps.icx.por.reqmgmt.webui.MyReqsCO	120.3.12010000.1

Flexfield References

No flexfields found on this page

⊞ **Translatable Items**

FIGURE 5-10. *The About this Page output for the iProcurement shopping page*

Let's consider logging in two scenarios: normal operational logging and special troubleshooting logging.

Each application instance has a specific role, such as the test instance used for configuration/ feature/fix validation, and the production instance for live business use. As such, the test environment will be used for much more troubleshooting, investigating problems encountered during the aforementioned validation. In addition, performance requirements and overall load on the production instance will be substantially different from that of other instances, again something that logging configuration may have an impact on. That is not to say that no troubleshooting will occur in production, but the permitted configuration changes may be restricted compared to what is permissible on other instances.

The trick here is to try to make sure the following actions occur:

- ■ The production instance is mirrored by another offline instance as closely as possible. Having a secondary instance for troubleshooting is exceptionally valuable, especially once you get into the realm of applying patches that add more debug code, test configuration adjustments, and investigate and verify data-fixes.

- ■ The normal operations logging that is configured is sufficient so that any serious problems are recorded in enough detail to point toward their cause.

- ■ The normal operations logging that is configured is not so expensive in terms of activity and resource consumption (I/O, CPU, memory, disk space, and so on) that it causes a noticeable effect on system performance. This is difficult to holistically assess, since one especially vital product or feature may write more log output than others and as such may be more severely impacted.

- ■ Enabling more detailed troubleshooting logging is a fast and painless process, without the need for involving too many additional parties (help desks, administrators, approving managers, and so on). This is more a matter of establishing an effective process than E-Business Suite functionality.

The normal operational logging, as found in the production instance, is one where configuration enables minimal general logging while still catching serious issues and errors. The troubleshooting logging, however, is set at a lower level with more general output as found in a test instance, plus the option to turn up the volume should the need arise. Let's now take a quick look at how this works in E-Business Suite.

E-Business Suite logging is predominantly based around what is sometimes called *FND logging*. That is not to say that exceptions do not exist: a huge amount of mature code in place uses several of the legacy logging mechanisms, since changing hundreds of lines of code just to adjust logging is a substantial risk with very little real reward. A few examples are the profile options starting with "OM: Debug" and "GL: Debug." That said, most of the products in the latest versions of Release 12 use FND logging.

As mentioned previously under the FND: Diagnostics Show Log feature, logging can be configured through accessing Oracle Applications Manager. This is an easy-to-use user interface that many administrators will appreciate. The older way of enabling FND logging still remains available, namely via the Profile Options. Underneath, both work in the same way, so it's just a matter of preference.

Figure 5-11 shows the basic logging profile options, as exposed in the Oracle Forms page. As you can see, the logging-related profile options (all starting FND: Debug) are listed and show the settings for the site, in this case indicating it's not enabled, the configuration for users accessing the Purchasing responsibility (which is also unset), and for the one specific user queried for (ERIK1) who does have logging configured.

Figure 5-12 shows the Oracle Applications Manager page for configuring FND logging, and it's easy to see the same data as the forms-based page, plus the Java settings and all other users as well. For example, JPALMER is clearly investigating something inside Oracle Enterprise Planning and Budgeting (which has the short code ZPB). The extra visibility provided by this page is important

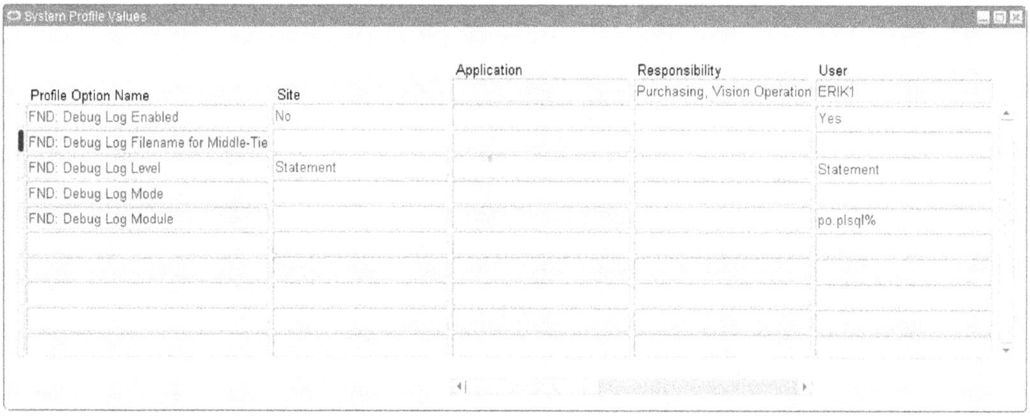

FIGURE 5-11. *The logging profile options shown in Oracle Forms*

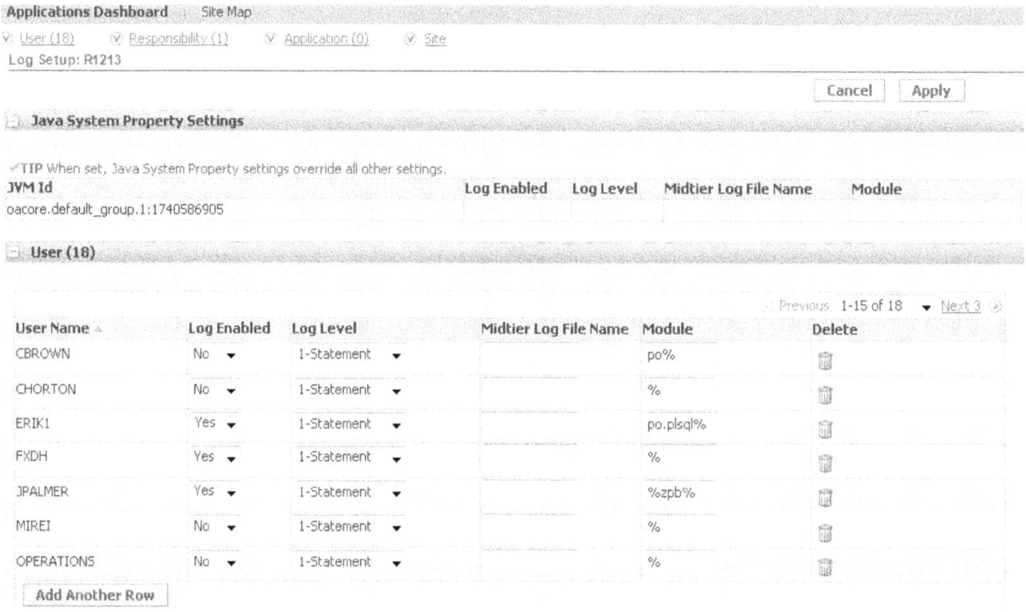

FIGURE 5-12. *The logging configuration shown in Oracle Applications Manager*

for the application manager to check and spot logging configurations that may be either invalid or need resetting.

Truly effective use of logging requires knowing what configuration to adjust to get the level of detail required to help identify the cause of the problem. While this may only require understanding what the Profile Options do and the appropriate values to set for each, it also requires the ability to interpret log output to make meaningful conclusions.

This can be tough. While errors in logs are usually easy to spot and perform basic research around (such as looking in the My Oracle Support Knowledge Base), the output from each log line from process execution often requires low level source code understanding, and therefore should be provided to Oracle Support.

We'll revisit logging in several of the later chapters, but if you want to know more about E-Business Suite FND logging configuration, please review Oracle E-Business Suite System Administrator's Guide—Configuration (E12893-04), which has an entire section devoted to the various types of logging and what each of the configuration options do. Since the exact usage of the log configuration parameters depends on what area of the system is being investigated, it is not especially sensible to include specific recommendations here.

Patching Functional Products   You can consider patching in both reactive and proactive work modes. First, when problems occur, the ability to quickly check for any related fixes is essential. This is available through a combination of actions in My Oracle Support: searching for knowledge articles, checking subsequent roll-up patches, and searching the patch repository.

Second, on the proactive side, it's sensible to keep a watch for solutions to key pieces of functionality. One way of doing this is to use My Oracle Support's knowledge of your system, such as the information collected by Oracle Configuration Manager and its clever way of knowing which relevant parts might be missing.

As shown in Figure 5-13, there are several resources in My Oracle Support that can help keep a watch for patches to functional features. These include

- Patch search has some powerful features, with the results being readily included in patching plans for analysis and implementation:

  - Search by Product or Family provides a detailed criteria choice, with results sortable by the last updated value, allowing quick visibility into the very latest patches.

  - Recommended Patch Advisor lists the patches available for one or more product combinations.

- Patch Recommendations, as shown in Figure 5-14, lists patches for the key system components and provides simple tools for planning their application.

- Upgrade Planner helps you understand what patches are needed to properly plan the step-by-step process of completing complex upgrades and updates.

- Patching Quick Links (not visible in Figure 5-13) is regularly updated with links to the latest information and catalog tools for displaying the most commonly used resources.

One slightly sneaky alternative method for finding fixes is to search both the patch and bug knowledge repositories for either error messages or code filenames that you know are involved in a key program or process. While not desirable for an everyday task, performed on a monthly cycle it may return some results that are of interest to your businesses core feature functions. This

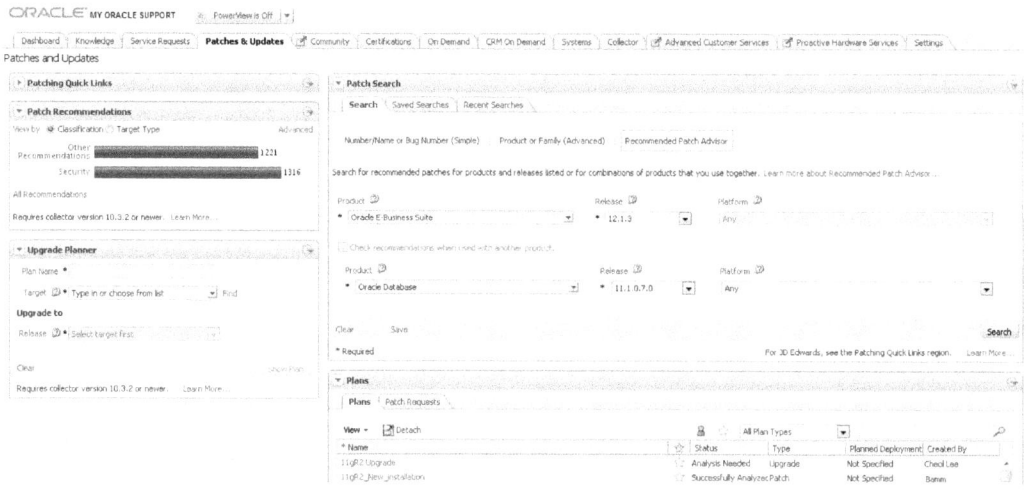

FIGURE 5-13. *Various features of the Patches and Updates tab in My Oracle Support*

is in addition to alerts and notifications we'll discuss next—and obviously, all error messages should be searched for in the Knowledge Base.

Working with My Oracle Support As just mentioned, My Oracle Support provides details on all known functional reliability issues, as well as a wealth of information on related troubleshooting and setups. The search mechanism in My Oracle Support is constantly evolving to be more intuitive, and now includes the intent or purpose of the search, such as looking for help during upgrades or during troubleshooting. The embedding of this multifaceted search capability adds another way of filtering the results so that they are more specific to the problem at hand.

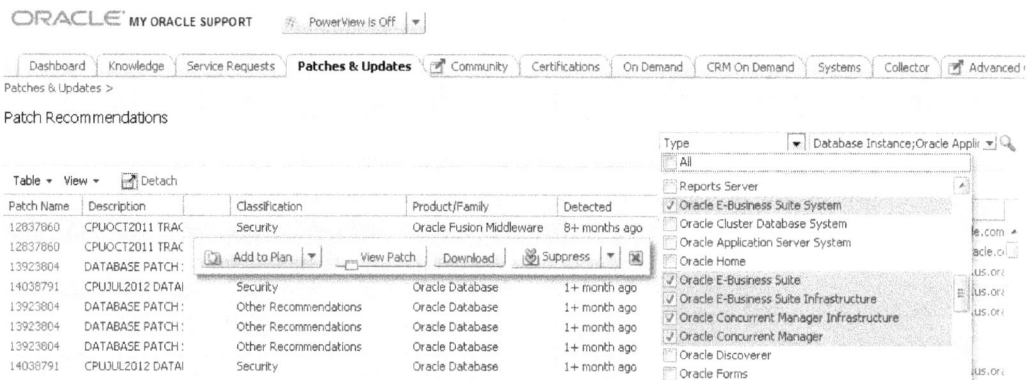

FIGURE 5-14. *Patch recommendations with options to filter the list and take various actions*

Here are some very basic recommendations for narrowing your search. During a simple test I ran, following these recommendations reduced a keyword search of "Negotiation Styles" from 177 documents down to just 7 relevant hits:

- Always choose your product carefully, going to the finest level of detail possible, ideally selecting the category or subcategory.

- Filter by release, so that the results definitely apply to you.

- Look at the document types and choose those that are most likely to be helpful. Look for fixes in "problem" type and explanations in "how to" types.

- Don't forget that there are great details in whitepapers and longer troubleshooting documents. Along with the product documentation, these are often worth bookmarking and checking through before running general Knowledge Base searches.

In addition, because we're considering functional reliability here, most of the major problems related to the use of the products are captured as knowledge articles, and if you use the My Oracle Support alerting mechanisms, you can be quickly notified of any new articles that apply to your most important areas of interest. This is shown in Figure 5-15, where I have set up my Settings page to inform me by e-mail of any new documents, SRs, bugs, or health recommendations of a few specific types for a few specific products, avoiding an overwhelming flood of extraneous information.

In addition to knowledge search and notifications, the My Oracle Support Community tab offers a central forum for Q&A, discussions, and knowledge sharing between all kinds of users, such as business users, technical experts, partners and consultancies, and Oracle staff. This free flow of information can really speed the resolution of general questions, as well as be a hotbed of many tips, tricks, and best practices. All information there is archived and searchable, traceable via RSS feed; the Community forum is fast becoming a great supplement to the Oracle Support service.

Another simple way of proactively keeping track of news and information is to follow the Oracle official @myoraclesupport Twitter account. While information is not specific to a product line, the most significant updates and details of Oracle's product support are shared. I imagine this kind of real-time and socially enabled engagement of support will only continue to evolve.

One final recommendation is to make sure you understand how to work effectively with Oracle Support. We'll revisit this in detail in Chapter 10, but here is a quick cheat-sheet list that can drastically reduce resolution time:

- Illustrate your problem with screen captures, numbered steps of actions taken, and as much detail as possible.

- Explain the background to the problem, whether or not it ever worked, and what's changed or different.

- Explain the impact of this issue to your business and any workarounds you're using.

- Include as many troubleshooting details as possible, such as Oracle Diagnostic output and the related logs.

- Take a little time to clearly present your details, including drawing attention to what you consider key information to the issue.

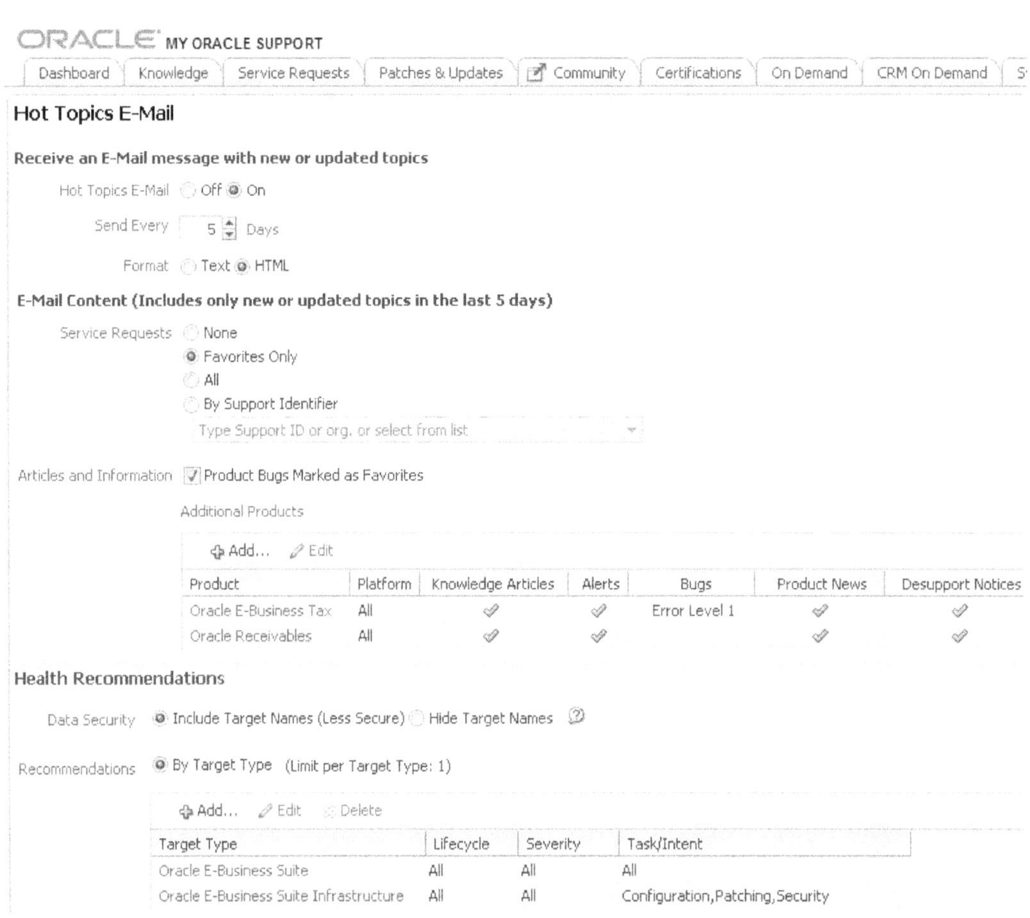

FIGURE 5-15. *Configuring My Oracle Support to send alerts when relevant new information becomes available*

Oracle Enterprise Manager   Oracle Enterprise Manager is the best-in-class administration tool for managing the complete Oracle technology stack across large-scale deployments. Indeed, the latest release includes not just organizational systems but the data center and cloud management as well. Oracle uses this same tool internally to manage its own cloud systems and services.

Basic Oracle Enterprise Manager doesn't require special licensing, so a large amount of functionality to help monitor failure on key components inside E-Business Suite (the database, host servers, and so on) is available without extra cost. This, however, is really only a generic portion of what Enterprise Manager is capable of, especially for E-Business Suite, with the installation of an extra management suite plug-in.

The Application Management Suite for E-Business Suite includes a host of specialized diagnostics, performance, monitoring, and management features, plus the Oracle Real User

Experience Insight (RUEI) product accelerator for E-Business Suite and the Enterprise Manager Configuration and Compliance features.

These are all great features, and we'll look at all of them in more detail in subsequent chapters, but this section is concerned with managing reliability of application business functionality, not the technology components. Nevertheless, there are some Enterprise Manager components and complementary solutions that can be integrated with E-Business Suite to offer useful capabilities.

Real User Experience Insight (RUEI) has evolved from the Moniforce acquisition and represents a powerful method of interrogating network traffic to understand what is happening at the user browser. It identifies exceptionally detailed page requests, performance information, errors, and a wealth of other data commonly available in hidden resources like network packets and message headers.

As shown in Figure 5-16, RUEI has easy-to-use visual dashboards of its data so that issues, exceptions, anomalies, and interesting patterns can be quickly identified. As concerns reliability management, this represents not only great background technical data for troubleshooting issues but also the opportunity to proactively monitor system activities for reliability problems.

RUEI contains a whole host of additional features such as session replay, where a problem can be repeated again and again based on the data collected. RUEI is used by some of the largest applications in the world and offers an E-Business Suite accelerator, which plugs into the RUEI framework so that it supports all its transactions and pages.

In addition to RUEI, there are a few Enterprise Manager plug-in products that offer similar insights into system activity that may be helpful in reliability management. One example is Business Transaction Management (BTM), which offers the capability of tracking and scrutinizing database activities that correspond to real application transactions.

Another is Business Activity Monitoring (BAM), part of Oracle Fusion Middleware. It shows details on Service Oriented Architecture (SOA) components, specifically how all Business Process

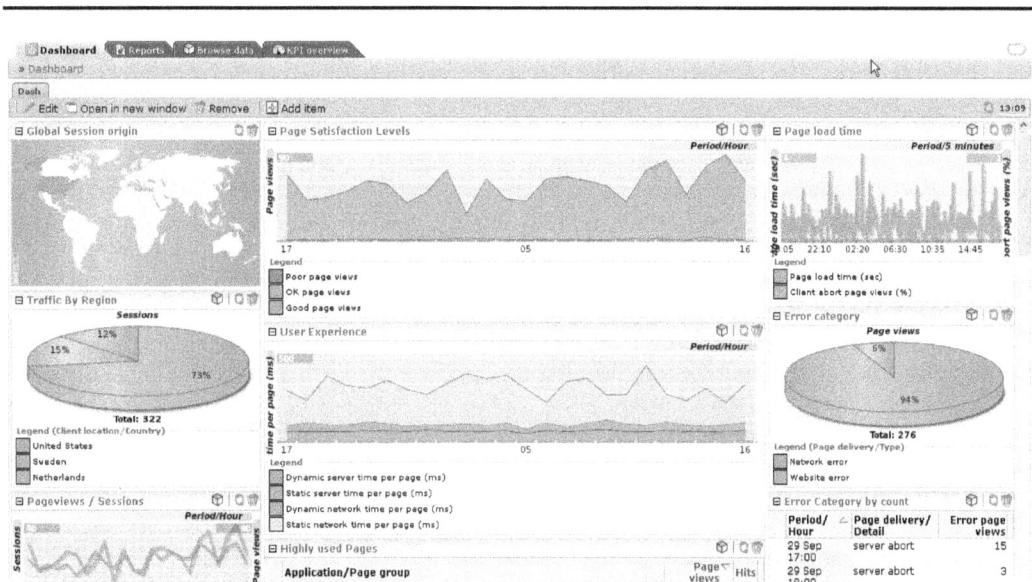

FIGURE 5-16. *The dashboard page of RUEI showing lots of rich usage information*

Execution Language (BPEL) activities are performing. While the need for this is a relatively recent addition to E-Business Suite with increasing integration through the standard Applications Integration Architecture (AIA) and all modern applications focused in this area, it is a logical enterprise application management addition.

Applications Technology Layer

Let's now look one layer deeper inside E-Business Suite to the Applications Technology Layer and consider the tools available for investigating reliability management, as well as avoiding and troubleshooting issues.

We'll cover the following items in this section:

- Oracle Applications Manager
- Oracle Workflow
- Concurrent Manager
- Oracle Forms
- OA Framework
- Business Intelligence
- Oracle Diagnostic Framework
- My Oracle Support: health recommendations and utility scripts
- Oracle Enterprise Manager

Oracle Applications Manager (OAM)   In the previous section we discussed how the FND Diagnostics feature redirects the E-Business Suite user into OAM screens for access to logs. This process, moving directly from business functionality into log files, isn't really a common situation and is really only recommended for a power-user or application manager who might be reproducing an issue. Most of the time, the application manager would go directly into OAM where log access is readily available.

Beyond logs, another reliability-related feature inside OAM is known as *System Alerts and Metrics*. This feature provides the capability to track applications' technology problems, such as failures in Concurrent Manager, Oracle Forms, or Workflow. Alerts are based around the use of the FND messages process (discussed previously). When the applications code is unsuccessful in using a component, it uses a failure message categorized as critical, error, or warning. As shown in Figure 5-17, when these messages are used, an *occurrence* of a specific alert is created and available for review in OAM.

OAM provides a few simple features to manage system alerts, including changing their status, adding notes, and saving them to the Support Cart for sharing. In addition, notifications (e-mails) can be triggered upon an occurrence of any of these alerts. In ITIL terms, this could be considered equivalent to the incident record.

Similar to System Alerts, Figure 5-17 also shows a Metrics tab. These are used to measure specific components such as Forms or Concurrent Manager, against which end user–defined exceptions can be set, ultimately providing a method to build custom event triggers for failure notifications and troubleshooting. This framework has existed for some time, but when compared with similar functionality of tools like Enterprise Manager, its practical application has limits.

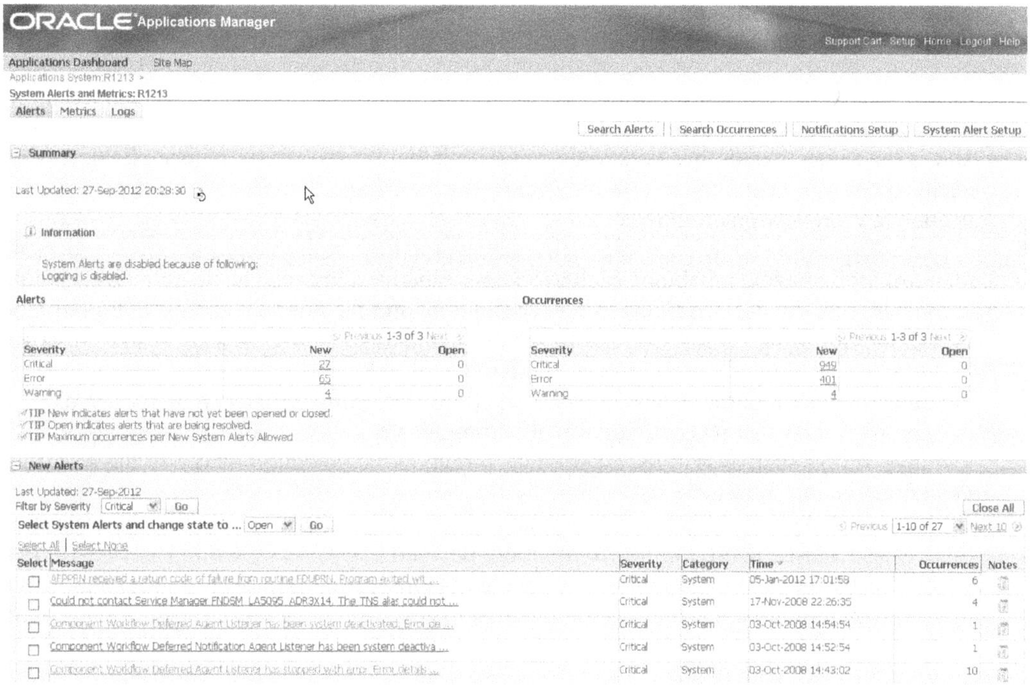

FIGURE 5-17. *The System Alerts page in Oracle Applications Manager*

The other area of OAM related to reliability is the *Debug Workbench*, available under the Diagnostics and Repair section of the site map. This is essentially a simplified method of configuring various debugging features. It applies specifically to Concurrent Programs and Oracle Forms only and has some useful configuration capabilities, such as being able to define a time period for which the debugging will start and stop and the selection of a user. As shown in Figure 5-18, it allows the setting of Logging, as well as SQL Tracing and the PL/SQL Profiler for analyzing database queries.

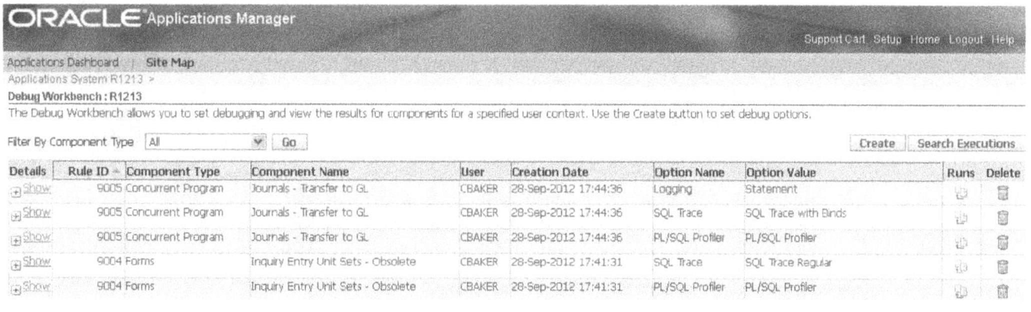

FIGURE 5-18. *Setting the tracing, logging, and profiler using the Debug Workbench*

While possible, enabling the debug configuration of forms and concurrent processing components outside of OAM is considerably more difficult; therefore, this represents a useful and much-simplified method. To clarify, this is not complete log and trace configuration, just a subset.

Oracle Workflow Troubleshooting As the engine for most of the process-driven functionality in E-Business Suite, investigating reliability issues inside Oracle Workflow is an important task. This is not to say that it's the Workflow engine itself that is unreliable—far from it. However, as each feature uses Workflow to execute its own business logic, if there is a problem, it is caught inside the Workflow environment.

Let's first review a few basics about Workflow and look at the tools and features inside the platform for managing reliability. Each Workflow execution instance is identified by a unique combination of the Item Type (the process definition) and the Item Key (an execution instance). Workflow runs using PL/SQL and database tables, and as such records a good amount of audit and execution log information in its own internal tables. Based on the Item Type/Item Key combination, much of the details of past executions, including errors, can be retrieved.

These troubleshooting tools are available through a number of different methods, including low-level scripts such as *WFSTATUS.sql*, which outputs an execution report, or the easy-to-use Workflow screens in OAM.

While OAM has some top-level summary pages that you'll see in several toolbox sections, there is also a search and drill-down into more detailed pages. As shown in Figure 5-19, once the Workflow instance has been found it's possible to launch the Workflow Monitor page. This rich applet provides a graphical view of the processing flow, including the ability to see the actions performed and the associated runtime data. The example in the figure shows the purchase order approval process, with the Document Complete Check Before Approval node selected and the result value of Yes. If the back-end code call had failed at this point, the monitor would show the error details.

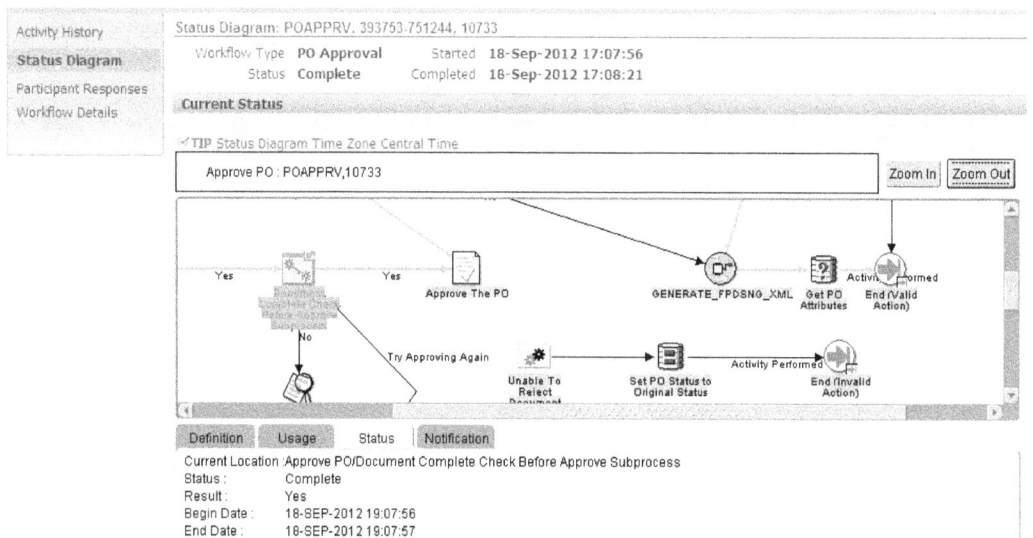

FIGURE 5-19. *Details from the Workflow Monitor*

Since Workflow processing is simply a structured mechanism for the execution of applications code, the usual troubleshooting techniques apply, such as enabling logging.

Oracle E-Business Suite's Workflow items can be further analyzed, but this requires low-level knowledge, such as using Workflow Builder for investigating the Workflow definition and the code calls behind it. It's also true that the majority of E-Business Suite installations include modifications to the standard Workflow items, and this capability is one of the more powerful features that allow it to be tailored to meet organization-specific needs.

Clearly, troubleshooting custom code requires knowing the standard tools available as well as the details of the customization. As such there is much more involved in using, administering and developing Workflow items, and the following documents are recommended for more information:

- Oracle Workflow User's Guide (E12906-04)
- Oracle Workflow Administrator's Guide (E12903-04)
- Oracle Workflow Developer's Guide (E12905-04)

We'll look at the internal components of the Workflow Engine later in this chapter, in the context of making sure they are performing effectively and are optimized.

Concurrent Processing Troubleshooting   E-Business Suite concurrent requests may occasionally fail but, just like Workflow, the Concurrent Processing engine is a mature and stable execution platform, and the problems are generally with the application program code it's running. Also like Workflow, when reliability issues occur, a working knowledge of the Concurrent Processing troubleshooting features is useful. On the whole this takes two forms.

The first process requires an understanding of what the concurrent request does—that is, what application program it calls. This can be discovered by looking at the program definition in the System Administration responsibility (under Concurrent | Programs). This details out the executable program called, the parameters used, configurations (including logging and tracing), and some summary statistics of use.

The second process is to lookup a problematic instance of the request and drill into the detail. This is possible via both Oracle Forms and (somewhat more intuitively) through Oracle Applications Manager. Figure 5-20 includes an example, and while this completed without error

FIGURE 5-20.   *Details of the PO Output for Communication concurrent request*

(see the status column), it shows all the detail recorded plus the buttons where access to diagnostic run data, logs for the request and the components, and the final output is all available. Again using OAM makes accessing all the important details much easier.

However, while the Concurrent Processing platform can be diagnosed by the features just mentioned, for specific program failures it requires knowledge of the related product and whatever troubleshooting it contains. An example might be a general ledger program that consistently fails: to investigate why it's failing, you'd need to set the general ledger debug mode on, which is done through a specific product profile option and is unrelated to Concurrent Processing.

Oracle Forms for E-Business Suite As illustrated by Figure 5-21, E-Business Suite provides a set of troubleshooting features that are specific to the Oracle Forms pages, accessible from the Help menu and secured by Profile Options.

These items are exceptionally useful for investigating both data and user interface issues, with the following recommended highlights for reliability issues.

- **General help items** The first three items in the Help menu provide content for assisting the end user. They should not be overlooked in the rush to access something more technical.

- **Diagnostics** A series of items for investigating the current form displayed:

  - **Display Database Error** Provides more detail on failure to change or insert data into the database. This is most often used for APP-FND errors where missing or unsupported data is being used by the form.

  - **Examine** Deconstructs the currently selected field in the form, giving its block name, field name, and value.

  - **Logging** Provides quick access to the Oracle Applications Manager pages for configuring and viewing the applications logs.

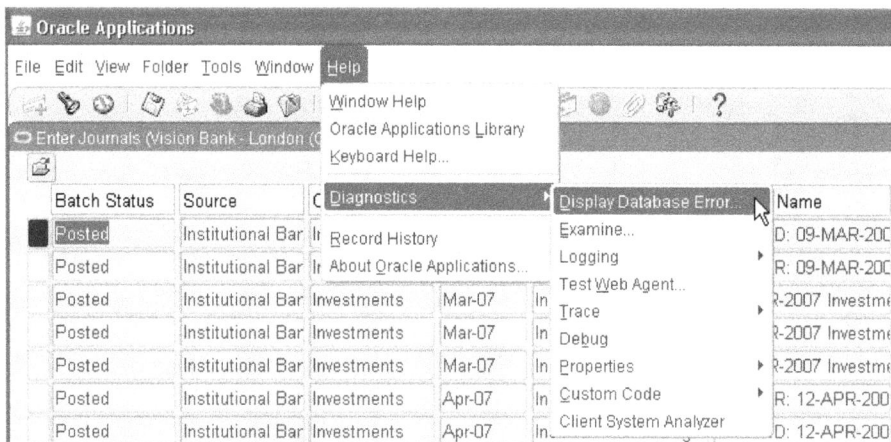

FIGURE 5-21. *Items in the Help menu available for Oracle Forms*

- ■ **Test Web Agent**   Calls the FND_WEB.PING utility that connects from Forms to the Application Server to return some database summary data. It's an older method to help troubleshoot problems launching OA Framework pages.

- ■ **Trace**   Provides the ability to set SQL Tracing on for the users session so details on database actions can be investigated. Since for these pages (unlike OA Framework) most of the logic is either in the form or as PL/SQL on the database, this is an important capability.

- ■ **Debug**   Not currently in use.

- ■ **Properties**   Similar to the Examine option, this shows the details of the object currently selected on a form. Its primary use is in customization of the form, known as Forms Personalization, and includes the ability to update an object's properties.

- ■ **Custom Code**   Also related to Forms Personalization, this provides comprehensive ability to change the way a form looks and works, including adding and removing fields.

- ■ **Client System Analyzer**   This tool runs an applet program to analyze details of the computer running the user session. It focuses on validating the required resources for running E-Business Suite, including memory, CPU, required software, and network connectivity.

- ■ **Record History**   Shows the database record details, including table name, who created and last updated it, and when it was last updated.

- ■ **About Oracle Applications**   Shows the login details, database details, forms server details, current form details, and version information.

OA Framework Diagnostics   I've already mentioned the diagnostic capabilities found in E-Business Suite OA Framework pages enabled by Profile Option FND: Diagnostics, such as the AboutThisPage output (shown previously in Figure 5-10). However, the Show Pool Monitor option is a little more technical in nature and therefore fits best in this section.

As shown in Figure 5-22, this page provides a sidebar of options offering insight into the runtime objects currently in use, Java system properties, session and memory usage, and related component versions. Most significant is the current Application Modules being used behind the currently active page, exposing clues on both the code objects involved and their performance.

Checking the tabs and data shown during issue occurrence can help validate both the system configuration as well as elements of the health of the related OA Framework components. You'll see this again in later chapters.

Reports, Intelligence, and Analytics   For the later releases of E-Business Suite, its analytics and reports features leverage three main components.

First, BI Publisher (BIP) provides services to generate static reports; including all those available within E-Business Suite for output and printing. Troubleshooting issues here commonly focus around standard applications logging as well as analysis of the Concurrent Requests (and its internal Output Post Processor) that are spawned to run reports.

Second, Oracle Business Intelligence Applications (OBIA) provide a complete set of prepackaged dashboards and analytical services for making decisions based on underlying E-Business Suite data. This is a separate product set to E-Business Suite, although it integrates directly into an instance.

AMs >

Application Module Pool Details

Application Module Instances

Instance ID	Availability	Username	Creation Time	Lock Time	Release Time	Timeout Time	Time To Create	View Links	View Objects	Nested AMs	Session id	Connection Logon Time	Jserv Session
0	Yes	CBAKER	Sat Sep 29 20:22:35 CEST 2012	Sat Sep 29 20:22:35 CEST 2012	Sat Sep 29 20:23:41 CEST 2012	N/A	1	0	81	10	16863395	2012-09-29 20:22:21.0	68c352b95ab0d23

oracle.apps.ap.oie.server.WebExpensesAM

Available	1
Unavailable	0
Creations	1
Removals	0
Checkins	1
Checkouts	1
Activations	0
Passivations	0
Referenced AMs Reused	0
Referenced AMs Reused Recycled	0

FIGURE 5-22. *The current Application Module Pool showing iExpenses objects in use*

Troubleshooting here is outside E-Business Suite entirely and focuses on the core components of the BI server, the Presentation services, and/or the database. The BI server has its own administration console with many troubleshooting features, together with its own logging process (focused around its NQQuery.log file), plus additional logs for the Presentation Server.

Finally, Oracle Business Intelligence Enterprise Edition (OBIEE) provides core technical services for the creation of new dashboards and analytics. This powers the OBIA product, so troubleshooting is essentially the same.

The product documentation has guides that cover administration and troubleshooting for BIP and the core BI components. For more detail, review the following recommended resources:

- **"Diagnostics and Performance Monitoring"**   Chapter 13 in Oracle Fusion Middleware Administrator's Guide for Oracle Business Intelligence Publisher (E22255-02)

- **"Diagnosing and Resolving Issues in Oracle Business Intelligence"**   Chapter 8 in Oracle Fusion Middleware System Administrator's Guide for Oracle Business Intelligence Enterprise Edition (E10541-05)

Oracle Diagnostic Framework   We looked at ODF as a vital tool for investigating functional reliability issues; however, it also contains tests that are aimed squarely at verifying the Applications Technology components. With so many components involved and tests constantly evolving with new releases and requirements, it would be unwise to list them here, but they can all be found in My Oracle Support's catalog note 421245.1, under the related release and, specifically, in the "Applications Technology" section.

As shown in Figure 5-23 taken from where these executed inside E-Business Suite, the tests are grouped based on their purpose and cover all significant core areas. Just as with the functional diagnostics, leveraging these tests has proven to make troubleshooting complex problems easier, and in turn speeds the resolution time.

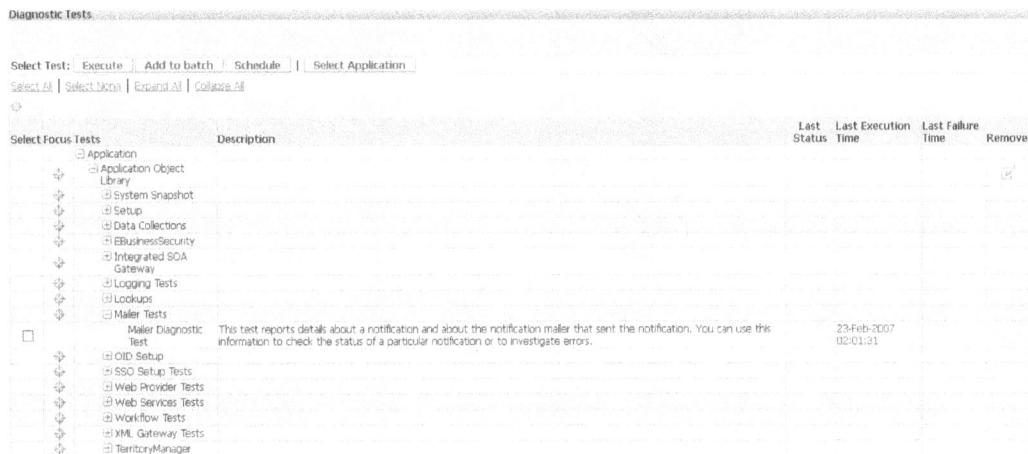

FIGURE 5-23.   *The technical diagnostic test categories under the Application Object Library product area*

My Oracle Support: Health Recommendations and Utility Scripts   My Oracle Support remains an enormous resource for information and utilities for troubleshooting problems, and it applies throughout the layers of the application. Previously, we looked at the functional resources available, but a wealth of tools are available for the Applications Technology, too. Two examples are health recommendations and utility scripts.

As shown in Figure 5-24, when Oracle Configuration Manager is implemented for E-Business Suite the information it collects is checked against predefined rules that verify settings are in

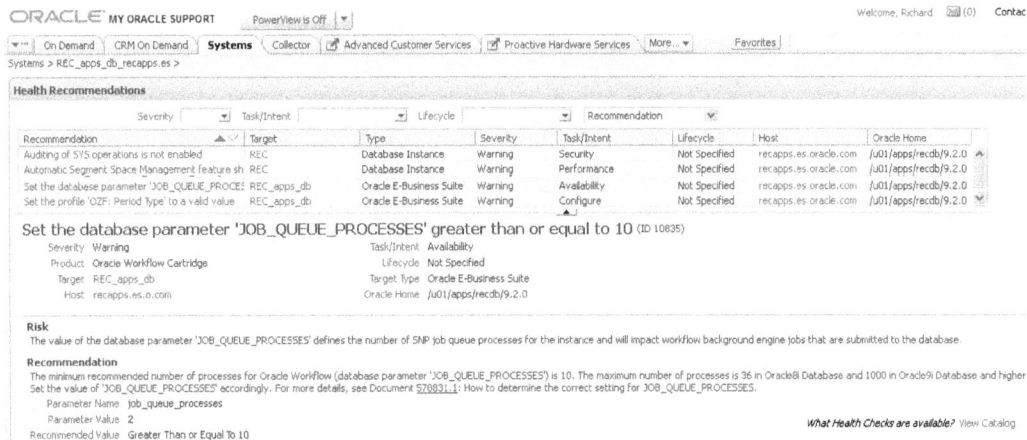

FIGURE 5-24.   *A health check identifying the database as having the JOB_QUEUE_PROCESSES value of 2, which is less than the recommendation for Workflow of more than 10*

accordance with Oracle's own recommendations. When a violation is detected, My Oracle Support highlights it and provides details on why it might be a problem and how to remedy it. This kind of proactive capability can save significant time and costs compared to addressing issues when they start affecting real business operations.

In addition to health recommendations and the embedded E-Business Suite ODF tests, there are utility scripts available that can significantly help troubleshoot specific reliability problems. E-Business Suite has many thousands of implementations, and all manner of Applications Technology problems have been addressed over its long history, with many requiring frequent and complex troubleshooting actions. Just as we discussed for functional troubleshooting, My Oracle Support also contains many general scripts that, while they may not be part of the ODF catalog (although they should be), they are useful in many situations.

Some examples include the monitor_jdbc_conn.sql script to monitor JDBC connections in E-Business Suite (Note 557194.1) and those in the Applications Technology Group Data Collection Script Repository (Note 742340.1). Since these are specific to each problem type, I recommend you search in My Oracle Support under the Knowledge tab using a related keyword and selecting the E-Business Suite/Applications Technology product and the Troubleshooting document type.

Oracle Enterprise Manager   Enterprise Manager is Oracle's primary system management tool, supporting the Oracle technology products by offering detailed administration functionality. This extends deep into management and monitoring, with features available to review all current and past availability and performance data and to catch the key symptoms of any reliability issues that occur.

In addition to its native capabilities, Enterprise Manager offers additional plug-in options to support specific Oracle products such as E-Business Suite. These form either a pack or a suite, depending on the range of features included, and for E-Business Suite there are several key components that significantly enhance the reliability management tools available.

As shown in Figure 5-25, with the addition of the Enterprise Manager pack (plug-in) for E-Business Suite the system understands all the key application-specific component details, such as those for Concurrent Processing.

We'll look at each of these in various contexts in the subsequent chapters; however, here is a summary with specific focus on their relation to investigating reliability issues:

- **Native diagnostics**   Including those for the database where all SQL throughput can be carefully analyzed to determine not only what was slow. It can also automatically analyze the explain plan and database configuration to determine why a statement was excessively slow and how it can be optimized.

- **Access and grouping of Oracle Diagnostics**   The E-Business Suite Management Pack for Enterprise Manager plug-in contains a central dashboard that has a Diagnostics tab under which it's possible to find and execute a range of the diagnostics tests available in the Oracle Diagnostic Framework.

- **Lifecycle Diagnostics**   In addition, the Enterprise Manager plug-in goes one step further and provides a broad set of additional diagnostics to run either individually or as a predefined pack in specific scenarios. These perform all the essential prerequisite checks and provide detail on potential issues in the environment. These diagnostics currently address problems in cloning, Setup Manager, Patch Manager, Customization Manager, or user monitoring.

ORACLE **Enterprise Manager** Cloud Control 12c

Enterprise ▼ | Targets ▼ | Favorites ▼ | History ▼

⬆ **UNIT4050-Concurrent Processing Service** ⓘ
⬡ Concurrent Processing Service ▼

Concurrent Processing Service: UNIT4050-Concurrent Processing Service

Home | Charts | Test Performance | **System** | Monitoring Configuration | Topology

System
UNIT4050-Oracle E-Business Suite (Topology)

Component Summary

Name	Type ▲	Status	Incidents ⚠	⊗	⊖	⚑
EBSSRV	Database Instance	⬆	0	74	0	0
UNIT4050-Apps Listener EBSSRV_ebssrv-APPL_TOP Context	Listener	⬆	0	0	0	0
UNIT4050-Core Managers for Concurrent Processing	Oracle Concurrent Manager	⬆	0	1	0	0

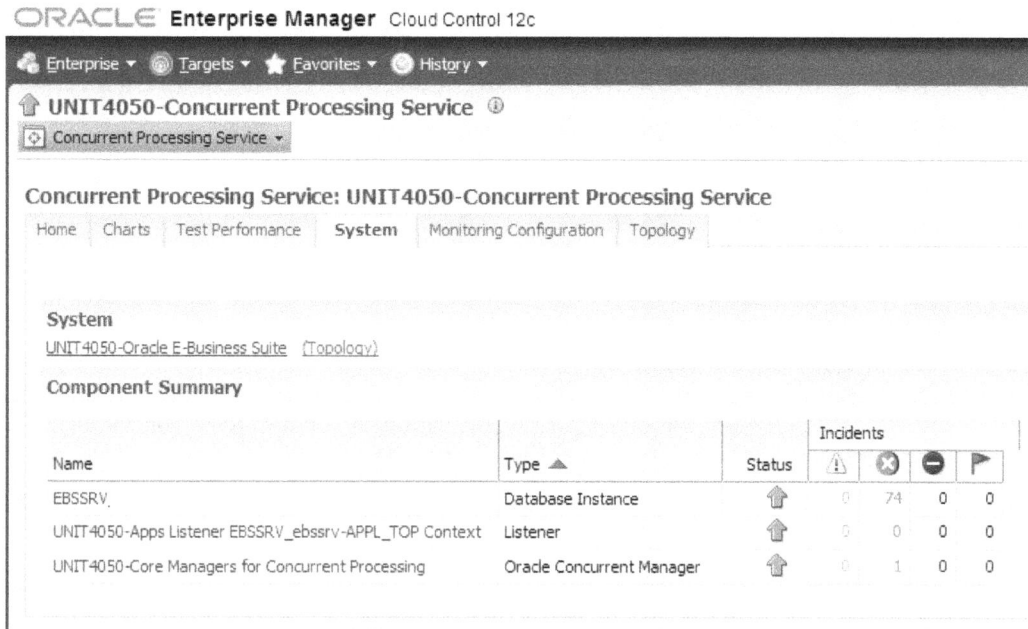

FIGURE 5-25. *The status of Concurrent Processing components as shown in Enterprise Manager*

- **Log Files** Access to the log files is available from Enterprise Manager's parent target menu. This provides an integrated log viewer that indexes all the log output from the related components across multiple files, allowing comprehensive result sets. Logs can be filtered and sorted by all their different attributes, including user, time window, component and module running, and as illustrated in Figure 5-26 the specific process identifier known as Execution Identifier (ECID).

- **Low-level performance data** Details from the host server and detailed JVM diagnostics are available to show how the execution platform was running and highlighting patterns and activities that might explain unexpected results.

- **Configuration management** Enterprise Manager's tools allow not only the collection of key metrics, but also their comparison between instances, change approval, change history records, an alerting and notification framework, and a compliance framework that checks their values against a wealth of Oracle recommendations. Configuration management support also extends to application setup data, where Enterprise Manager supports the extract and import of more than 300 data points from instances by calling standard E-Business Suite APIs and managing any transformations required.

- **Customization management** The E-Business Suite Customization Manager allows custom code to be registered in the system, allowing for detailed administration, versioning, compilation, and implementation using standard E-Business Suite patching.

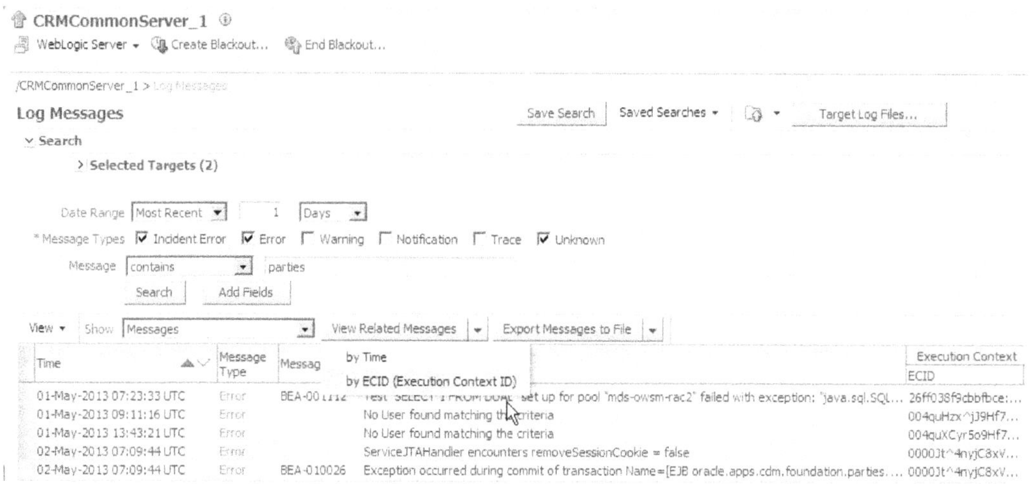

FIGURE 5-26. *Logs shown in Enterprise Manager*

■ **Patch management** With native integration with My Oracle Support, missing patches can be identified and then, with a standard process, can be analyzed and scheduled for application. This greatly simplifies the work of E-Business Suite patching, eliminating many command-line tools, adding more options, and providing a much clearer view of patching activities and history. Similarly, cloning of E-Business Suite instances can also be managed entirely from the Enterprise Manager interface.

Platform Layer

Having looked at reliability tools in the context of both E-Business Suite's Business Process and Applications Technology layers, let's complete our review by covering some tools related to the pure technologies underpinning the whole stack. For the sake of keeping the details easy to apply, we'll focus on the following tools, which are those that are most often relevant to managing reliability for E-Business Suite:

■ Problem and incident management

■ Oracle Forms

■ Java and the Application Server

■ The Database Server

■ Health Recommendations and the Compliance Framework

■ Remote Diagnostic Agent

■ Operating system, hardware, and networking

Problem and Incident Management Both the 11*g* Oracle Database and Fusion Middleware components have implemented a feature that automatically creates a snapshot of the system upon any serious failure. The platform for this is known as the Diagnostic Framework (DFw)—not to be confused with Oracle Diagnostic Framework (ODF), which is used for running diagnostic tests inside E-Business Suite.

This works by having a preregistered set of error conditions, defined as *problems*, configured within each system component. An example might be an ORA-0600 database error. When one of those problems occurs, the system calls a secondary process, known as the *Diagnostic Data Extractor* (DDE), which itself is configured to gather certain sets of information. The information captured is stored in a newly created folder in a standardized local file system, known as the Automatic Diagnostic Repository (ADR).

Each instance of a problem, or error, is an *incident*, and all the information collected is associated with a unique identifier, known as the *incident number*. Problems created and their corresponding incidents are exposed in various system management tools and utilities, such as the ADRCI command-line utility and, most significantly, in Oracle Enterprise Manager, as shown in Figure 5-27.

The information captured by an incident includes logs, trace files, system profile data, and various diagnostics appropriate to the component within which the error occurred. While E-Business Suite functional code does not raise incidents directly (unlike Fusion Applications), several of the technologies that underpin it do, such as the database and, especially important for Release 12.2, the Oracle WebLogic Server. With incidents offering an automated and rich set of diagnostic information that matches ITIL recommendations, it's reasonable to expect this capability to evolve and become a central resource for troubleshooting all serious reliability issues.

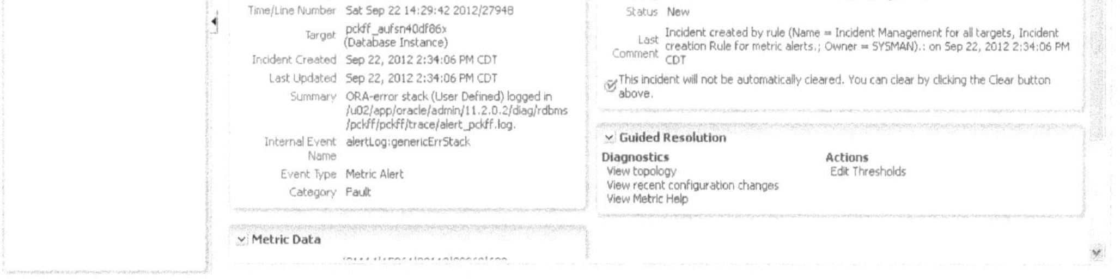

FIGURE 5-27. *Database incident 985595 generated by an error stack in the alert log*

Core Oracle Forms   While we have already mentioned Oracle Forms in the context of E-Business Suite, looking at the various features under the Help menu, let's now address this key component under the remit of managing its reliability as a part of the technology stack.

There are multiple methods of enabling Oracle Forms to produce additional diagnostic information as it performs its work delivering interaction with end users. This starts with a *Forms Runtime Diagnostic* (FRD), which is essentially an event log file generated by the Oracle Forms server. This can be enabled by appending parameters "record = collect" to the user-level profile options ICX: Forms Launcher or Forms Runtime Parameter. Alternatively, although not recommended, it can be enabled for all users by editing the forms configuration file appsweb.cfg.

In addition, *forms trace* is a newer feature that creates a similar event log but allows the specification of which events to trace. It also offers a little more detail in the output and they're generally easier to understand (after the binary is processed via a translation process). Forms trace is also enabled via the same profile options, most often by including the tracegroup parameter.

Finally, it is also possible to set Forms Servlet Logging to get output from the processes that handle the internal request traffic, offering more detail on sessions, network connections, and performance. This is done via settings in the appsweb.cfg file.

Details on all of these methods, the options available, and interpreting the output are available from My Oracle Support Note 438652.1.

Java and the Application Server   Let's look at some different methods for troubleshooting the Java Runtime Environment, which is entitled OACORE in E-Business Suite, and within which a substantial amount of the product code runs. If the code operates in a way that tries to violate the constraints of the execution container, such as leaking memory, the resulting failure may be captured by both the failure of E-Business Suite as well as the Java environment itself.

In addition, in some cases the environment itself might become unreliable, perhaps due to outside environmental influences such as networking, operating system, or hardware issues. A failure at this level will need many low-level logs, JVM traces, and associated diagnostics. An example is the JConsole tool in Figure 5-28 that can connect with the remote environment and help diagnose reliability issues. We'll visit this kind of tooling in more detail in our performance chapter.

As the figure shows, on occasion it will be necessary to dig past E-Business Suite into the native Java environment to complex diagnose issues. On the whole, this kind of work involves using the following best practice techniques. You'll see more of this in subsequent chapters.

- Investigate Java Server log and output files
- Investigate process threads
- Investigate the runtime configuration and parameters
- Investigate performance and resource utilization

From Release 12.2 onward E-Business Suite runs on the Oracle Fusion Middleware stack, which is essentially a move from the OC4J Java Server inside the Oracle Applications Server 10*g* to the equivalent 11*g* Oracle WebLogic Server. On the face of it, the same platform services are being used, but it is a different implementation of a J2EE Java Server, and they both come with very different management tools. This therefore affects the associated troubleshooting of any reliability issues.

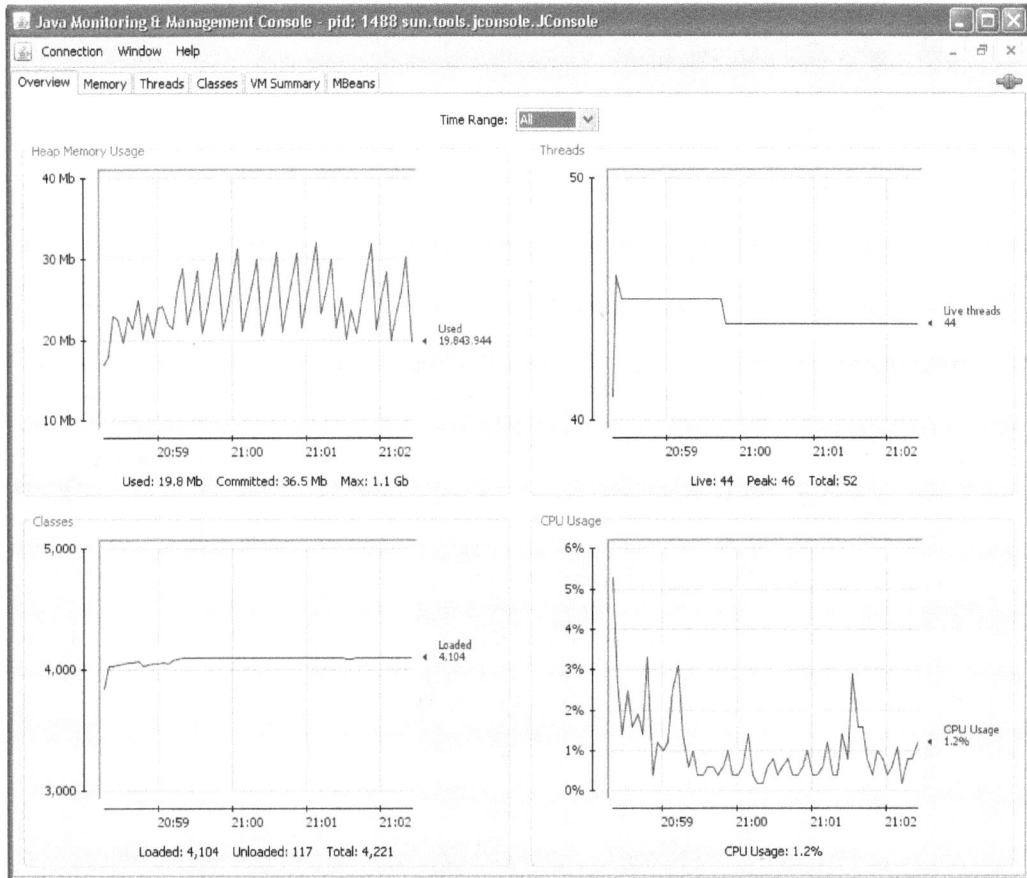

FIGURE 5-28. *JConsole showing JVM performance and resource information*

While going into masses of depth on both of these, or creating a delta between the two, is beyond the scope of this book, a complete breakdown of both of the features of both platforms is available in the following excellent documents:

- **For E-Business Suite 12.1**   Oracle Application Server Administrator's Guide 10*g* Release 3 (E10403-01):

  - Chapter 2,"Introduction to Administration Tools"

  - Chapter 5,"Managing Log Files"

  - Appendix H,"Troubleshooting Oracle Application Server"

■ **For E-Business Suite 12.2** Oracle Fusion Middleware Information Roadmap for Oracle WebLogic Server 11*g* (E14529-04):

■ "Learn About WebLogic Server System Administration"

■ "Monitor Your Domain"

■ "Troubleshooting"

The details in these two documents, plus many other texts of Java Server management, are more than adequate to execute upon the Java platform section of your own E-Business Suite reliability plan. Since the tools available for use here are not especially related to E-Business Suite, I defer more detail to those more appropriate resources.

The Database Server I've already mentioned enabling SQL Trace from inside E-Business Suite itself, but there may be a few occasions where you need to investigate reliability issues for the whole database platform itself. These should be few and far between, as this is the most mature of all of Oracle's products and is supported by the most advanced reliability features available anywhere. However, for the sake of completeness we'll review some of the more significant tools to use here.

The 11*g* Enterprise Edition of the Database Server used for E-Business Suite (12.1) contains a multitude of diagnostic tools, and while we'll revisit some of these in Chapter 7, I'll highlight just a few that may be occasionally useful in investigating reliability problems.

The following summarizes the most useful database tools for troubleshooting reliability issues and is laid out to mirror the menus shown in Enterprise Manager, as shown in Figure 5-29. (Incidentally, Exadata machine management is also very well supported.)

■ Database Instance

■ Diagnostics

■ **Support Workbench** Shows all DFw incidents and problems, with tools to investigate the information captured therein, and reports them to Oracle Support.

■ **Database Instance Health** Provides a simple overview page showing the following for the last 24 hours: incidents; ADDM data, including CPU, user I/O, and waits; and any nonincident alerts that were raised.

■ Logs

■ **Text alert log contents** Provides a search and viewer for the general database log file.

■ **Alert log errors** Provides a summary of any errors in the general database log file.

■ Performance

■ **Performance home** Gives a quick overview of the database and can quickly help determine if the symptoms of an issue being observed are causing a database problem. Similarly, the Top Activity page gives a bit more detail.

■ **ASH analytics and real-time ADDM** Offers detailed insight into the database activity.

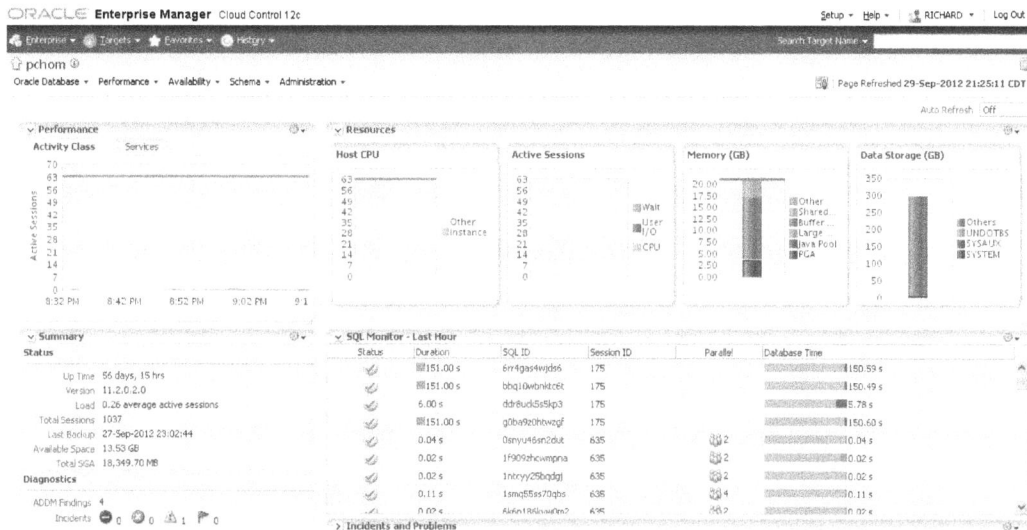

FIGURE 5-29. *Enterprise Manager's dashboard page for complete database management*

- **AWR report**   Gives a very comprehensive picture of recent system activity (time period snapshots can be specified), all composed into an easy-to-use HTML report.

- **SQL monitoring**   An active window of the statements running through the system, showing details on the slowest or most resource-hungry. The Search SQL option under the SQL submenu also allows a useful SQL statement lookup.

- Networking

  - Runs connection tests using command-line utilities like TNSPING or TRCROUTE as well as the Oracle Connection Manager Control utility (CMCTL).

  - Runs a loopback test from Oracle Net Manager.

To assist in leveraging these tools, it is worth reviewing the associated documentation for more details, including the Oracle Database Administrator's Guide (B28310-04), section 7, "Monitoring Database Operations and section 8—Managing Diagnostic Data." The Oracle Database Performance Tuning Guide (B28274-02) drills into much more detail as well.

Health Recommendations and the Compliance Framework   As mentioned and shown back in Figure 5-24 and here in Figure 5-30, Oracle Configuration Manager collects system configuration information, and you can allow My Oracle Support to process it and display any violations. The catalog of metric collections and associated health recommendations covers not only E-Business Suite components, but also many of the underlying technology components.

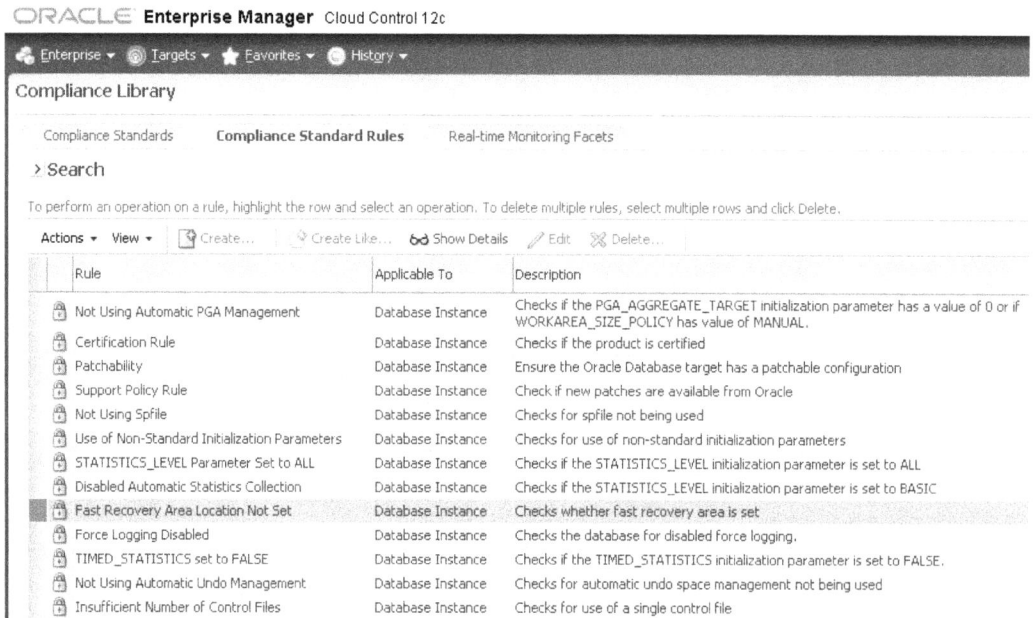

FIGURE 5-30. *Some compliance standard rules for the Oracle Database*

Similarly, Enterprise Manager also has a metric collection process, integrated with Oracle Configuration Manager in the latest releases, and offers a similar mechanism to verify the values found. This is found under the Compliance menu and is available for all of the target components that Enterprise Manager supports.

One extra feature to Enterprise Manager Compliance is that it not only supports recommendations shipped by Oracle, but also allows administrators to enter their own rule logic to add their own sets of validations. This means it can support implementation-specific checks, and together with the extended notification and reporting features, this offers an opportunity to use Enterprise Manager to catch the causes of reliability issues early, before they have much impact.

Another related feature inside My Oracle Support that sometimes gets overlooked is the certification database. E-Business Suite has many components in its technology stack, but only a certain set of them were designed and tested for use. Upon occasion a rather proactive administrator will apply a new update to a component before it has been properly certified, and while backward-compatibility is not always an issue, moving the technology stack away from the supported version, even slightly, may cause significant E-Business Suite reliability issues. As such, the certification tab in My Oracle Support provides features for quick verification of the component versions tested and supported for each E-Business Suite release.

Remote Diagnostic Agent (RDA)   As discussed in this chapter, there are diagnostic tools for each of E-Business Suite's core technology components. However, RDA represents a single process by which detailed component information can be collected, designed specifically for troubleshooting reliability problems. Through the execution of specific modules (or groups of modules known as *profiles*), RDA supports almost all of Oracle's technology products from the host server, the database, the middleware components, and E-Business Suite instance itself.

RDA is a mature tool, originally developed by the Oracle Support team, and is still used frequently today. It is a nonintrusive, read-only tool that collects technical data from configuration files and logs files. While a command-line tool at its core, RDA is delivered with most product installs and is exposed in various other diagnostic processes and tools, helping to add a complete system view. Examples include the ODF pages within E-Business Suite, the closely related Diagnostic Assistant that provides an interface for several command-line tools, and the packaging process involved in DFw's incident management.

The following is a list of the RDA modules that are used most often when investigating E-Business Suite issues and the technology products that surround them. Some of these only apply if those components have been implemented:

- **ACT**   Collects Oracle E-Business Suite application information.
- **ASIT**   Collects Oracle Application Server 11*g* installation information.
- **BI**   Collects Business Intelligence Enterprise Edition information.
- **BIPL**   Collects Oracle Business Intelligence publisher information.
- **BPEL**   Collects Oracle BPEL process manager information.
- **CFG**   Collects key configuration information.
- **DBA**   Collects Oracle RDBMS information.
- **LOG**   Collects Oracle Database trace and log files.
- **NET**   Collects network information.
- **OAM**   Collects Oracle Access Manager information.
- **OIM**   Collects Oracle Identity Manager information.
- **OID**   Collects Oracle Internet Directory information.
- **OS**   Collects operating system information.
- **PERF**   Collects performance information.
- **SES**   Collects Oracle Secure Enterprise search information.
- **SSO**   Collects single sign-on information.
- **WLS**   Collects Oracle WebLogic Server information.

More details on getting started with RDA can be found in My Oracle Support Note 314422.1.

O/S, Hardware, and Networking   While discussions at this level are down at the bottom of the E-Business Suite technology stack, you must consider the reliability of the physical components involved. From my own experience with E-Business Suite, I have spent many hours troubleshooting, analyzing each component, just to determine that the root cause was in the hardware.

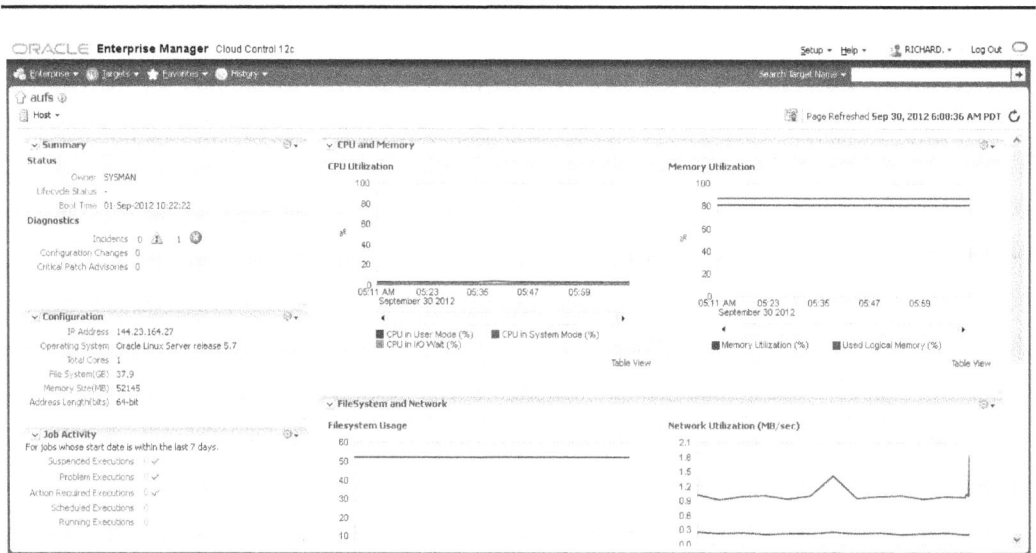

FIGURE 5-31. *Enterprise Manager's dashboard for the host server*

The good news is that these low-level components are usually supported by some of the best diagnostic tooling in the IT industry, which can make it relatively quick and easy for an administrator to verify the cause before handing it off to the infrastructure maintenance team. The challenge for most application administrators is to identify, understand, and implement access to this tooling.

Some simple examples include running utility programs like UNIX's *top* command, which monitors operating system activity like CPU, memory, disk, and I/O, or perhaps running the netstat and traceroute programs to check network connectivity.

The utilities and tools available vary with the platform being used, and the general recommendation is to invest some time with the related experts in your organization (or the platform vendor) to encourage access to tools that provide the basic information you can use to check for the most likely potential issues.

As I've mentioned already, Enterprise Manager is Oracle's complete system management tool, and along with E-Business Suite and all of its technology components, it also supports low-level platform target systems, including extensive performance and monitoring metrics for host servers and network connections. This is supported by the standard notifications and alerts features that inform the stakeholders should anything out the ordinary begin to occur.

Figure 5-31 shows the summary of the host target, with at-a-glance detail that can help you quickly spot if something in the low-level components is awry. From this dashboard it's possible to drill into more detail so you can view detailed configuration information, identify any compliance violations, view all log and core files, and review the networking and storage details.

Summary

Let's review the manifest table for this chapter to remind ourselves of the layers of E-Business Suite. Within each layer are the recommended tools for executing your reliability management solution.

Business Process	Applications Technology	Platform Technology
Online help	Oracle Applications Manager	Problem and incident management
Application messages	Oracle Workflow	Core Oracle Forms
Functional setup	Concurrent Manager	Java and the Application Server
Functional diagnostics	Oracle Forms for E-Business Suite	The Database Server
Functional scripts and utilities	OA Framework	Health recommendations and the compliance framework
FND: diagnostics	Business Intelligence	Remote Diagnostic Agent
Applications logging	Oracle Diagnostic Framework	OS, hardware, and networking
Patching functional products	My Oracle Support: Health recommendations and utility scripts	
Working with My Oracle Support	Oracle Enterprise Manager	
Oracle Enterprise Manager		

CHAPTER
6

An Availability
Management Toolbox

E nterprise applications like E-Business Suite are made up of many technology components but, although each comes with its own tools for maintaining the maximum availability of that component, few complement and cooperate together. Availability management is relatively simple: Keep all the dependent components running and accessible as much as possible. The challenge is that the dozens of different technologies spread across a complex architecture and deployment make it challenging to monitor and manage.

This can also be exacerbated by specialist enterprise architects and consultants brought in to determine organizational requirements and policies, but whose high-level designs are tough to implement based on the heterogeneous options available. This chapter aims to demystify the tools and options for managing availability of the key components of E-Business Suite, so that a holistic and complete monitoring and management implementation is possible.

The E-Business Suite documentation (Concepts Guide—E12841-04) has a section on high availability and focuses on the four main aspects mentioned next. We'll include these in this chapter, but will also add many more tools, techniques, and recommendations.

- **Patching** Tips and best practices to reduce the downtime required for patching. This includes merging patches, using shared APPLTOP and the Shared Application Tier File System, and distributed AD processing.

- **Database options** Such as *nologging*, the flashback database, and Oracle Data Guard.

- **Maintenance** Includes using stage and test systems effectively, E-Business Suite's own maintenance mode, and frequent maintenance windows.

- **Load balancing** Often closely related to high availability. While discussing generic hardware and networking architecture is outside the scope of this book, standard component implementations are usually recommended for E-Business Suite because it allows the use of various load balancing techniques based on the system needs and corporate standards. This applies for components in the middleware and the database; we'll look at this a bit more in the "Platform Layer" section later.

What Is Availability?

Strictly speaking, *availability* is a function of reliability, as logically a highly unreliable service will be frequently unavailable. In this book we separate them out, however, since in the real world it is more practical to use reliability to measure the *quality* of service, and availability to measure the *quantity* of service access.

In Chapter 2, we defined application availability as follows:

Ensure that all features are available whenever and wherever.

Primarily it is unscheduled downtime that is of most concern to the enterprise application manager, but even scheduled downtime should be kept to a minimum and not impact the business end users. This is especially true for modern multinational organizations and those that run around the clock. In addition, the advent of accessing enterprise applications through cloud computing and similar software-as-a-service hosted models also focuses attention firmly on availability management.

The commonly used term *continuous availability* implies no downtime at all, and therefore is either used with scheduled downtime excepted, or for specific system components that always have one instance available while others are taken offline.

Interestingly, while I just used the term downtime, there is a difference between uptime/downtime and available. The application might be running—hence up—but may be unavailable to end users because of a network issue, for example. A better term in this case is therefore *outage,* where the inferred expectation is that the system should be accessible but is not.

The impact of poor availability sometimes needs to be taken in context: a problem during peak usage is more significant than during a quiet time, for example. For some industries this can expand to cover seasonal activity, as when even a small problem during pre-Christmas trading for a retailer is much more costly than the same in the summer months. Similarly, the context might be the process through which the end user is accessing the system. For example, the fact that the Oracle Forms Server is down does not prevent access to similar functions through OA Framework pages. In this chapter, we consider tools that help us identify and manage unavailable components.

For our purposes in this chapter, assume that availability means general application accessibility, and therefore any problems or failures that are confined to one piece of functionality will be covered under reliability management.

Causes of Availability Issues

There are many reasons for unscheduled system downtime: an operator mistake, cleaners pulling out wires, random acts of nature such as lightning strikes. My favorite is the story of the original definition of system bugs from an incident in 1947, when a moth got stuck in a relay in an early computer system, causing a failure (both the log book and the moth are in the Smithsonian National Museum of American History). The more common events that may interrupt access to the application include

- Failure or unexpected process termination of software in the underlying software technology stack.

- Operating system process failures and terminations.

- Logically or physically severed network connections.

- Severe security breaches, resulting in intentional or unintended system isolation or shutdown.

- Physical resource depletion, such as memory, CPU cycles, disk space, bandwidth, or other capacities.

- Mistaken or deliberate reconfiguration of the applications or its components that stops widespread features from working. This might be technical configuration like maximum heap memory size, or functional configuration like the end-dating of a currency exchange rate.

- Failure in dependent, integrated, or related hardware systems and other physical components.

- Safety shutdown in system components due to unstable environmental factors, such as power interruptions and load fluctuations.

- Data center–wide environmental problems, such as natural and man-made disasters (too much or too little heat, flooding).

In an ideal world, *graceful degradation* (as part of theoretical fault tolerant design) would occur, where critical components continue to operate upon failure, albeit at limited capacity. Some of the hardware and the more mature technology stack components like the database may exhibit some similar behavior, but this rarely applies uniformly to all components that run the business functionality of E-Business Suite. As such, features tend to succeed or fail.

Measuring Availability

True availability measurement should be holistic and, as we've already discussed, the term *available* implies that tasks can be completed, although a severe problem might prevent this. If the application is up and can be connected to by end users, then in our definition it's available.

Measurements may be as simple as a proportion of expected uptime, such as 148/150 hours per week. Alternatively, this is often expressed as a decimal (0.9867) or, even more common as a percentage of availability (98.67 percent).

The exact value used may also be rounded to the nearest 9, such as 99 percent or "two nines," and therefore begins to be more of a guideline estimate than a precise measure, as illustrated in Table 6-1. Generally speaking, a level of five nines is considered close to the goal of obtaining high availability.

As the number of nines increases, so does the number of resources required to attain such availability. While for many businesses the point where cost outweighs benefits is just a few nines, web-centric businesses may have applications that are essential for handling both transaction throughput as well as customer loyalty; therefore true high availability will justify significant investment.

To measure availability, the measurement tool needs to be highly reliable and available— certainly more than the application it is measuring. It should also accurately collect details on any interruption to be able to categorize it. Normally this is done through simulation of user access and basic user actions (such as logging in), with all responses analyzed to signify success or a type of failure.

Since the targets and measurements of availability should be in factors of seconds and minutes, the term *high availability* (four or five nines) illustrates the need for automated service restoration, since human intervention is too slow.

It's worth noting that there are predictive models that calculate the probability of IT system failure over time, based on the many variables involved. Search Google for "Bayesian Theory," for

Availability Percentage	Downtime Per Year	Downtime Per Month
90 percent ("one nine")	36.5 days	72 hours
99 percent ("two nines")	3.65 days	7.20 hours
99.9 percent ("three nines")	8.76 hours	43.8 minutes
99.99 percent ("four nines")	52.56 minutes	4.32 minutes
99.999 percent ("five nines")	5.26 minutes	25.9 seconds

TABLE 6-1. *Measuring Availability with the "Nines" Method*

example. These mathematic models may have aspects of validity, but I have not yet discovered their practical application in managing enterprise applications.

All the measures taken are compared with the targets, objectives, and requirements set out in the availability section of the organization's service level agreement (SLA) for the enterprise application. This is the ultimate yardstick against which success and failure are measured.

Managing Availability

Availability solutions come in many different guises, and the right one to choose depends on a combination of the criticality of the system and the budget available. These two factors should be inextricably linked, as the high cost of any unavailability should justify the implementation of high quality preventative measures. Unfortunately, it's not always the case, which is why I mention them both explicitly here.

While the goal is always to eliminate any *single point of failure* by using failover to route additional requests to available resources, let's quickly review some of the more common concepts of ensuring availability.

- **Load balancing**   The capture of incoming requests that routes them evenly across multiple servers (hardware or software). This may be based on a preconfigured routing rule or resource availability, or it may happen more simply in a round-robin fashion. The load balancer will not assign work to an unavailable server, but will instead skip it and move around the system as appropriate.

- **Clustering**   The use of duplicate server nodes, with management software constantly monitoring their health status. This is normally done through a virtual heartbeat that probes each server to detect any availability issues. Once a problem is detected, traffic is either rerouted to another active server node already running the same application, or the application is started on another server and users are then redirected there. It should be noted that this might not always be seamless; for example, session information from before the point of failure may not get retained as the subsequent action is routed to an alternative server.

- **Redundancy**   An engineering term for the duplication of usually physical components (servers, disks) that means should one of them fail, all data and ongoing operations can be continued through automatically relying on the duplicate. There are two pure forms: active redundancy, which implies some automated artificial intelligence applied to solution determination, and passive redundancy, which suggests that excess capacity of the system can ensure service continues, albeit at an impaired level. Replication is similar to redundancy, although it's most commonly applied to data. Here multiple data stores are constantly synchronized so that loss doesn't occur. Often a master/slave model is used where data is changed in a batched load. However, active multimaster systems are increasing in popularity due to high-speed networks and reduced hardware and storage costs. Examples range from small individual disk mirroring to complete site level replication across geographies.

As suggested previously in the "Causes of Availability" section, an availability problem affecting the day-to-day business operation supported by E-Business Suite usually represents a significant problem for most organizations. Halting payroll midrun or interrupting manufacturing production processes are serious and costly. As such, advisory standards bodies such as ITIL do cover disaster recovery with their own product-agnostic process, policies, and procedures. Indeed, disaster recovery is the technology subset of the broader business continuity plan that helps ensure all operations continue in the face of threatening situations. We'll revisit this in more detail in our governance discussion in Chapter 9.

Availability Tools

This section provides details on tools for monitoring and managing the availability of E-Business Suite and its key components. As shown in Table 6-2, we again divide these into the three logical technology layers of the application, to aid their practical use.

Table 6-3 shows the same manifest items again but reordered into two simple categories based on their most common usage. The intention here is to offer a chapter index that applies to whatever situation you are currently in, as opposed to the general sequential reading structure given in Table 6-2.

Business Process Layer

Monitoring and displaying the precise availability of the features that support specific business processes, such as creating invoices or running payroll, is very complex to calculate as they depend on so many configuration settings, data values, program code modules, and technology stack components. This means that while this is the ultimate need, a complete holistic view of this type is rarely possible. However, there are a few tools in E-Business Suite that can give some top-down insight. Again, the focus here is to illustrate capabilities for the use of business users and domain managers, as well as for those that assist them such as help desks.

Oracle Applications Manager: Business Flows

It is possible to define a rudimentary business process flow in Oracle Applications Manager, based on the actions and applications components that are used to execute it. From this definition the system can then collect problems and performance data on the recent execution of that flow, highlighting any issues in the components that might be causing problems users might be facing.

Business Process Layer	Applications Technology Layer	Platform Layer
Oracle Applications Manager: business flows	Multiple instance availability	High availability architecture
Workflow Monitor	Reducing scheduled downtime	Oracle system alerts
Business Intelligence	Scripts	Enterprise Manager
Enterprise Manager	Oracle Applications Manager	
	Enterprise Manager	

TABLE 6-2. *Availability Manifest*

Monitoring and Troubleshooting	Managing
Reducing scheduled downtime	Workflow Monitor
Oracle Applications Manager	Oracle system alerts
Multiple instance availability	Scripts
High availability architecture	Enterprise Manager
Business Intelligence	

TABLE 6-3. *The Availability Toolbox Based on Use Case*

The example in Figure 6-1 shows the order-to-cash business process flow and would highlight any problems in its constituent components. The process includes creating a sales order, processing it through Workflow, picking items to fulfill it, organizing the delivery and distribution of those items, and finally, processing payment.

Depending on the focus on specific key business flows in an organization, this tooling is worth considering, as a little time spent decomposing the flow and modeling it in this way can enable an availability monitoring feature that is unavailable elsewhere in the application or the tools that surround it.

Workflow Monitoring

As the main engine behind executing multistep business processes in E-Business Suite, Oracle Workflow is a window within which blocking problems may ultimately cause functional availability problems. A simple example is that e-mail notifications for purchase order approval would not be sent out upon a down Workflow mailer component.

As illustrated in Chapter 5, Workflow processes can be analyzed retrospectively to troubleshoot problems. However, here we're more concerned with component availability.

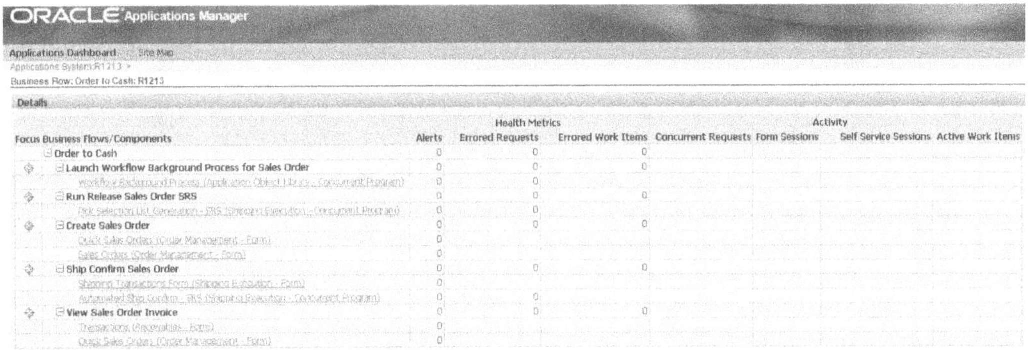

FIGURE 6-1. *The technical components of the order to cash business flow*

As shown in Figure 6-2, the Workflow System Status page accessible from Oracle Applications Manager provides an at-a-glance view of the status and availability of each of the main Workflow components, including notification mailers, agent listeners, service components, and background engines, as well as any purging of obsolete Workflow runtime data and control queue clean-up.

Although they look obvious, the possible status values used on this page should be given a little more explanation. First, if all instances of each component are running (or suspended) then the status will be Up. However, if any instance of the component is stopped-with-error or deactivated, the status will be Down. Finally, if no instances are found with either of these statuses, the status will be Unavailable.

Closely related to Workflow is the Approvals Management Engine (AME), a more recent addition for many of the E-Business Suite transactions. As a key component in the execution of business processing, the data flowing through this component needs to be efficiently handled and include careful monitoring for any systemic problems that result in widespread unavailability of document approval. Figure 6-3 shows the Approvals Management screen where failures in processing of any of the E-Business Suite approvals transaction types can be quickly interrogated. The example shows how the process to change a requisition has failed subsequent approval, and for ease of use the log can be cleared to keep data current, and the exception string contains the prepended timestamp.

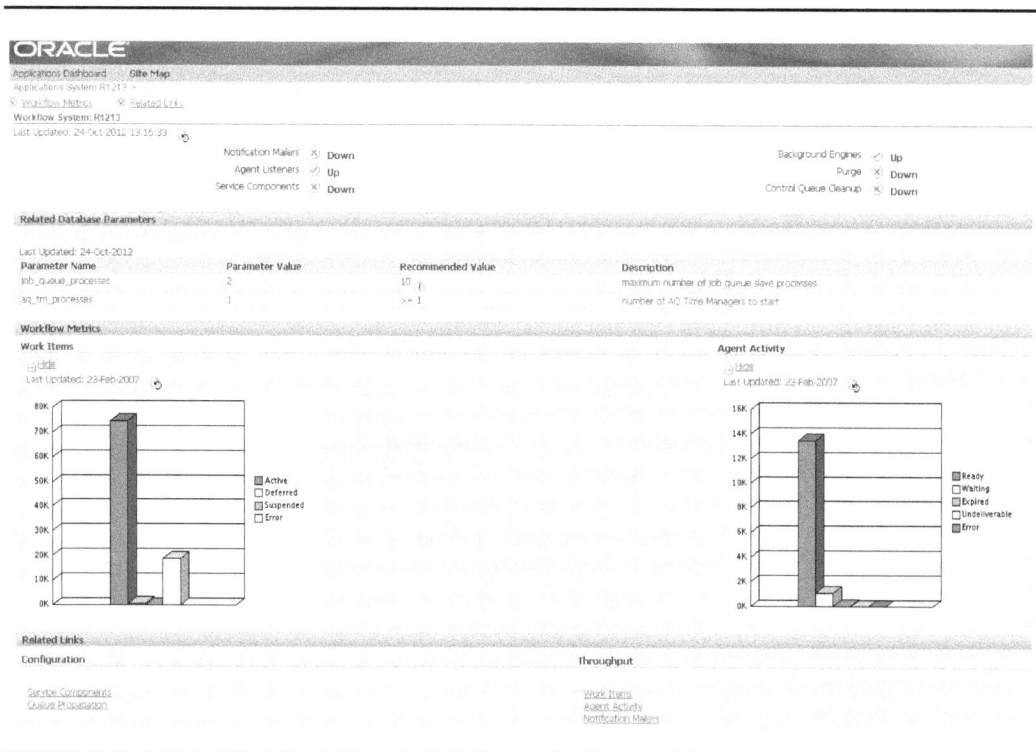

FIGURE 6-2. *The Workflow page from Oracle Applications Manager*

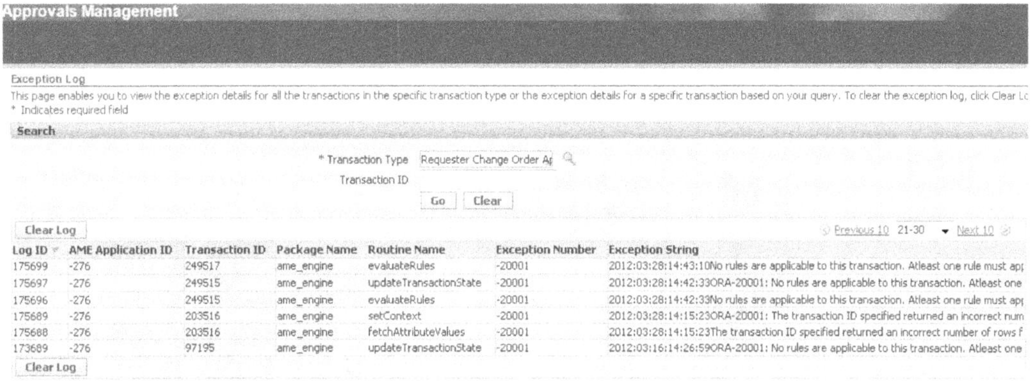

FIGURE 6-3. *The Approvals Management failure log*

In addition, monitoring the status and health of the following internal Workflow-related components allow for the preemptive avoidance of availability problems. Some of these components are available in pages under the E-Business Suite Workflow Monitor, but we'll discuss them in more detail in later chapters.

- Service components
- Notification mailers
- Agents and agent listeners
- Queues
- Web services
- Background engines
- Workflow data
- Business events

Business Intelligence

While slightly removed from an administrator's normal tool set, the powerful prebuilt dashboards in Oracle Business Intelligence Applications (OBIA) could be leveraged for additional insight into the performance and usage of the application. If there is a sudden drop in processing (or any dramatic change) that is out of sync with normal expected operations, it might be due to system problems, so the proactive applications administrator should be aware of this. As shown in Figure 6-4, metrics on transaction throughput and process usage may be useful to identify application issues.

Using carefully crafted privileges, system throughput and health information could be displayed without bombarding the administrator with reams of unsuitable information or exposing sensitive business details.

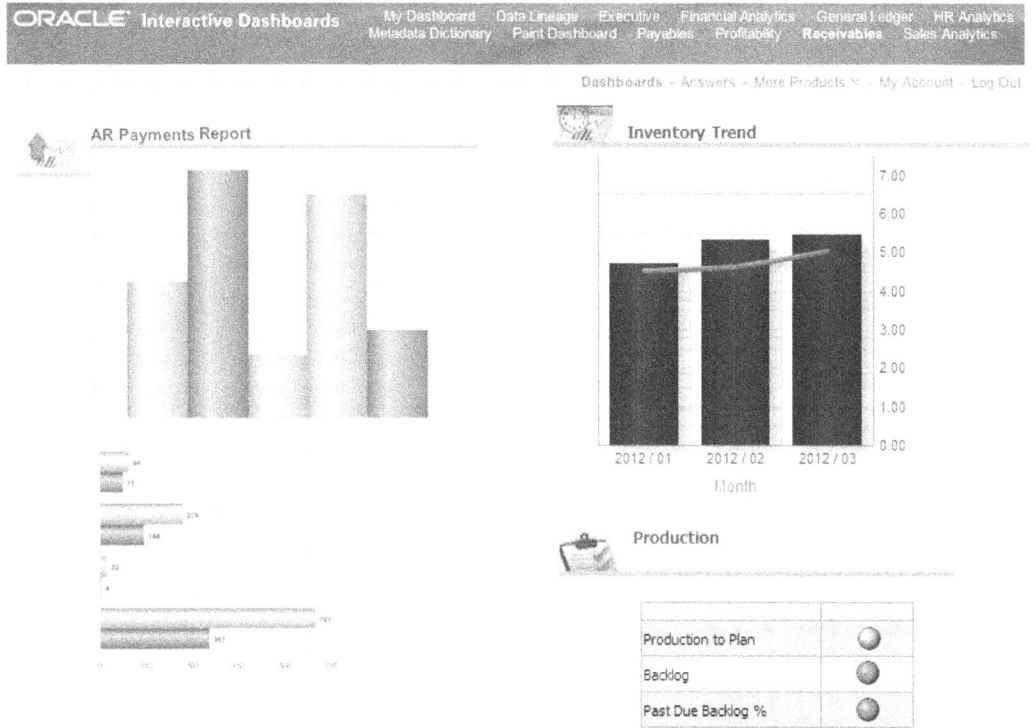

FIGURE 6-4. *OBIA regions and reports can be reused for functional monitoring*

In addition, the flexible development tools in the underlying OBIEE and BIP technology components mean that it's possible for basic status and processing data for business transactions to be made available for monitoring purposes, again without any sensitive business data exposed.

Figure 6-5 is based on the key performance indicators available in Enterprise Manager for Oracle Fusion Applications, and they illustrate how business processing statistics could be displayed so an insight into the functional system usage and health could be determined. While not currently a prepackaged option for E-Business Suite, it shouldn't take much effort to build a simple dashboard or set of reports that capture the most significant business processes (order capture, payments, or payroll, for example) and share significant patterns with those responsible for its effective service provision.

Enterprise Manager

Through the use of the Enterprise Manager's add-on Application Management Suite for Oracle E-Business Suite, the applications administrator can define a complete set of business transactions modeled internally as service level objects. As the name suggests, these are then available for managing service level agreements, and they can be used in many monitoring and management features.

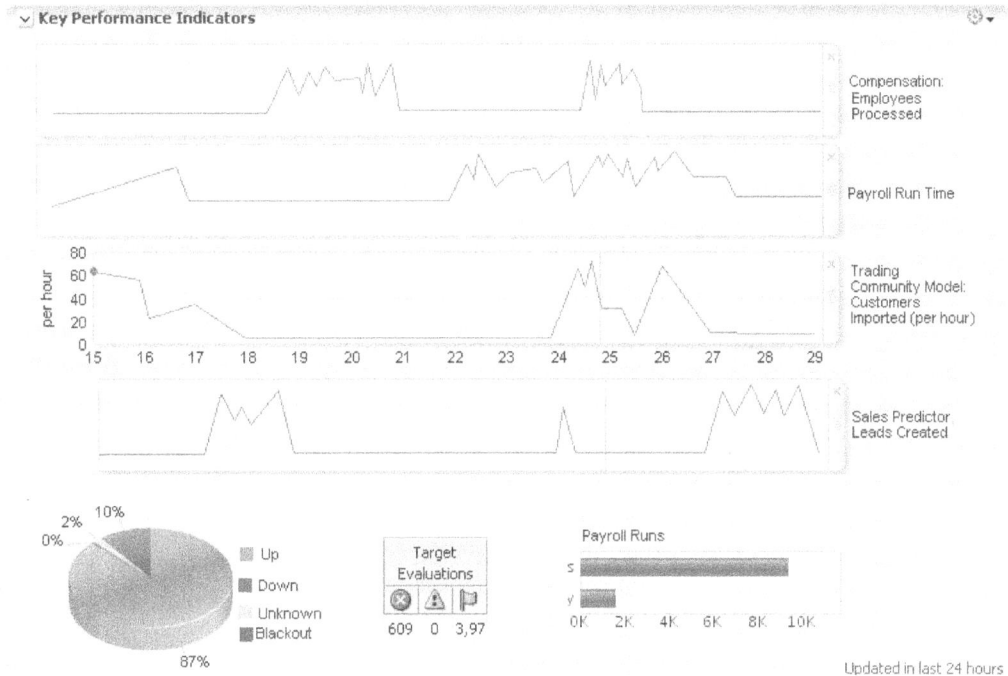

FIGURE 6-5. *Key performance indicators can aid visibility into functional availability*

Availability (and performance) information is available in several components inside Enterprise Manager; however, in the context of business processing, the most significant capability is the detailed end-user monitoring available through the Real User Experience Insight (RUEI) component.

As shown in Figure 6-6, this tool provides detailed dashboards and reports on what is happening at the client side through the use of network traffic sniffing. This means the context flow within which a user works is captured and any subsequent interruptions are monitored and recorded.

This tool can also create synthetic user monitoring, where predetermined user actions are registered and executed by the system. The resulting status and performance data is displayed, illustrating the availability level of the core process flows.

As with all of Enterprise Manager's features, the recorded metrics can be associated with configurable thresholds and, when violated, generate alerts and notifications. In addition, some remedial automated actions can be defined, such as restarting a failed concurrent manager so that job processes are not interrupted by what might have been a temporary issue. You'll see this in more detail in later sections.

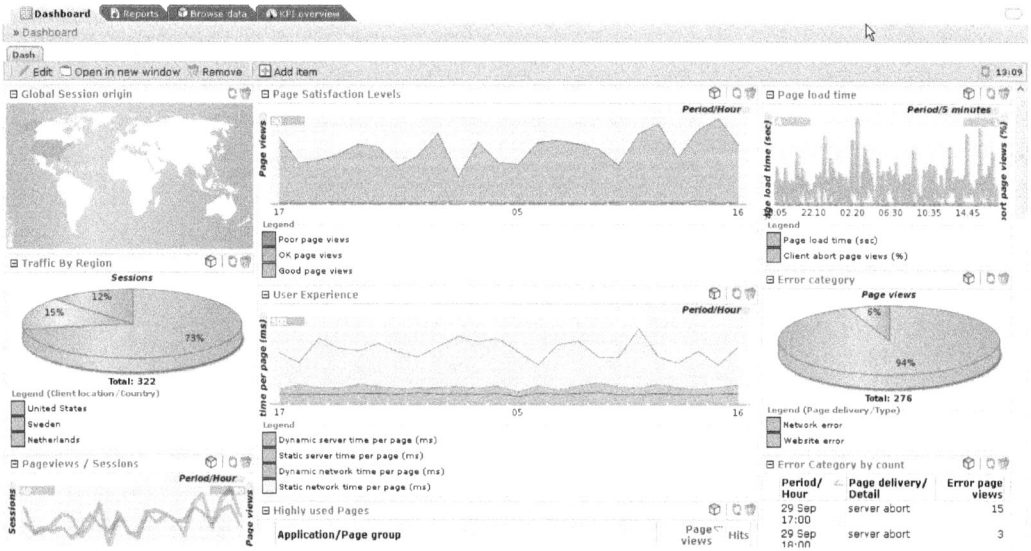

FIGURE 6-6. *The Real User Experience Insight dashboard*

Applications Technology Layer

Going down a level, let's look at the methods of monitoring and improving the availability of the application core technology components. I'll also include a few best practices points, including recommendations on managing multiple instances efficiently and actions you can take to reduce scheduled downtime. The following items will be the focus areas for this section.

- Multiple instance availability
- Reducing scheduled downtime
- Scripts
- Oracle Applications Manager
- Enterprise Manager

Multiple Instance Availability

In addition to the live production (PROD) environment that is used to support the daily business operation, there must be enterprise application instances for a multitude of other supporting purposes. The following is a basic list of the most commonly used additional instances, each of which should emulate or mirror the real production instance as closely as possible:

- **DEV** One or more instances used by in-house development teams for deploying custom code and related setups. Different projects might require separate development instances.

- ■ **TEST**   One or more instances with real data and users that are made available for the purposes of checking the results of changes such as upgrades, patches, reconfigurations, and extensions/customizations. These instances are normally stabilized for a specific time period and then refreshed, commonly from a production dataset. They may diverge into separate patch testing, user acceptance testing, and user training environments.

- ■ **PRE-PROD**   While not always used, it has been beneficial to have another instance that replicates the production instance closely, often known as a "gold" instance that remains safe for final validations of changes before moving them into the live environment. This is especially true when the test instance is subjected to destructive and rigorous tests that may cause it to diverge from a true mirror of production.

In order to manage four potentially different E-Business Suite environments, it makes sense to leverage whatever capabilities are most suited to your specific situation, as each capability can help save significant time and effort in specific situations.

First, installing a fresh E-Business Suite instance is no small matter, and while the modern rapid install process is mature and reasonably efficient, it takes many hours of work to set up and configure a new environment from scratch. The good news is that after initial implementation a fresh install is rarely used to set up a new environment. One new method is to use the Oracle VM Templates for E-Business Suite shown in Figure 6-7, as it allows anyone to lay down an E-Business Suite instance on a variety of hardware systems within minutes rather than hours. Since these are also available with the *vision* dataset, this is especially helpful for getting a system available to users for training, basic testing, and other demonstration purposes. In fact, these VM images are not intended for actual production use. However, for other purposes such as custom development, they can save significant time.

In addition to having an environment available, most of the time there is an instance available from which others should be created, usually the production environment where data and setups are their most current. This process is known as *cloning* and has been supported by E-Business Suite administrative (AD) functionality for many years. In its current form, E-Business Suite's *rapid cloning* requires creating a preclone configuration snapshot of the source system, copying files between machines, and then reconfiguring the target system from the snapshot. This is done separately for the Application Tier and the Database Tier, and involves the use of AD utility scripts, some manual steps, and some database functions. Cloning represents the most common method of creating additional E-Business Suite instances.

In addition, if you're using the Oracle Enterprise Manager plug-in for E-Business Suite, there is the option to use its *smart clone* feature. This advanced tool has been tested to cut E-Business Suite clone cycle times by up to 84 percent! As shown in Figure 6-8, it leverages Enterprise Manager's underlying provisioning framework to provide an easy-to-use interface for specifying exactly what the source system is and how the replicated target system will be configured. The process takes the user through a detailed sequence of steps so all required information is captured before launching (or scheduling) the related scripts to perform the work. There is also a monitoring page for smart cloning, showing scheduled, in-progress, and completed processes with detailed progress and status information available. In addition, Enterprise Manager has a customization management feature that allows extensions and customizations to be packaged, deployed, and managed as standard AD-compliant patches.

Cloning is a big subject with its own set of management challenges, but there are several utilities and best practices to consider that can help. One example is the Clone Log Parser (My Oracle Support Note 1447553.1), which checks all the logs from a clone for errors. For more

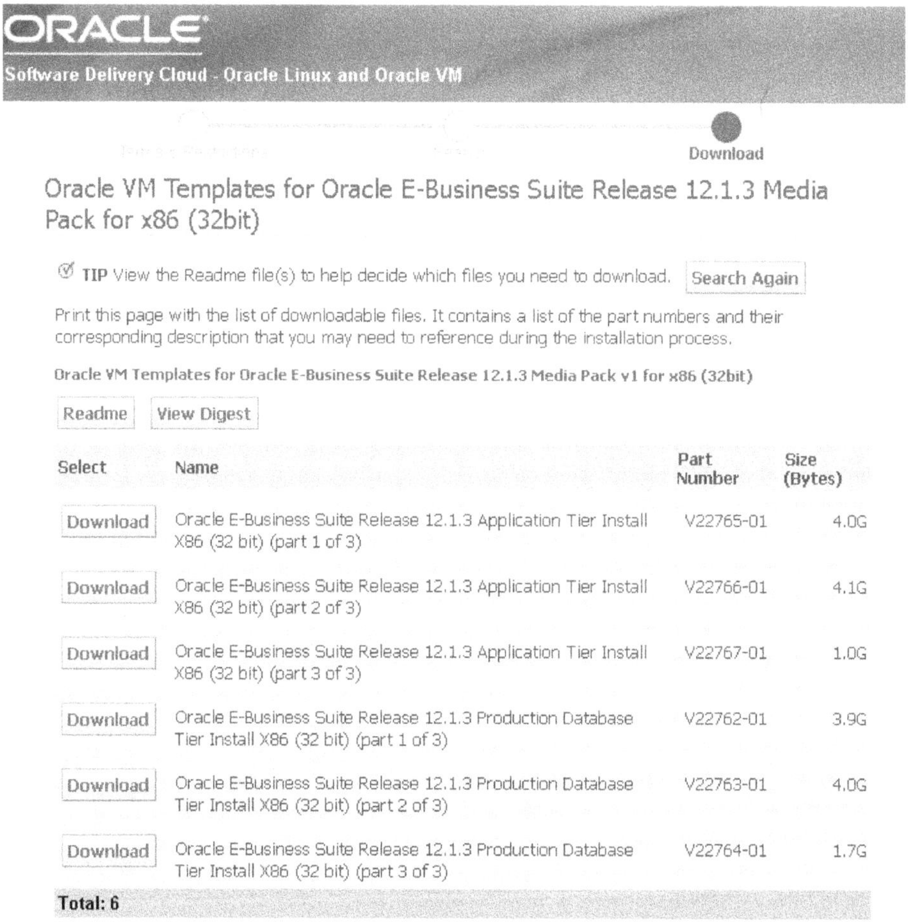

FIGURE 6-7. *Download the 32-bit VM template components for E-Business Suite 12.1.3*

detail, look carefully at the E-Business Suite Concepts Guide and in My Oracle Support for articles such as Note 406982.1, Cloning Oracle Applications Release 12 with Rapid Clone.

Reducing Scheduled Downtime

While availability is normally focused on managing unexpected outages, excessively long maintenance windows can also impact business user access to the system. As systems grow in size as do the maintenance tasks, this is something that works against the increasing need for 24 x 7 x 365 availability.

Because E-Business Suite is commonly used as an internal business system, it is not quite in the same league as websites and consumer Internet-based apps in terms of required uptime.

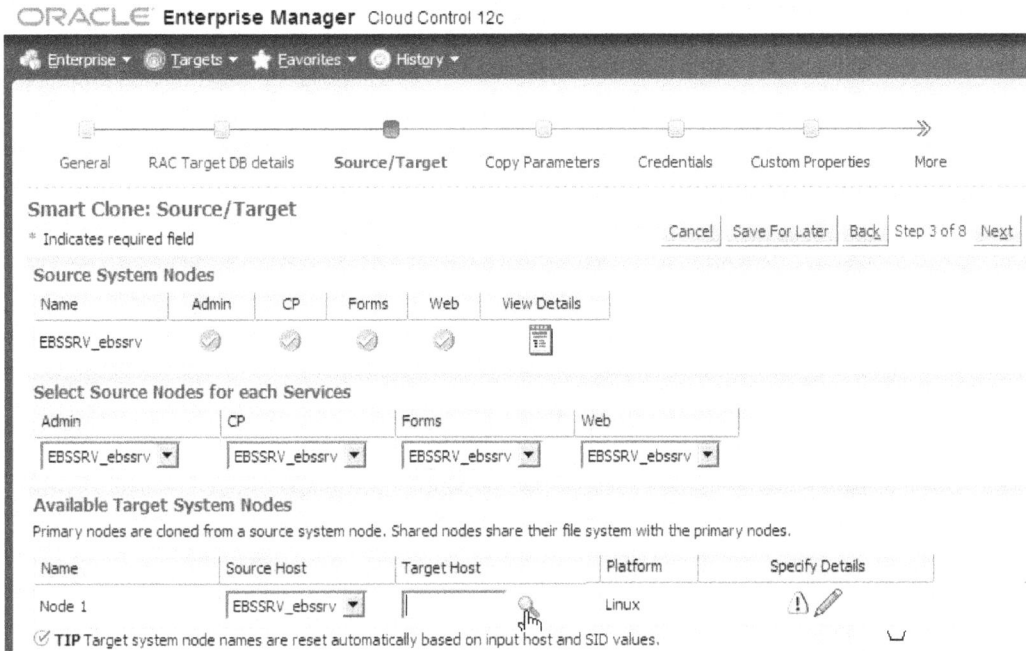

FIGURE 6-8. *Configuring the target system properties in the smart clone process*

However, with a user-base across multiple time zones and external users like suppliers and customers using web-driven integrations, it is not far behind for many organizations. Fortunately, there are multiple solutions that can be used to keep scheduled maintenance windows tight, and minimizing downtime is a focus area for the features coming in E-Business Suite Release 12.2 and beyond.

The following are some common activities performed during scheduled downtime. I'll offer some solutions to make them more efficient over the remainder of this chapter.

■ Taking system backups

■ Applying applications patches and updates

■ Applying Applications Technology stack patches and updates

■ Tuning, reconfigurations, purging, and other optimizations that require restart

■ Performing infrastructure hardware and networking maintenance

Before we start on the tips-and-tricks section, I want to let you know about a simple feature in Oracle Applications Manager for scheduling downtime, shown in Figure 6-9. This doesn't perform any work, but it does allow some simple scheduling and turns on a warning and the redirect for end users to a message and page to inform them of the maintenance window.

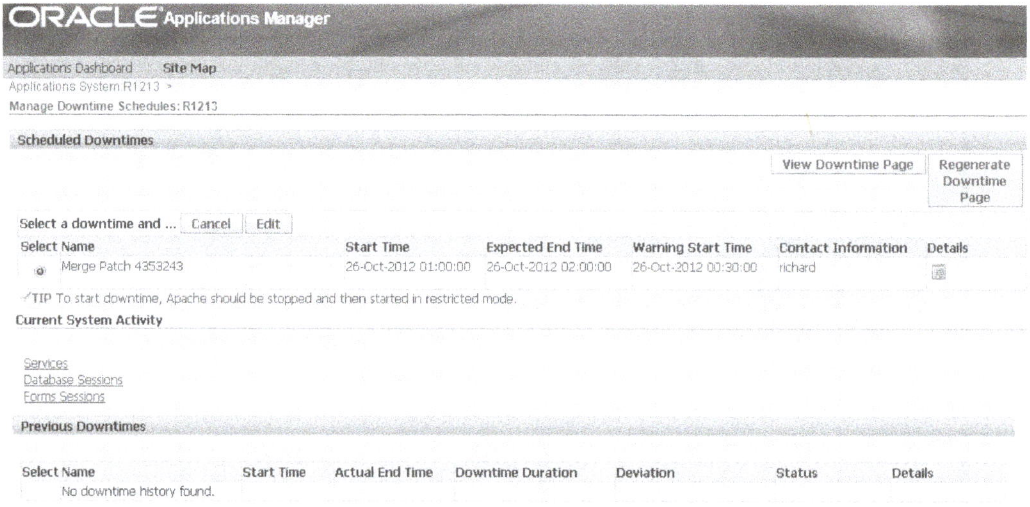

FIGURE 6-9.   *The Downtime Schedules feature in Oracle Applications Manager*

Efficient Patching

Patching takes the majority of the time of a maintenance window and requires lots of invasive work that could alter the system in an undesirable or unanticipated manner. As such, patching should be easily managed, simple, and effective, so that additional testing, problem resolution, and additional steps can be completed quickly and simply.

Patching the technology components is very different from the application, and we'll defer optimizing those outside E-Business Suite to the many, more specialized texts available. We'll also take for granted that you've applied the patch in the proper manner, reviewing the readme and adhering to all pre-, co-, and post-requisites. Using the extra features available within the application's AD Tools for E-Business Suite, it is possible to enable various options that can greatly improve patch application processing.

One popular example is merging compliant patches together, thus avoiding having to repeat and duplicate some of the administration work. This is done through the command-line program *admrgpch*, after which the consolidated patch can be applied as normal. The same thing is possible through the Oracle Applications Manager. Figure 6-10 shows how patches can be downloaded and merged together, ready for application through the Patch Wizard functionality. Another example is using the "apply = n" patching option, which allows the process to run through without doing the actual time-consuming work, while at the same time listing out all the items involved. This is useful to know when assessing downtime and testing schedules.

Another example of designing in effective patching to your E-Business Suite environment is to use a Shared Application Tier. This provides a deployment architecture where there is one APPL_TOP shared between system nodes, therefore, all related patches need only be applied once and not on each node. This can significantly reduce the repetition involved in patching large environments.

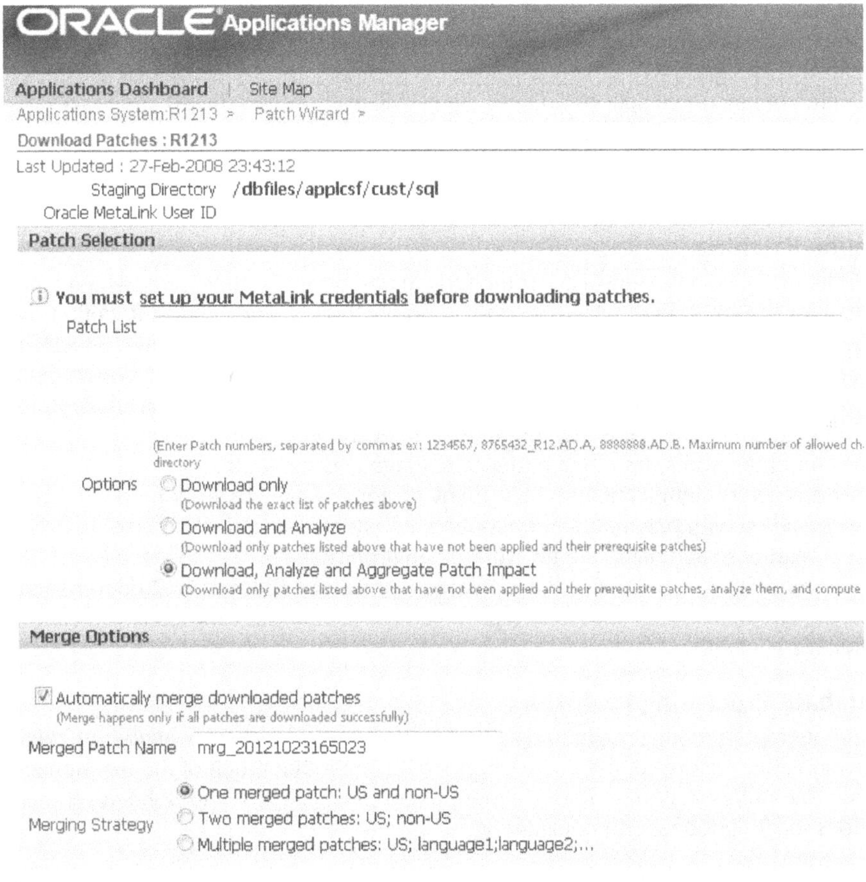

FIGURE 6-10. *Download and merge patches in Oracle Applications Manager*

Similarly, another deployment-related method of reducing downtime is to create a staged application instance, essentially a complete copy (clone) of the production system. Patches are applied to this stage environment APPL_TOP and database, then, once complete, the two systems are quickly synchronized.

The workers that the patch tool (adpatch) spawns can also be tuned so that the processing runs concurrently and is distributed across nodes in the system to optimize resource utilization. The tuning of the patching process is done through adjusting the input parameters when launching the patching process.

As mentioned before, try to keep your system current by making sure all Oracle recommended patches are applied. Ensuring the latest code is applied reduces the need for emergency or additional maintenance windows to fix known issues. It's easy to get the list of missing patches for your environment through Oracle Applications Manager's Patch Wizard or through My Oracle Support using the Collections tab.

A final recommendation is to look at Oracle Enterprise Manager's Application Testing Suite (ATS). Its automated functional and load testing features can significantly reduce the time required for the user testing that's needed after patching and larger application updates. Through the use of specifically designed ATS E-Business Suite accelerators, the embedded OpenScript tool allows the recording of functional actions (in both the HTML or forms interfaces) and makes that available for editing, extension, and then automated execution. Similarly, for load testing the tool also supports both Forms and HTML interface components and provides details on each page request of its performance and all other related system events. We'll look at this tool in more detail in Chapter 8.

Online Patching

Included in E-Business Suite 12.2 is the Oracle database 11g Release 2, which has a significant feature for the creation of near-zero downtime patching: Edition Based Redefinition. This feature allows a kind of snapshot of the applications database to be made online, which includes changes made by the patch to one edition and then a short cut-over time where everything is synced up.

As well as significantly reducing downtime, the side benefit of this is that while the cut-over period (outage) is small, it is also the same size every time, since no patch related processing is done—in other words, it's much easier to manage and schedule.

This is a very significant feature as many customers have to work hard to reduce maintenance windows filled with patching and upgrading actions, and when unexpected issues occur they cannot readily switch back to their working environment.

For more information on online patching, consult the Release 12.2 documentation. For a fully detailed explanation, see Chapter 19 of the Oracle Database Advanced Application Developer's Guide (E25518-06).

Database Processing Features

In our attempt to reduce the maintenance windows (and improve availability), it is worth looking at some native features of the database, since it is here that much of the maintenance activities occur. We will look at these items in more detail in Chapters 7 and 8; however, here are a few options that might be worth considering:

- **Advanced compression** Available in Database 11g Release 1 onward, this feature condenses data to significantly reduce the storage required, without affecting query processing time. A smaller database footprint means less disk read/writes and a lower overall storage requirement. With larger database instances fairly common to E-Business Suite, using this feature enables more data to be stored in faster to access and usually more reliable memory media (like flash), speeding up overall processing times for things like patches and PL/SQL compilation. It also helps reduce reliance on moving parts like storage disk drives.

- **Active Data Guard** Creates a standby database that is not just useful for failover, but also for offloading some of the work. In this context, it helps reduce maintenance windows as it eliminates the need for taking backups from the real production instance.

- **The Exadata Database Machine** Has been running E-Business Suite environments faster with less outages for dozens of customers. Its advanced processing power and memory-storage architecture has proven to complete the processing-heavy work commonly performed in maintenance windows.

Scripts and Oracle Applications Manager

Having looked at a few ways to improve availability by reducing scheduled downtime, let's switch gears a little and go back to looking at some more tools to help us monitor (and therefore manage) availability.

Most of the command-line utility scripts used for starting and stopping E-Business Suite and its application tier components can be passed the word "status" as a parameter, reporting back detailed information on current availability and health. The example given in Figure 6-11 shows the output for the Oracle Database Listener, including status, uptime, configuration basics, additional services, and a log for more detail.

These scripts are all found in the $ADMIN_SCRIPTS_HOME directory (which will have a different location on different tiers) and are regularly called by system administrators from their own management programs and custom tools to get real-time component information. Table 6-4 summarizes each of them.

For at-a-glance availability information, Oracle Applications Manager gives the best insight by far.

```
apr1213@petra:/r1213/oracle/R1213/inst/apps/R1213_petra/admin/scripts
[apr1213@petra scripts]$ adalnctl.sh status

adalnctl.sh version 120.3

Checking status for listener process APPS_R1213.

LSNRCTL for Linux: Version 10.1.0.5.0 - Production on 23-OCT-2012 18:53:33

Copyright (c) 1991, 2004, Oracle.  All rights reserved.

Connecting to (ADDRESS=(PROTOCOL=TCP)(Host=petra)(Port=1626))
STATUS of the LISTENER
------------------------
Alias                     APPS_R1213
Version                   TNSLSNR for Linux: Version 10.1.0.5.0 - Production
Start Date                22-OCT-2012 19:33:35
Uptime                    0 days 23 hr. 19 min. 58 sec
Trace Level               off
Security                  ON: Local OS Authentication
SNMP                      OFF
Listener Parameter File   /r1213/oracle/R1213/inst/apps/R1213_petra/ora/10.1.2/network/admin/listener.ora
Listener Log File         /r1213/oracle/R1213/inst/apps/R1213_petra/logs/ora/10.1.2/network/apps_r1213.log
Listening Endpoints Summary...
  (DESCRIPTION=(ADDRESS=(PROTOCOL=tcp)(HOST=petra.de.oracle.com)(PORT=1626)))
Services Summary...
Service "FNDFS" has 1 instance(s).
  Instance "FNDFS", status UNKNOWN, has 1 handler(s) for this service...
Service "FNDSM" has 1 instance(s).
  Instance "FNDSM", status UNKNOWN, has 1 handler(s) for this service...
The command completed successfully

adalnctl.sh: exiting with status 0

adalnctl.sh: check the logfile /r1213/oracle/R1213/inst/apps/R1213_petra/logs/appl/admin/log/adalnctl.txt for more

[apr1213@petra scripts]$
```

FIGURE 6-11. *Execution output from the apalnctl.sh administration script with the status parameter*

Script Name	Description
adapcctl.sh	OPMN-managed HTTP Server instances
adalnctl.sh	Oracle Database Listener
adcmctl.sh	Concurrent Managers
adformsctl.sh	OC4J Forms (nonsocket)
adforms-c4wsctl.sh	OPMN-managed FORMS-C4WS OC4J
adformsrvctl.sh	Native Forms (socket)
adoacorectl.sh	OPMN-managed OACORE OC4J instance
adoafmctl.sh	OPMN-managed OAFM OC4J instance
adopmnctl.sh	OPMN-managed processes
jtffmctl.sh	Oracle Fulfillment Server

TABLE 6-4. *Scripts that Give Availability Status Information*

Starting with an overall picture, Figure 6-12 shows the Applications dashboard that summarizes the current status of the main E-Business Suite components, with counts and drills available in more detailed pages. Next, Figure 6-13 shows the more detailed Application System Status page, with all of the E-Business Site components and their status, again the option to drill into more data.

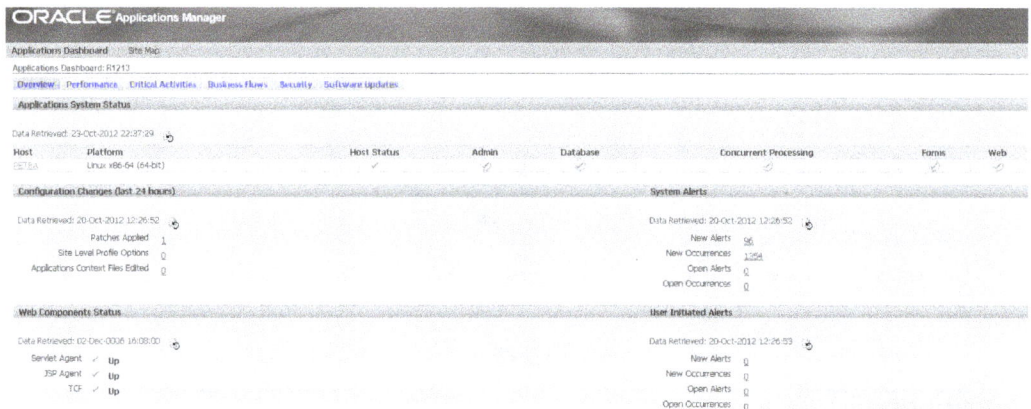

FIGURE 6-12. *The Applications dashboard page in OAM*

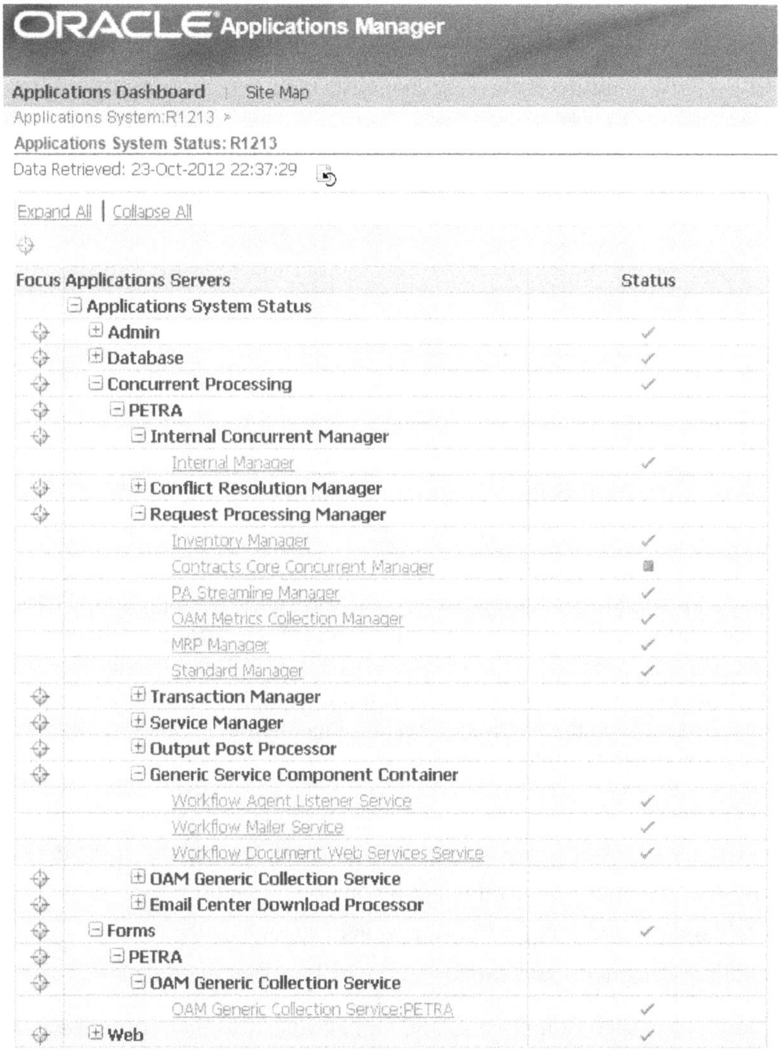

FIGURE 6-13. *The detailed System Status page in OAM*

In addition to these basic pages, as shown in Figure 6-14, Oracle Applications Manager has a whole selection of features categorized as related to availability. These are found from the site map, under the Monitoring region.

The first category is Hosts, and the subsequent page provides basic status information for the host hardware and all the key E-Business Suite components it is running, such as Web Server, Forms Server, Concurrent Managers, and the database. The page has various search and drill

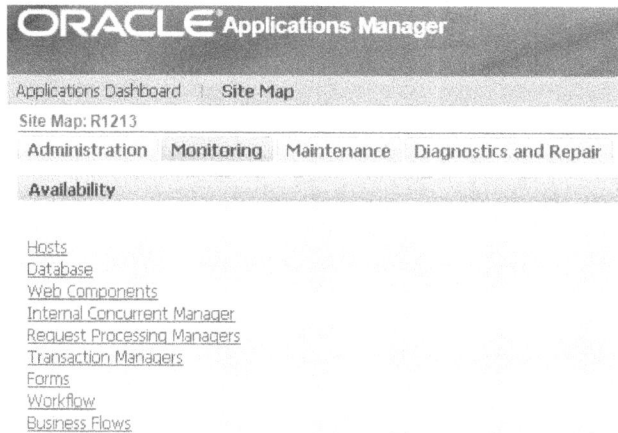

FIGURE 6-14. *The availability management features of Oracle Applications Manager*

capabilities with additional child pages as shown in Figure 6-15 for all the Concurrent Manager processes, including a drill on the AUDSID value to show related database performance.

The second link is Database, which provides a comprehensive page that starts with a basic availability summary at the top and then has multiple regions that can be expanded for more detailed interrogation on the status and health of its internal processes. As shown in Figure 6-16 this includes information on items such as:

- **Wait events**   Any processing that is delayed behind a dependent activity
- **Memory statistics**   How much memory the different parts of the database are consuming
- **System statistics**   General internal component performance metrics
- **Tablespaces and status**   Consumption of storage by the data
- **Rollback segments and extents**   Usage of uncommitted data

The third link is Web Components and contains basic availability and status information of the Forms and Web Servers in the environment, along with items like the summary of user and system alerts discussed previously, the status of the TCF socket server that connects internal web components, and the servlet and JSP agents that support OA Framework.

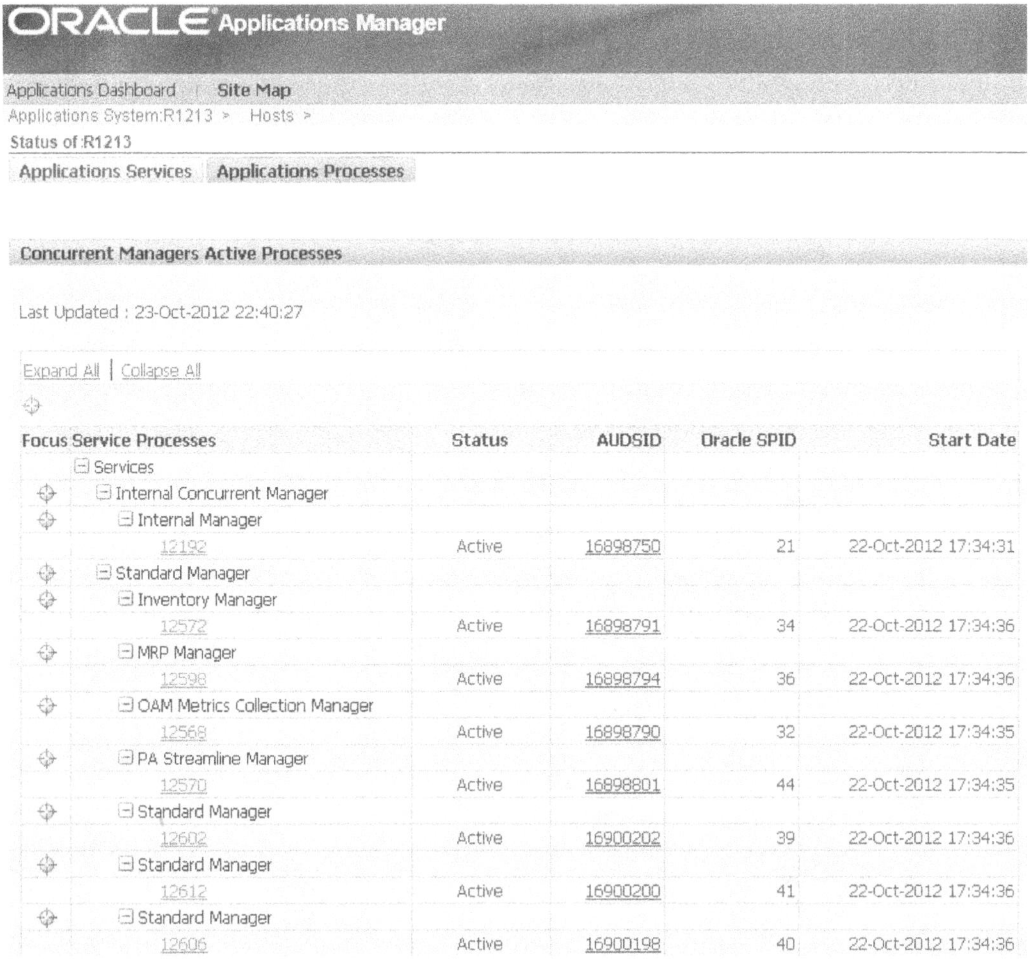

ORACLE Applications Manager

Applications Dashboard   Site Map

Applications System:R1213 >   Hosts >

Status of :R1213

Applications Services   Applications Processes

Concurrent Managers Active Processes

Last Updated : 23-Oct-2012 22:40:27

Expand All | Collapse All

Focus	Service Processes	Status	AUDSID	Oracle SPID	Start Date
	⊟ Services				
⊕	⊟ Internal Concurrent Manager				
⊕	⊟ Internal Manager				
	12192	Active	16898750	21	22-Oct-2012 17:34:31
⊕	⊟ Standard Manager				
⊕	⊟ Inventory Manager				
	12572	Active	16898791	34	22-Oct-2012 17:34:36
⊕	⊟ MRP Manager				
	12598	Active	16898794	36	22-Oct-2012 17:34:36
⊕	⊟ OAM Metrics Collection Manager				
	12568	Active	16898790	32	22-Oct-2012 17:34:35
⊕	⊟ PA Streamline Manager				
	12570	Active	16898801	44	22-Oct-2012 17:34:35
⊕	⊟ Standard Manager				
	12602	Active	16900202	39	22-Oct-2012 17:34:36
⊕	⊟ Standard Manager				
	12612	Active	16900200	41	22-Oct-2012 17:34:36
⊕	⊟ Standard Manager				
	12606	Active	16900198	40	22-Oct-2012 17:34:36

FIGURE 6-15.   *Host and its component availability*

The fourth link is Internal Concurrent Manager (ICM), which provides capabilities to both interrogate and administer this core component. As shown in Figure 6-17, this contains basic details plus buttons that reveal more detail such as more about its status, system processes, and the load it's currently under. It also includes the ability to quickly see the environmental parameters within which it's operating, such as sleep period, restart option, debugging, and logs, all the active and deactivated processes including a drill to the database session performance statistics, and access to the ICM log file contents.

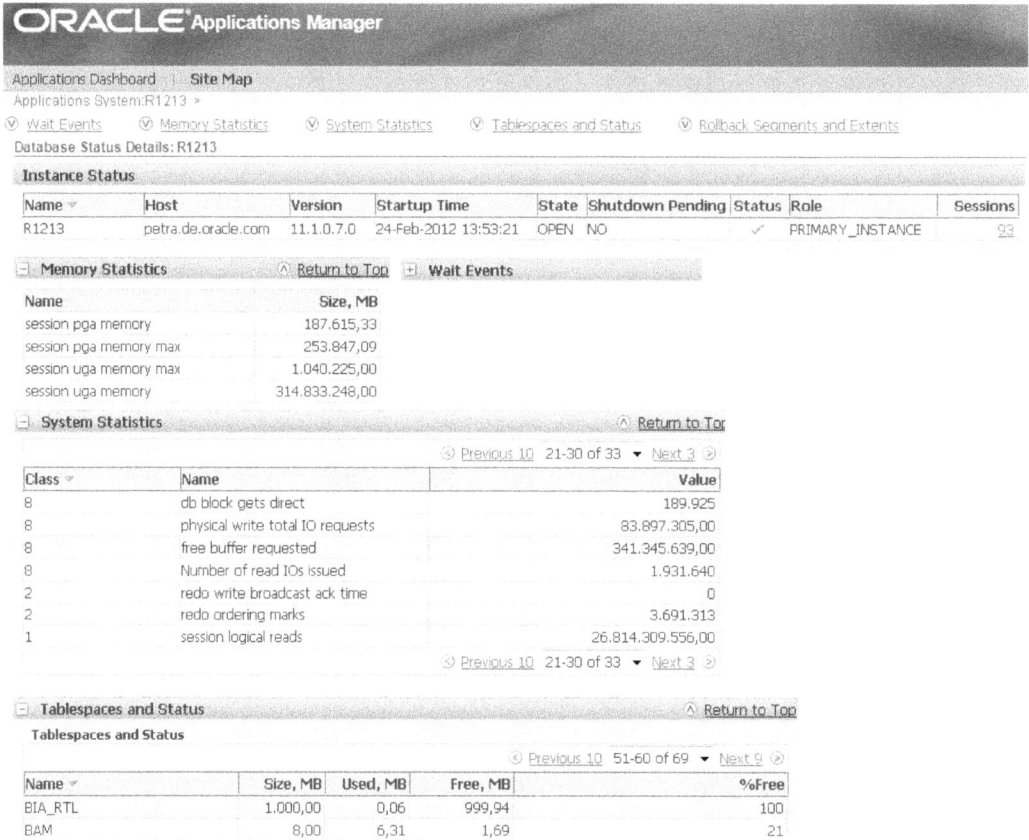

ORACLE Applications Manager

Applications Dashboard | Site Map
Applications System:R1213 >

ⓥ Wait Events   ⓥ Memory Statistics   ⓥ System Statistics   ⓥ Tablespaces and Status   ⓥ Rollback Segments and Extents

Database Status Details: R1213

Instance Status

Name ▽	Host	Version	Startup Time	State	Shutdown Pending	Status	Role	Sessions
R1213	petra.de.oracle.com	11.1.0.7.0	24-Feb-2012 13:53:21	OPEN	NO	✓	PRIMARY_INSTANCE	93

⊟ **Memory Statistics**   ⌃ Return to Top   ⊞ **Wait Events**

Name	Size, MB
session pga memory	187.615,33
session pga memory max	253.847,09
session uga memory max	1.040.225,00
session uga memory	314.833.248,00

⊟ **System Statistics**   ⌃ Return to Top

⊙ Previous 10   21-30 of 33 ▾ Next 3 ⊙

Class ▽	Name	Value
8	db block gets direct	189.925
8	physical write total IO requests	83.897.305,00
8	free buffer requested	341.345.639,00
8	Number of read IOs issued	1.931.640
2	redo write broadcast ack time	0
2	redo ordering marks	3.691.313
1	session logical reads	26.814.309.556,00

⊙ Previous 10   21-30 of 33 ▾ Next 3 ⊙

⊟ **Tablespaces and Status**   ⌃ Return to Top

Tablespaces and Status

⊙ Previous 10   51-60 of 69 ▾ Next 9 ⊙

Name ▽	Size, MB	Used, MB	Free, MB	%Free
BIA_RTL	1.000,00	0,06	999,94	100
BAM	8,00	6,31	1,69	21

FIGURE 6-16. *Database status and health information*

The fifth link is Request Processing Managers, meaning those concurrent managers that handle execution of the functional program code. As shown in Figure 6-18, this includes active and deactivated managers, standard managers, and those specific to certain product features, such as the Inventory Manager. It gives similar actions and process information as the Internal

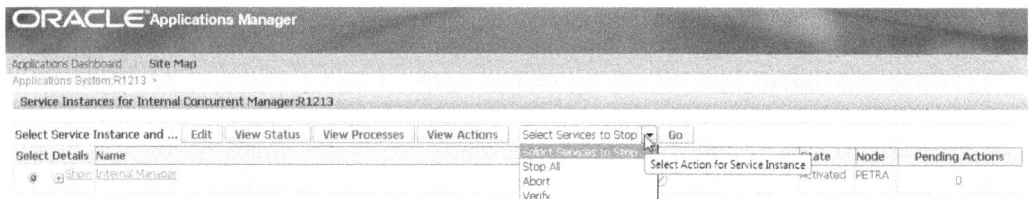

ORACLE Applications Manager

Applications Dashboard   Site Map
Applications System:R1213 ×

Service Instances for Internal Concurrent Manager:R1213

Select Service Instance and ...   Edit   View Status   View Processes   View Actions   Select Services to Stop ▾   Go

Select Details	Name			ate	Node	Pending Actions
⊙	⊞ Show: Internal Manager			ctivated	PETRA	0

Select Services to Stop
Stop All   Select Action for Service Instance
Abort
Verify

FIGURE 6-17. *Internal Concurrent Manager detail page with links and actions*

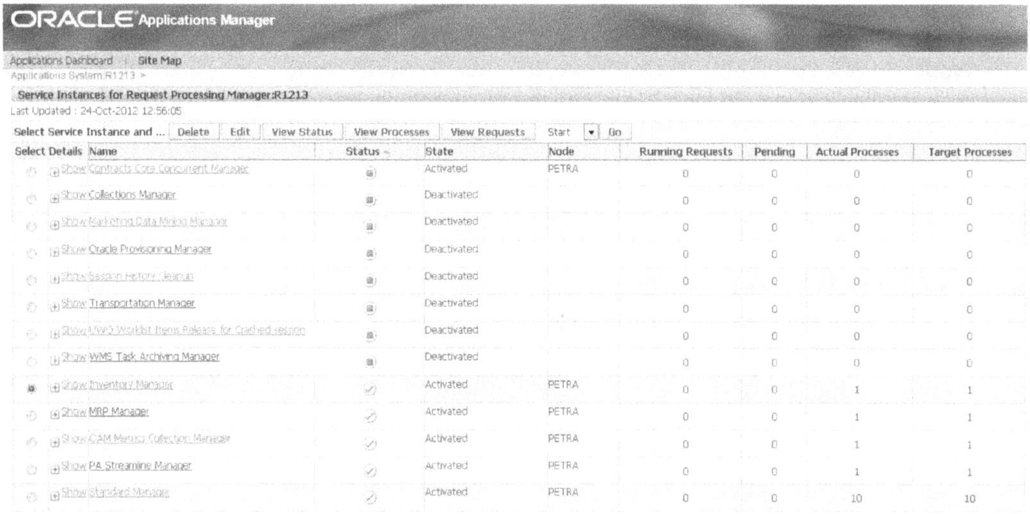

FIGURE 6-18. *Request Processing Manager detail with links and actions*

Concurrent Manager but logically includes detail on the functional requests they are running, such as counts, debug options, and access to both the manager's log and the related ICM log.

The sixth link is Transaction Managers and as shown in Figure 6-19 provides detail on the remaining set of Concurrent Managers, those that are designed to handle specific transaction processing. This provides similar status details as discussed previously, including processes, requests,

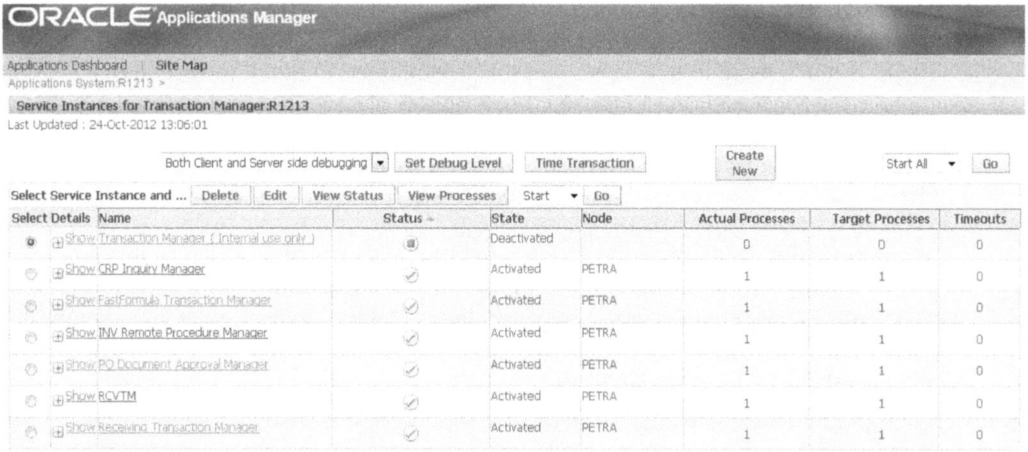

FIGURE 6-19. *Status of the Transaction Managers*

and log details, plus a few more details on enabling debugging. It also provides a Time Transaction feature that can be used to review the internal performance of invoking the components involved.

The remaining three links are Forms, Workflow, and Business Flows. We discussed both Workflow (see Figure 6-2) and Business Flows earlier in the context of availability management tools for the Business Process Layer, and the same details are accessed here. The Forms link provides brief details for the service instances for the Forms listener(s), including status and the processes running. All three of these show summary status information. For more details, the dedicated sections of OAM provide a richer set of information beyond monitoring.

Platform Layer

Since the majority of availability management is spending time and effort ensuring that the technology components underpinning E-Business Suite remain stable and healthy, this section forms a useful resource for such work. After all, a house built on a fragile foundation doesn't stay intact for long.

In this section, we'll first look at some basic technology platforms and architectures that are employed for achieving high availability, and then drill into the features available for implementing them. The section includes the following:

- **High availability architectures** Adopting the right approach
- **Oracle Alerts** Using automated notifications for data issues
- **Enterprise Manager** The best-of-breed Oracle management tooling

High-Availability Architecture

For the last few years Oracle has defined a set of products, principles, and best practices for achieving high availability for all of its products under the banner of Maximum Availability Architecture (MAA). Logically, this focuses around the database component, but it does include some recommendations for the Applications Tier component of E-Business Suite.

The MAA recommendations for E-Business Suite are summarized by the high-level diagram in Figure 6-20, showing how a combination of redundancy, load balancing, and Oracle's system management products can be used to implement a complete high-availability deployment.

There is much more to this topic, and this is explained in detail in several places. One example is the MAA section of Oracle.com, with lots of examples and case studies that may include a similar situation to that of your organization. Another set of useful resources is the Oracle Press books that explain full details on using specific key pieces, such as *Oracle Database 11g Release 2 High Availability: Maximize Your Availability with Grid Infrastructure, RAC, and Data Guard* (Oracle Press, 2011).

A complete discussion of all the components of a high-availability architecture like MAA and their application to all the components of E-Business Suite is outside the scope of the holistic management discussion in this book; however, here are a few general recommendations that may help you make the right choices for your specific needs. Some points were mentioned previously, but are included here for completeness.

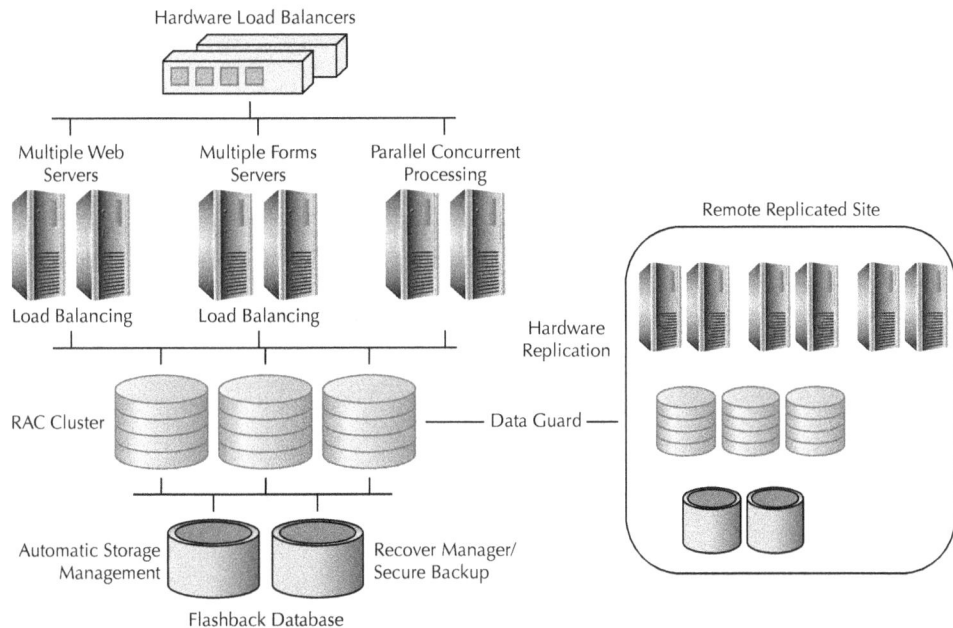

FIGURE 6-20. *The recommended MAA architecture for E-Business Suite*

Deployment options related to availability include

■ Eliminate all single points of failure. Look and test for them, and see what can be done to provide failover.

■ Ensure load balancing is done all the way through the system, from initial page requests (via hardware) to the network nodes, application servers, and the database. Also, ensure vendor load balancers are properly configured so they do not interfere with E-Business Suite connectivity. See My Oracle Support Note 380489.1.

■ Ensure the Web Server and the OC4J/WLS JVMs are set to include clustering/load balancing configuration based on your capacity plan and the expected system load.

■ Ensure Real Application Clusters (RAC) are deployed for all production database instances, along with the appropriate management tools. This not only improves performance, but due to inherent load balancing, it also aids disaster prevention should one node become unavailable.

■ Consider the Exadata machine for large, heavily used systems. In benchmarking and customer testing with E-Business Suite, it has shown significant transaction processing and user interface speed increases, along with other meaningful efficiencies like power consumption.

Recommendations for best practices related to availability include

■ Carefully consider the costs and risks of different outages, their probability of occurring (and look at reducing that), and the features of the components involved. Construct several business scenarios with real cost estimations to help justify spending on what seems like server and storage resources that remain idle most of the time. Also, look at ways of using these redundant resources to spread workload.

■ Carefully consider the time required for service restoration and data recovery. Sometimes it's possible to over-engineer (and over-spend on) a solution to a problem that may have little immediate business impact. Focus resources on the areas of most impact.

■ Test, test, and test. This is especially important if you're relying on services from external parties where things might change without your knowing. Run regular fire drills to make sure, in the advent of a problem, the expected contingencies still work.

■ Ensure change management is strong on the disaster recovery procedures and across the whole business continuity plan. Test them to prove it. Make sure you're kept informed of changes and are part of approval processes if required. When changes do occur, ensure the appropriate testing and documentation changes are included.

Oracle System Alerts

Oracle Alerts could have been included in the business process discussion, since seeded alerts are triggered from E-Business Suite functional activities such as creating a delivery receipt. However, there are also lots of predefined system alerts that get raised when a critical component becomes unexpectedly unavailable. Because they have the most value when passively monitoring for system problems, they are included here.

As a reminder, Oracle Alerts are natively focused on database actions and so don't contain coverage of outages for all components, such as those on the Web or Application Tiers.

The examples in Figure 6-21 include alerts for Workflow, for Concurrent Managers like AFPPRN, and violations to the monitored OAM metrics. As mentioned in the previous chapter, Oracle Alerts are customizable so that additional items can be constantly checked and any outages or violations can be immediately visible and reported as notifications.

Enterprise Manager's Oracle E-Business Suite Plug-in

With the E-Business Suite plug-in installed, the simplest place for managing availability of the complete E-Business Suite environment is the Services dashboard page, accessible from the top-level Targets menu. There is some duplication of purpose when compared to Oracle Applications Manager, but Enterprise Manager provides a best-of-breed technology management framework and applies and extends it for E-Business Suite. As such, the capabilities go far beyond what is possible in OAM alone.

As shown in Figure 6-22, with the E-Business Suite plug-in enabled, Enterprise Manager contains all the basic E-Business Suite components; each one defined as a service, including Concurrent Managers, Forms Servers, Web Components, and Workflow. You'll notice this page brings in not only statuses but also items like service level agreements based on metric monitoring, problems and incidents, and user-defined availability tests that can be set up, such as the login test shown.

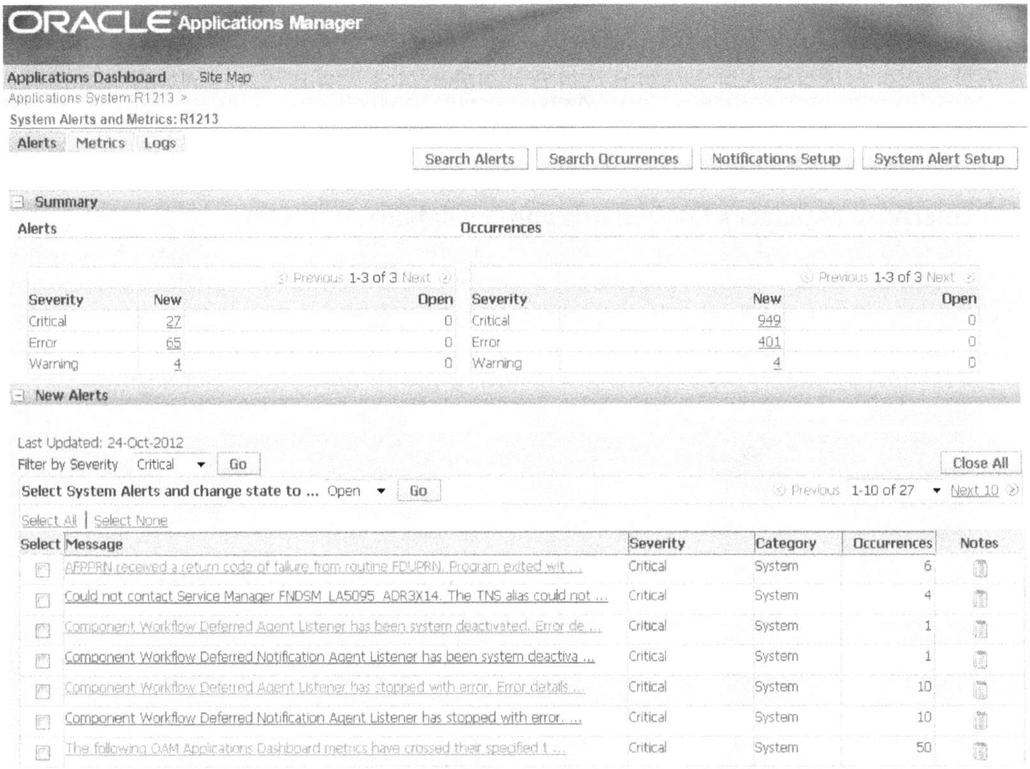

FIGURE 6-21. *System alerts in Oracle Applications Manager*

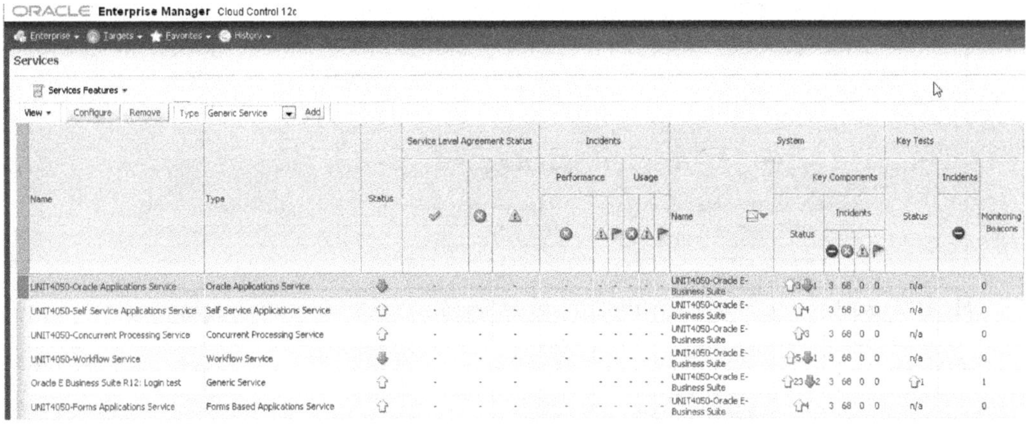

FIGURE 6-22. *The Services dashboard in the Enterprise Manager 12c plug-in for E-Business Suite*

In addition, if static reports are required, there are dozens under the Information Publisher Reports area, accessible from the Enterprise menu. This includes a whole section on monitoring, including reports like the top 20 most common alerts, alerts history, availability history, and availability metrics. These reports are useful when compiling data for reviewing availability management performance, such as when reviewing the parts of your application management plan. They can also be useful in managing service level agreements (SLAs), where hard data needs associating with the assessment reports.

Enterprise Manager's Dashboards and Availability Definition

The following sequence of dashboards from Figures 6-23, 6-24, 6-25, and 6-26 show how the Enterprise Manager plug-in provides at-a-glance availability information for all of the core

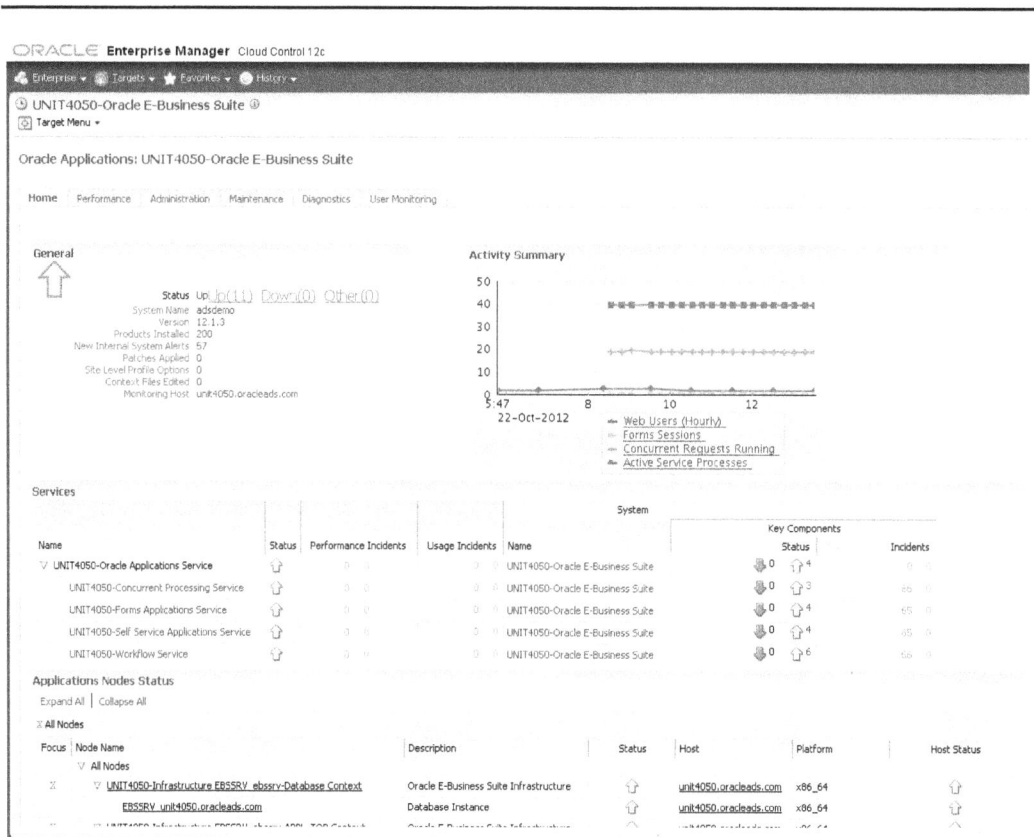

FIGURE 6-23. *The Home dashboard page showing status of systems, components, and services of E-Business Suite*

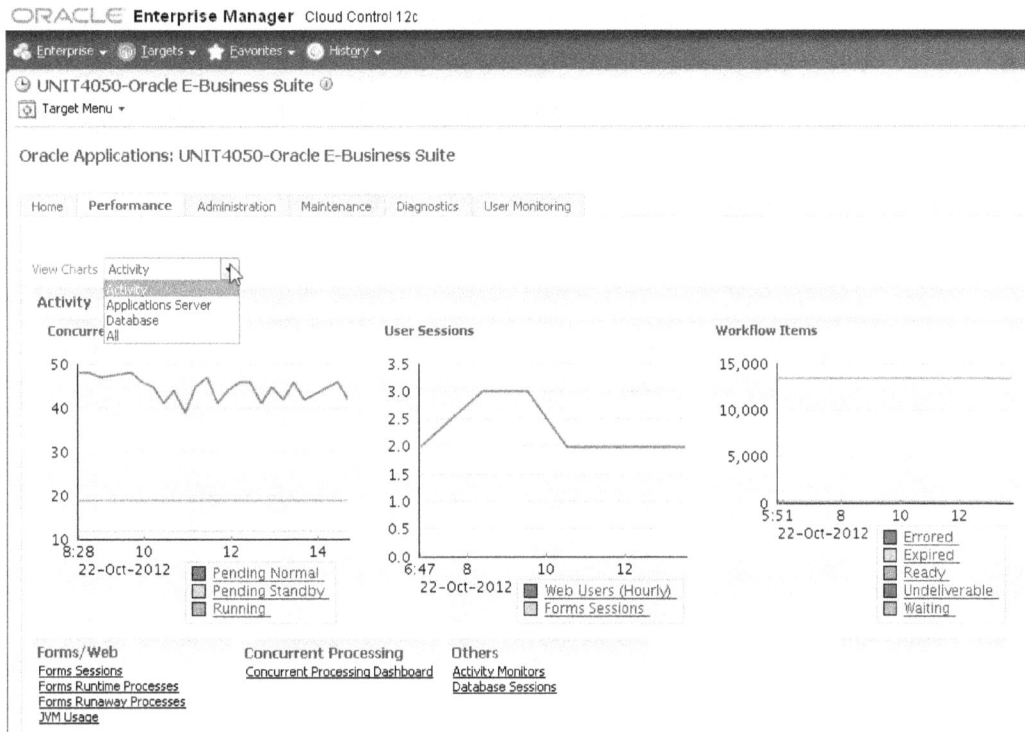

FIGURE 6-24. *Basic charts on performance metrics make it easy to spot availability issues*

components of E-Business Suite. These can be used to quickly review the availability of the related components either proactively or upon investigation of an issue.

Note that they include the links at the bottom of the page to more specific component pages, including those leading directly back to Oracle Applications Manager to execute diagnostic tests.

In addition to these dashboard pages showing basic status information, Enterprise Manager is flexible with what constitutes an availability issue, and it can be user defined. This is especially

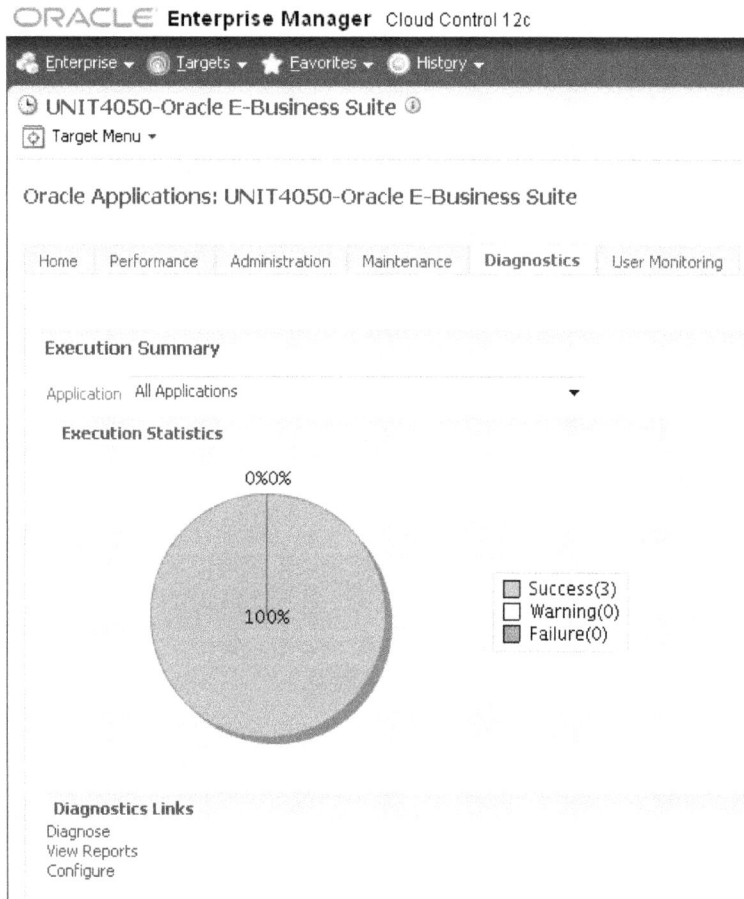

FIGURE 6-25. *The Diagnostics dashboard illustrating the Oracle Diagnostic Framework tests that have been run and their status*

useful for nonproduction instances, so a flood of alerts and notifications are not generated for noncritical systems or temporary issues with limited impact. Figure 6-27 shows how this is defined as deciding exactly what should be identified as a *key component*, and whether there must be more than one instance of those components available.

As mentioned before, availability definition also includes the use of user-defined monitoring known in Enterprise Manager as *beacons*, as well as custom *service tests* that can verify if something specific like a page, form, or function is up and available. More details on creating both of these is available in the Enterprise Manager documentation.

In addition to the features specific to E-Business Suite, the core technology components are supported by exceptionally powerful dashboards and reports of their own in Enterprise Manager.

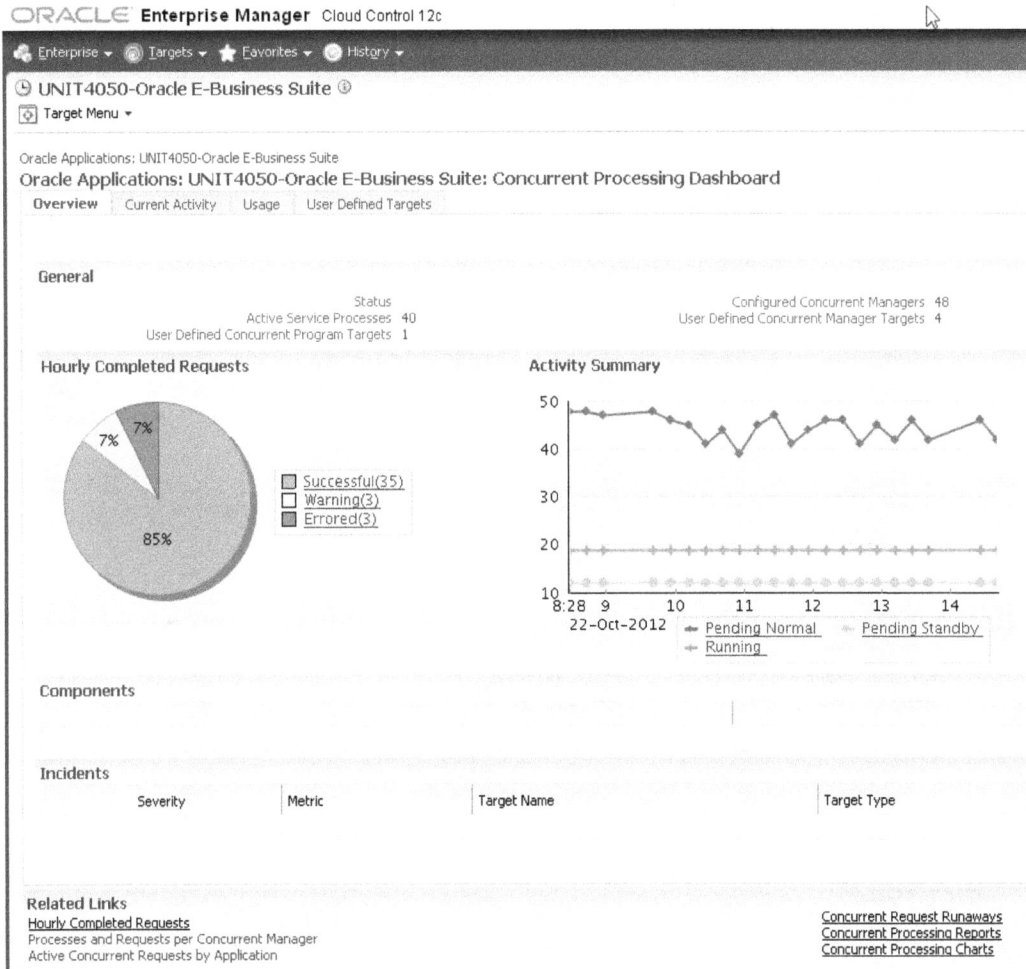

FIGURE 6-26. *The Concurrent Processing status, activity, and any incidents, along with related links for more detail*

Figure 6-28 shows the database management tools that include a wealth of analytics and features specifically for ensuring high availability. These tools also extend in the Application Server, where similar features exist. See the product documentation for each of these components for more details.

Although we looked at the various out-of-the-box alerts within E-Business Suite already, clearly Enterprise Manager extends this and provides more abilities to define thresholds, metrics, and notifications as part of the availability management infrastructure. You'll see this again in the upcoming chapters.

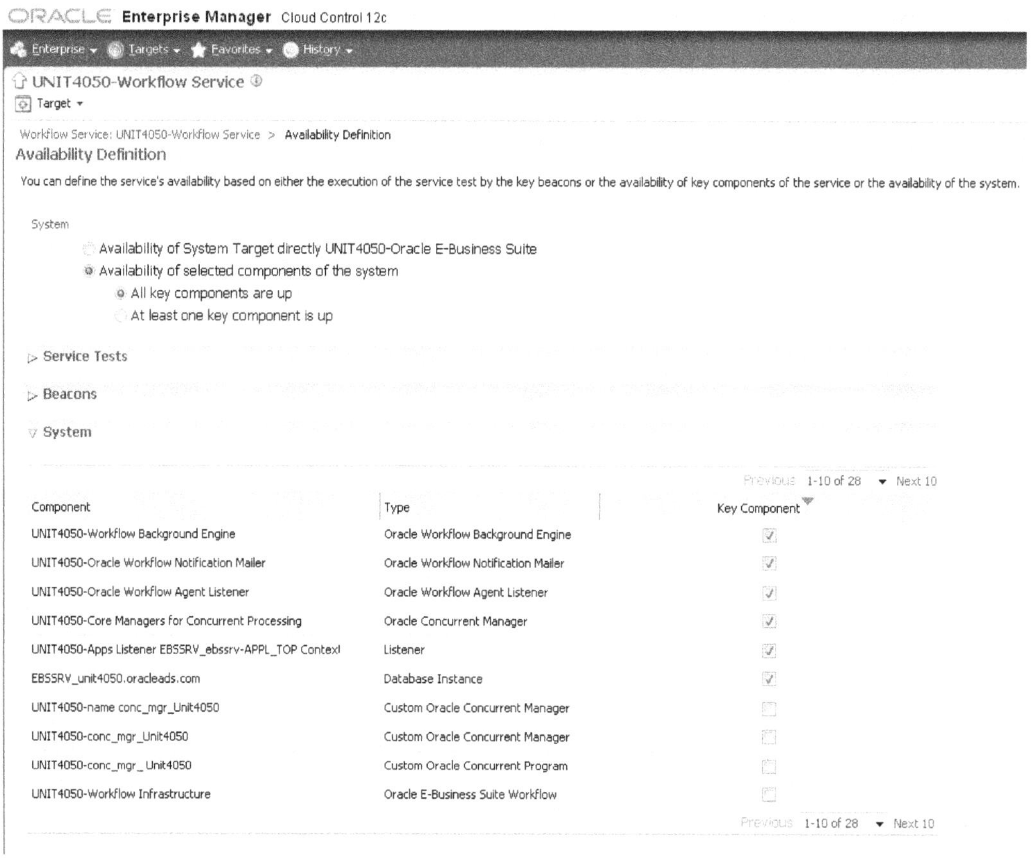

FIGURE 6-27. *Defining availability in Enterprise Manager*

Enterprise Manager's User Monitoring

Enterprise Manager's user monitoring is the powerful capability for reviewing availability and performance information by individual applications user. This feature is native to Enterprise Manager, but it makes particular sense for an enterprise application target, since problems are usually first reported in the context of a person being unable to perform a task (such as submitting an order), rather than a specific technology being problematic. This feature makes it easy to pin down either users affected by a particular problem such as slow SQL, or to search by username and see what components they are touching and which might be causing them problems.

The user monitoring page provides details from user sessions on the Concurrent Manager, Forms, Web, and Database nodes and details on their performance. It also includes (where possible) details on exactly what the session is doing, such as the active form or program name, and lists out all the activities related.

Figure 6-29 shows the user monitoring summary with the most active user sessions and links to drill into more detail, showing exactly what they are doing (concurrent jobs, forms sessions,

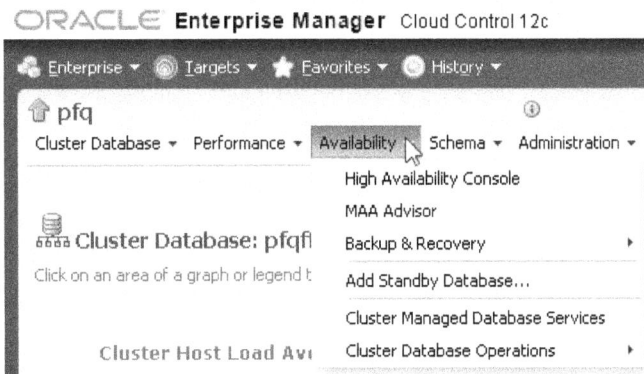

FIGURE 6-28. *Availability features specific to the Oracle Database*

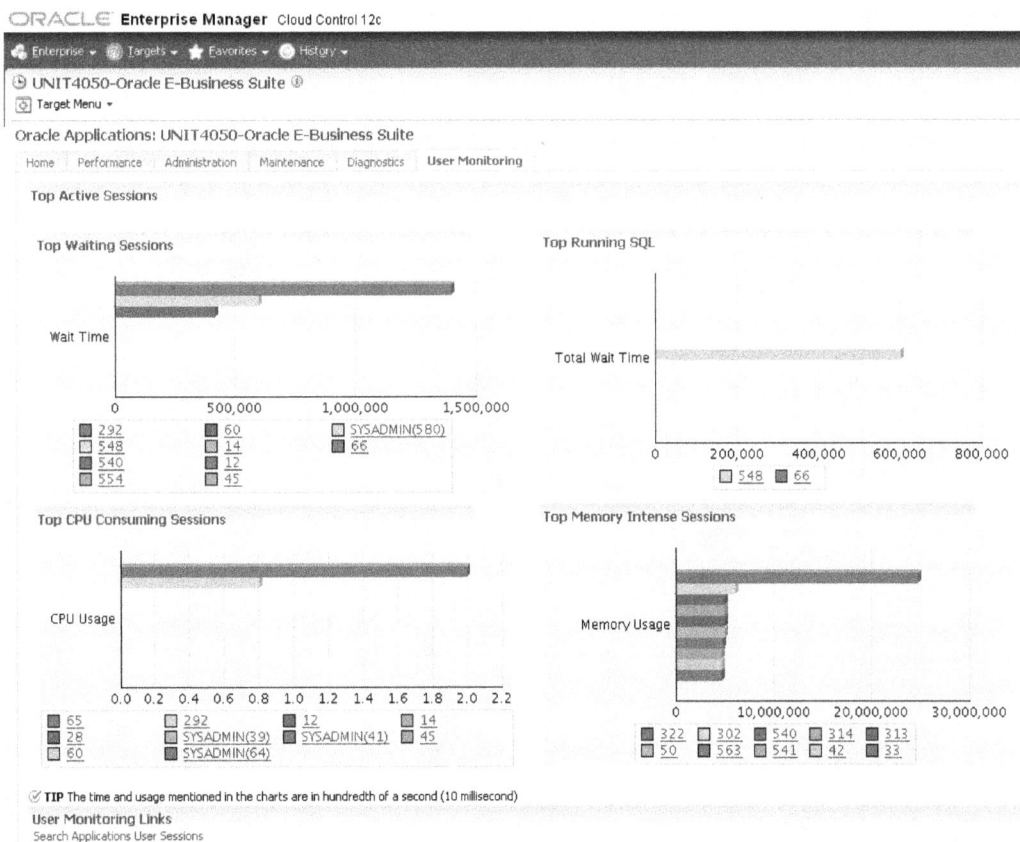

FIGURE 6-29. *Top activity with each bar representing a user process*

and so on). It also shows the Enterprise Manager core features that have more data, along with in-context analysis and diagnostics.

Enterprise Manager's Topology Viewer

Another easy way to get a quick view of the availability of the whole E-Business Suite system, and more importantly, what impact an outage on one component might have, is to use the Topology Viewer. This takes two forms, shown in Figures 6-30 and 6-31, respectively. The first is a graphical map view that shows the components as different node types in a diagram with links showing the relationships between them, along with their availability status emphasized. The second is a slightly clearer, more traditional table view that has some aspects of the hierarchy and relationships and includes the status of each component.

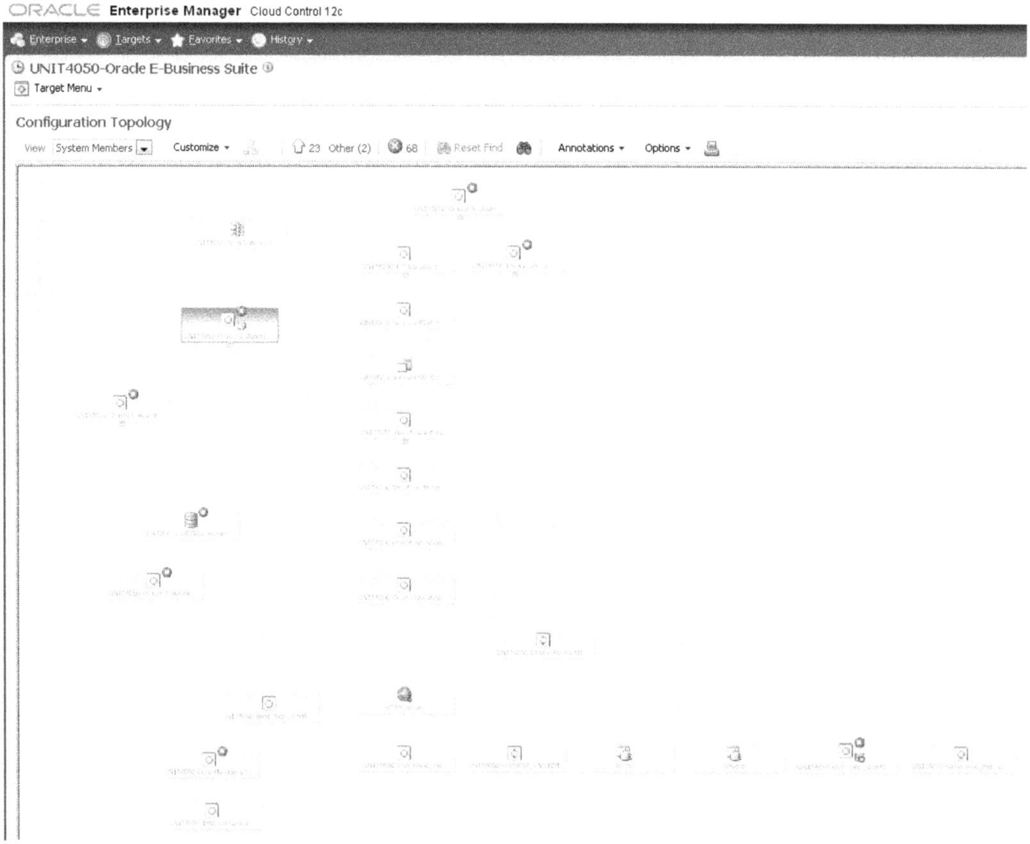

FIGURE 6-30. *The topology shown in the graph view*

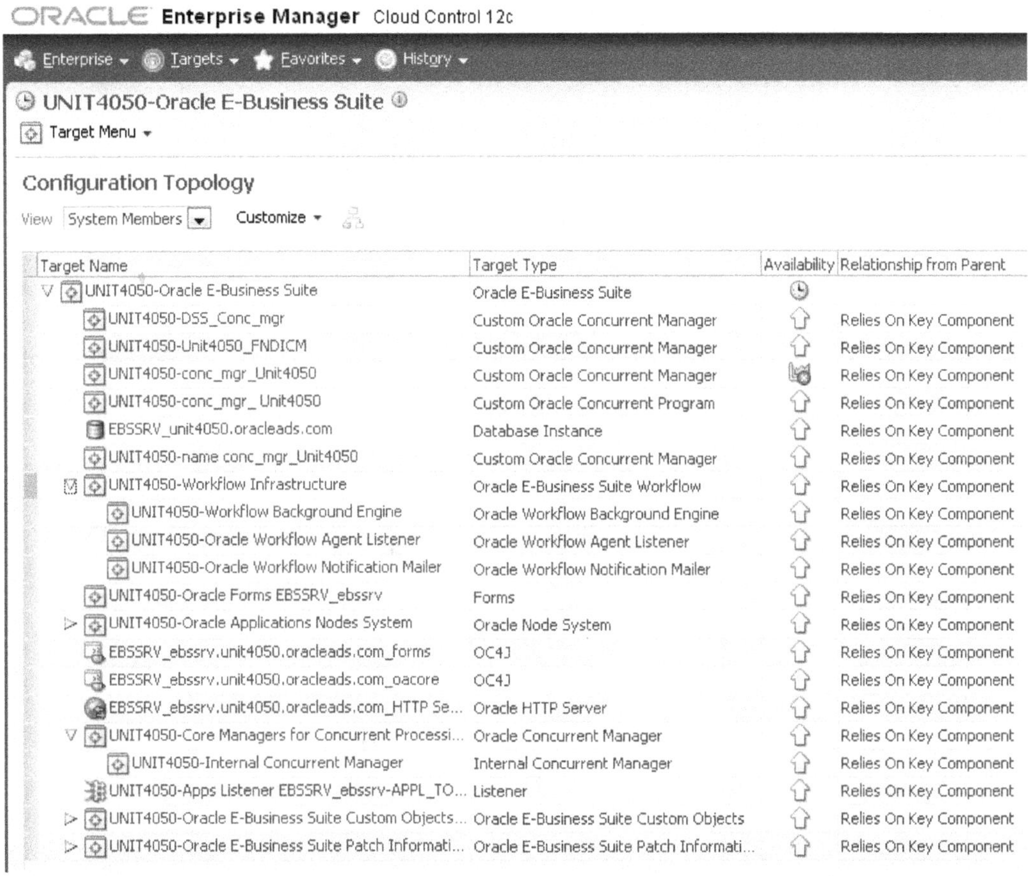

FIGURE 6-31.   *The topology shown in the table view*

Enterprise Manager's Metrics, Alerts, and Notifications

Enterprise Manager has over 60 predefined metrics specifically for monitoring E-Business Suite. This is a powerful and easy way to keep an eye on availability issues and be quickly notified of potential causes. All of these are configurable, so thresholds can be set that fit each particular instance, depending on its intended usage. This is a great way to avoid notification overload.

Figure 6-32 shows all of the metrics available are listed, with the selection of the internal system alerts. As you can see from the different categories of metrics, the support for monitoring E-Business Suite is well provisioned for by Enterprise Manager.

ORACLE **Enterprise Manager** Cloud Control 12c

Enterprise ▼ | Targets ▼ | Favorites ▼ | History ▼

⏱ UNIT4050-Oracle E-Business Suite ⓘ
⚙ Target Menu ▼

UNIT4050-Oracle E-Business Suite > All Metrics

All Metrics

Search | → |

View ▼

▽ UNIT4050-Oracle E-Business Suite
  ▷ Active Concurrent Requests by Application
  ▽ Activity
      Active Service Processes
      Concurrent Requests Running
      Forms Sessions
  ▷ Applications System Status
  ▷ Applications by Errored Execs
  ▷ Applications by Executions
  ▷ Applications by Pending Requests
  ▷ Applications by Running Requests
  ▷ Concurrent Managers Configured
  ▷ Concurrent Requests by Status
  ▷ Configuration Changes(Last 24 hours)
  ▷ Forms Database Sessions per Application
  ▷ Hourly Completed Requests
  ▷ Native Services
  ▷ **Oracle Applications Internal System Alerts**
  ▷ Processes and Requests per Concurrent Manager
  ▷ Programs by Average Running Time
  ▷ Programs by Errored Executions
  ▷ Programs by Executions
  ▷ Programs by Total Running Time
  ▷ Response
  ▷ Top Pending Requests
  ▷ Top Running Requests
  ▷ Top Scheduled Requests
  ▷ Top Users (Resquests Submitted)
  ▷ Users by Pending Requests
  ▷ Users by Running Requests
  ▷ Web Users (Hourly)
  ▷ Workflow Agent Activity
  ▷ Workflow Notifications
      Other collected items

Oracle Applications Internal System Alerts

Collection Schedule Every 15 Minutes
  Upload Interval Every Collection
    Last Upload 22-Oct-2012 13:56:52 CDT

Metric	Thresholds	Real Time Value
Last Update Date	Not Applicable	2012/10/23 06:10:57
New Oracle Applications System Alert Occurrences	Not Set	1086
New Oracle Applications System Alerts	Not Set	57
Open Oracle Applications System Alert Occurrences	Not Applicable	0
Open Oracle Applications System Alerts	Not Applicable	0

☑ Data shown in above table is collected in real time.

◀

FIGURE 6-32. *All metrics listed in categories, with the internal system alert example selected*

In addition, Figure 6-33 shows an example of the subsequent detailed metric page, with the performance and load on the web components from their user sessions. As you can see, the threshold values are not defined here. However, based on the capacity plan, it would be sensible to set an alert on the expected maximum number of concurrent web users.

Using this wide range of metrics takes a certain amount of skill and experience based on risk analysis that includes core E-Business Suite components, with some weighting towards those components your organization relies upon the most. That said, even setting up rudimentary metric measures can make sure many significant availability problems are caught quickly, before they cause too many detrimental effects.

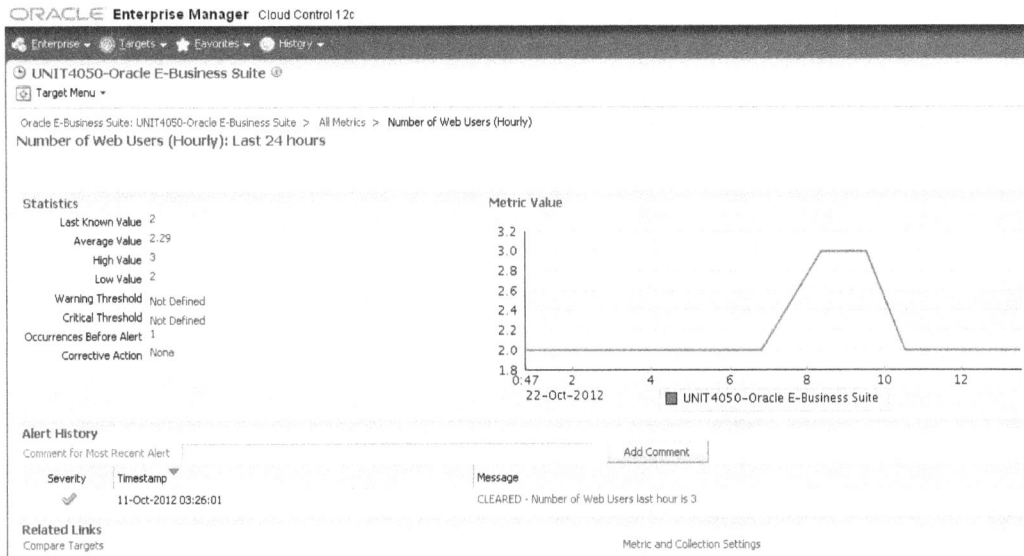

FIGURE 6-33. *Performance detail page for web user sessions per hour*

Summary

In this chapter, we covered the features and options available inside and around E-Business Suite for understanding and managing availability, providing a real-world way in which to act on whichever tooling and strategy you decide to use.

We covered the following main areas:

- **Availability**   Definitions, causes, measuring, and managing
- **Business Process**   How to check that your application features are working and available
- **Applications Technology**   How to ensure the application components are active and available
- **Platform Layer**   How to ensure your platform is set up for and provides high availability

High availability and disaster recovery are often equated to life insurance—you know you should have it, but it's hard to decide how much will be appropriate to invest, especially since you try very hard never to use it. Certainly, to even get a budget for them the accounting department will need return on investment estimates, risk analysis, upfront and maintenance costs, and all manner of other details that are very hard to nail down accurately, especially for resources that should be mostly idle.

The first step is to understand the features and options available to you, and based on that, run through the priorities and scenarios with those people most affected and best informed on the operational usage of E-Business Suite. From this collaboration you should be able to add authority and actual data to your availability management analysis and strategy. Don't forget, this is not a one-time activity; as mentioned in our application management model, all the plans should be revalidated on a cyclical basis to keep things accurate and optimized.

CHAPTER
7

A Performance
Management Toolbox

Performance is not just about speed, it's about efficiency, too. Enterprise applications like E-Business Suite are all about getting business tasks done correctly and effectively; this is the goal, not just how fast a technology component is running or a page loads. It's how quickly a successful payroll process runs or an order takes to book, not how fast a particular Web Server might be. Performance management is concerned with the sum of the parts.

Delivering high performance improves the user experience, improves company productivity, and contributes to better application adoption and more complete use of its features. Faster time-to-task completion also means more time to complete those less mundane and more creative tasks, again increasing the likelihood of increasing revenue/value. Put another way, costs can be saved as a lower number of hours and people are required to do the same tasks.

In these modern times new enterprise application delivery models, namely cloud computing or Software-as-a-Service (SaaS), are also driving a strong focus around performance management, perhaps more than ever before. Quite simply, if you are paying for a slow service, you're unlikely to be a satisfied customer. The expectations of social media systems and consumer apps have spilled over to enterprise applications, where similar responsiveness is beginning to be expected. Enterprise applications managers certainly have their work cut out for them.

One observation is that while people expect customer systems to be relatively fast, they often don't remember what the business task was like before there was a system to support it. Take checking product item details: if you look at the system now, all the attributes and data are presented, but in the past the clerk would have to get up from the desk, go to a file cabinet drawer, and thumb through files to get the product item details. This could have taken ten minutes or more, but users are now accustomed to immediate results irrespective of the past work involved.

What Is Performance?

In Chapter 2, we defined performance management as the following; while not overly scientific, this broad description satisfies multiple needs:

The ability to ensure that all work can be completed within an acceptable timescale.

The use of the word *acceptable* is deliberate, since performance is a relative term and is based on perception and expectations. You might expect your Google search results back in less than two seconds, but if your online payment submission takes twice as long, that is perfectly acceptable. Most modern applications are designed to set expectations by giving the user some kind of idea of what is happening behind the scenes via progress bars, hour-glasses and the like, thereby justifying a slower response for labor-intensive actions. In an enterprise application, the different system activities have different acceptable performance levels, such as batch programs for which an hour or more processing would be understandable.

This statement also focuses on *work*, namely the business tasks that need to be completed using the enterprise application. This means that the value calculation is firmly fixed on delivering operational benefits, rather than the performance of any specific IT components. An obvious and common example is where the Web Server and Application Servers are finely tuned to deliver lightning-fast results for basic user interface pages, but the back-end database, where much of the significant load occurs, has not been investigated and as such, data queries and processing may remain slow.

A well-managed enterprise application will have targets and service requirements (defined in the SLA) based on the performance of critical functional processes, such as order submission, payroll completion, or payment processing. These targets should be based on both business requirements and performance testing baselines to keep them both effective and achievable with the resources available.

In Chapter 2 we also defined three main types of performance issues, and this chapter will offer a whole host of capabilities, tools, and recommendations to address each of them:

- **Failures** Timeouts and errors that occur due to unresponsive actions
- **Peaks and troughs** Uneven load and unutilized capacity
- **Bottlenecks** Inefficient parts of an otherwise acceptable process

Cause of Performance Issues

Poor performance is a symptom of a problem and therefore the root cause may vary substantially. Examples include failing programs causing others to wait for a response, poorly configured components based on what is being asked of them, and overloaded hardware. For E-Business Suite specifically there are a number of areas where the majority of performance issues originate, and this chapter will look at the tools we use to diagnose them. First, let's run through those areas:

- **Database processing** It has been estimated that around 80 percent of E-Business Suite performance issues are database related. This includes metadata problems, inefficient application SQL statements, poor data quality, and bad database configuration.
- **Customizations** New code and data model extensions may not be immediately optimized for performance and may even disrupt existing structures and processing flows.
- **Changes in setup, configuration, and sizing** Evolution of business requirements and usage sometimes doesn't keep pace with the original capacity plans, and lack of foresight often results in problems when the system is used beyond the implementation design.
- **Infrastructure changes** This includes issues in the networking nodes and topology interconnects. A simple example might be badly distributed components, such as data files put on a node where access is not super fast.
- **Maintenance issues** When administration tasks are not properly completed on the right frequency, it can lead to performance problems from badly organized data and lots of old unused records.
- **PC issues** Sometimes overlooked are influences from older hardware specifications, browser version or setup, and other desktop operating system issues. Going forward, this will begin to include consideration of tablet PCs, smart phones, and other hybrid devices.
- **Functional configuration** E-Business Suite can be inadvertently set up in a way that may impact performance, such as an overly complex organization or HR structure that may increase related processing.
- **User expectations** I mentioned the open-ended nature of perception, but it could be said that if the system is not responding as expected then there is usually something that should be improved.

Measuring Performance

Performance measurement can be viewed in two ways: perceptive or quantified. Many performance complaints are based on the first, where end users are frustrated by what they see as an unexpected application response or slow task completion. Since this is based on their own perception of what is going on in the background, it might be a case of unrealistic expectations. More likely, the user's perception is based on some validity, and attributing metrics allows for a deeper analysis and usually some improvement. As such it's a combination of an appreciation of the perception plus quantified data that leads to strong performance management.

The distributed nature of the E-Business Suite management tools means performance metrics are of many different types and styles depending on the tool being used. The structure of this chapter is intended to help make it possible to understand the metrics and tools available for the area you are reviewing.

At the top level is the performance monitoring of individual transactions or business processes, such as order processing time. In addition, items like Workflow completion rates, slowest batch jobs, and core page response times are critical to end users. This top-level picture is essential to be able to show other departments exactly how well the system is performing, including using the related metrics in service level agreements. As mentioned before, this business view is not easy to build in a complex system like E-Business Suite, because, while technical metrics are prevalent, converting and linking them with end user tasks can be a challenge. We'll address some ways of doing this in this chapter.

For the next level down, the Applications Technology Layer, measurement is the technical data behind the business information. This includes items such as the speed of the page components (forms, OA Framework, reports), the Concurrent Processing components, and the approval and Workflow engines.

Finally, down deep in the technology layer, there are many dedicated performance measurements and tools and dashboards to go with them. The database is the obvious example, but most E-Business Suite components also have utilities and administration features that include throughput and response time metrics.

Managing performance requires the appropriate provision of scalability throughout the system. When done correctly, it enhances the platform so that the goals are rarely to make the system faster but instead to eliminate the likelihood of poor performance as system load increases. I mentioned several scalability features in relation to ensuring availability in Chapter 6, such as RAC and JVM clustering, and we'll consider many more in this chapter.

It is worth stating one more time that performance is relative, meaning that in order to truly analyze performance it is sensible to first collect a set of *baselines* that represent metric values for each component running at an acceptable level of performance. Some management tools allow you to do this, such as the AWR baselines you'll see later, whereas for many other areas this needs to be done proactively. This work should be considered part of the creation of the performance plan or even the service level agreements, as mentioned back in Chapter 2. It doesn't always have to be exhaustive, but you should define the most important features, processes, and components; run some tests with realistic datasets; and get an agreement from the various stakeholders on what constitutes acceptable performance levels. Oh, and don't forget to implement the related monitoring!

Managing Performance

As mentioned already and illustrated back in the previous toolbox chapters, the components for monitoring and managing of E-Business Suite are rather distributed, and the same scattered structure applies to managing performance. The capabilities are spread across simple dashboards and summary pages like OAM's activity monitors, shown in Figure 7-1, to more detailed component information available through the Enterprise Manager pages, and right down into the features, functions, and scripts available for the stack components.

So, since there is no single, centralized, performance monitoring console for use in managing the application, let's consider some recommended practices on bringing together the features and capabilities to establish effective performance management.

First, successful application managers approach performance management as an active task, taking ownership of this aspect of service delivery, just as they would for availability. This is much more effective than considering performance in a reactive fashion, scrambling to respond to complaints and resolve problems. In order to support this approach, it is advised to use a passive monitoring deployment, where silent management components automatically track metric data. Carefully consider the following related questions to help set this up in your environment:

■ Which components need performance monitoring, why, and at what frequency? This is usually influenced by what is known as important to a particular functional process, plus what is available for use.

■ What metric types should you use? This may be simple raw performance data or you may extend it to include calculated values that consider multiple variables at once. Metrics from key integrations and dependent infrastructure can be important too.

■ What values or threshold ranges should be set as acceptable or not acceptable for each key metric?

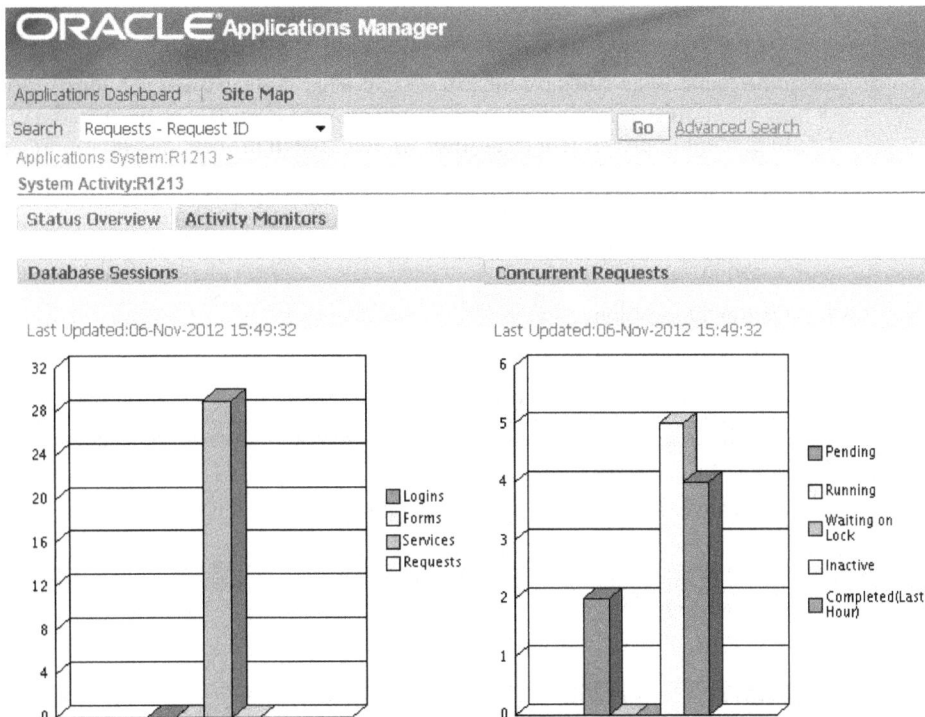

FIGURE 7-1. *Oracle Applications Manager's Activity Monitors dashboard*

- What types of violation reports and notifications do you need? What do you need as their contents, sending frequency, and severity levels? Who should they be sent to? Where, when, and how?

- What automatic remedial actions are possible, providing contingency measures like failover?

- How do you track performance trends and patterns? Examples include excessively uneven performance, slow degradation, or going over capacity.

Further, if a performance alarm is triggered, the subsequent reaction should be swift and effective so that the impact to users is limited and the extent and severity of the problem doesn't grow. As such there should be careful consideration of the tools, skills, and procedures required to manage and resolve the underlying problems. This ranges from items such as converting alerts to records in ticketing systems, granting access to troubleshooting tools (and their output), and most importantly, training related staff in performance analysis techniques.

Finally, to round off this section, here are some general best practices for getting and keeping your E-Business Suite in a state where performance management is more of an optimization project than wasting lots of resources on merely keeping things running and meeting the base-level expectations.

- **Keep the system up to date**   Performance fixes and improvements are released all the time. Making sure your systems are on the latest family packs and release updates is essential to avoiding hitting known issues.

- **Track all E-Business Suite recommended patches information**   Use My Oracle Support's patch recommendations, the recommended patch advisor, alerts and notifications, and specific patch lists such as that in Note 244040.1.

- **Keep the technology stack on the latest supported and certified versions**   One example of how much this can help is that by simply moving from 10g to the 11g database, a 10–20 percent improvement in E-Business Suite batch processing and report generation speed can be achieved.

- **Approach performance issues in the right way**   As taken from the excellent performance tuning whitepaper at www.oracle.com/technetwork/apps-tech/ebs-performance-tuning-part-1-470542.pdf:

  1. Define the problem clearly.

  2. Gather the right data to analyze the issue.

  3. Identify the root cause of the problem, and possibly gather additional data.

  4. Search for a known solution or workaround that addresses the root cause of the problem.

  5. If it is a product issue, pass on the right information to Oracle Support through the regular channels.

  6. Try to identify a temporary workaround to alleviate the issue until you get a permanent fix.

Performance Tools

This section provides details on tools for monitoring and managing the performance of E-Business Suite and its key components. We again divide these into the three logical technology layers of the application, to aid their practical use.

Business Process Layer	Applications Technology Layer	Platform Layer
Key performance indicators	Oracle Applications Manager	Enterprise Manager
Product-specific recommendations	Business intelligence and reports	User interface and client systems
Logs and traces	Workflow	Oracle Forms Server
End user experience	E-Business Suite Search	OA Framework and Java
	Applications data	Database
	Concurrent Processing	Network
		Hardware
		Integration and load testing

TABLE 7-1. *Performance Manifest*

Table 7-1 provides a sequential reading structure which is intended for educational or casual consumption. To complement this, the same content is given in Table 7-2, where it has been organized around how they might be most commonly applied to an existing system.

Monitoring and Troubleshooting	Managing
Key performance indicators	Enterprise Manager
Oracle Applications Manager	Product-specific recommendations
Business intelligence and reports	Workflow Oracle
User interface and client systems	Forms Server
Logs and traces	End user experience
Integration and load testing	E-Business Suite Search
	OA Framework and Java
	Applications data
	Database
	Concurrent Processing
	Network
	Hardware

TABLE 7-2. *The Performance Toolbox Based on Use Case*

Business Process Layer

Just like availability management discussed in the last chapter, monitoring and displaying the performance of the functionality that supports business processes is a complex process because it depends on so many configuration settings, data values, program code modules, and technology stack components.

This means that while supporting business task completion is the ultimate need, a complete holistic view of this type is rarely possible; however, there are a few tools in E-Business Suite that can give some of this top-down insight. Again, the focus here is to illustrate capabilities that apply to business users, department and domain managers, and those that assist them, such as help desks.

Key Performance Indicators

Key performance indicators also existed in the Availability toolbox, where the elements of important business features are monitored together and displayed in dashboards, notifications, and reports.

In Figure 6-1 in the last chapter, the Business Flows feature of Oracle Applications Manager allowed the definition of the key components of a business task flow (forms, pages, concurrent request, and so on), and shows how they can be monitored together to reflect items like health status and throughput rate—this is also useful for performance management. This is currently the closest to having business metrics available for E-Business Suite out of the box.

Similarly, Figure 6-5 showed how this could be taken to the next level using the OBIA solutions or custom business intelligence charts, dashboards, and reports, which could be put together based on simple transactional views and queries to provide additional performance related indicators.

Product-Specific Recommendations

Administrators supporting E-Business Suite often see performance issues as purely technical and immediately delve into investigating the stack components. Sometimes this can waste time, and it would be much better to start with a check for any known performance issues for the related functional process or product. Lists such as these are often available and include a mix of fixes in patches, nonpatch reconfigurations, and various other solutions that can help tune processing. Here are some general examples; others can be found in My Oracle Support by searching on performance and filtering by product and task, as shown in Figure 7-2:

- **Order Management**   Offering options to speed up processing, Notes 849060.1 and 130511.1
- **Financials**   Performance troubleshooting for account analysis and journal entries report, Note 983063.1
- **Financials**   Performance tuning in Subledger Accounting and Accounting Hub, Note 791049.1
- **Supply Chain**   Performance optimizations for Advanced Pricing and Shipping Execution, Notes 1397985.2 and 1393962.2

Logs and Traces

User performance is often best investigated by observation first, repeating the issue firsthand to see all the steps and the results, spotting any important nuances on the way. Often a second

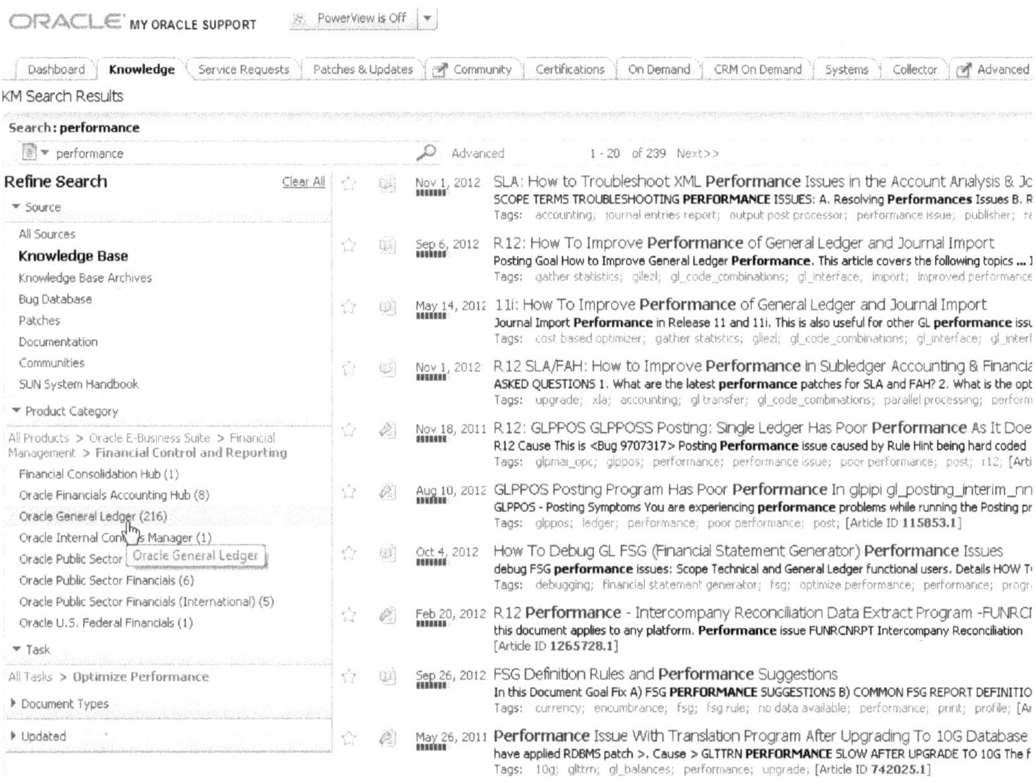

FIGURE 7-2.   *Finding performance improvements in My Oracle Support*

run-through is sensible for which additional levels of logging and tracing are enabled, so that there is more to investigate once the problem is verified. It makes sense to do this as a second test case, since often only after observation can the most appropriate debug settings be chosen. These options are secured by privilege and accessible only to certain roles, as mentioned before.

Using the FND: Diagnostics options, discussed previously in Chapter 5, with the appropriate profile option–based enablement, it is easy for the end user to set logging and tracing on themselves. This keeps the focus on the real task flow being performed, rather than spiraling off and investigating specific technology components. Once set, all subsequent actions and spawned processes inherit the logging and tracing settings and generate the associated output.

As illustrated in Figure 7-3, there are two options under the Diagnostics link in the top right of every OA Framework screen, with corresponding items in the Forms under the Help menu, as shown in Figure 7-4.

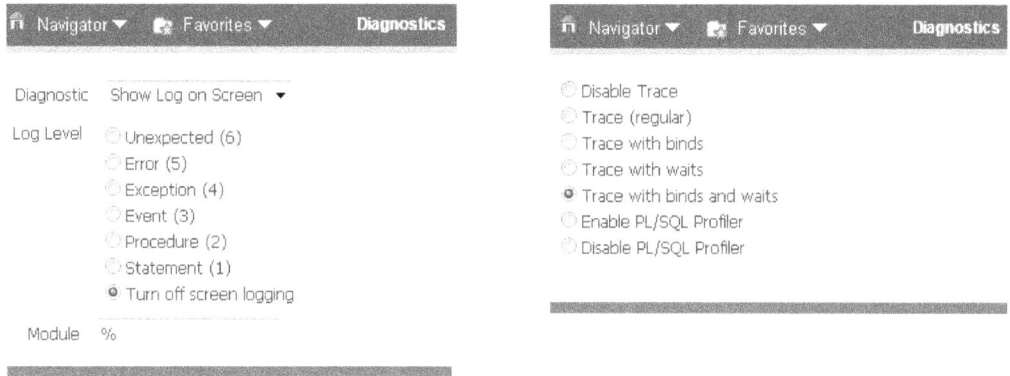

FIGURE 7-3. *The logging and tracing options from OA Framework pages*

In addition, the Show Log on Screen option available for OA Framework pages is frequently useful for problems related to one specific page, since it shows the exact server response and associated logs for each request. Checking these for activities and timings as you move closer to the performance problem is a useful diagnostic process.

For more detail on logs and traces, review Chapter 5, as well the specific documentation references provided by Oracle, such as Note 296559.1, Common Tracing Techniques within EBS; Note 117129.1, How to Get a Trace for and Begin to Analyze a Performance Issue: Basic Overview; and Note 296559.1, Tracing FAQ: Common Tracing.

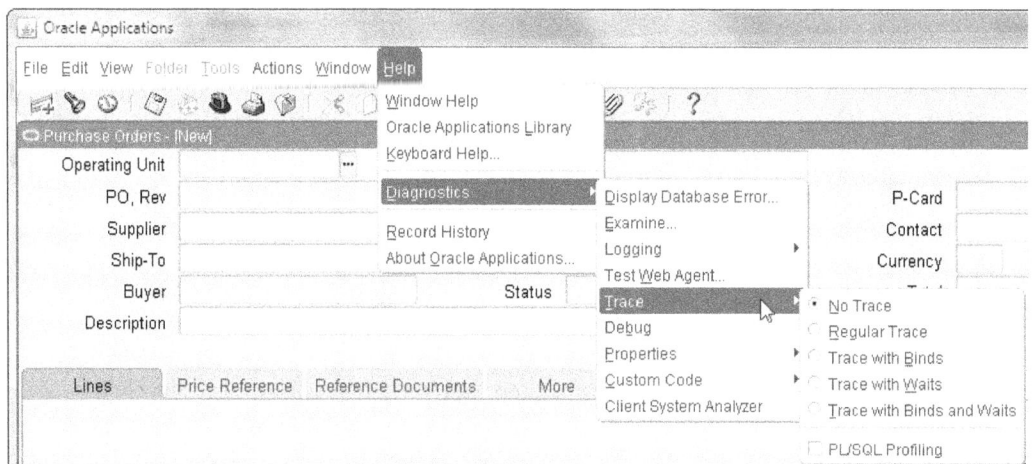

FIGURE 7-4. *The tracing options from Oracle Forms*

End User Experience

Ultimately, you need to know how your users are affected by the performance of the application, ideally highlighting slow areas before users even feel the need to spend time reporting it. Indeed, in an ideal world the performance of all the technical components should be measured by a single management platform, not by the end users.

Obviously, aspects of load testing prior to go-live highlight any relatively slow processes by running scripts that emulate user actions and measure both the system performance and reliability. This activity, however, is rarely repeated once the system is in place. While major changes like upgrades and hardware alterations may include some of this, it is worth keeping these tools on hand for use in less obviously significant events, such as increases in usage or application data imports.

The ideal of having a single dashboard for monitoring the performance of all technical components doesn't generally scale to large enterprise applications like E-Business Suite (although Fusion Applications come close), so you'll need to incorporate some other methods for capturing feedback about the end user experience.

There are two ways to approach this. The first is automating it with yet more software (don't groan just yet). Previous toolbox chapters already mentioned the Enterprise Manager component Real User Experience Insight (RUEI) and how it sits outside the application, monitoring the network traffic between the http server and clients, looking for clues as to how successfully page requests are satisfied.

As shown in Figure 7-5, the central RUEI dashboard page shows many rich components based on the monitored performance data. Each of the regions can be drilled into using the cube icon, going into the metric data underneath. The dashboard includes various ways of showing the number of page views based on request attributes like product module, user location, and user ID. It also shows problematic page responses, again differentiated by useful data such as the user's responsibility and the product module being used.

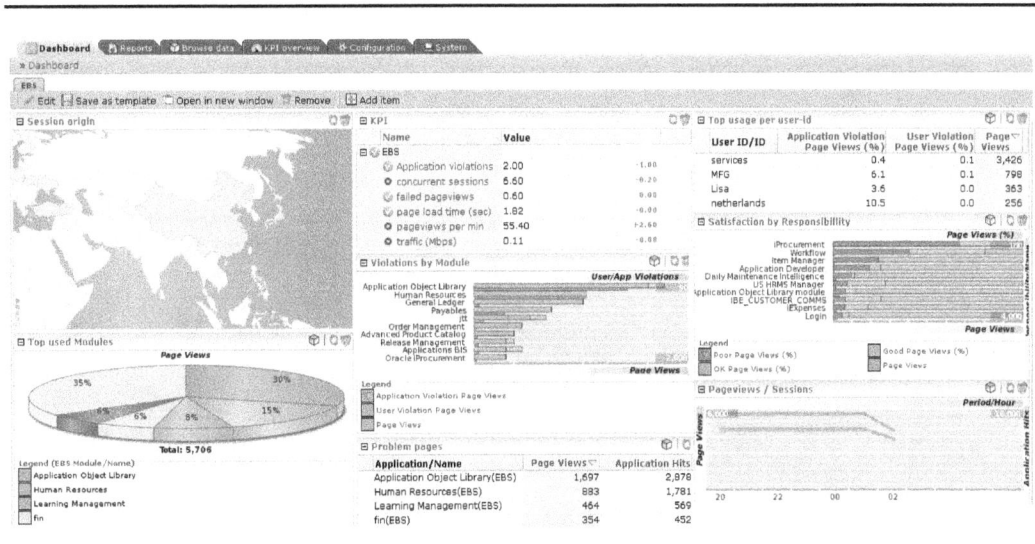

FIGURE 7-5. *RUEI dashboard for E-Business Suite*

A slightly more fine-tuned overview of the user experience is given by the KPI tab, providing a set of graphs for specific metrics. Figure 7-6 shows the seeded examples for E-Business Suite including overall traffic, successful and failed page views, other errors (violations), and the number of concurrent user sessions. For some metrics a target value is also set, such as "<= 12" for the Application Violations, illustrating how alerts and thresholds can be added to RUEI.

The next level of detail is available from the Reports tab, giving a wide variety of predefined reports that help identify performance levels, patterns, and trends in the data behind the user experience. As shown in Figure 7-7, these are grouped by type, providing overall reports together with ones for client-specific metrics, domain reports for specific network addresses, and server reports for specific back-end nodes. As you can see, the emphasis is firmly on performance data, such as total hits, page request volumes, page load times, back-end processing volumes, and any observed failures.

As illustrated on most screens, RUEI supports full customization and extension to the seeded data, reports, KPIs, and dashboards provided in the E-Business Suite plug-in. So, while RUEI is not deployed as part of E-Business Suite itself, when it is deployed it provides a complete and flexible solution for end user performance monitoring for all application systems.

The second method for verifying the end user experience is to quite simply ask end users. These should be formal surveys with a well thought-out focus. They should be short and simple to complete and include bias checks, quality controls, and even completion incentives. When done right they can provide fresh information, patterns, and insights into where users struggle and where they would most like to see improvements. This qualitative data is obviously harder to work with, but since we're providing a service (albeit an engineered one), there should be occasional consideration of how truly satisfied its consumers are. This may also have the desirable side effect of opening doorways between traditionally siloed departments, namely IT and the business, as information is seen to flow both ways.

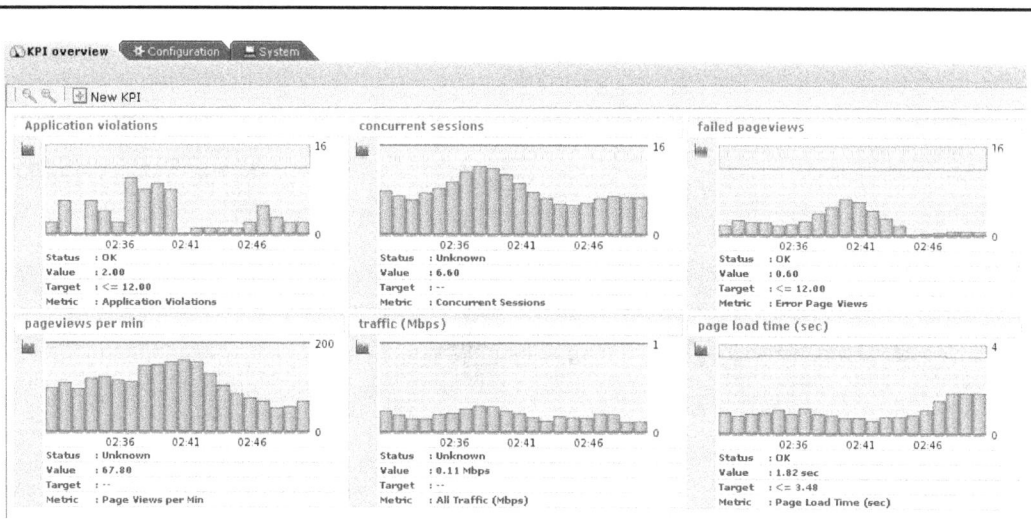

FIGURE 7-6. *RUEI's key performance indicators*

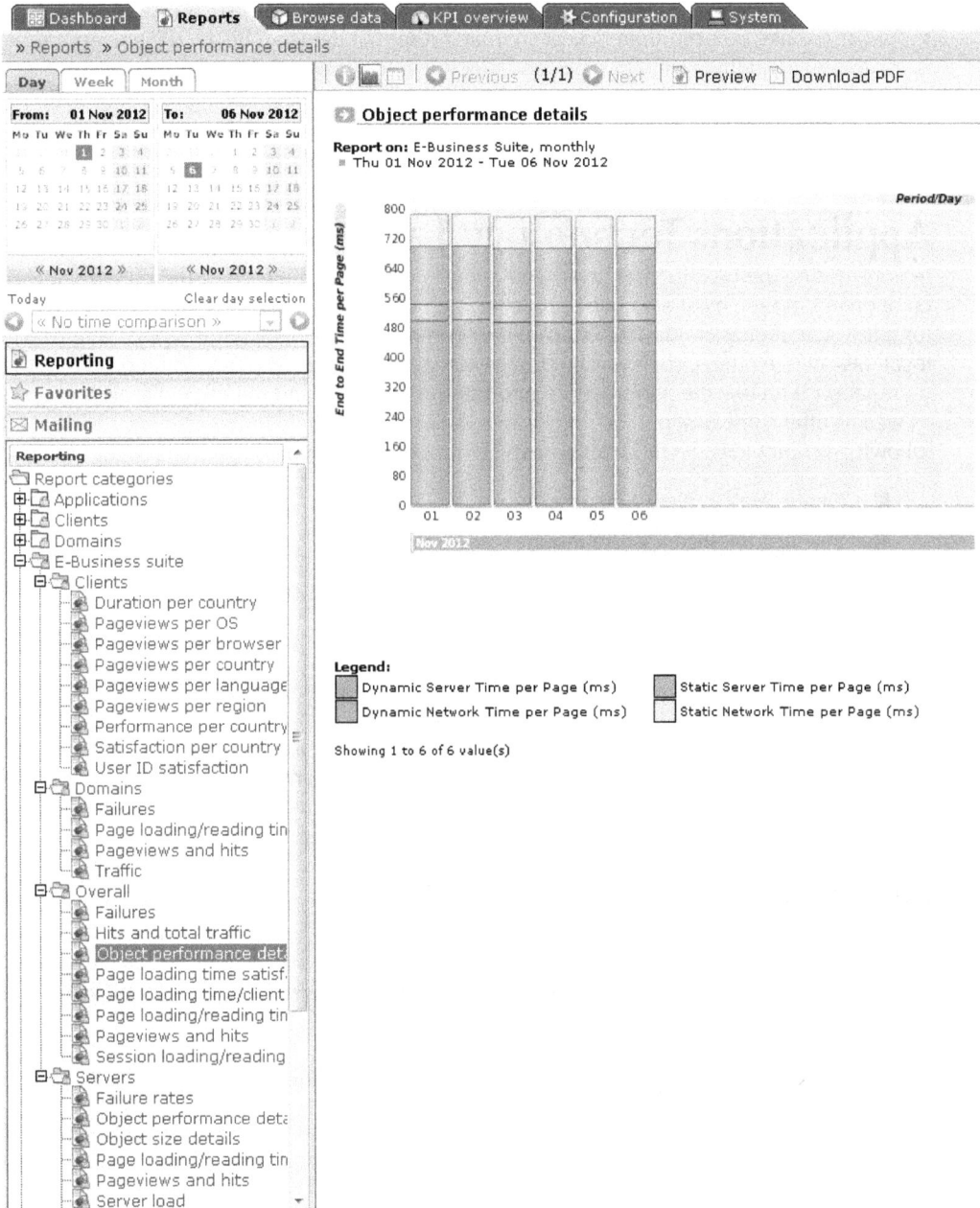

FIGURE 7-7. *RUEI's reports for E-Business Suite*

In addition to surveys and polls, it's important to analyze problem tickets reported to helpdesks for patterns of performance issues. As well as setting up such reporting tools, you should also make sure problem tickets are marked so that they can be accurately reported upon; for example, including problem types and functional focus area, investigation types performed with outcomes, and the cause and solution types and focus areas. Mining this information for insight to improvements is often laborious and therefore overlooked, but it's valuable and we'll discuss it more in the next chapter as well.

Applications Technology Layer

In considering the next logical layer, you need to understand which of the core technical components are the most effective to tune for high performance, since some areas are used only for a few specific tasks—say the MapViewer component for displaying service engineering locations—while others, such as Concurrent Manager, are used in many common processes.

Again, I'll review the performance information available and the related tools and features, as well as offer some best practice recommendations to help maximize efficiency and speed. The following list provides the technologies and components we will focus on throughout this section.

- Oracle Applications Manager
- Business intelligence and reports
- Workflow
- E-Business Suite Search
- Applications data
- Concurrent Processing

You may notice the absence of Enterprise Manager in this section. While it certainly gives performance information for application components in its many dashboard charts and graphs, most of its value comes from analyzing the core platform components of E-Business Suite, so I'll include it in the "Platform Layer" section at the end of this chapter.

Oracle Applications Manager (OAM)

As the broadest system management tool included in E-Business Suite, OAM contains some key capabilities that are specific to understanding and adjusting performance metrics. As shown in Figure 7-8, when you click the site map and choose the Monitoring tab, a small selection of features is listed under the Performance heading.

FIGURE 7-8. *Items related to performance in Oracle Applications Manager*

First, the SQL Activity link gives access to all recent SQL statements run through the application database. This includes details on physical and logical reads, sorts, and executions plus as shown in Figure 7-9, access to a graphical display of the full execution plan, which is useful for troubleshooting performance issues.

The next two links are related to Oracle Forms. The first provides a summary of all the specific Forms sessions, including each form being used and its performance against the database. The Forms Runtime Processes link provides more on each of the form's server components, including CPU percent usage and memory consumption. It's also possible to enable Forms Runtime Diagnostics (FRD) from this page, and the resulting file can be accessed from the process detail region. As a general diagnostic it's useful for slight and significant performance issues, many of which could be classed as reliability or, in extreme cases, availability issues. These two tracing features will significantly reduce performance themselves when enabled, and both depend on setting profile option Sign-On: Audit Level to the value Form. Also, an OAM generic collection service instance must be available.

The next three links are related to Concurrent Processing, with basic reports showing all requests by program or user, offering to drill into the request and the associated logs, manager logs, and output files. In addition the Programs Usage Statistics page offers a summary of all concurrent programs run with average, minimum, and maximum request completion timings. The variety of the charts available here is of interest to performance management, such as the visual comparison of requests versus the available processes to satisfy them, as shown in Figure 7-10.

ORACLE Applications Manager

Applications Dashboard | Site Map

Execution Plan for SQL Statement

SQL Statement

select /*+ ORDERED INDEX (r,FND_CONCURRENT_REQUESTS_N7) USE_NL (r p) NO_EXPAND */ r.rowid,r.request_id,decode(r.status_co
r.status_code),r.single_thread_flag,r.request_limit,r.requested_by,p.iprog_id,decode(r.crm_thrshld,null,-1,r.crm_thrshld),r.crm_tstmp
r.queue_method_code='B' and r.phase_code in ('P','R') and (r.phase_code='R' or ((r.status_code='I' or r.status_code='Q') and p.enab
r.concurrent_program_id=p.concurrent_program_id and p.queue_control_flag='N' and r.status_code between 'I' and 'W' order by de
r.request_id),r.request_id

Execution Plan

Cost	Card	Operation
–	–	SELECT STATEMENT
–	–	SORT ORDER BY
–	–	NESTED LOOPS
–	–	NESTED LOOPS
–	–	INLIST ITERATOR
–	–	TABLE ACCESS BY INDEX ROWID FND_CONCURRENT_REQUESTS
–	–	INDEX RANGE SCAN FND_CONCURRENT_REQUESTS_N7
–	–	INDEX UNIQUE SCAN FND_CONCURRENT_PROGRAMS_U1
–	–	TABLE ACCESS BY INDEX ROWID FND_CONCURRENT_PROGRAMS

Object Analysis Information

Table	Rows	Analyzed	Sample Size
APPLSYS.FND_CONCURRENT_PROGRAMS	11693	30-MAR-2009	11693
APPLSYS.FND_CONCURRENT_REQUESTS	1972	30-MAR-2009	1972

Table	Index	Rows	Distinct Keys	Analyzed	Sample Size
APPLSYS.FND_CONCURRENT_PROGRAMS	FND_CONCURRENT_PROGRAMS_U1	11693	11693	30-MAR-2009	11693
APPLSYS.FND_CONCURRENT_PROGRAMS	FND_CONCURRENT_PROGRAMS_U2	11693	11693	30-MAR-2009	11693
APPLSYS.FND_CONCURRENT_REQUESTS	FND_CONCURRENT_REQUESTS_N1	1972	1556	30-MAR-2009	1972
APPLSYS.FND_CONCURRENT_REQUESTS	FND_CONCURRENT_REQUESTS_N10	1972	68	30-MAR-2009	1972
APPLSYS.FND_CONCURRENT_REQUESTS	FND_CONCURRENT_REQUESTS_N11	1972	1599	30-MAR-2009	1972
APPLSYS.FND_CONCURRENT_REQUESTS	FND_CONCURRENT_REQUESTS_N2	1972	6	30-MAR-2009	1972

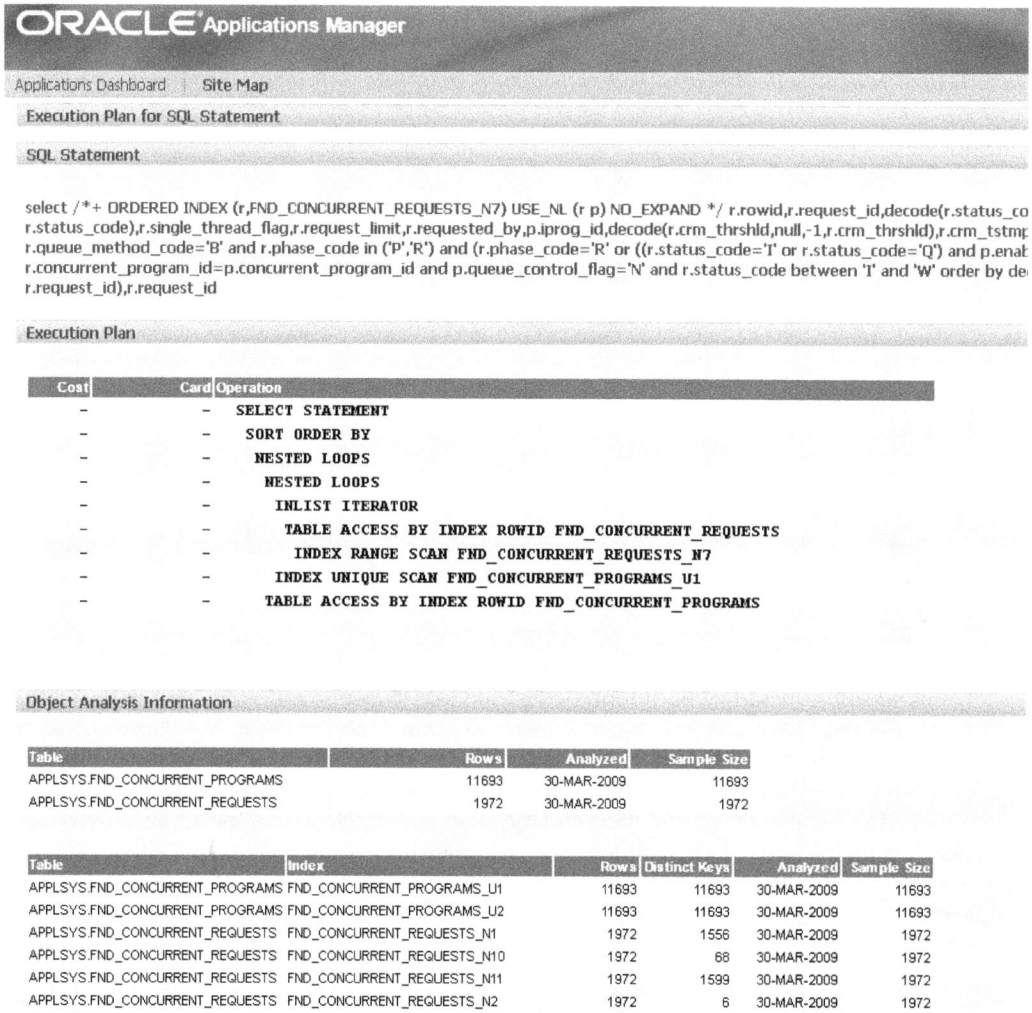

FIGURE 7-9. *The SQL execution plan accessible from Oracle Applications Manager*

The Concurrent Request Runaways page provides details on database connections that remain active but are associated with requests that are either completed or cancelled. The page summarizes the connection details and provides a button to terminate the process if required.

The last link under the performance region is Workflow, and it provides access to the pages that I'll cover in the related section a little later on.

One extra item to mention under the Oracle Applications Manager section is access to a selection of performance-related SQL scripts. Under the SQL Activity link mentioned previously,

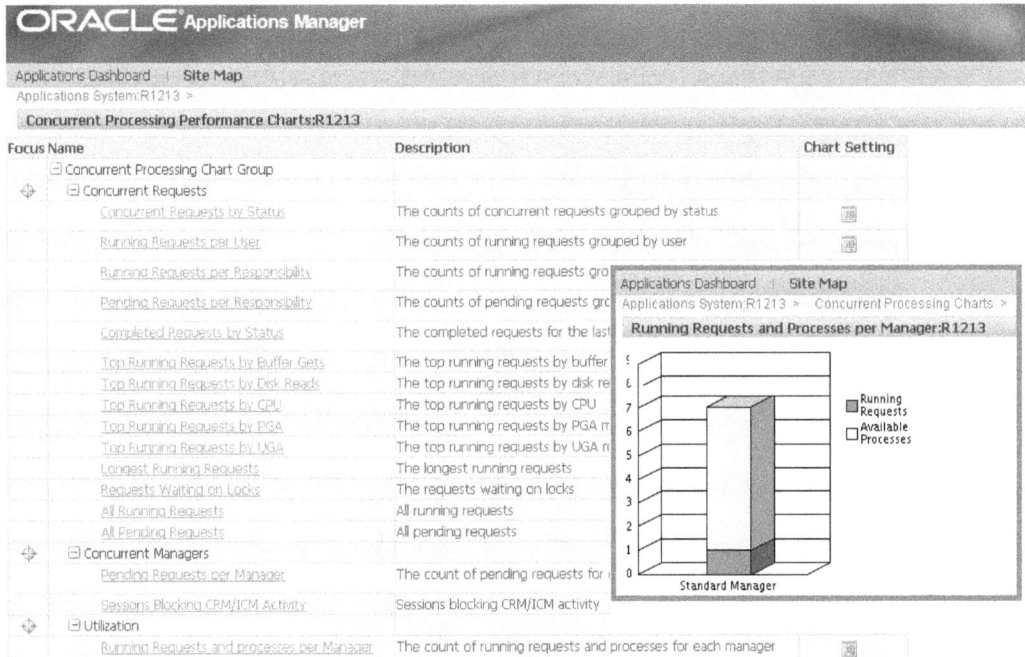

FIGURE 7-10. *Concurrent Manager performance charts*

there is a link *SQL Extensions* that displays various types of scripts available to run and the output reviewed. As shown in Figure 7-11, this includes basic database performance information along with a variety of other metrics and reports. While nowhere near as powerful as the database tuning capabilities you'll see later, these are E-Business Suite–specific, so they may reveal insights that generic tools often bury.

In addition to the performance links under the Site Map | Monitoring section of OAM, there is a dedicated Performance tab under the Applications dashboard. As shown in Figure 7-12, the resulting dashboard page gives a selection of metric values for current performance. All are hyperlinked, indicating a drill to more detail than just this top-level snapshot. We'll look at when and where to use these child pages and features as we look at the performance management of each of the components.

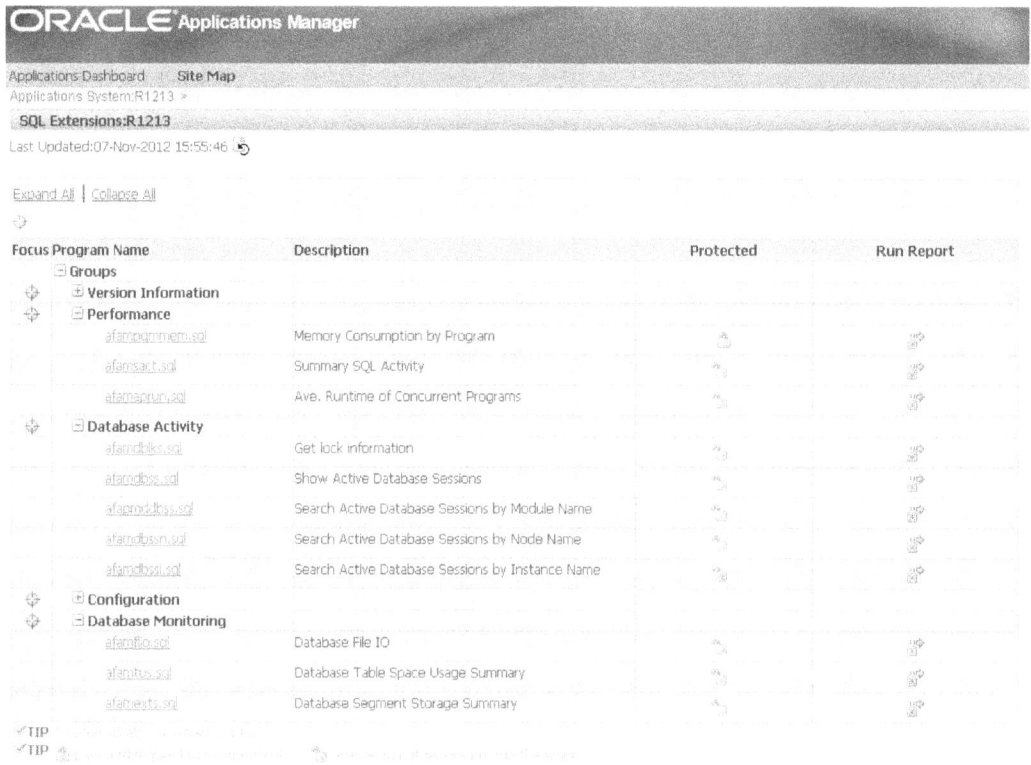

FIGURE 7-11. *Scripts available to run via the SQL Extensions page*

Business Intelligence and Reports

Managing the performance of the Oracle Business Intelligence Applications (OBIA) used with
E-Business Suite data is quite a complex and involved matter. The reason for this is that it's
primarily a standalone technology deployment that uses its own set of capabilities to provide
the rich dashboards and reports. As such, its performance management needs independent
consideration from E-Business Suite, albeit as part of the same overall management plan.

In more detail, the Oracle Business Intelligence Enterprise Edition (OBIEE) server components
that underpin the OBIA solution have evolved over time, and each one has its own set of
performance management tools and capabilities. For example, the older OBIEE 10*g* version had
its own Administration console with a dedicated performance monitoring capability. More on this
can be found in the related product documentation and examples given in Note 741495.1 for
collecting logs, plus the general performance troubleshooting Note 1096900.1.

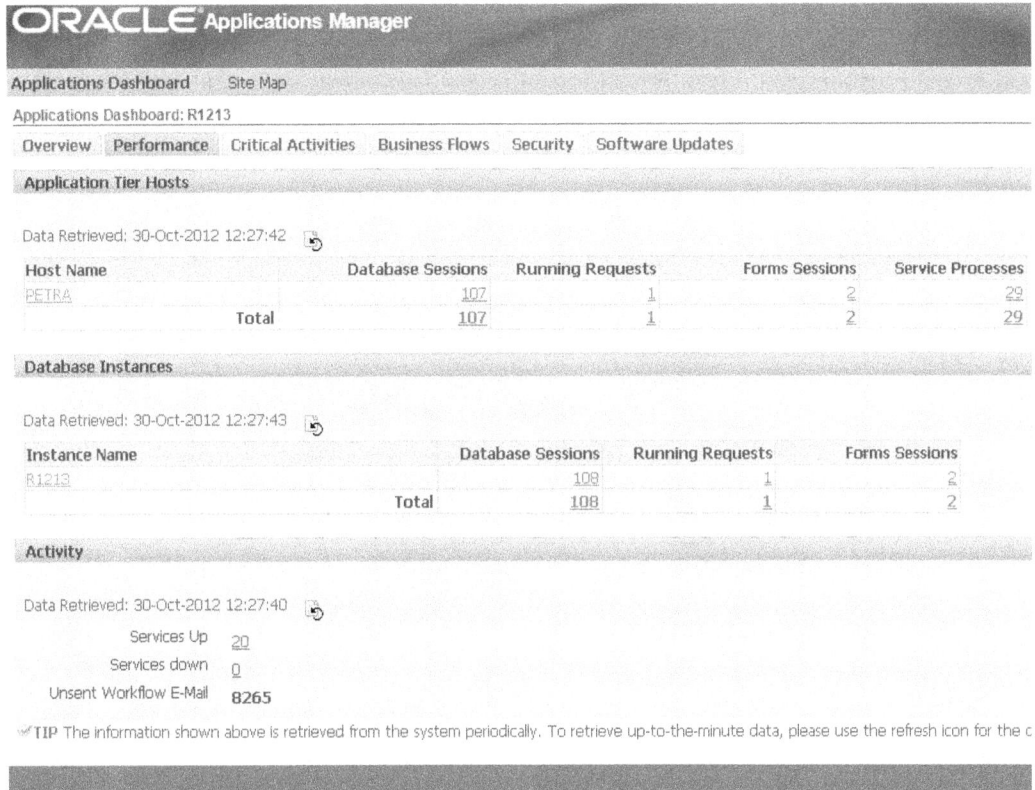

FIGURE 7-12.   *The Performance dashboard with summary info on each of the main technology components*

The later OBIEE 11*g* moved to a pure J2EE architecture and is managed via either the WebLogic Server Administration Console or by Enterprise Manager. This is illustrated by Figure 7-13, which shows the basic BI WebLogic server performance summary page in Enterprise Manager, in addition to which many more monitored metrics can be included using the Show Metric Palette feature.

More details on the 11*g* version can be found in Note 1333049.1, which contains an excellent whitepaper with lots of tips and tricks for getting the most from the performance tuning of the related BI components so that the dashboards and analytics functions that deliver business insights do so in a quick and efficient manner. If BI is not yet in use, the small performance overhead that often runs out of the box can be eliminated with a few manual steps, such as disabling the M$LOG seeded activities. Search My Oracle Support for details related to the products you are using.

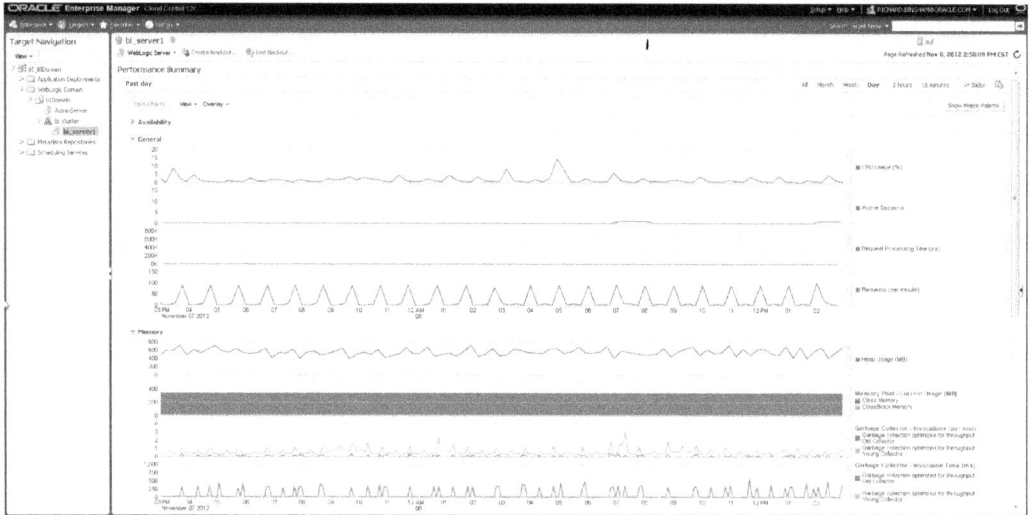

FIGURE 7-13. *OBIEE server performance summary from Enterprise Manager*

In addition to the OBIA components, the main print reports from within E-Business Suite are generated through a combination of the Output Post Processor and the BI Publisher component. The first is part of Concurrent Manager that we'll discuss later, and the second supports a few configurations related to performance tuning. Figure 7-14 shows the XML (BI) Publisher responsibility pages, and under administration there are some XSLT configurations that are intended to support performance optimization.

In addition, in the later versions (11g onward), BI Publisher has its own standalone console that can be used to run queries on reports, based on process performance and status values. The example in Figure 7-15 shows the detail of one report with its runtime execution information.

Finally, since these reports are embedded in the application, there are several environmental factors to consider as they can affect their efficiency, outside of the pure reporting technology itself:

■ The application code that validates the input parameters and launches the report

■ The logic inside the report, which may contain complex queries, recursive loops, and dynamic calculations

■ The quality of the application's functional and transaction data being reported upon

There are many other tips and techniques to managing performance of print reports, and I recommend you keep an eye out for fresh documentation, whitepapers, and notes. Search My Oracle Support specifically for any problematic reports; for example, Note 983063.1 for the subledger accounting reports. Also look for more general items like Note 1353325.1 for tuning scheduler parameters.

XML Publisher

| Templates | Data Definitions | Administration |

Configuration | Font Mappings | Font Files | Currencies

Configuration

Personalize Flow Layout: (PropertiesRn)
Personalize H Grid: (ConfigHGridRn)

Expand All | Collapse All

Focus Properties	Site Value
⊟ Properties	
⊞ General	
⊞ PDF Output	
⊞ PDF Security	
⊞ RTF Output	
⊞ HTML Output	
⊟ FO Processing	
Font mapping set	🔍
Currency format set	🔍
Bidi language digit substitution type	
Pages cached during processing	
Disable variable header support	▼
Add prefix to IDs when merging FO	▼
Use XML Publisher's XSLT processor	▼
Enable scalable feature of XSLT processor	▼
Enable XSLT runtime optimization	▼
Compress temporary files	▼
XSLT extension classes	
⊞ RTF Templates	
⊞ PDF Templates	
⊞ XLIFF Extraction	

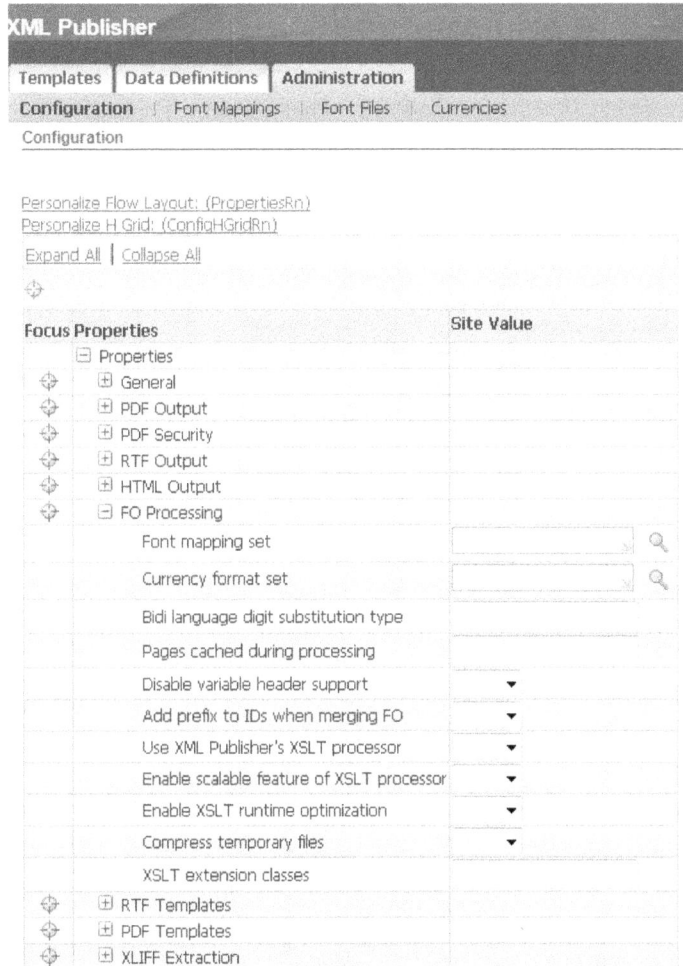

FIGURE 7-14. *Configurations for the BI Publisher*

Workflow

In simple terms, Workflow forms a platform upon which application logic executes sequentially. As such there are three types of performance issues commonly observed:

■ The Workflow platform (and its technical components) operates inefficiently.

■ The application logic that is called by Workflow is slow, halting the overall Workflow progress.

■ End user actions involved in Workflow are slow, again increasing overall progress time.

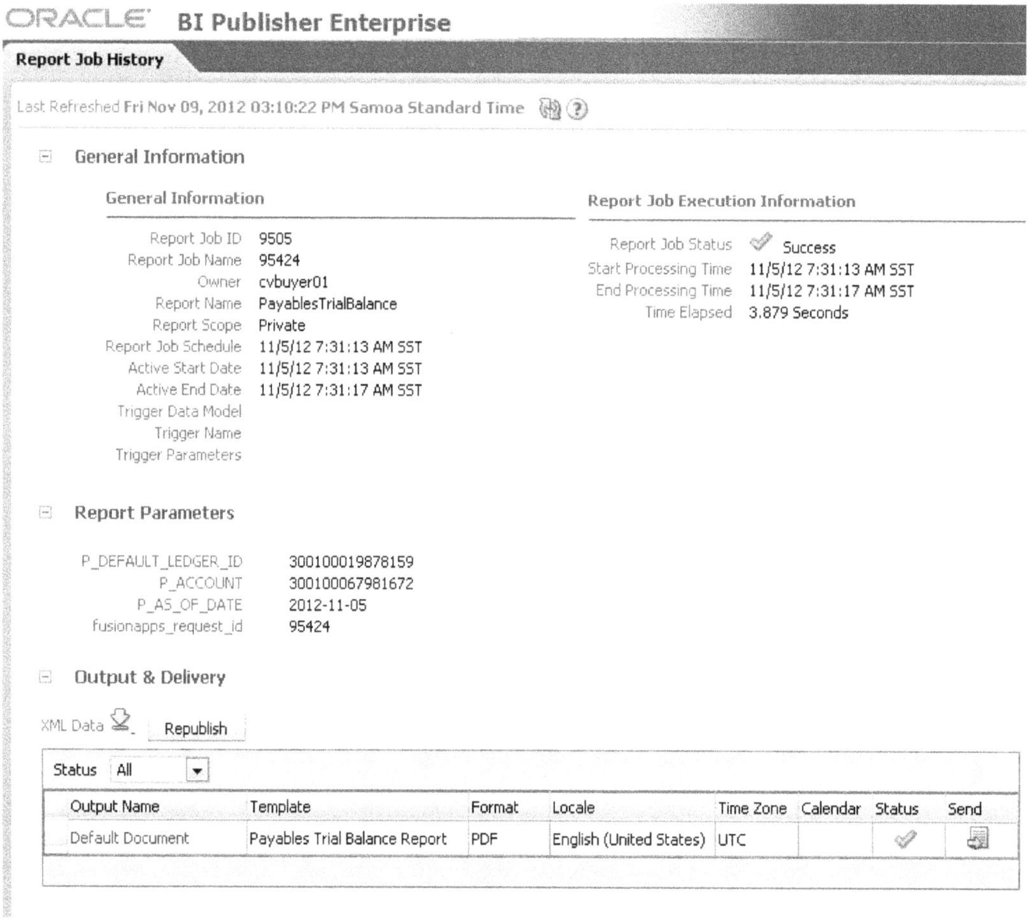

FIGURE 7-15. *XML Publisher report job detail*

Each of these points to different causes and solutions, but in most cases, E-Business Suite and its tools manage and monitor these through one single complete view. This simplifies things considerably and, based on each type of process, the detailed pages allow deeper analysis.

In addition to the seeded Workflow processes providing standard functionality, Workflow allows additions and extensions to be added with the hooks within its Workflow Business Event System. In simple terms, these are trigger points where a new Workflow process can be registered and associated with a particular action (user or internal) and spawns the execution of the additional process. More detail can be found in the Oracle Workflow User Guide (A95265-03), with a chapter devoted to the business events system.

In the System Administrator responsibility, under the menu Workflow: Administrator Workflow, there is the Business Events tab, as shown in Figure 7-16. This displays all seeded

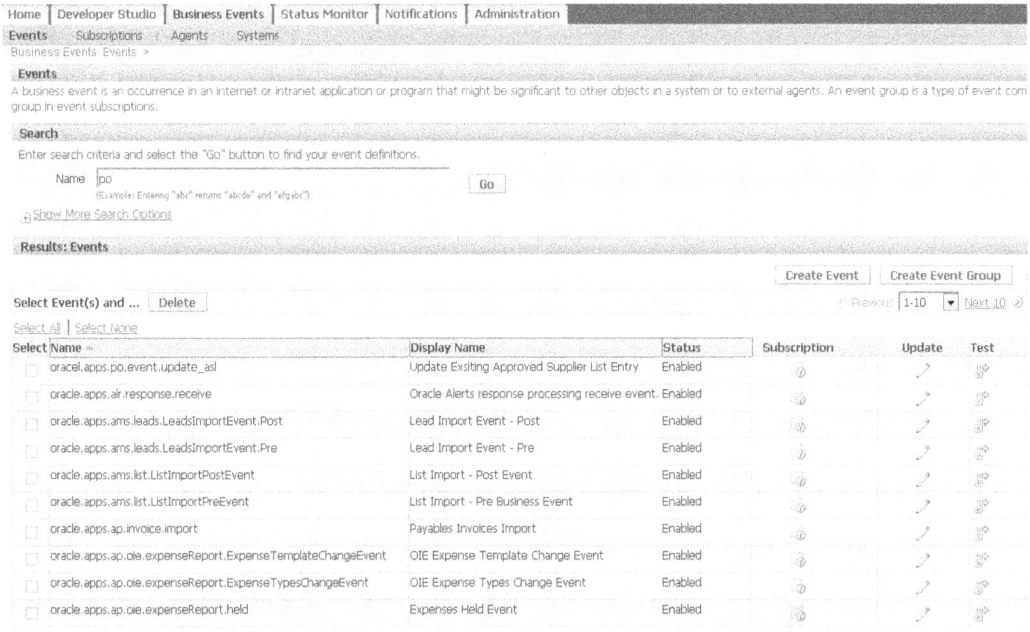

FIGURE 7-16.   *Workflow Business Events with monitoring and testing features*

events and allows you to see what is listening for each of them. These registered listeners are known as subscriptions and the page allows you to see some more detail and offers the option to enable/disable them if required. In addition, the test feature can be useful in diagnosis, as it accepts parameters and an XML payload, fires the event (via PL/SQL or Java), and returns status details. Knowing a critical event is responding and working is a good check.

Within E-Business Suite itself the Workflow responsibility has some useful pages that allow you to view executions (known as *items*) for specific time periods and types. As shown back in Chapter 5 in Figure 5-20, this has a powerful monitor view that graphically provides activities, statuses, and start and end dates and times. This is helpful if you know where the performance problem is, but it's too fine-grained a view to manage overall Workflow performance.

A more complete picture is available inside Oracle Applications Manager, however. As mentioned in Chapter 6, the Workflow page includes status values as well as metric data and charts on overall performance across E-Business Suite. As shown in Figure 7-17, this includes the number of Workflow items currently being processed and the status of the key agent components. The bars in the charts are clickable to switch to a view that shows just those items, plus the links at the bottom of the page allow a drill into specific Workflow item types and the various internal components for further investigation.

Workflow does have some options that can be carefully deployed to help maximize performance, and this is especially useful when specific high-volume, resource-intensive, or time-sensitive business processes have been already identified. Some of this is done inside the

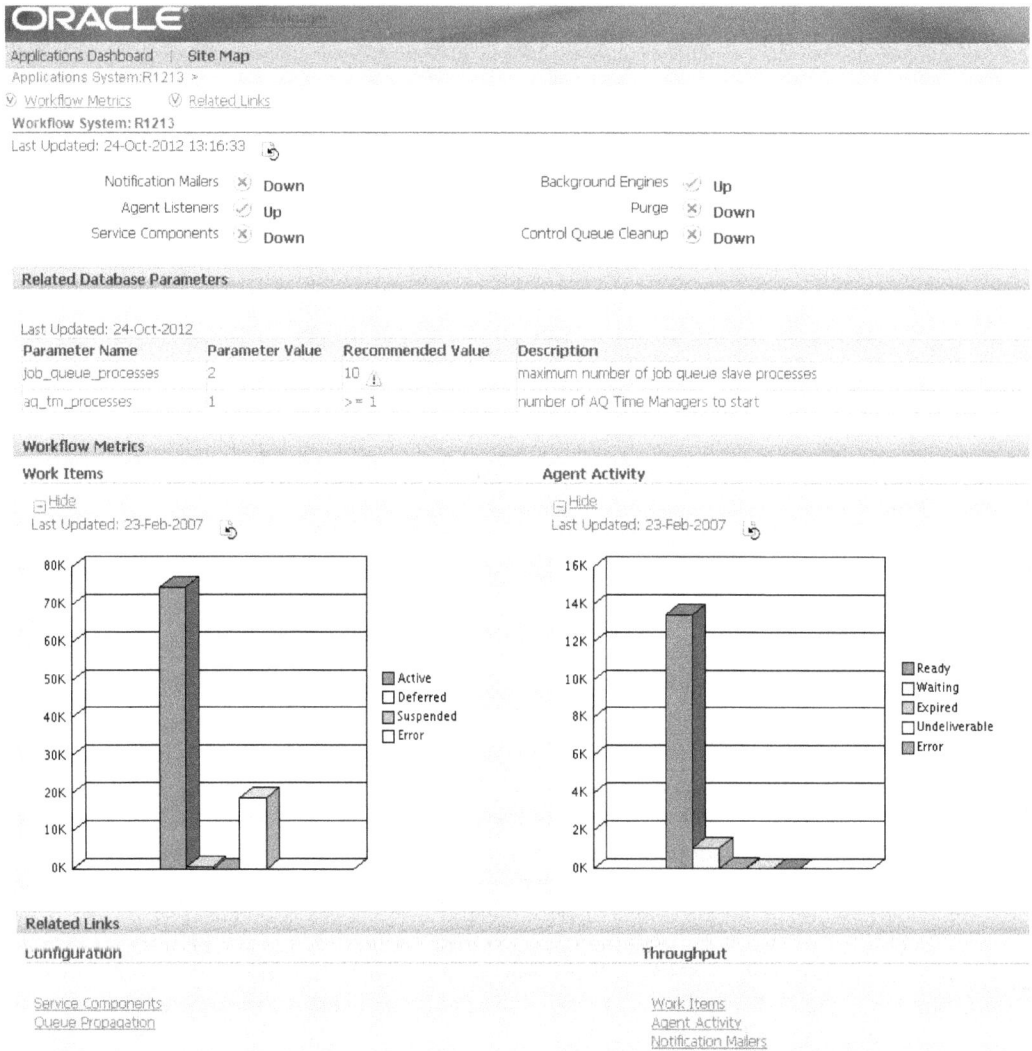

FIGURE 7-17. *The OAM Workflow dashboard page*

business process, where functional setups allow related Workflow tuning. Others are a little more generic, applying across the Workflow platforms configuration and use. Here are a few examples:

- **Process stuck workflows** There is an option for the system to automatically identify stuck Workflows, a process that is fairly resource intensive, requiring the execution of broad SQL queries on a frequent basis. As such, if this isn't useful, then it can be turned off by setting the background engine concurrent manager to have its Process Stuck value to NO. In its place, a separate background engine can be configured purely to handle the stuck processes and even dedicated to just those specific Workflows where this is important, set to run at an appropriate schedule, perhaps overnight.

■   **Online or deferred**   Another method of improving business processing performance is to use the deferred process for Workflow item types, where online wait times for synchronous processes are hurting user performance. Obviously this needs consideration on a case-by-case basis.

■   **Clean for speed**   A general recommendation is to keep on top of purging Workflow item data, as each execution leaves an audit trail in the system that eventually builds. The concurrent program, Purge Obsolete Workflow Runtime Data (program name FNDWFPR), should be submitted regularly to maintain a healthy record of Workflow data, keeping enough records that are of use while discarding others. This request has several parameters to help fine-tune the cleanup, including the option to run it for just one operating unit's data, choose a specific item type (or all), choose how many days from which to purge (age), and whether to schedule and repeat the request. This is available from either the forms Requests page or from within Oracle Applications Manager, as shown in Figure 7-18.

■   **A Workflow-ready database**   Since the Workflow engine runs on the database, there are some regularly recommended steps to help ensure maximum performance (the database performance monitoring tools we'll review later should also be used to look for Workflow issues).

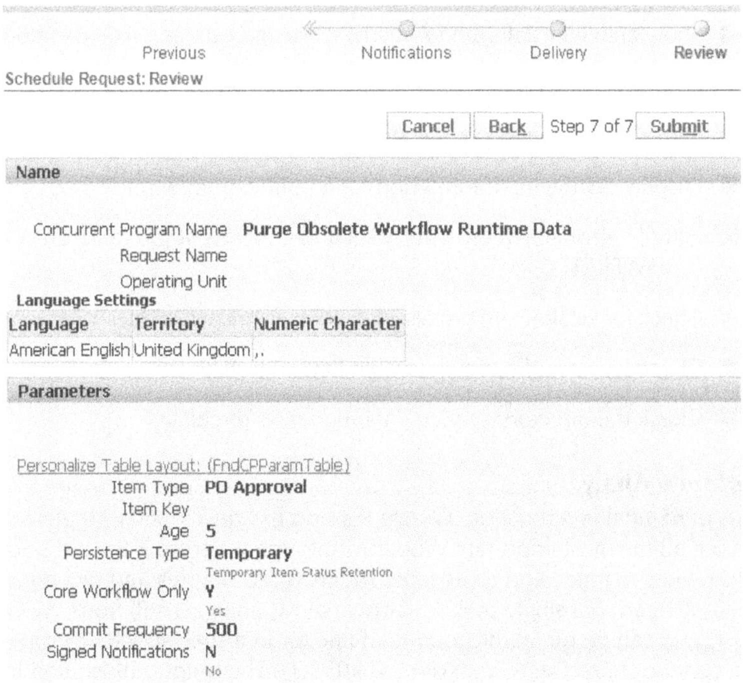

FIGURE 7-18.   *Submitting a Workflow purge for the PO approval item type*

- Configure for regularly run queries. While there are many database utilities to do this, one example is to run the E-Business Suite script in $FND_TOP/sql/wffngen.sql, which translates the regularly used activity function calls into static calls for more effective runtime use.

- Configure the technical components of Workflow, such as database objects, agents, mailers, Concurrent Managers, and queues. Examples are disabling the retention time on the Workflow queues or partitioning the runtime Workflow tables (see My Oracle Support Note 260884.1).

- **Workflow's scripts** In addition to OAM screens, there are standard scripts that can be used to interrogate Workflow performance. The list below is also detailed in the Oracle Workflow Administrators Guide (E12903-04), where there is also a small section on performance tuning.

  - Display the version of the Oracle Workflow server: wfver.sql

  - Display debugging information for an event: wfbesdbg.sql

  - Remove data from Oracle Workflow tables: wfrmall.sql, wfrmitms.sql, wfrmitt.sql, wfrmtype.sql, wfrmita.sql

  - Update translation tables: WFNLADD.sql

  - Enable/disable a language: wfnlena.sql

  - Run a Workflow process: wfrun.sql

  - Show activities deferred for the next background engine execution: wfbkgchk.sql

  - Display a status report for an item: wfstatus.sql, wfstat.sql

  - Show a notification's status: wfntfsh.sql

  - Display debugging information for a notification: wfmlrdbg.sql

  - Handle error activities: wfretry.sql and concurrent job Retry Error Workflow Activities (FNDWFRET)

  - Check for version and process definition errors: wfverchk.sql, wfverupd.sql, wfstdchk.sql

  - Check for invalid hanging foreign keys: wfrefchk.sql

  - Check the directory service data model: wfdirchk.sql

The Workflow Analyzer

After years of manual investigation, Oracle Support has developed a single comprehensive script that pulls out all the most important Workflow information from E-Business Suite, organizes it in an easy-to-review manner, and gives some rudimentary analysis and recommendations.

This is delivered as a single SQL script (workflow_analyzer.sql) from My Oracle Support Note 1369938.1, and can be run at the command line (or in a shell script) or from within E-Business Suite as a concurrent request (see Note 1425053.1). The output, illustrated in Figure 7-19, is in simple HTML format that includes rich graphics and tables, offering application administrators a quick and easy way to verify the health of all the Workflow components, as well as to identify

Workflow Analyzer Overview

Workflow Runtime Data Table Gauge

Your overall Workflow HealthCheck Status is in need of Immediate Review!
The WF_ITEMS Table has obsolete workflow runtime data that is older than 3 years.

We reviewed all 69,917 rows in WF_ITEMS Table for Oracle Applications Release 12.1.3 instance called R1213
Currently 61% (42,957) of WF_ITEMS are OPEN, while 39% (26,960) are CLOSED items but still exist in the runtime t

> **Note:** Once a Workflow is closed, its runtime data that is stored in Workflow Runtime Tables (WF_*) becomes obsolete.
> All the pertinent data is stored in the functional tables (FND_*, PO_*, AP_*, HR_*, OE_*, etc), like who approved what, for how m
> Remember that each row in WF_ITEMS is associated to 100s or 1000s of rows in the other WF runtime tables, so it is importan

Workflow Administration

Workflow Administrator Role

> **Warning:** The Workflow Administrator role (WF_ADMIN_ROLE) for R1213 is set to an Asterisk which allows EVERYONE access to
> This is not recommended for Production instances, but may be ok for Testing.
> Remember that the Workflow Administrator Role has permissions to full access of all workflows and notifications.
>
> **Note:** For more information refer to Note 453137.1 - Oracle Workflow Best Practices Release 12 and Release 11i

Show the status of the Workflow Error Notifications for this instance

Workflow Error Notifications by Type

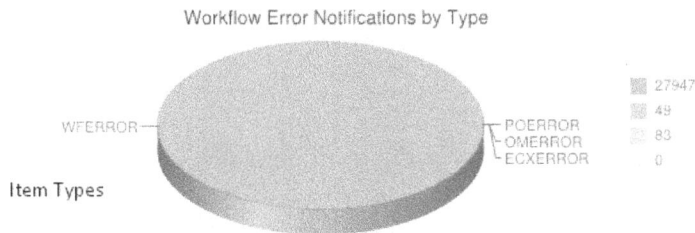

WFERROR	27947
POERROR	49
OMERROR	83
ECXERROR	0

Item Types

> **Attention**
> There are 28,079 Error Notifications of type (ECXERROR,OMERROR,POERROR,WFERROR) found on t

FIGURE 7-19. *Output example from the Workflow Analyzer showing obvious warning for an unhealthy Workflow system*

potential processing blockages or existing problems. The following is a summary of the main sections of the output:

- **Workflow Analyzer Overview**   Versions and configurations
- **Workflow Administration**   Setups, rules, errors, statuses
- **Workflow Footprint**   Volumes, averages, and counts

- **Workflow Concurrent Programs** Internal component activity, programs, statuses
- **Workflow Notification Mailer** Configuration and throughput
- **Workflow Patch Levels** Fixes and log information
- **Product Specific Workflows** Specialist information

Oracle E-Business Suite Search

Another technology that underpins several parts of E-Business Suite is the incorporation of Oracle's powerful search engines. Procurement has used the Oracle Intermedia search solution for a number of years, but Release 12 adds support for the Secure Enterprise Search (SES) solution for its global search, as well as for various in-product areas such as Enterprise Contacts and Product Management. With the latest releases, SES is already installed and requires just a little configuration before being ready for use. Obviously, as data volumes and usage grow, some maintenance and active management of search performance is inevitable.

E-Business Suite's Application Search Administrator responsibility includes some basic features available for its performance management. As shown in Figure 7-20, a task region under the Configuration tab includes the Optimize Indexes feature, which reduces data fragmentation that can occur as datasets grow and the related indexes begin to produce less efficient scans.

Also shown is the link to the Secure Enterprise Search administration login; it's this console that has the most configuration options for managing performance. One example is the partitioning of the search index over multiple disks, so that I/O can be done in parallel, increasing query response times for busy environments.

Chapter 12 of the Secure Enterprise Search Administrator's Guide (E21605-02) covers the detailed administration of these components and includes tuning advice for both the crawl and search components, such as managing the indexes, checking statistics, and managing their resources such as the JVM.

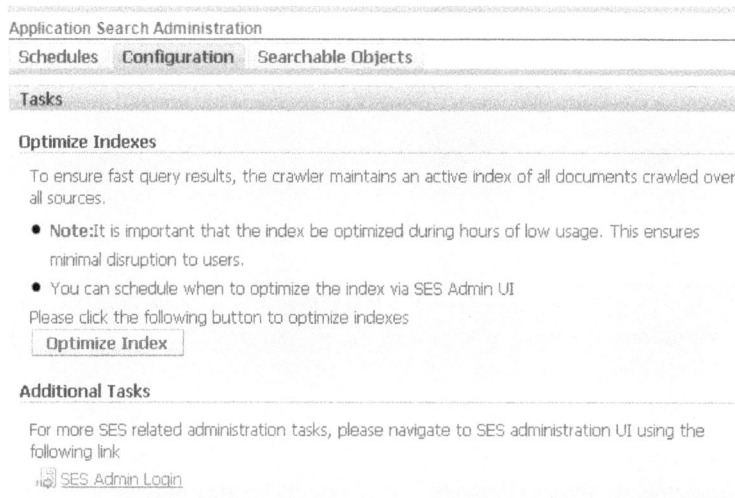

FIGURE 7-20. *Tasks in the Application Search Administrator responsibility for Secure Enterprise Search*

Application Data

This section is concerned with the effective management of E-Business Suite data so that it never becomes a cause of performance issues. We'll cover a few different general recommendations on managing and monitoring application data, but where specific application products or features use it in certain ways there may be dedicated management best practices that are available. For those processes important to your business, look for data troubleshooting or performance related documents on My Oracle Support; a good general starting point is Note 752322.1: Reducing Your Oracle E-Business Suite Data Footprint Using Archiving, Purging, and Information Lifecycle Management.

Data Quality Applications

The need for tools to manage application data is clear, and Oracle provides solutions for data that most commonly suffers from duplication, fragmentation, and abandonment. These tools act as central hubs that collect data from different application sources, provide cleansing services based on rules and standards, and then synchronize the fresh data back with the source systems.

Oracle's Master Data Management suite of applications currently includes the following products:

- **Oracle Customer Hub**   Based on Siebel but with prebuilt AIA integration with E-Business Suite
- **Oracle Supplier Hub**   Part of E-Business Suite's new Supplier Management product set
- **Oracle Product Hub**   A standalone solution with out-of-the-box integrations to E-Business Suite, Siebel, and other applications
- **Oracle Site Hub**   Native to E-Business Suite, providing solutions for managing complex and distributed enterprise locations

In addition to these application-based solutions, the Oracle Enterprise Data Quality product is more technical in nature and is used for tackling general custom data quality issues. It also has connectors available for applications, and it leverages ETL technology standards and best-of-breed data management products such as the Oracle Data Integrator.

Removing Old Data

As E-Business Suite captures, processes, and reports data, it grows in size (just as Workflow does, as mentioned in the last section) leaving residual records in structures such as interface tables. This data eventually needs cleaning up, since it takes up capacity and can slow down the exact same processes that created it. There are various methods of cleaning up this runtime audit type data, with several displayed in the Critical Activities tab, in Oracle Applications Manager, shown in Figure 7-21. The Modify Monitored Program List button displays other similar jobs for adding to this management dashboard, depending on which products and features are being used. Release 12 contains about 260 purge-related programs in total.

It's not only runtime audit data that can build to sizes that can affect performance, business data can also. This includes transactions such as expense reports or invoice lines, as well as setup data such as users and operating units. E-Business Suite is a mature product and has been used against most sizes of implementation over the years, but the natural evolution of business requirements and additional new product features means not all functions are well prepared to handle especially massive datasets.

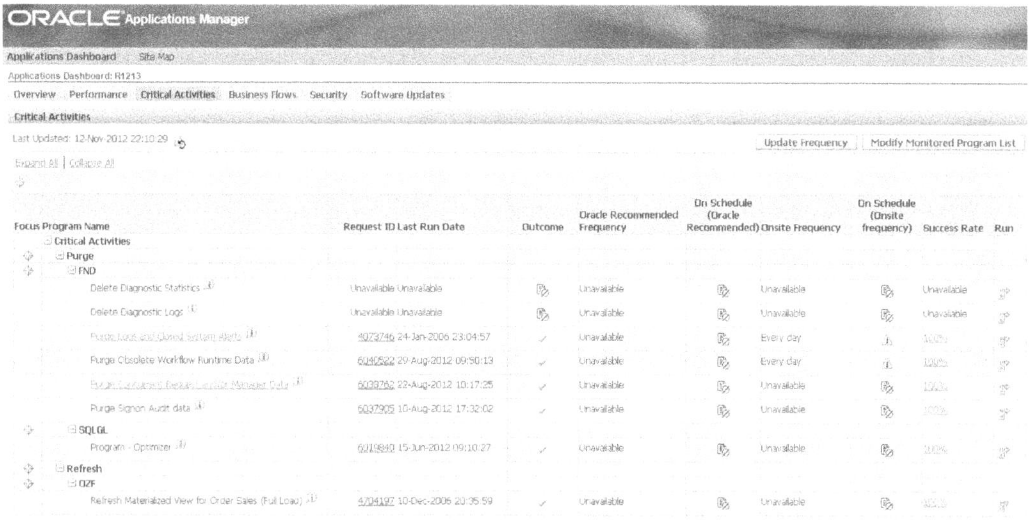

FIGURE 7-21. *The Critical Activities tab focuses on managing old data by purging*

Apart from raising service requests with Oracle Support, what else can be done to handle huge runtime data volumes? The most obvious thing is to adhere to best practices in archiving and purging old transactional and setup data. Oracle doesn't traditionally publish complete guidelines on this, mainly because it depends on regional and industry-specific regulatory and legal requirements that are impossible to centrally maintain for all customers globally. However, most product lines include programs and features with details in their own documentation.

The recommendation is therefore to make yourself aware of the requirements for each of the key data sets inside your E-Business Suite instance, and to ensure that the archive solutions you have implemented meet those needs effectively. This includes not just creating copies of data, but ensuring the clean removal of old archived data from the system without leaving orphaned or corrupted records behind. One additional tip is to carefully consider the new location of archived data, as often reports point at live transaction tables only and some custom reports may be needed to view the moved information.

Managing Metadata
Despite the cryptic title, the most common method of performing database metadata management is the well-known gathering of statistics. This process helps the SQL query optimizer produce an efficient execution plan. It does this by refreshing the statistics in the data dictionary so they accurately reflect the volume and distribution of the data in tables and indexes.

As such when E-Business Suite is being used in what could be deemed normal operations (average load and throughput), the guideline is to gather statistics about once a month. When fairly unusual activities such as a large volume of inserts or updates to data occur, statistics should be gathered again. Since data updates and inserts are rarely monitored in detail (unfortunately), statistics are often gathered when a performance issue is found as a potential solution, and it often helps. In addition, a prescheduled job to gather statistics should be set based on being triggered by any combination of the following: a period of low user activity, a certain time period since it was last run, or a regular event that it should coincide with, such as a data load or integration job.

Statistics are usually gathered for one or all schemas or specific tables, and it's important to use only the procedures in the E-Business Suite supplied FND_STATS package for this, or even easier the Gather Schema Statistics and Gather Table Statistics concurrent programs.

One extra recommendation is to not run this too often, especially not during peak periods, since it's a fairly resource-intensive task that itself can hurt overall performance.

The Oracle E-Business Suite Tablespace Model

Oracle first made this tablespace model available back in 11*i*10, and for Release 12 it is now the default deployment architecture for new installations. At a basic level, the E-Business Suite Tablespace Model converts any existing dictionary-managed tablespaces to new locally managed tablespaces. This active data management feature brings quite a few benefits related to overall performance, including:

- Consolidation of the overall number of tablespaces in an E-Business Suite instance

- Easier maintenance and reduced space usage as each database object is mapped to a tablespace based on its actual input/output characteristics

- The addition of Automatic Segment-space Management, which offers real-time tuning of several important schema object storage parameters

- More benefits gained from a Real Application Cluster (RAC) deployment

- Improved performance due to effects like increasing the block-packing that reduces the number of buffer gets

It also includes a Migration utility that guides you through the conversion process step by step. More detail on this is provided in the E-Business Suite System Administrator's Guide—Configuration (E12893-04) and in how-to notes on My Oracle Support such as Note 404954.1.

Concurrent Processing

Concurrent Processing represents one of the most significant areas for performance management, as E-Business Suite generally puts its most intensive workloads into concurrent requests for running in the background. This, together with the complexity and flexibility that the Concurrent Processing architecture offers means that it takes careful analysis to ensure that all the different concurrent requests are run in a way that maximizes efficiency and performance.

In this section, we will cover some of the main features and recommendations that can help comprise a high-quality Concurrent Processing deployment. In addition to the points provided here, at the end of this section there is a selection of the best references in which further detail and advice on Concurrent Processing can be found.

Monitoring Concurrent Processing Performance

As mentioned at the start of the "Applications Technology Layer" section, Oracle Applications Manager has a range of methods for monitoring Concurrent Processing, as shown as Figure 7-10's concurrent manager performance charts. In addition to graphic displays of data there are three standard reports, each of which provides a drill down into detail as required:

- **Concurrent Request Statistics by Program** Which programs performed best and worst
- **Concurrent Request Statistics by Username** Which users submitted which programs
- **Programs Usage Statistics** Which programs were used the most and how those programs performed

The last of these reports is shown in Figure 7-22, which gives the metrics for just one concurrent program, including the maximum, minimum, and average completion time in seconds, as well as other key values such as the number of times it was run and therefore the total time it spent executing. The collection of these metrics can also be reset to keep data recent and accurate.

As mentioned before, the Concurrent Request Runaways link is available under the Performance section of the Monitoring tab; if you click it, the system identifies any database sessions spawned from concurrent requests that have not been properly cleaned up once the job completes.

In addition to the Oracle Applications Manager dashboards and reports in this chapter, the System Administration responsibility lists out basic links to see both concurrent managers and concurrent requests next to each other. Clicking each of these brings back clear information about the current deployment and load on each of the managers, along with a flexible request search page that includes criteria on waiting and long-running requests. For the seasoned application administrator, these simple pages can be just as powerful as charts and graphs.

With the E-business Suite plug-in for Enterprise Manager installed, there is an extra layer of performance management capability available, with some items specific to Concurrent Processing. As you saw in Chapter 6, and repeated in Figure 7-23, there is a Concurrent Processing dashboard page that gives a simple picture of the throughput, with additional tabs that give more granular information on request activity (Figure 7-24) and general usage statistics for applications users. You'll also notice that the bottom right of the dashboard page has links to the same three statistics reports in Oracle Applications Manager, as mentioned previously.

Manager Deployment

The concurrent managers that service the requests submitted by the application are flexible in how many there are, how they execute, and what exactly they are used for. This allows each deployment to have the right architecture to satisfy whatever profile of requests are submitted

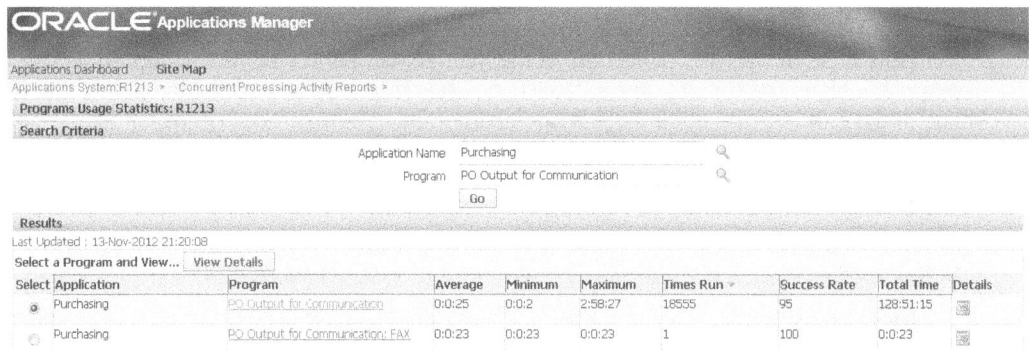

Select	Application	Program	Average	Minimum	Maximum	Times Run	Success Rate	Total Time	Details
◉	Purchasing	PO Output for Communication	0:0:25	0:0:2	2:58:27	18555	95	128:51:15	
○	Purchasing	PO Output for Communication: FAX	0:0:23	0:0:23	0:0:23	1	100	0:0:23	

FIGURE 7-22. *The Programs Usage Statistics report for the purchase order printing program*

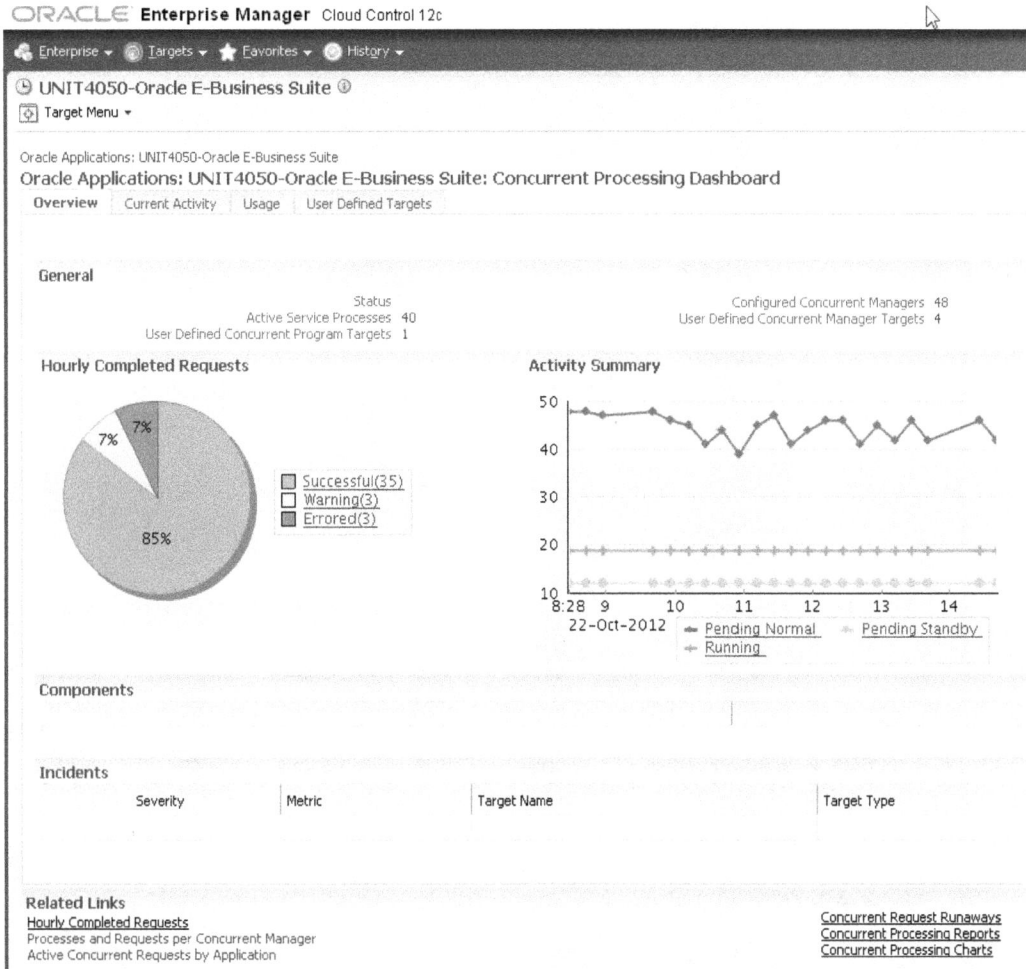

FIGURE 7-23.   *Enterprise Manager's Concurrent Processing dashboard*

most often. For example, one deployment might run payroll for 100,000 employees every two weeks but not create one single purchase order, whereas another might raise 10,000 purchase orders a month, pay just the 100 core headquarters staff through payroll, and use an entirely different application for the remainder of their wages.

By default there is just one Standard Manager deployed with E-Business Suite, and it will run all requests. This may be fine for many or indeed most features that have occasional use of Concurrent Processing and for relatively light loads that process quickly. As in the previous example, some specific product features may be used extensively by many users or for regular high-throughput operations, and as such a dedicated manager can be created to specialize in running one or more particular programs.

ORACLE **Enterprise Manager** Cloud Control 12c

Enterprise ▾   Targets ▾   Favorites ▾   History ▾

⏱ UNIT4050-Oracle E-Business Suite ⓘ
Target Menu ▾

Oracle Applications: UNIT4050-Oracle E-Business Suite
Oracle Applications: UNIT4050-Oracle E-Business Suite: Concurrent Processing Dashboard

Overview   **Current Activity**   Usage   User Defined Targets

Concurrent Requests by Status

Pending Normal	43
Pending (Standby)	12
Scheduled	6
Inactive (No Manager)	0
On Hold	0
Running	19

Hourly Completed Requests

Successful	32
Warning	4
Error	0
Successful Requests Rate(%)	88.88
Requests Warning Rate(%)	11.11
Requests Error Rate(%)	0

▽ **Concurrent Managers by Requests**

▽ **Top Concurrent Requests**

View   Running ▾

Request ID	Program Name	Short Name	Running Time	User Name	Manager Name	Phase	Status
10189672	Accounting Analysis Report	GLAAR	87.77	SYSADMIN	STANDARD	Running	Normal
10189684	Post Lines	GLPL	76.5	SYSADMIN	STANDARD	Running	Normal
10189693	Budget Summary Report	GLBSR	56.88	SYSADMIN	STANDARD	Running	Normal
10189405	Resource Planing Report	FNDRPR	47.32	SYSADMIN	MRPMGR	Running	Normal
10189645	Purge and Archive Orders	OEPAO	28.23	SYSADMIN	INVMGR	Running	Normal

Top Applications

View   Running ▾

Application Short Name	Application Name	Number of Running Requests ▾
SQLGL	General Ledger	16
FND	Application Object	1
OE	Order Entry	1

Top Users

View   Running ▾

User Name	Running ▾
SYSADMIN	19

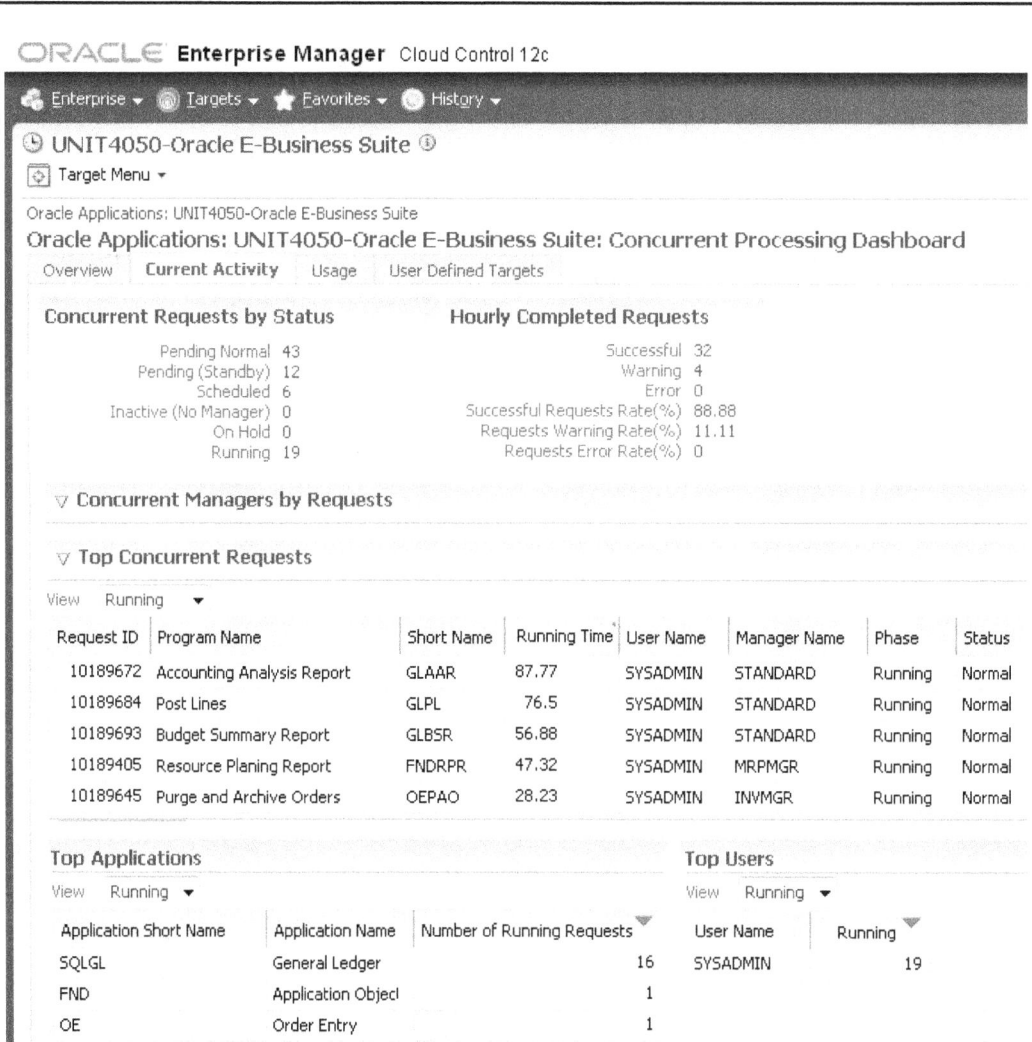

FIGURE 7-24.   *The Current Activity tab detail, as available under the Concurrent Processing dashboard*

The example in Figure 7-25 shows the Inventory Manager, which is a standard concurrent manager that has specialization rules listing only the programs for which it can be used. The same jobs are then excluded from the general standard manager. Specialized managers are often used for synchronous requests: a form launches a job as part of its processing and the user interface waits for the request results to then display. These requests need to complete quickly so that using dedicated managers make sense.

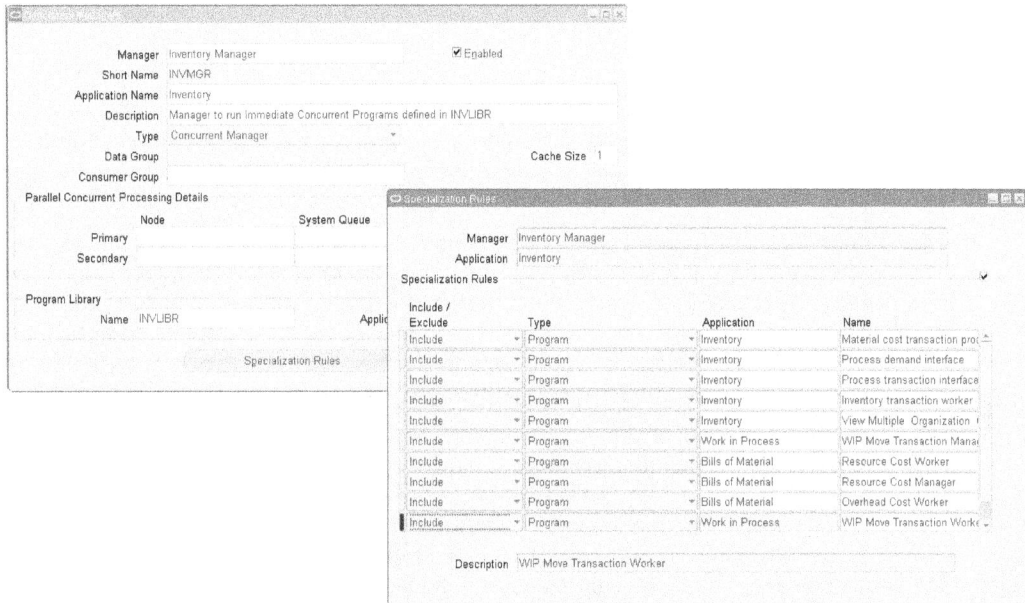

FIGURE 7-25. *The specialization rules for the Inventory Manager*

Managers can also be set to be dedicated based on other specific criteria, such as for one application product or even all requests from one particular user.

The temptation may be to create many dedicated managers. However, because each manager consumes additional memory and requires management and coordination with the others, adding managers is not without cost, and specialization is recommended only when high volumes and testing results confirm actual performance improvements. One general guideline is to reduce the number of normal managers to at most twice the number of processors. As a general guideline every additional concurrent manager requires about 20Mb.

Concurrent Configuration
In addition to getting the right number of managers, the managers and programs themselves can be configured so they run at optimal performance levels. To help with the different needs of different deployments, a variety of parameters can be tuned. The following are common parameters:

- **Sleep Seconds** Governs how long a manager waits until it rescans the queue for pending requests. Where many short running jobs occur, this should be set to a short time period to prevent backlog built, but for fewer larger jobs it should be higher so that the queue polling overhead isn't a wasted resource.

- **Cache Size** Allows managers to pick up multiple requests from the queue at once, reducing the polling. This is mainly useful when there are a large volume of short-lived requests.

- **Processes** Defines the number of operating system processes available for a manager to run requests in parallel. This needs to match with the capacity of the server to prevent overloading the system.

- **Workshifts** Determines when each manager becomes active over a specific time period. While most will need to be running all the time, there are cases when some specialist managers could be set to run differently. An example might be a resource draining high-volume print job, or perhaps a request that retries nonurgent failed transactions that are resource hungry (say like a purge), both are perhaps set to run overnight.

- **Profile Options** Several of the profile options starting with the word "concurrent" can be used to tune the way in which the managers operate. One example is Concurrent: Wait for Available TM, which should be set to a low figure to reduce unnecessary delays. Another is Concurrent: TM Transport Type, which governs the internal connections for organizing work. For this, the Pipes option is generally faster, however, it requires more configuration and administrative overhead than the alternative Queue option.

- **Conflict Resolution** As an internal component of Concurrent Processing, this option ensures that incompatible requests do not fight over the resources they both need. An example might be a request that reports on data that another request updates. Incompatibilities are predefined for E-Business Suite programs and, when two or more jobs are identified as incompatible, one request will remain in pending status until the other completes. This may be initially regarded as a performance block. It can be useful to check the incompatibilities for the slow job, along with the conflict resolution manager.

For more detail on these parameters, take a look at the E-Business Suite System Administrator's Guide—Configuration (E12893-04).

Cleaning Concurrent Processing

Just like Workflow, the Concurrent Processing platform uses lots of internal objects for scheduling work. As it runs, it also maintains an audit history, most of which is used in the reports discussed and diagrams shown so far. The audit history cannot continue unmaintained, and a few simple tasks exist that clean up the environment to prevent job scheduling and execution getting stuck behind internal parts that have to handle massive amounts of unused history data. There are three clean up related recommended actions to implement in a good performance management plan:

- **Purge** To clear old data from internal tables, use the concurrent request Purge Concurrent Requests and/or Manager Data (FNDCPPUR). However, this may not clear all logs and output files, so checking the file system manually is also recommended. The request accepts various parameters, with the recommended values being:

  - Entity = all

  - Mode = age

  - Mode Value = 10 (that is, keep the last ten days only, purge the rest)

  This request can take time, so it is recommended for use off-hours. Also ensure that you have the latest patches available for this program. Also somewhat similar is the CMCLEAN .sql script (see Note 134007.1), which clears and corrects problematic request statuses that have been known to prevent managers from working properly.

- **Defragment and statistics**   As mentioned before, gathering schema statistics can help the query performance for constantly changing records, and the concurrent manager internal tables are good examples. While this can be done specifically for concurrent request tables, for overall efficient use it is recommended to run the request with these parameters:

  - Schema Name = all

  - Estimated Percentage = 10–40

  - Backup Flag = NOBACKUP

  - History Mode = NONE

  - Gather Options = GATHERAUTO

  In addition, concurrent manager tables can become fragmented because they are active and then get purged The metadata may occasionally need fully refreshing, more than is done by gathering the statistics. This is done one table at a time, using the following basic process:

  - Move the table.

  - Rebuild the table's indexes.

  - Regather the table statistics.

- **Manage Logging and Tracing**   Excessive logging will cause performance drop thanks to the extra code calls and inevitable I/O. Silly mistakes do occur, like low level logging left on either for a user, a responsibility, or even at the concurrent program definition level.

Please refer to My Oracle Support Note: 395445.1 for an explanation of the relevant logging profile options and usage guidelines. The recommended default is to have the log level set to Unexpected (Level = 6) and to only change this to more detailed values at the user level. In addition, a quick tip is to run queries against the FND_LOG_MESSAGES table to check the logging traffic and consider truncating it as needed.

It should also be mentioned that inadvertently setting SQL Tracing can also affect performance, and this feature should be used sparingly and specifically. The resulting trace files can be quite large and should also be archived or cleaned up on regular intervals to free up disk resources.

For concurrent jobs the proper way to use logging is via the profile option Concurrent: Allow Debugging, which enables the Debug Options section on the request submission page. This means the log writes for just one request at a time. Concurrent logs are stored in the filesystem directory set by environmental variables $APPLCSF/$APPLLOG and the concurrent request output is in $APPLCSF/$APPLOUT. Finally, don't forget that the concurrent managers themselves generate internal logs, which should also be properly maintained.

Concurrent Reports
One of the most frequent tasks for Concurrent Processing is the generation of reports. These are normally generated by a combination of program logic and the Output Post Processor working with BI Publisher. As such these additional components can also be tuned for performance.

The Output Post Processor is a dedicated concurrent management and like the others should be deployed and configured based on the expected load. In addition to configurations and number of managers, it supports multithreading (one per process) and setting the processes parameters field can improve throughput.

In addition, BI Publisher itself, as well as the report programs it runs, has configurations and performance best practices, as reviewed previously in this section.

Concurrent Affinity

Concurrent affinity is a relatively new feature, available from Release 12.1.3 onward, which aids processing by leveraging better efficiency in RAC deployments. This allows all related programs to be associated with the same compute node in the RAC environment, thereby reducing the cross-node activity that can slow performance. An example might be when transaction inserts occur on Node1 only, and the associated Workflow background program that processes these transactions should also be set to run on Node1.

As you'd expect, this is most beneficial for database intensive programs like those often run as concurrent requests. However, it has also been proven that associating other application components (forms, and so on) to specific RAC server nodes can also improve performance.

Concurrent affinity is set up for each concurrent program within the Define Concurrent Program form, under the Session Control button and in the Target Node and Instance fields. More information is available in My Oracle Support Notes 1359612.1 and 1129203.1.

Parallel Concurrent Processing

Parallel concurrent processing allows multiple distributed hardware nodes to run concurrent managers, so that request processing can run in parallel when required, providing better resource utilization and greatly improving performance by eliminating wait times. It also has the benefit of increasing fault tolerance so that should one node fail, additional nodes are available to run requests. It also helps avoid any incompatible programs queuing up behind each other, as mentioned earlier.

Each of the nodes running concurrent managers can be configured so they are optimized for batch processing, while at the same time visibility of the whole Concurrent Processing system remains simple and centralized. This works through the use of the Generic Service Management (GSM) component, which fires the Internal Concurrent Manager and assigns specific nodes to the concurrent managers. Primary and secondary nodes can be configured to increase specialization and offer directed failover, although in later releases these are not mandatory.

As mentioned in the section "Concurrent Affinity," the nodes can also be used to support specialization of specific programs so they are dedicated to run on specific managers on specific nodes.

More detail on the options and steps for implementing Parallel Concurrent Processing can be found in the Oracle E-Business Suite System Administrator's Guide—Configuration (E12893-0).

The Concurrent Processing Analyzer

Just like its sister the Workflow Analyzer, this innovation from Oracle Support provides a tool that analyzes the concurrent manager configuration and operation and creates a troubleshooting report output. This report can also be used to proactively investigate the health of the system, such as checking performance. It includes the following:

- Analysis of the concurrent environment, including all internal components, versions, and patches.
- Concurrent system configurations, including all related application and database setup parameters.
- Concurrent request summary, including history and current throughput, backlog, and performance
- Recommendations for concurrent best practices, offering alerts and solutions.

The tool itself is simple noninvasive SQL script (cp_analyzer.sql) and outputs a single HTML file of results in an easy-to-review format. The section of output shown in Figure 7-26 illustrates just how easy this is to interpret. This script-based deployment and HTML output also means that past executions can be stored and it offers simple comparison of the results over time that can help with performance analysis.

FIGURE 7-26.   *Part of the Concurrent Processing analyzer that shows clear purge recommendation*

The script for the Concurrent Processing Analyzer is available from Note 1411723.1, and the following is a summary of the output.

- E-Business Applications Concurrent Processing Analyzer Overview
  - Total Purge Eligible Records in FND_CONCURRENT_REQUESTS
  - E-Business Suite Version
  - Concurrent Processing Database Parameter Settings
  - Concurrent Processing Environment Variables
  - E-Business Suite Profile Option Settings
  - Applied E-Business Suite Technology Stack Patches
  - Known 1-Off Patches on Top of E-Business Suite Technology Stack Rollups
- E-Business Applications Concurrent Request Analysis
  - Long-Running Reports During Business Hours
  - Elapsed Time History of Concurrent Requests
  - Requests Currently Running on a System
  - FND_CONCURRENT_REQUESTS Totals
  - Running Requests
  - Total Pending Requests by Status Code
  - Count Pending Regularly Scheduled/Non-Regularly Scheduled Requests
  - Count of Pending Requests on Hold/Not on Hold
  - Listing of Scheduled Requests
  - Listing of Pending Requests on Hold
  - Listing of Pending Requests Not on Hold
  - Volume of Daily Concurrent Requests for Last Month
  - Identify/Resolve the Pending/Standby Issue, if Caused by Run Alone Flag
  - Tablespace Statistics for the fnd_concurrent Tables
- E-Business Applications Concurrent Manager Analysis
  - Concurrent Managers Active and Enabled
  - Concurrent Manager Processes by Workshift
  - Active Managers for Applications That Are Not Installed/Used
  - Total Target Processes for Request Managers (Excluding Off-Hours)

- Request Managers with Incorrect Cache Size

- Concurrent Manager Request Summary by Manager

- Check Manager Queues for Pending Requests

- Check the Configuration of OPP

- References

Concurrent Processing Further Reading

The following My Oracle Support notes contain many tips, tricks, and best practices for the performance management of Concurrent Processing. These notes are in addition to the setup and implementation documentation in Chapter 7 of the E-Business Suite System Administrator's Guide—Configuration (E12893-04):

- **Note 1359612.1**   Webcast: E-Business Suite—RAC and Parallel Concurrent Processing

- **Note 1367676.1**   Webcast: E-Business Suite—Concurrent Manager Performance

- **Note 164085.1**   Enhancing and Automating Oracle Applications Concurrent Processing

- **Note 1057802.1**   Best Practices for Performance for Concurrent Managers

- **Note 1304305.1**   E-Business Concurrent Processing Information Center

- **Note 171855.1**   Diagnostic Script to Diagnose Common Concurrent Manager Issues (CCM.sql)

- **Note 1399454.1**   Tuning Output Post Processor (OPP) to Improve Performance

Platform Layer

In this section we'll cover the lowest level technologies and components that the applications administrator will normally be required to consider as part of performance management, both in planning and in day-to-day tasks. Just as in our other toolbox chapters, if the base platform is not performing well then it is unlikely that the application is. However, knowing where to start and what to do when taking the leap from applications and its own technology down into the core base technologies can be daunting.

Here are the topic areas most relevant to the E-Business Suite performance management that we will cover in this section:

- Enterprise Manager

- User interface and client systems

- Oracle Forms Server

- OA Framework and Java

- Database

- Network

- Hardware

- Integration and load testing

The Oracle Enterprise Manager Plug-in for Oracle E-Business Suite

As an overall advanced management solution, let's consider a few of the performance-related features available, before drilling down into individual platform components.

Performance Dashboard

The main E-Business Suite Performance Dashboard in Enterprise Manager, also mentioned previously in Figure 6-26, shows charts for general activity, applications server activity, database activity, or, as you can see in Figure 7-27, all of them together.

This is a comprehensive performance overview where spikes or patterns are clear and obvious. Also, the legends for each chart can be clicked to see the underlying data within their own specialist Enterprise Manager pages. Also of note are the links at the bottom of the dashboard page that mostly drill into the pages you've already seen in Oracle Applications Manager—except the JVM Usage link that opens another Enterprise Manager page, which we'll discuss later.

Performance Metrics

As illustrated in Figures 6-32 and 6-33 of Chapter 6, there are many metrics available in Enterprise Manager, and a good quantity of them are useful for performance monitoring. Examples include those related to Concurrent Processing, broken down by variables such as status, completion rates, users, and programs. In addition, more general data like page response times, web user traffic, and component activity also exist. Each metric can be used to build alerts with respective notifications or other actions triggered upon breach of the configurable threshold values.

Taking the proactive monitoring approach one stage further, service level management is available as a feature of Enterprise Manager, so that performance requirements can be modeled and the associated metrics reported upon. This might include a set of capacity utilization reports to ensure resources are appropriate at all times.

User Monitoring

Also mentioned in the last chapter (and shown in Figure 6-28), the User Monitor page shows current and historic performance data, where again patterns and anomalies can be readily identified and investigated. The information available includes a summary of CPU usage, memory usage, and database queries and waits. Since processes may be spawned from internal application activities, end user login names are not always available; hence the proliferation of process ID values. As shown in Figure 7-28, each of the data points can be clicked for more detail on that particular activity.

User Interface and Client Systems

User interface and client systems information could have logically been put under the Business Process Layer, but as it's the first step in the technology flow, I've included it here. Let's consider the usability of the application, sometimes known as user experience (UX). Oracle has a large team of UX experts that work across all applications products to fine-tune the user interface so that it improves productivity by leveraging latest design methodologies and display technologies.

With the advent of web and mobile apps, the ease-of-use expectations of all users have evolved, and the opportunity for increasing efficiency and adoption for enterprise applications is huge. As such, user experience could be considered part of a truly holistic performance management plan, and for those planning extensions and customizations, this should definitely be part of the design and testing process.

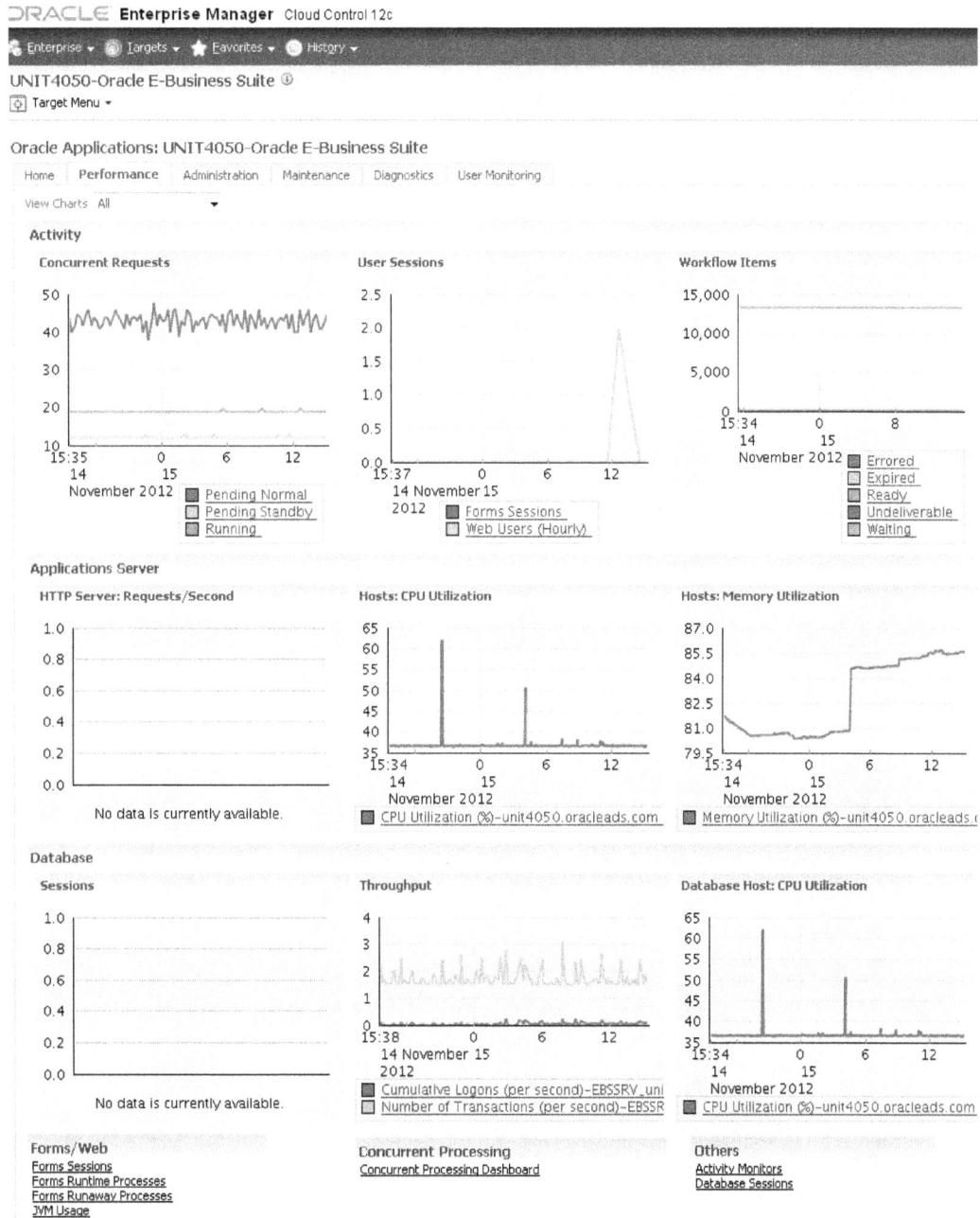

FIGURE 7-27.   *The complete performance review from Enterprise Manager*

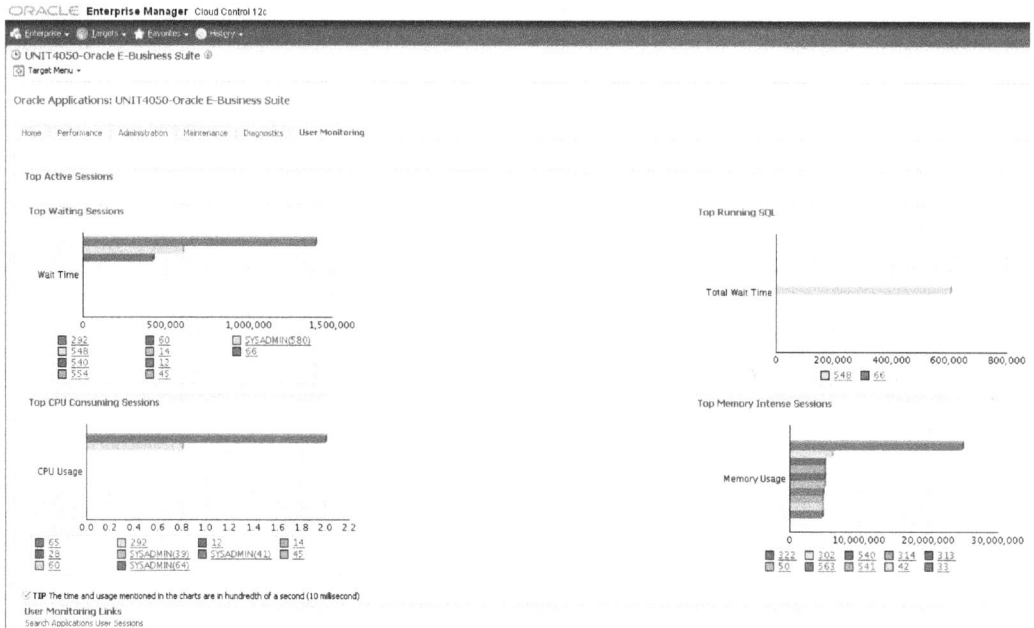

FIGURE 7-28.   *User Monitoring Dashboard showing performance data by end user and/or the process ID*

In Oracle E-Business Suite 12.1.3 there are several new features that originate from the user experience team's input, and this will continue to evolve in subsequent releases. Some examples of these are

■   Inline attachments where users can add, update, and delete within the transaction page directly

■   Navigational improvements to the main menus

■   Implementation of type-ahead/auto-suggest on search fields

■   More embedded analytics, such as charts and graphs within dashboards and related pages

More information about Oracle's UX team, their initiatives, and the products in which they are available can be found at www.oracle.com/ux.

In addition to the design of the forms and pages, the software running on the client machines should also be reviewed for performance. This comes in three versions: first, the Java version that the Oracle Forms client uses, second, the browser version used for OA Framework based pages, and third, the Microsoft Office version used for client desktop integration features. All of these should be standardized and must comply with the certified and recommended versions for use with E-Business Suite. Details can found in My Oracle Support under the Certifications tab and in the useful Note 380482.1: Oracle E-Business Suite Release 12 Technology Stack Documentation Roadmap.

There are two other useful resources for reviewing end user system performance, a knowledge resource and a utility program.

First, Note 557259.1 provides the whitepaper, "Oracle E-Business Suite 11*i* and 12 PC Client Performance," which takes a pragmatic approach to considering how to get the best performance from existing client machines, thereby helping reduce the need for costly upgrades and replacements.

The second resource is the E-Business Suite Client System Analyzer, which is essentially an applet that runs to collect information. This is launched from any of the Oracle Forms pages, under the Help menu, within the Diagnostics item. As shown in Figure 7-27, the data collected is available in the browser upon completion, but it is also uploaded back to E-Business Suite and made available to administrators in Oracle Applications Manager under the Client Configurations page.

One item to note is that this applet originates from Enterprise Manager, but it does not require Enterprise Manager at all since it is embedded within E-Business Suite (from 11.5.10). As shown in Figure 7-29, the information collected by this simple program is quite comprehensive, including information about the following, which can be useful in client performance reviews:

- Network and browser, including latency measure, bandwidth, and configurations
- Hardware, including CPU detail, RAM memory, I/O, and disk sizing
- Operating system, including version, properties, and configuration details
- File system, including type, mount points, and capacity
- Other installed software, including product name, vendor, version, and install details

For more detail on the Client System Analyzer, see My Oracle Support Note 277904.1.

Oracle Forms Server

In the section "Applications Technology Layer," I demonstrated how Forms Server activity is summarized by OAM within the links to Forms Sessions, showing what is currently being used by end users, as well as Forms Runtime Processes, the components servicing those sessions. This was explained in the "Oracle Applications Manager" section.

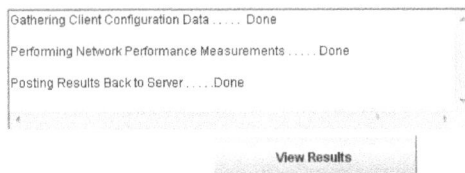

FIGURE 7-29. *The Client System Analyzer*

In terms of the core Oracle Forms server, the platform is so mature that it is mostly optimized out of the box, but there are a few areas of configuration that can be used for performance tuning.

First, the choice between socket and servlet mode remains one determined by implementation factors, and in some cases performance gains can be found. Generally speaking, socket mode is the fastest but is also less flexible, so it is dependent on the needs of the whole system. My Oracle Support Note 177610.1 explains more on this area.

Next, there are a few options in Forms that, while useful in some situations, they can add a performance overhead. Following are some examples of these options:

- **Enable Forms Dead Client Detection using the FORMS_TIMEOUT parameter** Checks for Forms sessions that are no longer being used and cleans them up. While sensible, the process adds overhead.

- **Review the use of Forms diagnostic parameters** These offer several enhancements to failure management, however, may also add performance overhead. See Note 1494442.1.

- **Assess configurations that validate and manage database connections** Connection tuning can have benefits but should be used to ensure addition capabilities are regularly required. Examples are profile "FND: Enable Cancel Query" (see Note 138159.1) and Forms parameter FORMS60_RECORD_GROUP_MAX.

It makes sense to have tools to measure the network trips between the client forms applet and the server size forms runtime process. You can implement specific PC-based network monitoring tools, or you can alternatively include the "netStats = true" parameter in the profile option ICX: Forms Launcher (in socket mode only), which gives detailed network timings output.

OA Framework and Java

Managing the performance of E-Business Suite web technologies is a complex task, and capable experts have written dozens of papers about it. Back in 2000, there was even a 900-page *Oracle Applications Tuning Handbook* published by Oracle Press—while an excellent resource, it is now mostly outdated. As with most technology, the real difficulty comes in satisfying the implementation-specific requirements. This section is written so that administrators can understand which areas and actions to focus on. It is therefore not necessarily exhaustive in depth, but it is complete and easy to consume.

Let's begin with a quick reminder of how the OA Framework-based process works, again from a basic high-level perspective. Figure 7-30 shows how page requests go from the Web Server

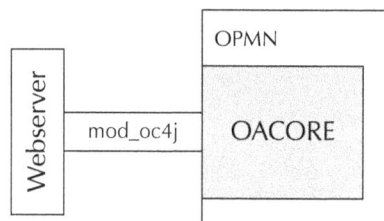

FIGURE 7-30. *High-level flow of non-Forms page requests in E-Business Suite 12.1*

through the mod_oc4j module and on to the Application Server running the OACore OC4J Java Server instance. In the background, the Oracle Process Manager (OPMN) makes sure things are kept running, providing automated restart if required.

This is a simplistic view, since some or all of these components may be configured and deployed in specific ways based on different requirements, but generally speaking this is the flow. From Release 12.2 onward the components change slightly because the application server is WebLogic, but the flow is generally the same.

This section provides an overview of the best Java performance management tools available for E-Business Suite, and illustrates which key metrics and features should be used. The focus is on management rather than troubleshooting, where much more lengthy advice and recommendations are required. That said, there are some short lists of the best references available at the end of several sections that provide more detail.

Dashboards and Consoles

Oracle Applications Manager is not a specialist Java Server management tool; it was designed specifically for the E-Business Suite components and doesn't offer much detail in terms of Java performance diagnostics.

The Java Server (for Release 12.1.x it's OC4J as part of the Oracle Application Server 10.1.3.4) is deployed as part of the Rapid Wizard install for E-Business Suite (see Note 376811.1), meaning that it comes without its visual administration console, Oracle Application Server Control (which is part of Enterprise Manager). This is unfortunate, as this tool contains an advanced view of all the web components therein. While the rapid install provides the same components, as well as the required command-line scripts to manage them, the user interface console does have some useful performance management features, such as:

- Graphs showing usage of CPU and memory resources by OC4J versus other active applications, as well as OC4J heap usage
- Statistics on database connections and transaction activity, JVM usage, JSP and servlet requests, and EJB methods
- A query system for most-requested JSPs, servlets, and EJB modules
- Access to logs and configurations

This is remedied for E-Business Suite Release 12.2 onward as the Java Server changes to WebLogic, which has its own Fusion Middleware Control console with the same types of features to help manage the Java environment.

To get Java tools for Release 12.1.x, one option is to use the Enterprise Manager plug-in for E-Business Suite, discussed before. This provides useful pages for checking performance information and, as with all metric data, associated alerts and notifications. Figure 7-31 shows the JVM Usage screen, available from the E-Business Suite plug-in Performance Dashboard, which provides details on the OACORE related JVM's deployed (one in this case), and their current CPU and memory utilization. It also includes counts and status information on the loaded objects and connections, with a drill for more details.

As well as benefiting from E-Business Suite specific features, leveraging Enterprise Manager also provides support for the native OC4J Java server, including its performance monitoring. The

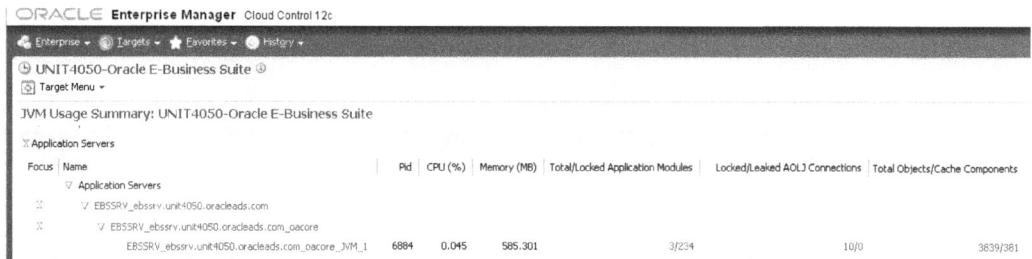

FIGURE 7-31. *Visibility to the E-Business Suite JVMs via the Enterprise Manager plug-in*

example in Figure 7-32 shows the Enterprise Manager dashboard page for the JVM target type, with status, basic configurations, and the response and load graph. You'll notice this has a menu at the top for OC4J, which includes management features and access to metric data. Also displayed on this page are any incidents created for the JVM and the host server. The page additionally shows that the host is outside the compliance score threshold, suggesting it is not configured as Oracle recommends. This demonstrates how using Enterprise Manager adds much more value than just improving information visibility.

On this same page is the Performance tab, which gives a much more detailed view of the JVM utilization. Figure 7-33 shows this page, with data and charts for key items like resource usage,

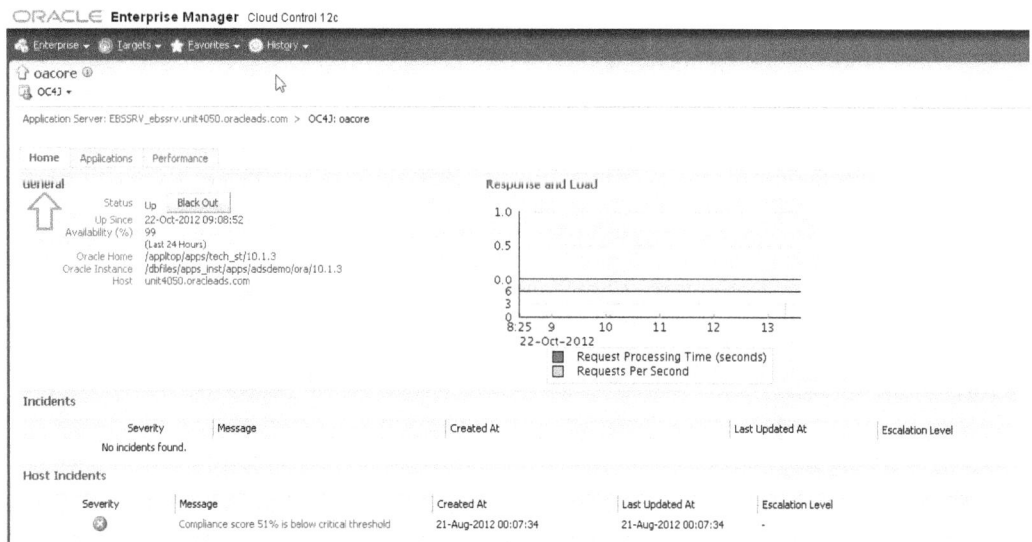

FIGURE 7-32. *The OC4J target page in Enterprise Manager*

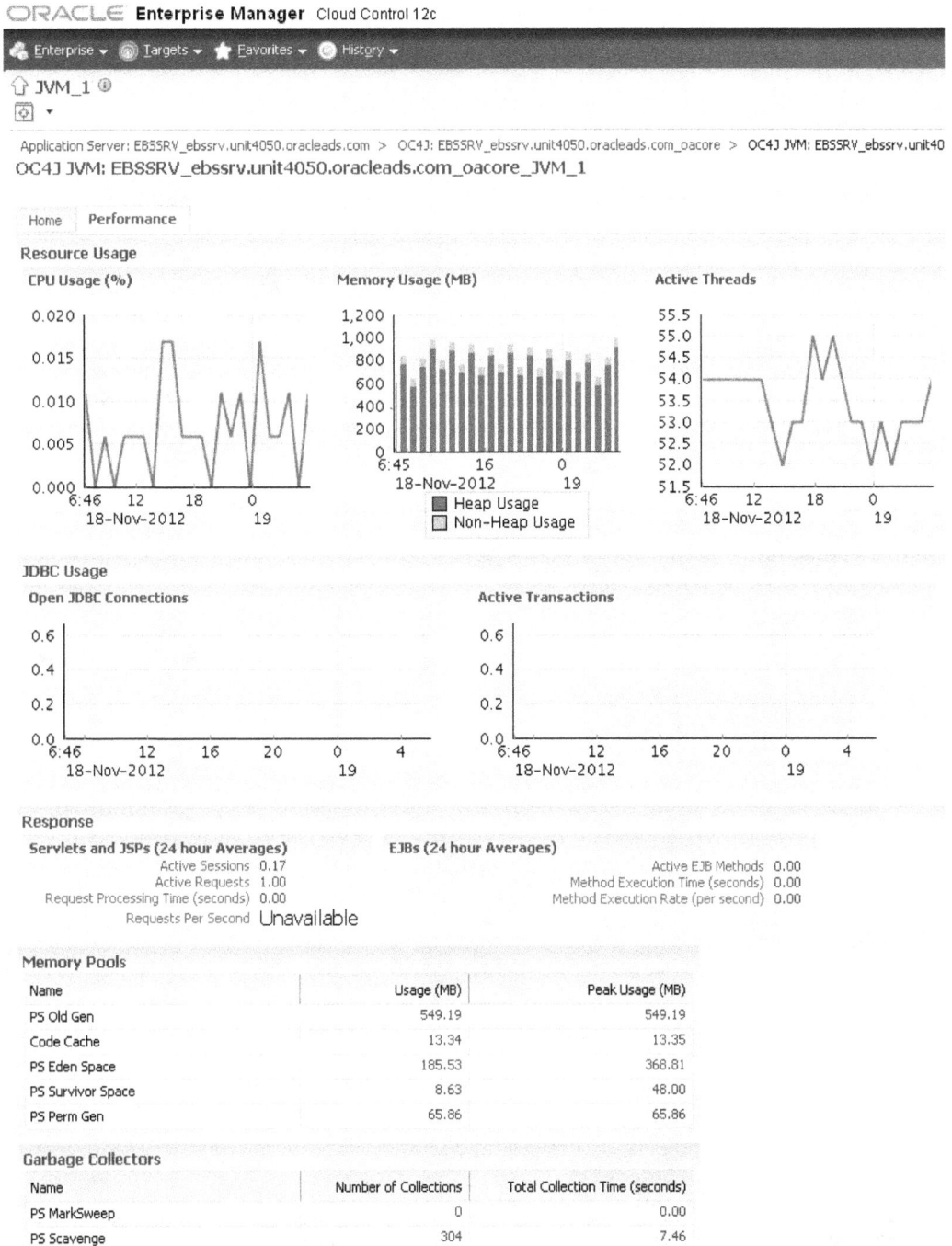

FIGURE 7-33. *The Performance tab for the OC4J JVM target*

connection usage, response times for the different component types, as well as JVM internals like memory pool usage and garbage collection.

For even more detail on JVM performance and analysis, Enterprise Manager 12c Cloud Control offers a feature called JVM Diagnostics, as shown in Figure 7-34. This sets up local agents that monitor each JVM instance and provide detailed reports and data on activity history; it also includes many additional tuning features.

Pool Monitors

Pools provide a predefined set of resources that are initialized and ready for use. When needed, an API is used to retrieve a resource from the pool. Once the use is complete, it is safely returned back for another process to use. The resources in the pool are managed as a set, exposing usage and simplifying administration. There are a number of technologies that use resource pooling, but we'll begin with the application module pool used by OA Framework to manage data in memory.

Oracle Applications Framework provides a few pages with information for use in performance management. We discussed troubleshooting for this in Chapter 5; however, there is a variety of information available, such as component status, properties and parameters, active pools and sessions, versions, and a variety of metrics. Figure 7-35 shows a few such metrics from the Show

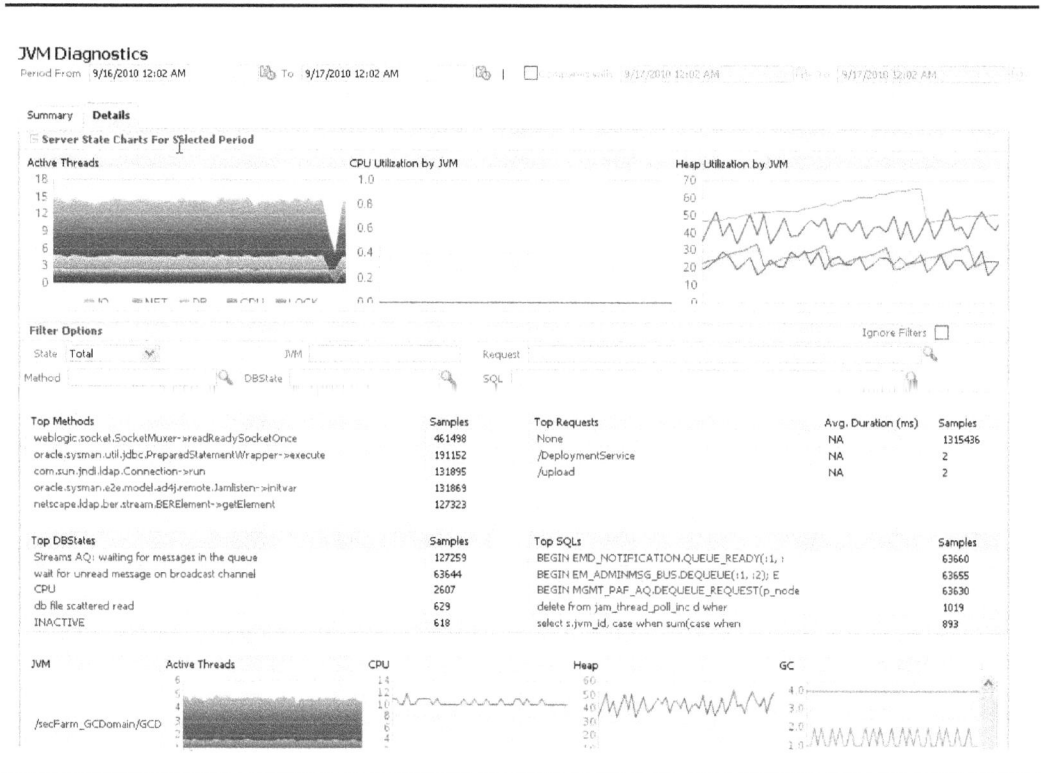

FIGURE 7-34. *A summary page from the advanced JVM Diagnostics feature*

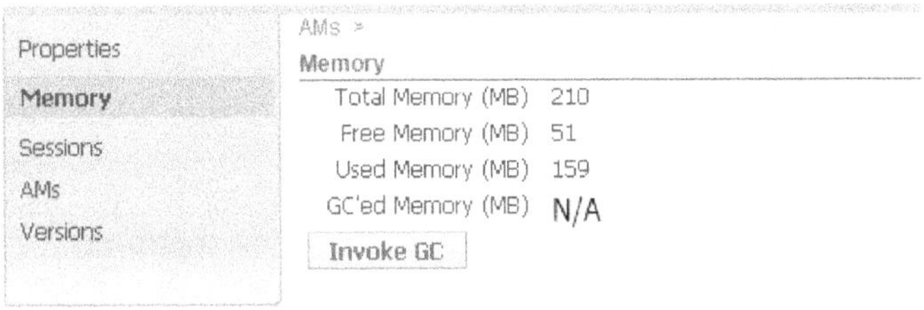

FIGURE 7-35. *Current JVM memory usage as shown in the Show Pool Monitor page*

Pool Monitor page available from a list of values under the Diagnostics link in any OA Framework page (with profile FND: Diagnostics = Y).

Back in Chapter 5, Figure 5-24 showed the application module (AMs) detail page accessible from the same diagnostics link, and how it can be used to see what OA Framework objects are currently in memory and some of their details, such as view objects, sessions, status information, and various timestamps.

Middle-tier resource consumption will also be influenced by the settings used for the application module and Connection Pooling. Please refer to My Oracle Support Note 395445.1 in the section entitled "Application Module Pooling." A detailed explanation of application modules and connection pooling can be found in the related section of the OA Framework Developer's Guide (Note 394780.1), which goes into the mechanics behind the pooling architecture for BC4J and AOL/J JDBC connections, including mechanisms for monitoring and tuning custom application modules and JDBC connections.

Another key performance resource for E-Business Suite is the database connection pool. This can also be actively interrogated and monitored and is often important to review for performance management, looking for things like waiting connections and exhausted resources.

The AOL/J Database Connection Pool Status page, available from the System Administration responsibility under Diagnostics, is a simple yet well used way of gathering such information and, as shown in Figure 7-36, it shows the configurations and lots of real-time statistics for these types of connections.

More detail can be found in the OA Framework Developers Guide, in the section on JDBC Pooling, as well as in the useful whitepaper in Note 278868.1.

Java Configuration

JVM parameters and configuration do vary by both deployment type (test, production, and so on) and the overall objectives set for the instance, including of course its performance targets. These targets apply throughout the technology stack but are especially important in the Java layer, where a substantial proportion of the processing load executes. Fortunately, there are a host of different Java configuration options available, and the list below introduces some of those most commonly used by E-Business Suite in relation to performance. As mentioned already, Oracle Applications

petra.de.oracle.com:8000/OA_HTML/jsp/fnd/AoljDbcPoolStatus.jsp

AOL/J Diagnostic Tests

ORACLE
E-BUSINESS SUITE

AOL/J Database Connection Pool Status
November 19, 2012 4:55:23 PM CET

Configuration Tips

Pool Created: Nov 15, 2012 1:30:44 PM CET

Configuration Parameters

FND_JDBC_MAX_CONNECTIONS: 500
FND_JDBC_BUFFER_MIN: 1
FND_JDBC_BUFFER_MAX: 5
FND_JDBC_BUFFER_DECAY_INTERVAL: 300
FND_JDBC_BUFFER_DECAY_SIZE: 5
FND_JDBC_USABLE_CHECK: false
FND_JDBC_CONTEXT_CHECK: true
FND_JDBC_PLSQL_RESET: false

Current Statistics

available connections: 4
locked connections: 6
leaked connections: 0
connections currently being created: 0
pool size counter: 10
clients waiting: 0

Lifetime Statistics

request: 8156
request successful: 8156
request timed out: 0
connection creation failed: 0
connection created: 89
connection created by thread: 82
connection creation by thread failed: 0
connection destroyed: 79
connection destroyed by thread: 77
closed connections: 2
abandoned connections: 0
removed available connection 0
pool at maximum size: 0
buffer empty: 7
context mismatch: 2393
not usable: 0

FIGURE 7-36. *The AOL/J Database Connection Pool Status page*

Manager, AutoConfig, and the Show Pool Monitor pages are the places to check and manage these values.

- **Deployment architecture**   The capacity plans for the instance, coupled with benchmark tests, may dictate that the Java environment needs scaling up to provide resources to handle the request volume and throughput that will be expected. Increasing the number of OACore JVMs using clustering techniques and even setting the memory sizing is a complex matter that often requires extensive testing, tuning over time, and specialist expert input.

- **Garbage collection**   While garbage collection is a low-level configuration, when set incorrectly it can have obvious effects. Generally speaking, while it seems logical to increase JVM heap size to provide more available memory, it causes garbage collection to take longer, ultimately causing pauses in the application. Thus, while the administration overhead might be more, increasing the number of JVMs each with a smaller heap may prove more beneficial.

- **Hardware Scale**   The general recommendation is for one JVM (OC4J instance) per CPU on the hardware, allowing little bottleneck between the two. Oracle has suggested that having two CPUs per JVM would be an even better configuration, although cost becomes a factor here.

- **Concurrency Scale**   Similarly a rough guideline is to have one OACore JVM per 80–100 active users. This is a broad recommendation since it may depend on the load from what those users will be doing.

- **Memory Configuration**   As a broad guideline for detailed JVM memory configuration, the following is regularly recommended for E-Business Suite 12.1.x when using the 11*g* database version. More details can be found in Note 362851.1.

  - Xmx = 1024M

  - Xms = 512M

  - MaxPermSize = 256M

  - NewRatio = 2

- **A small JVM for Forms**   The OC4J instance that is used for Oracle Forms (servlet mode) doesn't do much processing work, so it is recommended that one instance should be sufficient for 100–250 concurrent users. The instance can also be set with a smaller heap size, as processing is not long lived or resource hungry, such as Xmx of 256M and Xms of 128M.

- **Disable OAFM**   The third and final OC4J instance for E-Business Suite (after Forms and OACore) is OAFM, which is used for special features only, including MapViewer and SOA processing. If these features are not used, this can be disabled entirely. See My Oracle Support Note 763658.1 for more details.

- **Keep up to date**   Use the latest certified version of the Java runtime, currently JDK 1.6, and watch for later updates so that additional native performance benefits are available. See Note 455492.1 for details.

General Recommendations

Java performance management for E-Business Suite is so context sensitive that prescriptive advice and many specific tips, tricks, and techniques often get lost in the noise of all the possible situations and requirements. So here are some of the more commonly used techniques to ensure Java performance is good, well managed, and well monitored:

■ **Use caching**   When static page elements and JavaScript libraries are cached locally, it can significantly reduce network calls. You can do this by turning on the mod_expires feature in the HTTP Server, done via E-Business Suite's AutoConfig tool. Similarly, the application server can be provisioned with advanced caching tools. Caching capabilities also include the Java Object Cache (see Note 455194.1) and the Oracle Application Server Web Cache (see Note 380486.1), both of which support E-Business Suite Release 12 onward and can offer significant performance management features and solutions.

■ **Set user timeouts**   For example, setting the session timeout value to 30mins has been proven to improve resource utilization because users frequently forget to logout properly. More examples of this are given in the "User Sessions" section in the Oracle Application Framework Developer's Guide (Note 394780.1).

■ **Set user limits**   You do this most commonly through profile option FND: View Object Max Fetch Size, which, when set at site level (defaults to 200) means all users can only return up to this number of rows from SQL queries, avoiding broad queries that can use up resources.

■ **Gather data**   When problems occur, it's good to know the tools available, such as the best management console pages described previously, plus lower level tools like getting thread and heap dumps as described in Notes 833913.1 and 835909.1, respectively. Keeping a handy reference of the tools available in your environment can be invaluable and a real time-saver.

OA Framework and Java Further Reading

The following selection of documents and notes provide more detail on Java and OA Framework–based components and the tools and techniques available for their performance management. Most have been called out already in this discussion but are repeated here for an easy-to-use reference.

■ **Note 362851.1**   Guidelines on Setting up the JVM in Apps E-Business Suite 11*i* and Release 12

■ **Note 567551.1**   Configuring Various JVM Tuning Parameters for Oracle E-Business Suite 11*i* and Release 12

■ **Note 462550.1**   Generate JVM Heap Dump in E-Business Suite 11*i* and Release 12

■ **Note 1108093.1**   Oracle E-Business Suite Java Caching Framework Developer's Guide, Release 12

■ **Note 380489.1**   Using Load Balancers with Oracle E-Business Suite Release 12

■ **Note 828157.1**   Useful Articles for the Oracle E-Business Suite Technology Stack for Technical Consultant/DBA

■ **Oracle Application Framework Developers Guide**   AOL/J and OAF Caching

- **Oracle E-Business Suite Administrators Guide**:

  - Administering Oracle HTTP Server and AdminAppServer Utility

  - Oracle Application Server with Oracle E-Business Suite

Database Performance Management

In this section, we'll look at the tools, techniques, and recommendations for ensuring that the database at the heart of an E-Business Suite instance is efficient and well managed. This includes but is not limited to the generic topic of database performance tuning. We'll also include many key concepts along with other E-Business Suite specifics.

As part of a prepackaged application, the database management for E-Business Suite has a special context that much of the traditional database management texts do not include. This means not all the native approaches, features, and configurations are applicable when compared with a home-grown application. One example is SQL statement tuning, where changes to the queries inside E-Business Suite code are not recommended.

Database Dashboards and Monitor Consoles

As you've seen in many screenshots, Oracle Applications Manager does include database level performance statistics and information. For example, the overall Performance dashboard shown previously in Figure 7-12 shows basic database performance information, and the detailed Concurrent Processing pages include a drill into the database session performance data of particular request.

In addition, there is a dedicated Database Status Details dashboard with all the key statistics that can help in reviewing configurations, resources, and managing performance. Figure 7-37 shows this page, with basic information at the top (including a drill into sessions), current data on wait events, internal activity in the system statistics region, tablespace resources available, and rollback segments and extents.

In addition, just as we saw for Oracle Application Server, when you implement Enterprise Manager in your E-Business Suite environment there is a whole host of additional features, reports, and analytics available for use in performance management. As mentioned, Enterprise Manager requires a separate installation and is not provided by Rapid Wizard, although where they exist all the equivalent scripts and programs are there in the E-Business Suite database ORACLE_HOME.

As you might expect, Enterprise Manager has extensive support for database management, providing the broadest and most complete set of capabilities compared with any of the myriad of other technology components it manages. Most of these can be used effectively to offer superior management of the E-Business Suite database.

As shown in Figure 7-38, there is a dedicated performance menu item for the database target type, with a host of features available. These are discussed in more detail throughout this section:

- Prebuilt monitoring dashboards showing the most important metrics

- Submenus of SQL and Automatic Workload Repository–related tools

- Access to proactive performance analysis tools known as advisors

- Tools to help with real-time serious problems

- Analysis tools to trace problematic sessions

- Database replay feature for reviewing recent activities in detail

ORACLE Applications Manager

Applications Dashboard   Site Map

⊙ Wait Events   ⊙ Memory Statistics   ⊙ System Statistics   ⊙ Tablespaces and Status   ⊙ Rollback Segments and Extents

Database Status Details: R1213

Instance Status

Name ▼	Host	Version	Startup Time	State	Shutdown Pending	Status	Role	Sessions
R1213	petra.de.oracle.com	11.1.0.7.0	24-Feb-2012 13:53:21	OPEN	NO	✓	PRIMARY_INSTANCE	103

Wait Events   **Memory Statistics**

⊙ Previous 1-10 of 15 ▼ Next 5 ⊙

Name ▼	Total Number of Waits
smon timer	1
rdbms ipc message	11
pmon timer	1
pipe get	6
fbar timer	1
VKTM Logical Idle Wait	1
Streams AQ: waiting for time management or cleanup tasks	1

System Statistics   ⊙ Return to Top

⊙ Previous 1-10 of 33 ▼ Next 10 ⊙

Class ▼	Name	Value
128	background timeouts	90.074.029,00
128	messages received	38.615.672,00
128	messages sent	38.615.669,00
128	spare statistic 3	0
64	cell physical IO interconnect bytes	4.783.610.575.360,00
40	gc local grants	0

Tablespaces and Status

Tablespaces and Status

⊙ Previous 1-10 of 69 ▼ Next 10 ⊙

Name ▼	Size, MB	Used, MB	Free, MB	%Free
XDB	65,00	54,81	10,19	16
WCRSYS_TS	3,00	1,69	1,31	44
UNDO_TBS	3.686,41	2.553,34	1.133,06	31
UDDISYS_TS	22,00	19,13	2,88	13
TS_SIM_X	50,00	0,06	49,94	100
TS_SIM	50,00	0,06	49,94	100
TS_SALES_DATA_ENGINE	50,00	0,06	49,94	100
TS_SALES_DATA	50,00	0,06	49,94	100

Rollback Segments and Extents   ⊙ Return to Top

⊙ Previous 1-10 of 12 ▼ Next 2 ⊙

Name ▼	Extents	Size, MB	Optimum, MB	High Water Mark, MB	Wraps	Extends	Status
_SYSSMU9_1228296233$	36	272,12	0,00	484,68	708	504	ONLINE
_SYSSMU8_1228296233$	31	232,12	0,00	477,12	666	472	ONLINE
_SYSSMU7_1228296233$	31	226,12	0,00	437,43	658	471	ONLINE
_SYSSMU11_1271325623$	21	152,12	0,00	312,43	462	311	ONLINE

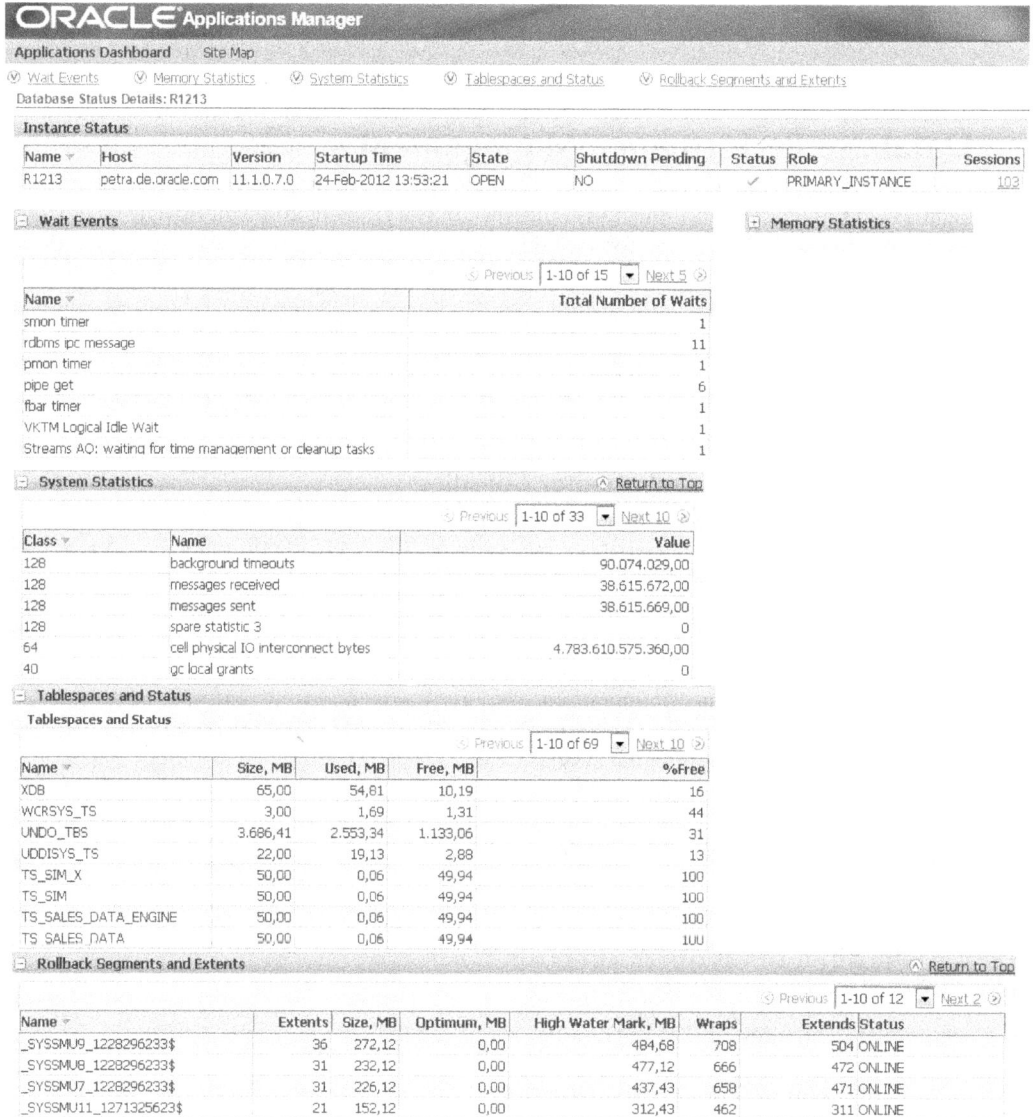

FIGURE 7-37. *Oracle Application Manager's Database Status Details dashboard*

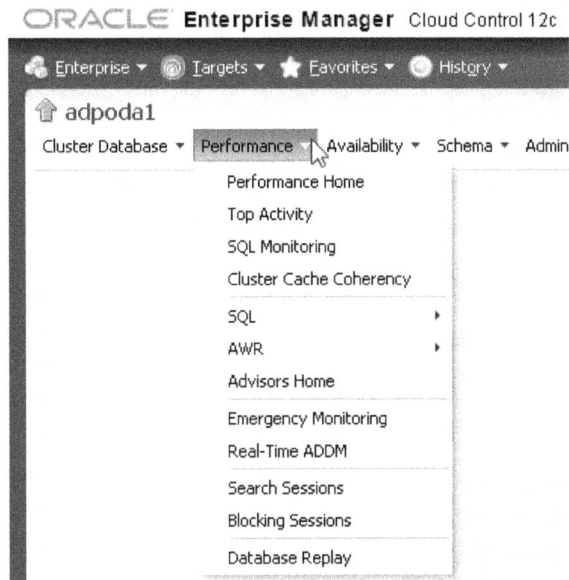

FIGURE 7-38. *The extensive performance features available in Enterprise Manager*

The first two items from the menu, Performance Home and Top Activity, are shown in Figures 7-39 and 7-40, respectively. The Performance page shows a system load overview with tabs to more detailed information on I/O, parallel execution, and any component services used. As you can see, this page shows recent data (against the default hourly baseline), but it can also display past snapshot periods. The various links and buttons provide quick access to detailed features should problems be identified on the dashboard. The Top Activity page shows more detailed information for a set period, indicated by the shading in the chart. This includes the most active SQL statements and sessions, both of which are clickable to see the exact statement and activities being performed at that time.

In addition to predefined dashboards and reports, Enterprise Manager exposes all metrics for use as required; it also supports metric extensions for defining your own critical monitoring values and allows the incorporation of those into custom pages, reports, and notifications also. More details can be found in the Oracle Enterprise Manager Cloud Control Administrator's Guide (E24473-20) in Chapter 8, "Using Metric Extensions."

Turning to slightly more invasive management features, the Administration menu in Enterprise Manager offers features like the Resource Manager that may be used with E-Business Suite. This tool allows the creation of *plans* that are sets of directives that specify how resources, such as maximum execute time or CPU, are allocated. These plans are then assigned to specific groups of users who have a similar usage profile. While this may be seen as rather a strong enforcement technique, setting upper limits this way can prevent problems that could affect the system as a whole. It can also be used to guarantee resources for critical activities or users.

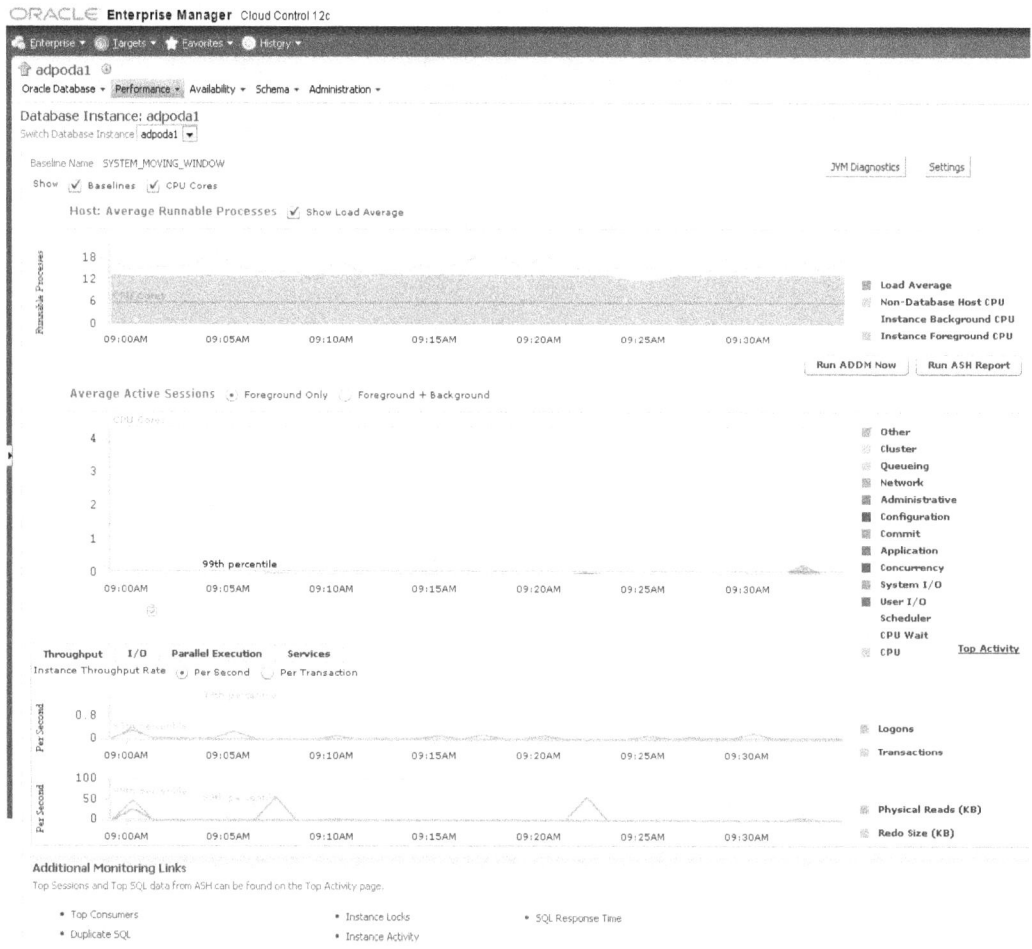

FIGURE 7-39. *The Performance Home dashboard*

We hit on a few database performance diagnostic tools back in our reliability toolbox in Chapter 5. We'll revisit those with a bit more focus this time and add a few more than are proven to be essential for a complete E-Business Suite database performance management plan.

Database Performance Diagnostics

As mentioned at the start of this chapter, around 80 percent of performance issues for E-Business Suite are caused by problems at the data level; therefore, application administrators should be familiar with the related database analysis tools.

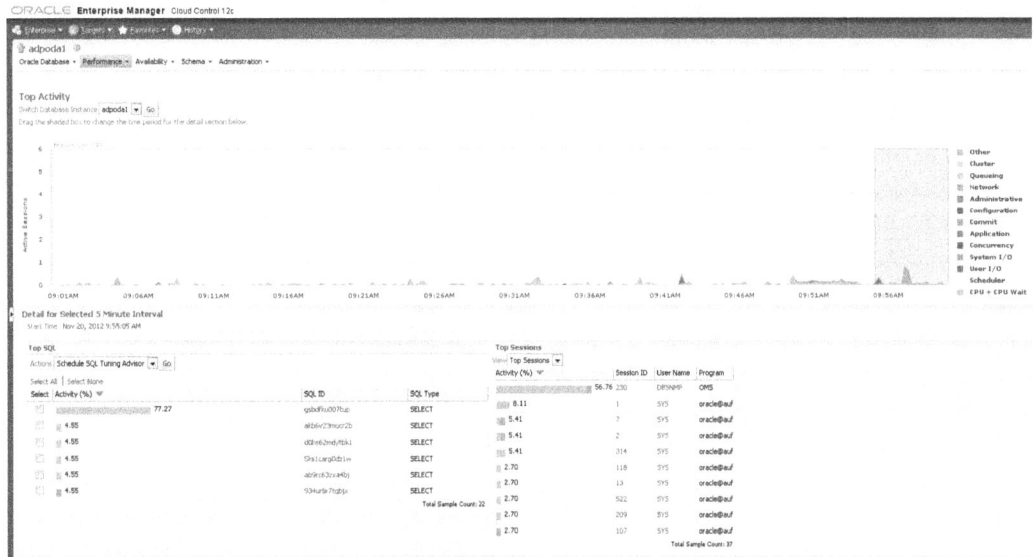

FIGURE 7-40.   *The Top Activity dashboard*

All E-Business Suite actions performed on the applications database can be logged to a file, generally known as a database trace. Understanding what queries, inserts, updates, or deletes occurred during the user's problematic actions often provides an insight into what data and activity might be contributing to the issue.

Enabling this requires configuration, and as explained in section "FND: Diagnostics" of Chapter 5, the Set Trace Level option turns this on for one user for all OA Framework pages they visit, and it performs an equivalent action for the user's Oracle Forms session, under the Forms Help | Diagnostics menu shown previously in Figure 5-21. It is generally recommended that you set the user tracing with binds and waits included in order to obtain a more complete output.

Tracing creates what is known as a raw trace file, and without a great deal of expertise and a strong eye for detail it is tough to interpret. However, several tools exist that convert and enhance it to create a more usable output. One example is TKPROF; the first image in Figure 7-41 shows the raw output while the second image shows the interpreted output. Another example is the TRCANLZR utility program.

In addition to a log of activity, errors that have occurred are captured in the database alert log file. This file has details of system level process events and any failures. It is a rich resource that captures many attributes in time-stamped log lines.

If the problematic query is known, there is another tool that can be used to diagnose that particular statement, creating a detailed report on its execution. This is the SQLT or SQLTXPLAIN tool and its use is detailed in Note 215187.1.

Finally, if the performance issue occurs for a specific period of time, the PL/SQL Profiler may be of use. This is also available for applications users to enable themselves, recording all the queries run through the system for later analysis. For more details on this, see My Oracle Support Note 808005.1.

```
apr1213@petra:/r1213/oracle/R1213/db/tech_st/11.1.0/admin/R1213_petra/diag/rdbms/r1213/R1213/t...  ⊡  □  ⊠

PARSING IN CURSOR #108 len=340 dep=1 uid=65 oct=3 lid=65 tim=1353428372511130 hv=38
07685801 ad='9446aee8' sqlid='d2t4farjg9b59'
select to_char(CODE_COMBINATION_ID), nvl(ENABLED_FLAG, 'Y'), nvl(SUMMARY_FLAG, 'N')
, to_char(START_DATE_ACTIVE, 'YYYY/MM/DD HH24:MI:SS'), to_char(END_DATE_ACTIVE, 'YY
YY/MM/DD HH24:MI:SS'), SEGMENT1, SEGMENT2, SEGMENT3, SEGMENT4, SEGMENT5 from GL_COD
E_COMBINATIONS where CHART_OF_ACCOUNTS_ID = :FND_BIND1 and CODE_COMBINATION_ID = :F
ND_BIND2
END OF STMT
PARSE #108:c=0,e=111,p=0,cr=0,cu=0,mis=0,r=0,dep=1,og=1,plh=0,tim=1353428372511129
BINDS #108:
 Bind#0
  oacdty=02 mxl=22(22) mxlc=00 mal=00 scl=00 pre=00
  oacflg=13 fl2=0001 frm=00 csi=00 siz=48 off=0
  kxsbbbfp=2a98627000  bln=22  avl=03  flg=05
  value=101
 Bind#1
  oacdty=02 mxl=22(22) mxlc=00 mal=00 scl=00 pre=00
  oacflg=13 fl2=0001 frm=00 csi=00 siz=0 off=24
  kxsbbbfp=2a98627018  bln=22  avl=04  flg=01
  value=13799
EXEC #108:c=0,e=1187,p=0,cr=0,cu=0,mis=1,r=0,dep=1,og=1,plh=1623987546,tim=13534283
72512495
FETCH #108:c=0,e=37,p=0,cr=3,cu=0,mis=0,r=1,dep=1,og=1,plh=1623987546,tim=135342837
2512568
STAT #108 id=1 cnt=1 pid=0 pos=1 obj=35936 op='TABLE ACCESS BY INDEX ROWID GL_CODE_
COMBINATIONS (cr=3 pr=0 pw=0 time=0 us cost=2 size=40 card=1)'
STAT #108 id=2 cnt=1 pid=1 pos=1 obj=35944 op='INDEX UNIQUE SCAN GL_CODE_COMBINATIO
NS_U1 (cr=2 pr=0 pw=0 time=0 us cost=1 size=0 card=1)'
FETCH #108:c=0,e=1,p=0,cr=0,cu=0,mis=0,r=0,dep=1,og=0,plh=1623987546,tim=1353428372
512618
CLOSE #108:c=0,e=6,dep=1,type=0,tim=1353428372512661
====================
```

FIGURE 7-41. *First image showing the raw trace output and the second showing the same after it was run through TKPROF (continued)*

```
apr1213@petra:~

*************************************************************************

select to_char(CODE_COMBINATION_ID), nvl(ENABLED_FLAG, 'Y'), nvl(SUMMARY_FLAG,
   'N'), to_char(START_DATE_ACTIVE, 'YYYY/MM/DD HH24:MI:SS'),
   to_char(END_DATE_ACTIVE, 'YYYY/MM/DD HH24:MI:SS'), SEGMENT1, SEGMENT2,
   SEGMENT3, SEGMENT4, SEGMENT5
from
 GL_CODE_COMBINATIONS where CHART_OF_ACCOUNTS_ID = :FND_BIND1 and
   CODE_COMBINATION_ID = :FND_BIND2


call     count       cpu    elapsed      disk      query    current       rows
------- ------  -------- ---------- --------- ---------- ---------- ----------
Parse        1      0.00       0.00         0          0          0          0
Execute      1      0.00       0.00         0          0          0          0
Fetch        2      0.00       0.00         0          3          0          1
------- ------  -------- ---------- --------- ---------- ---------- ----------
total        4      0.00       0.00         0          3          0          1

Misses in library cache during parse: 0
Misses in library cache during execute: 1
Optimizer mode: ALL_ROWS
Parsing user id: 65      (recursive depth: 1)

Rows     Row Source Operation
------- ---------------------------------------------------------
      1   TABLE ACCESS BY INDEX ROWID GL_CODE_COMBINATIONS (cr=3 pr=0 pw=0 time=0 us
 cost=2 size=40 card=1)
      1    INDEX UNIQUE SCAN GL_CODE_COMBINATIONS_U1 (cr=2 pr=0 pw=0 time=0 us cost=
1 size=0 card=1)(object id 35944)


*************************************************************************
```

FIGURE 7-41. *First image showing the raw trace output and the second showing the same after it was run through TKPROF*

In addition to these tools, Enterprise Manager exposes other powerful features for diagnosing performance management issues: there is a whole submenu of items related to diagnosing SQL query issues, as shown in Figure 7-42. While editing E-Business Suite code is not possible, checking the data to find the root cause of a poorly performing query is essential. From this menu, I recommend you consider the SQL Performance Analyzer and the Search SQL options. The first provides a detailed analysis of a SQL Tuning Set, which is a collection of specific statements run during a specific period. Figure 7-43 shows the entire list of advisors, including the SQL Performance Analyzer, available for running against SQL tuning sets.

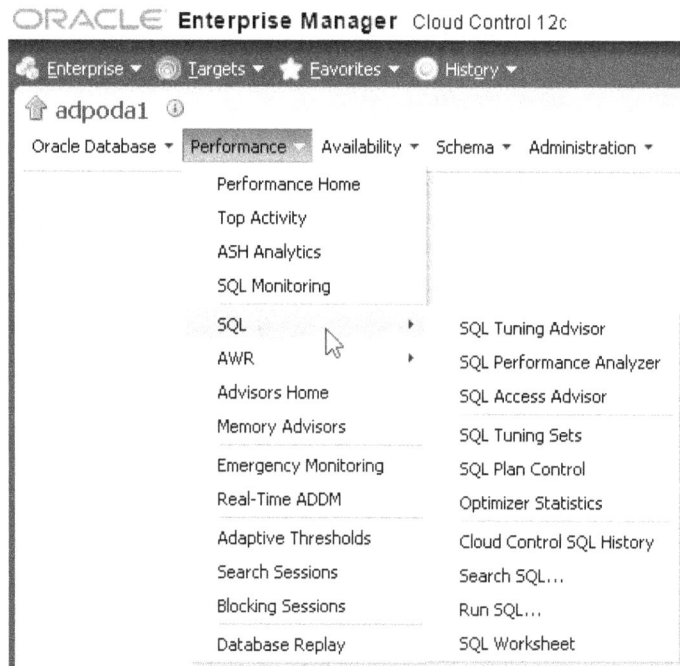

FIGURE 7-42. *Performance submenu of features for diagnosing SQL*

The Search SQL option can help you quickly find problematic SQL statements run by E-Business Suite, since often there are so many internal queries run by the various components that the one issued by the application get lost in the noise. Once the problematic query has been determined, it's possible to drill into more detail such as locks, waits, and execution plans without even having to run traces at all.

Finally, since I mentioned errors at the start of this section, it would be remiss not to mention the fact that all occurrences of database (ORA-) errors are captured as incidents by Enterprise Manager. These are associated with various diagnostics such as traces and logs and displayed on the various dashboard pages. When clicked, the problem details are displayed with error messages, diagnostic output files, and options to review, analyze, and even upload to Oracle Support.

Don't forget to use the database information in combination with diagnostics from the functional process issuing the queries. This includes the Forms Runtime Diagnostics (FRD) trace (Note 445166.1) and, for reports, the Reports Client Process Trace commonly enabled from a check box in the associated concurrent request (Note 111311.1). Similarly, it makes sense to cross-reference database diagnostics with visibility into the runtime hardware performance, such as the operating system's performance data from both the application server and the database host machines. This granular information, such as details on CPU and memory consumption at the process level, has often been required to aid diagnosis; tools for this include the OS Watcher tool, described in My Oracle Support Note 301137.1 and the "Hardware" section, later in this chapter.

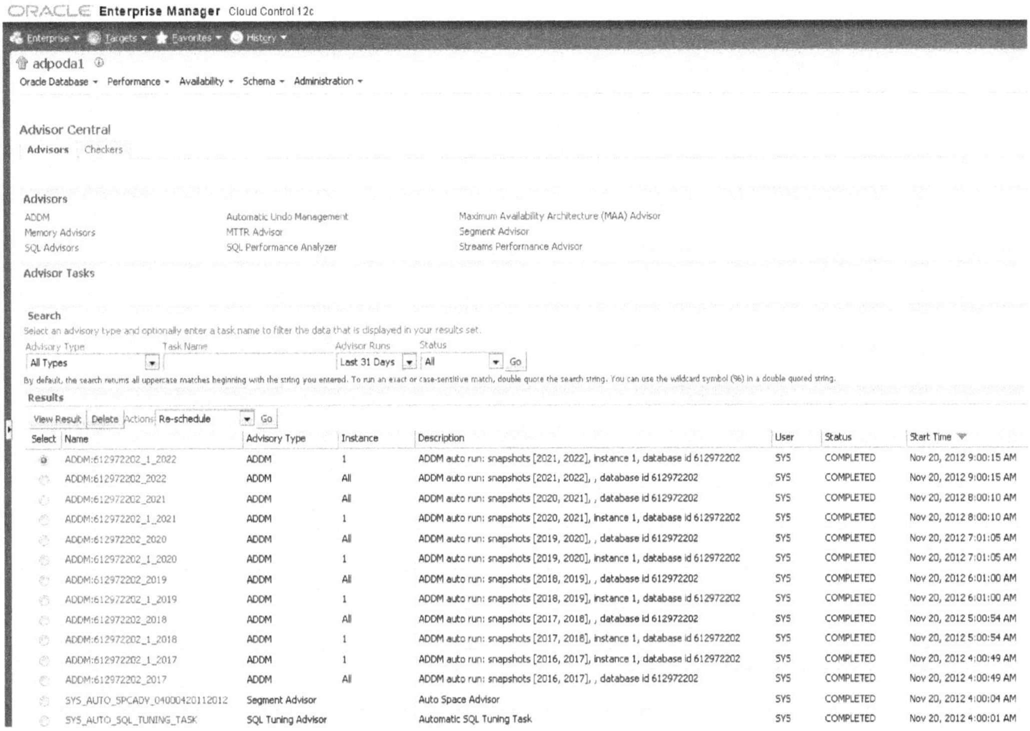

FIGURE 7-43. *The various advisors available for running against SQL statements*

In addition, there are two essential My Oracle Support notes that offer exact steps on using the tools mentioned, one for basic issues and another for more in-depth performance issues:

- **Note 1121043.1** Collecting Diagnostic Data for Performance Issues in Oracle E-Business Suite
- **Note 1362660.1** Gather Enhanced Performance Diagnostics for Oracle E-Business Suite

While these notes are not specific to database use, this is where the majority of issues occur and, therefore, the content focuses on this area.

Automatic Workload Repository (AWR), Automatic Database Diagnostic Monitor (ADDM), and Active Session History (ASH)

The Automatic Workload Repository (AWR), Automatic Database Diagnostic Monitor (ADDM), and Active Session History (ASH) tools are relatively new to the Oracle database, but they bring enormous benefits to performance management and problem troubleshooting. This section describes them at a high level and offers resources to find out more.

From the 11g version onward, the Automatic Workload Repository keeps a record of performance data based on a standard baseline or regular snapshots, which by default are taken at hourly intervals. The principle is that by comparing the data it can be easier to identify anomalies, trends, and patterns. Each baseline and snapshot can be viewed as a report, launched either from the command line via awrrpt.sql or from within Enterprise Manager, as shown in Figure 7-44. The output is available in the page or can be downloaded as a file. This rich resource includes large amounts of data for each of the following sections:

- Report Summary (as shown in the figure)
- Wait Events Statistics
- SQL Statistics
- Instance Activity Statistics
- IO Stats
- Buffer Pool Statistics
- Advisory Statistics

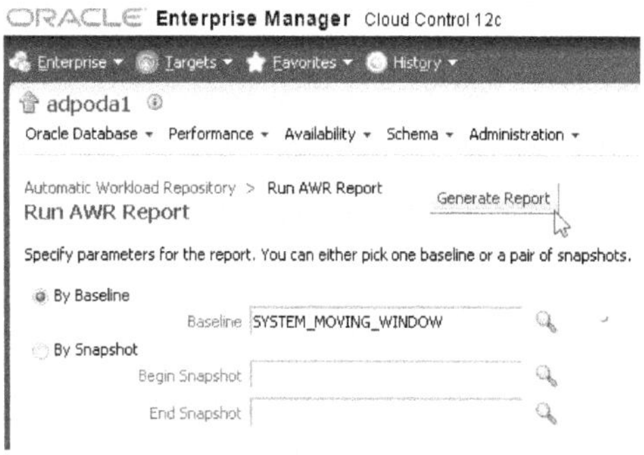

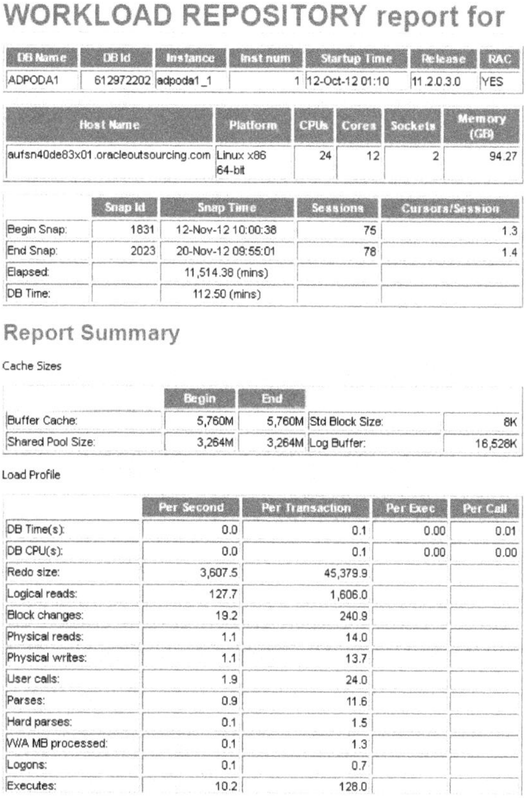

FIGURE 7-44. Generating the AWR Report from Enterprise Manager

- Wait, Undo, and Latch Statistics
- Segment Statistics
- Dictionary and Library Cache Statistics
- Memory Statistics
- Streams Statistics
- Resource Limit Statistics
- Shared Server Statistics
- All init.ora Parameters

With such detailed performance information available, the next step is diagnosis. Manually checking the output for clues is often required, but there is a tool that automates much of this: the Automatic Database Diagnostic Monitor (ADDM). This tool can reveal the symptoms of known issues and perform diagnosis, providing corrective recommendations. Like AWR, it can be run from the command line via addmrpt.sql or, more commonly, from Enterprise Manager. It supports issues related to CPU, memory, I/O, resource intensive SQL, PL/SQL and Java, Real Application Clusters, and configuration. These two tools together also have the benefit of being available at runtime, reducing the need to reproduce complex and severe issues.

Active Session History (ASH) is somewhat similar to AWR in terms of collecting system activity and performance data; however, it does this for individual database sessions, creating a more granular collection than AWR, which runs for the whole database instance. The benefits are that this data is available for more context-sensitive problems where it affects only a single activity or user, or where it occurs for only a small period of time. It has a report that can be run either as a script (ashrpt.sql) or from Enterprise Manager, where the ASH Analytics detailed capability (under the Performance menu) helps diagnosis.

This is a high-level overview of these features, and more detail can be found in these essential resources:

- **Note 748642.1** How to Generate an AWR Report and Create Baselines
- **Note 250655.1** How to Use the Automatic Database Diagnostic Monitor
- **Note 1438123.1** Extract Additional SQL Information from ASH, AWR, ADDM, and V$SQL_PLAN
- **Oracle Database Performance Tuning Guide** E16638-05

E-Business Suite Configuration and Scripts

While the database that runs E-Business Suite is deployed through Rapid Wizard and set up through AutoConfig, it remains a vanilla Oracle Database. This is beneficial for many reasons, including more standardization, reduced dependencies, and the fact that it includes the latest tools and features for use with E-Business Suite (after certification, of course). That said, there are certain parameters that are recommended for use with E-Business Suite, and Oracle offers guidelines on the values to use, based on either known problems or optimizations.

The current E-Business Suite database configuration is exposed in multiple places, but, as shown in Figure 7-45, only Oracle Applications Manager provides both the current settings alongside the recommendations, highlighting any that do not match.

ORACLE Applications Manager

Applications Dashboard | Site Map

Complete List of Init.ora Parameters

Recommended/Mandatory Init.ora Parameters: R1213
Last Updated : 20-Nov-2012 18:08:30

Filter [Name ▼] [contains ▼] [   ] [Go]

Previous 1-25 of 57 ▼ Next 25

Parameter Name	Current Value	Recommended Value	Mandatory
O7_DICTIONARY_ACCESSIBILITY	FALSE	FALSE	TRUE
_index_join_enabled	FALSE	remove	TRUE
_schema_progression_cost	2147483647	remove	TRUE
max_dump_file_size	UNLIMITED	20480	FALSE
nls_language	american	remove	TRUE
plsql_code_type	INTERPRETED	NATIVE	TRUE
query_rewrite_enabled	true	remove	TRUE
sga_target	1073741824	x=2147483648	FALSE
shared_pool_reserved_size	41943040	>=62914560	FALSE
shared_pool_size	419430400	>=629145600	FALSE
timed_statistics	TRUE	remove	TRUE
undo_tablespace	UNDO_TBS	APPS_UNDOTS1	TRUE
_b_tree_bitmap_plans	FALSE	FALSE	TRUE
_fast_full_scan_enabled	FALSE	FALSE	TRUE
_like_with_bind_as_equality	TRUE	TRUE	TRUE
_optimizer_autostats_job	FALSE	FALSE	FALSE
_sort_elimination_cost_ratio	5	5	TRUE
_system_trig_enabled	TRUE	TRUE	TRUE
_trace_files_public	TRUE	TRUE	FALSE
aq_tm_processes	1	1	FALSE
background_dump_dest	/r1213/oracle/R1213/db/tech_st/11.1.0/admin/R1213_petra/diag/rdbms/r1213/R1213/trace	OS dependent	FALSE
compatible	11.1.0	11.1.0	TRUE
core_dump_dest	/r1213/oracle/R1213/db/tech_st/11.1.0/admin/R1213_petra/diag/rdbms/r1213/R1213/cdump	OS dependent	FALSE
cursor_sharing	EXACT	EXACT	TRUE
db_block_checking	FALSE	FALSE	FALSE

TIP: The rows that deviate from recommended values are marked with warning icons.
Parameters with recommended value as 'remove' need to be removed from the init.ora file.

Previous 1-25 of 57 ▼ Next 25

Complete List of Init.ora Parameters

FIGURE 7-45. *Oracle Applications Manager's validation of the E-Business Suite database configuration*

For detailed explanation of these parameters and the recommendations, see My Oracle Support Note 396009.1, Database Initialization Parameters for Oracle Applications Release 12 (for 11*i*, see Note 216205.1). In addition, there is an equivalent script for checking these same database parameters for use with E-Business Suite. SQL script bde_chk_cbo.sql is available for download from Note 174605.1.

While we're on the topic of scripts, there are some similar troubleshooting SQL scripts that are commonly used in performance issues. Most have been around for a long time but are still applicable in Release 12. These can be useful tools for quickly gathering core performance data. The following scripts are regularly used by Oracle Support today:

- **coe_stats.sql** Automate CBO Stats Gathering Using FND_STATS and Table Sizes (Note 156968.1)

- **bde_session.sql** Expensive SQL and resources utilization for given Session ID (Note 169630.1)

- **bde_last_analyzed.sql** Verify the CBO Statistics (Note 163208.1)

Use Database Features

In addition to the reactive tools and features we're discussed so far, a high-quality performance management plan includes adopting the best possible features and deployment options available, and with the Oracle database there are many. Here are the most important recommendations to consider implementing that give proven performance improvements with E-Business Suite:

- **Real Application Clusters**   Oracle strongly recommends production E-Business Suite databases be deployed on RAC architectures because they offer unparalleled performance and failover capabilities.

- **Oracle Applications Tablespace Model (OATM)**   This is a best practice for ensuring much better resource management (with it, 400 tablespaces becomes just 12, reducing storage space).

- **Automatic Storage Management and Automatic Memory Management**   This simplifies memory sizing, resource administration, and configuration tasks, a great benefit for over-stretched enterprise application managers.

- **Advanced Compression**   This reduces E-Business Suite table sizes up to a factor of four without sacrificing any noticeable query performance increase. This reduces storage, I/O, and network overhead, at the same time increasing the performance of many concurrent batch requests (payroll, order to cash, and so on).

- **Database Partitioning Option**   This organizes data storage by usage, which makes practical sense and has been used to improve E-Business Suite query performance for both analytics and transactional data. More details are in Note 554539.1.

Database Further Reading

The following list includes important documents that require more low-level detail to complete and implement many of the recommendations offered here, especially around reactive troubleshooting of performance problems. Some are specific to E-Business Suite, whereas others provide more detail on native capabilities that are fully supported. At first glance, this list might seem inordinately short, but the documents mentioned are comprehensive and provide additional resource references where needed:

- **Note 1121043.1**   Collecting Diagnostic Data for Performance Issues in Oracle E-Business Suite

- **Note 1362660.1**   Enhanced Performance Diagnostics for Oracle E-Business Suite Release 12.1.3

- **Note 169935.1**   Troubleshooting Oracle Applications Performance Issues

- **Note 744143.1**   Tuning Performance on E-Business Suite

- **The Oracle Database Performance Tuning Guide**   E16638-05

Network Management

Network Administration is not traditionally part of an E-Business Suite Application Management Plan, however, the delivery of a reliable, available, and high-performance service assumes a stable and effective network. As such the strong dependency means network management should not be taken for granted and a certain amount of visibility and involvement in its administration is essential.

This section reviews the tools most commonly used to get information about the networks involved in an E-Business Suite deployment, however as a key stakeholder there should be a regular liaison with the network management staff, which may include use of their specialist tools also.

Common Networking Tools

First, there are a host of common items that are used in trying to understand the performance of the connections between the E-Business Suite nodes, servers, and components. It is worth listing these out here, since some are often ignored or forgotten in what is often an urgent panic to understand what is going on.

- **Client Utility Programs**   Often useful to get basic connection data. Common examples are:

  - **Ping/TraCert**   For getting performance timings of a network roundtrip to the application server host machine.

  - **Traceroute/PathPing**   To see the network nodes and devices between the client and the E-Business Suite host server.

- **Firewalls and Proxy Servers**   There are various types of intermediary nodes filtering traffic based on rules that can sometimes change, alerting the flow. These tools have useful management consoles and usually maintain detail logs.

- **Network Acceleration hardware**   Again often with logs and consoles for checking traffic and performance.

- **Security**   Changes in protocols and equipment have often been attributed to changes in performance, and testing is recommended to properly manage user expectations.

- **Operating Systems and Java**   The native software upon which the E-Business Suite runs should be kept up to date including any fixes or improvements to its networking capabilities.

- **HTTP Server logs**   The access_log can be set to include timestamps, which can be useful for page request/response tracking.

Forms Network Test

Accessed via the System Administrator Responsibility, under Application, there is an item called Network Test. This provides a single form, shown in Figure 7-46, which runs an Oracle Forms round-tip process a number of times, and displays the timing results.

The most useful are the latency values, under the sample data section, and where one-way values over 3ms and round-trip values of more than 300ms are considered above average. The throughput region to the right of the form represents the bandwidth capacity measurement, which may be fairly meaningless on its own and is normally used in comparative analysis.

Be clear, this data is specific to the Oracle Forms performance, not the network alone, as it includes some internal processing. As mentioned, the data is generally used to compare different locations and over different time windows, so that performance issues can be identified and diagnosed.

The Client System Analyzer

In the "User Interface and Client Systems" section earlier we looked at this tool and mentioned the fact that in addition to supplying information about the PC client, it also performs some

FIGURE 7-46.   *The Network Test utility form for measuring client-server response times*

network performance tests. As shown in Figure 7-47, this is effectively a single latency and bandwidth testing output. It is different to the Forms Network Test however, since it does not include the internal forms processing, being just a round trip from browser to the Web Server. Again the recommendation is to use the results in a comparative manner, rather than delve too deeply into specific result values.

Common Networking Recommendations

The following is a short bullet list of best practice tips and advice for managing E-Business Suite network performance. Some may seem rather obvious, however, they still frequently get missed or ignored, resulting in unnecessary and costly problems.

- Server nodes should be connected to each other by fast connections on the same network switch.
- Use caching features (discussed already) to help speed up page delivery times.
- Ensure client hardware is up to date and configured properly, especially at remote locations.
- Consider implementing load balancing to reduce the effect of node outages

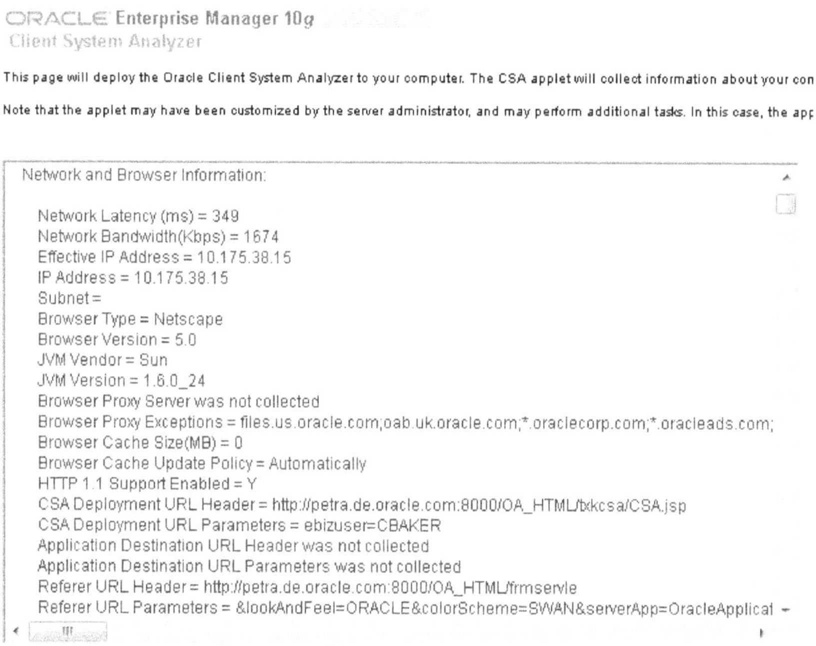

FIGURE 7-47. *Example output from the E-Business Suite Client System Analyzer*

- Look at SQL*Net connectivity (e.g. Note 69591.1) and JDBC connection pool tuning options.

- Review the whitepaper Oracle E-Business Suite Network Utilities: Best Practices in Note 556738.1.

Finally, it is important to proactively consider all remote client types that might be added to the user base. These days many different types of connections are possible and E-Business Suite supports users from many different backgrounds, including infrequent users, mobile users, and external users. Each remote connection type will give different performance results, such as LAN vs. WiFi vs. VPN vs. Satellite. Again, setting baselines and expectations is crucial to managing performance.

Hardware

There are many resources for understanding the performance management of servers and other hardware components, so again here we will provide some known best practices and recommendations that apply specifically to E-Business Suite.

Indeed, beyond minimum sizing, there are no real special hardware requirements for E-Business Suite (that currently supports nine different operating systems), therefore, generic hardware performance management and tuning techniques are all valid.

■ Make sure servers are properly managed and monitored, with a watchful eye on operating system metrics and resource consumption in all three tiers of E-Business Suite. In addition to the hardware vendors tools, operating system tools, and third-party utilities, consider again using Enterprise Manager as it contains a range of features and data that support management of host systems, as shown in Figure 7-48. Including this along with the E-Business Suite Management plug-in means all information and tools are available in one place, greatly simplifying the overall process.

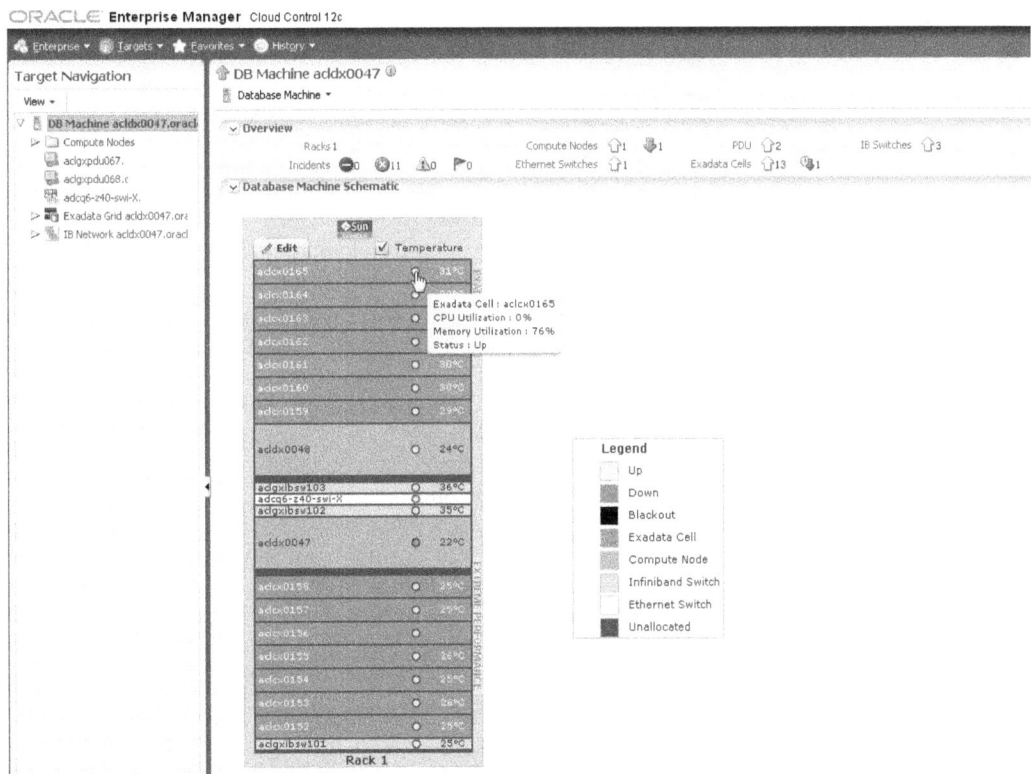

FIGURE 7-48. *The Oracle Exadata hardware as managed by Enterprise Manager*

- Consider the Oracle Exastack (currently Exadata, Exalogic, and Exalytics) hardware options, as discussed in the whitepaper in Note 1460742.1. These run E-Business Suite instances faster all around the world today, and benchmark tests have proven significant benefits against standard hardware, including:

  - Forms: 3x better response time and 2x better scalability

  - OA Framework: 8x better response time and 2x better scalability

- As mentioned before, use load balancers to improve performance across the topology. This has been discussed and see Note 727171.1 for more details.

One extra consideration in performance management that rarely gets a mention is that performance tuning a system means not only a faster application, but also lower hardware resource requirements and lower power consumption—thereby lower operating costs. As systems scale using the best performance management tools that deliver tuning improvements can pay for themselves quickly.

Integration Performance

There are many functional processes in E-Business Suite that support integration with external systems, such as automatically sending transactions to trading partners so they can act upon them quickly. Should these integrations run slowly they may in turn hold up the overall completion of the task.

This usually works at two levels: online and offline. First, in online integration problems the synchronous transmitted documents are a slow response, no response/timeout, or a failure message back. Here investigation from producer system, through the network, to consumer destination (and sometimes back again) is required, commonly through various component logs and tracing utilities.

The second level, offline, is asynchronous with external systems being sent documents to consume, get an acknowledgement response, which in turn triggers a business processes and the result of which is sent back into E-Business Suite via a callback. An example might be the Advanced Shipment Notice sent back sometime after a purchase order is received, to tell the purchaser when the goods will be delivered. The management of these integration processes requires similar steps already described, however, is normally less immediately technical, as the first stage is to check the success of the business processes itself.

E-Business Suite contains three integration solutions that use different technologies and support different document types. When used, each should be included in the performance management plan and be supported by the provision of monitoring tools. These are EDI Gateway, XML Gateway, and SOA Gateway, and more detail on the tools available can be found in the related product documentation guides on docs.oracle.com.

Load Testing

As a mature solution Oracle E-Business Suite has several in-house and third-party testing products available for running manual and automated performance and load testing cycles.

While support for HP's popular Winrunner testing tool has now ended, the replacement QuickTest Professional (QTP) has the following E-Business Suite Test Starter Kits available for immediate use:

- QTP Test Starter Kit for Release 12.1.1   Patch 8408886
- QTP Test Starter Kit for Release 12.0.4   Patch 6845309

In addition the Oracle Applications Testing Suite includes products for Load Testing—offering scalability, performance and capacity tests; Functional Testing for automated business process and regression testing; and Test Manager—for process management, automated test execution, and defect tracking. While these features are designed for use with any application, there are E-Business Suite accelerators available that provide out-of-the-box capability for immediate use.

While only briefly discussed here, much more on load testing can be found on Oracle.com and in the excellent E-Business Suite Technology Blog, such as this related post: http://blogs .oracle.com/stevenChan/entry/oats_ebs_certified.

Summary

Performance Management is tough, even more so for E-Business Suite, a broad enterprise application with a technologically diverse architecture. However using a holistic approach that considers all levels, situations, and requirements, coupled with knowledge and access to the array of tools available, it is not insurmountable.

In this chapter we again broke down the application into its three logical layers and picked apart each, focusing on monitoring and managing the performance of the key application components, as well as identifying those areas where an active approach is most significant. Here is the manifest repeated again as a reminder of what we covered.

Business Process Layer	Applications Technology Layer	Platform Layer
Key Performance Indicators	Oracle Applications Manager	Enterprise Manager
Product Specific Recommendations	Business Intelligence and Reports	User Interface and Client Systems
Logs and Traces	Workflow	Oracle Forms Server
End User Experience	E-Business Suite Search	OA Framework and Java
	Applications Data	Database
	Concurrent Processing	Network
		Hardware
		Integration and Load Testing

Finally, for handy reference here are again the key notes for performance troubleshooting in E-Business Suite.

- **Note 1121043.1** Collecting Diagnostic Data for Performance Issues in Oracle E-Business Suite
- **Note 1362660.1** Enhanced Performance Diagnostics for Oracle E-Business Suite
- **Note 244040.1** Oracle E-Business Suite Recommended Performance Patches
- **Note 69565.1** A Holistic Approach to Performance Tuning Oracle Applications Systems
- **Note 214088.1** Oracle Applications System Administration Scripts
- **Note 1340493.1** How To Trace Performance Issues
- **Note 864226.1** How Can I Diagnose Poor E-Business Suite Performance
- **Note 169935.1** Troubleshooting Oracle Applications Performance Issues

CHAPTER
8

An Optimization
Management Toolbox

I t sounds easy: stop the moaning and complaining and starting making improvements. The problem is that getting free time to look at what changes to make is often a luxury. However, unless you start, even in a small way, time will always be limited and management-by-crisis will be unlikely to change. Ask yourself how long you want to carry on like this—one more quarter, one more year, or indefinitely? Sometimes a quick thought about the future of your role is enough to drive a little change.

You might be surprised, but almost everything in E-Business Suite can be optimized, and far too often great opportunities to tweak and improve go unnoticed. This chapter gives some interesting examples, and I hope it will at least get you thinking and researching to find out what you may have missed. Another way of thinking about optimization is to rebrand it as *innovation*, a term today's corporate management love more than any other.

Opportunities for improvement exist throughout the technology stack, from base to summit, including on the server/storage hardware, O/S, and web and application servers; in networking, databases, Concurrent Manager and other managers, Workflow, the topology, security, integrations, forms, reports and intelligence; you can even optimize user activity. Covering all of this in full detail would create a chapter far too large to be of practical use, so instead we'll look at the themes and areas that I have found to be most effective for E-Business Suite.

What Is Optimization?

While related, this chapter is not just a repeat of the performance chapter, since optimization is much more than that. Reliability, and as shown in Figure 8-1 availability, performance, and governance can and should all be optimized, plus here we'll also take a holistic look at areas and methods beyond the essential management components, so that the complete solution has a solid core, complemented by an optimized infrastructure and key relationships.

Back in Chapter 2, we defined optimization as:

To ensure that the software helps meet the organizational objectives.

You might think this general statement sounds like the intent of the E-Business Suite instance as a whole, or perhaps the job definition of the Application Manager. While that's true, more specifically, optimization is the ability to continuously take progressive steps to strive toward this same goal.

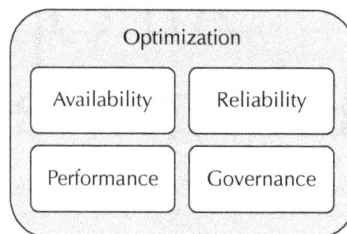

FIGURE 8-1. *Optimization is part of improving all aspects of application management*

This kind of work is never more applicable than now, where organizational objectives can change and pivot quickly. Therefore, optimization management also includes ensuring that enterprise applications remain as flexible as all other business support services.

If the preceding three objectives (reliability, availability, and performance) have been managed in the manner proposed in this book, then there *should* be more time and resources available for optimization, and that in turn further magnifies the benefits of delivering effective application management. This includes real business benefits such as driving user productivity, increasing process and task efficiency, and delivering new business insights.

I hope this begins to illustrate how our five dimensional application management plan is just like Aristotle's famous quote, "The whole is greater than the sum of its parts." Indeed, like so much in life, success breeds success, as the model will feed itself by the use of each of its internal parts: as reliability management is improved, then so becomes availability, and in turn performance and optimization. Done correctly, none of the parts are independent.

Causes of Poor Optimization

The easiest way to look at causes of poor optimization is from the negative: how inaction limits what is possible. A poorly optimized application is therefore usually a result of the following mistakes, as repeated from Chapter 2:

- Not running improvement projects
- Ignoring any future planning
- Static and unmanaged configuration, extensibility, and customization
- No involvement in system design
- No effort to reduce costs
- No effort to realize supplier efficiency

Using this list, we can fairly easily infer what we are trying to achieve by optimizing the system in a way that is proactive in nature, through a conscious and dedicated set of tasks.

Measuring Optimization

At first, optimization might seem tricky to measure, especially if it's mostly reactive—addressing problems as they occur—and not currently a categorized management task. This chapter aims to inspire something more.

Measuring optimization should be kept relatively simple: record the current situation and what you'd like to see, summarize the attempts to improve it, and record the end result. It doesn't have to be extensively detailed, and for practical purposes it's better if it has short concise status and goal statements.

The methods to employ are specific to each type of task; for example, performance optimization is reliant on representative metrics sampling, and security optimization needs a sound summary of the vulnerability, risk, options, and verification testing. Overall optimization needs to be an iterative process as illustrated in Figure 8-2, and needs clear goals and associated metrics that establish criteria for success and a way to measure progress.

Attempts to optimize might not always produce exceptional results; some might be small improvements, some subtle or context-sensitive, and some result in no change or even make

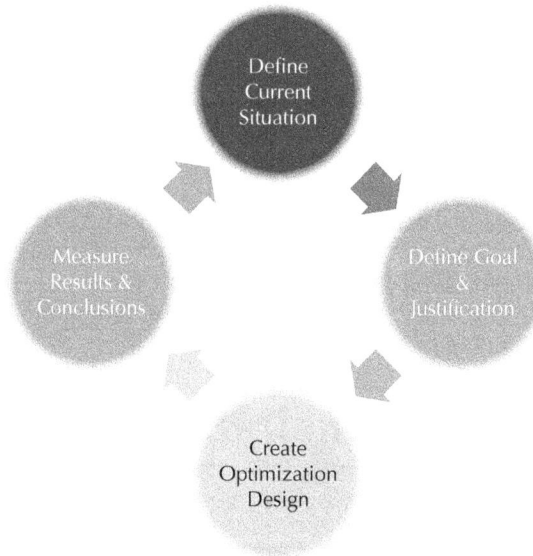

FIGURE 8-2. *Measuring optimization based on a cycle of understanding where you are, what you're trying to achieve and why, executing a design, measuring the results of changes and making conclusions*

things worse! I recommend you record everything precisely, so it's clear that a valiant effort was made, no one else repeats the same mistakes, and all lessons are shared.

I also recommend that you use cumulative optimization by layering discrete projects over each other. For example, you might decide to improve the performance of one particular concurrent request, and during investigation some options are discovered that apply to other requests also, or even across the whole Concurrent Processing system.

Despite the excitement, incremental optimization is better so that discrete achievable changes are applied to the most critical areas first, and the success is properly verified, followed by a second iteration with a slightly different focus and its own analysis, verification, and documentation phases. It's tempting to become overzealous and bundle in extra changes that seem beneficial, but in my experience the creep in scope regularly causes disruption, cost escalation, and unachievable goals.

As you might think, there are strong links with project management and change management here, and I recommend you reuse what currently exists, finding a place for your application optimization management tasks within organizational standards, processes, and tools. If they don't exist or if they are not deployed in respect to application management, then optimization can be a good driver to help get what you need.

Managing Optimization

While I have already mentioned six causes of poor optimization, and thereby some focus areas, these can be further distilled into some high-level core goals that optimization management addresses. Using these during discussions with business stakeholders allows them to air their needs without leading into second-stage implementation considerations.

Optimization should focus on improving system productivity and efficiency so its users can do more with what they have in less time. In addition, it should allow extend capabilities, adding new services that bring additional value to its users.

Since optimization objectives mostly originate from business user requirements, the Application Manager often needs to translate these into related system actions, such as determining how to deliver a faster transaction creation time or simplify an overly complex approval process. This requires a considerable knowledge of the components involved, so it is necessary to distill focus to just a few key areas. Many of the tools and techniques we'll discuss in this chapter help with this.

Optimization projects also need proper management and control, and the essential task is to balance two factors: dedicating the appropriate time and resources and maintaining a focus on the appropriate business operations and the overall application management plan. This is outside the scope of this book and requires that you consider your own prioritization and task planning techniques.

One final extra recommendation is to ensure optimization work is well publicized, especially where relationships and dependencies on other teams is involved. If you don't, it can cause complete failures, such as optimizing a reduced-priority business feature, or improvements based on invalid assumptions about a dependent platform. Bringing together all parties involved and discussing the options available significantly increase the likelihood of optimization success.

Optimization Tools

Table 8-1 gives an overview of the many different concepts, tools, and techniques we'll consider for implementing an optimization management plan. You'll notice this table contains several less technology-related aspects than the other E-Business Suite management toolboxes. While the underlying work is no doubt technical in nature, the focus is firmly on identifying ways to deliver real business value.

Business Process Layer	Applications Technology Layer	Platform Layer
Uptake new features	Business Intelligence	Technical architecture
Optimize for new usage	Extending features	Simplify maintenance
Personalize for productivity	Application's data health	Health checks and technical compliance
Functional tasks	WebCenter	Hardware and networking
Functional configuration and change management	Caching framework	Watching the watchman
Proactive support	Integration	
	Workflow	
	Concurrent Processing	
	Alerts and notifications	
	Setup and implementation	

TABLE 8-1. *The Optimization Toolbox Manifest*

In addition, Table 8-2 shows the same manifest items but reordered into two simple categories based on their most common usage. The intention here is to offer a chapter index that applies to whatever situation you are currently in, as opposed to the general sequential reading structure given in Table 8-1.

Business Process Layer

This chapter moves the focus beyond better management of what you have to evolving the overall system to better meet the needs of its users. Optimization is a general intent, and there is some gray area between deploying tools and techniques for better management and performing dedicated optimization. The obvious example is tuning for performance.

While we'll repeat a few items from previous chapters, there are many areas where optimization opportunities are rarely recognized and not seized upon as much as they could be. Realistically, who is going to drive that if not the Application Manager?

Uptake New Features

New product features are released all the time, many bringing real business benefit, so they need to be proposed and scheduled for implementation as soon as possible. In my experience, the information flow between those who are made aware of new software releases (and its content) and those who benefit from what they contain is often broken, or at least not as fluid as it could be. This is where an optimization focus helps.

Monitoring and Troubleshooting	Managing
Health checks and technical compliance	Uptake new features
Alerts and notifications	Optimize for new usage
Application's data health	Personalize for productivity
Functional configuration and change management	Setup and implementation
Proactive support	Integration
Watching the watchman	Extending features
	Functional tasks
	Technical architecture
	Business Intelligence
	Simplify maintenance
	WebCenter
	Workflow
	Concurrent processing
	Caching framework
	Hardware and networking

TABLE 8-2. *The Optimization Toolbox Based on Use Case*

I recall being involved in the initial launch of E-Business Suite Release 12 and being asked again and again why people should upgrade. In the end, the single most powerful reason was to leverage the new features to better support business operations. I was told that the Advanced Procurement product family alone had more than 200 new features between Releases 11.5.10 and 12.

In fact, the release content document for the later release (Note 561580.1) shows that E-Business Suite Release 12.1 provides 19 entirely new products over Release 12.0. These documents are exceptionally valuable in understanding new features.

In addition, for every E-Business Suite product and release there is a "release notes" type of document, each of which contains a standard content structure with a section entitled "What's New," listing exactly what has changed. An example is Note 1102798.1, for Self Service HR, which has a table of seven enhanced (i.e., optimized) features available in release 12.1.3 including support for processing reverse termination and the ability to view entitlement balances in notifications. Perhaps in an ideal world there would be a single master list of new features for all products, but optimization should focus around the benefits to just the most critical business features first. As such, the breakdown in these notes by product is helpful.

Another example of looking for new features is a solution called E-Business Suite Extensions for Endeca (Release 12.1.3), which illustrates how uptake of an existing feature inside one release can deliver significant business benefit. With the addition of a few patches and some configuration, the following areas of E-Business Suite are significantly enhanced by Endeca's powerful in-memory support for displaying and searching structured and unstructured data, implemented with a relatively seamless merging of the two user interfaces:

- Field service
- Channel revenue management (trade management)
- iRecruitment
- iProcurement
- Project management
- Enterprise asset management (see Figure 8-3)
- Order management
- Manufacturing Execution System (MES) for discrete manufacturing
- Item master (PIM)

In addition to features contained in new releases and add-on capabilities like Endeca, E-Business Suite already contains a wide range of features that complement the core functionality and should be considered to both increase functional capability and also often help consolidate and automate similar existing processes. Here are a few general examples that are native to E-Business Suite and integrated in all the places their use makes sense:

- **Approvals Management Engine**   For centralizing approval chains and rules
- **iSurvey**   For collecting extra data in a standard way using prebuilt scripts
- **Enterprise contracts**   For supporting all manner of agreements
- **Employee self-service**   To get more work done at the point of origin, such as distributing basic HR functions

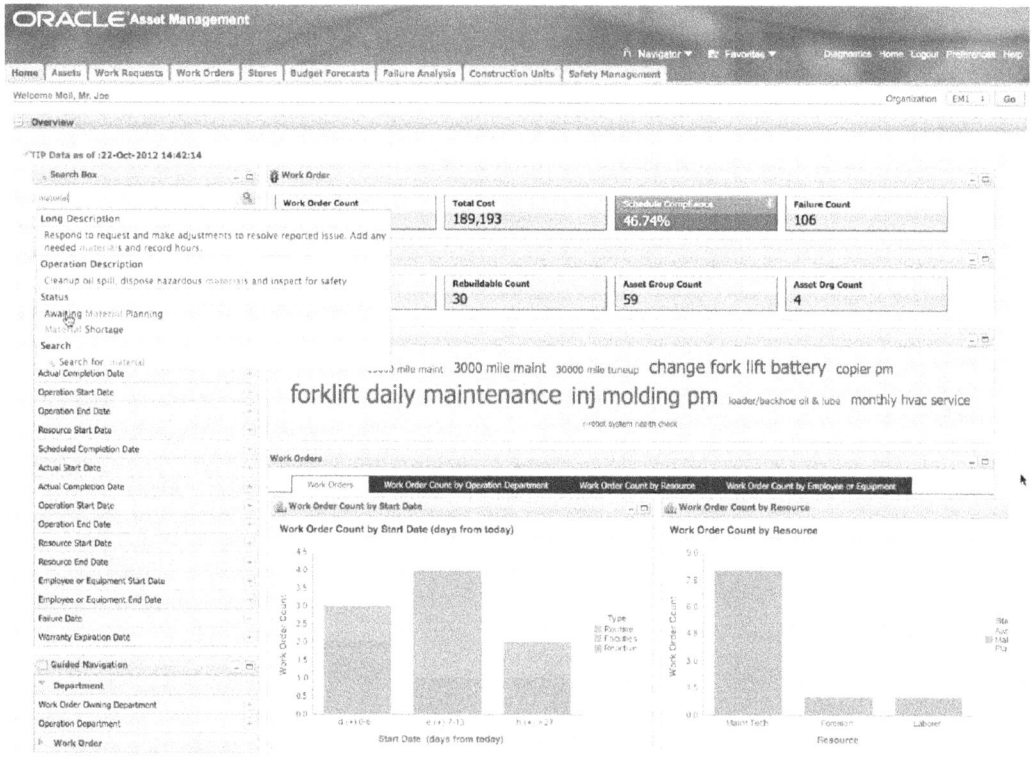

FIGURE 8-3. *E-Business Suite's Enterprise Asset Management screen significantly enhanced with new, more efficient tools from the Endeca extension*

- **MDM solutions** For centralizing data management, including products such as Product Hub, Customer Hub, Trading Community, and Supplier Management
- **Built-in integration** For sharing transactions and business data through features like EDI, SOA, and XML Gateway

Optimize for New Usage

Unlike the monolithic ERP suites of old, enterprise applications are no longer separate from the rapid pace of technical innovation. Modern organizations want all their IT services to mirror the evolving technology landscape, and the expectations of consumer systems like apps and online stores are transferred to back-end systems.

Enterprise applications are expected to be "easy to learn." This is an interesting phrase, as it implies these applications should not be any less complex or powerful, but that they should be more intuitively designed around task requirements and user profiles, leveraging modern visual and interactive features. This is at the heart of the Oracle User Experience team that has begun to influence capabilities in E-Business Suite 12.1.3.

The obvious example of a change in usage profile is the support for mobile devices, such as phones and tablets. Out-of-the-box solutions right now are limited to specific E-Business Suite products such as CRM sales and field service, but this is a strong area of focus going forward, and many organizations are starting to leverage integration with the powerful mobile capabilities inside Fusion Applications.

As system administrators of a large enterprise application, we commonly need to consider the management and optimization of E-Business Suite globalization, especially as the business grows into new markets. Globalization covers many features within E-Business Suite that help support its users in different countries and regions. The national language support (NLS) offers dozens of languages available to install in addition to the U.S. English base. In addition *localizations* provide country-specific features and extensions for many E-Business Suite products. These run on the native support in the middle-tier and database for broad character sets, ensuring complete and accurate information is always used. Indeed E-Business Suite is in use in more than 150 different countries. For more details on what is available, see the product guides on http://docs.oracle.com or review the Globalization Guide in My Oracle Support Note 393861.1. In terms of optimization, some of the extra features enabled to support globalization come with some overhead cost, such as applying patches for each language, so the Application Manager must review the requirements, costs, and ongoing usage and make adjustments accordingly. Management of instance globalization is available in Oracle Applications Manager under the License Manager, offering various functionalities and reporting options.

Another slant on new usage is how increasingly the E-Business Suite solutions are extending their user base outside of traditional "processing departments" into other occasional-usage areas, such as senior management analytics, self-service features for infrequent and temporary workers, and capturing and integrating information from external trading partners. This is another area of substantial industry growth where the most progressive organizations are taking opportunities to differentiate themselves.

A similar recommendation is to make use of the product features that support the outsourcing of business services and the creation of single centralized departments. One example is to set up a single purchasing department for all regions (rather than one per region), which allows for more effective and efficient standardized buying processes and greater savings from using single high-volume/high-discount supplier agreements (see Note 296364.1).

Finally, an area related to the centralization activities mentioned is consolidation. For example, moving to a single global instance of E-Business Suite rather than having several similar applications solutions across different centers and departments. This helps eliminate complexity and removes duplicated costs. The stock phrase "standardize and consolidate" is very much at the forefront of modern IT optimization efforts, and there are opportunities even in E-Business Suite administration. Consolidation is something we'll discuss again in our consideration of cloud computing in Chapter 11.

Personalize for Productivity

E-Business Suite supports a broad set of personalization options, from setting the corporate look and feel to removing unnecessary fields. However, there is a fine line between personalization and extensions, and some personalization ultimately requires extension, such as adding an extra field to a page. For clarity, we'll discuss these two separately, but in real-world implementation there is some gray area between them.

Personalization is all about tailoring the user interface to more closely fit with the requirements of a specific user or set of users. The more the application looks and works in a way that is relevant to the users' needs, the more productive they will be. Obviously, application features are built with a specific job role in mind, but between organizations these roles differ. Adding this malleable veneer allows for greater optimization.

Since the E-Business Suite user interface is split into OA Framework pages and Oracle Forms, we'll discuss the personalization options of each, as unfortunately they are completely different.

OA Framework Personalization

OA Framework personalization provides the ability to redefine the properties for E-Business Suite's pages and regions and the components they contain, such as fields, labels, and buttons. The personalization works by storing the changes as a separate metadata record and applying it over the standard base definition at runtime. This implementation has the benefit of allowing personalization to usually remain patch and upgrade-proof.

True OA Framework personalizations that apply to a set of one or more users are created based on two parent values: the *level* and the *context*. The level represents when the personalizations will be applied to the users' session and are comprised of seven standard values. Site, responsibility, and user levels are the most commonly used, but here is the full list:

- **Function**   Applies based on the security function granted to the user
- **Industry**   Applies based on an industry categorization value
- **Localization**   Applies based on the user preference for their regional locale
- **Site**   Applies for all users in the system
- **Organization**   Applies when using pages in the context of a specific organizational business unit
- **Responsibility**   Applies when using one specific responsibility value
- **User**   Applies for one named user only

The personalization context sets more criteria about where the changes will apply—that is, it specifies exactly what you are personalizing. This is illustrated in Figure 8-4 and these contexts include

- **Scope**   What is being personalized
- **Document name**   The internal object (the XML file) where the changes will apply
- **Site**   Whether or not it applies at the site level also
- **Organization**   What organization it applies to
- **Responsibility**   What responsibility it applies to

The last three of these equate to the values set in the level and serve as a reminder as to where this personalization will appear.

In addition to the personalizations that are intended to be specific to a group of users, another set applies in a much broader manner, setting properties and values that determine how products work for all users. These are called *administrator personalizations* and include the following:

- Changing product branding (image), region header icons, and the cascading style sheet (CSS) to personalize the look and feel
- Hiding or showing regions and items and changing their layout

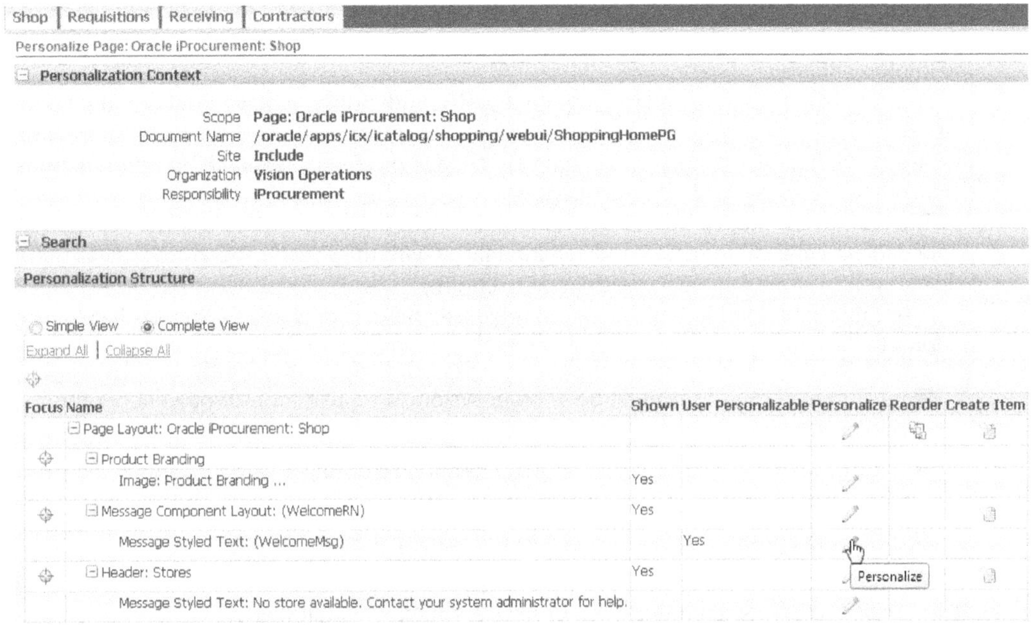

FIGURE 8-4. *Personalizing the iProcurement home page showing the context and options available for different fields*

- Including or excluding descriptive flexfield segments
- Defining the default sorting, filtering, and number of rows displayed in tables
- Changing the item default values, labels, and region headers
- Defining tips (inline help) for items

Finally, one last level is *system personalizations*. As you'd expect, it applies everywhere and to every user. These are supported by a combination of OA Framework options and administrator functions. They include more options for customizing the look and feel of the application and the setup of responsibilities, as well as for adjusting the logos, default texts, and many standard lists of values used.

More detail on the features of personalization that can be used to optimize the user interface for better productivity can be found in Oracle Application Framework Personalization Guide (E12646-04).

Oracle Forms Personalization

While a few personalization options are available to end users, such as managing their own folders or adjusting items in their Top Ten List, changing the look and feel of E-Business Suite forms is something users generally need administrative help with.

Since a substantial amount of the core functionality remains accessible through Oracle Forms, it is sensible to include the options for equivalent usage fine-tuning. Like OA Framework personalization, a successful Oracle Forms personalization project requires some teamwork. A combination of end users and business analysts help highlight the areas of concern, with application administrators explaining the options available and performing technical aspects of the implementation.

Forms personalization used to be quite invasive and mostly achieved through the Forms Designer development tool and the CUSTOM.pll library for injecting new code. This changed in Release11*i* with a new option to declaratively change properties, execute built-in functions, display new messages, and add menu entries.

The Forms personalization is found under the Help | Diagnostics | Custom Code menu, and while declarative it still requires a strong familiarity with the way Oracle Forms works under the skin, as well as some familiarity with PL/SQL coding.

A simple example of how this can optimize user tasks is to change forms so that users can perform the following extra actions, all of which personalization supports:

- Launch a URL—this might be another system, a related tool, or other supporting information.

- Run a function or a stored PL/SQL procedure, returning a value for use in the page, such as a calculation.

- Call the custom PL/SQL package to run some extra processing.

- Raise a forms trigger that automatically performs some action upon a particular event, such as opening another form or even running a default query.

- Show additional messages to help the user, providing extra information or alerts. An example is shown in Figure 8-5.

- Perform extra validation on data entered, enhancing consistency and reducing mistakes.

- Hide a field or even a whole tab, helping simplify the user interface.

Details on using the Forms personalization features can be found in Oracle E-Business Suite Developer's Guide (E12897-04), the whitepaper in Note 395117.1, and the walkthrough in Note 1534116.1, together with some useful-to-know limitations described in Note 420518.1.

One other small feature related to forms is that they can be set up to be available to users in read-only mode. This has been used by many organizations to expose important information to those that need it without running the risk of improper use. For more details on setting this up, see the example in My Oracle Support Note 566713.1.

Active Personalization Management

From my work in Oracle Support, I found that personalization is a powerful feature but if it's not controlled, it can become excessively used by many different users in many different ways.

While only occasionally responsible for problem and performance issues, there is always some overhead in terms of storing each personalization and applying them at runtime. As the number of personalizations increase, so does the overhead. Adding a certain amount of control and standardization (a.k.a. consolidation) is recommended as it helps make the end user experience consistent and enhances system management.

In E-Business Suite the functional administrator responsibility contains an option to manage all the personalizations done for OA Framework regions and pages (for Forms this can be done via an FNDLOAD export). As shown in Figure 8-6, it's possible to search and see which areas are personalized, change the personalization and level, and even import and export them between instances.

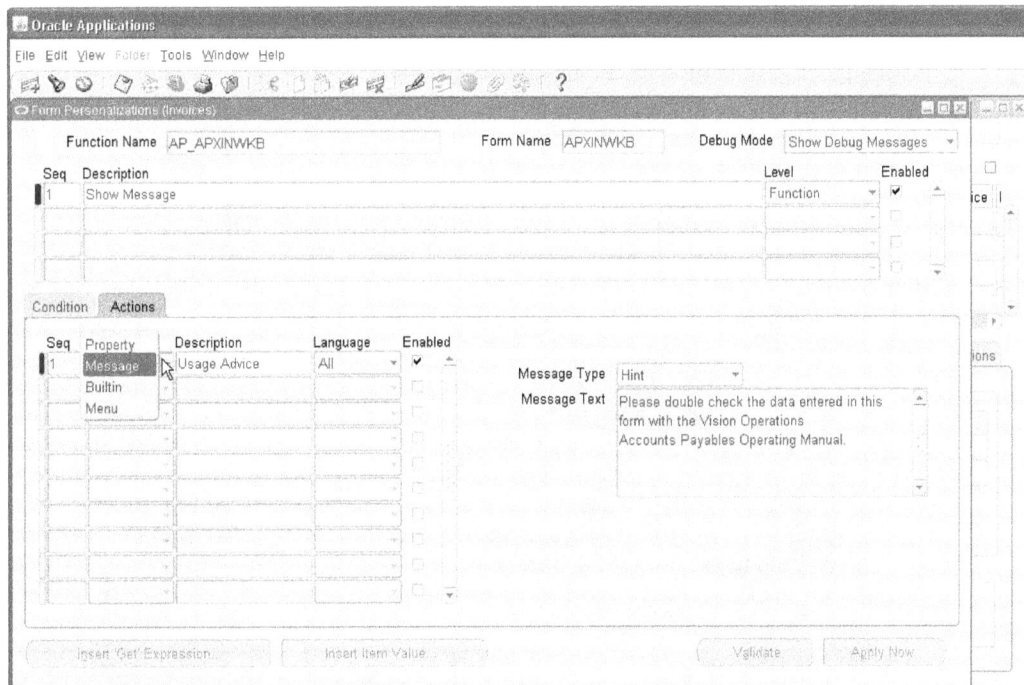

FIGURE 8-5. *Adding a new message to the Invoices form using personalization*

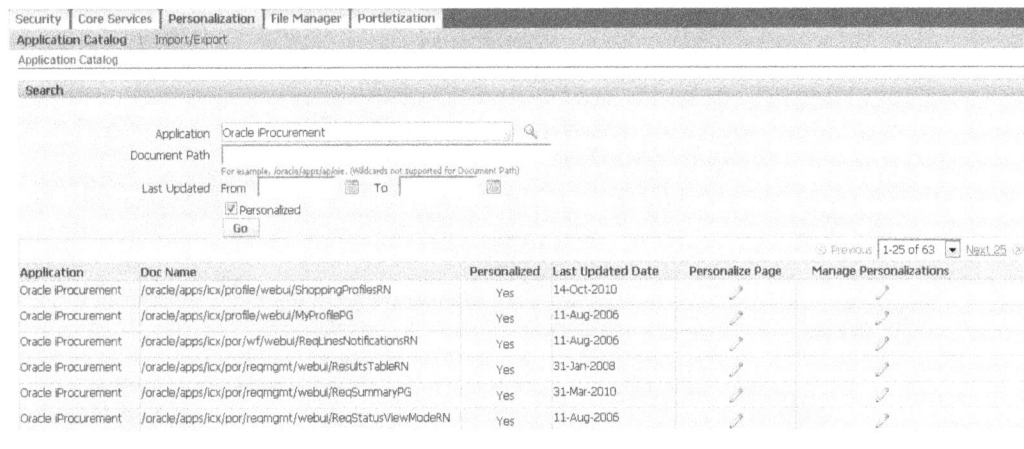

FIGURE 8-6. *Reviewing current OA Framework personalizations*

Personalized and Extended Help

Enterprise application UIs are evolving, such as those available in Oracle Fusion Applications, however the goal remains to make the applications more productive by improving their efficiency and adding better capabilities. So, while next generation UIs seem increasingly easier to use, as features become richer, training and online help still remain important. Even Fusion Applications have extensive embedded and online help to guide users, as well as strong features that support extending and tailoring it.

In E-Business Suite, adding help content to explain and demonstrate how your implementation uses features in specific ways that can improve system usage, reduce mistakes, and generally make uptake more effective.

All the features to support customization of the help are available from the Help Administration menu under the System Administration responsibility.

The basic process for changing or adding help is to load a new or changed HTML file into the database. Existing content can be downloaded first and adjusted or brand new files can be added. The system also supports the loading of new GIF images, PDF documents, and custom Cascading Style Sheets. The help system has its own method of linking and cross-referencing different sections and files, broadly based around HTML anchors.

Once files are loaded you can use the Help Builder applet, illustrated in Figure 8-7, to adjust its access. This allows drag-and-drop changes to the tree hierarchy shown in the index page, adjusting the existing nodes, or adding new ones.

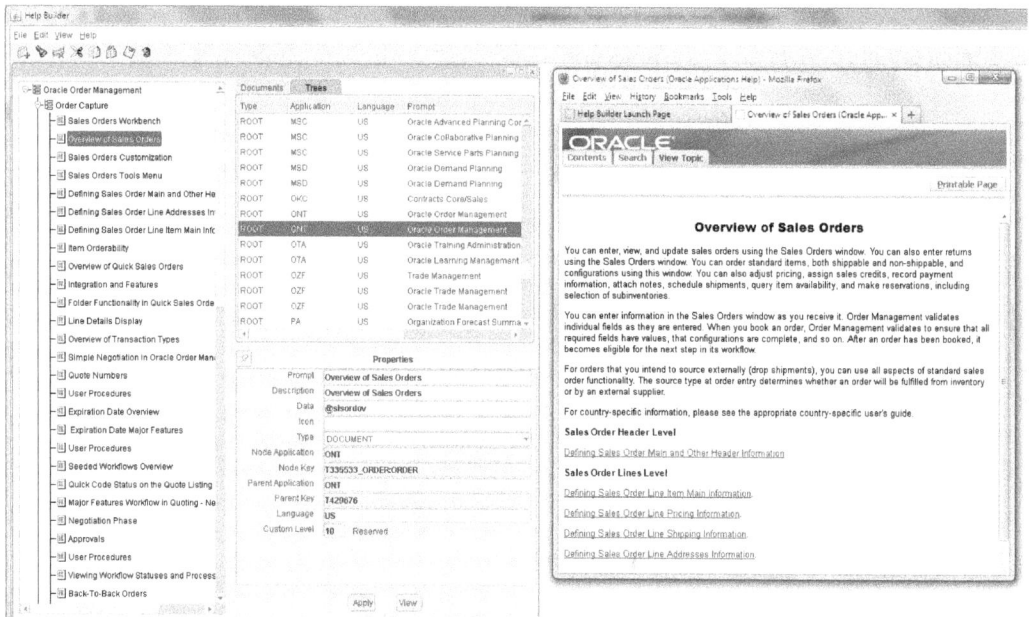

FIGURE 8-7.   *The Help Builder applet shows the structure; when you click the View button, content appears in the right-hand browser window*

More details on changing help content can be found in the Oracle E-Business Suite System Administrator's Guide—Configuration (E12893-04). For more extensive capabilities, Oracle Tutor provides features for the creation of additional content and its implementation within E-Business Suite for specific user roles. More detail is available within the Oracle Tutor documentation.

More Invasive Personalization

The only drawback to custom help is that it relies on the user going to the help screens in the first place, an action which is not guaranteed to happen. It's not always the most productive option either, as it relies on reading through static text and retrying operations. A much better solution is to improve the user interface itself, adding tweaks that enhance the ease of taking the right action the first time.

This is possible by adjusting the text fields shown on the page and used in the responses shown when something isn't quite right. You can do this by adjusting Messages and Look-ups, under the Core Services section available to the Functional Administrator responsibility. These adjustments are often done at the start of an implementation, adding organization-specific terms rather than running the system with only the seeded base data. This gives you the opportunity to revisit the processes and pages that are proving the most challenging, and to optimize what is shown to end users.

The example in Figure 8-8 shows the extra text added to a message (the second sentence), giving end users a way to move forward with a problem situation, thereby slightly increasing productivity. Similarly, Figure 8-9 shows the Item Type lookup and how its text and meaning

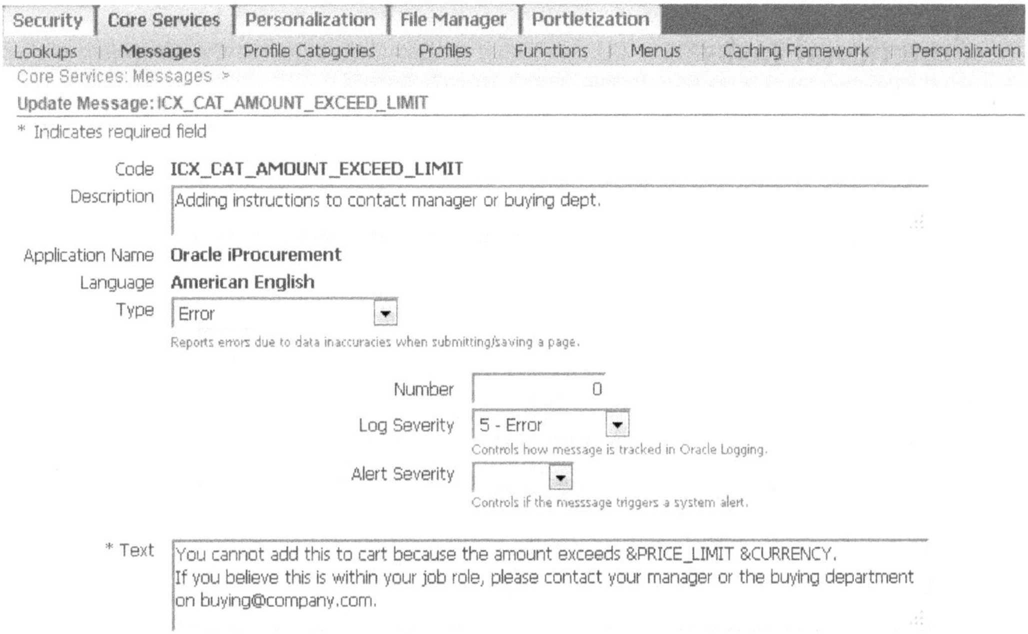

FIGURE 8-8. *Adjusting a standard message to better fit with an organization*

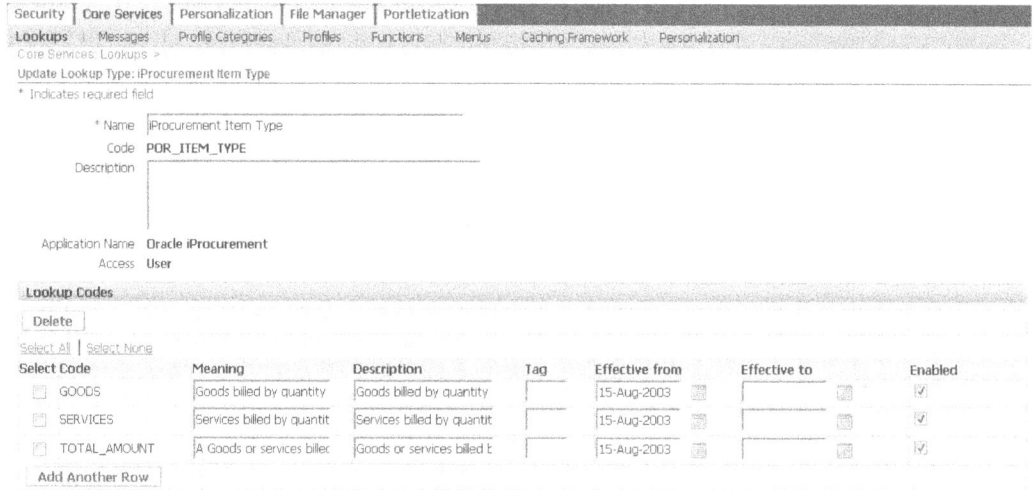

FIGURE 8-9. *Adjusting a standard lookup to better fit with an organization*

values can be adjusted to fit better with organizational terms and nomenclature, while retaining the standard functionality associated with the fixed code field.

Functional Tasks

Most of the functional processes in E-Business Suite can be adjusted to fit the way an organization operates. This is usually done on implementation only, missing an opportunity to reoptimize the system upon changes in business objectives and priorities such as mergers and organizational changes.

Generally speaking, the enterprise applications manager needs to be aware of the most business-crucial or problematic processes, so they can begin to review options for optimization. This might be the top five items from each of the following:

- The processes most crucial to the business operation, often measured by financial loss upon failure

- The processes, features, and functions that are used the most

- The processes that are slowest to complete, based on realistic expectations

- The processes that often require extra assistance, such as help desk tickets or online help usage

- The processes that are used less than was originally expected

- The processes easiest to change and adjust

The processes most often optimized are from Workflow, not far behind are concurrent request sets as well as reports and business intelligence pages. I recommend you run a review of what processes are most eligible quarterly, at least verifying that the items on the lists above remain correct, thereby ensuring all priorities remain correctly aligned.

As the most commonly tailored area, let's take a look at some available options in Oracle Workflow. Shown in Figure 8-10 is a simple example of optimization is the effective use of Workflow Vacation Rules, where business document approvals are sent on to other people for immediate action rather than left incomplete when people are unavailable. This basic practice is regularly overlooked, frequently causing the build-up of approvals and even processing timeouts resulting in stuck transactions.

Similarly straightforward but also often overlooked is the Worklist Access option shown in Figure 8-11, which allows users to set up a delegation process so that employees can complete actions assigned to others.

You could argue that excessive use of these features might indicate that the approval hierarchy setup being used is incorrect and needs adjusting. Either way, however, a balanced use of appropriate features makes for an optimal solution.

Taking Oracle Workflow in more depth, most organizations will review each standard process and determine if the steps apply to their organization. If not, they make adjustments to it and reimplement the customized files. While this process is part of most E-Business Suite initial implementations, understanding and regularly reviewing the key workflow processes based on changing business operations is a recommended optimization technique.

Opening the Workflow item in the client Workflow Builder tool (see Note 261028.1) allows for a detailed review with domain experts to identify optimization candidates. You should also review the executions of the Workflow processes to understand how it runs. Look for slow or overly complex parts that don't add any important functionality. Fortunately, there are several

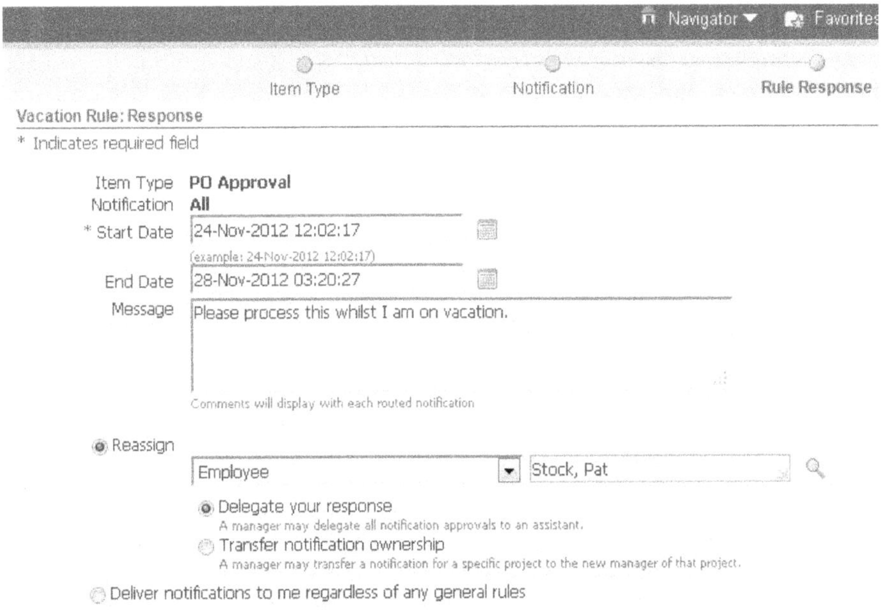

FIGURE 8-10. *Setting the Workflow Vacation rule*

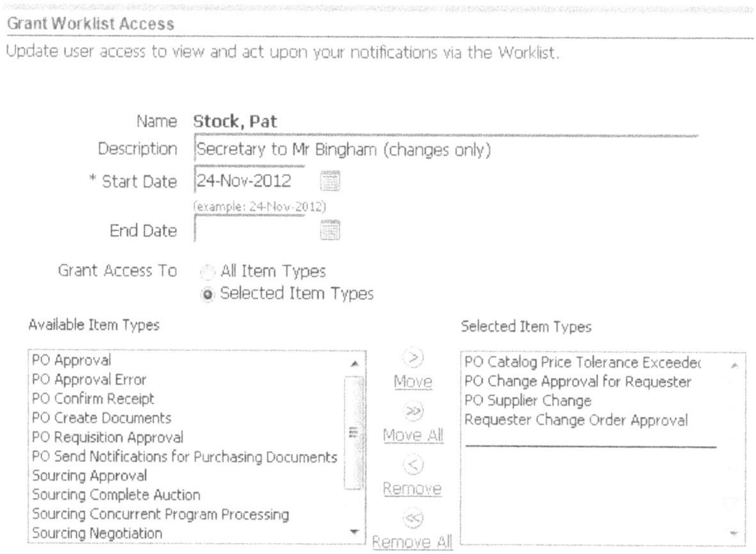

FIGURE 8-11. *Granting Worklist access to delegate approval for purchasing change workflows to Pat Stock*

Workflow monitoring tools to help, as discussed in the previous chapters, especially the Workflow Monitor applet, which displays the execution in the same graphical way as the builder, making comparison easy.

Each workflow is specific to the business functionality it supports and therefore a detailed analysis of one example would not be representative. Instead, here are key areas where Workflow optimizations are commonly beneficial:

- Overly complex processes, beyond what the business needs
- Process switches that in reality always route one way
- Nodes that always return the same value
- Notifications generated and sent that bring no real value
- Nodes where an extra notification would be helpful
- Adding nodes to ensure errors or nonresponses are caught and progressed automatically
- Nodes that make calls to code that is slow to complete
- Notification content that should better meet the needs of users

As an example, Figure 8-12 shows a small part of the PO Approval process, illustrating complexity that may be a candidate for simplification. For example, you could adjust the flow so that the complex order signature processes are not used if not required by the business.

Oracle Workflow is generally well supported by E-Business Suite Diagnostics, and there is extensive documentation in the E-Business Suite Administrators Guide—Maintenance (E12894-04) and its own Oracle Workflow Administrator's, Developer's, and User Guides.

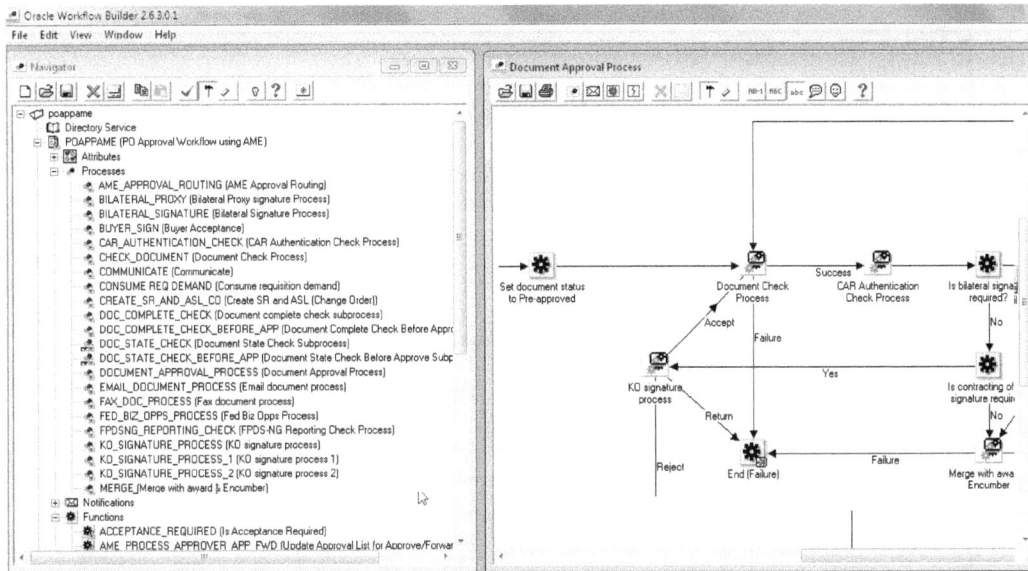

FIGURE 8-12. *Workflow Builder showing a section of the PO Approval workflow*

Functional Configuration and Change Management

One aspect that is hard to keep track of and is rarely done well is the proper management of functional configuration and setup. Often this is done through maintaining a gold instance image and then locking down access to the configuration screens so settings cannot be changed. However, this does not constitute proper configuration management.

One potential solution is the use of iSetup, but with its limited breadth and, more specifically, its setup phase scope, iSetup is not a complete configuration management solution. With the E-Business Suite Plug-in for Enterprise Manager the overall solution is expanded enormously. As shown in Figure 8-13, this includes the display and comparison of configurations such as system setups, patches and context files, core configuration files, the technology stack, and Concurrent Processing and Workflow components.

There are also third-party solutions that do include the extract of E-Business Suite functional setup data for management and comparison purposes. These also often support more detail in terms of context, such as showing the configuration for one operating unit, organizations, or sets of books.

Another method of reviewing and validating functional setup is through the use of the diagnostic tests inside E-Business Suite. The catalog contains a set of diagnostics categorized as health checks that are intended to capture setup and transaction data and to look for potential problem causes and symptoms. The Release 12 catalog is provided in My Oracle Support Note 421245.1. These diagnostic tests are limited in terms of configuration management features, but as illustrated in Figure 8-14, they do represent a useful focused collection and validation capability. Even at a basic level, the output from these tests can be stored for later manual review-and-compare purposes.

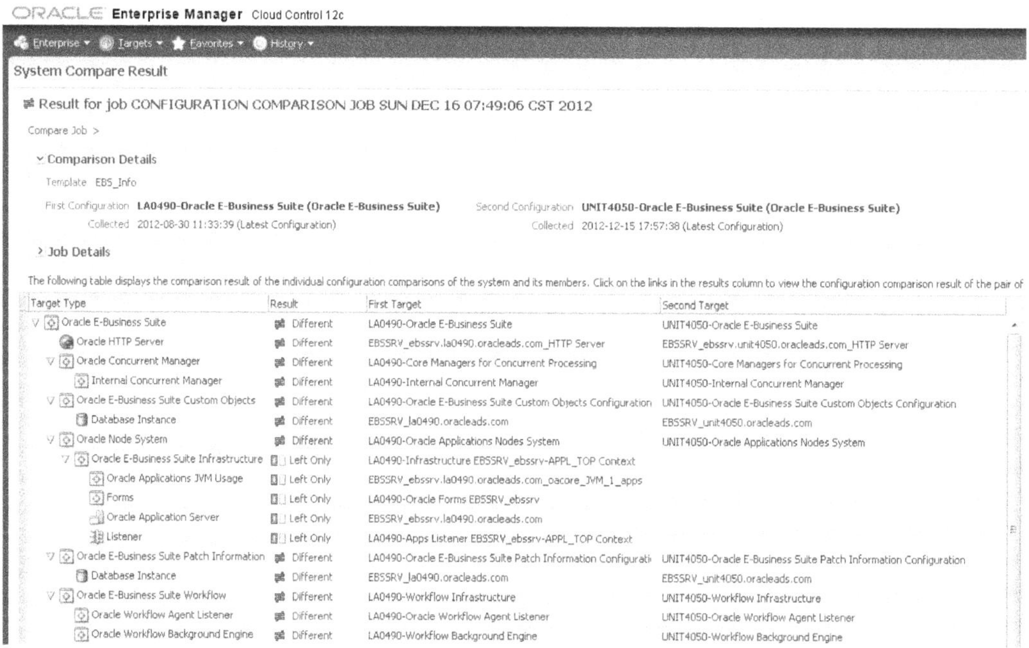

FIGURE 8-13. *The Enterprise Manager configuration compares features of two E-Business Suite instances, easily showing differences with links to drill into details*

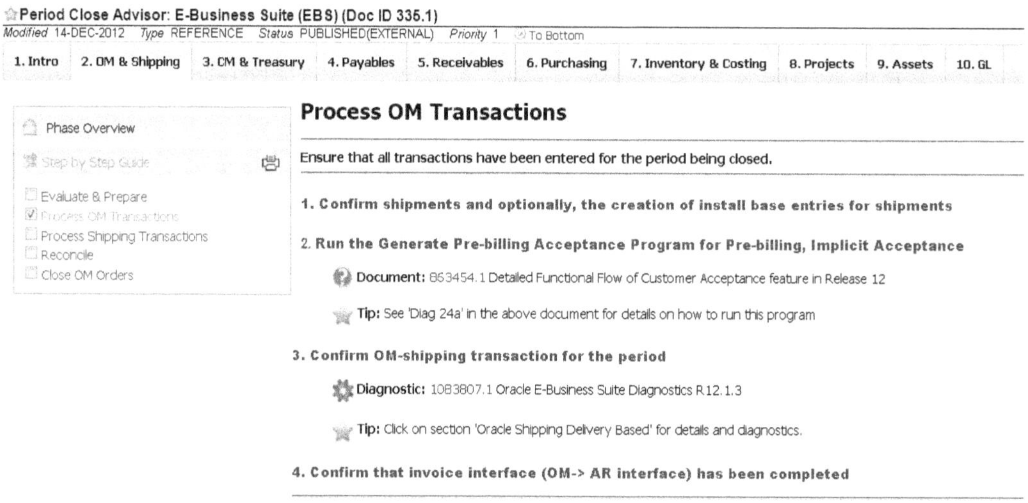

FIGURE 8-14. *The My Oracle Support Period Close Advisor (Note 335.1), showing how diagnostic tests are integral to effective functional health checking*

Remember, change management is a process that is implemented by one or more tools. A wealth of information exists on this, but at a minimum a formalized set of phases should include *proposing, approving, testing, applying*, and *recording* all functional changes. The change management procedure should be logical and clear, and it should be supported by an implementation that is transparent and simple to use. Sometimes optimizing the process is required, and even something basic is better than nothing at all.

Proactive Support

Beyond items such as Oracle Configuration Manager and its associated change management and health recommendation features discussed already, My Oracle Support contains other options that offer early warnings that help you identify areas for potential optimization:

- New alerts created for patches and important information like certification changes
- New articles published on product areas of critical focus, such as FAQs and usage recommendations
- Product newsletters
- Focused knowledge such as the *Get Proactive* type content consisting of advisors and their related information centers (see Note 432.1 for more details)
- Solutions to common mistakes and known problems
- Changes in the support for the technology stack components or changes to features therein
- Patch recommendations tools
- Details on new and forthcoming product features or changes to be aware of
- New and updated tools for gathering diagnostic information, such as Remote Diagnostic Agent
- New Oracle services that may resolve serious issues or offer improvements

Of special mention are Oracle Communities (http://communities.oracle.com), the modern way to engage with both Oracle Support as well as peer organizations. This includes the opportunity not only to get answers to questions on dozens of specialist forums, but also to share and consume experience and knowledge on optimization. Categories exist for all the E-Business Suite product areas, as well as a good amount of technology-related items, including Install and Patching, Concurrent Processing and Workflow, Customizations, and as shown in Figure 8-15, the E-Business Suite Technology Stack.

As an Oracle employee I should also mention the expert services provided by Advanced Customer Services and Oracle Consulting, both of which are constantly evolving their offerings to fit customer needs. For E-Business Suite, this includes post-live services such as specialist reviews for optimizing performance, reliability, configuration, and diagnostics. For details on the current packaged services or where to go to discuss specific needs, please visit the Oracle website.

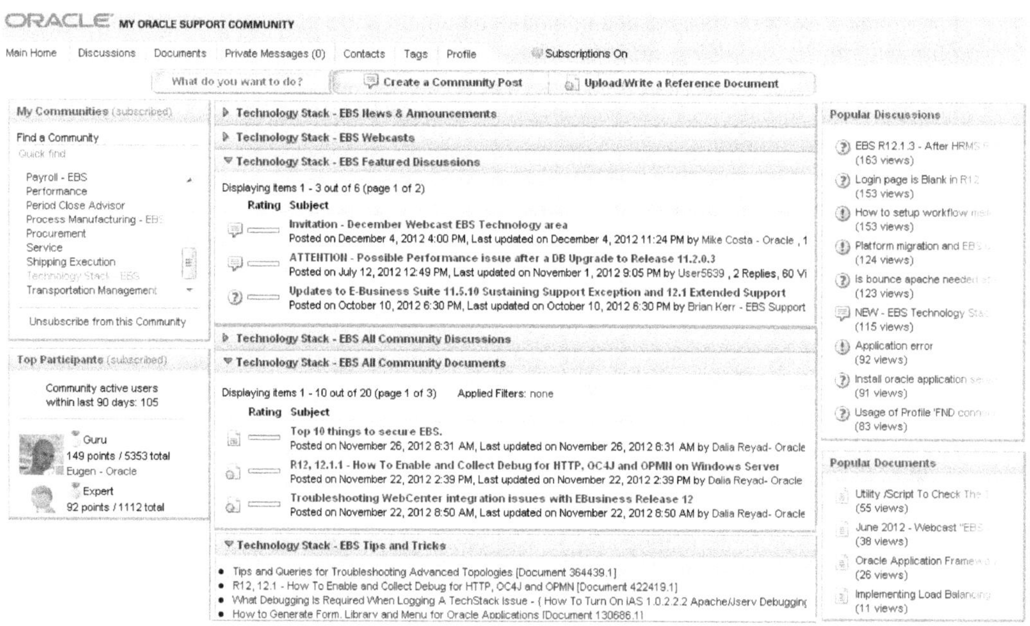

FIGURE 8-15. *Regions showing news, webcasts, discussions, and documents from the My Oracle Support Community for the E-Business Suite Technology Stack*

Applications Technology Layer

Going down one level, optimizing the technical components that support business features is a logical way to make improvements, and certainly some of these provide maintenance options and tools for exactly this purpose. Others might not immediately offer improvements in base functionality, but this section highlights steps that can be taken that regularly provide significant results.

Business Intelligence

Business Intelligence, encompassing both reports and analytics is often an area prime for optimization, where a few improvements can help deliver significant gains. Examples include adjusting the content and style of dashboards and reports, making them run faster, making them easier to access, and expanding the entire intelligence catalog, the features, and their capabilities.

Solid BI solutions are essential for IT departments to deliver measurable business value back to key stakeholders such as senior management. Oracle Business Intelligence Applications (OBIA) is a solution worth considering because it adds a substantial value layer over the top of your existing E-Business Suite.

I recently worked with an organization who had built substantial operational dependency on the older Discoverer technology for reporting against their E-Business Suite, but they were never satisfied by its implementation. So much evolution occurred in BI since their original choice that it reached the point where the gains from moving to an OBIA solution would be quickly realized.

One of the extra benefits was the consolidation of the piecemeal custom solutions they had built themselves (which included dozens of reports and data layers), into a single standardized capability that delivered what they needed out-of-the-box, along with a flexible architecture for taking things to the next level.

Another example of how integrating a best-of-breed solution can deliver business value from raw E-Business Suite data is the use of the Hyperion products. These leverage OLAP technologies with prebuilt application integrations, offering enterprise performance management for Financials. They contain solutions in the areas of profitability and strategy management, planning, budgeting and forecasting, financial period closing and reporting, and master data management. The example in Figure 8-16 shows the related Enterprise Planning product with budgeting reduction plans run against real data to show the forecasted savings.

Another BI-related optimization that we'll discuss later is Oracle Exalytics, a hardware server tuned specifically to the BI components that has its own in-memory database technology to greatly enhance what is possible for reporting and analysis of Oracle Applications data. This could be considered prebuilt optimization, out-of-the-box ready to support many concurrent users and the back-end data crunching involved for datasets like that from a well-used E-Business Suite instance. For more details see oracle.com or My Oracle Support Note 1427996.1.

While there may be additional up-front costs involved when you adopt new products, even only slightly extending the capabilities of what you already have and using the dormant E-Business Suite data can often bring quick returns. In addition, these products are often already in use somewhere in the organization but not used to their maximum capability, so another tip is to review feature adoption figures.

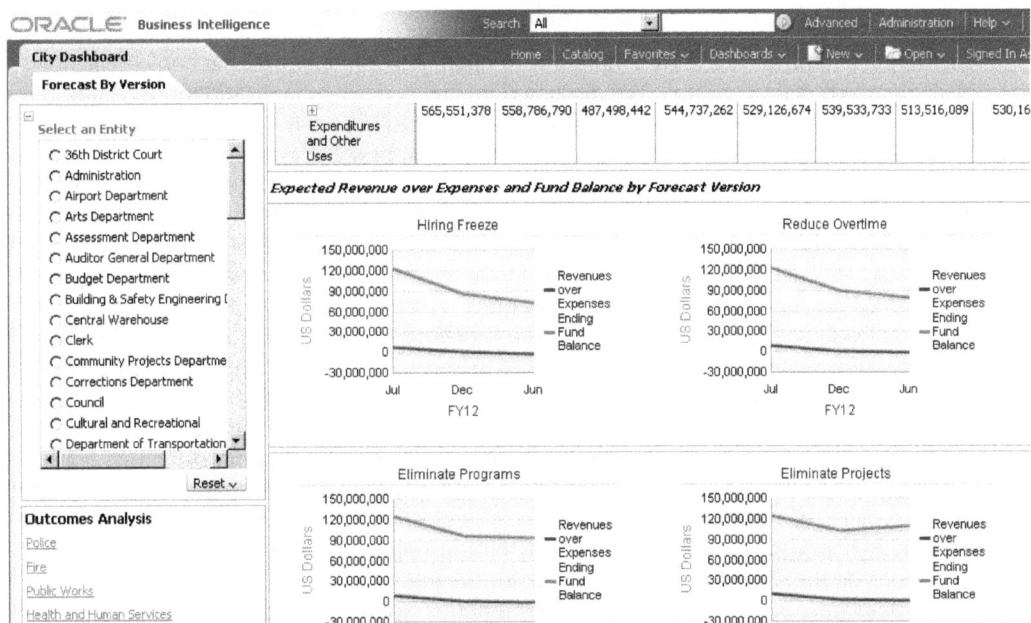

FIGURE 8-16. *The Enterprise Planning BI product, showing information for budgeting plans and forecasts against real application data*

One great illustration of the value BI data brings to enterprise applications is how this is done in Fusion Applications. Oracle focused on embedding more analytics inside the product pages to deliver insights exactly where business users work, not in a separate page or system. This highlights the fact that rich information exists in the applications system, and the real value comes when insights are delivered in a way that is simple, accessible, fast, and often automated.

Finally, as the reporting workhorse inside E-Business Suite, Oracle BI Publisher can also be optimized. Using the same thinking we've been using throughout this chapter, report content may be fine-tuned, as can the places and ways in which it is made available. It can be as simple as speaking to the business users and understanding how they work, what they need to see, and where they need to see it. Details on customizing BI Publisher reports is provided in Oracle Fusion Middleware Report Designer's Guide for Oracle Business Intelligence Publisher (E22254-03).

Extending Features

One step beyond personalization is extension, which is the ability to add to the standard features in E-Business Suite. Most organizations use the extension capabilities to make the functionality match their own industry- or company-specific requirements more closely. Extension used to be a one-time activity, but modern organizations constantly adapt to new market conditions and operating methods, so E-Business Suite now needs to be the platform upon which these can be made.

As always, it's a good idea to first explore the flexible product configuration options, to ensure that similar features and options don't already exist and that changing the functionality is worth the cost of creating and maintaining an extension.

Probably the most often used standard extension is the implementation of Dynamic Flexfields (DFF). DFFs offer the addition of extra fields to forms and pages and the subsequent processing allows organizations to add to what they deem essential extra information to existing records. The success of this capability is again illustrated by its adoption (and extension) in Fusion Applications. This therefore represents a fairly simple way to optimize (or reoptimize) the implementation to better meet the needs of the business. We discussed flexfields in Chapter 1, and more details can be found in the Oracle E-Business Suite Flexfields Guide (E12892-04).

Extensions go all the way into adding new pages, new concurrent programs, and new code. However, there is a standard method to do this for E-Business Suite that offers the main advantage of using prebuilt tools and options, making development faster and more reliable. Using the standard extension methods also makes the resulting solution easier to maintain and support. A more detailed discussion can be found in either the E-Business Suite Developers Guide (E12897-04) or the excellent Oracle Press book written by my ex-colleague Vladimir Ajvaz (and Anil Passi) titled *Oracle E-Business Suite Development and Extensibility Handbook* (2009).

E-Business Suite also now includes more support for Fusion Middleware technologies, and many of them are available for use in extensions. Of particular interest are the Service Oriented Architecture (SOA) components where Web Services and BPEL flows are exposed for simple integration with other applications and systems. In addition, the support for Oracle Applications Development Framework (ADF) in E-Business Suite means that additional rich modern user interface pages can be built on the latest technologies, which also includes support for mobile devices. ADF is also the technology used by Fusion Applications, and it makes sense to build extensions on the same platform to prepare for the future.

Remember, consolidation is a popular method of optimization and both poor documentation and siloed departments often lead to duplicated extensions being built. Where good application management is implemented, this overlap should be evident, and some small reengineering projects can quickly reduce extension volume and complexity.

Applications Data Health

Optimizations need balance, so while I've advocated adding flexfields to better support business needs, you shouldn't use more than is needed, as everything nonstandard raises costs. In this section, I recommend getting and keeping the application data trimmed and tidy, so that what is needed is available without too much waste or too many expired records that add complexity and slow things down.

One logical suggestion is to take each of the high volume or critical functional areas and conduct a data usage review. As mentioned in the previous chapters, Enterprise Manager has some great tools for doing this. Based on a comparison between the user's and administrator's expectations and the actually review findings, there may well be optimization options available. The following are some examples of what these options can accomplish:

- Archiving of old functional data and transactions, condensing bloated tables down to a manageable size. Each E-Business Suite product has specific programs and features for archiving its own transactions and data. To be clear, archiving is different to purging, as the latter deletes records entirely.

- Cleanup of old setup data and expired seed data. An example might be removing all those "do not use" look-up items from lists of values.

- Better management of the unstructured data associated with E-Business Suite. One example is the repository of attachments associated with various documents and transactions. Another might be the image files that can be associated with various entities, such as products and people. Over years of use these may benefit from a little optimization.

- Purging system records, such as Workflow and Concurrent Manager, as discussed in previous chapters.

- Maintaining the database APPS schema. This includes gathering statistics using adadmin or a SQL script like advrfapp.sql and recompiling any invalid objects.

- Scheduling the execution of crawl jobs and index optimization to keep Secure Enterprise Search source data up to date.

- Maintaining the objects and data behind the various solutions being used. This ranges from tasks such as merging suppliers, customers, and products to BI-related tasks such as refreshing materialized views, managing Essbase cubes, and clearing ETL jobs for OBIEE.

In addition to these common maintenance tasks, the applications administrator is in a prime position to propose the adoption of Master Data Management tools and solutions, some of which might already exist but be under-utilized. These tools bridge the gap between functional and data management, and their adoption can significantly improve data quality and consistency, as well as reduce redundancy and duplication. We'll discuss MDM more in Chapter 9.

WebCenter

WebCenter is a product suite comprised of four main solution areas: WebCenter Sites provides powerful website creation tools, WebCenter Portal allows the creation of composite applications and mash-ups, WebCenter Social provides broad sets of collaborative tools, and WebCenter

Content provides content management. While any of these could be deployed and manually integrated with E-Business Suite, it is the Portal and Content solutions that have native connections.

As illustrated in Figure 8-17, E-Business Suite supports the use of its pages and features for exposure as WebCenter portlets inside custom web pages and composite applications. This is especially useful for building a centralized access point for all of an organization's applications or building access to specific capabilities for specific purposes, such as enquiry screens or simplified transaction creation.

The general process is for E-Business Suite and WebCenter instances to share the identity management and single sign-on security deployment, and with a little setup (E-Business Suite must be registered as a portlet producer), the access is assigned to users via E-Business Suite menus, and the pages are built around OA Framework pages and WebCenter.

In addition, there is a WebCenter Content solution known as the Oracle E-Business Suite Adapter for WebCenter, which exposes the advanced content management and collaboration features to business end users. This enriches the standard functionality and, where a matching requirement exists, it can be a powerful optimization.

WebCenter is another cornerstone of Fusion Applications, and this is further evidence that adopting this technology reduces the learning curve later on and allows for the potential porting of custom solutions to the next generation of applications.

For more details, see the WebCenter Developer's Guide (E10148-18), section 55, "Integrating Other Applications," or for details on installation and setup, see Note 1074345.1.

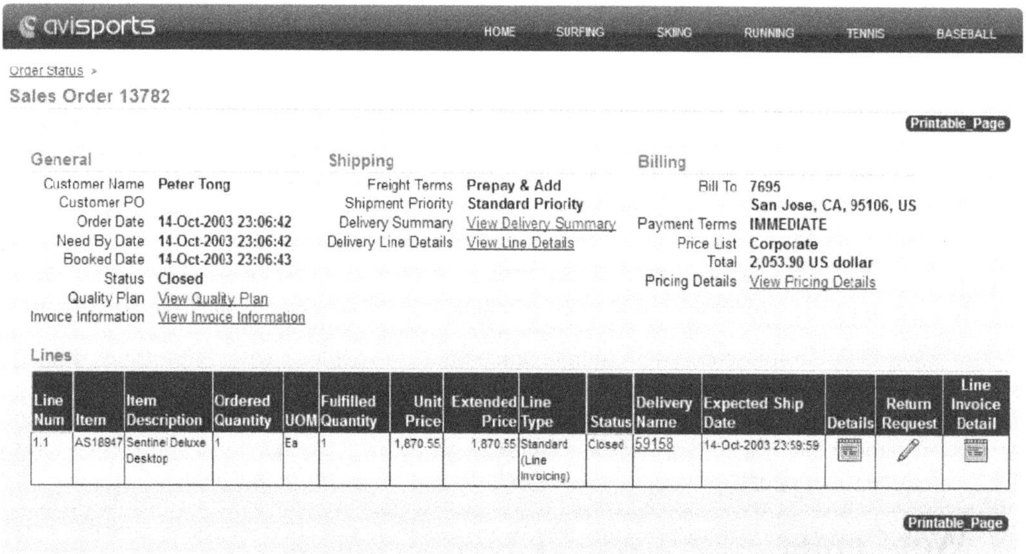

FIGURE 8-17. *The fields and table are part of the Order Management page from E-Business Suite, here contained inside a custom WebCenter portlet as part of a composite custom application*

Caching Framework

In addition to using the caching technologies from the middleware, E-Business Suite has its own internal caching feature that stores pages and query data in cache objects, reducing the round trips required for frequently repeated requests. A simple example of this caching is the way that when you assign yourself a new responsibility you often need to log out and back in to see the changes.

Cache management is accessible from the Functional Administrator responsibility and provides configuration options and the ability to create new caches. It is recommended that this feature be used for measurement (via enabling statistics) and identification of cache misses before any caches and configurations are changed.

Figure 8-18 shows the list of caches for the iProcurement product; when Statistics Collection is enabled the table shows usage details.

If you have any problems with caching, contact Oracle Support; however, general information on caching technologies and the framework can be found in the Oracle E-Business Suite Java Caching Framework Developer's Guide in Note 1087332.1.

Integration

Enterprise applications like E-Business Suite used to be considered almost monolithic, capable of running almost all organizational operations without any major dependency on other systems. This has changed substantially since the enterprise application is no longer about manual data entry and processing as these parts are now mature and mostly automated. The focus is now more on data presentation, decision support, and business planning execution.

As such, integration solutions are part of almost every implementation of E-Business Suite, and a multitude of options are available. It is true that many E-Business Suite integrations are based on longstanding options, such as interface tables, and checking these for errors and orphaned records remains an exceptionally important task.

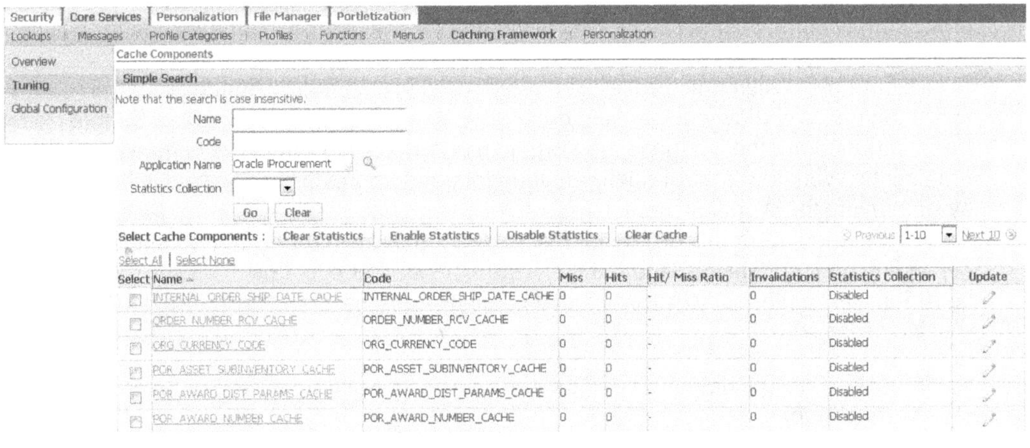

FIGURE 8-18. *The actively cached components with buttons for taking additional optimization actions*

The current gold standard from Oracle is known as Applications Integration Architecture (AIA), providing a standards-based method for implementing prebuilt integrations, either as direct integrations or process-integration-packs (PIPs), for specific features and specific application products. There are dozens of these solutions available, with a commonly used example being the Order to Cash Integration Pack for Siebel CRM and Oracle E-Business Suite Order Management. This solution essentially allows orders taken from Siebel to flow into E-Business Suite for fulfillment and payment processing. AIA leverages the same Fusion Middleware technologies used by Fusion Applications, therefore it is another opportunity to not only optimize your business capabilities, but also take a step toward the future.

As I've mentioned in other chapters, there are several other integration options within E-Business Suite and each of these should be regularly reviewed for optimization opportunities, because the faster and more reliable documents flow in and out of the system, the more effective the whole business process becomes. As a reminder, the following are the solutions I've discussed:

- **eCommerce Gateway** Supports the generation of ASCII text EDI documents and sends to trading partners or secondary EDI translators. When used it contains several optimization options, including a selection of reports to review all activities as well as inbound document status forms and a seed data reconciliation to resynchronize with system changes.

- **XML Gateway** Supports the generation of XML documents for sending to trading partners or hubs. Workflow's Transaction Monitor provides detailed insight into activity and usage for potential optimization.

- **Integrated SOA Gateway** Supports the use of Web Services for various integration purposes. It provides access to what was known in 11*i* as the E-Business Suite Integration Repository (iRep), containing information on all the APIs and various published hooks for integrating with E-Business Suite.

Oracle Workflow

As mentioned in the section "Functional Tasks," Workflow controls much of the multistep processing within E-Business Suite, and is therefore a key target for optimization for business processes, acting as the rails upon which they run.

It's both the design time process (items exposed via Workflow builder) and the runtime execution (the Workflow engine), and quite often both, that can be optimized. Simple examples I've mentioned in other chapters are purging workflow data to improve engine performance, running the Workflow control queue cleanup job, and improving an ineffective business process by simplifying the Workflow item.

As you know from this discussion, Workflow implementations and configurations vary depending on requirements, and if those requirements alter over time it makes sense to revisit both. Some examples of Workflow internal configurations that could be adjusted to better support specific needs are

- Workflow queues have configuration values for Maximum Retries, Retry Delay, and retention.

- Workflow Background Engine is a concurrent program (FNDWFBG) that has parameters including minimum and maximum threshold, which is the number of hundredths of a second this program may consume.

- Most Workflow agents/listeners have inbound and outbound configurations, such as Max Error Count, Thread Count, Processor Read Wait Timeout, and Process Loop Sleep.

- Workflow mailers can be configured in great detail, including support for setting various connection timeouts, maximum message fetch size, and SSL enablement.

In addition, based on the Release 12 adoption of Generic Service Management (GSM) containers for running Workflows internal Java programs, scaling out is now easy by adding more instances of the container. Similarly, additional concurrent processors (or dedicated specialized managers) can be added to support overloaded workflow background engines.

There are a variety of methods for optimizing core workflow, and the business drivers should guide you to which area to focus on to prevent wasting time on investigations that may bring little final value.

One other item to consider is that Workflow is supported by multiple technical components that together service the end user functionality, and as such improvements may lie in more appropriate use of these supplementary areas. One example is Oracle Business Rules (OBR), which offers an interface with Workflow's internal business events system, allowing comprehensive support for developing detailed conditional logic.

Similarly, the Approvals Management Engine (AME) runs as another complementary service for building approval lists. This works based on detailed parametric calculations made against a set of predefined rules, such as routing approval to manager levels 1 and 2 when a purchase order total is more than $999. AME also processes the responses and passes the result back to the appropriate part of the originating workflow. Of course, the conditions, rules, and attributes used in the logic must remain up to date, and a periodic effort to review these with subject matter experts is strongly recommended. In Chapter 9, we'll look at AME and how it works with Oracle E-Records to allow electronic signatures on documents and transactions that can help optimize security.

Like most components, OBR and AME have general configuration settings that can be tweaked. The screenshot in Figure 8-19 shows the AME general configuration page and how values can be set as default or per transaction type.

Configuration Variables
To use any of the default configuration variables value in your transaction type, leave the specific Transaction Type variable field blank and click Apply.

Transaction Type POS Supplier Approval M   Go

General Configuration Variables

Variable Name	Description	Default		Transaction Type	
Administrator Approver	An Administrator who should be notified in case of any exceptions in Approvals	SYSADMIN			
Allow All Approver Types	Whether Approvals Management allows all approver types	No			
Allow All Item Class Rules	Whether Approvals Management allows to create subordinate item class rules	No			
Allow For Your Information Notifications	Whether Approvals Management allows For Your Information notifications	Yes			
Distributed Environment	Whether Approvals Management runs in a distributed-database environment	No			
Production Functionality	What types of production-rule functionality are allowed	No production rules			
Purge Frequency	How many days temporary Approvals Management data ages	15			
Record Approval Deviations	Whether to record approval deviations or not	No			

| + Rule Priority Modes |
| + Forwarding Behaviors |

FIGURE 8-19. *AME's general configuration settings for the Supplier Approval process*

Concurrent Processing

Deciding on the number, distribution, and configuration of concurrent managers is a popular method for optimization, since the jobs these processors run tend to be the largest number-crunching processes inside E-Business Suite.

Here are the top four optimization actions to consider.

- Implementation of parallel concurrent processing for a truly scalable multinode architecture.

- Use of specialized concurrent managers to be dedicated to specific important and high-volume programs.

- Utilizing dedicated resources (for example, RAC compute nodes) for running specific manager types and programs.

- Verifying manager utilization. In addition to alleviating overloaded managers and improving throughput performance, reclaiming under-utilized resources from inappropriate setup can provide useful extra capacity, or at least a simplification to the system, which is a considerable optimization in itself.

It's important to remain cognizant of what is hurting the business users, or what remains most critical and therefore worth tuning, especially as business priorities change. As mentioned already, all of this should already be part of the E-Business Suite SLA management process.

Look for configuration recommendations for the specific programs and dedicated managers of importance to your system, such as how the receiving transaction manager requires at least three processes (as explained in Note 404336.1), plus more general adjustments needed, such as switching to pipe network mode in RAC deployments.

Alerts and Notifications

It's one thing to devote time and effort into tweaking the various components with the aim of optimizing E-Business Suite, but it's another to know which ones will make the biggest difference. This requires active monitoring, which means frequently checking the monitoring pages, tables, and graphs looking for peaks, troughs, and patterns—an arduous task that's not an effective use of time. Much better is passive *monitoring-by-exception*, where rules and limits are set on regularly sampled metrics and any violations trigger an appropriate reaction. There are several capabilities within and around E-Business Suite that offer this kind of functionality.

You can start simply by implementing a base set of alerts in key business areas, such as when capacity plan limits are close to being exceeded, or there's a marked increase (or sudden drop) in processing throughput and backlog. These are warnings, not errors, so it's not reliability or availability management we're considering, but rather an opportunity to improve and optimize *before* things go wrong.

Oracle Applications Manager's System Alerts and Notifications

Embedded inside E-Business Suite are several features that offer the ability to set up the automated capture of particular types of events and the subsequent spawning of notifications.

Under the System Alerts link is a page that offers several related features, along with access to log files. The Alerts tab provides a dashboard-type page showing the instances of any predefined problems in the system, so actions can be taken to resolve them and close the alert out, similar to a traditional support incident ticket.

System alerts are defined based on the E-Business Suite message dictionary database tables and generated by the internal logging API. The most significant messages are set up so that the process already knows this requires recording as a system alert.

It is also possible to configure your own messages in E-Business Suite, and you can turn on or off their ability to raise system alerts in the same place. The rules for a message to raise a system alert are that the logging must use the *unexpected* severity level, and the message must have the following two attributes set:

- Category is: System, Product, Security, or User
- Severity is: Critical, Error, or Warning

Figure 8-20 shows the System Alerts page, with summary counts of alerts of each severity, the occurrences of each distinct type, and a listing of the latest alerts. Notice the buttons for related search and setup options. As illustrated by the list, both functional processes like Oracle Forms and concurrent requests can raise alerts, as well as technology components like Workflow agents and internal managers. All alerts sit in the system for review and manually close out once they're addressed.

In addition to the preconfigured System Alerts, it is also possible to create custom notifications to be triggered when a particular action is performed. This requires manual configuration, which depends on detailed knowledge of the key system components and processes. It is therefore recommended that you begin with a simple setup for a handful of vital components and follow it with regular review and extension as the usage and management plan matures.

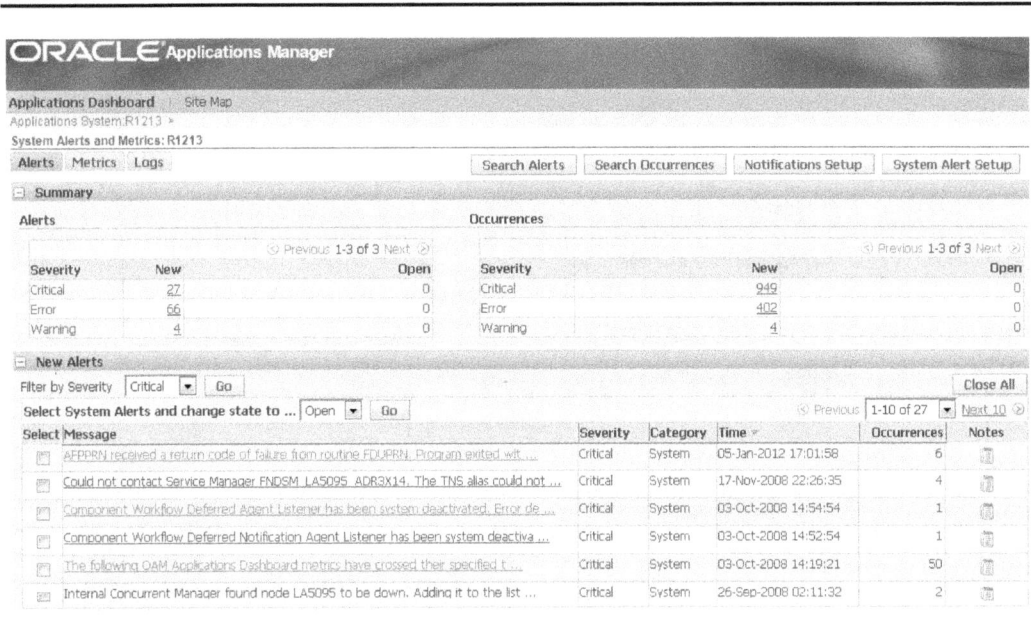

FIGURE 8-20.   *The System Alerts dashboard page showing summary data with new occurrences listed that can be drilled into for more information*

As illustrated in Figure 8-21, a notification (e-mail) can be defined around a specific object, in this case the Create Releases concurrent program. Upon failure, an error-type notification will be sent to a specified user for appropriate action.

More on creating and using System Alerts can be found in the E-Business Suite Developer's Guide (E12897-04).

Enterprise Manager's Monitoring and Metrics

With the E-Business Suite plug-in installed, or even if you use Enterprise Manager to manage the technology stack alone, a whole host of powerful management capabilities are available that can help quickly identify areas that would benefit from optimization.

First, for most components there is a monitoring template available, which is a predefined set of metrics and thresholds than can be quickly deployed and configured. The small selection of templates are shown in Figure 8-22, illustrating support for core E-Business Suite components like Workflow and Concurrent Managers, as well as all the key technology stack pieces. Monitoring templates can also be extended or adjusted as required.

Many of the metric threshold values in the seeded monitoring templates contain just logic to raise an alert if the component status is down, with the other criteria values left blank. This is intentional

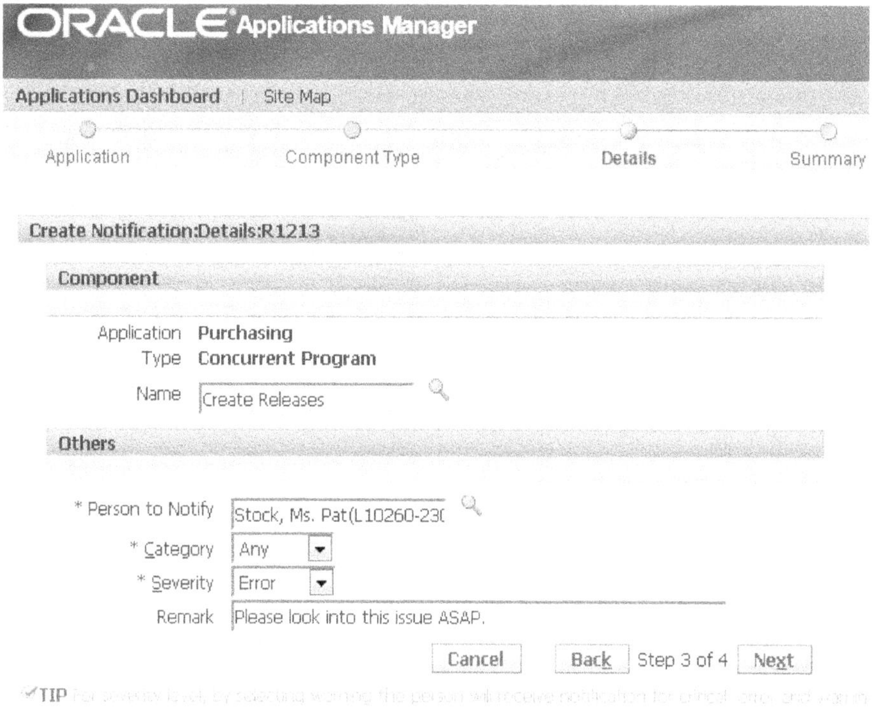

FIGURE 8-21. *Notification creation for the Create Releases concurrent program*

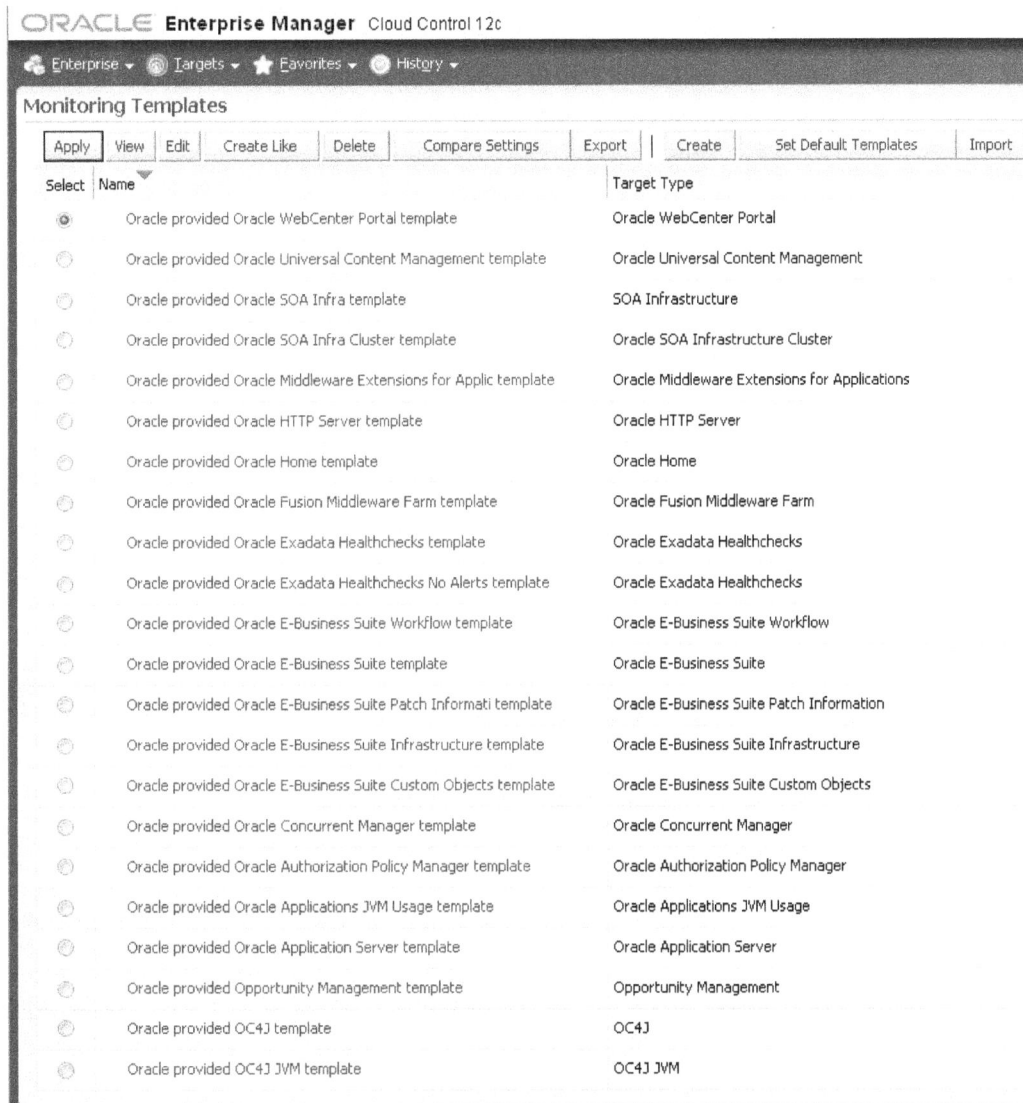

FIGURE 8-22. *A small selection of all the monitoring templates available for an E-Business Suite system, with buttons offering detailed management features for easy use, such as Create Like and Export/Import*

since each implementation differs and setting generic values based on general assumptions would mostly result in annoying notifications. As such it is an important management task to go through these setting the appropriate values for each instance. The example in Figure 8-23 shows a WebLogic Server template with the thresholds properly set up with examples such as checks for a down response status every 2 minutes, the number of stuck threads, and the server response time.

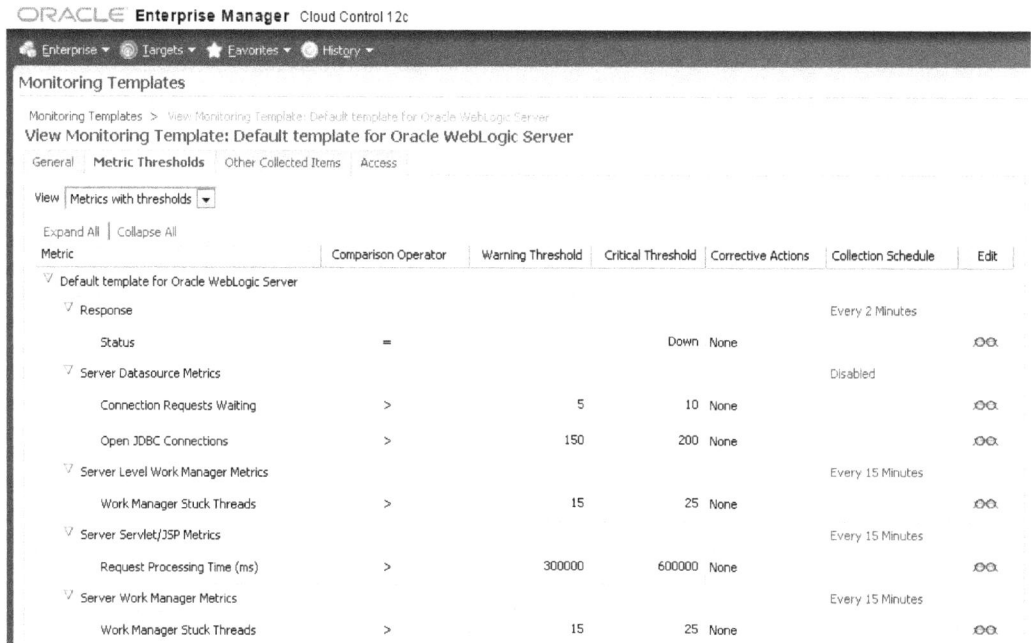

FIGURE 8-23. *A small part of the standard monitoring template for WebLogic Server, with related thresholds and metric collection schedules*

Similarly the same metric-based thresholds can be defined outside of a monitoring template. This is done in the type of screen shown in Figure 8-23, and there are dozens of metrics available for E-Business Suite as discussed in previous chapters. Figure 8-24 shows a small sample as they are from the initial deployment, with thresholds as yet undefined in this system. As you can see, they include attributes for components where logic can be easily added, such as simple alerts for exceptional peaks in concurrent requests running, forms sessions, web users, and errors in workflow.

In addition to the existing metrics in the system that are set up for collection and threshold validation, it is possible to use the Enterprise Manager target discovery process to set up new

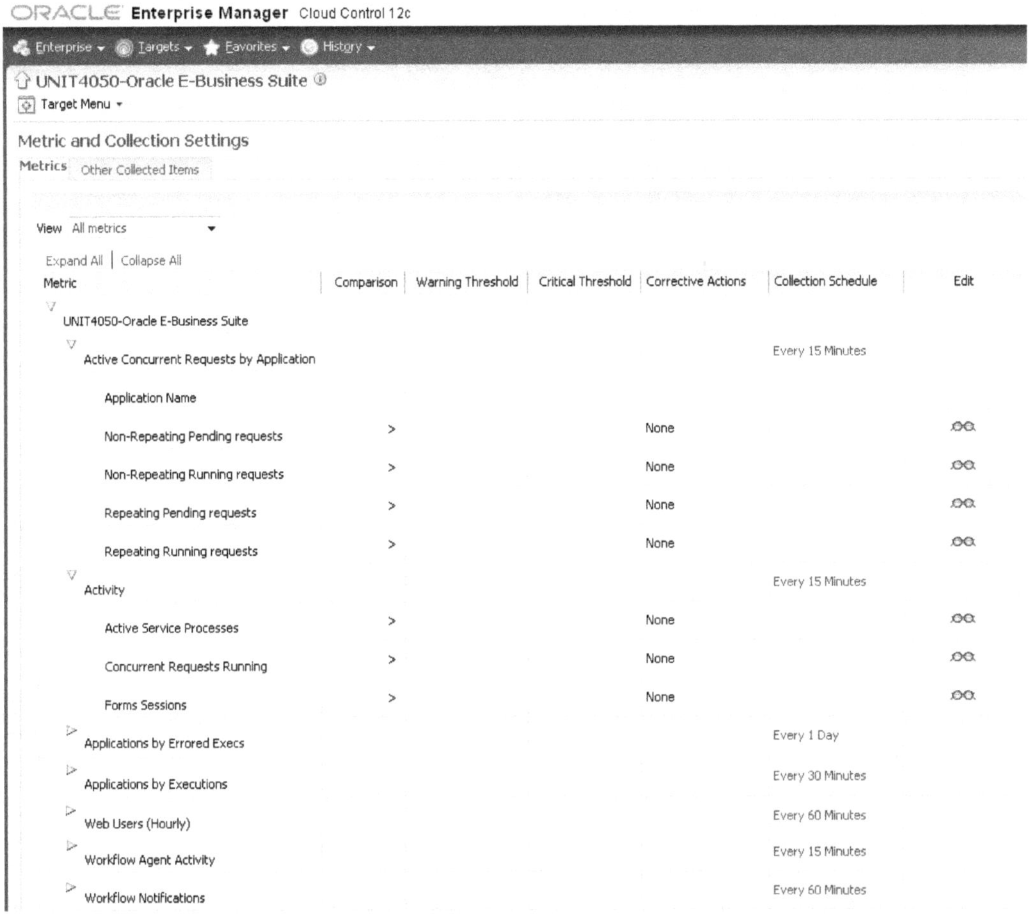

FIGURE 8-24.   *A small sample of the thresholds available for E-Business Suite metrics*

metrics, specifically for measuring and optimizing performance. The example in Figure 8-25 shows the setup screen for the Concurrent Processing service target and the creation of a new metric to measure the number of connections refused for the related listener component. This simple metric, or something more complex using an aggregate function, can then be configured with a threshold so that alerts and notifications are generated.

One step beyond configuring existing monitoring for performance measurement is to set up completely new data sources and brand new associated metrics. This is possible in the Enterprise

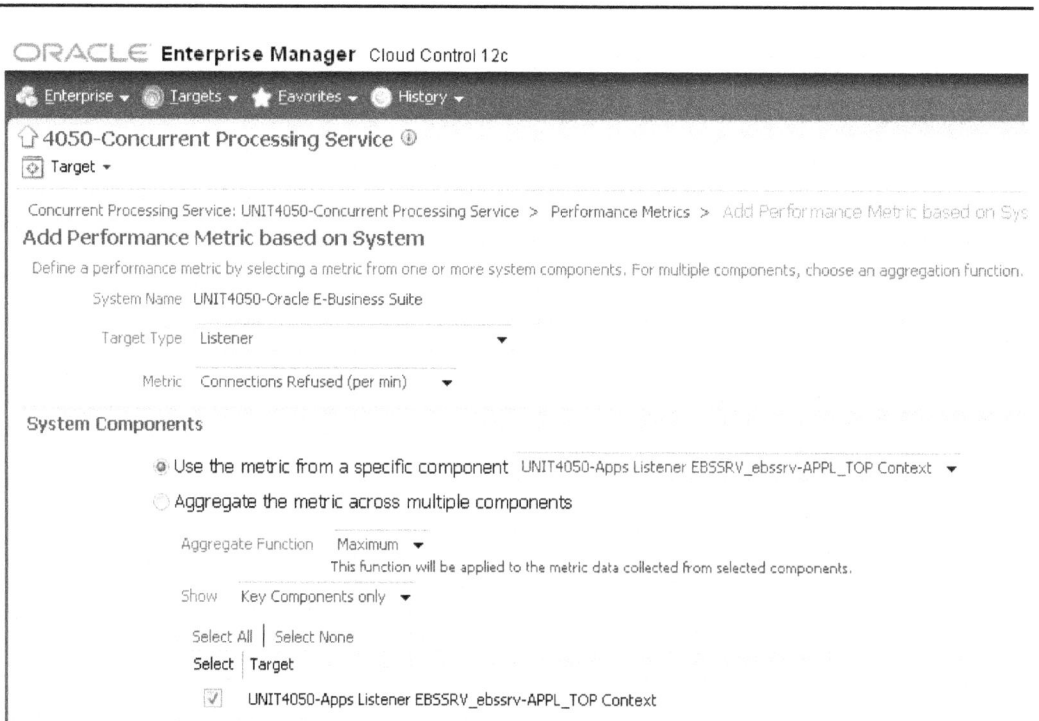

FIGURE 8-25. *E-Business Suite performance metrics can be added based on data already available in Enterprise Manager*

Manager feature called Metric Extensions (known as User Defined Metrics in the previous release). The helpful one-page graphic shown in Figure 8-26 illustrates how the process works. First, creation is often defined by linking to the execution of custom queries or scripts. Next, testing is done to ensure notifications are triggered as expected. Finally, the new metric is published either as a standalone or as part of a template, associated with one or more target types.

A simple Metric Extension example could be a Concurrent Processing Down metric where no Internal Concurrent Manager (ICM) database session exists, or perhaps an Invalid Objects Exist metric that is fired after running a query on the APPS schema. Scripts that scan logs and output files for certain significant value and patterns are another common usage.

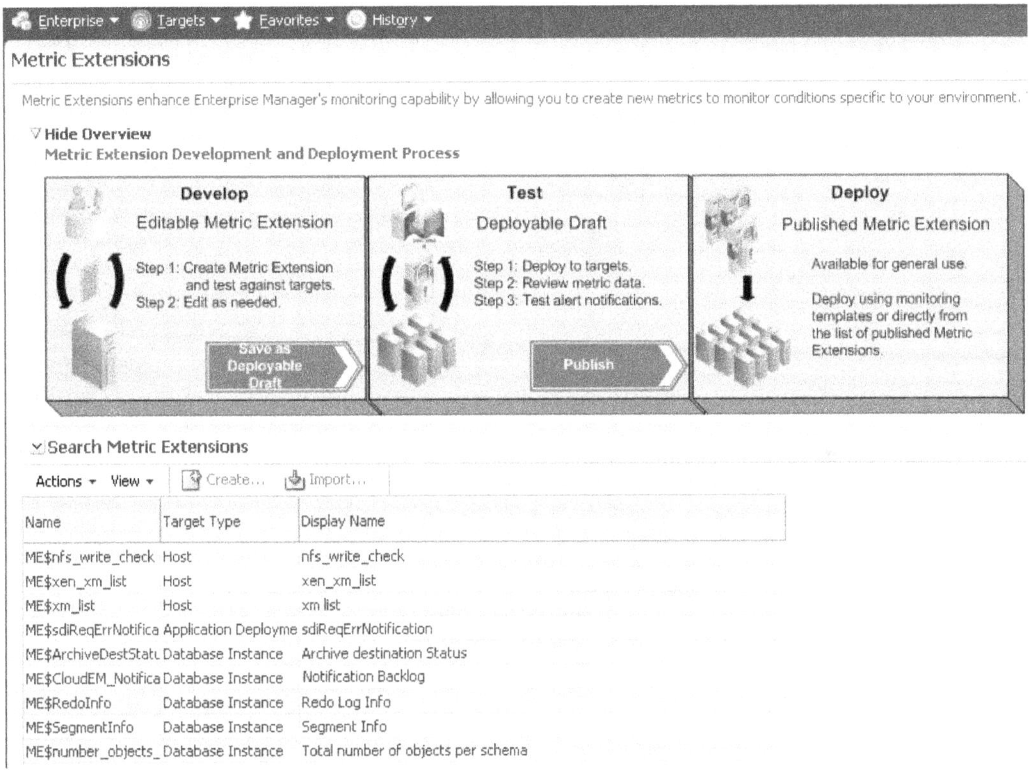

FIGURE 8-26. *Metric Extensions allow additional custom metrics that can be added based on any data source available, such as logs, scripts, and queries*

Finally, Enterprise Manager allows the configuration of rules that define exactly what happens when a problem incident occurs in the system. As shown in Figure 8-27, these are defined as incident rules, and the rule set contains logic rules and the targets that they apply to. The example shows three basic rules defined that details what should happen if an Enterprise Manager agent (the process that monitors the target) is unavailable, if there are fatal events for any of the target types in the list (Generic Service, Oracle HTTP Server, Database Instance, Listener, and so on), and if a metric threshold has been violated and the associated alert event is categorized as Critical, Fatal, or Warning. As you can see, the Action Summary shows what is then triggered, including sending e-mails, creating an incident (a type of diagnostic system snapshot), and calling the auto-ticketing external system to raise a help desk ticket.

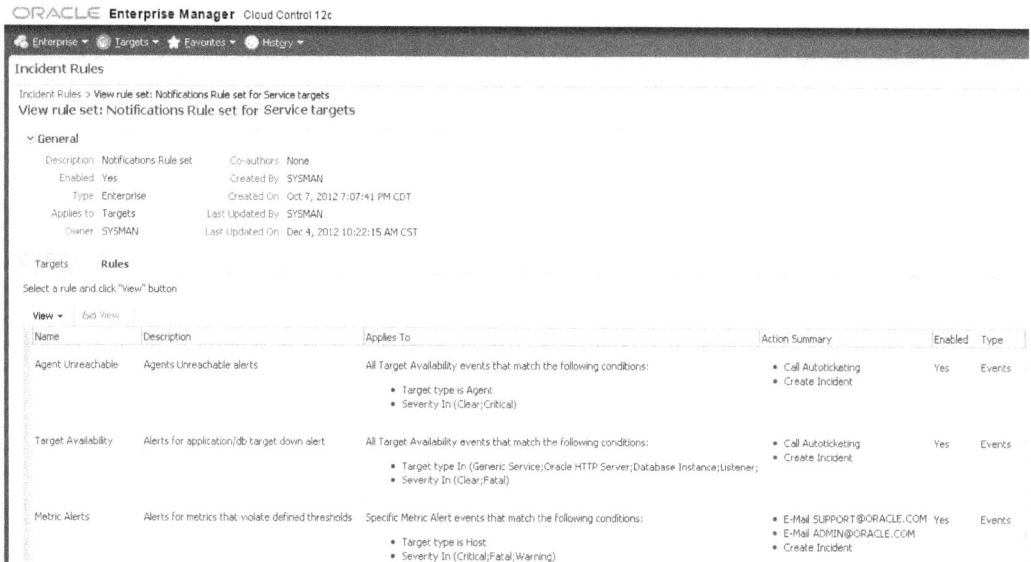

FIGURE 8-27. *The Incident Rules page shows how both the system component status and a metric threshold violation can trigger various actions*

Oracle Alerts

Oracle Alerts allows the creation of logic that notifies administrators and managers when something unexpected is found in the E-Business Suite database, such as odd transactions, bad job statuses, and errors. These can be triggered immediately upon certain events (usually table inserts or updates), or used as data collections with queries run periodically to allow later measurement. The alerts, once triggered, run a query to gather associated data and then fire one or more actions, such as sending e-mails or running scripts.

As shown in the example in Figure 8-28, an event alert can be used not just for technical optimization such as checking for problematic statuses, but also for key functional activity in the E-Business Suite system. The figure shows that the General Ledger journals table has an alert configured so that when any exceptionally large value update or entry is made, an appropriate functional manager is informed via e-mail notification with full details.

Oracle Alerts are entirely database focused but, since little E-Business Suite data is anywhere else, it remains a useful tool for tracking and managing optimization. More detail on its capabilities and use can be found in the Oracle Alert User's Guide (E12951-04).

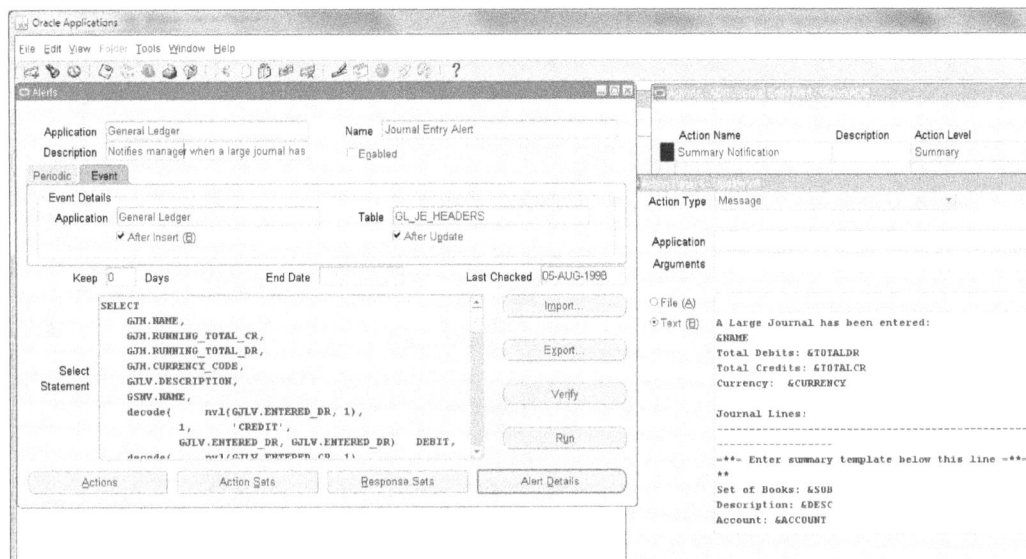

FIGURE 8-28.   *An Oracle Alert defined to notify managers for high-value ledger posting*

Setup and Implementation

While this book isn't focused on E-Business Suite installation or implementation, some related tools are worth mentioning because to perform optimization you need to know what you have, how it's currently configured, and where to make the adjustments.

The following is a short list of E-Business Suite technology layer tools related to setup that represent features and capabilities that have proven useful when considering optimization-based projects:

- **Oracle iSetup**   This is the preferred tool for functional implementation for key core application products; it contains reports and review screens that may be useful for optimization.

- **AD tools**   The Applications DBA toolset is extensive and has many tools for adjusting the system as required during an optimization project.

- **AutoConfig**   The key E-Business Suite configuration tool is exposed in an extremely clear way in Oracle Applications Manager, offering insights and simple access for optimizations. Figure 8-29 shows a small example section.

- **Profile options**   As the main E-Business Suite setup mechanism, there are a multitude of profile options that might result in optimizations for specific products or across the whole system. One example might be user session limits like ICX: Session Timeout and ICX: Limit Time for managing the resources held up by inactive user sessions.

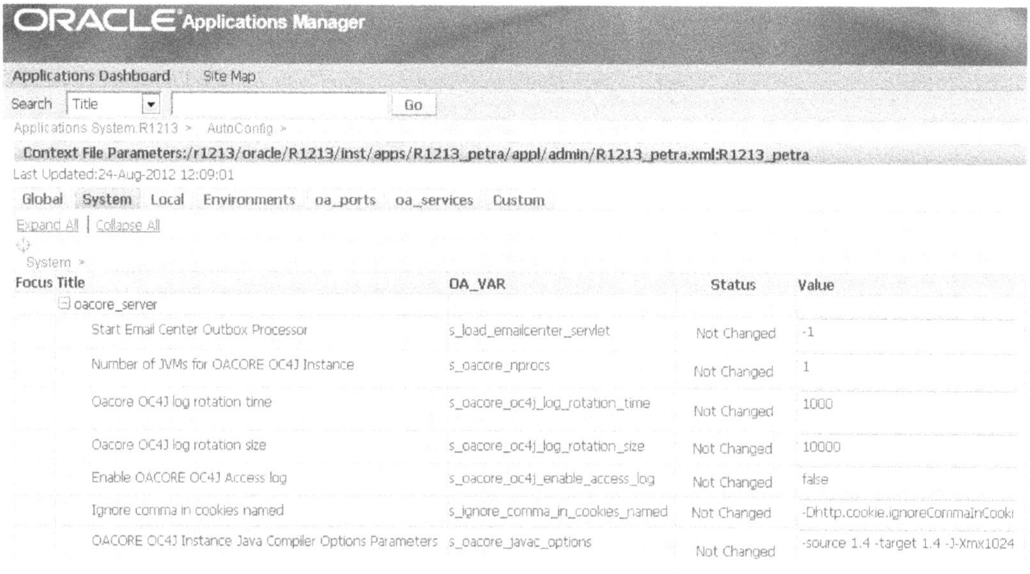

FIGURE 8-29. *Oracle Applications Manager allows you to review, compare, and edit the AutoConfig context file where many potential optimizations may lie, including Forms, Concurrent Processing, Workflow and Java configuration*

- **Seed Data Comparison Report**   This report provides a comparison of seed data from one release to another, such as 12.1.1 to 12.1.3. The intention is that any adjustments or dependencies that have been made on seed data in one instance are accounted for prior to upgrades that might cause problems. Seed data is not just things like units of measure; it includes lots of different product components. As shown in Figure 8-30, this is a prebuilt HTML-based report supporting all E-Business Suite product families. In the figure, one Financials product is chosen (GL), and the right-hand pane shows a summary with links to drill down into the detail. The report is exceptionally comprehensive (800MB unzipped) and goes right down into low-level differences, including the content of the actual seed data definition (.lct files). Download and more information can be found in Note 1327399.1.

EBS ATG Seed Data Comparison Report

Reference: Please refer to MOS Note: 1327399.1   FAMILY: Financials (FIN)

Summary statistics of Differences
Generated on: 23-Jun-2011

Summary of differences across Releases

Product	12.1.3 Vs 11.5.10.2			12.1.3 Vs 12.0.4		
	Added in 12.1.3	Removed in 12.1.3	Changed in 12.1.3	Added in 12.1.3	Removed in 12.1.3	Changed in 12.1.3
AMW	1084	-	153	2	-	14
AP	1665	11	702	437	24	202
AR	2439	24	1263	665	2	342
AX	608	59	229	77	2	25
CE	1016	3	91	98	-	33
CUA	1	-	1	1	-	-
FA	1226	30	626	592	2	92
FUN	947	-	-	29	-	97
FV	373	17	690	110	-	60
GCS	1579	-	5	335	1	56
GL	2581	66	1006	285	246	276
IA	21	-	14	13	-	4
IBY	1110	-	181	127	-	45
IEX	619	1088	813	172	1	111
IGC	217	1	554	56	-	20
IGI	1030	34	845	289	34	295
IGW	6	1	16	1	-	2
IMC	107	15	98	4	-	5
IPM	1	-	-	1	-	-
ITA	162	-	-	1	-	5
JA	8044	2	96	425	20	451
JE	306	7	302	97	-	76
JG	316	7	212	54	-	64
JL	914	5	358	329	-	48
ALL**	1865	9	387	402	1	166
TOTAL	38402	2664	12572	7402	739	3755

Detail statistics of Differences for product GL
Generated on: 23-Jun-2011

Difference report for 12.1.3 Vs 12.1.1

Datatype	GL		
	Added in 12.1.3	Removed in 12.1.3	Changed in 12.1.3
BIP Defns Temps	1	-	2
Concurrent Programs	5	-	9
Descriptive Flexfields	-	-	-
Diagnostics	-	-	1
Functions	-	-	-
Key Flexfields	-	-	-
Lookups	-	-	1
Menus	79	-	162
Messages	20	-	-
Printer Styles	Not striped by application: No differences		
Profiles	-	-	-
RSG Metadata	-	-	-
Report Manager Components	-	-	-
Report Manager Contents	-	-	1
Report Manager Integrators	-	-	2
Report Manager Layouts	-	-	1
Report Manager Mappings	-	-	1
Report Manager Parameter Lists	-	-	2
Report Manager Security Rules	-	-	-
Request Groups	-	-	-
Request Sets	Not striped by application: Differences		
Responsibilities	-	-	-
UMX Roles	1	-	-
Value Sets	Not striped by application: Differences		
TOTAL	106	0	182

FIGURE 8-30. *A section of the Seed Data Comparison Report for the General Ledger product, showing the differences between 12.1.3 and other releases*

Platform Technology Layer

Explaining how to optimize the whole technology stack running under E-Business Suite would require a whole series of books, so in this section we'll focus on the tools and techniques that are most often successful for the customers my colleagues and I have worked with.

Remember, we must always focus on delivering against organizational objectives and improvements, and not spending hours tweaking the technology for its own sake. We're looking for opportunities like reducing complexity, increasing capabilities, enhancing productivity, and facilitating deeper business insights. This requires translation to convert the needs of the user community into actions on the technology components, and this chapter will try to offer help.

From the combination of E-Business Suite's complex execution and the fact the platform technology layer introduces some software and hardware engineering disciplines, the optimizations here are most commonly categorized as *tuning*. This makes sense since efficiency is often the main reason for trying to improve the technology stack.

Technical Architecture

Don't let the words "technical architecture" make you panic. I am not suggesting that you completely disrupt your E-Business Suite instance by changing the deployed architecture just to realize something such as slightly faster concurrent requests. It is true, however, that it can make sense to consider adjustments or extensions at major system lifecycle milestones.

For example, when performing a major upgrade, you should revisit the application management plans and the Service Level Agreements and consider whether now is the time to also make some improvements based on predicted future requirements, such as scaling out. Similarly, later releases often come with new options that meet current requirements, such as implementing single-sign-on for better security management.

Here are some options to consider that are supported by E-Business Suite and proven to deliver significant optimizations. This list is broad and goes far beyond topology changes. However, it represents a practical method of offering inspiration, which is much better than either repeating information better explained elsewhere or omitting key areas all together.

- **Use E-Business Suite's architecture features** For example, use staged and shared applications tier file systems, or implement the E-Business Suite Tablespace Model.

- **Scale out** Adopt an RAC database deployment or increase the registered nodes or the number of component server instances like Forms and OC4J.

- **Adjust the Concurrent Processing architecture** Do this with options such as Parallel Concurrent Processing or by adding specialized managers.

- **Implement caching** Do this with Java Object Cache, Oracle Application Server Web Cache, or the embedded E-Business Suite options such as the Oracle Universal Connection Pool.

- **Add load balancing** This is available as hardware options for user requests, as well as inside software components like OC4J and WebLogic, Oracle Forms, and database with RAC.

- **Increase database options** For example, use advanced compression, database partitioning, DataGuard, and ASM.

- **Data management** Do this with MDM, archiving and Information Lifecycle Management (ILM), and even simple actions like properly gathering statistics as detailed in "Query Optimization in Oracle E-Business Suite" in the Oracle E-Business Suite System Administrator's Guide—Configuration (E12893-04).

- **Harden security** Use Identity Management, Single Sign-on, Database Vault, Transparent Data Encryption (TDE), and DMZ deployments.

- **Use virtualization and advanced cloning** Use the E-Business Suite features and templates to get additional instances available with shorter lead times and lower resource needs.

- **Extend Business Intelligence** Deploy advanced features like BI Applications to deliver better services to end users.

- **Deploy Enterprise Manager** Ideally, include the E-Business Suite plug-in, although even the core components bring significant features for better system management.

Simplify Maintenance

Maintenance is where 70 percent of IT budgets gets used, but it rarely brings any noticeable improvement to the system, although historically it was considered a necessary cost. With new features and technologies, the profile of maintenance was changing, and E-Business Suite is beginning to adopt more components that are self-aware and that can automatically handle regular maintenance activities with little or no intervention.

We discussed ways of reducing system downtime in Chapter 7 as a way to improve performance. Simplifying maintenance also enhances the Application Manager's productivity, so it falls under optimization. While there are many activities that can or must be done during maintenance windows, for simplicity's sake we'll discuss the most common three: running backups, applying patches, and making upgrades.

Backups

Backup procedure is commonly predetermined by corporate IT policy and is usually based around the existing processes, tools, and services in use. In Chapter 6 we considered how many of the technology stack components offer features that can be used to facilitate quick backup times, reducing or eliminating the need for taking the system offline. These are mostly centered around component redundancy and many of the database high-availability features such as Automatic Storage Management, Secure Backup, and Oracle Data Guard. In addition, using preconfigured hardware such as the Oracle Database Appliance can significantly simplify administrative tasks.

E-Business Suite itself does not offer much in the way of features for backups, except perhaps the option of a Staged Applications Tier, allowing processing to move between nodes so that online backups can be taken.

Patching

Patching is an area that significantly improves with E-Business Suite Release 12.2 and the new online patching feature. This is based on leveraging the Edition-Based-Redefinition feature of the 11g Release 2 database, which greatly optimizes patching, reducing patch downtime to a consistently short switchover period.

Prior to this, there were some longstanding basic features and options that are frequently ignored or unappreciated, repeated here for review.

- **Merge patches** Use AD tools (admerge) or the equivalent option from Oracle Applications Managers Patch Wizard. This was discussed in Chapter 6; details are available in My Oracle Support Note 1077813.1.

- **Run AD Administration (adadmin)** Use a defaults file that has your own standardize inputs predefined, reducing the keying and potential mistakes. Also run this in noninteractive mode for common tasks, as it considerably speeds execution if it doesn't have to print to the screen.

- **Use the Patch Manager feature** This is available in the Enterprise Manager plug-in for E-Business Suite. It supports all the standard features of patching (adpatch) but it does so via simple Enterprise Manager pages in an easy six-step process as shown in Figure 8-31. It includes integration with My Oracle Support to find and get patch files, allows multiple instances and multiple patches to be applied in one go, and even supports custom patches through the Customization Manager feature. Reporting and patch run information pages are available, increasing visibility of what happened when for effective system management.

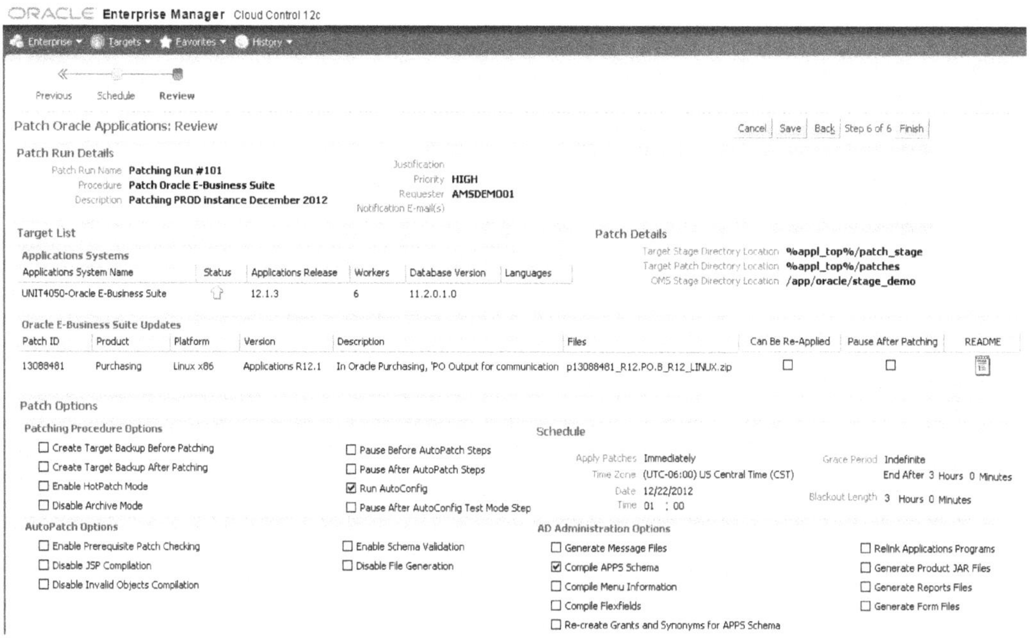

FIGURE 8-31. *Summary of a patch request ready to be submitted. Note the various flexible options that would be tough to recall and review using the command-line equivalent*

- **Use the Job Timing Report** This is available through Oracle Applications Manager or the AD command-line tools and provides a variety of detailed administration and patching information, reducing the need to dig into large log files for information. As illustrated in Figure 8-32, it includes patch job statuses, restart attempts, failures, and time spent on each phase. Similarly, the AutoConfig Performance Profiler script (adconfig.pl) can be useful for identifying performance improvements.

Upgrades

Upgrade policies are commonly governed by existing organizational practices or defined after initial installation and seemingly frozen. These policies can often benefit from regular review to make sure the most effective options and processes are still being used.

In addition to the excellent documentation in the E-Business Suite Administrators Guide—Maintenance (E12894-04), a helpful resource filled with best practice recommendations is the Maintenance Wizard. This is an installable product feature and provides screens that guide you through the upgrade of Oracle E-Business Suite, say from Release 11*i* to 12. In addition to upgrades, it also supports the installation of Release Update Packs (RUPs) and Maintenance Packs and assists with major updates to the applications database.

The Maintenance Wizard leverages information from numerous manuals and guides to provide you with a comprehensive view of all the activities required during an upgrade. From this it dynamically filters the necessary steps based on criteria obtained directly from analyzing the

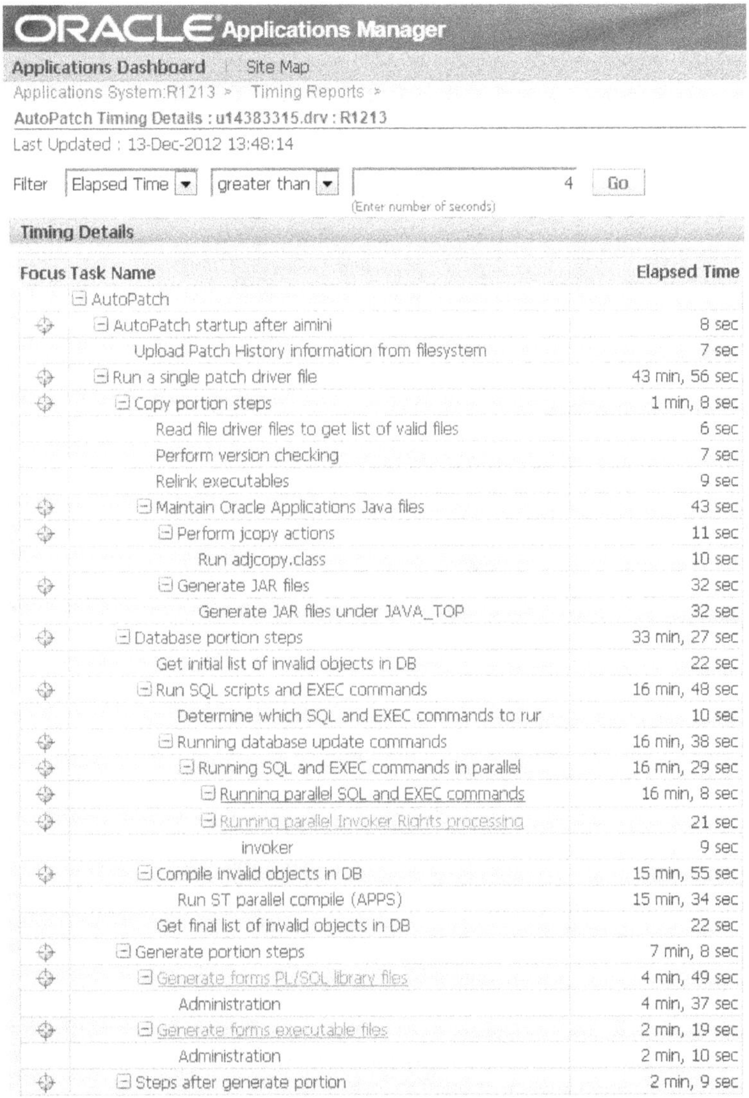

FIGURE 8-32. *An example Job Timing report for one patch run, showing detailed activities, status, and timings*

E-Business Suite instance it is installed upon. The result is a step-by-step instruction report, as shown in Figure 8-33.

Maintenance Wizard also exposes various upgrade utility features for investigation and troubleshooting and can also automatically execute many of the core tasks, reducing the overhead and the possibility of errors or accidental step omission. For more details and the download, see Note 215527.1 in My Oracle Support.

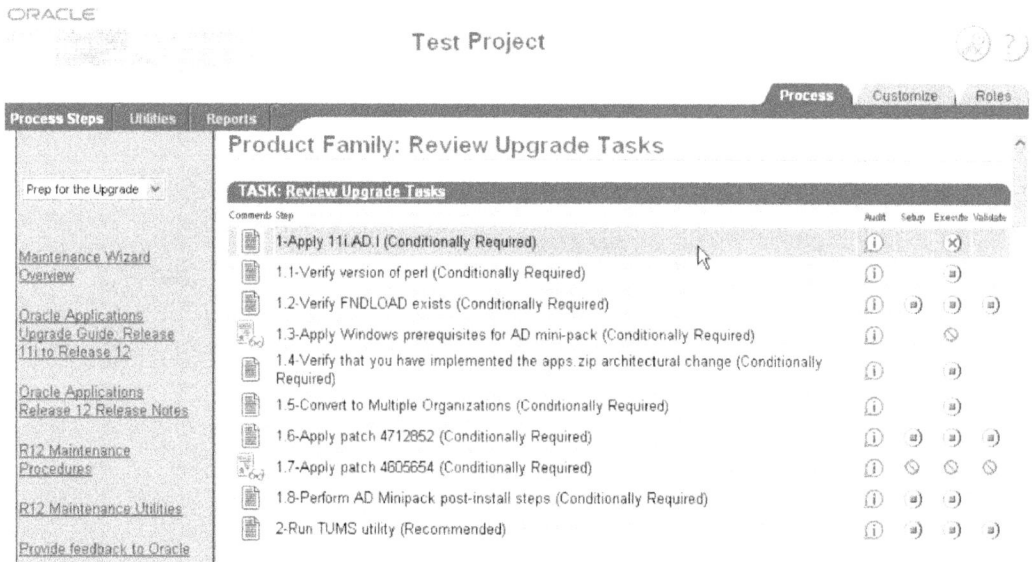

FIGURE 8-33. *The Maintenance Wizard feature with a list of required upgrade tasks and options to execute where appropriate*

System Testing

Another arduous but inevitable task is facilitating testing after patches and upgrades to check for issues and regressions. Thankfully, this is another area where new technology and automation brings enormous optimization opportunity, and there are solutions available specifically for E-Business Suite.

The Oracle Enterprise Manager plug-in options include a set of testing products known as the Oracle Applications Testing Suite (OATS), which offers a set of core functionality based around the OpenScript tool for testing any custom application, plus prebuilt accelerators to support Oracle's own application products like E-Business Suite.

Figure 8-34 shows the Oracle OpenScript client tool that runs scripts for functional testing or load testing purposes. Each test is a sequence of steps recorded directly from a user performing them in an E-Business Suite instance. The figure shows an example in the left pane: each step, starting from login, navigating to General Ledger, and entering a journal is shown. The right pane shows details of what is occurring, and the bottom of the screen shows a log of the last time the test was run and the time to completion. These results can be expanded in greater detail, as can the test script itself, by clicking the Java Code tab to allow full customization features.

The OpenScript client also supports loading data from Oracle Real User Experience Insight (RUEI) from any recorded transactions it has captured. This is a great method for testing and verifying performance issues. Using this automation reduces testing times substantially. For example, E-Business Suite administrators have reported going from 270 hours for manual testing to just 21 hours using functional testing and the OATS accelerators for Oracle E-Business Suite.

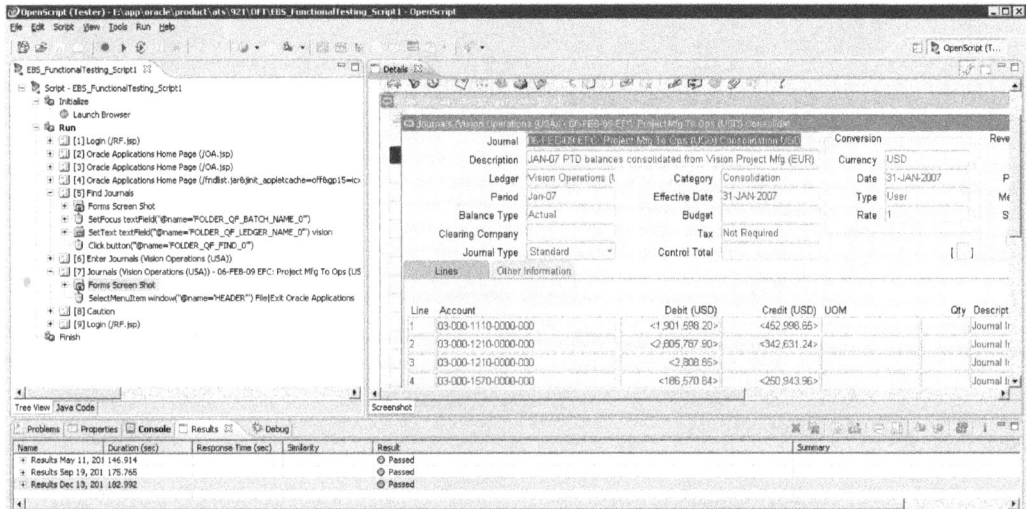

FIGURE 8-34. *Testing entering a journal in E-Business Suite*

Another useful feature of the testing suite is the Oracle Data Masking Pack, available as part of the Enterprise Manager plug-in. This tool scrambles sensitive data as part of running a clone job, resulting in a new instance with data that is safe for all users to view. Prebuilt masking templates are available for E-Business Suite, and they can be extended and adjusted as required. We'll cover more on E-Business Suite security and the potential optimization in Chapter 9.

Health Checks and Technical Compliance

I mentioned health checking earlier, but only in the context of functional setup and data. There is a different set of tools that specialize in the validation of technology configurations, such as Remote Diagnostic Agent (RDA) and Enterprise Manager's Compliance Management feature.

RDA provides a framework within which product-specific scripts are run that interrogate files and other repositories to collect all the most essential configuration data. This is then displayed in an easy to review HTML format. There is explicit support for E-Business Suite through the use of the ACT module in RDA, which is runnable from both the command line and the Oracle Diagnostic Framework user interface. Figure 8-35 shows just the top of the output with the table of contents, illustrating how exceptionally detailed this report is.

This rich resource can provide a simple way to access comprehensive technical information and therefore is useful in optimization projects. More details on RDA can be found in Note 314422.1. Also, keep a look out for integration with new tools like the Diagnostic Assistant (DA) for Release 12.2 onward with the Incident Packaging process in Enterprise Manager.

Going further, Enterprise Manager has become the de facto standard for managing the Oracle Technology components and supports the presentation of configuration information as well as checking that it is inline with Oracle's recommended usage. This is done through the use of logic-based compliance rules that validate collected configuration values.

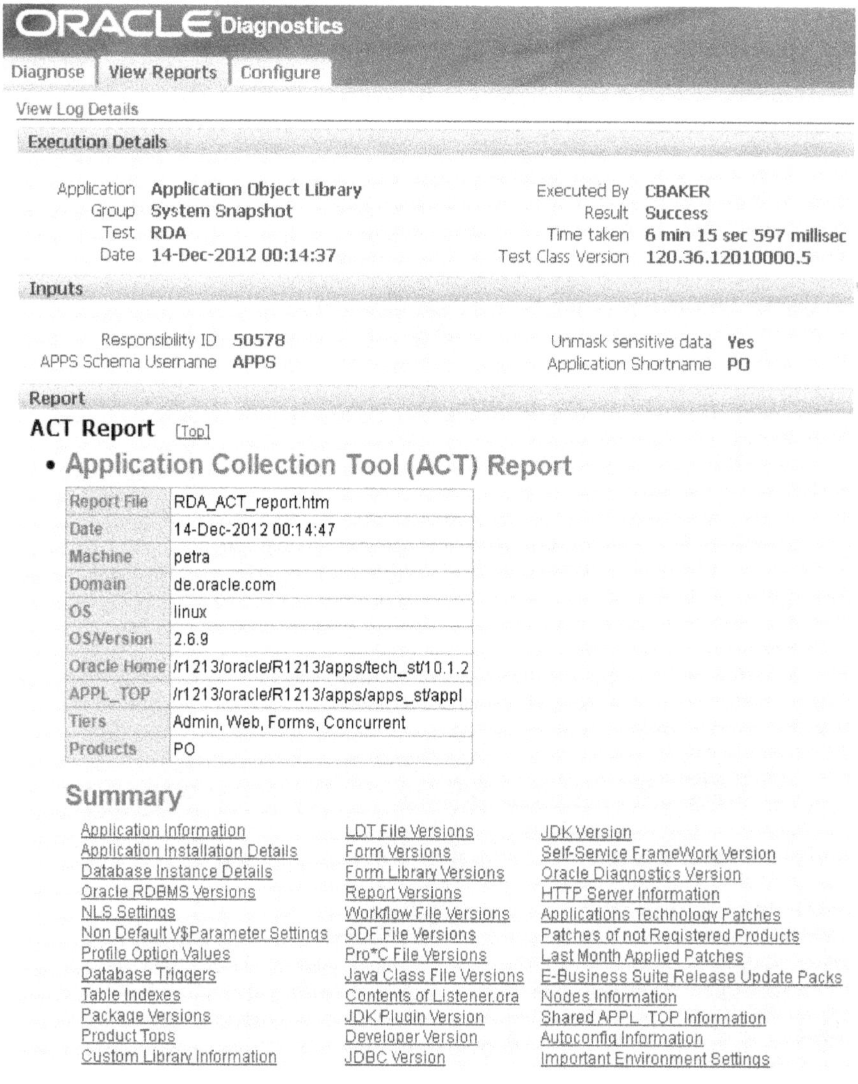

FIGURE 8-35. *Remote Diagnostic Agent output for the E-Business Suite ACT module*

These rules are grouped into compliance standards, usually based around a product or technology, and these standards are further put into different compliance frameworks that commonly represent different use cases in which configuration checks might vary, such as production versus test instances, or specific regulatory requirements. This is shown in Figures 8-36 and 8-37, which show the compliance standards and rules for the Oracle Database.

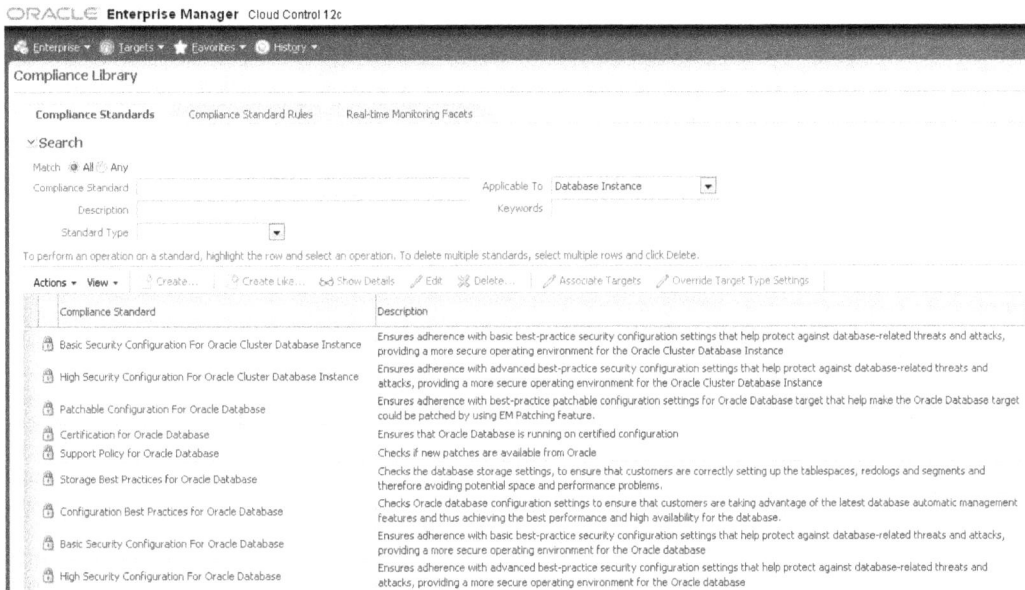

FIGURE 8-36. *A few of the compliance standards available for the Oracle Database*

Oracle already provides hundreds of these rules across a large proportion of its technologies, and it includes the ability to dynamically download new rules from a central server as soon as they are available. The real power of this feature comes where organizations also enhance it with custom rules that enforce their own boundaries, best practices, and guidelines.

Hardware and Networking

While not intended to be a big part of this software management book, with Oracle's move into physical servers and storage it seems remiss to not consider optimizing hardware. I've already mentioned using the Oracle Exa-machines for improving performance and Enterprise Manager's support for host systems. Tools like these allow for numerous optimizations, including lower storage resources, reduced power consumption, and greater fault tolerance. Interestingly, Oracle itself uses the Exa-machines to power the on-demand and Oracle Cloud.

A production-ready E-Business Suite environment requires many different hardware devices to support the distributed topologies required for optimal performance, security, redundancy for failover, and load balancing. Each server node will differ based on the tasks it performs; therefore, including hardware optimization effort is useful. In addition, between the application hosts are the various physical network components (firewalls, proxies, routers/switches, and so on), and these are also strong candidates for potential optimization.

I won't go into too much depth here, but I'll discuss a couple of general recommended principles proven useful for managing enterprise applications.

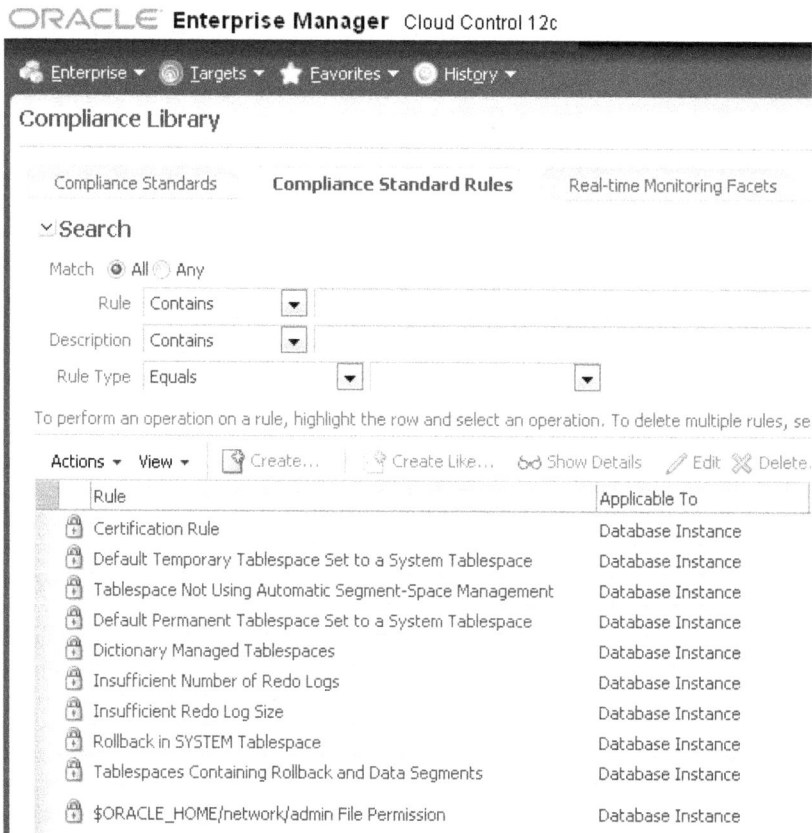

FIGURE 8-37. *A small selection of the 205 rules that reside across the compliance standards for the Oracle Database*

Optimizing the Stack

Throughout this book we have advocated approaching E-Business Suite Management with particular goals in mind: reliability, availability, performance, or governance. The optimization of hardware should be done in the same way, to improve a particular service for end users, such as tighter security or faster processing time.

The simple graphic in Figure 8-38 highlights that while an E-Business Suite instance uses most of the Oracle technology stack, the management of all components—from functional applications to virtualization and hardware—needs to be brought together and optimized with a clear intent. This is essential as it means the related projects are specific, discrete, and controlled, with results that are measurable.

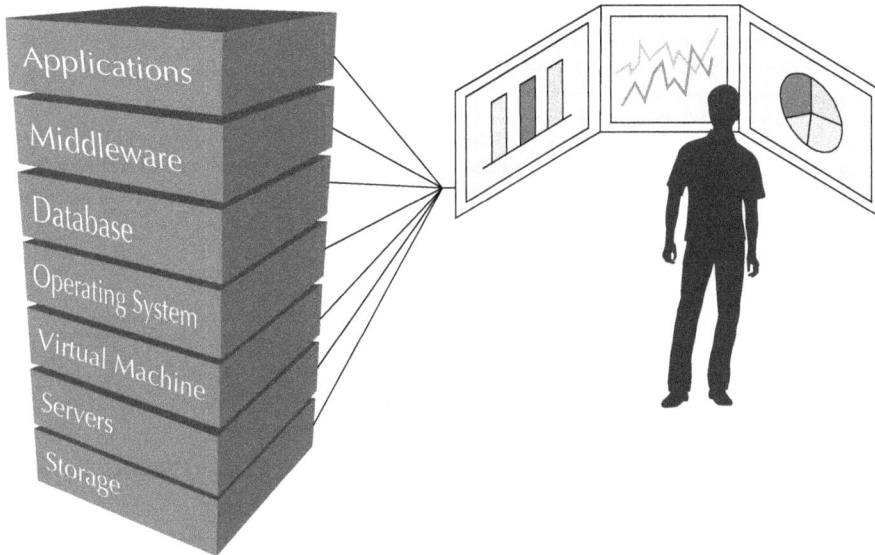

FIGURE 8-38.   *Optimizing the whole stack, always based on a specific purpose*

Component Lifecycle

The only time hardware components should require dedicated management is when they are nearing the end of their life. As mentioned in Chapter 3, each physical component has a lifecycle and will ultimately require repair or replacement to remain effective, certified, and supported.

This can be done intelligently, integrated with the implementation of other optimization projects so that complementary changes are coordinated across hardware, software, and business operations. Such a combined change is crucial, as when these elements fall out of sync with each other, the potential synergies and opportunities are lost and problems occur. All too often, technical adjustments are designed based on outdated business expectations, wasting time and money. Communication, coordination, and regular reviews are essential for truly effective application management.

Resource Management

Resource management is often combined with middleware, database, and general performance; it's crucial that hardware and networking resource consumption and utilization are measured, analyzed, and subsequently managed.

Although the hardware offers resources to the layers above it, it has its own part to play in how efficiently those resources are distributed and scaled based on demand. For example, SQL queries are made as efficient as possible by the cost base optimizer inside the database; however, the actual response time the end users see will vary depending on the resources, capabilities, and health of each physical compute node and the connections between them.

Where resource consumption is high (after all, the goal is to have a well-used application), even slight latencies can quickly scale to become noticeable by end users. The pursuit of hardware optimization is an important task, and despite the significant expertise required, it shouldn't be ignored by Application Managers by assuming other teams will or have already tuned the machines appropriately.

All hardware and operating system vendors offer management tools, and it is strongly recommended that Application Managers work with the specialists involved to set up some basic dashboards and interrogation utilities so that monitoring and management is possible. Many times I have worked on E-Business Suite issues where, after top-down analysis through the functional and application layers, we finally determined the root cause to be a resource constraint or networking bottleneck.

Some of the tools that may be made available to the applications manager are listed here, and while some will add processing or administrative overhead, their use can offer significantly higher levels of effective application management.

- Read-only access to the operating system, with execute privileges on utility programs
- Custom web forms and pages that execute specific back-end shell scripts and report the back data
- Dashboard pages with portlet regions showing real-time data from various tools and scripts
- Secured access to features within the full hardware management tools

While some of these basic elements might work in a limited fashion, Oracle Enterprise Manager Ops Center shown in Figure 8-39 is the most powerful solution available, offering the same capabilities I've detailed for application management, but for the hardware and operating system components. This includes configuration and compliance, performance monitoring, problem capture, automated diagnostics and troubleshooting utilities, and threshold-based alerts and notifications. Although specific to managing the base system platform, it is integrated with Enterprise Manager Cloud Control for complete stack management. Its ease of use and automated system analysis makes it an exceptionally good candidate to consider for optimizing the technology platform.

Networks and Clouds

With access to enterprise applications being expanded to a new set of user profiles, management planning needs to keep up with the new breed of possibilities, requirements, and options. The trend remains toward more remote access options over a multitude of different network types, using a range of different client devices. This really stretches the traditional Application Manager and makes their network management process increasingly important.

The enterprise applications market, including E-Business Suite, is showing a clear increase in cloud-based deployments, including the entire application (Software-as-a-Service) and, more recently, running over an outsourced base technology platform (Infrastructure-as-a-Service). It's essential that application administrators still have the tools and information they need to support their end users, and careful analysis of different service provider management features is strongly recommended. We'll discuss this more in Chapter 11.

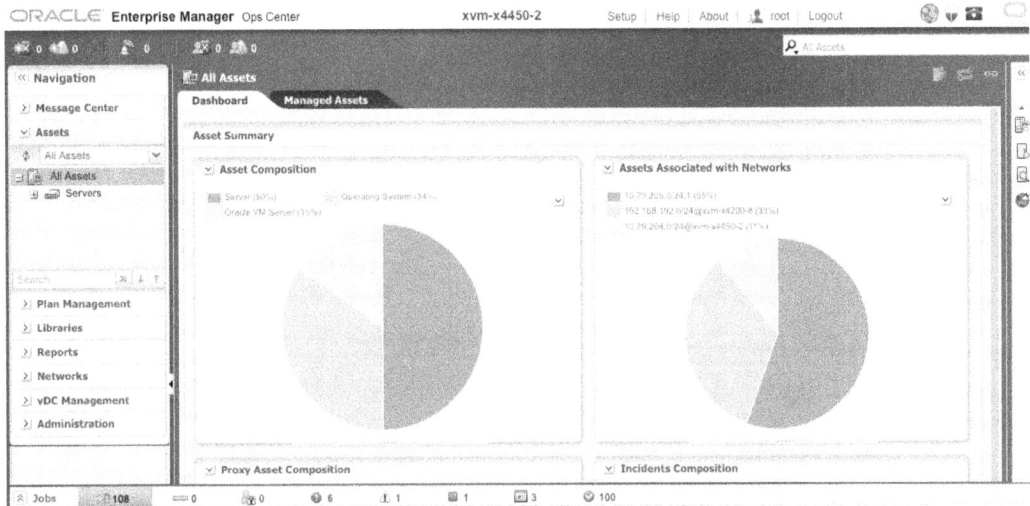

FIGURE 8-39. *The Assets dashboard in Enterprise Manager Ops Center 12c*

Watching the Watchman

One final word on optimization: sometimes optimizing the management tools is a great method to quickly realize significant improvements. Being able to identify issues early, understand the components involved, and get to the root cause efficiently helps to make application tuning relatively simple, even for a complex system like E-Business Suite. Indeed, many times it is a functional manager or administrator who needs to make the required change, such as a profile option, but it's the Applications Manager who needs to help by analyzing why a process is slow, what the components involved are, how they are configured, and what the underlying processes are doing.

Therefore, it's essential to make sure that the management tools are not only complete, but also operational, accurate, and efficient. I've seen several E-Business Suite environments with performance issues that turned out to be caused by incorrectly configured tools that checked dozens of system components every second, resulting in far too much information collection, overloading networking and shared resources. Similarly, I have seen E-Business Suite situations where incorrectly deployed diagnostics fail with errors, slowing not only the resolution of the original problem, but also creating more work and generally adding to everyone's stress levels.

Therefore, I recommend you regularly review the catalog of management tools and their capabilities, and run some simple tests to make sure everything works as expected. Executing such tests can be automated to save time, plus they may also be done in combination with similar introspection tasks, such as running Service Level Agreement reporting and reviews.

Summary

In this chapter, we looked at dozens of tools and techniques for adding a layer of continuous improvement around our E-Business Suite application management plan. This holistic approach brings a focus to what we are trying to achieve and plugs the gaps between the traditional system management categories so that results are complete and cohesive.

The following table summarizes the items we covered in this chapter.

Business Process Layer	Applications Technology Layer	Platform Layer
Uptake new features	Business Intelligence	Technical architecture
Optimize for new usage	Extending features	Simplify maintenance
Personalize for productivity	Application's data health	Health checks and technical compliance
Functional tasks	WebCenter	Hardware and networking
Functional configuration and change management	Caching framework	Watching the watchman
Proactive support	Integration	
	Workflow	
	Concurrent processing	
	Alerts and notifications	
	Setup and implementation	

CHAPTER
9

A Governance
Management Toolbox

After the corporate scandals and market collapses of the last decade, the need for corporations and other organizations to implement strong governance and compliance processes has become essential. For many industry sectors, adherence to regulatory standards is commonplace (such as Generally Accepted Accounting Principles - GAAP), and are increasingly part of legislative requirements, such as Sarbanes-Oxley (SOX), Payment Card Industry (PCI), Health Insurance Portability and Accountability Act (HIPPA), Statement on Auditing Standards (SAS) 70, and the various elements of the International Organization for Standardization (ISO—not an acronym but the greek word for equal).

The evolution of IT governance has accelerated in this environment, and as a facilitator of business process execution, IT operations also need accountability to ensure its resources best serve consumers, remaining focused on organizational objectives and delivering an auditable return on investment. Not surprisingly, both the Information Technology Infrastructure Library (ITIL) and the Control Objectives for Information and Related Technology (COBIT) frameworks discussed in earlier chapters include many aspects of governance in their recommendations.

As a subset of IT governance, application governance for a system like E-Business Suite must inherit all of the parent values, as well as deploy the controls and measures to its end users and administrators. This is another complex management area with many distributed options to consider. This chapter will guide you through where to focus and what is available.

What Is Application Governance?

Governance is control, and just as in human society, there are laws that influence how the elements of a system operate and its overall success in any one organized environment. In addition, and especially in human society, those laws need enforcement to help those in authority govern their communities successfully.

In Chapter 2 we defined application governance as follows:

To ensure that features and data are available only to authorized users.

Application governance has two focus areas that need control: functional features and application data. Our definition mentions the availability of these, which in this context could be synonymous with general access control, but it also includes ensuring those items are appropriate and compliant with overall business rules and organizational policies. As you'll see from the different types of tools in this chapter, addressing governance from these angles ensures nothing is left to chance and that management quality will reign supreme.

As ultimate system custodian and guardian, the Applications Manager needs to understand the following four key aspects of governance. Some or all these responsibilities are also commonly part of other specialist roles, or they can even be the responsibility of a cross-discipline team.

- **Security** This is the obvious central focus and includes the assurance that there is reliable user access to appropriate features and functions and resilience to intrusion.

- **Data quality** Applications data must be curated and stewarded to ensure its completeness and accuracy.

- **Change management** The system must not be compromised by inappropriate or unverified changes.

- **Information gatekeeping** This is the protection and channeling of information based on requirements, ensuring that the right person has access to the data they need to perform their tasks. This includes meeting the organization's immediate and future regulatory, legal, risk, environmental, and operational information requirements.

Causes of Failed Governance

As you learned in the last chapter, sometimes the best way to look at these less scientific application management disciplines is to focus on what we're looking to improve, thereby automatically achieving positive results. This is not a method by which to set targets, but purely to help illustrate how application governance success is influenced. As such we will cover the following examples in this chapter:

- Unstructured and distributed security policies
- Policies that are poorly supported by complex procedures and hard-to-use tools
- Lack of reporting and analytic capabilities on system usage and security
- Lack of collaboration between IT and business operations, leading to a lack of ownership
- Lack of dedicated resources for monitoring and measuring application performance
- Poor on-boarding and exit procedures for people and assets
- Poor and/or fragmented change control and configuration management
- Poor disaster recovery and backup solutions, causing delays and potential data loss

Measuring Governance

Industry Analysts performed some research and found that application governance still has a relatively low level of adoption in business organizations, with only around 20 percent of those sampled engaged in dedicated IT governance activities, with extra cost cited as the main barrier. Interestingly, the research also concludes that the benefits gained by those 20 percent outweigh the costs involved, and therefore their recommendation is for simple entry-level uptake steps to realize some immediate value. This chapter will offer some methods for doing just that.

As with other toolboxes in this book, there is no sliding scale against which to measure your adoption and use of governance methods. However, simply reviewing your application management plan against the basic requirements discussed in this chapter should offer a method for making at least an estimation.

One method of measuring governance is to consider the extent to which the industry standards are known and applied, commonly through third-party certification. This may be at the organizational or personal levels, as most governance frameworks are taught through and measured by a certification program. ITIL is a good example, where several levels of professional certification are available that help ensure governance concepts and methods are well understood and are being used.

The first step is to review the list in the previous section to see if your implementation is guilty of any of the causes of poor governance. Then, using the rest of this chapter as a guide, you can determine which types of solutions to implement to help close those gaps.

Once the measures are in place, governance management becomes a matter of monitoring the usage and success (or otherwise) of the solutions put in place.

Managing Governance

Different roles in an organization need governance solutions. The networking manager isn't interested in the throughput of order transactions or expense payments but will want to know if particular IP addresses are causing excessive traffic. Another, more functional, role might be the *data steward,* who focuses on application data management and therefore needs a good understanding of the context of the system records so they can be managed in the appropriate way. I recommend you build solutions around the most critical requirements, most commonly from finance, HR, and security business functions.

During system implementation, a good proportion of the project should be related to ensuring governance solutions are deployed and configured, but even during normal operation, active management remains important. Throughout this chapter we'll look at all kinds of solutions, some of which can be used immediately and others that require planning before use, such as when they are part of an upgrade project.

In addition, in Chapter 11 we'll look at the evolution of your E-Business Suite deployment, which also includes taking your governance solutions forward. One interesting aspect to bear in mind is how the use of cloud computing will affect your governance needs and how you should match the right provider and a modular adoption program with the existing and future governance needs of your organization.

You might think governance is mostly centered on reporting and analytics for use in something like a service level agreement (SLA). While this is a strong practice, in this chapter we'll also look at the tools available for upstream implementation of problem prevention systems and the downstream ability to react effectively should issues occur. The complete governance solution needs a dedicated effort interwoven with all aspects of system management.

Governance Tools

The tools in and around E-Business Suite for implementing application governance range vastly, from recommended technical configurations, product features, to whole architectures and management solutions that need dedicated deployment. Some of the recommendations in this chapter should be considered part of building and evolving your governance plan, whereas others can be considered during the cyclical review process, similar to optimization.

As with the previous toolbox chapters, Table 9-1 provides a sequential reading structure which is intended for educational or casual consumption. To complement this the same content is given in Table 9-2, but this time organized around how they might be most commonly applied to an existing system.

Business Process Layer	Applications Technology Layer	Platform Layer
Governance, risk, and compliance	Technical customization governance	Identity management
Managing customization and personalization	User management	More security best practices
Functional features	Basic security best practices	Database governance options
Configuration management		Audit
Change management		Networking
Data governance		Integration
Oracle Diagnostic Framework		Enterprise Manager compliance standards

TABLE 9-1. *The Optimization Toolbox Manifest*

Monitoring and Troubleshooting	Managing
Oracle Diagnostic Framework	Governance, risk, and compliance
Technical customization governance	Managing customization and personalization
Basic security best practices	Functional features
More security best practices	Configuration management
Audit	Change management
Networking	Data governance
Integration	User management
	Identity management
	Database governance options

TABLE 9-2. *The Governance Toolbox Based on Use Case*

Business Process Layer

In controlling, protecting, and monitoring E-Business Suite through application governance, it is ultimately in the standard business features, functions, and data where the related solutions need to manifest themselves. Unlike a few of the other toolboxes that are more technology driven, application governance offers many of the most successful options at this first functional layer, right within E-Business Suite products and features themselves. This is not to say technology options are not powerful—but controlling E-Business Suite successfully must be done in the right context, and much of this can only occur in the application itself.

In addition to the extra tools detailed in this chapter, my first recommendation is that you revisit the E-Business Suite products you use and review the implementation options and setups to look for additional governance capabilities. The following are areas with low-hanging fruit that quickly provide governance improvements after the review of legacy settings in need of update:

- **Self-service applications** User access to core functions should be carefully controlled and regularly tuned to fit business operations.

- **User registration and management** System user records must contain complete and accurate details, and they must be provisioned with the right capabilities. This applies to both new and existing business users and system administrators.

- **Approvals management** Outdated rules and hierarchies may expose greatly increased risks.

Oracle Enterprise Governance, Risk, and Compliance (eGRC)

Oracle has a suite of products known as Enterprise Governance, Risk, and Compliance (eGRC) that enforces controls directly in Oracle E-Business Suite so compliance can be achieved through normal daily operations. This integrated approach helps increase financial integrity, reduces risk, and optimizes stakeholder value. While an additional product, this solution is designed to provide a complete solution for business governance and should be considered by all organizations, especially those where regulatory and legal compliance is of high priority.

eGRC provides a method for running dedicated projects and plans to ensure that the application includes adherence to regulatory compliance standards, exposes interdependent risks between products and their records, and provides flexible controls automation.

The eGRC suite sits as a standalone product suite but integrates natively with E-Business Suite (and PeopleSoft). It is comprised of the following four components:

- **Oracle Applications Access Controls Governor** Documents, manages, remediates, and enforces access policies for effective segregation of duties.

- **Oracle Configuration Controls Governor** Enforces application and data integrity, monitors configurations, audits changes to configurations, and ensures accurate reporting.

- **Oracle Enterprise Transaction Controls Governor** Continuously monitors policies, controls, and transactions to detect suspicious business activities.

- **Oracle Preventive Controls Governor** Prevents unauthorized changes to critical application data and setups and enforces real-time policy changes at a granular application level.

The eGRC solution adds a valuable platform upon which a more secure, controlled, and compliant E-Business Suite instance is run. This includes many high-value items, including the automation of many manual administrative processes that enforce consistency and reduce mistakes. The eGRC solution also has aspects of embedded configuration and change management not readily exposed as a feature in the standard products. In addition, it extends the support for auditing and assessment, providing detailed testing and regulatory reporting based on most popular compliance standards. Finally, eGRC products provide detailed risk management and analysis capabilities so that corporate strategy, projects, policy, and procedure management can be developed and managed based on legal and regulatory compliance standards.

The Fusion GRC solution offers similarly powerful capabilities, illustrated in Figure 9-1, together with the benefits of an optimized user experience and numerous options and features for a rich and visual preemptive solution for financial compliance and operational risk management. Fusion GRC also supports IT governance, following internationally recognized standards such as COBIT that focuses on regulatory compliance, ITIL that offers general IT management recommended practices, and the ISO-related standards such as ISO/IEC TR 90005:2008 for system life cycle management and the popular TickITplus assessment used in the UK.

By implementing Fusion GRC alongside E-Business Suite, companies can deploy the leading governance capabilities across their organization without disrupting their core business system. One healthcare organization who did this reported a 25 percent reduction in the number of hours required by its internal audit team and a 40 percent decrease in paper trails and paperwork.

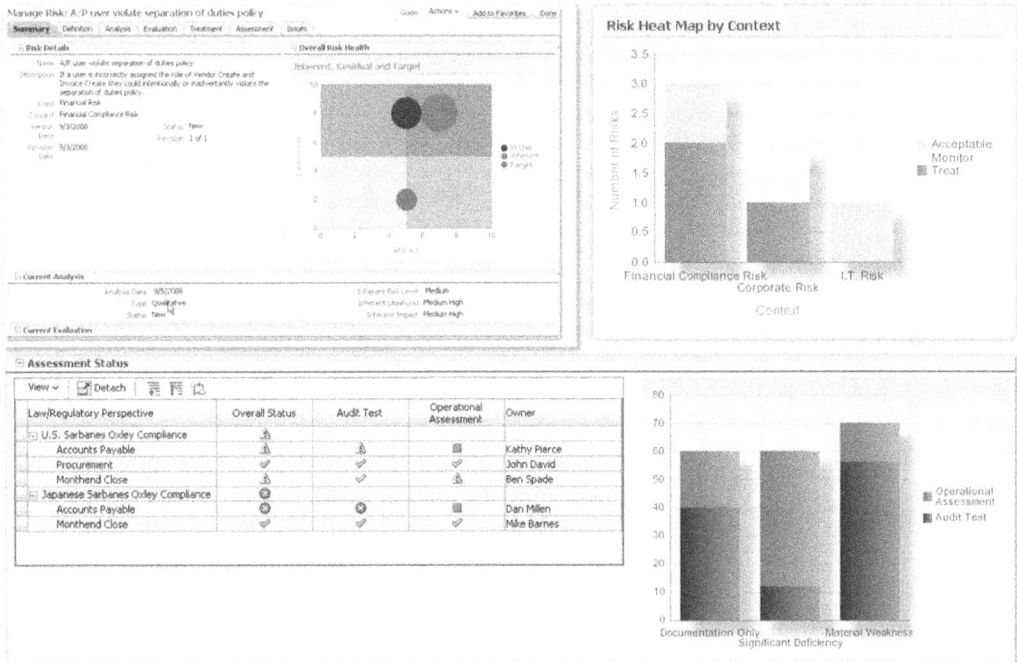

FIGURE 9-1. *Fusion GRC's rich solution for financial compliance and risk management*

A valuable resource for use in establishing and operating an effective GRC solution for E-Business Suite is the book entitled *Governance, Risk, and Compliance Handbook for Oracle Applications* (Packt Publishing, 2012) by Nigel King and Adil Khan, both of whom are industry experts with more than 30 years combined experience. Somewhat similar to the book you have in your hands, it goes beyond the traditional product descriptions and usage guidance, adding full explanation of the principles, concepts, and industry best practices. It also includes many detailed examples and recommendations throughout, with particular topic highlights including:

- **Governance**   An in-depth coverage of corporate, IT, and security governance, including strategy-based topics, such as overall policy development, communication, reporting and control.

- **Risk management**   Information about creating a risk management program, including performing risk assessment and control verification.

- **Compliance Management**   Coverage of cross-industry, cross-regional laws and regulations, industry-specific laws and regulations, and region-specific laws and regulations.

To maximize real world learning, the book examples are built around a fictional company, illustrating how to build complete governance processes.

Managing Customization and Personalization

In the last chapter we briefly discussed the capabilities and technologies involved in managing customization and personalization and how a degree of control is strongly recommended. Implementing that control is a governance task and should be embedded early into the design and development process. Here are some best practices to consider:

- Establish what degree of personalization is available to different user roles.

- Inform stakeholders of the risks and costs associated with system changes, extensions, and customizations.

- Define and enforce development and deployment standards.

- Review the approval processes for deploying new code and system changes and employ prerequisite checks before running deployment.

- Establish audit and reporting processes for deployed changes and extensions.

- Establish the maintenance plans, processes, and responsibilities for supporting changes and extensions.

- Manage and maintain detailed records of all customizations and extensions.

These practices may sound like they would incur large overhead costs that could be skipped, but so many times I have encountered issues that hurt business operations and took days to resolve, impeded or caused by poorly managed customizations. A little up-front effort can offer huge dividends later on.

I have yet to see an off-the-shelf tool that provides detailed customization management support for a specific enterprise application, and while there are many types of source code control and version systems, none offer support for E-Business Suite code specifically. Oracle Forms Developer and the OA Extension for JDeveloper provide the required libraries, connections, and utilities but offer little in the way of either enforcing standards or offering management capabilities. Because of this, the Applications Manager needs to work with the development team (or partners) to determine the management process, usually based on existing practices and systems. Where none yet exist, it's an opportunity to revisit governance and take steps to begin its implementation.

For more detail on the Oracle recommended development guidelines for E-Business Suite see the following documents:

- Oracle Application Framework Developer's Guide—Chapters 8 and 9 on Standards and Extensions
- Oracle E-Business Suite Developer's Guide (E12897-04)—the sections on Overview of Coding Standards and Customization Standards
- Oracle E-Business Suite User Interface Standards for Forms-Based Products (E12900-03)

Functional Features

Many E-Business Suite products have embedded features that help ensure the validity and control of their critical transactions and data. Some of this is essential to the correct operation of the core parts of E-Business Suite, whereas others are based on industry standards against which organizations must adhere. A good example is Oracle Electronic Records, used as a legally binding digital equivalent to having a handwritten approval signature on a document. I won't list all these features in this chapter, but I do recommend that you consider and share the content of new releases of your key product set, as important new governance capabilities are regularly added.

E-Business Suite products also contain safeguard options for controlling user input, so that mistakes in data entry and system use are reduced or, ideally, made impossible. Some examples are lookups and flexfields. In addition, some products implement their own features to control use of their specific functionality, such as the information templates in procurement that add an extra page to orders for capturing additional required information. This kind of control could be seen as another way of ensuring governance.

Similarly, personalizations and extensions should be used to disable or hide certain fields or to create default values, reducing the possibility of mistakes, deliberate or otherwise. An example might be an additional mandatory attachment for uploading required complimentary material documents, such as product schematics or certification documents.

While this detailed level setup is mostly the domain of a functional manager, it is essential that the options and capabilities are thoroughly researched. It is often only the Applications Manager that is in a truly holistic position to be able to review high-level requirements and has enough broad expertise to understand and present the best technical and functional solutions.

Configuration Management

Maintaining system control depends on a platform of good information management. Each E-Business Suite instance runs according to its setup data, and while there is no single place for configuration management of both technology and functionality, there are several solutions that can together provide a similar capability:

- ■ **The AD Configuration Report**   This low-level utility is generated from a SQL script (adutconf.sql) and as shown in Figure 9-2 contains a simple yet useful summary of the E-Business Suite instance setup. It includes data on tablespace and rollback segment usage, products registered and their versions, and NLS settings. While it contains no management features per se, the comprehensive report is a quick and reliable way to access all basic setup data.

- ■ **AutoConfig**   Traditionally done at the command line, as illustrated in Figure 9-3 Oracle Applications Manager now provides a simple and convenient view of the whole E-Business Suite configuration. While AutoConfig is mainly based on technical components, it is specific to E-Business Suite and provides the most complete source of configuration management available.

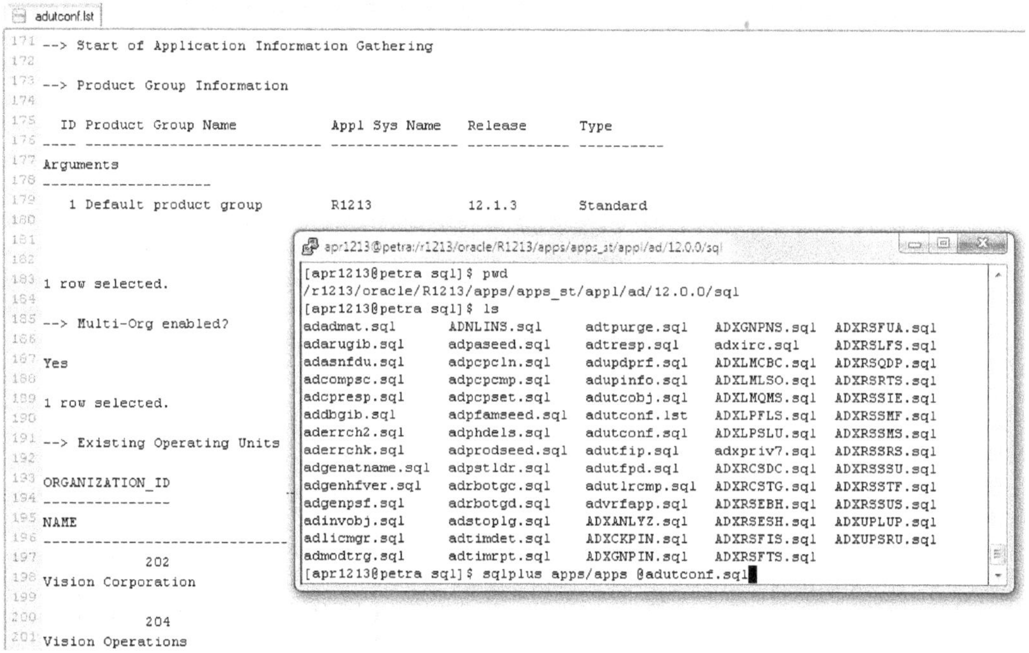

FIGURE 9-2.   *Running the adutconf.sql script is a simple way to report on basic configuration data*

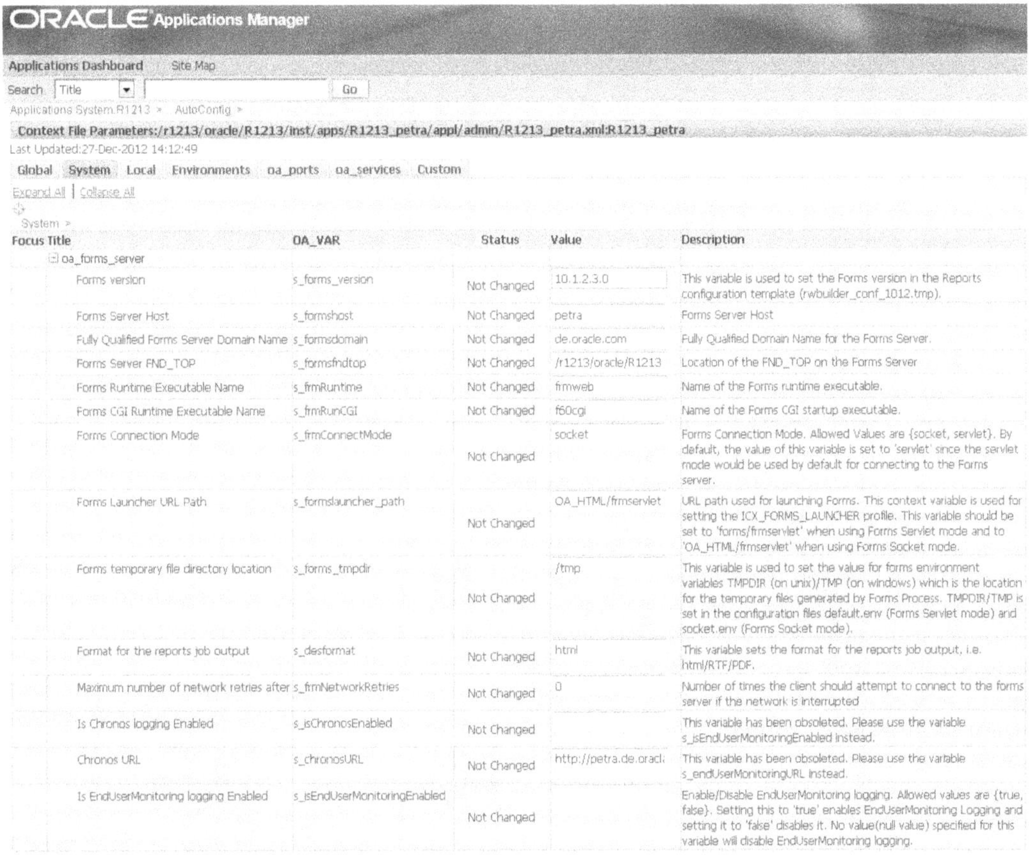

FIGURE 9-3. *AutoConfig configuration as displayed in Oracle Applications Manager*

■ **My Oracle Support's Oracle Configuration Manager** This feature runs a small program that collects a predetermined set of data from the system and uploads it to a secure database. The data is reuploaded only upon change and as shown in Figure 9-4 is used for basic configuration search, display, and comparison, as well as to form the basis for health and patch recommendations. For more details, click the Collector tab in My Oracle Support, or see Note 548815.1. Going forward, its combination with Enterprise Manager via the forthcoming harvester feature enriches the dataset substantially and provides more capabilities.

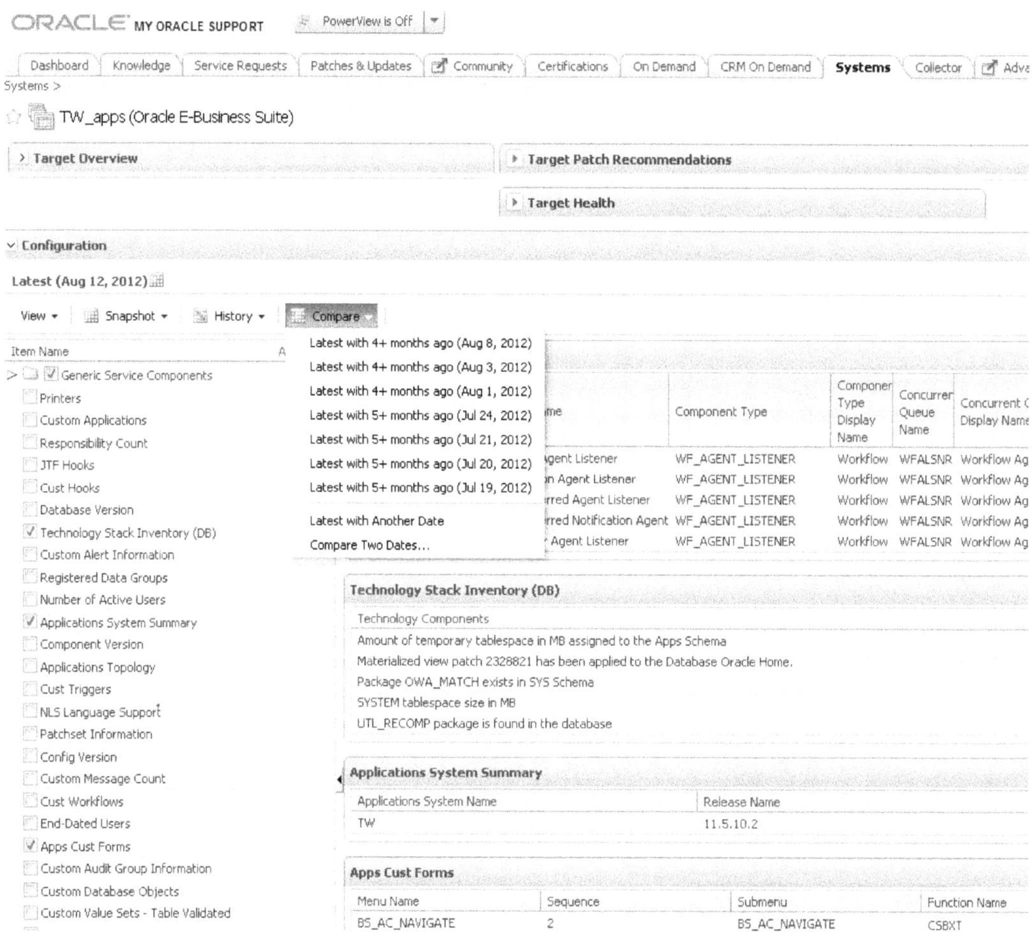

FIGURE 9-4. *The My Oracle Support configuration data for an E-Business Suite system showing the varied data that is collected, plus the history and compare reporting features*

- **E-Business Suite iSetup** The iSetup product can be used to review and manage functional configuration. Relevant to governance is the Reports tab that allows for review of the setup for selected objects within a data snapshot, such as the current accounting calendars. It also allows you to run comparisons between snapshots to help identify anomalies.

- **Enterprise Manager's E-Business Suite Plug-in: Setup Manager** This tool extends and enhances iSetup by providing a project capability within which one or more data extracts can be managed and redeployed. This leverages the rich coverage for functional setup (Figures 9-5 and 9-6) with some simple yet powerful management options (Figure 9-7) such as chaining prerequisites, transforming data, and running comparisons.

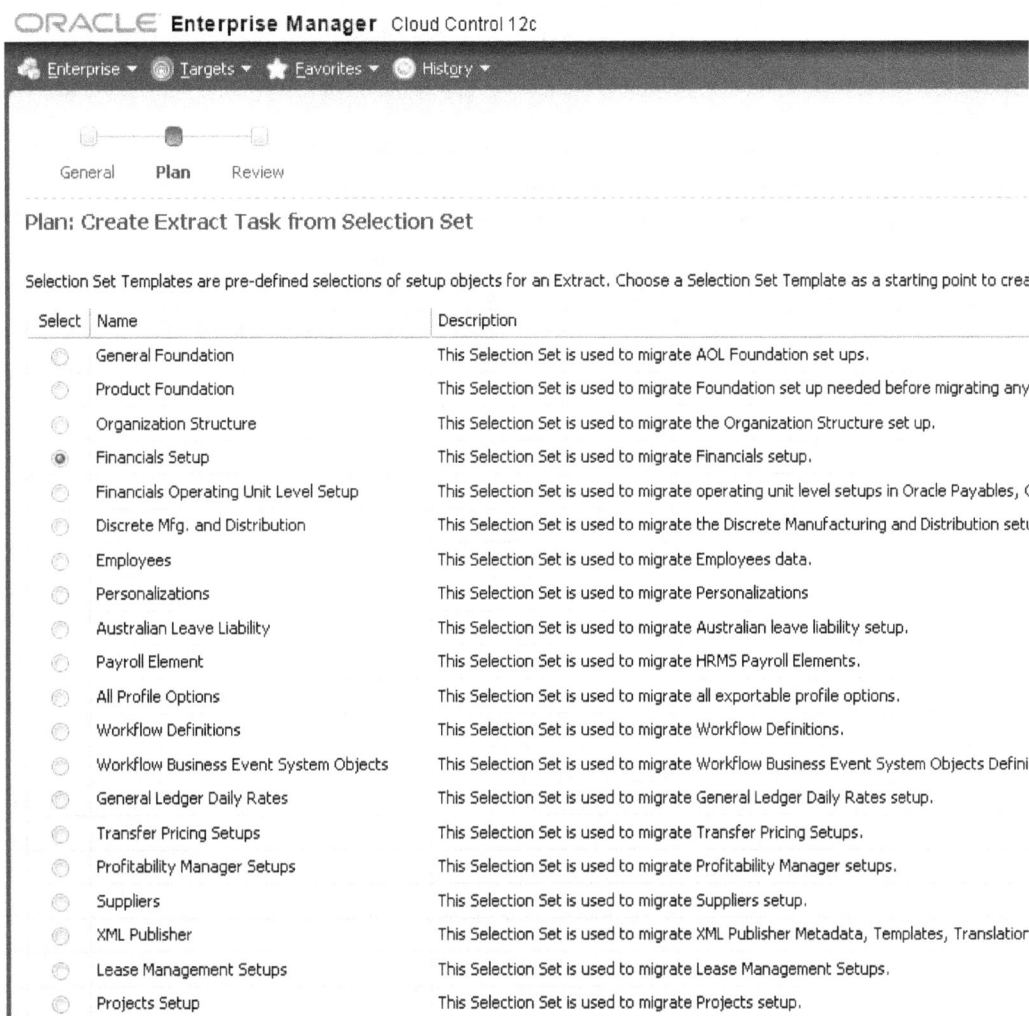

FIGURE 9-5.   *The product areas upon which functional setup data can be extracted and managed in Enterprise Manager*

- ■ **Enterprise Manager**   Even without the E-Business Suite plug-in deployed, there is a rich configuration management capability that supports all the main technology components of E-Business Suite. With E-Business Suite Release 12.2 moving to run on Fusion Middleware and beyond to Fusion Applications, the need for rich technical configuration management becomes ever more important. As shown in Figure 9-8, Enterprise Manager offers broad support for the technology stack including saving data, historic reporting, and comparative analysis.

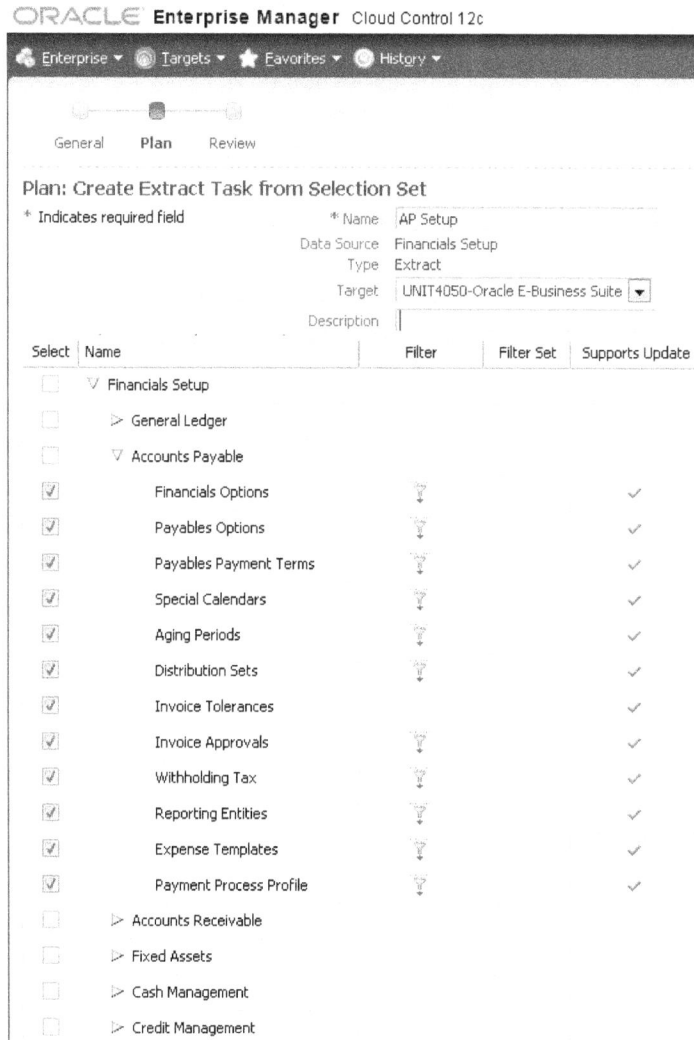

FIGURE 9-6. *The detailed Account Payables setup objects selected for extract, upon which various functions and reports can be performed*

Change Management

As mentioned in Chapter 6, having a gold image of the system and its current configuration is an essential application management basic. However, those static settings occasionally stop providing what the business needs.

System changes are often part of an optimization project, such as improving performance or hardening security, although changes such as patches are a common outcome of reliability issues. As such, change is inherently essential to effective application management.

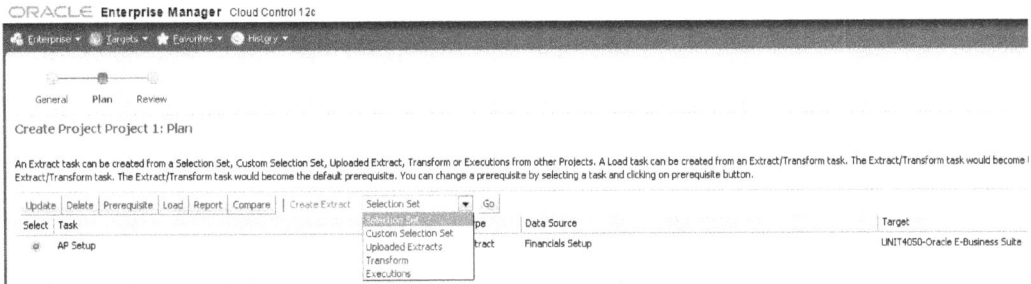

FIGURE 9-7. *The different types of extract and how the project plan can be changed, executed, set as a prerequisite, or reported upon and compared. Also note the options for loading and transforming existing extracts*

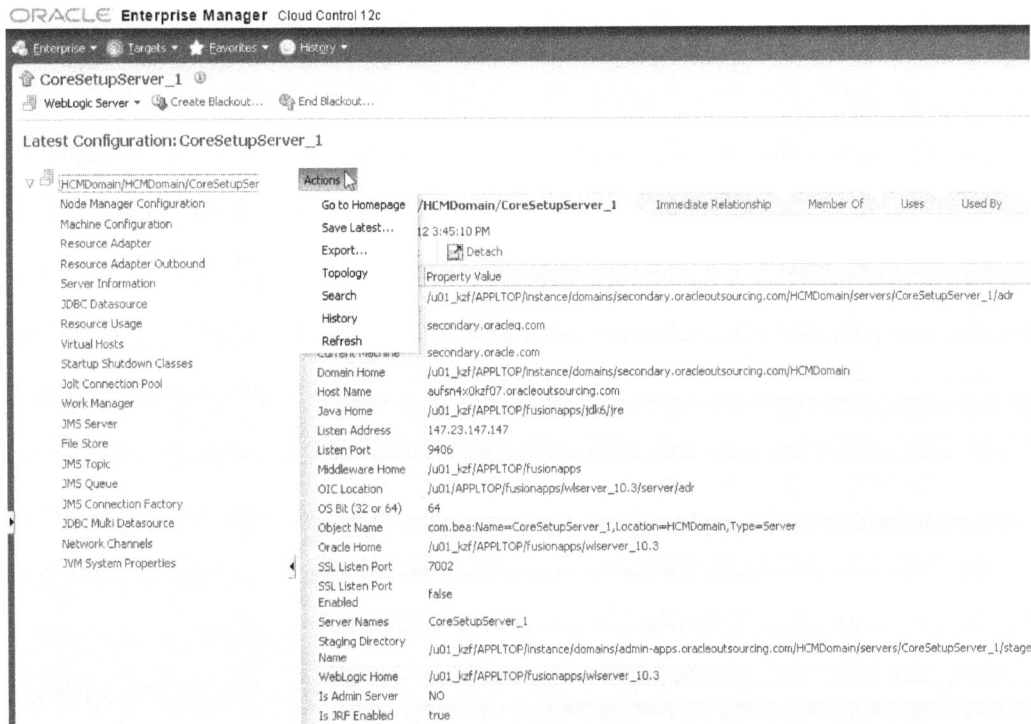

FIGURE 9-8. *Enterprise Manager's configuration screen for WebLogic targets, with its rich set of menu actions*

This emphasis is not necessarily on change for its own sake—even the mature E-Business Suite can be destabilized by invalid changes—but since change is inevitable and necessary, the goal is to ensure it is properly managed. This involves using an agreed set of standardized methods, processes, and procedures so that all changes are properly verified, authorized, implemented, and recorded. If nothing else, remember these four steps.

Change management is a whole IT service management discipline in itself, with the various methodologies proposing slightly different steps and practices. In reality, having a grasp and method of implementing the basic principles is usually enough for an enterprise application like E-Business Suite. A good start is reviewing the IT change management Advisor in My Oracle Support Note 301.1, which is based on the ITIL standards.

I already mentioned that some of the tools that support configuration management include features of change management too, usually through the storage and display of historic records and comparison features. The menu items in Figure 9-4 for Oracle Configuration Manager and Figure 9-7 for Enterprise Manager show these kinds of options.

The closest E-Business Suite comes to offering change management is via the AutoConfig management pages in Oracle Applications Manager. Figure 9-9 shows the basic page with the AutoConfig files, plus options for comparing files when several are available. It also shows the file change history, which itself has a feature for comparing it to the current active configuration in use. While simple, these are useful utility features for keeping control of the underlying E-Business Suite configuration.

One more step is to leverage the Enterprise Manager E-Business Suite plug-in and its set of change management features, as shown in Figure 9-10. The first section of this dashboard shows the Change Approval Requests, a feature based on a framework that provides a single-level approval for any configuration or code change, with strong auditing capabilities. The second section is a simple interface to the Patch Manager feature, which has powerful recommendations, search, and scheduling capabilities. The final two sections, Customization Manager and Setup Manager, round off the potential areas of system change with their own capabilities, which we've discussed in previous chapters.

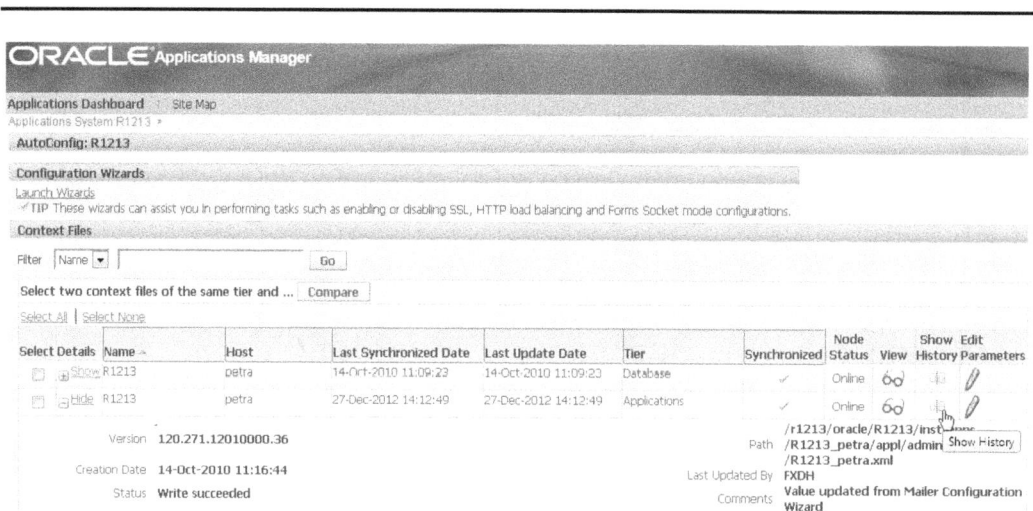

FIGURE 9-9.   *The AutoConfig management page with Compare and History features available*

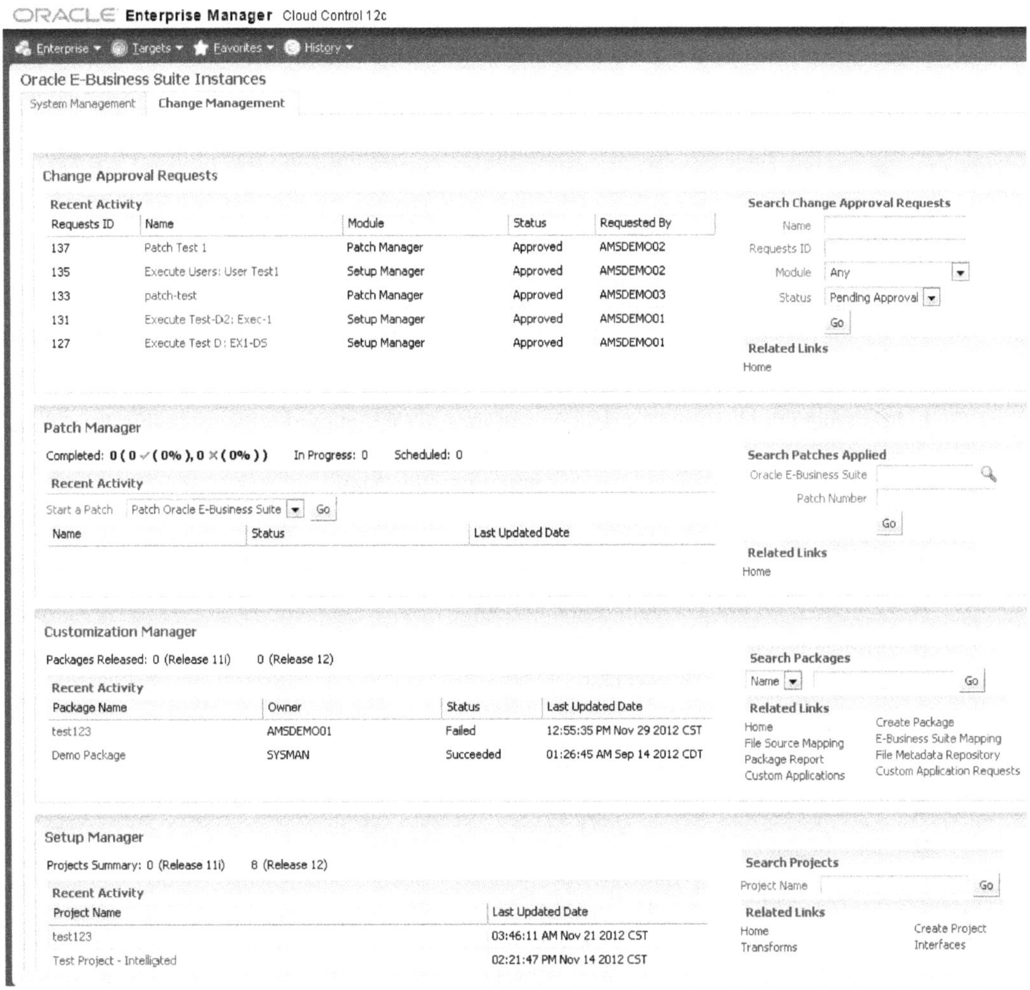

FIGURE 9-10. *Enterprise Manager plug-in change management features*

Another Enterprise Manager feature that can be leveraged to power change management is the Compliance Framework. This offers both a set of recommended configurations for much of the Oracle product range, plus a method for defining your own rules based on your own operating environments. We'll look at this in more detail right at the end of this chapter, since it currently focuses on technical configuration data.

One final point to note is that central to the governance of change is validation through testing. The solutions we've discussed from the Oracle Applications Testing Suite should be considered, as they can greatly reduce the costs involved in validating system changes and have no detrimental effects to critical business features.

Data Governance

Controlling application data so that it remains clean and accurate is of the utmost importance. This is compounded by the fact that modern deployments of enterprise applications like E-Business Suite are commonly connected to dozens of integrated systems, accepting input from sometimes thousands of different users. Therefore data quality should not be assumed; it requires a dedicated effort. There is also a context to what constitutes data quality, as some areas like product inventory are primarily focused on accurate unique records, whereas others like customer hub include ensuring valid relationships between a hierarchy of data such as contacts and addresses.

The data governance discipline goes so far as to recommend that a formal strategy be implemented to guide corporate behaviors toward the effective management of enterprise data. This includes establishing data management procedures, roles, responsibilities, policies, and control metrics. Data governance is one small part of overall IT governance, itself a component of enterprise information management. More detail on these general topics can be found at www.oracle.com/goto/EA-Welcome.

To implement the key parts of data governance, Oracle provides the following Master Data Management products. These span multiple business domains, each offering features and analytics to help ensure their respective datasets remain healthy. Many of these support multiple source system types, including E-Business Suite.

- Oracle Customer Hub
- Oracle Data Relationship Management
- Oracle Enterprise Data Quality
- Oracle Fusion Customer Hub
- Oracle Fusion Product Hub
- Oracle Higher Education Constituent Hub
- Oracle Product Hub
- Oracle Site Hub
- Oracle Supplier Hub

The example in Figure 9-11 shows a dashboard from the E-Business Suite 12.1.3 product for Supplier Management, illustrating how various key performance indicators and metrics are analyzed and displayed to help administrators and domain managers ensure their core application data remains clean and accurate.

These products run data gathering and standardization processes followed by full consolidation through a cleansing process with both built-in and extensible rule-based logic. In addition they also offer the opportunity to enrich data, pulling additional information from internal or external sources. Finally, the data is transformed as required and shared back to the original systems to become the more complete system of record. Increasingly, and with Oracle's acquisition of Silvercreek, these MDM systems include more semantic capabilities, matching and improving more and more varied data, allowing new technologies to increase the power of what they can deliver back to the business operation.

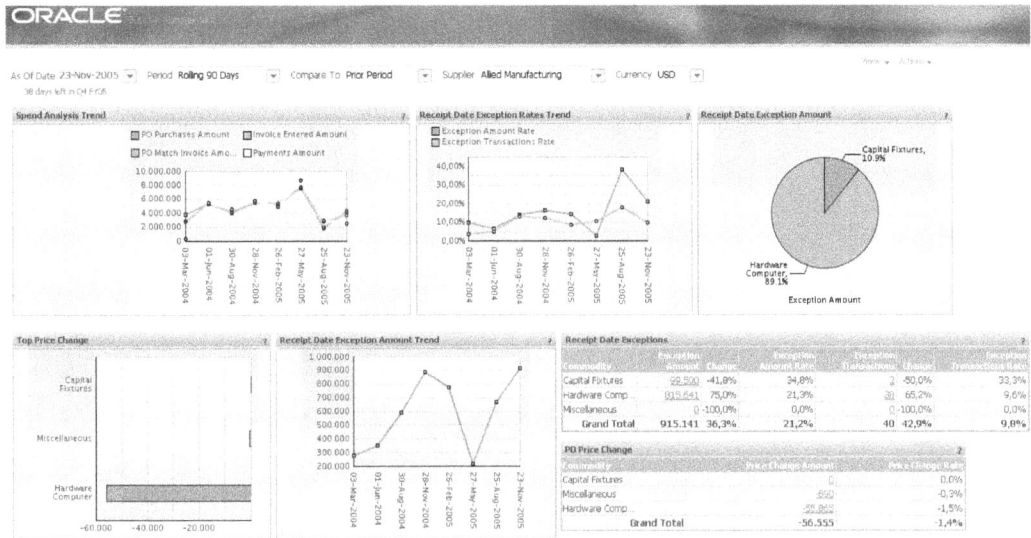

FIGURE 9-11. *The Supplier Manager dashboard showing trends and data changes for key operational data*

Obviously, full information and data governance goes beyond the data quality aspects of MDM and those we discussed in Chapter 8; for E-Business Suite, the full implementation should also include a combination of corporate policies and procedures that support the legislative, regulatory, and risk requirements of the business, together with a strong job role-based deployment—something we'll look at in a later section.

Oracle Diagnostic Framework

Since we're still reviewing tools and techniques at the Business Process Layer, using E-Business Suite Diagnostics is another way of reviewing the system to look for evidence of governance issues. This is not intended as a governance tool, but details of transaction, data, and system status and health can prove useful. For example, auditing the output from diagnostic tests can provide low-level insights for review and offline storage as a snapshot record.

There are many data collection type diagnostics for use by functional experts in reviewing specific datasets. An example might be the header of the test that shows the configuration settings for a product, or the profile option settings currently in use. In addition, there are tests with more built-in validation; especially useful are those that highlight potential compliance-related issues, such as inconsistent records, security concerns, or implementation issues. One simple example is where an administrator runs a diagnostic test to show all users with the System Administrator responsibility and is then able to quickly identify and remove any he or she hasn't approved. Figure 9-12 shows some other examples related to security, the related technical components, and Workflow users.

FIGURE 9-12. *The E-Business Suite Diagnostics for the Applications Object Layer (FND) application containing various security checks that are available in addition to the functional tests for each product area*

Applications Technology Layer

Unlike the other toolbox chapters, this chapter on governance focuses more on the Business Layer. However, it is the underlying technical components that ensure the information and functions available are appropriately controlled. Since E-Business Suite maintains a certain amount of its own technical components in the Applications Technology Layer, it can be helpful to understand which are especially important and what options, features, and recommendations exist for use with application governance.

Technical Customization Governance

As a tribute to my past in Oracle Support, I want to be clear that we're discussing customizations that are compliant with E-Business Suite, done with the provided tools and standard mechanisms. We are not discussing nor recommending the deployment of homegrown standalone applications or programs on the E-Business Suite technology stack. While this might seem like a tempting reuse of core technologies, it disrupts the E-Business Suite instance in often unforeseen ways and is never recommended.

The first tool for helping manage customization is the E-Business Suite Data Model Comparison Report. This is a set of reports that have been run against standard E-Business Suite environments and show all the differences between data models from one release to another. This report is intended to verify how a customization will operate in an upgraded environment, although it remains a manual task to trawl custom code for dependencies (where not properly documented).

Currently, the reports compare Releases from 11.5.9 up to 12.1 against the current 12.1.3 release and will continue to set the current release as the comparison baseline. Figure 9-13 shows the top of a sample output for the Accounts Receivable product, comparing Release 12.0.6 to 12.1.3. The table of contents shows how it includes tables and changes in items like indexes, views, and PL/SQL packages. The report includes not just objects added or removed, but also changes such as field lengths, column orders, data precisions, and changes to SQL statements. More details can be found in My Oracle Support Note 1290886.1.

The second similar utility is known as the E-Business Suite Seed Data Comparison Report. This report was discussed in detail in Chapter 8; but to summarize, it provides a way to spot data entity changes between two instances of different release versions. It includes messages, lookups, flexfields, menus, responsibilities, and concurrent programs. Its use in customization governance is through leveraging the information it contains to help preverify that all customizations are appropriately future-proof, both as a preupgrade step as well as part of a proactive approach to new customization development.

Another part of governance for E-Business Suite customization is ensuring that the changes and extensions being implemented support the Oracle standards, ensuring the result is robust and compliant enough to work well alongside the standard code. This is particularly relevant as new technologies such as Business Process Execution Language (BPEL), Applications Development Framework (ADF), and even Application Express (APEX) are now being used to enhance E-Business Suite.

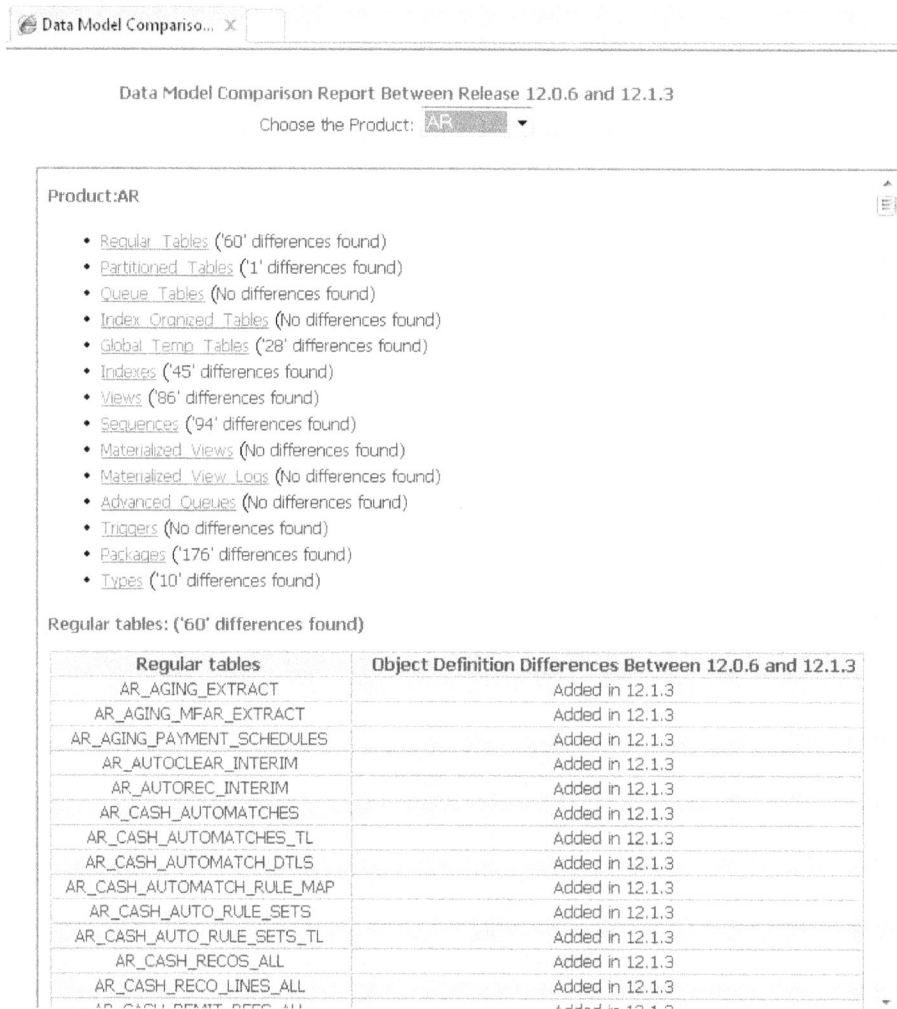

FIGURE 9-13.   *The top of the Data Model Comparison Report for 12.0.6 and 12.1.3*

To help with this, beyond documentation, is the new E-Business Suite Software Development Kit (SDK) for Java. This provides useful features that help custom J2EE applications easily and safely connect with the E-Business Suite security system, user sessions, and database data. More detail on using these features can be found in Note 974949.1.

Finally, Enterprise Manager's plug-in for E-Business Suite offers a Customization Manager feature. This provides a standardized method for deploying custom code into E-Business Suite. This creates AD-compliant patches and then runs them into the standard tools (including Enterprise

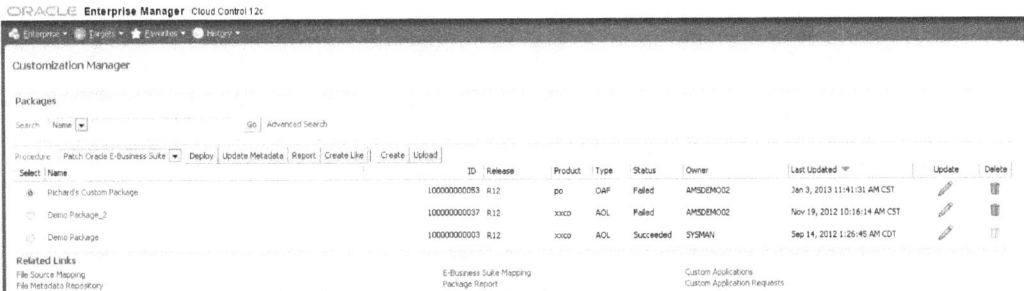

FIGURE 9-14. *The Customization Manager home page with features for building and reporting on packages to deploy custom code in E-Business Suite in a standardized and controlled manner*

Manager's Patch Manager) for installation, ensuring consistency and that standardizations are followed. Figure 9-14 shows the home page for Customization Manager with the variety of features to build a package of custom code for deployment, and Figure 9-15 shows an example package with two custom files that have been deployed.

User Management

User management consists of three principal components: *authentication* to verify the user's identity, *authorization* to allow the user access to the resources they need, and an *audit trail* to track activity.

Introduced in Release 12, Oracle User Management is a centralized product for managing E-Business Suite users and roles and focuses on simplifying and standardizing what was previously a fragmented, multistep and multiform process. It also allows the delegation of user management to functional administrators in each business domain, reducing the need for dedicated resources for this kind of work.

The product allows the creation of new people and new user accounts, password reset, user disabling options; it also has its own reporting. It uses roles to grant or revoke access to products and features. The solution sits over the standard E-Business Suite responsibility-menu-function internal structure, which makes administration and day-to-day management (and therefore governance) much easier.

This framework is based on the standard Role Based Access Control (RBAC) principal, where security is modeled on the job functions within the organization, against which users are then associated. This means users have access only to what they need to perform their work. As illustrated in Figure 9-16, these predefined roles are all carefully defined based on the principle of *segregation of duties*, where no one role includes more than one business function; for example, the purchasing role shouldn't include payment functions as well. For more details, see My Oracle Support Note 950018.1 and the recommended whitepaper found in Note 1537100.1.

User Management also provides more self-service options such as user registration, self service access requests, approval processing, and safe delegation facilities, all of which help reduce administrative bottlenecks. There is a more detailed discussion on using Oracle User Management in the System Administrators Guide—Security (E12843-05).

FIGURE 9-15. *An example custom package that has been deployed through Enterprise Manager*

Security Concepts

Lets start with an introduction to some security fundamentals.

Application security is an approach or process, a way of considering every part of the application deployment and configuration. It's also evolutionary, as it improves through review and fine-tuning and adjusting where either the business need arises or reacting to changes in the application and its usage.

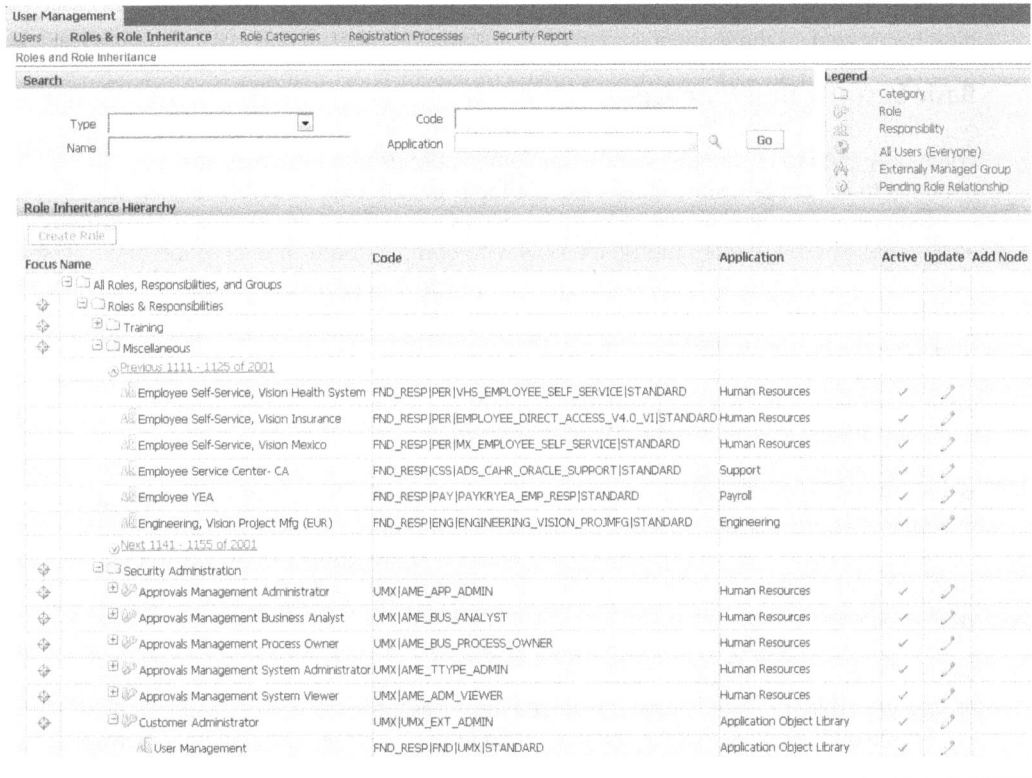

Focus Name	Code	Application	Active	Update	Add Node
All Roles, Responsibilities, and Groups					
Roles & Responsibilities					
Training					
Miscellaneous					
Previous 1111 - 1125 of 2001					
Employee Self-Service, Vision Health System	FND_RESP|PER|VHS_EMPLOYEE_SELF_SERVICE|STANDARD	Human Resources	✓	✎	
Employee Self-Service, Vision Insurance	FND_RESP|PER|EMPLOYEE_DIRECT_ACCESS_V4.0_VI|STANDARD	Human Resources	✓	✎	
Employee Self-Service, Vision Mexico	FND_RESP|PER|MX_EMPLOYEE_SELF_SERVICE|STANDARD	Human Resources	✓	✎	
Employee Service Center- CA	FND_RESP|CSS|ADS_CAHR_ORACLE_SUPPORT|STANDARD	Support	✓	✎	
Employee YEA	FND_RESP|PAY|PAYKRYEA_EMP_RESP|STANDARD	Payroll	✓	✎	
Engineering, Vision Project Mfg (EUR)	FND_RESP|ENG|ENGINEERING_VISION_PROJMFG|STANDARD	Engineering	✓	✎	
Next 1141 - 1155 of 2001					
Security Administration					
Approvals Management Administrator	UMX|AME_APP_ADMIN	Human Resources	✓	✎	
Approvals Management Business Analyst	UMX|AME_BUS_ANALYST	Human Resources	✓	✎	
Approvals Management Process Owner	UMX|AME_BUS_PROCESS_OWNER	Human Resources	✓	✎	
Approvals Management System Administrator	UMX|AME_TTYPE_ADMIN	Human Resources	✓	✎	
Approvals Management System Viewer	UMX|AME_ADM_VIEWER	Human Resources	✓	✎	
Customer Administrator	UMX|UMX_EXT_ADMIN	Application Object Library	✓	✎	
User Management	FND_RESP|FND|UMX|STANDARD	Application Object Library	✓	✎	

FIGURE 9-16. *Oracle User Management showing the predefined roles and their hierarchy*

Application security comes in two parts: the first is a set of three goals that help define what we are trying to manage; the second is a set of three complementary controls with which providers such as Oracle build products, tools, and features.

The goals of security are *confidentiality, integrity, and availability*. Confidentiality is the principle of keeping private data private. Integrity provides assurance that all data changes are authorized and audited, promoting consistency and preventing leaks or corruption. Finally, availability ensures that systems and data are accessible when needed, including the mitigation of related causes such as code bugs, poor role provision, and insufficient capacity management.

The controls of information security are authentication, authorization, and auditing. Authentication confirms you are who you say. It provides proof of identity, often using multiple factors such as something you know (pin number), something you have (electronic token), and something you are (a fingerprint). For applications this is usually more simple, such as proper password strength configuration plus an audit of failed-login attempts. Authorization defines what you are allowed to do. In modern application systems (including E-Business Suite Release 12 onward), it applies a role-based access control concept, defining what you need for the duties in your job role rather than complex personal grants, ensuring that the least amount of privilege is provided to reduce risk. Finally, auditing is capturing a record of system activity and access to trace issues and eliminate their causes. Often a legal requirement in case of prosecution, application audits are often based on database fields and system log lines. What is interesting is that the audit records themselves must be secured, as the sensitive and internal information they contain may be useful to attackers.

Basic Security Best Practices

Now that you have a basic grasp of the key elements, let's consider some simple methods commonly used to ensure the security implementation is as effective as possible. Then we'll continue to look at E-Business Suite specific tools and advice.

The first recommendation is to keep the deployment of security tools and platforms as simple as possible. These are often high-tech tools with complex built-in encryption and obfuscation capabilities, but the way in which each tool is applied and the overall architecture should be, at a high level, relatively easy to understand. Generally speaking, complexity adds risk, such as increasing the possibility of leaving gaps in coverage or introducing conflicts between multiple solutions.

The next step is to make sure you continue to question all assumptions when it comes to security reviews. Taking for granted that a part of the system has the necessary security controls without verifying it increases the risk of problems.

A well-known recommendation is to create a layered security architecture. Often referred to as defense-in-depth, like an onion when one layer is peeled back, this type of architecture doesn't expose the whole, just one section. Using this and putting the less sensitive items in the outer layers is common sense. Applying solutions in this way also simplifies the administration, since each component has a clear purpose and set of resources it applies to. Using a segmentation approach, system components can be broken apart to make them not only safe but isolated in case of a breach. The security layers should extend beyond software solutions also, into the network infrastructure and even out into physical security, system management policies, and general procedures. This structured approach greatly increases the resilience of the application.

Testing and verifying that the security procedures and safeguards put in place work as intended is critical. For security this could include the use of independent assessment and certification for additional hardening and increased piece of mind. Testing security should also be ongoing, most likely as part of the optimization discussed in the previous chapter.

As with physical security, a complete security management solution includes mitigating risk and not just attack prevention. The important factors to bear in mind are either to reduce the frequency or likelihood that a related problem will occur, or reduce the impact of the problem should it occur (and ideally, to do both). Risk management is another topic that should be reviewed, and once identified and assessed, each distinct risk should be eliminated, mitigated, or accepted. The outcome of security risk assessment work needs to be documented, communicated to all stakeholders, and regularly reviewed, especially when circumstances change. Threat modeling provides good methodologies that can be used to review the system and potential problems.

E-Business Suite Basic Security Best Practices

Having discussed generic principles, the following is a small set of E-Business Suite specific recommendations. Although they may be generally well known, they do still occasionally get missed. Please also see the next section for more on complementary technical security tools, techniques, and recommendations.

- Set up default security assignments for all types of users, including temporary workers and external users.
- Base new responsibilities and roles on the seeded ones, copying them and then applying changes, retaining the originals. Retire any nonrequired seeded responsibilities.

- Document the security architecture clearly so that it can be quickly understood by new participants. This includes not just the technical security tools and solutions but also the functional deployment, such as how Multi-Org Access Control (MOAC) is being used.

- Use change management (including approvals) to help keep the security documentation accurate and up to date.

- Use the E-Business Suite product implementation guides to find out exactly what menus/functions apply to which features.

- Ensure all custom code adheres to all security standards, reusing existing utility APIs and services where possible.

- Review profile option settings, especially those delivering significant features assigned to specific users.

- Ensure audit features supply real information that can be acted upon. Also make sure expired audit data is purged properly.

- Set user and session timeout profile options—ICX: Timeout and ICX: Session Timeout.

- Set password expiration via the concurrent program FNDCPEXPIRE_SQLPLUS, and set case sensitivity via the profile option Sign-On Password Case. Passwords must remain strong but not so hard to remember that they get written down, and while regular expiration is good, it shouldn't be so frequent that users forget or resort to weaker passwords.

- Ensure the following documents are regularly reviewed to properly understand the concepts, principals, and implementation options:

  - The general introduction to security options in Oracle E-Business Suite Concepts (E12841-04).

  - The main security guide in the Oracle E-Business Suite System Administrator's Guide—Security (E12843-05). This is essential reading and should be used as a frequent reference, especially regarding changes upon upgrades and new releases.

  - Several vital security-related utilities detailed in Oracle E-Business Suite System Administrator's Guide—Configuration (E12893-04).

Platform Technology Layer

Implementing application governance also requires configuring the technology stack components to enable the features that support the top-level goals. Without a controlled and well-managed platform it is impossible to deliver a comprehensive solution, as core requirements will be omitted. It is vital that the lowest-level governance options are used in addition to in-application options, since policy violations and system attacks often bypass the upper application layers.

This section focuses on options for enhancing both data and function security in E-Business Suite, so that what data can be accessed and what can be done to it are controlled. We'll also consider how governance should be extended to areas of the application ecosystem, such as integrations, and how tools can be used to embed validation so that best practices are and remain implemented.

Authentication Through Identity Management

While E-Business Suite maintains its own security implementation, it is now possible to integrate it with Oracle's industry leading security products, enabling a whole set of advanced features and the adoption of standards-based solutions. In addition, as you'll see in the next chapter, Fusion Applications extends these capabilities even further, providing a modular identity management implementation.

At a high level, E-Business Suite can be integrated with Oracle Access Manager to provide centralized user authentication management, most importantly including support for Single Sign-on. Underneath this runs Oracle Internet Directory as the LDAP server for storing user data, although the solution can be configured to work with third-party LDAP products as well.

As illustrated by Figure 9-17, the process works through the use of two intermediary agents, an AccessGate component that integrates the E-Business Suite to a WebGate server, itself part of Oracle Access Manager. This ensures all traffic runs between the systems properly, once the initial setup and synchronization of users and roles has been completed. More details are available in My Oracle Support Note 975182.1.

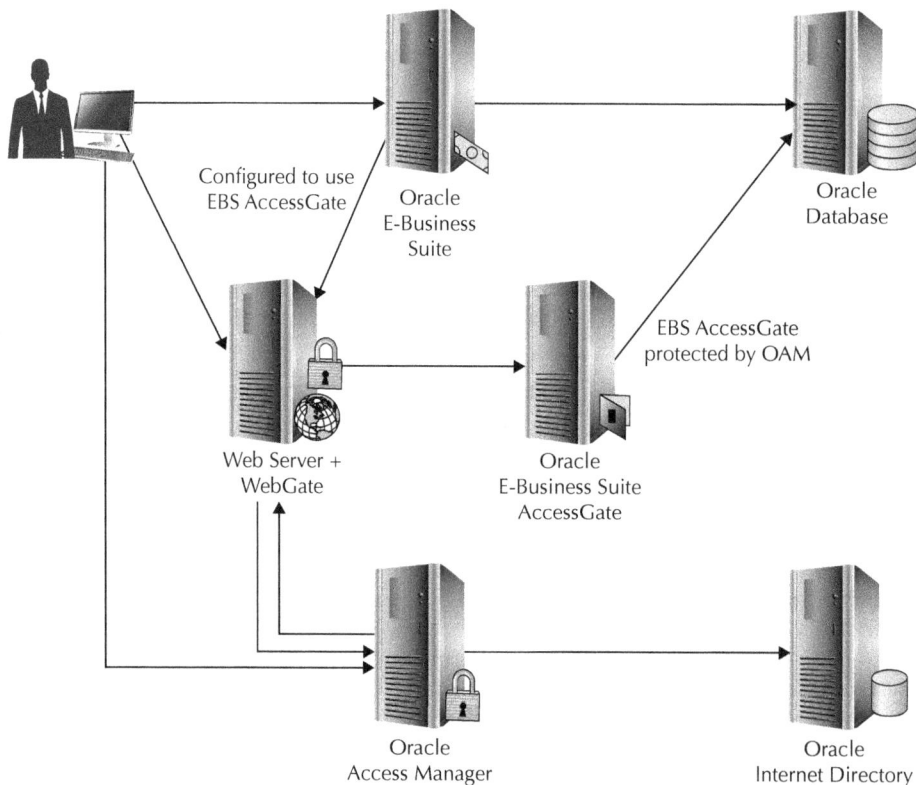

FIGURE 9-17. *The components involved in an E-Business Suite deployment of Oracle Access Manager*

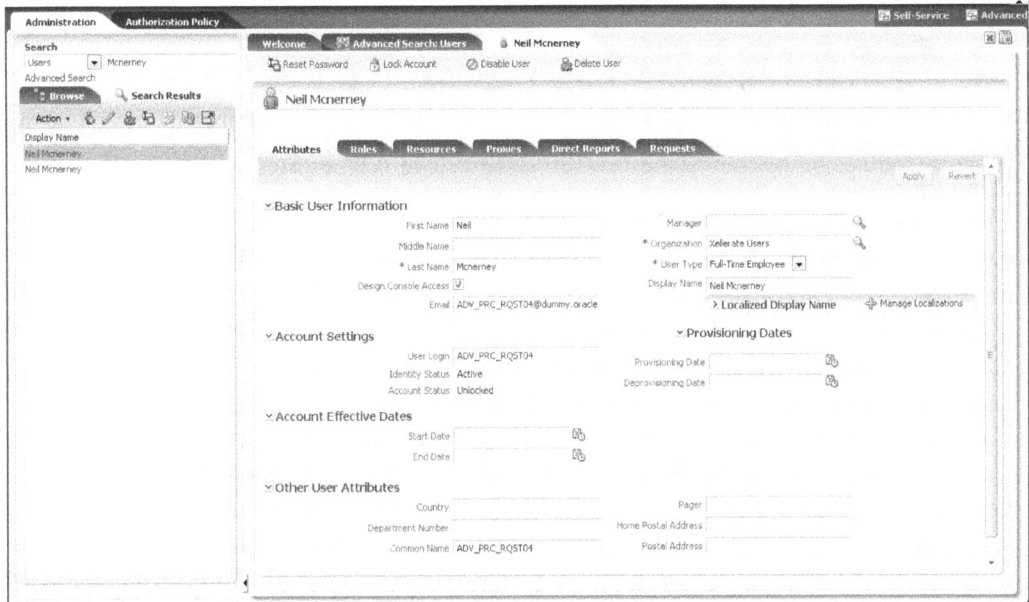

FIGURE 9-18.   *The administrative console of Oracle Access Manager, showing a detailed user record and the features available*

Oracle Access Manager, as shown in Figure 9-18, is an easy-to-use solution with many of its own features, including both administrative and self-service consoles. It has many features that help support user governance, such as extensive audit and compliance reporting that supports most of the standard regulatory requirements.

With, E-Business Suite user role access needs to be combined with complete system records, such as ensuring that the user has an appropriate employment record assignment within Oracle HRMS. Therefore it is a combination of technology and business solutions that provide full governance management.

For more detail on using Oracle Access Manager with E-Business Suite, take a look at the section of the E-Business Suite Administrators Guide—Security or My Oracle Support Note 1388152.1.

Technical Security Best Practices

The following is list of more technical recommendations that have proven to help E-Business Suite administrators govern over their instances in an effective manner, using both embedded features and general best practices. For more details, see Note 403537.1—Secure Configuration Guide for Oracle E-Business Suite.

■ Make sure the O/S on each machine is patched and securely configured.

■ Make sure the networking hardware (firewalls, proxies, and so on) is securely configured.

- Keep up to date on critical patch updates (CPUs) and maintenance packs, and watch for security alerts in My Oracle Support.

- Activate server security options such as ModSecurity and review secure connection to attachment storage.

- Disable any seeded system users that are not required and change all default passwords. Use the default password scanner script from Note 361482.1.

- Retire any inactive application user accounts quickly.

- Ensure passwords are updated along with your corporate standards and ensure that passwords are strong. See Note 457166.1 for implementing hashed passwords.

- Avoid the liberal use of diagnostic options and other admin features; see Note 946372.1 for guidance.

- Carefully secure the E-Business Suite admin pages, as many expose sensitive information. See Note 1334930.1 for details.

- Actively monitor for all security violations and breach attempts, both deliberate and accidental. This includes use of various governance tools, including specialist Intrusion Detection Systems (IDS).

- Mask the data used in test and development environments. Enterprise Manager has a Data Masking Pack for E-Business Suite that scrambles over 1000 columns of PII data, including about 65 percent of HRMS data, while allowing dummy values to remain so testing doesn't fail. This is essential for clones of production data that find their way into open and less-secured test and development environments.

- Control data exports as much as possible, and control data access that isn't through the user interface, such as via APIs, web services, and SQL connections.

- If exposing your E-Business Suite to external users via the Internet, implement a DMZ configuration based on My Oracle Support Notes 287176.1 and 380490.1.

Database Governance Options

As the standard platform for storing application data, E-Business Suite or otherwise, the Oracle database comes with a host of features for implementing additional governance, most of which have been certified with and have options for E-Business Suite. These include:

- **Database partitioning**   To enable true information lifecycle management
- **Virtual private database**   To add additional column-level security
- **Database vault**   To help protect against inappropriate DBA access to business data
- **Transparent data encryption**   To secure data at rest for whole tablespaces or for specific columns.

Reviewing these options is strongly recommended for all production E-Business Suite environments, as they can quickly and easily add powerful underlying governance capabilities with no perceivable alteration to the business application at all. For more details look at the Oracle Database documentation, especially the Security Guide (E10575-08).

Auditing

Although mentioned in passing several times we have not yet reviewed the options and features available for implementing a full auditing capability in E-Business Suite. With this kind of auditing we are looking to protect data, maintain valid data accessibility, track usage patterns, and protect the business. These are broad goals, so let's add a bit more meaning by looking at a few ways this can be done.

First, you need to verify that users are performing only operations that are required by the business, as defined by their role. To do this you need metrics and records that you can monitor, ideally in real time, with notifications sent should any violations (or attempts at violation) occur. You also need to meet any regulatory or compliance demands, ideally without the administration effort of defining and setting up dozens of rules.

Another key aspect of auditing is making sure that the metrics and records being stored include those most critical for the business and are focused on the most risk-sensitive areas. This can vary between industry and organization, so looking at the data being audited is an important step. Of course, there are many generic areas, such as logins, system changes, setup changes, and deployed customizations, but decisions must be made as to which sensitive business processes and data to track. Some organizations might wish to focus on payment processing jobs, others on order approvals profiles, and others on access to personnel records. Building an overall audit strategy for the application is recommended.

There are several layers of auditing possible, with in-application audit, in-database audit, and advanced database audit options.

First, E-Business Suite offers two main embedded auditing features, Sign-On Audit and AuditTrail. The first supports tracking Oracle Forms users' activities, both online and historically as illustrated in Figure 9-19. It is enabled by a system profile option and therefore can be enabled at various levels, including for a particular responsibility or a user.

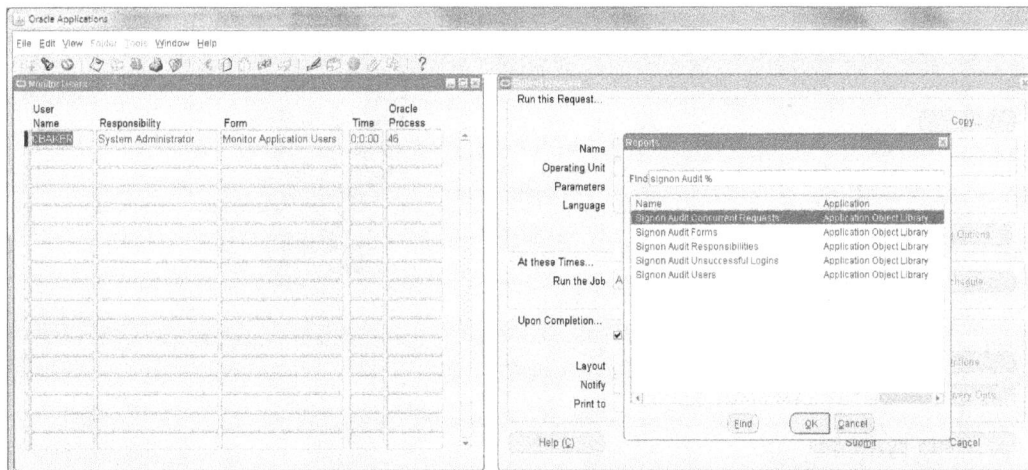

FIGURE 9-19. *The two main outputs from the Sign-On Audit option for tracking customer activity are the live Monitor Users form and the five reports on historic data*

In addition, E-Business Suite's AuditTrail feature provides a record of all data changes made, when, and by whom. This requires the creation of audit groups, made up of the sensitive applications tables or columns that require monitoring. The system then implements the appropriate database triggers to capture audit records into new shadow tables. Although there are seeded audit reports available, the creation of custom reports is encouraged based on specific needs and the data in the shadow audit tables.

For further details on both audit features, see Oracle E-Business Suite System Administrator's Guide—Security.

While these options cover a reasonable amount of auditing for E-Business Suite, for particularly sensitive data it can be more effective to enable low-level auditing, right down in the database itself. In its basic form (Release 11g and higher), this is enabled by setting the related AUDIT_ initialization parameters for the database instance. This powerful feature centers around three main database audit trails: first, failed login attempts; second, the recording of privilege changes; and third, the auditing of database object changes. Specific items like tables and views are enabled for auditing with support for criteria-based auditing, which allows focus on the most important areas without affecting the entire system. In addition, the audit database features shown in Figure 9-20 can also support networking and operating system audit records.

All database audit output can be either kept in basic database audit tables, or fed into the separate and secure Audit Vault repository. This consolidates audit data away from transactional data and offers alerts and notifications, attestation and archiving, along with prebuilt reporting that includes support for the common compliance regulations such as SOX and PCI.

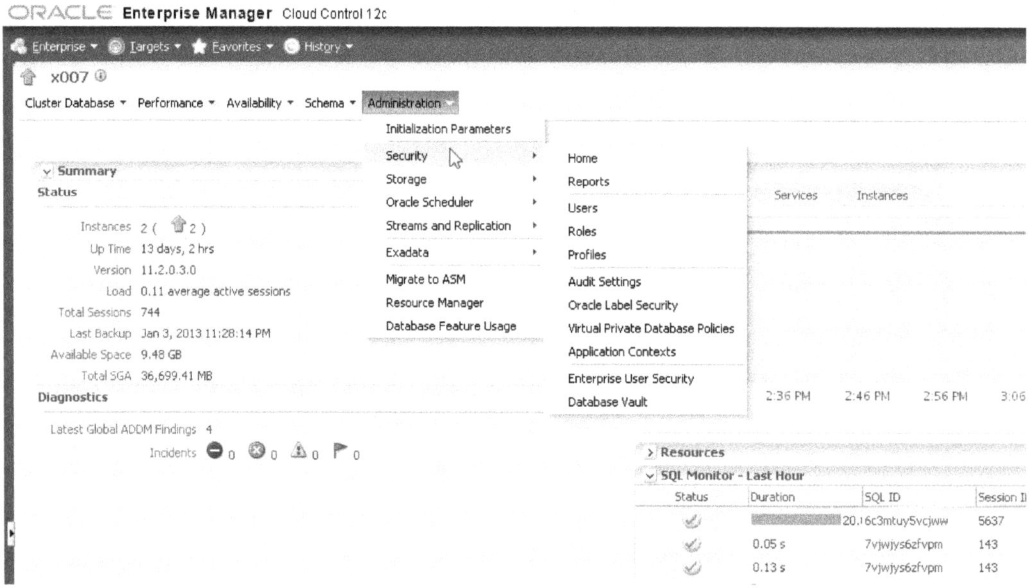

FIGURE 9-20. *The Audit Settings menu item in Enterprise Manager's Database Control management console, along with the other governance-related menu options*

More details on database auditing can be found in Chapter 7 of the intuitive Oracle Database 2 Day and Security Guide (E10575-08) or Chapter 9 of the standard Oracle Database Security Guide (E16543-14).

Networking

The connections to E-Business Suites physical and virtual servers and other technical components must be well governed to avoid unauthorized access. This may have already been implemented by IT networking or security teams as part of the original deployment, usually based on existing company policies. However, there are some standard recommendations specifically for E-Business Suite that are worth reviewing by the applications administration even after specialist teams have done their job.

The applications topology must be designed and maintained with security in mind and, since change is an inevitable, many new features or altered business requirements demand adjustments to the original design. As we'll discuss in the next section, E-Business Suite integration requirements often change, which affects system access. As new networking and communication channels open up, the applications administrator needs to ensure and verify that they are secure and remain well governed. While this book doesn't cover detailed implementation design, there are resources available for more detail and recommendations, such as Note 380490.1 for using DMZ.

The most common method of hardening the networking inside E-Business Suite is to implement Secure Sockets Layer (SSL) for the communication between the nodes, as well as to and from the user client machines. This is a commonly recommended task, and as it can be quite tricky for the initiated, Oracle Applications Manager has a set of Configuration Wizards that make it relatively simple. Figure 9-21 shows the available wizards for Release 12.1.3, and Figure 9-22 shows the steps for implementing basic SSL between the E-Business Suite nodes. For more detail on the options and tasks involved in managing SSL for E-Business Suite, see My Oracle Support Note 376700.1. One example of why this wizard is recommended is that certain applications such as iRecruitment still use the SYS.UTL_HTTP package to make web-to-database connections, and as such, the HTTPS connection fails unless the database Oracle Wallet is updated with the SSL certificate.

In addition, internal connections between the database nodes are not sent over the HTTP protocol, usually on proprietary TNS, which can also be secured to improve governance. This is possible using the Advanced Networking Option (ANO), which encrypts traffic sent to/from the TNS Listener. This feature is part of the Advanced Security Options (ASO) available with the Oracle Database, and although the software is included with E-Business Suite Release 12, it

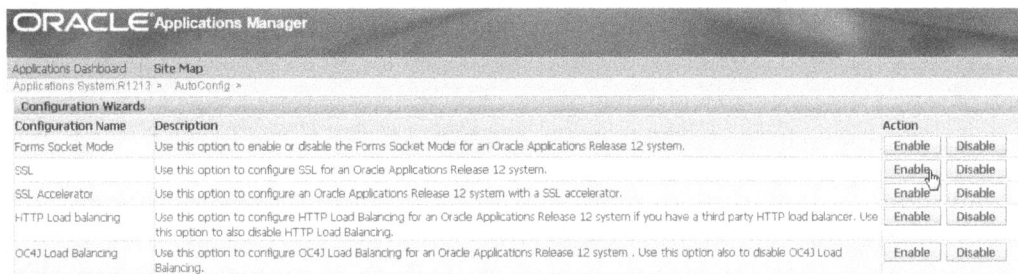

Configuration Name	Description	Action	
Forms Socket Mode	Use this option to enable or disable the Forms Socket Mode for an Oracle Applications Release 12 system.	Enable	Disable
SSL	Use this option to configure SSL for an Oracle Applications Release 12 system.	Enable	Disable
SSL Accelerator	Use this option to configure an Oracle Applications Release 12 system with a SSL accelerator.	Enable	Disable
HTTP Load balancing	Use this option to configure HTTP Load Balancing for an Oracle Applications Release 12 system if you have a third party HTTP load balancer. Use this option to also disable HTTP Load Balancing.	Enable	Disable
OC4J Load Balancing	Use this option to configure OC4J Load Balancing for an Oracle Applications Release 12 system . Use this option also to disable OC4J Load Balancing.	Enable	Disable

FIGURE 9-21. *The Oracle Applications Manager Configuration Wizards, including options to implement SSL over the nodes, as well as the option to use SSL accelerators*

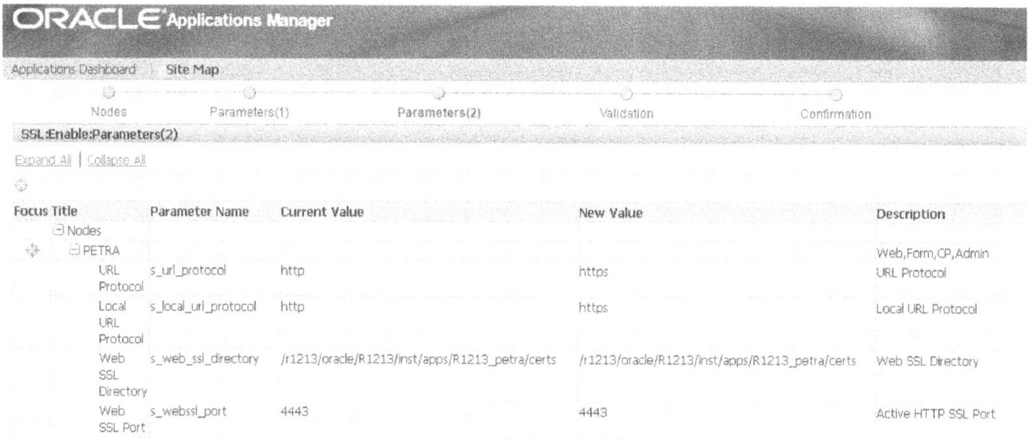

FIGURE 9-22. *The SSL Configuration Wizard that allows the entry of basic parameters and then makes the adjustments required. Once complete, AutoConfig runs and the Web, Forms, Concurrent Processing, and Admin nodes can then communicate securely using HTTPS*

requires licensing. More details can be found in Note 391248.1. As well as encryption, the TNS Listener process itself has configuration options that can help with governance, such as advanced logging options, IP address restrictions, and administrator controls.

Integration

The features in E-Business Suite help organizations run their business operation, and therefore are exceptionally critical, containing processes that can halt real-world tasks as well as information and intellectual property that is highly sensitive. Exposing this system to users and systems outside the organization is by definition high risk—or at least it would be without proper governance.

Integration governance is about ensuring that each integration is well designed and its quality and robustness is well tested. It needs to be secure, and this needs physical verification. Additionally, the integration needs to allow control should problems occur, and it should be linked with monitoring features so those controls can be used before the impact becomes too great. The obvious example is the processing of purchase orders sent from external customer systems electronically. While E-Business Suite has a queuing mechanism for this, if processing fails without controls a huge backlog may occur, eventually consuming resources and potentially overloading the system.

The most common method of E-Business Suite integration, XML Gateway, allows business transactions to flow in and out of E-Business Suite. In terms of governance, it includes many configurations and controls, as well as dashboards and reports on processing. For example, Oracle Transport Agent (OTA) component supports once-only message sending, username and password message authentication, and both client and server certificate authentication over SSL. More details on the capabilities and options are available in the Oracle XML Gateway User's Guide (E12954-04).

A more modern approach to building custom integration is to use Web Services as part of a standard Service Oriented Architecture (SOA) solution. SOA governance is a relatively new topic introduced as a result of general confusion and widespread failure to design, build, and implement effective SOA-based enterprise applications. With the flexibility and power of Business Process Modeling and the open and independent nature of Web Services, many organizations struggled to build consistent and well-architectured, large-scale integrated applications. As such, a set of recommended practices was established to make sure SOA projects limit complexity by following clear standards and good practices. This is implemented through the use of enforceable SOA governance policies. Since these are generic, I won't go into more detail here, but many resources exist on the topic. More details including overviews, documents, and podcasts can be found on oracle.com by searching for the Oracle SOA Governance Resource Kit.

E-Business Suite itself offers the Integrated SOA Gateway product for implementing the technical components required to deploy composite applications, namely Oracle BPEL Process Manager. It also offers some prebuilt solutions for quick implementation of commonly requested integrations, including the following:

- Oracle Price Protection
- Complex Maintenance, Repair, and Overhaul
- Oracle Transportation Management
- Advanced Supply Chain Planning
- Product Information Management

Just like XML Gateway, these integrations need governing, including adding security. Fortunately, Integrated SOA Gateway already supports the industry standard username and Security Assertion Markup Language (SAML) token-based Web Service security (WS-Security). The product also provides the Integration Repository (iRep), a tool for discovering and understanding the published integration points across all E-Business Suite products. While not specifically security-related, good governance requires a deep understanding of the system components to ensure all controls and management capabilities are correctly implemented, and this is where the Integration Repository excels. As shown in Figure 9-23, it includes details of Web Services and XML gateway maps, as well as traditional integration APIs like business events, Java classes, PL/SQL packages, and E-Business Suite interface tables.

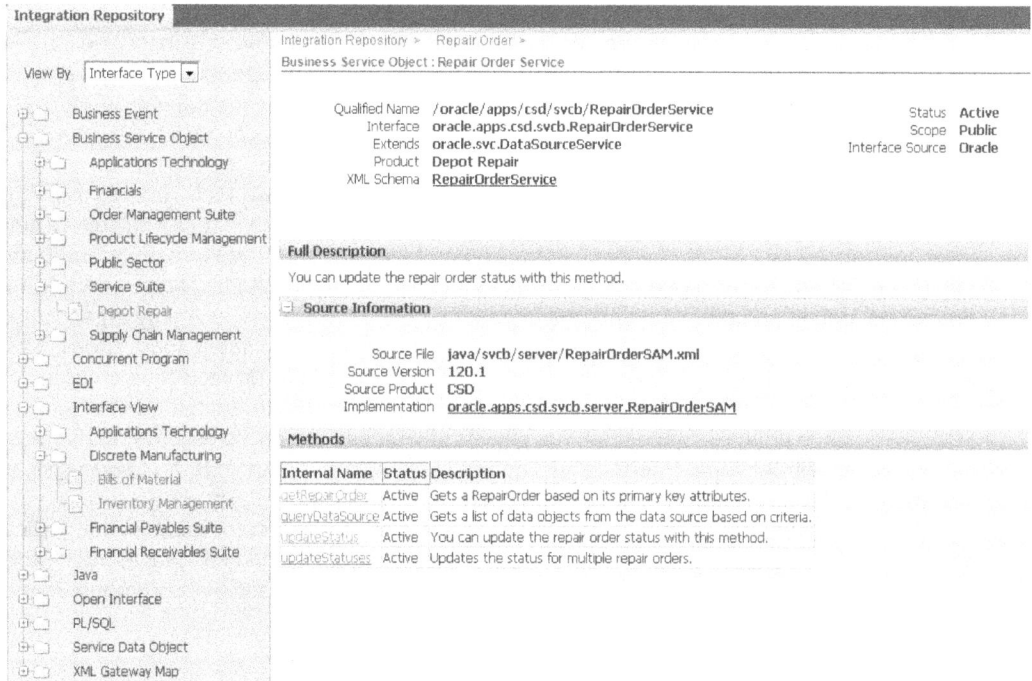

FIGURE 9-23. *The Integration Repository tool showing details on a published Web Service for use in implementing custom integrations*

Enterprise Manager Compliance Standards

Wouldn't it be great if there was a feature that already knew about governance recommendations and checked that your systems had them implemented? Fortunately, there is: Enterprise Manager Compliance. Not only does it come preseeded with nearly 2000 rules, it also allows you to define your own, providing a solid platform for governance validation.

As the name suggests, the intention of Enterprise Manager Compliance (also discussed in other toolbox chapters) is to monitor the technology components for configuration that could be considered outside of recommended usage.

Figures 9-24 and 9-25 illustrate the out-of-the-box security compliance standards and rules available that help the Application Manager monitor the system configuration for settings that could open it up to governance-related issues such as unauthorized data access. As shown, each compliance standard consists of dozens of detailed rules that constantly check the runtime deployment, configuration, dependencies, and version levels. As you can see from the Keywords column in the table, there are dozens of rules that are focused on security checks. Simple examples shown include checking that well-known seeded database accounts are expired and locked and that configuration files are accessible only to the right operating system user and group. Rules currently cover most of E-Business Suites platform and is an area that will continue to evolve.

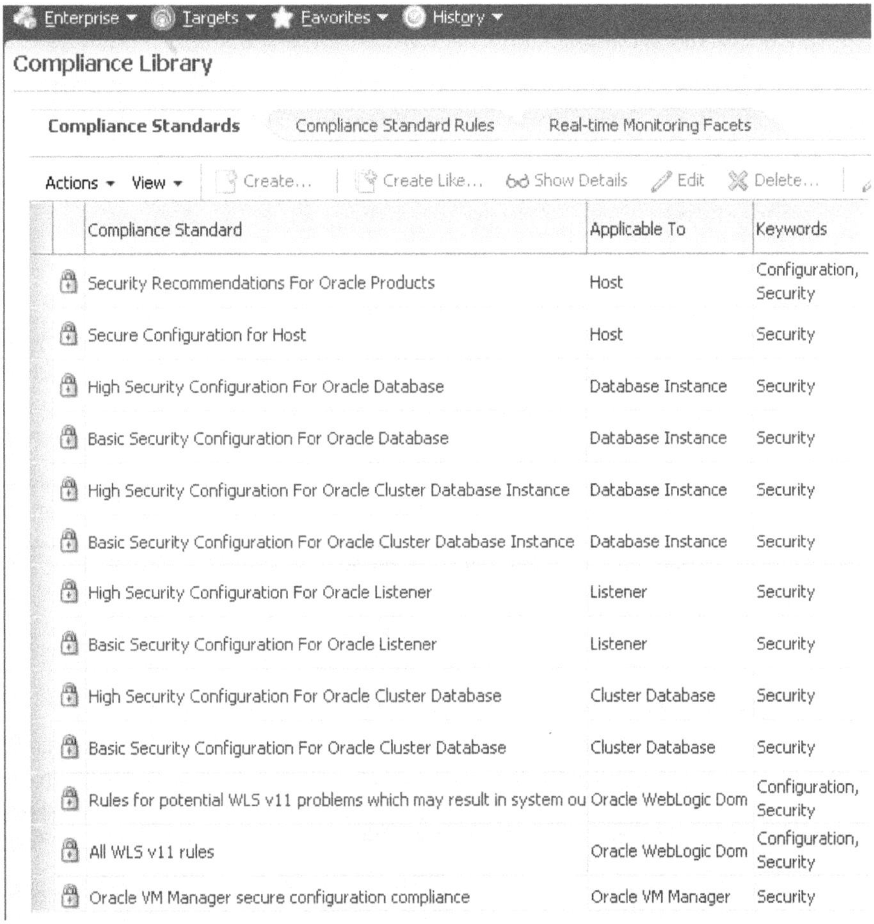

Compliance Standard	Applicable To	Keywords
Security Recommendations For Oracle Products	Host	Configuration, Security
Secure Configuration for Host	Host	Security
High Security Configuration For Oracle Database	Database Instance	Security
Basic Security Configuration For Oracle Database	Database Instance	Security
High Security Configuration For Oracle Cluster Database Instance	Database Instance	Security
Basic Security Configuration For Oracle Cluster Database Instance	Database Instance	Security
High Security Configuration For Oracle Listener	Listener	Security
Basic Security Configuration For Oracle Listener	Listener	Security
High Security Configuration For Oracle Cluster Database	Cluster Database	Security
Basic Security Configuration For Oracle Cluster Database	Cluster Database	Security
Rules for potential WLS v11 problems which may result in system ou	Oracle WebLogic Dom	Configuration, Security
All WLS v11 rules	Oracle WebLogic Dom	Configuration, Security
Oracle VM Manager secure configuration compliance	Oracle VM Manager	Security

FIGURE 9-24. *The list of 17 compliance standards that are related to checking the Oracle technology products for security concerns*

Compliance Library

Compliance Standards	**Compliance Standard Rules**	Real-time Monitoring Facets

> Search

To perform an operation on a rule, highlight the row and select an operation. To delete multiple rules, select multiple rows and click Delete.

Actions ▾ View ▾   Create...   Create Like...   Show Details   Edit   Delete...

Rule	Applicable To	Description
Webcache Initialization File Owner	Database Instance	Ensures Webcache initialization file (webcache.xml) is owned by Oracle software owner
Oracle Agent SNMP Read-Only Configurati	Database Instance	Ensures Oracle Agent SNMP read-only configuration file (snmp_ro.ora) is owned by Oracle softw
Oracle Agent SNMP Read-Write Configural	Database Instance	Ensures Oracle Agent SNMP read-write configuration file (snmp_rw.ora) is owned by Oracle soft
Oracle HTTP Server mod_plsql Configuratic	Database Instance	Ensures Oracle HTTP Server mod_plsql configuration file (wdbsvr.app) is owned by Oracle softw
Oracle HTTP Server Distributed configurati	Database Instance	Ensures Oracle HTTP Server Distributed Configuration Files permissions are limited to the Oracle
Oracle HTTP Server Distributed Configurat	Database Instance	Ensures Oracle HTTP Server distributed configuration file ownership is restricted to the Oracle sc
Oracle Agent SNMP Read-Only Configurati	Database Instance	Ensures Oracle Agent SNMP read-only configuration file (snmp_ro.ora) permissions are limited to
Oracle Agent SNMP Read-Write Configural	Database Instance	Ensures Oracle Agent SNMP read-write configuration file (snmp_rw.ora) permissions are limited t
Oracle HTTP Server mod_plsql Configuratic	Database Instance	Oracle HTTP Server mod_plsql Configuration file (wdbsvr.app) permissions are limited to the Orac
Oracle Agent SNMP Read-Only Configurati	Database Instance	Ensures Oracle Agent SNMP read-only configuration file (snmp_ro.ora) permissions are limited to
Oracle Agent SNMP Read-Write Configural	Database Instance	Ensures Oracle Agent SNMP read-write configuration file (snmp_rw.ora) permissions are limited t
Oracle HTTP Server mod_plsql Configuratic	Database Instance	Oracle HTTP Server mod_plsql Configuration file (wdbsvr.app) permissions are limited to the Orac
Access to STATS$SQL_SUMMARY Table	Database Instance	Ensures restricted access to STATS$SQL_SUMMARY table
Access to STATS$SQL_SUMMARY Table	Cluster Database	Ensures restricted access to STATS$SQL_SUMMARY table
Well Known Accounts	Database Instance	Ensure well-known accounts are expired and locked
Well Known Accounts	Cluster Database	Ensure well-known accounts are expired and locked
Limit OS Authentication	Database Instance	Ensures database accounts does not rely on OS authentication
Limit OS Authentication	Cluster Database	Ensures database accounts does not rely on OS authentication
Secure Os Audit Level	Database Instance	On UNIX systems, ensures that AUDIT_SYSLOG_LEVEL is set to a non-default value when OS-lev
System Privileges to Public	Database Instance	Ensure system privileges are not granted to PUBLIC
System Privileges to Public	Cluster Database	Ensure system privileges are not granted to PUBLIC
Use of Database Links with Cleartext Pass	Database Instance	Ensures database links with clear text passwords are not used
Use of Database Links with Cleartext Pass	Cluster Database	Ensures database links with clear text passwords are not used
Core Dump Destination	Database Instance	Ensures that access to the core dump files directory is restricted to the owner of the Oracle soft
Core Dump Destination(Windows)	Database Instance	Ensures that access to the core dump files directory is restricted to the owner of the Oracle soft
Oracle XSQL Configuration File Permission(	Database Instance	Ensures Oracle XSQL configuration file (XSQLConfig.xml) permissions are limited to the Oracle sol

FIGURE 9-25. *A small section of the compliance rules related to improving product security, as identified by their tag*

Summary

In this final toolbox chapter we considered the many different dimensions to application governance and the options and features available to address them through the layers starting from a business focus, moving into the applications technology, and going deep into the technology components underneath. We looked at many techniques for adding additional controls and measures as well as low-level options that will address many of the root causes of governance concerns.

The following table summarizes the items we covered in this chapter.

Business Process Layer	Applications Technology Layer	Platform Layer
Governance, risk, and compliance	Technical customization governance	Identity management
Managing customization and personalization	User management	More security best practices
Functional features	Basic security best practices	Database governance options
Configuration management		Audit
Change management		Networking
Data governance		Integration
Oracle Diagnostic Framework		Enterprise Manager compliance standards

CHAPTER
10

Getting and
Staying Healthy

The chapter takes a holistic look at application health and includes the topics that have so far fallen outside of our five core application management tenets but are nonetheless important intermediaries and complementary elements. Think of a car: it can deliver good performance and be efficient, reliable, and well-equipped; however, unless it's driven properly and looked after carefully, its parts will deteriorate to the point of eventual failure.

You may be considering outsourcing your enterprise application management or adopting cloud-based deployment, and therefore you might wonder if you should skip this section. I wouldn't recommend it, for one simple reason: you need to know what the team looking after your application should be doing.

Application Health Viewpoints

Let's first take a look at how you might review the application's health, as a system like E-Business Suite is so large that it can be hard to decide where to start.

The Principals

If you are managing E-Business Suite based on the five principles we've discussed in the previous chapters, you will have most of the key aspects covered. Use the tables in each toolbox chapter to see what tools are available for monitoring and managing reliability, availability, performance, optimization, and governance. Figure 10-1 acts as a reminder.

The Layers

In the toolbox chapters, we discussed E-Business Suite in terms of the three layers: the Business Process Layer, the Applications Technology Layer, and the Platform Technology Layer. By addressing each of these and considering their health, some productive and beneficial tasks can be quickly completed. As an example, consider these questions:

- Is the way in which users complete their tasks using the application satisfactory? Is the software an inefficient fit? Perhaps a change of process, procedure, or system setup might align the real world activities with the software better.

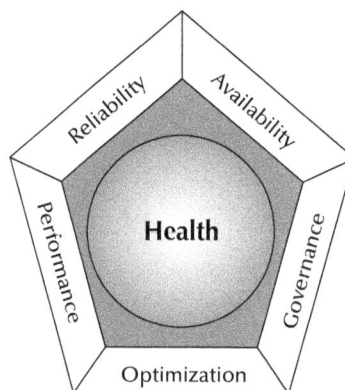

FIGURE 10-1.   *Review the five toolbox principals of enterprise application management*

■ Is the application technology struggling to support any specific functionality, and is its data well organized? Perhaps changes in use mean the maintenance plans need reviewing. An example might be failures in approvals processing or optimizing the storage of unstructured attachment data.

■ Is the technology platform operating well and is it up to date? Are there additional patches, versions, or options that E-Business Suite supports that will bring improvements?

The Priorities

While breaking down the application into manageable layers makes sense, it still doesn't give you anything small enough to analyze in detail, as each area is still vast, covering multiple technologies and capabilities. A better approach would be to identify a list of the top business processes and then analyze each to understand how they work and how their health can be monitored.

As an example, here are the main processes and components for purchase order submission:

1. Submission can start via multiple methods such as an Interface Table import, form-based submission, OA Framework-based submission, or the AutoCreate process triggered from Requisition Approval.

2. There is a complex order validation process that runs various Java and PL/SQL procedures to confirm all the parts are complete and accurate. If successful, the record is submitted to the database.

3. The order is submitted for approval. This is usually automated and managed by an involved Oracle Workflow process.

4. The approval may then invoke the Approvals Management Engine (AME) or use the traditional internal process to get the list of approvers.

5. Once approvals are successfully completed, the order may be sent out to suppliers automatically, as a PDF report using XML Publisher via Workflow e-mail notification or integrated fax, or as part of an EDI or XML Gateway integration.

If you understand the key processes at this level, it's quick and easy to see which components need to stay optimized, and should any problems occur, investigations are more focused. This knowledge is not easy to retain, but there are plenty of product documents and troubleshooting guides in My Oracle Support to help you break down your most important business process flows.

Monitoring

We brush our teeth and regularly visit the dentist as preventative measures to avoid the pain that would occur if we didn't. You might think our alerting systems are adequate alone, informing us of signs of poor health, however at this point the damage has already started. It is similar in application management, where waiting for problems to occur is far from the best approach.

We discussed many monitoring tools in the preceding chapters, and these should be incorporated into a monitoring infrastructure. Remember also, you need to accept qualitative input, including all forms of feedback from end users about how they perceive the health of the application based on their use to complete business tasks. This can be quite different from measuring the technology and software alone.

The term "monitoring" infers accessing a real-time picture of current system performance. However, it's important to support this picture with historic data also, so that current symptoms can be matched to patterns and trends, as in the case of slow health deteriorations or an annual seasonal peak.

Monitoring also needs to be supported by diagnostics, and by that I mean you must have a method of drilling into the data and components behind the metric to understand it. If a metric changes unexpectedly, the questions that need to be answered are what, where, how much, when, and why?

Another critical ingredient that makes monitoring practical is automation. The monitoring system needs to understand what might represent early warning signs of a problem. Should one of these signs be recognized, the system needs to trigger both alert notifications and where possible, a remedial action. You've seen how Enterprise Manager excels in this area.

The big hurdle in creating a world-class monitoring platform is cost. The tools and resources required to professionally monitor all the components of a large enterprise application through one single system are substantial, and this additional cost can be hard to create a business case for when the main justification is outlining horrendous problems no one wants to consider possible. On the flip side, trying to propose potential productivity improvements to a healthy system is almost as difficult. My advice is to add as much real data as you can find, such as past system maintenance costs and any specific problems that could have been either avoided or had their impact reduced by better monitoring. I've found some good general material in the Enterprise Manager marketing content, which includes numerous case studies of organizations that have measured improvements.

One other aspect of creating an effective monitoring solution that often gets overlooked is that the work is not only about looking at your own system, but also about tracking new information and useful resources. Here are some examples, with many more shown in Figure 10-2 available Oracle.com:

■ In Chapter 5, we discussed some of the My Oracle Support features including the Hot Topics settings that can provide notifications upon the publication of new alerts, newsletters, and knowledge articles, along with any patch recommendations available for your systems.

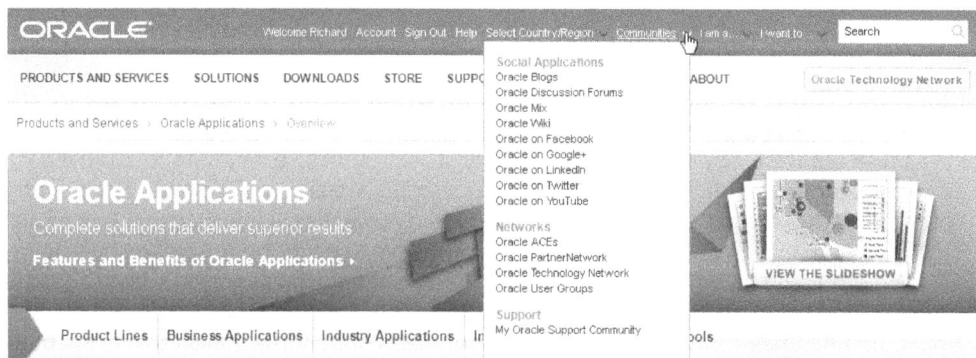

FIGURE 10-2. *A sample of the many communities and resources from which you can learn a wealth of tips, tricks, and recommendations*

- In Chapter 8, we discussed the use of My Oracle Support Communities (http://communities .oracle.com) and how they are a great place to learn and share experiences and to pick up recommendations both from Oracle and from other organizations running the same systems as you.

- The Patch Advisor tool integrates Enterprise Manager and My Oracle Support to offer lists of patches that can be immediately validated and applied within a single tool. This also works with Oracle Configuration Manager's Health and Patch Recommendations, which show patches (and other solutions) that will resolve known issues identified as applicable in scanned systems. Even the My Oracle Support portal contains a range of features (complex saved searches, recommendation lists, alerts, patching plans, and so on) to help you identify specific solutions and verify their suitability for use.

- Oracle Applications User Groups, both those focused on one industry as well as the generic or regional groups, represent a rich and collaborative community of like-minded folk that openly share advice and experiences.

- Applications-related social media channels, blogs, forums, and partner sites publish many best practices and recommendations. One example is the applications technology blog at http://blogs.oracle.com/stevenChan/.

Understanding Health Resources

Not all resources are the same, both in terms of their attributes and properties and their criticality to your organization. Obvious items like enough memory and CPU resources are essential, but as you go into data storage, security configurations, and disaster recovery options, the usage becomes more subjective. The trick to managing application resources is to identify and understand each of them carefully, and then to dynamically judge which gets attention based on a consolidated set of priorities universally agreed upon by all stakeholders.

The Past Is the Key to the Future

Allocation (and reallocation) of system resources is usually based on a multitude of factors and influences. First and foremost is the current consumption and performance data, and as I've shown in the toolbox chapters, this is available from multiple sources.

Many make decisions based only on the current system state, but unless you are fighting an immediate problem, that view alone can be quite shortsighted. It is better to also consider historic records because usage patterns and trends often provide insights and data-backed justification to what may be about to happen. In addition, plans and strategies for system usage (and therefore resource consumption) should be accessible and integrated so that resourcing is based on a long-term view and includes incorporation of items that support future projections and requirements.

Capacity Planning and Forecasting

The goal for a capacity management plan is to minimize the discrepancy between underutilized resources and unsatisfactorily fulfilled requests.

Effective capacity planning is not achieved by stockpiling resources, but today's application management environment is also driven by cost-effective IT spending. As such once the usual tasks of determining the resources required to meet short- and long-term capacity requirements is complete, the primary activity becomes researching and validating ways to optimize resource consumption, thereby reducing the resource requirements as much as possible.

Can resource requirements be predicted to avoid potential exhaustion? There is no silver bullet, especially when it comes to something as complex as E-Business Suite and all its features, options, configurations, and flexibility. However, a few simple, well-tested techniques can help you formulate a sensible approach.

First, it's important to meet with the business management team and carefully go through the pertinent business plan sections and related projects with enough clarity that the business plan can be applied and extrapolated to formulate the requirements from and influences upon the enterprise application. In addition, the IT management must be consulted so that infrastructure changes can also be accounted for in the capacity plan. This focuses work on the access to resources, rather than the actual need for them.

Finally, capacity can be estimated as a result of benchmarking using automated load and performance testing tools, such as those that exist in the Oracle Applications Testing Suite. These include the setup and execution of standard scripts as well as the various ways to make requests to the system, including virtual users. The resulting hard data should be used in quantitative analysis and as an input into recommendation and planning calculations.

This approach is also reflected in Information Technology Infrastructure Library (ITIL version 3), where capacity management is viewed as having three core elements:

- Business Capacity Management, which ensures that the focus remains on fulfilling business goals

- Service Capacity Management, where the ITSM approach to the provision of IT is used to ensure the agreed upon capabilities and performance is maintained

- Component Capacity Management, where specific technology pieces are validated as having optimized resource availability and utilization rates

Using these items as inputs, you should attempt a risk analysis cycle, looking at the impact of the best- and worse-case scenarios, and consider appropriate mitigation strategies. This should result in a range of problems and matching solutions and be used to get a general agreement (with sign-off) on the probable outcomes and the appropriate plan.

Similarly, you should create a contingency plan, in case a severe situation arises due to unforeseen circumstances. These predictions are best guesses most of the time, and although testing and trials are ideal, the nature of many resources means that there is often a lack of opportunity, capability, and enough accurate information to do many detailed tests. A robust backup plan should also include some layered solutions, where tolerance ranges are used to identify specific scenarios that can be weathered up to a point, after which remedial activities kick in. This kind of preparation and planning should already be part of your basic capacity management automation, via items such as load balancing and failover.

The first mitigation strategy should be to look at improving resource consumption efficiency, rather than just throwing costly resources at a problem. This is not always easy to do, and it takes discipline, effort, and lots of time. This work can also be exceptionally technical in nature requiring specialist skills. The Application Manager must help identify candidate areas for capacity review and use their own system expertise and business knowledge to help analyze the process flows and their resource utilization needs.

Resource Profiles

As mentioned, not all resources are equal, and it may be important to factor in the time it takes to acquire and implement additional capacity and capabilities.

Some changes are automated and immediate, such as the auto-extend tablespace feature in the database, while others such as hardware improvements might require installation and setup, followed by a system or component restart.

Other capacity-related adjustments need even more planning, such as scaling-out application servers or changing the security capabilities. These types of adjustments often require more extensive configuration changes and therefore post-implementation testing before being released to users.

The capacity plan should therefore reflect the implementation profile of all the key resources and help support the practical deployments of optimization projects and system evolution.

Service Usage Profiles

Often traditional DBAs and systems administrators assume that all application users are pretty much the same, and inflict roughly the same load on the system. This is an assumption that really needs to be validated because I have seen how changes in the use of the application can cause unanticipated problems.

As new users are added to an application, it can be helpful to analyze and record what activities they will commonly perform, and therefore the kind of system overhead they will represent. Invoicing clerks who mainly create transactions, for example, will have a different usage profile from that of sales representatives who occasionally query lead contacts and submit orders. This contrasts with the profile of a business development manager who runs many detailed reports and uses complex ad hoc analysis tools.

Although the performance overhead of a user profile can be a difficult value to quantify, some attempt should be made, and the results discussed with business and IT managers so that everyone understands the system impact. With this information the application system can then be tuned to match demands, and the process of managing the user base should be efficient with fewer costly oversights.

Also worth considering are changes in the application features that originate either from upgrades or changes in business operations. As features are implemented or existing features are used in new ways, the resource utilization can also change.

For example, some e-Business Suite CRM and manufacturing products include powerful predictive modeling features that use very different technical components (and therefore resource requirements) to most simple search and transaction creation pages. Combine this with the fact that some features are also accessible to potentially unlimited user-base sizes, and it illustrates how usage profiles can be dramatically varied and have a real effect on resource consumption.

Elastic Capacity

A relatively new innovation in application management is the ability of the system to autonomously move resources around (in a dynamic scale up and down) to whatever service needs them at any point in time. This is important based on the fact that around 80 percent of hardware resources are underutilized most of the time, and it is made possible by using abstraction and virtualization with very clever management software running in large data centers.

The benefit is that every individual application system no longer needs to be provisioned with dedicated resources based on what its peak load might be. This substantially lowers both operating and implementation costs.

For E-Business Suite, this is more of a generic discussion on the hardware and data center provisioning. We'll discuss this a little more in our next chapter related to moving to the cloud.

Good Health Saves Money

As mentioned in earlier chapters, Industry analysts Gartner and IDC have recorded that on average a business organization spends over 70 percent of the IT budget on maintenance, and you might assume this is an average amount of maintenance. While already regarded as too high, imagine the cost escalation if it included an application system running an outdated configuration, unpatched and ancient component versions, unsuitable connectivity, over-bloated storage of archive data, and disorganized metadata. The proportion of the budget would be even higher thanks to inefficient performance, poor reliability, and most likely, serious availability issues.

Despite the all-too-common tendency to avoid testing and maintenance costs by leaving the application on what is considered a "stable" version, the better-the-devil-you-know argument tends to fall down after a while.

IT managers are under pressure to ensure that cost efficiency is at the forefront of their operation, and having persuasive arguments supported by hard data is essential to get the green light for implementing health optimization projects and solutions. This should include calculations of all benefits, such as increased efficiencies, reduced resource requirements, and disaster avoidance. These are certainly hard items to quantify, however calculated estimates and probabilities should be used whenever possible, as often any realistic data is better than none at all.

When the hard sell fails due to the high upfront cost that forms an insurmountable barrier for optimization projects, the solution is to be smarter. Either find a more cost-effective alternative using creative approaches or consider an incremental approach that starts at a low cost and that delivers quick wins that prove the project's worth. If this doesn't work, go back and build a better business case and a more thorough justification, perhaps based on the experience of others, for example. In my experience, nothing is more persuasive than illustrative examples.

Healthy Processes and Procedures

Remember, it's not just the machinery that needs to work but also the complete operation that supports it, its inputs, the operating environment, and what happens to its outputs.

As such, the processes, procedures, infrastructures, people and teams, communications, and all other related factors surrounding the enterprise application also need to be optimized for health. A simple example is that even if the system raises an immediate alert that a component has failed, unless that alert is routed to the right person (or process) with sufficient actionable information, and that person (or tool) has the access and expertise to take the appropriate remedial action, the alert has little real value. Even better than a simple alert like an email, a well-optimized system might instead execute an automated remedial action, such as OPMN's Web Server process restart.

While it is tempting to draft process and procedure diagrams and flow charts and to avoid the validation of regular realistic testing, unforeseen factors often make the proposals not worth the paper they are printed. Don't wait until disaster strikes to check if the recovery process and procedures work—and they should work quickly. Demand the same of your business critical partners too, especially when they manage key parts of your operating infrastructure.

Be a Superhero, Not a Target

The enterprise Application Manager sits at the central gateway between business users and the IT department and is therefore the go-to person for both sides. This can be quite a burden, as business users may complain incessantly about every last frustration, and corporate IT may cite their own constraints and push back on ideas and resource requests. It can seem like the walls are moving inward from all sides.

The challenge is how to be smarter so that the business regards you as an advocate and facilitator, and the IT team considers you a sanitized way of ensuring their services match real business requirements. I myself have been in a similar position for some time. Having spent many years working with and supporting E-Business Suite customers, I built up a certain reputation internally for my troubleshooting expertise, proactive knowledge sharing, and attempts at addressing longstanding challenges with new ideas. I then took an opportunity to use these skills in working with product development on designs for and implementation of the diagnostic capabilities for Fusion Applications. This worked out well because customers and support teams need a product that is easy to support, and product managers and developers need to understand the real-world challenges faced in diagnosing enterprise applications issues. I had the domain knowledge to help translate requirements between the teams, review and validate solutions, and help enhance the communication between the systems users and its back-room technicians.

Because of experiences like these, I have found the tricks and techniques illustrated in Figure 10-3 have helped me move proposals and requirements into delivered solutions. In truth, most are general tips for working effectively across teams, but I believe these are worth spelling out. Ultimately, however, your own work style, personality, and role within the organization will dictate how you adopt these.

- **Use clear communication**   Communicate openly and clearly what you have done and plan to do next (and when), and outline any challenges and constraints you encountered. Most importantly, make clear the reasons for the steps you have decided upon, as well as the expected outcomes.

- **Be positive and resilient**   Remain focused, positive, and upbeat in all follow-up communication, and at the same time be resilient and determined to achieve results.

- **Establish channels**   Maintain channels to officially record business requirements with the teams involved. Log requests in the appropriate format for the recipient, ensuring that you'll add value to the raw request by suggesting approaches or adding considerations. Also, set up a method for creating follow-up discussions and review, and if required, escalation.

- **Set expectations**   Set realistic expectations clearly with all parties, and try to propose adding targets and deadlines to move things forward.

- **Be data-driven**   Focus on collecting facts and data to support all requests and justifications. Try not to use subjective arguments or one-off individual opinions.

FIGURE 10-3.   *Five tips for heroic enterprise application management*

Quality Information In and Out

The quality and format of the information flowing through the enterprise application management process is important to get right. When you don't, system knowledge and therefore health often fail. Take system usage, for example. If the Application Manager is oblivious to the fact that a large import of transactions occurs on the tenth day of every month (say, from an integrated system) with processing kicked off by a specific user every time, a monitoring system set up to review only average loads would not notice this. As a result, the potential for optimizing is lost.

This also works the other way, where the "black hole" that is the IT department remains a mystery to the business users they ultimately serve, and system improvements and problem resolution go mostly unnoticed and therefore unappreciated. Even more common is the way seemingly unjustified and sudden system changes made by IT impact business users, causing frustration that could have been avoided with a few brief warnings and explanations.

The modern enterprise IT landscape has come a long way since the Enterprise Resource Planning (ERP) systems of old and the Application Manager has a unique opportunity to adopt and take the lead in the new information revolution. Today's workforce of Generation Y and Millennials expect a wide range of information to flow efficiently to them based on a very small amount of personalization and filtering effort. This sets the communication bar higher for traditionally siloed departments.

The nature of communication has also changed. With a deluge of textual information in e-mails, blogs, wikis, and websites, modern workers require and appreciate condensed and visual information, so they can quickly recognize key messages and patterns. As such the information shared, especially for business users, need not be fine-grained or overly technical, as a combined summary or general trend is enough to share the messages. Think of the way a car dashboard contains only a few general dials and lights, amalgamating information inputs from dozens of sensors across the car. This method should be embraced as an opportunity to shine rather than as a complex challenge.

Sharing information, especially when automated, has another huge benefit: it can reduce workload. Providing an information buffer between the Application Manager and the people he or she supports can absorb and address many of the common incoming questions, concerns, and requests.

Some examples of great information to openly share include:

- **Current and recent performance trends**   Including availability summary data
- **Past and active optimization projects**   Including health improvements implemented and a results summary
- **Throughput and system workload summary**   Including who and what is contributing load to the system
- **Recent and planned patches and updates**   Focusing on justifications, new features added, and known issues avoided
- **Upcoming maintenance**   Including when and why downtimes may occur, reducing frustration and emphasizing the improvements that will result
- **Change management reports**   Possibly including another method of sharing optimizations, applied patches, or other configuration adjustments—with the emphasis on sharing the purpose, justification, and resulting benefits of changes
- **Feedback polls**   Including a focused method of sampling and surveying users, which is a useful information inflow mechanism

Effective Housekeeping

Like cleaning your teeth and physical exercise, most health-related activities don't offer much in terms of immediate benefits, but done regularly they avoid the painful consequences of neglect.

In the preceding toolbox chapters we went over the activities required to effectively manage E-Business Suite. In this section we'll consider what to do when. As such we'll split the recommendations into two separate cycles, broadly illustrating the frequency with which they should be done. Just like the "little and often" advice given by fitness coaches, the key message here is consistency and repetition.

Clearly, the actual usage depends heavily on the profile of the system, since a large throughput may require more regular cleanup activities than a lightly loaded one.

It should also be clear we're not including active system monitoring here, as this should either be immediately triggered upon symptomatic event detection or accessible through daily queries and data checks. The focus here is similar to cleaning the entire house rather than doing something as frequent as, say, washing the dishes. Nor are we talking about longer-term activities like data archiving or optimization projects; they would be more akin to redecorating our metaphorical house.

Cycle 1

Cycle 1 includes regular maintenance activities that should be considered important enough to be scheduled weekly or perhaps biweekly:

- Check for increases in nonfatal errors in important areas, such as database errors or workflow items.
- Look for patterns in E-Business Suite System Alerts.
- Run and review key security and audit reports.
- Ensure system backups or equivalent online services run consistently well.
- Summarize and support investigations into recent system issues (availability, performance, reliability, governance).

Cycle 2

The items in Cycle 2 are no less important than those in Cycle 1, but, based on system capabilities and requirements, they don't need to be completed quite as often. In practice it is not a case of waiting until the last two days of the month to run all the tasks in Cycle 2. The only effective way to complete the following long list is to run these tasks throughout the period, as illustrated in Figure 10-4, ensuring an appropriate interval between repetitions. Setting this up is the toughest

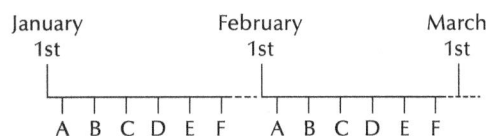

```
        January          February          March
          1st               1st              1st
           |                 |                |
           |_____ _|_____ |...
           | | | | | | |     | | | | | | |
           A B C D E F       A B C D E F
```

FIGURE 10-4. *Embed consistent and repetitive maintenance and health checking*

part, and the best advice is to start simple and incrementally, adding additional (rewarding) activities when the opportunity arises.

- Analyze and purge concurrent process and workflow runtime data.
- Check for new patches and alerts for technology and functional areas.
- Collect schema statistics and optimize indexes, such as that for Secure Enterprise Search.
- Purge logs beyond automated rotation and archiving, based on your file retention policy.
- Purge expired audit data based on retention standards.
- Consider validating failover and contingency plans.
- Assess resource consumption and capacity plans.
- Review configuration and change management reports.
- Review governance reports with domain experts.
- Review system usage reports, including workload and throughput distribution.
- Ensure the root-cause solutions to recent issues are applied and verified.

Watch for the Unexpected

We've mentioned how a healthy system is well monitored, triggering alerts and actions when something starts to deviate from optimal performance. The challenge of this is that it's rather reactive: waiting for a problem to occur is never the best approach. It's best to treat the cause, not the symptoms. As such it remains prudent to devote a little time to look for early warning signs of problems.

A good method to do this is to keep an eye on hardware utilization and consumption. Let's take disk space as an example. You can't know or remember where every last piece of output from an enterprise application like E-Business Suite might go, and there are not enough tools to automatically track these distributed and disparate accumulations. Some varied examples include Oracle Forms output, Concurrent Manager's logs, diagnostic test output, Web Server and Application Server logs, and the various E-Business Suite functional product-specific outputs. Sampling and recording disk space consumption across the filesystem is recommended. The result should include both general background noise and highlight unusual consumption, such as a process stuck in a recursive loop, a sudden workload change, and alterations to system configuration.

It therefore pays to keep an eye on the health of the supporting infrastructure and the ecosystems integrated with the application system, as spotting changes and symptoms early may help avoid subsequent problems.

Making It Fun

This section might seem a little far-fetched at first, but stay with me, as it might at least offer a little inspiration. The recent trend in software application design is to enhance the level of user engagement, with the aim to increase productivity as well as enrich the overall experience and resulting actions. This is mainly driven by a desire to mimic the success of consumer apps, where the runaway popularity of relatively small and simple applications provides important lessons for enterprise applications.

With these kinds of incentive-based approaches becoming part of modern enterprise applications, it makes perfect sense that it trickles through to the management processes and tools. Here are some examples of engagement activities based on incentive and collaboration principles:

- Apply gamification techniques with feedback, rewards via badges, leveling-up concepts, and comparative performance via leader boards

- Adopt visualizations and rich methods of displaying trends, patterns, and exceptions in complex data and analysis

- Consider how to mine the massive data sources available, such as logs, database records, and audit records. This is Comparable to the big data methods of handling and interpreting huge datasets

- Leverage collaborative tools for sharing and collecting information, as well as running cross-team projects where contributions may come from many distributed sources, such as technical and business specialists

- Get into social media by using messaging and publishing techniques for sharing and collecting ideas and information such as instant messaging and chat, blogs, wikis, and communities, which all represent easy-to-use methods that can be deployed internally to enhance the interaction opportunities across traditional department boundaries

- Get out and meet real people in the same position as you by joining, for example, the very active Oracle User Groups that hold numerous local and international events and meetings where everyone is invited to share lessons learned and find out how others approach common challenges

Help Desks and Support

Enterprise IT help desks are often used to support core business applications like E-Business Suite, as the majority of the business users and operations rely upon them. The level of enterprise application support offered by the help desk will vary between organizations, and commonly a few support specialists will exist providing some level of technical expertise, with the functional equivalent usually occurring among the end-user community.

The Application Manager should have collaborative processes and responsibility boundaries clearly defined between them and the help desk, enhancing the effectiveness of the business user support. As such they should be intimately engaged with the help desk, sharing skills and knowledge to encourage preventative steps that ensure the workload is appropriately distributed. This section provides a few recommendations on setting up and maintaining a health application help desk.

Help Desk Tools and Capabilities

We've looked at many systems, tools, scripts, and utilities, all the while assuming the use was by a fully privileged application owner, and so far we've given little consideration to limitations of access. As I already recommended offloading some of the monitoring, managing, and even troubleshooting workflow to the IT help desk team, they'll need connection to both the tools and the training required to use them properly.

The extent to which offloading the work applies varies by a number of factors, including the volume of requests and remittance of the IT help desk, its skills levels, and the available capacity.

Where uptake of management tasks is possible, the access to the following broad resources needs considering, as it may contribute to the final decision of who has responsibility over what.

- **Oracle Applications Manager**   Requires a new system administration type user and role (responsibility) within E-Business Suite. Not all forms and pages support view-only mode, which opens up potential risks.

- **Enterprise Manager**   Includes support for fine-grained user management, including role-based access control. Careful testing will be required to ensure items like notifications, alerts, configuration data, diagnostics, and monitoring and performance data remain accessible at the right level.

- **Filesystem**   It's unlikely that help desks will have low level access for running scripts and commands, but I have seen workarounds such as utility features made safely available in a custom web application (CGI script), with built-in safeguards.

- **My Oracle Support**   This is a useful resource that help desks may well benefit from. It includes user management features, where information consumption through the knowledgebase and communities is typically granted. However, the ability to raise service requests and more proactive support features like Oracle Configuration Manager and patch/health recommendations is retained only for Application Manager users.

Let's now consider some of the best ways to turn the IT help desk from a necessary evil to something that is regarded as effective and efficient and that enriches the overall service delivery.

Approach

There is a definite personal profile that suits the role of someone who provides technical support. While one would hope that this profile is already prevalent in the IT help desk staff already, it is explicitly detailed here to help you pick out those that are more likely to be successful, either for special projects or in maintaining the existing collaboration. An IT staff person should be

- **Systematic**   IT staff members should have a clear, logical, and progressive work style.

- **Motivated**   Staff should need little additional encouragement to devote significant effort, especially when responding to upset or frustrated users.

- **Decisive**   Staff should have the ability to make and execute on a specific path of investigation.

- **Attentive to detail, accuracy, and precision**   Staff should understand that complex systems require careful handling of investigative information.

- **Creative and inquisitive**   Staff should know that sometimes nonstandard methods are required to understand brand new issues.

- **Determined, persistent, and enthusiastic**   Staff should have enough focus and drive to wade through investigations and determine the true root cause and the best resolution.

In addition to the preceding qualities, IT staff should be able to do the following:

- **Use conjecture, hypothesis, and probability**   To formulate ideas on what could be the most likely factors and causes.

- **Spot assumptions and implied information**   To quickly acknowledge and assess information from unverified sources.

- **Check biases and be self-aware** To identify and address any potential misdirection or expertise limitations related to ongoing investigations.
- **Apply Reasoning** To appreciate the facts and influences behind new information and make logical conclusions.

You'll notice I have not mentioned technical skills and knowledge. While they are exceptionally useful, as the well-used (somewhat cliché) management directive suggests, you should "hire for attitude and train for skill."

Next, let's dig a little deeper into support and help desk operations, breaking down the key parts of the resolution process for enterprise application support. What follows are recommendations based on my experience of more than a dozen years in resolving software problems, many of which related directly to E-Business Suite.

Problem Identification

It has been measured that in customer services it takes about 10 percent of the overall resolution time to capture the problem and another 40 percent to fully understand it. This is a good chunk of time, so it is worth focusing on ways to speed things up.

I have seen many skilled and experienced people skip collecting basic information that later turns out to be central to the cause of the problem. This is often because of their enthusiasm to delve into deep technical analysis or an overzealous drive to hunt for quick-win solutions. Despite the fact that enthusiasm and expertise are important to problem solving, time can be wasted chasing red herrings and diverging off on tangents when you don't take the time to understand the problem fully.

Before even looking for potential solutions, you should try to define the problem in a clear and structured manner. This technique is often called "framing a problem," because it defines the boundaries, focus, and extent. In defining the problem, there are a few questions to ask that help gather the full picture of the issue.

- When does the problem occur? When did it start, when did it last happen, and does it happen only at certain times or in performing certain operations?
- How does the problem occur? What are the precise steps taken to reproduce it? If it cannot be reproduced, what was done previously and what might be different now? Also, what still works that is in a similar area?
- What is the extent of the problem? What is affected? Is it all or some users, transactions, or product features?
- What does the problem look like? How is it manifested, and what are the exact details of any errors, warnings, or incorrect results?
- What is the impact of the problem? How and why does this issue cause challenges in completing business tasks? Can the impact of the problem be worked around using alternative steps?

In addition to capturing this information, I recommend you discuss the problem directly with the parties involved, since often small throwaway comments can be critical to resolution. This is especially important for high-priority problems where contextual information and clues might save valuable hours or days of investigation. Examples include small changes to the system, its data, or its use that fall outside formal change management records and therefore are not common knowledge.

If you have worked with Oracle Support, you will most likely have experienced Oracle Diagnostic Methodology (ODM—see My Oracle Support Note 312789.1), a technique for ensuring that the key parts of the problem are captured throughout its lifecycle. You may have noted this begins with similar issue clarification and verification steps. Indeed, a famous quote from Charles F. Kettering, world-renowned inventor and holder of 186 patents, states, "A problem well-defined is half solved."

Problem Analysis

Once you've identified the problem, the next step is to figure out what might have caused the symptoms you observed, so the problem can be solved once and for all. Consider how an ineffective doctor might give out cough suppressants when he should be treating bronchitis with antibiotics. Root cause analysis is a complex area with many possible factors involved and several potential causes. This work involves not only a logical mind, but also many subtle skills based on the vague recollection of a past experience. That said, a few process-based recommendations have proven to significantly and consistently improve average resolution time and solution accuracy, leading to a better maintained and healthier system.

As shown in Figure 10-5, once the problem has been understood and recorded the next step is to consider all the elements and facts and begin to construct a hypothesis on what influences may be involved. This will require some investigation, and you may have to go over the factors and components related to such a problem. The strongest theories should be recorded with reasoning as to what makes them more probable. This approach helps avoid assumptions (such as not checking setups), just as the well-known Occam's Razor states that among competing hypotheses, the one that makes the fewest assumptions should be selected. Next is the analysis and research cycle, after which the meanings behind results obtained are interpreted based on the problem definition, and a conclusion is formulated.

This is also illustrated in more detail in Figure 10-6, where each proposal is analyzed based on research data to see if it is truly the cause of the issue. This process includes gathering further

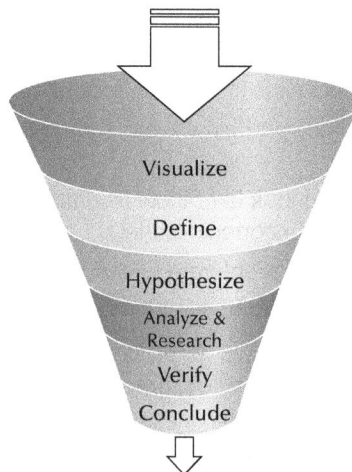

FIGURE 10-5. *The enterprise application troubleshooting process*

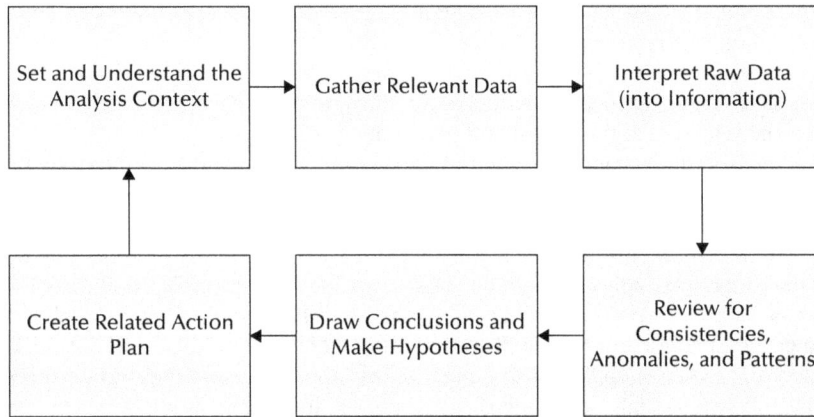

FIGURE 10-6. *Basic problem analysis steps*

evidence with which to make more insightful interpretations. This kind of discrete and progressive approach helps keep action plans tight, manageable, and relevant; avoids a drift of focus; and becomes exceptionally helpful when handling multiple problems at once. A methodical and systematic advancement is also facilitated by clear and logical documentation, including details on what was tested, what the expectations were, the results of the test, and the conclusions. This should include negative or inconclusive information as well, not just the activities that prove a theory right, since when actions go unrecorded it seems to the parties affected that nothing was attempted.

As an example, one simple and well-used method of problem solving is to use questioning techniques, such as repeatedly asking why until the external layers are removed to reveal the heart of the problem. Looking at the problem and asking insightful questions about what you observe helps ensure a careful and progressive analysis. There is in fact a "Five Why's" general purpose problem-solving technique, based on the fact that five repetitions of "why?" is usually enough to get to the root cause of most issues. While it's a basic technique, it demonstrates these elements of critical thinking, and they should be strongly encouraged.

When teaching these ethereal techniques, I've found that analogy helps considerably. Although software troubleshooting is often compared to the medical profession that diagnoses based on symptoms, I also like the analogy of forensic science, whereby following the available evidence and the timeline of events and studying internal relationships among components, you can piece together investigative threads.

Technical Skills

As you can interpret from Figure 10-6, completing several parts of the investigative process will require technical expertise. The second step is the gathering of relevant data to help investigate the issue. This requires a strong understanding of the process in question, the components involved, the execution flow, and precisely how to configure these to create more diagnostic output.

The next stage involves taking this new raw data and transforming it into meaningful information. This requires skills in understanding the output by first recognizing which parts are important, and then being able to identify their true meaning. For example, log files are sometimes filled with hundreds of often irrelevant lines from utility code that perform tasks such as checking security privileges, with the odd line here or there including cryptic messages from business logic execution. From this point, the information is assessed and based on the level of understanding conclusions are made that direct the next steps.

In fact, even before this analysis cycle begins, coming up with the list of potential hypotheses requires significant technical knowledge. Similarly, experience is required to be able to conclude which route will lead to the fastest and most effective solution.

The key is to understand the different parts of the system and how the basic processes work, from page submission to end result. This basic knowledge is essential for all kinds of application management tasks beyond simple error troubleshooting including change verification, setup validation, data problems, and clearly set expectations on process performance boundaries.

In my experience, although training classes provide a good introduction to technical knowledge, nothing beats hands-on experience. Of the many excellent support team members I have worked with, a good number came with a history of implementation projects and business operations that provided real experience in running the systems and processes they now support. This helps formulate likely potential causes and good avenues to investigate as it is easier to interpret potential effects of system changes, especially where past attempts have left painful memories.

One simple way of quickly getting this kind of real-world experience is to run a test case. The act of running through the steps in order to attempt to reproduce a problem frequently illustrates a factor or influence that would have not been otherwise obvious. Running a test case early in the resolution process is strongly recommended, and often helps you visualize the problem so it can be properly understood; it sets the context upon which cause hypotheses are often built.

Since E-Business Suite has business data at its core, you must understand the related data models and how transactions are defined and processes through them. This is not confined to memorizing complex structures and queries however, as there are many different tools to help you sift through the volumes. Some examples include building a script library, using documentation such as the Electronic Technical Reference Manual (eTRM at http://etrm.oracle.com), enabling database tracing techniques, and leveraging data collection type diagnostic tests. Other recommendations for effective troubleshooting using database records include reducing datasets down to manageable volumes by extracting only the significant parts, comparing records by looking for differences and patterns between transactions, using health checking tools to spot corruption or anomalous values, and reviewing system monitoring records such as query performance.

Customer Skills

In a role external to Oracle, I am an assessor for the U.K. Institute of Customer Service. I teach best practices and validate that customer support staff exhibit what it takes to deliver exceptional customer service. Surprisingly to some, we regard "our customer" not only as the consumer of our products and services, but anyone with whom we interact—colleagues, managers, subordinates, suppliers, or partners. This helps staff focus on what we call the *holistic approach* to customer service, where everyday work practices focus not only on the fee-paying customer but also on internal interactions within the organization, addressing corporate goals, personal development, and overall growth. Reducing the need to "switch-on" the right approach helps ingrain the principles all the quicker and deeper.

Obviously, technical customer service is a broad topic, and going into depth is outside the scope of this book. However, there are a few simple tips to bear in mind when making sure your E-Business Suite support operation is as effective as possible:

- Set the expectations of all parties involved as early as possible, and maintain them constantly.
- Ensure communication is open and honest, and most important of all, frequent.

- Define clear action plans, and for long-running issues make regular summaries that clarify the current status of an issue, where it's heading next, and the purpose behind it.

- Ensure collaboration across teams is based on agreed-upon protocols with some semblance of similar expectations around responses.

One final point on the subject of customer service skills is that everyone loves to deal with people who have a positive, upbeat, can-do attitude. Try to seek these people out, encourage them with recognition and reward when possible, and most of all, lead by example.

Documentation Skills

The ability to record information clearly is an often-overlooked skill, and one I believe is central to effective application support. When all definitions, actions, results, facts, observations, and relationships are clearly laid out, then determining the differences, similarities, and patterns between them becomes much easier. This ultimately leads to faster and more accurate solutions.

I have seen both quickly resolved issues where stakeholders have parted amiably with respectful thanks to all involved and long-running issues filled with frustration and escalation from all sides. The following few points make the difference between the former and the latter:

- Use formatting and style that is clear, with an easy-to-understand layout.

- Document only relevant information, removing any superfluous detail that would otherwise obstruct analysis.

- Categorize and organize information clearly, by type, technology, or other logical grouping.

- Record the corresponding result for every action, making it clear which ones match up.

- Record observations with reference to the relevant raw data and factual evidence.

Support Resources

The right tools can make or break a team that is trying to support a complex enterprise application such as E-Business Suite. They're the difference between a cost-effective and efficient operation and one where requests back up because resolution is laborious and therefore slow.

As shown in Figure 10-7, the following list includes four essential areas that should be focused upon when looking to provide help desks with the resources they'll need to operate effectively. Oracle's own CRM help desk solutions are built around many of these components.

- Complex technical systems are impossible to effectively diagnose without the appropriate tools and instruments. This applies whether it's a modern car, the human body, or an enterprise application. A strong library of tools must exist that is usable and has a readily understandable output. We've looked at what E-Business Suite has to offer out of the box in our reliability toolbox in Chapter 5. While some of these tools are quite advanced, a subset like the health checkers can be used for a quick triage of known issues. Delegating some of this work to run proactively can free up time for more valuable work, such as executing on outstanding tasks that lie within the optimization or governance plans.

- Ensuring a consistent method of working and properly documenting all support issues is a hugely beneficial asset. Reference materials and systems that initially train and then continuously validate adherence to (and evolution of) these standards might seem like overkill, but they do bring significant rewards, especially in larger organizations.

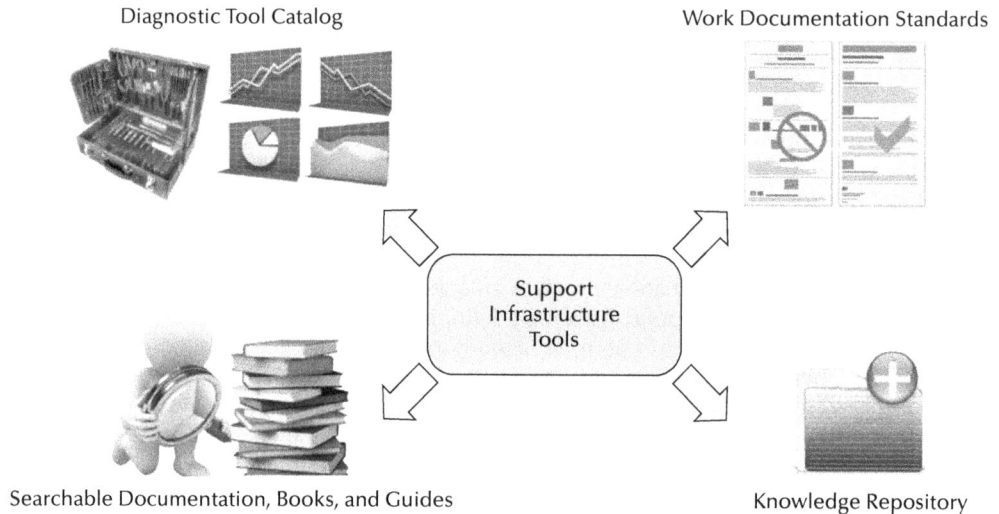

FIGURE 10-7. *Four important resources for encouraging help desk success*

■ Content that documents how the system should be implemented, configured, managed, and used must be readily at hand to the help desk team. E-Business Suite is such a vast system that it is hard for nonspecialized staff to recall this information on-the-fly, so it must be instantly accessible to explain the features, validate issues, set the context, and verify use. Often such content exists in different formats and different places, resulting in some being ignored and time wasted due to misinterpretations, assumptions, and not following the guidelines.

■ Knowledge repositories generally exist to supplement the preceding items in this list, and they offer a way of recording past experience, tips and tricks, known challenges, and other information that can solve or significantly aid resolution. Access to tools like this, commonly as an extension of a broader corporate or IT knowledge system, and the procedures that ensure its continuous evolution, is another strong recommendation. In today's connected world this may start with, or be supplemented by, an online community-based service, such as My Oracle Support.

Final Tips for Healthy Application Management

Although this whole chapter has been filled with recommendations on operating effective application management, there follows a few more suggestions that didn't fit into the previous sections that I am very reluctant to leave out.

Project Management

Project management sounds like it is going to be complex and perhaps overbearing, but my advice here is to use a logical and advancing process in completing initiatives and the tasks therein. In application management it is easy to get distracted and side tracked and never return to an incomplete project, or to waste significant time and effort figuring out where things were left and redoing work you've already completed.

Being organized and dedicating and prioritizing your resources to get things done is the key to project management. I use a simple lifecycle flow of setting objectives, creating a strategy with an implementation plan, executing the sequential tasks, monitoring results, and adjusting where needed. This plan improves success rates, promotes quality and thoroughness, and makes reporting, justifying, auditing, and accountability easier. More tips can be found at the Project Management Institute at www.pmi.org.

One elemental way to remember to stick to this kind of structured approach is to draw or print the diagram shown in Figure 10-8, known as the Demming wheel. This is a simple way of taking a situation and progressively moving it toward improvement. The idea is that this is not a one-time iteration, and each cycle makes one or more improvements. The elements consist of the initial planning of objectives and defining processes for achieving them, implementing and executing, checking and analyzing results, and finally determining any corrective or improvement-related next actions.

Reusable Templates and Automation

Life as an Application Manager is much easier if you can embed as many standardized and automated processes as possible in the system setup and management infrastructure. From availability alert notifications, capacity warnings, performance bottleneck alerts, and new patch information to reliability errors, there should be no need to waste time manually checking the many different places for the information that you know is always important; it should flow in. The productivity gains from this need no explanation.

Similarly, processes in system management should be templated as much as possible, from the details captured in new enquiries and problem reports to the process of cloning and executing patches. Where well-tested and optimized processes and structures exist, they should be reused. The consistency provided by this approach reduces mistakes, offers opportunities for continuous improvement, and facilitates getting the benefits of full service level management.

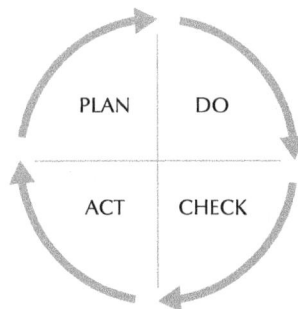

FIGURE 10-8. *The Demming wheel*

Dedicated Training

Run and maintain a training program for the different levels of engagement with your enterprise applications. As illustrated in this book, the multitude of concepts, features, and tools that exist to support E-Business Suite are extensive, and often organizations maintain multiple systems of similar size for various different purposes.

As different people engage with various aspects of managing these environments, they must be familiar with the basics to help avoid mistakes and inefficiencies. Assuming everyone has the required knowledge and expertise is a dangerous game, and while building a training program requires upfront investment, it doesn't have to be very formal and will pay off very quickly.

An Oracle E-Business Suite Checklist

The following checklist is intended as a quick-and-dirty guide for Application Managers to compare against their management infrastructure and see if they have everything covered. While this would ideally have been used on initial system implementation, it can also be very effective to review before running upgrades and similar evolutionary phases, as these represent opportunities to adjust and deploy any missing related management parts.

The tasks listed here are deliberately left at a high level, so they can be reapplied in the context of your operating environment. However, most of these tasks have been covered to some degree in this book and are supported by additional references to specialist material. This should act as a simple guide for your journey to a healthy application management infrastructure.

Should your application deployment (or related parts) be hosted outside your own data center, consider how these items are provided for by your current service provider, and help them optimize accordingly.

Reliability

- Set up failure monitoring and alerting infrastructure and tooling.
- Set up and configure diagnostic tools.
- Set up logging and tracing configurations and guidelines.
- Set up internal help desk processes for incident management.
- Set up a proactive issue avoidance plan.

Availability

- Set up regular maintenance plans and tooling.
- Set up emergency plans, including failover, contingency, problem resolution, and escalation processes.
- Set up backup and disaster recovery plans and resources.
- Set up a hardware lifecycle plan, including upgrades, replacements, and so on.
- Set up instance type (Dev, Test, Prod etc.) provision plans, including related resourcing and usage profiles and monitoring.
- Set up complete systems integration management, for both internal and external components.

Performance

- Set up a complete performance monitoring plan with priorities, targets, and thresholds.
- Set up a capacity management plan, including scalability and lifecycle consideration.
- Set up automated alerting infrastructure and tooling.

Optimization

- Set up budgetary and cost management plans.
- Set up configuration management process and tooling, including customization management.
- Set up application management resourcing, including people, time, tasks, and priorities.
- Set up improvement reviews of cross-organization stakeholders, content, and frequency.
- Set up supplier/partner capabilities, engagements, and monitoring.
- Align all plans and strategies with those from the business operations.

Governance

- Set up system security (all aspects, including violation rules and processes).
- Set up a data management methodology.
- Set up all required audit and reporting tooling.
- Set up an application software lifecycle plan (upgrades and so on).
- Set up a change control process and tooling.
- Set up patching and application testing methodology and tooling.

Summary

This chapter covered a broad range of tips and tricks that help to turn the hard, scientific toolbox content into a dynamic and polished operation. We started by defining application health and looking at ways to address and approach it as a task-based discipline. We then considered how to measure and assess health with qualitative and quantitative measures that facilitate control and results-based progression.

From this, we considered the other side of the coin, the softer process-based health aspects, and how your management can be tuned to induce positive emotions in its consumers, as well as how to avoid the traditional information black hole of corporate IT. We also looked in detail at the best ways to address ill health and how to handle problems effectively so systems are quickly restored to optimal service.

In the next chapter we look to the future and consider how to take you from your Release 11*i* or Release 12 deployment of E-Business Suite into a clearer understanding of your options going forward, such as how to properly prepare for a move to (or toward) Oracle Fusion Applications. The future for Oracle Applications, and its management in particular, is very bright indeed.

CHAPTER
11

Being Future-Ready

350 Oracle E-Business Suite 12 Tuning Tips & Techniques

Business complexity is ever increasing and with it, so is a strong reliance on software applications to help execute efficient business operations and enhance competitive advantage through information insights. As data volumes explode, it's up to software applications to do something meaningful with the inflow. Indeed, it's been recorded that managers waste about two hours a day looking for information, and half of what they find has no value at all.

Because of this, the traditional model of Enterprise Resource Planning (ERP) is becoming outdated, incomplete, and somewhat redundant. Businesses are now in need of enterprise applications that contain the very latest capabilities and support today's dynamic business models. These capabilities include being able to do the following:

- Intuitively capture all required business data at its source. The days of manual data input are long gone, along with the latency in accessing real-time information.

- Process transactions automatically, based on flexible business rules.

- Visually display business performance trends and patterns through powerful yet easy-to-use analytics.

- Raise alerts upon unexpected business activities, supported by a choice of ready-made remedial flows, including options for collaboration.

This short chapter guides you through some features and options to help you make sure your E-Business Suite deployment supports this type of next-generation evolution.

Usability Drives Productivity

Many years ago Oracle formed a User Experience team to look at improving the ease-of-use for all of their products. With the acquisition of application companies such as PeopleSoft and Siebel and the inception of Project Fusion, this team built a great store of knowledge and went on to lead the way in ensuring the next generation's solutions were as engaging as possible. This work was so instantly successful that it was clear that existing product lines could also benefit.

In 2007, Oracle looked at how to improve the user experience in E-Business Suite, with a goal to boost productivity. Initially there were concerns that radically changing the technology or architecture of Oracle Applications Framework might introduce instabilities or backward incompatibilities, which would be unacceptable to the huge user base and a threat to the otherwise stable platform.

What resulted was a clever combination of new features that safely extends existing features, plus a method to embed radically advanced user interface components, such as analytics and ADF regions. The first set of obvious improvements was in Release 12.1.3 and included items like type-ahead (or look-ahead) search, inline lists of values, drop-down navigation options, and as shown in Figure 11-1, the ADFX function that can point to a region of an ADF page. These initial improvements were measured as delivering up to three-fold productivity improvements and were well received by enthusiastic customers. As such, more usability improvements are on their way, and now all new E-Business Suite features are designed, built, and tested against user experience design patterns. More details on Oracle's User Experience team and design patterns can be found at www.oracle.com/usableapps.

Another way of improving usability and productivity of your E-Business Suite is by integrating it with products that already have these capabilities built-in. I've mentioned a couple of times the options for using Endeca solutions embedded into EBS. Endeca's powerful in-memory database

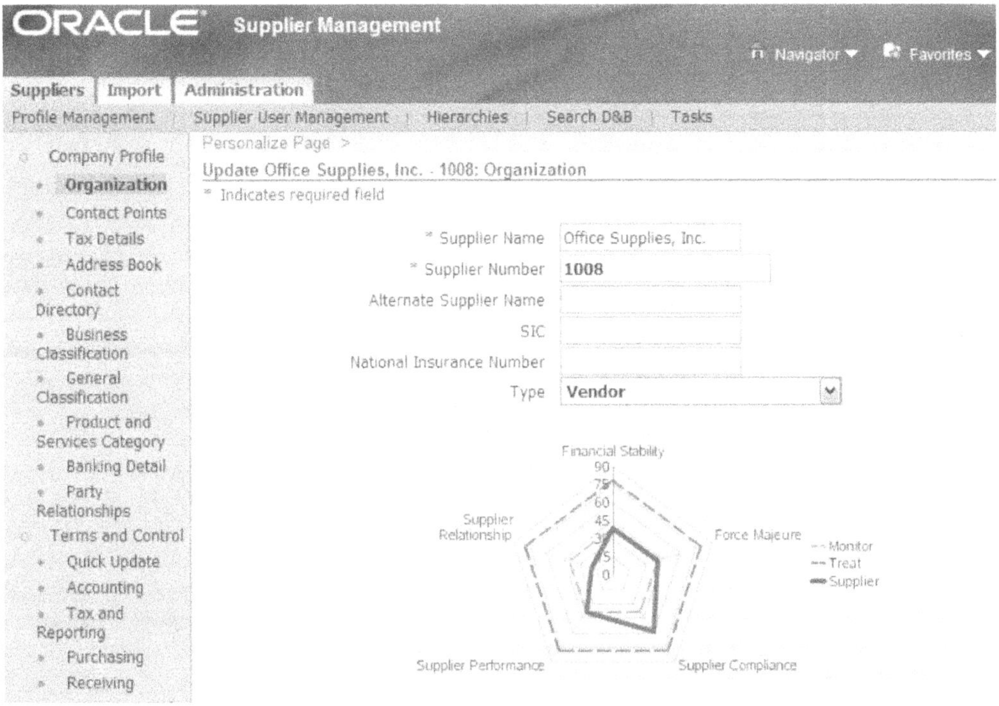

FIGURE 11-1. *An ADF component (the diagram) embedded inside the standard EBS pages as a custom region*

offers super-fast browsing and searching over massive structured and unstructured datasets, with the benefit of an intuitive, rich, and visual user interface.

This extension improves productivity and information insight while also simplifying IT because the need for separate Online Transaction Processing (OLTP) databases and a data warehousing infrastructure for analytics is removed—the in-memory database pulls live data from the base transactions. The beauty of this solution is that it inherits many E-Business Suite standards, such as security, because it runs inside a standard container.

Endeca already covers some significant areas where complex data and lack of visibility regularly leads to inefficiencies. Example processes where Endeca solutions already exist are in order management (shown in Figure 11-2), procurement and inventory, asset and project management, and CRM field service.

Almost all companies running E-Business Suite tailor its features to better fit their own business needs, from customizing workflows, changing the user interfaces, to making it work with various extensions. While tools that do all this have existed for a long time, such as Oracle Forms and Reports Developer, AD Utility features, Workflow Builder, and the Oracle Applications Framework plug-in for JDeveloper, the custom solutions tended to be strictly either inside E-Business Suite or integrated with one of the standard mechanisms like Interface Tables or XML Gateway.

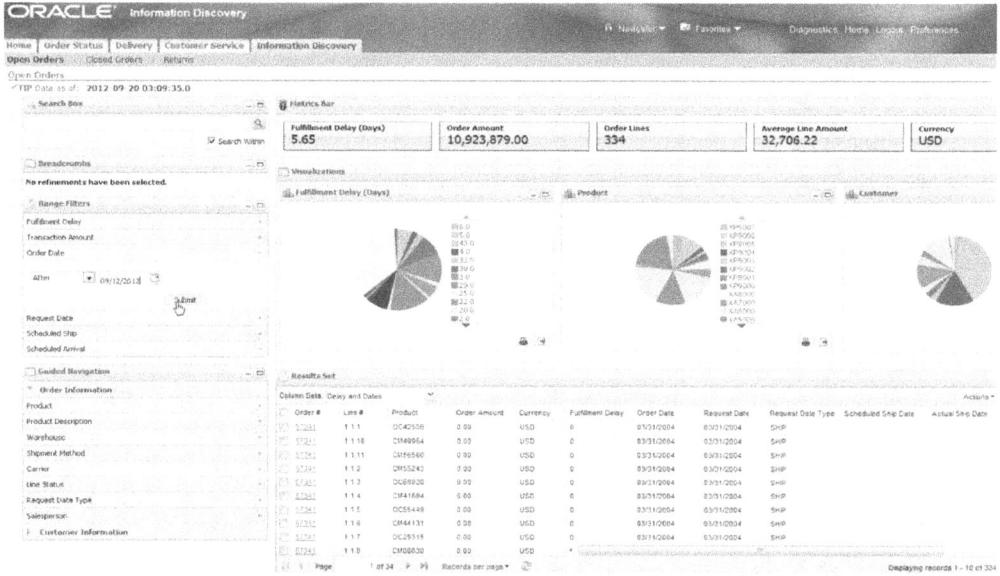

FIGURE 11-2. *Oracle Order Management with the Endeca solution indicating order processing metrics for a specific period, with a broad range of other search and guided navigations available to quickly identify business concerns*

With the continued adoption of middleware technologies, this has been further extended by the E-Business Suite SDK for Java. This is the latest evolution of what started out as a single custom PL/SQL package (CUSTOM.pll), then, with Release 11.5.10, evolved into a new Personalization framework, and now has this additional capability. The SDK offers Java developers the options to access both E-Business Suite data and stored procedures (via AppsDataSource) and the active E-Business Suite user sessions (via Java Authentication and Authorization Services). This means additional functionality can be more seamlessly integrated with the standard features, ultimately delivering better usability and a more productive workforce. More details on the SDK are available in My Oracle Support Note 974949.1.

Adopting New Technologies

Moving forward with your business means moving forward with your enterprise applications, and there are already a number of opportunities to include the latest technologies with the existing releases of E-Business Suite. Examples include Oracle Applications Express (APEX) for rapid database application development, Oracle Data Integrator (ODI) for sharing large sets of data, and Oracle WebCenter for managing collaboration, dashboard portals, and file attachment features. In addition, we'll discuss two more features particularly worth highlighting, as they illustrate options that deliver business value as well as prepare the business operations and IT teams for running enterprise applications on the most modern technology.

First, Oracle's BI Applications leverages Oracle Business Intelligence Enterprise Edition (OBIEE) to deliver the very latest in analytical, dashboard, and reporting solutions with native out-of-the-box support for an E-Business Suite back-end. As illustrated in Figure 11-3, empowering users by delivering business data and metrics in a readily consumable way significantly improves the opportunity for better management and deeper insights. Unlocking this kind of information from within the enterprise application is a longstanding dream of many business managers, and with BI Applications this is readymade.

Second, while E-Business Suite has a long and productive history of supporting business process management and execution through Oracle Workflow, this technology has now evolved into a nonproprietary industry standard platform that delivers many more advanced capabilities, namely BPEL and the other components of Service Oriented Architecture (SOA). While reengineering all the existing workflow processes in E-Business Suite into these new technologies is pointless, there is a method of deploying and leveraging these technologies for extensions. There are currently two main options.

The first option is to set up the E-Business Suite product called Integrated SOA Gateway. This installs the Oracle BPEL Process Manager technology and integrates it with E-Business Suite's own internal tool previously known as the Oracle Integration Repository (iRep). As shown in Figure 11-4, the clear information means the end result is integration that is modernized and simplified, as touch-points are wrapped by standard web service containers, allowing them to be easily invoked by external systems.

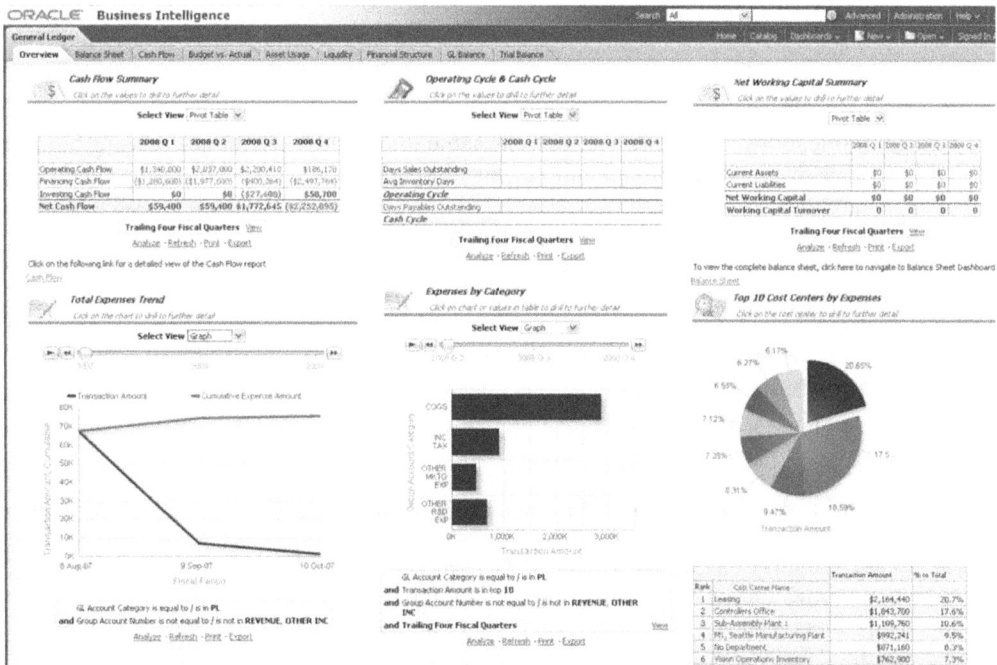

FIGURE 11-3. *The rich General Ledger Overview dashboard in Oracle BI Applications*

Integration Repository						

Interface List : Sales Order

View By Product Family ▼

Interface Source All ▼   Scope All ▼   Go

Export

Name ▲	Internal Name	Product	Type	Source	Status
CreateAndMaintainSalesOrders	oracle.apps.ont.services.oexoeord.s	Order Management	Java	Oracle	Active
Event For XML Integration Collaboration History	oracle.apps.ont.oi.xml_int.status	Order Management	Business Event	Oracle	Active
Event for Genesis Outbound Acknowledgment	oracle.apps.ont.genesis.outbound.	Order Management	Business Event	Oracle	Active
INBOUND: Cancel Purchase Order XML Transaction	ONT:CPO	Order Management	XML Gateway Map	Oracle	Active
INBOUND: Change Purchase Order XML Transaction	ONT:CHO	Order Management	XML Gateway Map	Oracle	Active
OUTBOUND: Purchase Order Acknowledgment (855/ORDRSP)	EC:POAO	Order Management	EDI	Oracle	Active
OUTBOUND: Purchase Order Change Acknowledgment (865/ORDRSP)	EC:POCAO	Order Management	EDI	Oracle	Active
Order Management Acknowledgments Open Interface	ECEPOAO	Order Management	Open Interface	Oracle	Active
Order Management Acknowledgments Open Interface	ECEPOCAO	Order Management	Open Interface	Oracle	Active
Order Management Sales Orders Open Interface	ECEPOCI	Order Management	Open Interface	Oracle	Active

View By list (left panel):
- Advanced Planning
- Applications Technology
- Contracts Suite
- Discrete Manufacturing
- Financial Globalizations Suite
- Financial Payables Suite
- Financial Receivables Suite
- Financial Services Applications
- Financials
- Human Resources Suite
- Interaction Center
- Marketing Suite
- Marketing and Sales Suite
- Order Management Suite
  - Advanced Pricing
  - Configurator
  - Order Management
    - Sales Agreement
  - Release Management
  - Shipping Execution Common

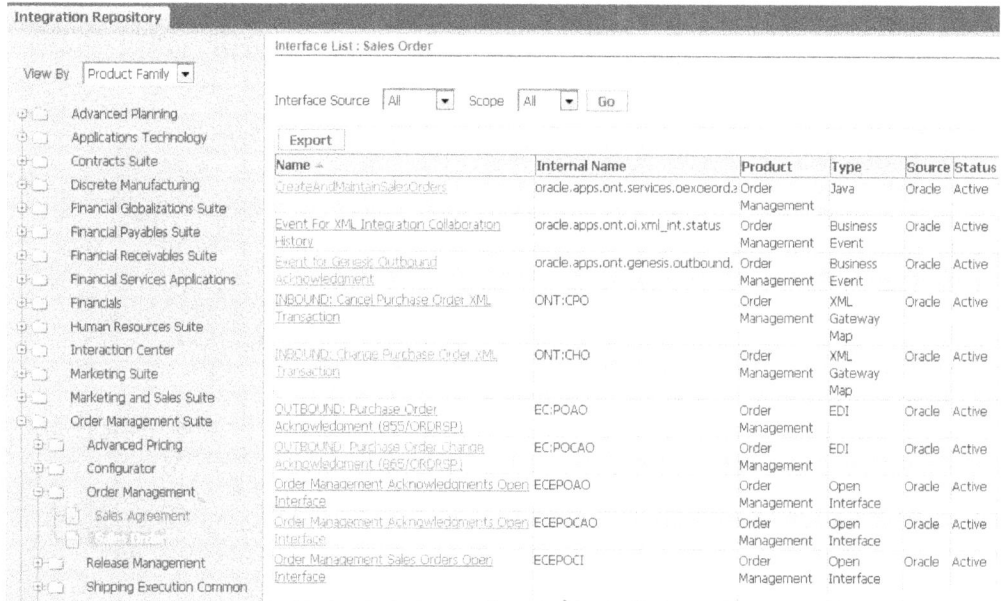

FIGURE 11-4. *E-Business Suite's Integration Repository showing the different integration options for sales orders with the parameters required for use*

The second option is to set up the Fusion Middleware option called the SOA Adapter for Oracle Applications. This delivers much the same improved integration solutions but from the other end, by making the external middleware able to communicate with the standard E-Business Suite integrations, as defined in iRep and shown in Figure 11-5. This then allows for the creation of custom solutions for E-Business Suite in JDeveloper or SOA Suite.

To illustrate the power of these types of improvements, in Release 12.1.3, iRep details the following wide selection of integration options available within E-Business Suite:

- 1200 PL/SQL APIs
- 1400 Business Events
- 147 Interface Tables
- 214 Concurrent Programs
- 140 XML Gateway integrations and another 24 in eCommerce Gateway for EDI

To add a little reality into this discussion, there are a few areas where these latest integration tools need some consideration. First, the information on E-Business Suite's internal workings has, like the product, evolved over time. While the newest sources like iRep have the most up-to-date content, they can be well supported by some of the more in-depth but older documentation. My advice is to look for useful content wherever you can find it.

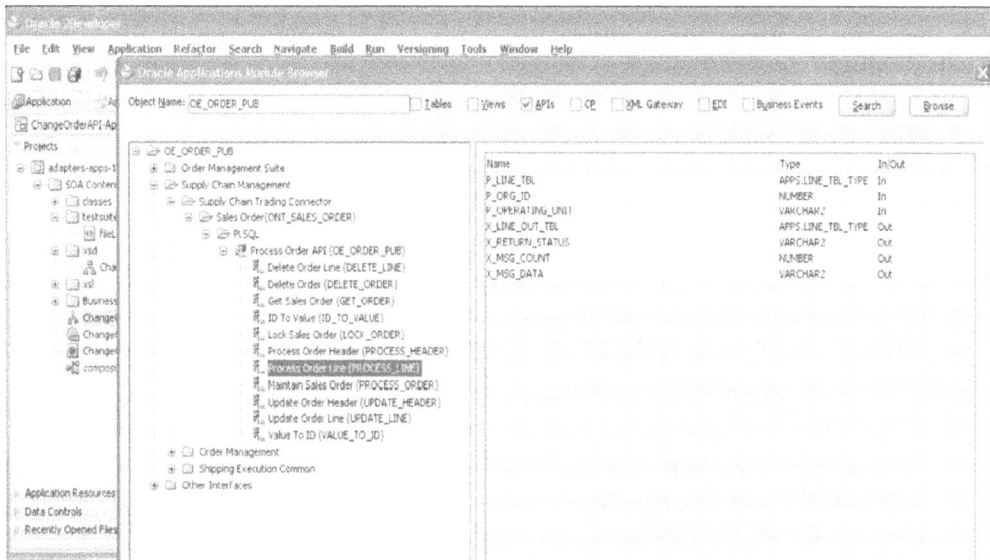

FIGURE 11-5.   *The JDeveloper Module Browser Wizard allows the selection of E-Business Suite integrations from iRep for design-time development*

Second, where integration requires that you go beyond the standard APIs available, there is a tendency to attempt to meet the requirement using whatever methods possible. This results in low-level customizations to objects that may change over time, causing failure in the dependent code. Sometimes the cost of this outweighs the feature benefits that it added.

Oracle E-Business Suite Evolution

As is made clear by the Applications Unlimited commitment made by Oracle several years ago, all the applications product lines, including E-Business Suite, will continue to be developed and enhanced for years to come. This means that new releases will not only include bug fixes, but will also add new features, new products, and the adoption of new technologies.

E-Business Suite Releases 12.1.3 and 12.2 are prime examples of this, where the product has evolved significantly both functionally and technically. While on initial inspection it might seem odd to be continuing to compete with sister product lines like JD Edwards, PeopleSoft, and Siebel, the truth is that these products are not going away anytime soon, and the more advanced they become the shorter the jump over to Fusion Applications will be when that time comes. To illustrate this point, here are a few examples of new features in E-Business Suite Release 12.2 that also exist in Fusion Applications:

- Release 12.2 includes Fusion Middleware components, such as SOA Suite and WebCenter.
- Release 12.2 moves the Java Application Server architecture from OC4J to the more advanced capabilities of WebLogic.
- Release 12.2 moves from the extended Apache HTTP Server to the standard Oracle server.

- Release 12.2 offers better technology control and management through the inclusion of Enterprise Manager Fusion Middleware Control and the WebLogic Administration Console.
- Release 12.2 adopts the 11*g* Release 2 of the Oracle Database, leveraging its advanced capabilities such as edition-based redefinitions to support online patching.

With Fusion Applications now released, it's clear that, while it lacks the functional breadth of E-Business Suite, it is evolving at a rapid pace and closing the gaps where the need is most obvious. Ultimately, there will be a convergence of sorts, where Fusion grows to be functionally equivalent to E-Business Suite, and E-Business Suite runs on similar technologies. That said, the E-Business Suite pages and forms are not going to be rewritten in ADF, and the stable base code of E-Business Suite will remain that way. It's the extensions and new features that will be the focus when considering taking up and benefiting from these new Fusion-related technologies.

Interestingly, there were some precursor niche products written using an early Fusion techstack, commonly referred to as *Fusion Edge* products. These modern features run alongside the traditional E-Business Suite products, and have already proven the benefits and opportunities available by reengineering enterprise features using the latest technologies.

In addition to technology, Fusion Applications seized upon the opportunity to redesign many of the standard business functional processes, especially those that evolved somewhat organically in E-Business Suite. This resulted in many simplifications and optimization opportunities, as advanced features added later to the E-Business Suite product are native in the design, plus it includes more effective implementations used by other equivalent applications product lines. Fusion is therefore a most appropriate name.

The differences in Fusion Applications range from increasing task completion efficiency, thanks to a simpler and more intuitive interface, to reducing the complexity of many of the back-end processes. For example, compared to E-Business Suite, Fusion Procurement takes fewer steps for a user to raise a requisition, and the back-end processes (and related setup) to automatically create it into a purchase order are also greatly simplified.

The Fusion Applications Roadmap

Since its initial release in 2011, much has been written about Fusion Applications that directly and indirectly recognizes some of the benefits it has over the existing Oracle Applications product lines. The outpouring of writing has also begun to include advice and experiences about using the different adoption options, as the uptake gains momentum. When and how to successfully move to Fusion Applications remains somewhat open to interpretation; the right approach depends on a number of organization-specific factors. We'll discuss building a strategy shortly, but here are a few points to consider:

- Making the most of consolidation opportunities, including hardware and existing application
- Improving the alignment of business strategy with the applications portfolio
- Modernizing the IT infrastructure, including more options for mobile and social capability, plus ensuring the continuation on fully certified and supported platforms
- Adopting new technical capabilities offered by the latest technologies
- Adopting new business capabilities offered by the functional products
- Simplifying and standardizing opportunities, such as using open-standards technologies and eliminating high-overhead customizations

- Creating better budget visibility by leveraging service and subscription models

- Starting small and cherry-picking the features worth having, such as getting ROI quickly

- Cleaning the business system using Master Data Management solutions, so when the move happens it has quality information going in

I hear often a lot about the "upgrade" process and having to reset some expectations. There is currently no upgrade process to move from any Applications Unlimited products to the Fusion Applications equivalent. This is because Fusion Applications is a new product line with a new technology stack and different applications code. As such, moving to Fusion Applications requires a fresh implementation, although there is some support for migrating (importing) legacy data. Obviously, the effort and resources required to do this kind of reimplementation are significant, and already the Software-as-a-Service or cloud-based options are popular alternatives that offer revolutionary alternatives.

Oracle has in fact recommended six potential Fusion Application strategies to consider, ranging from no immediate adoption to full suite deployment, with several flavors in between. These strategies are not mutually exclusive, and some products might fit with one model whereas others will fit with a different one. Here are the key points in more detail:

- **No change**

  - Don't adopt Fusion Applications but keep your existing applications on the latest releases. This helps protect the current investment and allows you to continue to realize value without having to forget about the future since it will inevitably incorporate Fusion technologies.

- **Standalone Fusion**

  - Adopt Fusion products but without any integration to existing applications. The use of discrete standalone Fusion Application products is possible and can suit many business needs.

  - Adopt Fusion Applications and retire existing equivalent application products. Here data is migrated into the new system. This is sometimes called a rip-and-replace strategy, although most products can be deployed incrementally.

  - Adopt Fusion Applications where there were no existing application products. This would be suited for a rapidly growing company requiring the latest Enterprise Application suite.

- **Coexist**

  - Adopt Fusion Applications with some loose integration. An example might be data that is initially imported during setup into the Fusion Application and periodically refreshed. Master Data Management is an example, and this method can add new functionality without the overhead of creating and maintaining full integration.

  - Adopt Fusion Applications with tight integration. Here the real-time sharing of data between systems is implemented. Examples are products like Fusion Distributed Order Orchestration which analyzes, decomposes, and routes orders from a capture system like Siebel, to the appropriate downstream fulfillment system like E-Business Suite Order Management.

Fusion Applications Coexistence

Due to the modular nature of Fusion Applications, specific products and features can be adopted on an ad hoc basis and integrated with existing Oracle Applications like E-Business Suite. This includes support for on-premise, on-demand (private cloud), and SaaS (cloud) based adoption. In simple terms, it presents a simplified opportunity for an incremental migration path and the ability to leverage the advanced capabilities of Fusion Applications, all without large up-front implementation costs.

In principle, there are essentially two types of coexistence, although in reality there is some intermingling during deployment. The first is a *packaged coexistence scenario*, where both ends of the integration are already instrumented with code that will communicate with each other when the appropriate setup is completed. The second is a *coexistence-enabled scenario*, which requires the implementer to build some of the integration, although it is based on published outlines and APIs as hooks into and out of Fusion Applications. We'll look at both of these in more detail, but first, let's preface this section with a short mention of the main catalog tool for understanding how you might be able to integrate your existing E-Business Suite application with Fusion Applications.

Oracle Enterprise Repository (OER)

The Oracle Enterprise Repository (OER) tool is basically like the aforementioned Integration Repository (iRep) from E-Business Suite, but it's supercharged with both more depth and breadth of content from Fusion Applications. It also includes many useful features to help you find what you need. Currently, it contains over one thousand integration assets, consisting of many asset types such as Web Services, Schema Definitions, SOA composites, business events, and interface tables. It also contains a wealth of electronic Technical Reference Manual (eTRM) information, such as information on database tables and views, flexfields, profile options, and reports.

A public instance of OER, shown in Figure 11-6, is currently available from https://fusionappsoer.oracle.com.

The content in OER is specific to the integration asset type, but common details are items such as message definitions, methods and operations, security privileges, dependencies, and detailed implementation documentation, all of which make this a very valuable resource.

Packaged Scenarios

Completing only some limited configuration to get a complex system-to-system application integration working is a huge cost and time savings when compared with traditional methods that also involved extensive coding. In addition in these scenarios the integration process that runs is fully tested and is supported by Oracle.

At a basic high-level, E-Business Suite requires the implementation of an integration capability, to which linking with Fusion Applications is done using standard mechanisms such as Oracle Data Integrator and SOAP-based Web Services. An example for E-Business Suite is Application Integration Architecture (AIA), which benefits from being a well-proven solution and uses the same common business object definitions as Fusion Applications (such as the structure and data attributes of a purchase order), as well as the same technologies for both ends of the integration, reducing the general likelihood of problems.

Let's look at the example of integrating with Fusion Talent and Compensation Management with Applications Unlimited HRMS. This is sometimes referred to as HR2HR coexistence, however, this name is being retired in preference for expansion of a universal file-based loader approach. In this solution, E-Business Suite (or PeopleSoft) always retains the system-of-record

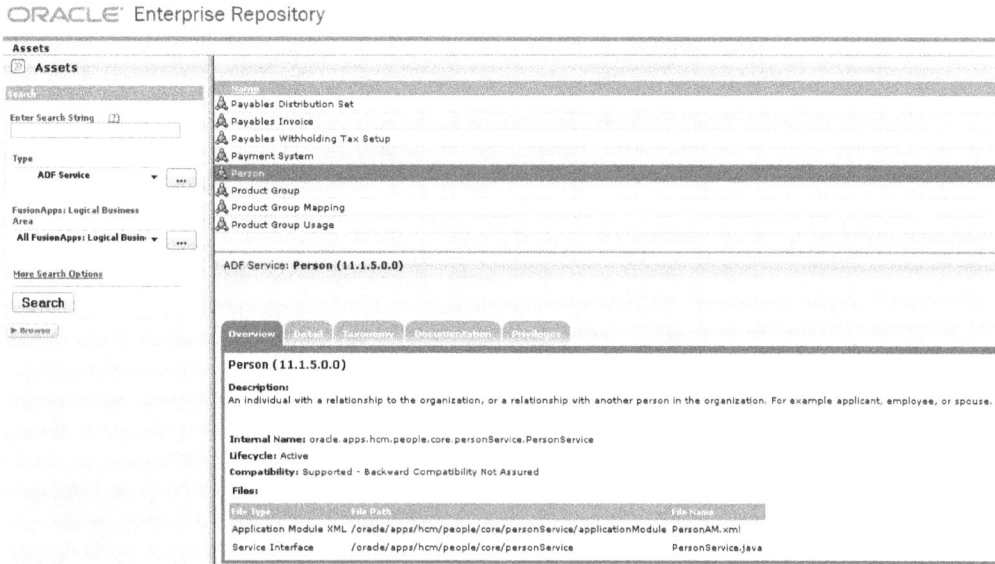

FIGURE 11-6. *The Person Web Service shown in OER, with overview and detail under each tab*

(or source of truth) for the core HR data, but an initial extract and data load is done into the Fusion database, consisting of people, jobs, organizations, and compensation details. Once complete, ongoing synchronization is performed with fresh profile information coming into Fusion and any changes in compensation shared between both systems. The Fusion system is then used for its advanced capabilities under talent review, goal and performance management, and analytics. It then becomes the system-of-record for the talent data, synchronizing back to E-Business Suite any changes to compensation such as bonuses and promotions. As illustrated in Figure 11-7, it now becomes a rich new business tool for detailed compensation analysis, planning, and allocation. This coexistence solution works through a combination of data mapping (processed via ODI) and loader programs fed by secure file transfer, and therefore supports both on-premise and cloud deployments.

Each packaged integration works in its own way, some using pure Web Service invocations, many through file-based export and import and others focusing more on ODI data transformation and movement. In addition to the HCM integration mentioned above, the following prepackaged integrations are available:

- Fusion Accounting Hub to E-Business Suite, PeopleSoft, and JD Edwards Financials
- Fusion Project Portfolio Management to Primavera P6
- Fusion Distributed Order Orchestration to Siebel Order Capture, E-Business Suite Order Management, JD Edwards Order Entry

As mentioned before, OER contains details on hundreds of published integration options, so while the packaged scenario list will continue to grow over time, integration is part of the Fusion

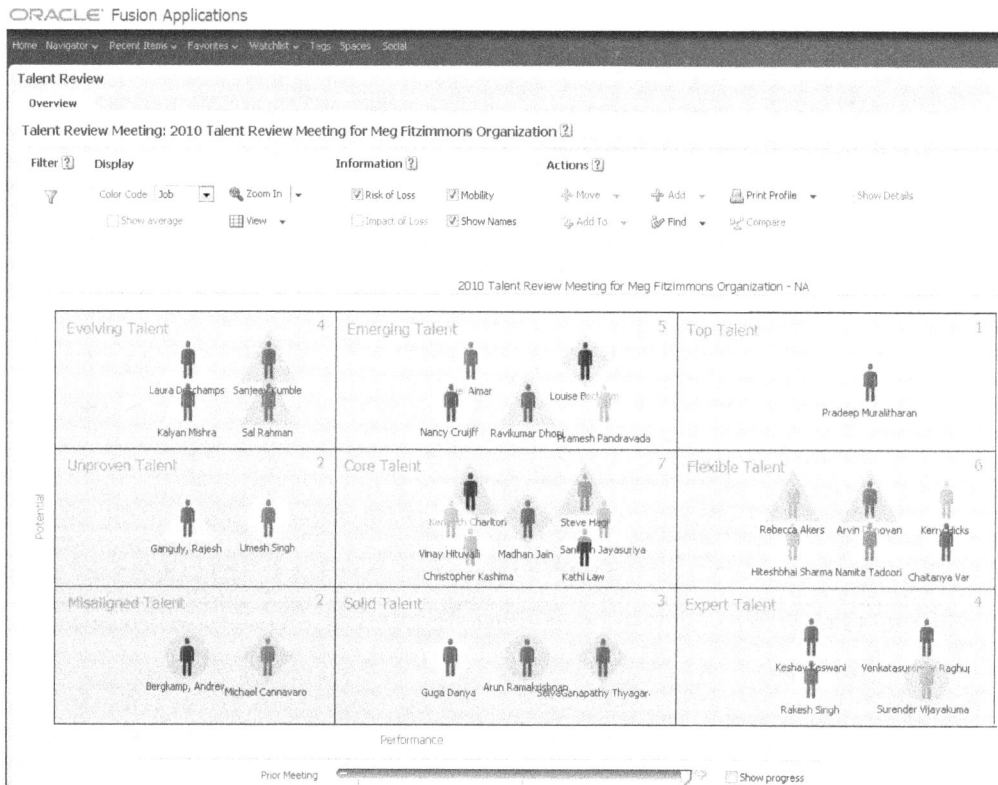

FIGURE 11-7. *Powerful and intuitive features of Fusion HCM includes alert summaries for compensation policy violations, with embedded actions and modeling options*

Applications DNA thanks to its implementation of open standards architectures like SOA and Web Services.

Enabled Scenarios

In addition to pre-prepared integrations, there are other popular functional business processes where complete integration solutions are *almost* packaged. This exposes more features of Fusion Applications for use, again without the requirement for a complete system migration or implementation. These scenarios are all supported by a set of APIs for the tasks involved, detailed out in OER as illustrated in Figure 11-8, and require some implementation effort to enable the flow. Some examples include the following:

- Fusion Territory Management to E-Business Suite, Siebel, and PeopleSoft CRM

- Fusion Incentive Compensation to E-Business Suite and PeopleSoft HCM, and to E-Business Suite, PeopleSoft and Siebel CRM

- Fusion Spend Analysis, Sourcing, and Contracts to E-Business Suite and PeopleSoft Requisitioning

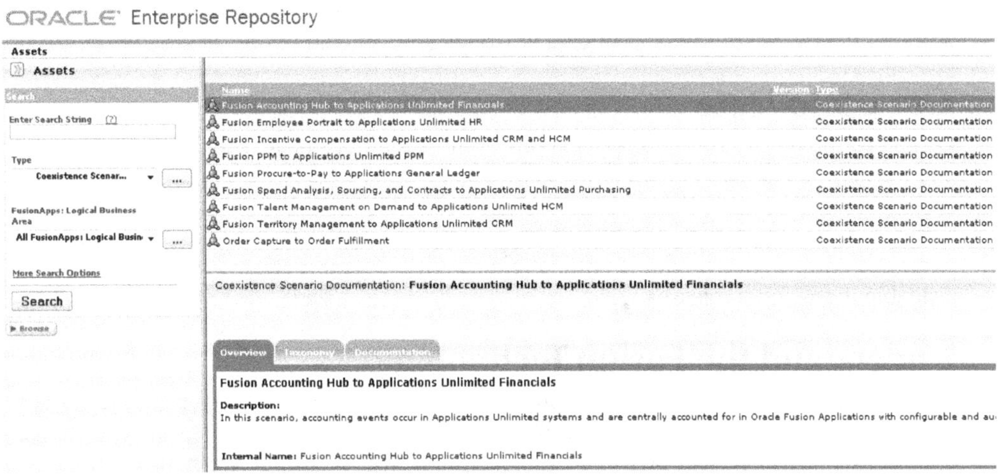

FIGURE 11-8. *The coexistence scenarios are detailed in Oracle Enterprise Repository, where under the Documentation tab both, functional and technical flow diagrams, explain the processes involved*

How to Build Your Strategy

I've already mentioned some of the options that allow you to get started building a roadmap from E-Business Suite to Fusion Applications, but there are several well-recognized steps that can be taken right away to begin any of these journeys.

However, I am not suggesting you rush into moving to Fusion Applications if your existing application features support your current operation satisfactorily. The term *disruption* might have become fashionable in the technology industry, but it remains high-risk and unpopular in more traditional business circles, especially where not necessary. Nevertheless, moving forward with your Application Management Plan is an essential part of the optimization toolbox from Chapter 8.

The following sections include actions that are worth considering to help get you started.

Take Stock

It is often hard to make a good application management plan when you do not have a solid grasp of where you are right now. The sheer magnitude of the components, their complex dependencies, and often, their outdated business expectations make it tough to understand what might be appropriate system changes. As such, the first step is to review your enterprise application's footprint, along with its related technologies. It is common that expensive niche solutions and old inactive requirements are the low-hanging fruit ripe for the picking. Often it is helpful for the resulting inventory to include related items like security solutions and the most critical business data and processes. From a clear starting position all subsequent changes are more likely to be progressive improvements.

Another part of this process is ensuring that your applications and enterprise IT department remains correctly aligned with your business operation. This is an ideal opportunity to undertake this substantial yet critical review task, and stakeholders must analyze and verify that the tools they have remain optimized for task completion in the various job roles to which they are intended for use. Going further, the strategies and plans of Enterprise IT must remain parallel to those for the overall business, reducing any divergence, assumptions, and bad prioritization.

Get Up to Date

Constantly moving to the latest applications releases is an overhead, but the benefits are also well documented. Especially related to this discussion is the fact that there is no current software upgrade from E-Business Suite to Fusion Applications. It is an entirely new application and as such requires a new implementation. The saving grace is that your data can be migrated, but only when the current data model is compatible for Fusion Applications, something that's only available in the latest releases.

Understand the Fusion Technology

Get familiar with the Fusion Applications technology by starting to use it now. Apart from those components introduced in the latest E-Business Suite releases, additional Fusion Technology options exist to satisfy your business needs, as illustrated in general in Figure 11-9. Some of the options for E-Business Suite include the following:

- Optimizing user productivity by including Oracle WebCenter portlets and information mash-ups

- Delivering more reporting and analytics using OBIEE, OBIA, and BI Publisher tools

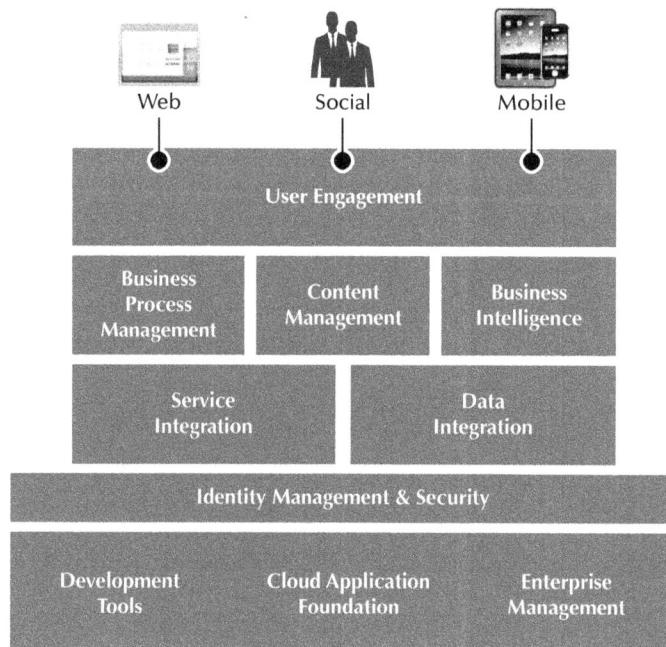

FIGURE 11-9. *Broad categories of the Fusion Middleware components*

- Managing attachments and documents using Enterprise Content Management (ECM)
- Incorporating the Google-like search of Secure Enterprise Search
- Embracing SOA-based and modern message-based integration capabilities
- Enhancing security through implementing single sign-on and Oracle Identity Management

You might also consider the benefits of the advanced application management features of the Fusion platform, something we'll discuss at the end of this chapter. One example we've mentioned throughout this book that has an equivalent in Fusion Applications is centralizing your Applications Lifecycle Management with Enterprise Manager's plug-in for E-Business Suite.

Consolidate

Generally speaking, fewer components usually means a lower cost. These might be legacy Enterprise Applications yet to be retired, specialist systems that are no longer required, or multiple instances of E-Business Suite deployed regionally that could be centralized into a single global instance.

Another important item to consider is your customization portfolio. These tend to grow over time, and reviewing them fully often leads to retirement, or some replacement with less costly equivalents. In addition to simple rationalization of customizations, it's also an opportunity to rethink the past strategy of when and how to use customization because the need to support a key business requirement may be different now.

One more suggestion around consolidation is to look at your application data. This also grows over time and, while purging and archiving can clean up processing records and basic transactions, there is often obsolete data in a system, especially around functional setups. With data migration and reimplementation potentially on the horizon, leveraging some of the Master Data Management techniques and solutions in E-Business Suite (or Fusion Applications) can improve data quality and prepare you for better information management in the future.

One final word on consolidation. When planning the evolution of your Enterprise Applications, leveraging outsourcing of system administration and cloud-based deployment models will inevitably come up. Obviously, calculating the ROI from moving an on-premise application to the cloud is very tough to do beyond procuring hardware and software licenses, but those organizations that have introduced service-based subscription seem to be reporting positive results. As this segment of the industry evolves, it seems logical to expect the catalog of options to expand, the implementation and integration processes to simplify, and other positive benefits of increased competition.

Understand the Fusion Functionality

Just as taking stock of your current situation helps plan its evolution, you also need to understand the options available to you in enough detail to make informed decisions. A simple example is how there is no point for a consumer-packaged goods organization in considering the earlier releases of Fusion Applications when the manufacturing functionality was not released.

As such, it's important to spend some time understanding the features of Fusion Applications and to look for opportunities through either improved or brand new business functionality. You'll probably want to do this before your competitors do! There are many methods to do this, and a simple start is to review the Oracle website and look for the product data sheets, whitepapers, online demos, and of course the detailed documentation.

In addition, the most popular choice today is to use just a few products from the Fusion Applications suite either loosely integrated or as standalones available through the Oracle Cloud. This lowers costs and is a careful way to instantly get business benefits without significant risk and disruption to your existing IT infrastructure. Visit http://cloud.oracle.com for more detail on the features available.

Share and Learn

Over the last few years, the Oracle community has become more vibrant than ever, and with social networks helping drive more collaboration, there has never been a greater opportunity to benefit from the experience of others, or to contribute yourself.

When considering a bold move like evolving your Enterprise Application, it's unlikely that anyone wants to make the same mistakes others already have, or to run into known issues that could have been avoided. Therefore, taking time to understand the experience of others is strongly recommended. There are multiple resources you can use to do this:

- Many Oracle Conference papers are based on real-world implementation experiences. Look at past and upcoming Oracle OpenWorld content catalog for examples.

- Work with your Oracle sales team to get customer references and follow them up.

- Engage with system integrators, partners, and Oracle consulting services who have worked on similar projects in the past.

- Engage with a local, regional, or international groups to find out about other members who might be willing to share their experiences.

Fusion Applications Manageability

Since this book is about managing E-Business Suite, it makes sense to conclude with a brief discussion about how application management has evolved in Fusion Applications and what there is to look forward to. If and when you decide to take this to the next level of understanding, please consider reading the equivalent book to this one, entitled *Managing Oracle Fusion Applications* (Oracle Press, 2011), also written by me.

Enterprise Manager

First, out-of-the box Fusion Applications are deployed with Enterprise Manager Fusion Applications Control, the primary tool for monitoring and managing the entire system. This is very similar to the Fusion Middleware Control available in E-Business Suite Release 12.2 and contains most of the same benefits and is tailored specifically for the needs of Fusion Applications. Similarly, Enterprise Manager Cloud Control is the big sister of these tools. While it requires its own deployment, it contains a powerful plug-in for Fusion Applications, along with many equivalent features to those illustrated in this book. Because all other components of the Fusion Technology stack are also supported by Enterprise Manager, and illustrated in Figure 11-10, there is finally a single one-stop-shop for the majority of applications monitoring and management.

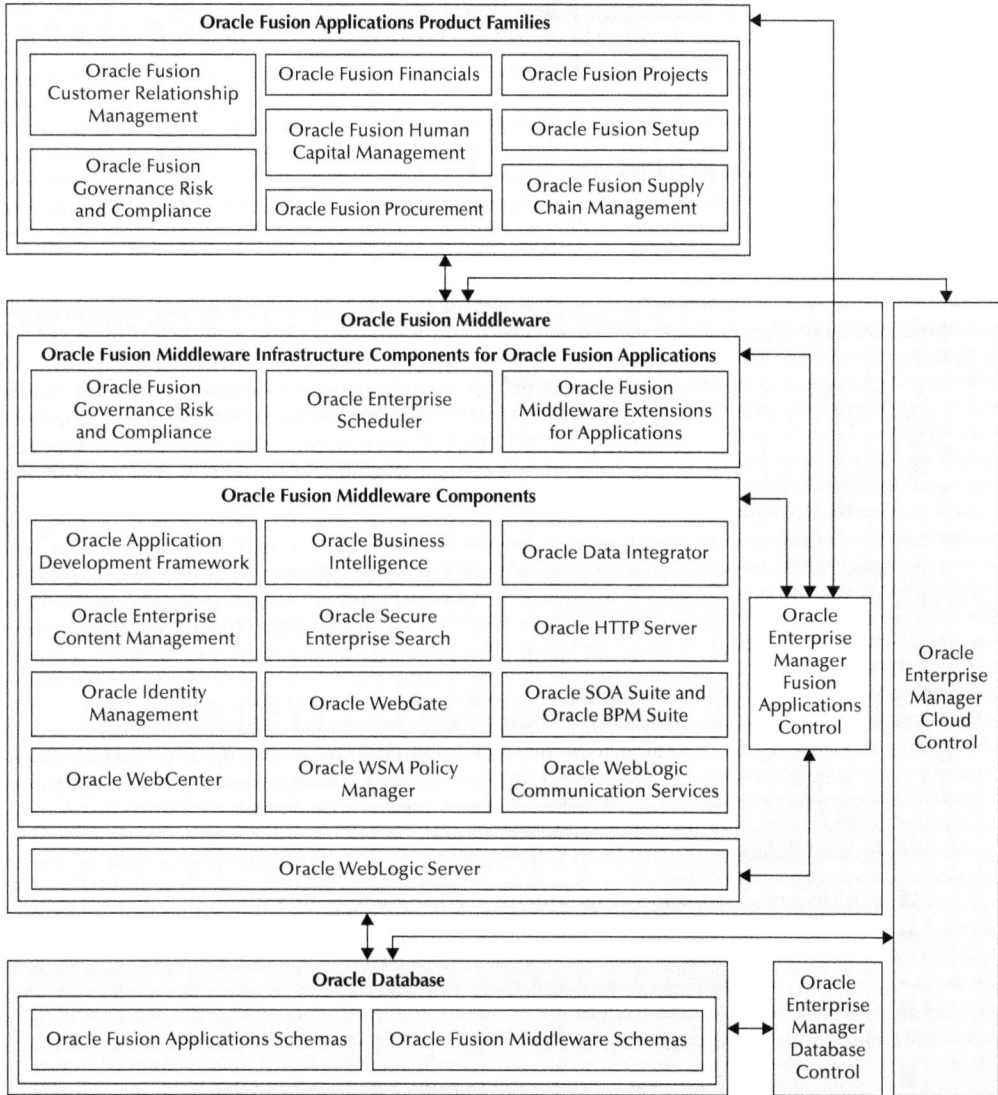

FIGURE 11-10. *The Fusion Applications products sit over Middleware and Database, with Enterprise Manager available across the board*

Common Platforms

Throughout this book, I've mentioned the fragmented set of tools and features for troubleshooting E-Business Suite, something especially prevalent between products, where different options and mechanisms are used for common system administration items such as configuration, logging, and tracing. This is greatly improved for Fusion Applications, since all architectures and common capabilities were standardized and controlled during design. Logging is a good example, where Fusion Applications implements the now gold-standard logging style known as Oracle Diagnostic Logging (ODL), the same one used by the 11g+ Database and most of Fusion Middleware. This creates rich logs in a standard format that can be parsed through easy-to-use tools like Enterprise Manager.

Problem Management

Like both the Database and Fusion Middleware, Fusion Applications implements something known as the Diagnostic Framework (DFw). This is a subsystem that is used whenever a serious failure occurs, essentially capturing a snapshot of the system at that point in time. This means that the days of end users subjected to ugly technical errors and cryptic catch-all failure messages are finally over. When a problem occurs in Fusion Applications, the end user gets either a descriptive product message that tells them how to resolve the problem, or in extreme circumstances, they get a reference Incident Number with which they can follow up with their help desk. This facility is inline with the IT Service Management industry standards on problem management, such as these in the popular ITIL framework.

Incidents themselves contain a rich and context-sensitive range of diagnostic information including multiple log files based on different filters, such as process thread, time interval, technology component, and the user's click history. There are also lower-level Java server diagnostics, such as thread dumps and JVM profiler traces. There is configuration data from related components, and an incident can even trigger a functional diagnostic that provides business setup and transactional data analysis. An incident is therefore a complete resource that prevents the need to repeat issues to collect more information, a benefit sometimes referred to as "first failure diagnosis."

DFw and Problem Management are also embedded inside Enterprise Manager, and therefore the help desk or system manager is immediately alerted to incident creation and has multiple resources at their disposal to begin troubleshooting. Figure 11-11 shows the Incident Manager page for the Fusion Procurement product family, and for each incident a multitude of options are available, including the following:

- Drilling down into the diagnostic files to perform analysis

- Adding more diagnostics from related technology components, such as database reports and traces

- Basic ticketing system operations that can also be easily integrated with more fully functional help desk systems like Siebel Call Center and Remedy

- Matching against similar incidents and problems to identify patterns

- Viewing recent configuration changes for the related system components

- Searching My Oracle Support for matching solutions without leaving Enterprise Manager

- Packaging the incident files and creating a new SR (or updating an existing one), again without leaving Enterprise Manager

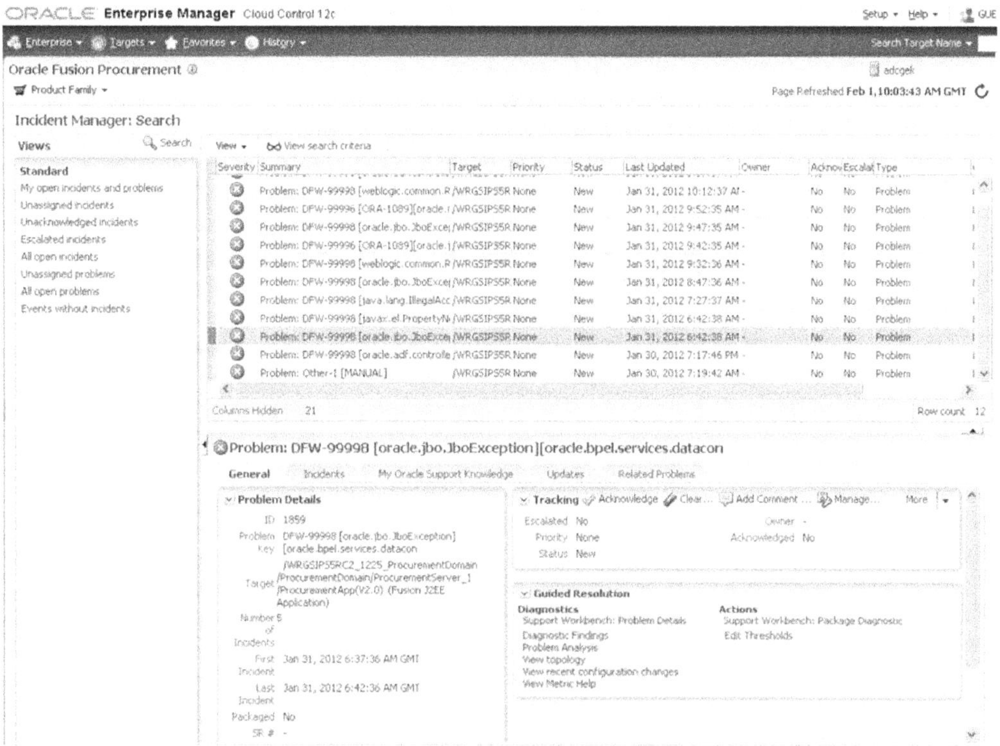

FIGURE 11-11. *The Incident Manager page within Enterprise Manager*

Summary

In this final chapter we took a glance ahead to see where the evolution of E-Business Suite is going, as well as how and why formulating a strategy for the future can bring both short- and long-term benefits.

We started by looking at how we can improve productivity through new options, such as embedding ADF regions and Endeca extensions in E-Business Suite. Next, we considered how to leverage additional solutions for E-Business Suite based on the very latest technologies such as OBIEE and advanced integration. We also reviewed the key features of E-Business Suite 12.2 and how it moves us naturally to a state where the jump to Fusion technologies is not quite so large anymore.

We laid out some recommended options for building a roadmap toward Fusion Applications, with a focus on explaining the popular method of adopting the parts that can deliver immediate business value, known as coexistence scenarios. We then looked at some of the key elements to focus around in building your own evolution strategy.

We finally ended somewhat poetically with a glimpse into the future of enterprise application management, and explained how the platforms, capabilities, and tooling have finally come together to form a coherent and complete application management solution. Indeed, to substantiate this bright vision of the future, when setting up our back-end support system for the enterprise applications offered in the Oracle Cloud, I was part of the team that implemented the very same Enterprise Manager solutions, proving once and for all that the ultimate test of your product is to use it yourself.

APPENDIX

Further Reading

A
s discussed in Chapter 1, this appendix includes a simplified summary of the E-Business Suite products, with a table devoted to each of the product families.

Common Applications Components

These products exist with the sole purpose of supporting the functional products of E-Business Suite. They perform a range of common tasks, execution platforms, and utility functions that are used by one, many, or all of the features.

Product	Description
Alert	Tool for creating custom notifications of specific events from, or patterns found in the application database.
Approval Management Engine (AME)	Definition of rules against which various E-Business Suite products execute their approval processes. AME is an integrated product that is called based on specific parameters (approval type, amount, and so on) and generates the list of applicable approvers for the subsequent notification processing.
Common Application Calendar	Common calendaring system for use across an organization. Logically, it's integrated into many E-Business Suite products, such as HRMS for work scheduling and shifts and Oracle CRM Sales for booking customer appointments. It uses industry standard calendaring protocols and can integrate to Outlook and other systems.
Configurator	Tool for building configuration models (rules and capabilities) for setting up specific features or products. For example, you can use it with Oracle Bill of Materials to configure a complex product assembly. A complex product that includes several technical elements like data model knowledge, user interface development, and deployment and unit testing.
Contracts	Contract management infrastructure for use in Oracle Sales Contracts, Oracle Procurement Contracts, Oracle Service Contracts, and Oracle Project Contracts. Includes contract authoring tools and document management capabilities.
Diagnostics Framework	Application product that provides over 400 diagnostic tests for troubleshooting E-Business Suite.
e-Commerce Gateway	Manager of the communication of transaction messages between trading partners, focused on the EDI protocols.
E-Records	Platform for the creation and management of e-signatures and e-records to be applied to various transactions to comply with industry practices and legal regulations.
iSetup	Data migration and reporting tool for moving data between instances (export/import) and comparing. Currently supports core setups (FND) as well as HRMS and Financials products.

Product	Description
Trading Community Architecture	Single data model for recording parties, their locations and contacts, and the relationships among them. The standard data model for suppliers, customers, and other entities used across E-Business Suite.
Web Applications Desktop Integrator	Provides integration between Microsoft Office and E-Business Suite, used across many products, with special ties with Projects, HRMS, and Financials. Also used to perform offline presentation and analysis of data and often to reload the results back.
Workflow	Routes business process functions based on predefined rules. Used across E-Business Suite especially for controlling processes that include approvals, notifications, and sequential steps for completion. Has a custom development interface (Workflow Builder) to adjust rules and processes as needed.
XML Gateway	Integration tool used across E-Business Suite for sending XML messages between internal products and also external systems (for example, "Send order to supplier"). Contains support for many seeded message types, plus tools to extend the capabilities.

Customer Relationship Management

The Customer Relationship Management family of applications provide a single, global basis of information that ensures all selling channels are aligned with corporate objectives. This comprehensive product set also includes extensive service management applications providing information-driven customer service capabilities

Product	Description
Customer Data Librarian	Manages the quality of customer data, including consolidation, cleanliness, and completeness. Data is held in the Trading Community Architecture (TCA) Registry and is part of the Customer Data Management product set.
Advanced Inbound/ Outbound Telephony	Provides extensive call handling capabilities, including routing and reporting. It has integration with Oracle Marketing (outbound), Oracle TeleSales, Oracle TeleService, and Oracle Advanced Collections, as well as adapters and an SDK for the additional integration of telephony solutions. It forms a technical platform for E-Business Suite CRM, especially for Oracle Interaction Center.
Advanced Scheduler	Does planning and assignment of tasks to field service technicians, including service calls, as well as regular tasks like inspections and maintenance. It uses rules based on extensive setup, constraints, and other parameters to calculate the optimal schedules.
Content Manager	Provides full lifecycle management for all kinds of custom content (documents, video, images, and so on), stored in a shared repository for use with products such as Sales, Marketing, and E-Commerce.

Product	Description
Customer Interaction History	Common tool for capturing customer contact activities, both directly or through integration with other products like Call Center.
Customers Online	Provides creation and management of customer records as part of the Oracle Customer Data Management (CDM) product family.
E-mail Center	Used for management of all official e-mails with customers, partners, suppliers, employees, and other entities that interact with an organization.
Field Service	Used for scheduling and dispatching tasks to field technicians and monitoring the progress and status of those tasks to completion. Integrates closely with Spare Management and Advanced Scheduler products.
Interaction Blending and Interaction Center Server Manager	Allows management of servers that deliver media (Web callbacks and outbound telephony) to help desk agents. Integrates with related CRM products like Call Center.
iStore	Provides creation and management of custom web stores for creating customer orders. Integration with Web Analytics, CRM Products (for example, iSupport), and of course, Order Management for processing.
iSupport	Self-service customer support product focused on reducing calls by delivering services and knowledge articles online. Integrates with call center and other CRM products.
Knowledge Management	Provides creation and management of knowledge documents and offers integration to many CRM products like iSupport, TeleService, and Field Service.
Leads Management	Provides management of the prospect-to-sales conversion, offering a staging area for quality processing, qualification, and prioritization before being assigned to sales teams.
Marketing	Manages the planning, budgeting, execution, and tracking of product marketing initiatives. Integration across many CRM products, including Leads Management, Sales, and Telesales.
Mobile Field Service	An extension of Field Service product, specifically supports mobile service technicians (via laptops, mobile devices, and voice). Helps them receive schedules and report on progress, material, expense, and labor.
Mobile Supply Chain Applications	Enables use of application features via wireless radio frequency devices that can be hand held, wearable, ring scanner systems, and lift truck mounted. Integrates to most Supply Chain applications and contains its own technology and server for communication.
One-to-One Fulfillment	Provides a centralized mechanism for managing document and notification delivery to customers. Generally used with CRM products.

Product	Description
Partner Management	Manages partners who sell product through indirect channels. Includes extensive integration to Sales and other CRM products.
Price Protection	Specialist product (high tech, mostly) that provides management of transactions that affect how price changes by customer or supplier may influence product availability. Integrates closely with Oracle Channel Revenue Management.
Proposals User	Provides creation and management of proposals, including documents to aid in selling a product or providing service to a customer. Includes Sales, Telesales, and Marketing product integrations, plus Content Management for storage.
Quoting	Provides management of customer quotes across all sales and service channels. It integrates closely with Sales, Contracts, and TeleSales.
Sales	Product set comprised of core sales process management features to support customers, contacts, and leads and opportunities, as well as subproducts Sales Offline, Sales for Handhelds, and Sales Contracts. Integrates with many products, including Territory Management, Trading Community Architecture, Quoting, Inventory, Service Contracts, Order Management, Proposals, Partners, Projects, Incentive Compensation, and Marketing.
Scripting	Guides customers and agents through decision flows (such as making sales calls) using predefined scripts. Comprised of Script Author, Scripting Engine, and Scripting and Survey Administration. Integration includes TeleService, iSupport, and Marketing Online.
Supplier Ship and Debit	Specialist product that allows distributors to sell at a special price and manages the associated difference. Integrates closely with Channel Revenue Management, as well as Order Management, Advanced Pricing, Receivables, Payables, and common integration tools like e-Commerce and XML Gateway.
TeleSales	Manages the sales cycle from prospects to booked orders. Integrated across CRM products, including TeleService, Sales, Order Management, and Interaction Center.
Territory Manager	Assigns sales objects (customers, opportunities, leads, and so on) to resources (people) based on a set of business rules. Includes integration across the CRM sales products.
Universal Work Queue	Provides a core framework for managing different types of work generated in a customer call center. Integrates with CRM products such as TeleSales, TeleService, and Sales Online.

Financials Product Family

The E-Business Suite Financials family supports industry standard accounting processes such as credit-to-cash and procure-to-pay, with a focus on improving efficiency and productivity, shared services, and integrated performance management.

Product	Description
Accounts Receivable Deductions Settlement	Provides management of claims and deductions, commonly between manufacturers and retailers, such as claim compensation for damaged goods or process promotional deductions. Process flow from Creation, Assignment, Approval, Research, Settlement, and Reporting.
Advanced Collections	Provides management of the collection of outstanding payments, with features to support delinquency, broken promise, executing collection strategies, and associated reporting.
Advanced Global Intercompany System	Manages the process of creating, settling, and reconciling intercompany transactions (that is, within a single legal entity).
Asset Tracking	Deploys and reports on assets wherever they are located. This includes integration to Purchasing, Projects, Inventory, Assets, Payables, and Install Base.
Assets	Manages company assets (normally physical items). This includes maintenance, leases, depreciation, retirements and transfers, budgeting, and other reporting. Integration to Purchasing, Inventory, and other financial products.
Bill Presentment Architecture	Manages the content of bills presented to customers (print and online). Includes integration capabilities beyond receivables for custom data to be included in bill delivery.
Cash Management	Provides overall management of cash flow through the business. It includes reconciliation between transactions and bank accounts and across many other related products (Payables, Receivables, Payroll, and Treasury). It also includes a forecasting component.
Credit Management	Makes and implements credit decisions for customers and prospects. Includes defining criteria and policies, risk management, and processing via workflow and approvals components. Has integration to/from various products, especially Receivables.
E-Business Tax	Sets up and maintains the transaction tax across the system. Obvious integrations to most product areas as well as third-party tax systems.
Enterprise Performance Foundation	Provides a framework of rules and a single repository of data to support the Corporate Performance Management product set. Close integration with many products, especially General Ledger.
Enterprise Planning and Budgeting	Allows control of the processes in, and analysis of, financial planning, budgeting, and forecasting.

Product	Description
Financial Consolidation Hub	Brings together financial data from disparate sources to create a single, global view of financial information across the entire enterprise. It forms part of the Corporate Performance Management product set.
Financial Services	Focuses on Transfer Pricing and Profitability Manager. Now (as of Release 12) based on Enterprise Performance Foundation that itself is part of the Corporate Performance Management product family.
Financials RXi Reports Administration Tool	Helps meet statutory and other reporting requirements for custom content and layout.
General Ledger	Contains the central account cycle process and forms a central repository of all financial activity for reporting and analysis.
Grants Accounting	Extends Oracle Projects to provide tracking of grants and funded projects from inception to final reporting. Integrates to Subledger Accounting, Labor Distribution, and Grants Proposal.
iAssets	Self-service tool; finds assets and manages their transfer. Includes approval (via AME) and workflow notifications.
Internal Controls Manager	Related to the Governance, Risk and Compliance product family; provides documentation features, test internal controls, and the ability to monitor ongoing compliance.
Internet Expenses	Self-service entry of expense reports; uses Workflow for approval and reimbursement policies compliance. Contains close integration with Payables for processing.
iReceivables	Self-service product for customers; runs bill inquiries, disputes bills, pays invoices, and reviews current account balances. Native integration into Receivables.
Lease and Finance Management	Provides management of leases, from origination to contract termination and asset disposition. Tight integration with General Ledger, Assets, Inventory, Payables, Order Management and Receivables products, as well as CRM modules.
Loans	Provides creation and servicing of financial loans. Integrates to HRMS and Resource Manager, General Ledger, Receivables, and Payables.
Payables	Provides complete management of and reporting on the processing of invoices and related payments. Core part of Financials family with integrations with all products related to purchasing items.
Payments	Provides a funds capture and disbursement engine that integrates Payables invoices, bank transfers from Oracle Cash Management, and settlements from Receivables. Also supports integrations to third-party systems.

Product	Description
Profitability Manager	Highlights which areas of the business are profitable and which are less. Part of Corporate Performance Management, built on the Enterprise Performance Foundation for data discovery, it leverages data warehousing and Discoverer tools.
Project Billing	An extension to Oracle Projects; allows the setup of rules for revenue and invoicing of projects, performs revenue and invoice management, and hands off the related processing through integration with Oracle Receivables.
Projects	Supports the management of resources and funds to support complex projects, like construction and aerospace. It has various subproducts such as Project Contracts, Project Costing, Project Management, Project Portfolio Analysis, and Project Resource Management. Integration focus on Financials, but supply chain products include projects support for resource allocation.
Property Manager	Provides management of property assets and commitments, including components under Lease and Space Management. Integration includes General Ledger, Payables, Receivables, and Human Resources, as well as third-party solutions for CAD and CAFM.
Public Sector Budgeting	Allows Public Sector organizations to prepare and maintain budgets, including support for personnel services, general operating, and capital budget components.
Public Sector Financials	As an extension to other Financials products (General Ledger and so on), provides specialist support for Encumbrance Account Analysis, Funds Available Inquiry, Funds Available Detail Report, and Governmental Accounting Standards.
Receivables	Performs the process of managing outgoing payments. This is done via a Receipts Workbench, a Transactions Workbench (for processing invoices, debit/credit memos, credits, charge-backs, and adjustments), and a Bills Receivable Workbench.
Report Manager	Provides centralized functions to support reporting, primarily focused on Financial and Accounting needs.
Subledger Accounting	Previously implemented as a Set of Books; supports the management of financial structures required for full enterprise accounting. It is essentially part of General Ledger and integrates across financials.
Transfer Pricing	Provides advanced accounting for implementing a matched rate transfer pricing. As part of Financial Services, it includes integration to other products Profitability Manager and Enterprise Performance Foundation.
Treasury	Allows management of cash flows, foreign exchange and money market deals, risk, and bank relationships and settlement.

Human Resource Management System

E-Business Suites human capital management family offers core HR features that supports global organizations, extensive workforce management, broad talent management and development features, and extensive analytics and reporting.

Product	Desciption
Human Resources Enterprise and Workforce Management	Product set; supports all aspects of the HR function, including Human Resources, Payroll, Self-Service Human Resources, Performance Management, iRecruitment, Time & Labor, Learning Management, Advanced Benefits, and HRMS Intelligence.
Human Resources FastFormula	Creates complex formulas using words and basic mathematical functions. Used to check values, generate values, add value to reports, and so on. Used in Payroll and various other products. Includes native integration and can be called from custom API hooks.
Human Resources Management Systems Compensation and Benefits Management	Includes overall HRMS setup set of products, including Compensation Structures, Salary, Grades, and Pay Administration, Compensation and Awards Management, Leave and Absence Management, Setup for Health and Welfare Management, Administration for Health and Welfare Management, and Payroll Earnings and Deductions.
Human Resources Workforce Sourcing, Deployment, and Talent Management	Contains Recruitment and Hiring, People Management, and Talent Management.
Incentive Compensation	Manages the compensation plans for salespeople, including cash and other tangible rewards.
Labor Distribution	Schedules, creates, corrects, and certifies labor cost distribution without a timecard system. Integrated with Human Resources, Payroll, General Ledger, Projects, and Grants Accounting.
Learning Management	Provides management of education through a unified learning delivery system to employees, customers, and partners. It's closely integrated with the Talent and Performance Management and passes data to Oracle Financials and Order Management.
iRecruitment	Self-service product; allows prospective candidates to search available vacancies, view details, and upload enquiries and resumes to begin the application process.
Time Capture	Previously called Time and Labor; provides self-service creation of timecards plus various approval rules and related routing for processing. Integrates heavily with products with a time capture feature, such as Oracle Projects.

Supply Chain Management

The Supply Chain Management family of applications integrates and automates all key information-driven value chain processes, from design, planning, and procurement to manufacturing and fulfillment.

Demand Signal Repository	Collects demand data, analyzes it, and helps identify issues and opportunities. It leverages data warehousing techniques and performs integrations using SOA. It includes integration to Point-of-Sale systems and other data sources.
Advanced Planning Command Center	A dashboard layer over the Advanced Planning applications (Demand Management, Real-Time Sales and Operations Planning, Strategic Network Optimization, Advanced Supply Chain Planning, Distribution Requirements Planning, and Inventory Optimization); provides demand planners, supply chain planners, inventory managers, and a unified analysis tool. Has BPEL-based integration to execute on results. It also leverages Oracle Business Intelligence and WebCenter technologies to provide personalized what-if modeling and team collaboration capabilities.
Advanced Pricing	Provides an engine that can execute complex calculations to generate item prices. This includes creation of price breaks, discounts and promotions, surcharges, and price agreements. Integration focuses on Oracle Order Management but can include CRM products.
Advanced Supply Chain Planning	Allows the creation of plans that decide when and where supply items should be best deployed across an organization. A multitude of parameters are used to build and execute plans to derive the most effective distribution. Integration occurs across the Supply Chain products, especially Oracle Purchasing and Inventory.
Bills of Material	Provides creation and management of lists of items that can be assembled to form a new product. Primarily used by Oracle Manufacturing and Oracle Order Management products.
Capacity	Plans and executes product supply so that inventory capacity is sufficient to meet your production requirements.
Channel Revenue Management (previously called Oracle Trade Management)	Plans, executes, and administers payment for trade promotions, used by manufacturer dealing with extensive and complex customer agreements. It is a parent product that includes smaller products: Oracle Accounts Receivable Deductions Settlement, Oracle Channel Rebate and Point-of-Sale Management, Oracle Supplier Ship and Debit, and Oracle Price Protection.

Collaborative Planning	Communicates, plans, and optimizes supply and demand information between trading partners (customers and suppliers). It integrates with Oracle Advanced Supply Chain Planning, Oracle Demand Planning, and Oracle iSupplier Portal as well as third-party systems.
Complex Maintenance, Repair, and Overhaul	Provides complex equipment maintenance management, including scheduled and unscheduled maintenance visits, component monitoring, job scheduling and routing, labor time collection, cost collection, inventory management, and maintenance document management. It integrates with a range of other products, including Oracle Counters, Install Base, Inventory, Quality, Advanced Supply Chain Planning, Purchasing, Warehouse Management, Order Management, Enterprise Asset Management, and Customer Support, was well as specialist third-party product Enigma 3C.
Contract Lifecycle Management for Public Sector	Manages the procurement processes specifically for the regulations inside U.S. federal agencies.
Cost Management	Costs and values all Inventory, Work In Process, and Order Management or Purchasing transactions. Includes detailed reporting and integration with the Financial products, such as General Ledger.
Demand Planning	Manages forecasts for future demand and generates associated tactical, operational, and strategic business plans. It's integrated with Inventory Optimization, Collaborative Planning, and Advanced Supply Chain Planning, and it collects data from many sources, such as Sales.
Demantra	A large (acquired) product set; provides detailed demand management solutions, including analytics, planning, forecasting, and modeling.
Depot Repair	Manages the entire one-off repair process and routine maintenance tasks. Includes integration to many products, such as Knowledge Management, Scheduler, Contracts, Install Base, Field Service, HRMS, Inventory, iSupport, Order Management, and others.
Engineering	Manages engineering change orders and materials disposition. Includes integrations through manufacturing products and Inventory and Bill of Materials.
Enterprise Asset Management	Manages, schedules, and plans maintenance procedures for assets and rebuildable inventory items. Includes extensive integration with other products, with mandatory installation of Inventory, Bills of Material, Human Resources, Cost Management, Manufacturing Scheduling, Quality, and Work In Process.

Flow Manufacturing	Contain features that support the entire flow manufacturing process, from line design and balancing to production execution.
Global Order Promising	Provides an order promising calculations based on current and projected demands and supplies across a supply chain, stating when a customer order can be fulfilled (delivered). Tight integration to Order Management and CRM products exists, but it has flexible integration options, both inside E-Business Suite and as a stand-alone.
Install Base	Provides lifecycle tracking for inventory product items. Is used with many of the supply chain related products.
Inventory	Provides management of product items, including item attribute data, lots and serial numbering, physical stock levels, locations and transfers, and planning and reporting.
iProcurement	Self-service product; allows and manages the internal request for products or services (requisitions).
iSupplier Portal	Self-service tool; allows suppliers to view and enter details on purchasing documents to aid the buying/selling process. Integrates to Purchasing, Payables, and some supply chain applications.
Landed Cost Management	Manages estimated and actual landed cost for an item purchased from a supplier (including shipping, storage, and other fees). Integration includes Purchasing, Receiving, Payables, Cost Management, and Advanced Pricing.
Manufacturing	Product set; provides management of item manufacturing operations. Includes support for Discrete, Process and Flow-based methodologies and includes Execution System, Operations Center, Scheduling, Product Development, Quality and Regulatory Management, and Subcontracting.
MRP Master Scheduling	Provides advanced planning and scheduling capability for inventory management and manufacturing production. Integrates across Supply Chain products.
Order Management	Provides management and processing of customer orders, focused on high-volume transactions and fulfillment. Central supply chain product with integrations both on order capture, pricing and item management, fulfillment, and financial reporting.
Product Information Management	Provides management of product item data, including the construction of item catalogs. Integration occurs where item data flows in or out.
Production Scheduling	Advanced engine; provides production schedules for discrete manufacturing environments. Integrates closely with Advanced Supply Chain Planning and manufacturing products.

Purchasing	Manages the procurement process, converting requirements into supplier orders. Includes aspects of receiving items as well as integration to payables for invoice reconciliation and payment.
Quality	Manages the checking of products for quality compliance. Includes managing nonconformance and dispositions, corrective actions, auditing. Close integration with other supply chain and manufacturing products such as Inventory and Work In Progress.
Rapid Planning	Part of the Value Chain Planning product set; provides support for special situations where supply chain plans need expediting. It has close integration with Global Order Promising and Advanced Supply Chain Planning.
Release Management	Provides electronic collaboration with customer systems to calculate demand and ensure on-time delivery of goods to customers. It analyzes customer planning, shipping, and production sequence schedules and synchronizes them with sales orders, sales agreements, and forecasts. It includes use of both e-Commerce Gateway and XML Gateway integration products.
Service Contracts	Provides contract authoring and management for warranties, service usage, subscription services, and service agreements. Integrations include Inventory and Order Management.
Service Fulfillment Manager	Offers a specialist extension of SCM features for telecommunication providers, ISPs (Internet Service Providers) and similar, specifically for order capture, order activation, and network administration and operation. Offers close integration with both Inventory and Order Management.
Service Parts Planning	A component product of Value Chain Planning; offers spares demand and supply forecasting, service parts planning, and overall spares management. It is dependent on Field Service Spares Management and Depot Repair, plus integrated with Demantra Demand Management, Order Management, Procurement, and Inventory.
Supplier Management	Provides management of Supplier records, including data quality, qualification, performance assessments, and tracking compliance with corporate and legal requirements. Integrates its data with Purchasing, Payables, and other products.
Telecommunications	Comprised of two products, Telecommunications Billing Integrator and Telecommunications Service Ordering; manages telecommunications companies' orders and services. Allows integration between E-Business Suite core products (financials, order management, and so on) to third-party specialists systems, mainly via XML Gateway, workflow and advanced queuing.

Transportation Management	Combines planning and execution with freight payment, inbound freight logistics, and freight rating and routing. Includes integration to Order Management, Shipping Execution, Payables, Warehouse Management, and Purchasing.
Warehouse Management	Contains all aspects of material handling for warehouses, manufacturing facilities, and distribution centers. It includes resource management, configuration, task management, advanced pick methodologies, and value added services. It also features integrations to mobile devices (RFID and so on), as well as many other Supply Chain products.
Web Analytics	Offers a flexible tool for tracking and reporting on E-Commerce website activity, logically focused around the iStore product. Also includes integration to Marketing.
Work in Process	Includes support for discrete, project, repetitive, assemble-to-order, flow, and lot-based jobs. It includes extensive reporting and integration across other manufacturing and supply chain products.

Index

R

X

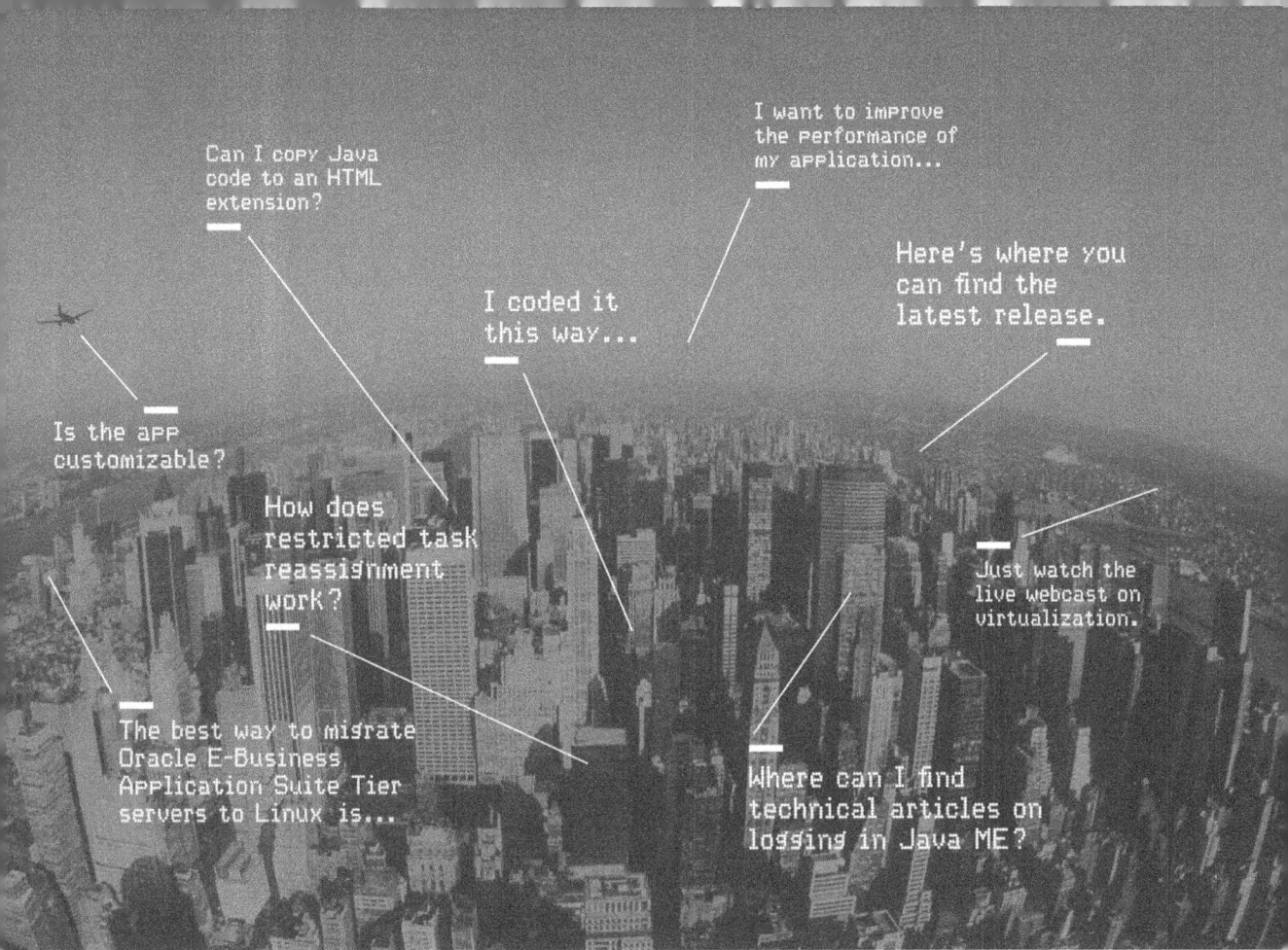

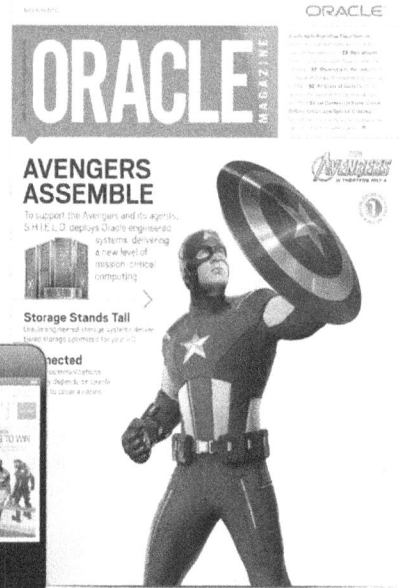

Reach More than 700,000 Oracle Customers
with Oracle Publishing Group

Connect with the Audience
that Matters Most to Your Business

Oracle Magazine
The Largest IT Publication in the World
Circulation: 550,000
Audience: IT Managers, DBAs, Programmers, and Developers

Profit
Business Insight for Enterprise-Class Business Leaders to
Help Them Build a Better Business Using Oracle Technology
Circulation: 100,000
Audience: Top Executives and Line of Business Managers

Java Magazine
The Essential Source on Java Technology, the Java
Programming Language, and Java-Based Applications
Circulation: 125,000 and Growing Steady
Audience: Corporate and Independent Java Developers,
Programmers, and Architects

For more information
or to sign up for a FREE
subscription:
Scan the QR code to visit
Oracle Publishing online.

ORACLE®

www.ingramcontent.com/pod-product-compliance
Lightning Source LLC
Chambersburg PA
CBHW080139220326
41598CB00032B/5109